THE
ENIGMA
OF
SUICIDE

George Howe Colt

A TOUCHSTONE BOOK
Published by Simon & Schuster
New York   London   Toronto   Sydney   Tokyo   Singapore

TOUCHSTONE
Simon & Schuster Building
Rockefeller Center
1230 Avenue of the Americas
New York, New York 10020

1   3   5   7   9   10   8   6   4   2

1   3   5   7   9   10   8   6   4   2   Pbk.

Library of Congress Cataloging in Publication Data
Colt, George Howe.
The enigma of suicide / George Howe Colt.
p.   cm.
Includes bibliographical references and index.
1. Suicide.   I. Title.
HV6545.C596   1991
362.28—dc20   90-19859
CIP
ISBN 0-671-50996-9
ISBN0-671-76071-8 Pbk.

Grateful acknowledgment is made for the following permissions:

Extract from *The Poems of Stanley Kunitz, 1928–1978,* by Stanley Kunitz, copyright ©
1971 by Stanley Kunitz. By permission of Little, Brown and Company. Extract from *The
Children of Night* by Edwin Arlington Robinson (New York: Charles Scribner's Sons, 1897),
courtesy of Macmillan Publishing Company, A Division of Macmillan, Inc. Extract from
Suicide Solution, words and music by John Osbourne, Robert Daisley and Randy Rhoads,
copyright © 1981 Essex Music International, Venice, CA. Used by Permission. Extract
from *The Savage God* by A. Alvarez. Published by George Weidenfeld and Nicholson, Ltd.
Extract from *The Vital Balance* by Karl Menninger, copyright © 1963 by Karl Menninger,
M.D. Reprinted by permission of Viking Penguin, a Division of Penguin Books USA, Inc.
Extract from *The Collected Poems of A.E. Housman,* copyright © 1936 by Barclays Bank
Ltd. Copyright © 1964 by Robert E. Symons. Copyright © 1965 by Holt Rinehart and
Winston, Inc. Reprinted by permission of Henry Holt and Company, Inc. Extract from
Wanting to Die by Anne Sexton, copyright © 1966 by Anne Sexton. Reprinted by permis-
sion of Houghton Mifflin Co. Extract from "Perhaps Love," lyrics by John Denver, copy-
right © 1980 Cherry Lane Music Publishing Co., Inc. International Copyright Secured. All
Rights Reserved. Used by permission.

CONTENTS

PREFACE

SEVERAL YEARS AGO, not long after I started the research for this book, I attended a conference in Boston on "Suicide: Assessment and Management." My notebooks soon became filled with information about warning signs, risk factors, mother-infant bonding, and countertransference hate. It was a good conference, less dry and more practical than many I had attended on the subject. "Empathy with despairing people requires the therapist to give up the psychological distance between himself and the patients he might ordinarily like to maintain," said one psychiatrist, a dapper fellow in a bow tie. "We must meet the patients in the howling desert where the unfinished business of early childhood has left them." On my right a middle-aged psychologist in a pin-striped suit copied the statement verbatim into his leatherbound notebook. There suddenly seemed to me to be something slightly absurd about hundreds of psychiatrists, psychologists, and social workers sitting in a thickly carpeted hotel ballroom under ten-foot crystal chandeliers and being exhorted to meet the patient in the howling desert. As the conference ended and we walked out, I wondered how many of us were prepared to do so.

It was a Friday night in January, and the Boston streets, still shiny with the afternoon's rain, were crowded with honking cars. Everyone was in a hurry to get home and begin the weekend. In the subway station a thin young man with a saxophone played "Summertime." But the evening was chilly, the subway trains were running late, and as the platform filled, the waiting commuters grew irritated. "Get us home!" shouted a bearded old man.

After the subway finally arrived, it traveled only one stop when a voice over the loudspeaker informed us that the electricity had been shut off between this station and the end of the line. Buses would deliver us to our destinations. Grumpy and impatient, the crowd spilled back into the streets. "What is it?" called out passers-by. "Is it a fight? Did somebody die?"

I found a seat on the bus near the back. Behind me two young men complained loudly about having been forced off the subway. Suddenly they stopped talking and turned to look out the window. The flickering blue lights of police cars mingled with spotlights at the far end of a side street. Word filtered through the bus that the subway line had been closed down because the tracks, after coming above ground, passed a cathedral from whose steeple a young man was threatening to jump.

"They got the whole street blocked off," said the older of the two boys behind me. "Fire trucks, police, and everything."

"Shit, man, if he really wanted to do it, he'd just run up there and jump," said the younger boy disdainfully. He gave a high-pitched giggle. "Hell, I say go ahead and jump, but not on *my* time."

The older boy hesitated a moment and then, his voice quieter, said, "Why does he want to do that? Why does he want to die?"

"He don't wanna die," said the younger boy. "He just wants to get his face on TV."

They laughed, but the older boy fell silent again. "Ever think of doing something like that? I don't understand it."

"I'd *never* do it," said the younger boy. "I mean I like the hell out of living."

"Maybe he got no reason for living," said the older boy.

"Then go ahead and jump," said the younger, recovering some of his bravado. "Or do it alone—go home, turn on the water, and slit your wrists. Get it done and let the rest of us go home. We got places to go."

"People to see," said the older.

"Drugs to do," said the younger. He giggled, the other boy joined in, and they began to talk about their plans for the evening. At the next stop they got off the bus, jostling each other, laughing as they disappeared into the night.

When the bus reached the end of the line, I persuaded my brother, who had been waiting there for me in his car, to drive back into Boston. I wanted to find out what happened to the man on the steeple. By the time we returned to the cathedral, however, the crowds were gone. A lone police car was parked in front. The officer told me that a drunken twenty-year-old man who had broken up with his girlfriend had climbed the scaffolding surrounding the steeple and stayed there, 150 feet up, for seventy minutes before policemen, firefighters, and two priests managed to talk him down. He had been taken to the hospital for psychiatric observation. Now, saying he had to file his report, the sergeant excused himself and drove off.

The cathedral was in a rough-looking neighborhood whose streets were dark and deserted. The night was quiet except for the sporadic clatter of the subway, which, back in operation, swept by overhead. I looked up at the steeple and tried to imagine where the jumper might have stood.

Then I noticed a man about fifty feet away from me, staring at the cathedral, his arms resting on the iron fence that surrounded the churchyard. I walked over and asked him whether he'd seen what had happened. No, he said, but he had heard about it. His voice was quiet and listless. He wore old jeans, a flannel shirt, and a blue parka that was shiny with dirt. Shocks of gray hair stuck out from under his black wool cap. His face was thin and his beard was flecked with white as if he'd just drunk a glass of milk. I guessed he was in his late thirties.

I shook my head. "Thank God he didn't jump," I said.

"Yeah," said the man. He asked me if I was a reporter. I said no but that I was writing a book on suicide.

"Oh." He looked over at me. "I'm a prime candidate."

"Why?" I asked.

"Because . . . things get you down," he said. I must have looked confused because he added, "There is an entire group of people in this country that gets put down, kept down, and ignored."

"By whom?"

"By everyone. By the federal government, by the laws, by big business." He saw that I wasn't convinced. "I'll tell you what happened to me. I used to be a *person,* with an office and a degree and an apartment and a car and a life. I was making $30,000 a year. I had a girlfriend, but she was a married woman and when her husband found out, he came to my house and punched me out and . . ."

As we stood side by side gazing up at the church, he told me of the breakup with his girlfriend, of financial troubles, of legal difficulties, of friends pulling away, of life in his cramped apartment, of his deep depression. As the story unraveled I had the sinking feeling that this could be a long evening, and I was cold because I'd left my jacket in the car, where my brother waited with the engine running. "And I was committed to a mental hospital," he was saying. "Once you've been in there, our society says you're no good." He paused. "I have no money. I have no job. My life is ruined. But don't worry, I'm not going to run up there and jump now." He shook his head. "But I think about killing myself every day."

"What do you do when you feel like killing yourself?"

"I call a prevention center."

"Do they help?"

"Sometimes, yeah."

I shivered. "You're freezing," he said. He reached over and touched me lightly on the back. I shivered again but not from the cold. He took an almost empty pack of Marlboros from his jacket pocket and offered me one. I shook my head, and he lit one for himself. He took a puff on his cigarette and began to talk more about his broken life in the same leaden, expressionless voice.

In the years since then, I have thought often of that evening. My encounters with the psychiatrists, the boys on the bus, and the lonely man at the cathedral gate raised many of the questions that this book attempts to explore. Between

1 and 2 percent of all Americans die by suicide, and some 4 or 5 percent make a suicide attempt at some point in their lives. Very few of us have not known someone, however distantly, who has taken his or her own life. In the course of writing this book, I talked with several hundred people who had intimate experience with suicide—people who had made attempts, family and friends of people who had killed themselves, psychiatrists, social workers, members of the clergy, biologists, hot line volunteers. But perhaps more surprising were the hundreds of other people I met in the course of my daily life who ended up telling me their stories. These included a middle-aged Scandinavian woman sitting next to me on a train, who told me she'd been so depressed she had tried to hang herself with a belt earlier that year; a young minister I met at a restaurant who was about to take over a small Virginia parish in which there had recently been several teenage suicides; a woman at a bus stop whose mother, a cancer patient, was considering taking a fatal overdose; a man I met at a party who believed that anyone who *hadn't* considered suicide must not have explored the true meaning of life; a psychiatrist haunted by thoughts of a patient who had killed herself eight years earlier; a young artist who told me that one evening shortly after she had moved to New York City she was eating dinner when the body of an upstairs neighbor fell past her window.

When I began the research that led to this book, I was surprised by the sheer volume of writing on the subject. As I turned from a seventeenth-century clergyman's sermon on the sin of suicide to a neurobiologist's paper on serotonin imbalance to a philosopher's defense of the right to suicide to a novelist's description of a character's suicidal depression, I was struck by how fragmented and lacking in context the literature on suicide seemed. Each book or paper approached the subject from a different perspective, and reflected little knowledge of—or interest in—any insights from outside its own narrow focus. This parochialism was true, too, of the majority of mental health professionals and researchers I interviewed, many of whom were completely unaware of related developments even within their own fields. It is true that as our knowledge of suicide has deepened we have come to realize that the subject involves many different disciplines. Yet it seems to me that a preliminary understanding of suicide is incomplete without some familiarity with all avenues of exploration.

This book is an attempt to bring some of those different vantage points together. It endeavors to put current thinking about suicide into a historical perspective by tracing the way people have thought and felt about the subject during the last four thousand years. It explores the various motives and meanings that suicide may have had to the persons who killed themselves and the explanations offered by so-called experts. It discusses who commits suicide and why certain people and certain groups are more vulnerable than others. It also explores the range of suicide and self-destructive behaviors, including those that do not immediately end in death: alcoholism, Russian roulette, and so on. It looks at the methods of suicide and the meanings those methods may have. It also describes the problems faced by those left behind after a suicide and how they deal with them.

Most people feel that suicide is a tragedy that should be prevented. But how can we prevent it when our understanding of its causes is still imperfect? This book attempts to describe the state of the art of suicide prevention today, in crisis centers, therapists' offices, hospitals, and the halls of government. It also raises the question of whether there are some suicides—those of terminally ill people, for example—in which intervention is inappropriate.

The book opens with a discussion of adolescent suicide. In 1983, as I started my research, a rash of teenage suicides in Plano, Texas, drew the national media's attention. Indeed, the rate of adolescent suicide had nearly tripled since 1950. Suddenly, magazines, newspapers, and television shows trumpeted the "national epidemic" of suicide that seemed to plague upper-middle-class suburbs. And though I was aware that even at its highest the rate of adolescent suicide remained lower than for other groups, I was intrigued by the issues it raised—and by how many of them were the same issues that had been raised for centuries in many different cultures. And so when eight adolescents in the tri-county area north of New York City killed themselves during a four-month period in 1984, I decided to investigate the so-called Westchester cluster. Although every suicide is unique and suicide has different meanings and motives for different groups, according to age, race, religion, and so on, a detailed examination of this particular rash of suicides serves as an introduction and exploration of some issues inherent in all suicides. By beginning with a look at how suicide affected one age group in one area in one year, I hope to offer a window into the larger subject of suicide.

Whenever I told people I was writing a book about suicide, they asked whether I had had a suicide in my family. They were, I think, surprised when I told them the answer was no. I, in turn, was surprised at their assumption that my interest in the topic must have been compelled by some intimate personal experience. After all, what other subject touches so intensely on so many aspects—ethical, psychological, biological, cultural—of human life? Who could not be interested in such a subject? As I worked on the book, I also recalled the times that suicide had touched my life in various ways and with varying degrees of seriousness—my early fascination with Hart Crane, Sylvia Plath, Anne Sexton, and other suicidal writers; the vow I made with my best friend, when we were both caught up in the romantic angst of being sixteen, to swim out to sea and drown if we were still alive at twenty-five; the alcoholism that has frequently blighted my family tree; the pain and confusion I felt in college when I learned that a classmate had jumped to his death from a dormitory window. And although I have never thought seriously of taking my own life, I remember the occasional sudden urge to find out what would happen if I swerved my car into the opposite lane; the desire to find a way to stop living—without dying—when a relationship of many years broke up; the years of excessive drinking in college and graduate school that I realized only later were an expression less of collegial bonhomie than of fear and loneliness.

Certainly, these were relatively tame encounters with self-destruction, no more and probably no less than most people I know have experienced. And I describe them to show not that I am closer to the subject than other people, but that the subject has touched all of us in some way—and to suggest that even the most extreme suicidal depression is but an extension of feelings most of us have had at some point in our lives. By the end of my research I had also come to believe that any of us, if sufficiently pushed by genes, bad luck, ill health, or a combination of these factors, might be drawn to the precipice. Part of my purpose in writing this book is therefore to chip away at some of the barriers our culture erects between "normal" people and "suicidal" people—barriers that I believe we erect from the fear that the difference is so slight.

———————

As the man at the cathedral talked, part of me wanted to stay, to find a place to talk with him over cups of hot coffee, not because I thought he was going to climb the steeple and jump, not because I believed I could get him his former life back, but because he was lonely and depressed and had asked for help. But I saw the evening stretch out before me, filled with the sadness of his life and the dullness of his voice. I thought of my brother waiting in the car, of the drive out to the cozy suburbs to the well-lighted house where dinner was waiting. I thought of how callous the young men on the bus had sounded to me, and my guilt prodded me to stay. But already my brain was furnishing my heart with excuses: This man was probably crazy; this man *wasn't* crazy, and he didn't need my help; I was exhausted after a long day at the conference.

He may have sensed my thoughts, for when I shivered once more, he said kindly, "You're cold. You should go home." He said good-bye, turned, and began to walk away. "Take care," I said. Then, because that sounded lame, I added, ". . . of yourself." I took a step toward the car. "Take care of yourself," I called once more. I opened the door and slid into the warm car. Then I turned and watched him stuff his hands into his pockets and walk away from the church into a dark side street.

1

ADOLESCENT
SUICIDE

—◆—

I

JUSTIN

JUSTIN CHRISTOPHER SPOONHOUR
OCTOBER 10, 1969
10:20 A.M.
7 LB 20 IN

THE GOLD LETTERING stands out against the cover of the white photograph album, now beige with age, coffee-spattered, and held together by tape. Inside, 114 snapshots, with captions written by the proud mother, lovingly document Justin Spoonhour's first few years. *Justin was less than three hours old:* a picture of "Boy Spoonhour" in his hospital bassinet, a white blanket covering all but a puckered face with a pale shadow of hair. *First day home:* his mother, Anne, breastfeeding. *At a month, he was easy to shop with—but where do you put the packages:* Justin asleep in a supermarket shopping cart. *About four and a half months—getting very fat and sassy:* Justin snug in a comfy chair, a grinning, diapered Buddha.

Slowly, in the album's pages, the prunish infant becomes an energetic, red-cheeked child moving happily through a succession of milestones: Justin's first Christmas; Justin sitting up; Justin learning to crawl; Justin's first tooth; Justin standing; Justin beaming *(Working on teeth five and six);* Justin's first birthday; Justin's first step; Justin's second Christmas; Justin standing on a chair *(Pausing for a souvenir photo atop Mt. Everest—I did it all myself).*

From the beginning, Justin Spoonhour was treated like a little adult. "We never talked baby talk to him," says his father, Giles. "We always talked English." Justin responded in kind: His first word was "McGovern" (his parents had volunteered for the senator's 1972 presidential campaign), and his first sentence was "MerrillLynchBullishAmerica." He was raised on a diet of "Sesame Street" and "The Electric Company." Even after he learned how to change channels, he spurned cartoons and stayed tuned to the educational television station. The Spoonhours' house in Putnam Valley, New York, was crammed with books, and Justin was reading before he entered kindergarten.

At elementary school, Justin's precociousness was not the only thing that set him apart from his classmates—there was also his appearance. Justin seemed to have a permanent rumple. His blond hair often hung down to his shoulders, uncombed; his shirts were untucked, his clothes unironed, his sneakers untied, and his fly frequently unzipped. He suffered from a bedwetting problem until the age of eleven. Doctors prescribed an antidiuretic, but it helped only temporarily. His parents set an alarm clock in his bedroom so he could go to the bathroom in the middle of the night, but by then it was often too late. The problem embarrassed Justin, and Anne and Giles didn't want to make him more self-conscious by questioning him. So each morning Anne would check his sheets and remind Justin to take a bath before school. Occasionally he forgot. At school he became a target for teasing: "Justin, you greaseball, did you ever hear of soap?" To his classmates the issue wasn't that Justin was messy so much as that he was peculiar. One morning he arrived at school wearing a three-piece suit for no apparent reason. At lunch the other children giggled and discussed how "stupid" it was. And even though he had worn a suit, they noticed, his hair was still uncombed.

Justin dismissed the teasing with a cutting remark or a simple "shut up." He never got into fights; he just walked away. At recess, while his classmates played, he usually sat alone, and when the class split into groups for an activity, Justin was always left out until the teacher chose a group for him. He was rarely invited to his classmates' houses, and although his parents encouraged it, he seldom brought anyone home from school. Justin's few friends tended, like him, to be on the fringes of grade school society: a foster child with a wild temper; a chubby boy with glasses and an attaché case; a shy boy who stuttered. On the rare occasions that Justin did bring home a friend, they inevitably quarreled and ended up playing alone. While his grades were good, Justin's marks for "cooperation" were low. "It wasn't so much 'Justin doesn't get along,'" says Anne, "as 'Justin doesn't even relate.'"

Anne and Giles weren't as concerned as some parents might be that their son was "different." They were "different" themselves. Their three-bedroom home in Lookout Manor, a small, isolated neighborhood, had a somewhat anarchic air. Four or five cats had the run of the house, dishes often went unwashed, and tilted pictures were likely to remain that way. "Housekeeping," admits Anne, "was not a high priority." Giles and Anne had no rules about dress or hair. They dressed casually themselves and paid little attention to what was in or out of style. "Giles and Anne were nonconformist from the word go," says a townsperson. "And they chose to live in a community where conformity is the watchword."

Putnam Valley, fifty miles north of New York City, had been settled by farmers in the eighteenth century. By the early twentieth century it was principally a summer resort. After World War II, when newly built highways made commuting to Manhattan possible, people moved into the summer houses and lived there year-round. Today, Putnam Valley is a conservative, largely middle-class bedroom community of about ten thousand people (the population doubles in summer), many of whom commute to Manhattan. Although Putnam Valley is growing, its residents are spread over a wide area, and the community still has a rural feel. The commuter train doesn't stop there, and the closest thing to a town center is Oregon Corners, a group of shops clustered around a four-way intersection. "This is a very small town," says the town librarian. "There's a great deal of interaction among citizens and a great deal of knowledge about one another." As the local newsweekly, *The Community Current,* observes, "There are no secrets in Putnam Valley."

Anne grew up in Putnam Valley in the early fifties. Her parents were what some townspeople would call "senior hippies." Her father, who managed a millionaire's estate, wore his hair in a ponytail, and their house was a haven for stray cats, hitchhikers, and runaways. Local schoolteachers still remember Anne as an exceptionally gifted student. They also remember how willful and independent she was. At various times she wanted to be a veterinarian, a rodeo rider, a Formula 1 race car driver, a police officer. After two years as a drama student at Ithaca College, she returned home to live with her parents and work at a nearby department store. Every Monday night she drove to the Friars of the Atonement Seminary in Garrison to play the flute in their folk masses. There she met Giles Spoonhour, a tall priest with a surprisingly soft voice, blue eyes, and a sudden, booming laugh. "He was very different from most men I knew—better read, better spoken," says Anne. "He was more tolerant and compassionate. And he wanted to make changes in the world." She and Giles talked earnestly about religion, politics, and Vietnam, and found they agreed on most counts. They even shared a passion for science fiction.

Giles was the oldest of three brothers raised in a conservative Catholic family in Chicago. As his son Justin would be, Giles was a precocious, somewhat withdrawn child. He planned on becoming a mechanical engineer, but halfway through the Illinois Institute of Technology he met an elderly woman who ran a Catholic retreat outside the city. Their long philosophical talks convinced Giles there was more to the world than engineering, and despite opposition from his parents, he entered the priesthood. However, after thirteen years as a theology student, parochial school teacher, and parish priest, Giles became disillusioned with the orthodoxy of the church. He wanted to marry and have children. By the time he met Anne he had decided to leave the priesthood. Several months later Giles left the seminary, and he and Anne were married.

Settling down in Putnam Valley, the Spoonhours put their political convictions into practice. As a social worker in Peekskill, Giles counseled troubled families. Anne became a reporter for Putnam Valley's weekly newspaper, writing spirited articles and editorials. They were active in the Democratic Club and belonged to a discussion group that explored new directions in Christianity. Although Giles had left the priesthood, he continued to perform weddings and baptisms as a member of the Federation of Christian Ministries, which stirred up gossip and occasional criticism in the strongly Catholic town. While Anne was admired for her energy and conviction, she had too much substance for those in town who concentrated on style. "Anne uses long words and doesn't do small talk," says a friend. "At eleven in the morning people want to talk about their shopping, their mothers-in-law, and their children. Anne wants to talk about the plight of the American Indian." After reading an article in *Newsweek* about the problems of ethnic and handicapped adoptees, Giles and Anne decided to adopt at least one "hard-to-place" child. Three years after Justin was born, his parents adopted Leah, an eighteen-month-old black albino girl from Louisiana. She and Justin soon developed a fierce sibling rivalry.

If their classmates were encouraged by their parents to achieve in grades and sports, Justin and Leah were encouraged to become independent, morally responsible individuals. "We assumed they would go to college, but they were going to be whatever they bloody well wanted to be," says Anne. "We encouraged them not to just go with the herd. We wanted to bring them up as reasonably pacifist and humane people." She pauses. "Do you encourage a kid to be a conformist for the sake of his own happiness, or do you cross your fingers and hope he has enough strength of character to tolerate the kind of singling out he's going to get if he's different—and maybe survive it to be happy later on?"

When Justin was eight, he told his parents that he wanted to join the Cub Scouts. They bought him a blue uniform and drove him back and forth to den meetings. But Justin didn't like it. "He really wasn't into making like a little Indian and doing crafty stuff and being a cub and a bear and a wolf and a Webelo and all that junior fraternity stuff," says Anne. "I don't know how much of that attitude he may have absorbed from me because I was not an organization person. Boy Scouts are great for kids who are going to be back slappers and chummy and rah-rah all their lives. But for somebody who is being raised as an individual, somebody who really wants to do things of significance or do nothing, that's not where it's at." After a half-dozen meetings, Justin stopped going.

Justin seemed more interested in creating his own world than in fitting into any preexisting social structure. Far more fascinating to him than the nature hikes and knot-tying of the Cub Scouts were the cosmic realms of Middle Earth or outer space. In his reading, Justin was drawn to fantasy and science fiction. He devoured books such as Madeleine L'Engle's *A Wrinkle in Time,* and when his fourth grade class was assigned the first volume of C. S. Lewis's *Chronicles of Narnia,* he quickly went on to finish the rest of the series. Then he read and reread Tolkien's *The Lord of the Rings.* He spent his allowance on comic books—*Superman, Superboy,* and *Legion of Super-Heroes.* He saw the film *Star Wars* several times and decorated his room with posters of Luke Skywalker and Darth Vader, and with models of intergalactic spacecraft.

Although Justin had few friends his own age, he got along well with the younger children in his neighborhood, and they often played war in the woods across the street from the Spoonhour house. Unlike school, this was a society in which Justin was the leader. He made himself the general, and his "soldiers" admired the elaborate worlds he created, complete with secret salutes, codes of conduct, and court-martials. When Justin chose to do something, he threw himself into it, planning it down to the last detail, and when others didn't fit in the way he'd imagined—if a neighborhood soldier didn't carry out orders according to military protocol—he could get exasperated and angry. He had a clear sense of how he felt the world ought to operate. Anne remembers taking him for a riding lesson and seeing him get thrown from the horse. "He grabbed the reins and started to get back on, but first he looked the horse in the eye and very reasonably explained, 'Now listen, horse, you're not supposed to do that because I'm supposed to be the boss and I'm on top!' "

Justin spent most of his time alone in his room at the rear of the house, reading or listening to the radio. From his mother he inherited a taste for folk and classical music, which developed into a passion for Bach, Mozart, and, above all, Beethoven. His favorite piece of music was the Ninth Symphony. Justin's room, cluttered with bric-a-brac collected at flea markets, was usually a mess, his bed rarely made, his clothes on the floor, his baseball gloves and archery bows in a corner. Justin had built his own bookshelves where he kept his Narnia set, Tolkien books, Peanuts comic books, *Mad* magazine anthologies, Plato's *Meno, 2500 Insults,* Asterix comics, *The Encyclopedia of American History,* and the *World Book Encyclopedia* his parents had bought when he was five. His library overran the shelves into boxes on the floor; whenever his parents couldn't find one of their own books, they knew where to look. On one wall was a huge Confederate flag an uncle had given him. On another wall was an old map of Putnam County. Justin covered a third wall with aluminum foil, partly to brighten and partly to warm the poorly insulated room. On his door Justin posted a sign:

DO NOT DISTURB
DO NOT ENTER
TRESPASSERS WILL BE SHOT
5 CENTS TO ENTER

Justin's affinity for spending time alone was encouraged by the demands of the Spoonhour household. When Justin was three, Giles took a new job as a drug counselor in New York City, a two-hour commute each way. By the time the children were stirring at 7 A.M., he was usually gone. Anne worked odd hours at the newspaper, was trying her hand at writing novels, and served as a volunteer on the town's ambulance corps. Giles's and Anne's community activities kept their schedules erratic, and one or both of them were often busy in the evenings. "There was a certain amount of running in and out and coming and going," says Anne, "but we tried to make it a point to schedule a couple of meals a week together." If she and Giles weren't going to be home for dinner, Anne left a casserole for the children to heat up. If that wasn't possible, Justin and Leah were capable of fixing themselves something to eat. Justin had been cooking since he was seven and enjoyed it. Sometimes, however, it was as if four self-reliant grown-ups were sharing the house at Lookout Manor.

Justin and Leah were treated as adults partly from the necessity of their parents' schedules and partly because that was the way their parents had been raised. "I was not spanked, I was reasoned with," remembers Anne, "and I tried to do the same with Justin." Anne proudly recalls being complimented by a woman who'd seen her in school with Justin and Leah. "She was very impressed because I was explaining things to the kids as though they were adults." Giles also tried to reason with his children, but occasionally his temper would explode. "When I was in a disciplining state of mind, I had a tendency to get very loud," he says, "and I know that this was scary for Justin and Leah." A sports fan who got so excited he would shout himself hoarse at games, Giles coached some of the town's recreational teams. In Justin's sixth grade year, Giles coached him in midget basketball. Justin, who was not naturally athletic, played second string. "I tried not to single him out for special consideration or special criticism," says Giles. "I tried to treat him like all the other boys." Yet several parents remarked at how much more exacting he was of Justin. One woman got quite upset at baseball games because Giles yelled at Justin if he struck out.

Yet there were many moments of family happiness. At unexpected times Justin would sneak up behind Anne and give her a hug. "You're a good little mommy," he'd say. Giles and Justin occasionally threw a football, played chess, or went swimming in nearby Lake Oscawana. His mother often invited him along when she drove into Oregon Corners on errands, and they talked earnestly about politics or ecology. On weekends the Spoonhours picked apples and strawberries together, browsed flea markets, went to church, and occasionally ate out, sometimes at a restaurant, sometimes at McDonald's or Burger King. And though Justin usually went to his room after dinner, sometimes the family watched "M*A*S*H," with Giles's laughter booming over the rest, or went to a movie. Or they would be out driving in Anne's beat-up '69 Chevy Nova, with the sound track to *Peter Pan* on the tape deck, and she and Leah and Justin would belt out, "I Won't Grow Up."

At school Justin was a step ahead of most of his classmates—at least in the subjects that interested him. The consensus on his report cards was, "Brilliant but doesn't try." Some things came easily to him, and he invested little effort in those that didn't. When his grades slipped, he could usually buckle down in time to get his accustomed B average by semester's end. But unlike his classmates he didn't agonize over grades. In sixth grade, because of his high I.Q., Justin was placed in an accelerated program for gifted children. While others in the project lorded their status over their classmates, Justin didn't seem to care; he skipped assignments, floundered through the program, and was not asked back the following year. When it appeared Justin might be held back a class because his grades were so poor, Giles and Anne took him to a psychologist. Justin was placed in a group with other youngsters who lacked what the school tactfully called "socialization skills." They met once a week to play games, talk, and eat pizza.

Though Justin had few friends his own age, he got along well with adults. At school he sought out the company of teachers, with whom he had vigorous philosophical discussions about ecology, nuclear disarmament, and the state of the world. What his classmates saw as "different," many adults saw as "special." Lora Porter, the Putnam Valley librarian since 1965, never thought of Justin as peculiar, perhaps because she, too, as she says, is considered "a bit of a kook." Justin, who felt at home at the library from an early age, delighted Porter by asking her to recommend books for him. The summer after Justin's seventh grade year, Anne would drop him and Leah off at the library on her way to the newspaper office. They spent the day there, reading and helping out at the children's story hour. "I always sort of knew they hadn't had breakfast," says Porter, "so I'd send Justin to the store down the road for some rolls and oranges."

Like many others, Porter treated Justin as an adult. "There was no other way to treat him." When she became embroiled in a controversy over whether a fundamentalist group should be allowed to use the library for meetings, she talked about it with Justin. "His mother had written some strong articles in the paper supporting my civil liberties position. Justin had read them, and he brought up the subject when he came to the library. Though he was very young, he discussed the issue with the understanding of a mature mind. I remember him saying, 'I guess you really have to take a stand.' "

Justin and Leah became the official library puppeteers, putting on shows for children during vacations. Starting with theatrical kits, Justin designed and embellished sets for a series of fairy tales. For *Rumpelstiltskin* he found some straw and sprayed it with gilt to resemble the gold the dwarf spun from straw. He and Porter had lengthy deliberations about lighting techniques and sound effects. "We discussed the shows as if we were Mike Nichols and his producer," she remembers. Using the library's elaborate puppet theater, Justin, Leah, and two of Leah's friends performed *Puss in Boots, The Three Little Pigs,* and *Hansel and Gretel* for flocks of small children who sat on the floor in open-mouthed awe. Justin, working several puppets at once, expertly adapted his voice to each character. When the play was over, Lora Porter asked the puppeteers to step out from behind the red velvet curtain. When Justin heard the applause, his face always broke into a huge smile.

As Justin entered adolescence, the contrast between him and his peers grew still sharper. At Putnam Valley Junior High, Justin's class gradually sifted into cliques. "There were three groups," explains one of his classmates. "There was the cool group, the burnouts. They were the kids who were the first to start smoking, drank a lot, used drugs, talked back to teachers, and spent a lot of time in detention. Then there was the sort of easygoing group—not trying to be tough, not real burnouts, a little bit academic. Then there were the losers—kids who couldn't do sports, who were ugly, or who didn't really care much about anything. Maybe they liked one another, but nobody liked them. And then there was Justin. He was a group in himself."

Justin obviously wasn't cool, and he was too intense to be in the easygoing group. He didn't qualify for the losers' group either. He wasn't ugly—a girl in his class grudgingly admits that, combed and washed, "he would have looked just as good as anybody else." Although he didn't excel in sports, he wasn't hopeless. And though he cared about many things, the things he cared about were, to his classmates, the wrong things. He preferred chess to checkers, cats to dogs, archery to soccer. He preferred reading to hanging out at the Jefferson Valley Mall. After school, when most seventh grade boys were playing ball, Justin was one of three males to sing in the school chorus. While his classmates' Walkmans were tuned to rock, the radio in Justin's room was tuned to classical. In music class when the students were asked to present reports, virtually everyone chose rock bands and snickered as they stood in front of the class playing tapes by Prince, Black Sabbath, or The Cars. Justin chose Beethoven. He brought in an armful of articles and books, played a recording of a piano concerto, and clenched his fists with passion as he described Beethoven's work.

In junior high "cool" boys wore concert jerseys with pictures of rock groups, Harley-Davidson T-shirts, designer jeans, and Members Only jackets. Justin wore flannel shirts, jeans that were usually too baggy and too short, and black dress shoes or dirty white high-top sneakers with the laces untied. Once when his mother bought him a pair of designer jeans, Justin made sure to cut off the label before wearing them. While the athletes preened in shorts and T-shirts in gym no matter how cold the weather, Justin wore a stained oversized sweatsuit. Whatever he wore was unironed, untucked, often unwashed, and sometimes backward. His classmates hurled insults: "Wash your hair." "Is that the only shirt you own?" "You smell." "Why do you listen to that classical crap?" "Get a life." Justin would shrug off their taunts, which made his tormenters all the madder. Justin wasn't like them, but he didn't seem to *want* to be like them. Says one classmate, "He brought most of this stuff on himself by not trying to fit in."

Even when Justin tried to fit in, he was not allowed. In seventh grade he persuaded the track coach to let him be team manager. He traveled with the squad to their meets, cheered for his classmates, and kept careful records of their times. Justin was proud of his position, and he had letters put on the back of his sweatshirt that spelled out "Track Manager." But while the team admitted Justin did a thorough job, he remained an outcast. "Theoretically, he was part of the team, but nobody really liked him," says a team member. "On bus trips he sat up front with the coaches or by himself because he knew nobody else would sit with him, or if he sat with somebody, they'd just give him heck all the way there or hold their nose or something like that." Justin managed the team for two years. Eventually, the letters on his sweatshirt started to fall off, and it read, "   CK   AG R."

There were occasional moments of acceptance: when Justin made a difficult move in a basketball game; when he had a solo in the school chorus. In seventh grade, after a minor hip operation, his classmates clamored to borrow his crutches, and suddenly Justin was the center of attention. But after two weeks the crutches were gone and so was the attention.

Mike LoPuzzo was the closest thing to a friend Justin had. Although he was considered part of the easygoing group, Mike himself was a little different—for his music report in seventh grade, Mike had chosen to explicate the genius of Frank Sinatra. He dressed neatly, wore his hair short and cleanly parted, and carried a briefcase to school. He was earnest, tolerant, and precocious, qualities not highly prized by his peers. But because he was a big, strong fellow, he wasn't teased much. He had watched the kids badger Justin since fifth grade when his family moved to Putnam Valley from the Bronx, and although he had occasionally chimed in, he felt sorry for Justin and admired the way he handled the situation. In seventh and eighth grades, when the class divided into groups for a project, Mike didn't groan like the others when the teacher put Justin in his group, and they occasionally talked about school, movies, and books. Sometimes Justin brought in collections of Doonesbury cartoons to show him—Justin was partial to Zonker, a long-haired, leftover sixties type. Mike found Justin interesting to talk to and liked his dry sense of humor. But, says Mike, they never ate lunch together, talked on the phone, or saw each other outside school. "Justin never said a word about his parents or his home life," says Mike. "He never talked about girls or about problems. He never talked about his personal life, and he never asked me about mine."

Nor did Justin ever talk about being teased. "It never seemed to bother him—he was always a happy-go-lucky kind of person," says Mike. "He would just put his head down and say, 'Aaargh.' No matter how all the students were down on him, he always seemed to bounce back." Mike once asked Justin why he didn't wash his hair. "If you washed and combed it, then people wouldn't bother you," he said. Justin shrugged, and Mike didn't press it. "To me it seemed like such a simple solution, but to him maybe it was symbolic," says Mike. "Maybe he was trying to send the world a message: 'Does physical appearance matter that much? What's important is inside.' Besides, Justin had more important things to worry about, like Beethoven and Shakespeare."

But even Mike admits that he may have drawn back a little from Justin: "Sometimes I was afraid that other people would treat me like they treated him." In May 1983 the eighth grade took its annual four-day trip to Washington, D.C. "We chose roommates before we went down," says Mike, "four to a room. Me and two friends were together in one room. Naturally, nobody wanted Justin. I think he was just hoping for someone to ask him, so I said, 'Yeah, come on with us.' " When they arrived at their hotel after the four-hour bus ride, everyone was excited and rambunctious. "We started messing up Justin's bed," says Mike. "He'd make it up, and then we'd pull it apart again. We got a little carried away. Justin was on the verge of tears. I'd never seen him that upset before. We kept apologizing, but he wouldn't talk to us. Later I went over to him and said, 'Geez, I'm sorry, Justin, we were only kidding around. We didn't mean to hurt your feelings.' He said it was all right, and we shook hands." It was the only time Mike ever saw the teasing get to Justin.

Giles and Anne were aware that Justin was teased. "It had come up a couple of times in conferences," says Anne, "but I had not bothered to go to them for a couple of years. I got tired of hearing the same thing that my mother heard about me and what I'm sure Giles's parents heard about him, and what every parent under the sun hears in conferences: 'Your little bastard isn't working up to his full potential.' Well, I say if he isn't disruptive in class, let's let it go. If he stares out the window, well, so did Edison. For that matter they thought Einstein was retarded." At his son's basketball games, Giles overheard jokes about Justin's bedwetting and his sloppy clothes. He once saw one of

Justin's teammates throw a basketball at him on the sidelines. At home Giles would ask him about the teasing, but Justin would dismiss it, saying, "Ah, they're just idiots."

Justin's eccentricities exasperated even his teachers. He was often late to class, rarely raised his hand unless the topic interested him, and turned in careless work. "I think some of the teachers had almost the same attitude that we kids did," says one of his classmates. "They wanted to avoid him. They wouldn't go out of their way to call on him or make him comfortable. When Justin didn't turn in his homework in English class, the teacher would get mad at him. There was another kid who didn't do his assignments either, but the teacher laughed at him because he was really lovable. But Justin wasn't, so she'd get annoyed. In homeroom my friend and I came in late almost every day. The teacher would smile and shake his head. But when Justin was late, he'd get pretty perturbed." And although some teachers welcomed Justin's extracurricular attention, others were less receptive. "Justin always tried to hang around with the teachers, maybe because he had no friends," says a classmate. "Some of them would sort of ignore him, or they'd wave him off—like 'not this kid again.' They didn't treat him badly, but they treated him like an outsider just as much as the kids did."

And yet Justin seemed to relish being different. As treasurer of the Grace United Methodist Church Youth Group, he concocted elaborate fund-raising schemes such as breakfasts and bake sales while the other five children planned football games, video parties, and trips to the beach. When one of his ideas was rejected, Justin immediately tried to devise another project that would meet with their approval. The group expected Justin to hatch grand ideas; it was a running joke that Justin always wanted to be president of something. Justin often seemed to delight in dissenting just for the sake of testing his peers. When everyone else voted for an adventure movie like *Superman* for a pizza and video party, Justin fought for a classic Western or *Star Wars* although they'd all seen it before. One time when the group was planning the music for a party, Justin said he wouldn't attend because he liked only classical music. After all the arguing, however, Justin usually went along with the majority.

"He had his clashes with his peers, but on the whole I think he related rather well," says Marion Cox, pastor at Grace United Methodist and leader of its Youth Group. "I don't think he had an enemy in our group. There were times when he would take the opposite tack from everyone else and just push and push and push, and the kids would get down on him. But it was never unfriendly. They'd just say, 'Oh, that's Justin.' " Cox had moved to Putnam Valley a few years before and was still getting settled in the community. "He and Justin got along famously," says Anne Spoonhour. "Justin was aware that Reverend Cox was something of an outsider." Justin appreciated Cox's corny jokes, and he liked to tease him that his sermons were too long and "dry as dust." Cox, who was married but had no children, took something of a paternal interest in Justin. "He was a very lively boy with an impish sense of humor," says Cox. "He liked to test you. But just as you were about to get exasperated, he'd have a twinkle in his eye as if to say, 'Now really, don't take it all *that* seriously.' "

During the summer after the eighth grade, Justin spent a week at a Methodist youth camp near Stone Ridge, New York. It was his first time away from home. The dozen campers slept in lean-tos and cooked their own meals. Justin loved it, but he came on a bit strong at first, giving orders just as he did as "general" of his neighborhood army. The night before the campers returned home, the pastor who led the camp held a small communion service. As part of the service he told the campers, "Before you take the sacraments, if you feel there's something you need to say to someone because you haven't understood him rightly or perhaps you mistreated him in some way, now is the time to apologize." There was a pause, and then all eleven campers lined up in front of Justin.

The next fall Justin entered ninth grade at Putnam Valley Junior High. In the previous year he had grown rapidly. "Every time I looked up, he seemed to have grown another inch and put on another ten pounds," says Giles. At five-eleven and 140 pounds, Justin was gangly but broad-shouldered. The features on his round face had grown larger and sharper. When Lora Porter saw him at Christmastime, she noticed how much he looked like his father. Anne bought him a new sports jacket, brown corduroy with elbow patches, size 20 collegiate.

That same fall Leah entered seventh grade. Although her appearance—a tall, skinny body topped by a pale face and a shock of frizzy white hair—made her a more obvious target for teasing than her brother, Leah possessed a certain sheer nerve that drew people to her. She quickly found herself at the center of a tight circle of friends; whatever the "norm" was that Justin wasn't part of, Leah was at its core. While Justin ate alone at lunch in his last year at the school, his sister, in her first year, was surrounded by giggling friends. Unlike Justin, Leah was often asked home by her friends, and they frequently visited the Spoonhour house for afternoons and sleepovers. Justin would arrive home to find Leah and her cronies gossiping to a background of Michael Jackson, AC/DC, and Kiss. He would groan and yell at them to keep quiet. "You're weird," the girls would answer. "Why don't you go read a book," Justin replied scornfully. "Don't you do anything with your head except wear hair on it?"

Justin and Leah's rivalry had always been strong, though no worse than that of other siblings their age, Anne and Giles thought. They were intensely competitive playing board games, and at Youth Group meetings they occasionally argued. Justin needled Leah about her marathon telephone calls, her cooking, and her taste in books and television, while she teased him about his taste in TV. Their musical preferences were a particular problem; their parents finally decreed that they must alternate afternoons in control of the stereo. Genuine love lay beneath the teasing, Anne believes.

Justin seemed to be making slow social progress of his own. That summer his psychologist had agreed that Justin didn't need the socialization group anymore. And while Justin had no real friends, he had a small circle of what Anne calls "associates" with whom he played Dungeons and Dragons, a fantasy role-playing game. Given the basic instruction manual for his thirteenth birthday, he quickly became an avid player. He spent long hours alone in his room filling stacks of notebook paper with maps, sketches of new characters, and equations calculating the characters' chances for survival. He occasionally played the game with a few people at recess or at lunch. Although Justin rarely used the telephone, since discovering "D and D" he might call a classmate to discuss a character he had just created or to make plans for a D and D session. In October for his fourteenth birthday he asked his parents for a D and D party. A half-dozen boys arrived at noon and stayed through the evening, poring over battle plans at the dining room table, filling up on pizza and popcorn, and taking occasional breaks to throw a football in the yard.

Justin had another way to step out of his own world into one over which he had more control. He had grown up listening to his parents' recordings of *West Side Story* and *The Fantasticks,* and had attended several Broadway shows on school trips or with his parents. After seeing *Can-Can* on the eighth grade trip to Washington, D.C., Justin said, "When I grow up, I want to be rich enough to be a Broadway producer so I can revive all the good old musicals." He also talked about an acting career. In eighth grade he played the title role in the school production of *Whatever Happened to Ebenezer Scrooge?,* a contemporary sequel to Dickens's *A Christmas Carol.* He threw himself into the character of the crotchety old miser, wearing his nonprescription spectacles offstage, nattering on in his "Scrooge" voice. "When he got a role, he took it very seriously," remembers Anne. "He would truly identify with the character." Although Drama Club was hardly the cool thing for Putnam Valley boys, his classmates had to admit that Justin was talented.

In ninth grade he was cast as a curmudgeonly senator in *Outrageous Fortune.* Playing opposite him was Diana Wolf, a classmate who had also been in *Scrooge.* "At first it was like I didn't want to shake his hand, but the drama teacher took me aside and said, 'He's different—just give him a chance.'" Diana and Justin got along fairly well. In *Outrageous Fortune,* Justin had some trouble with his lengthy role, particularly with one long speech. "He knew his lines, but he was so nervous he'd start stuttering and garbling the words," says Diana. "He'd get frustrated and ask to start again." She and Justin devised a remedy. "At one point he was supposed to be showing me something in his briefcase, so we taped some of his lines in there." Opening night did not go well for Justin. Before the curtain he wanted to make his hair neat for the show. He went from cast member to cast member asking to borrow a comb. Each of them said sorry, he didn't have one. Onstage, recalls Diana, "he messed up so badly we all had to cover for him." When his mother saw the production, however, she was impressed. "Most of the kids acted the way eighth and ninth graders act—flat line readings with a lot of hesitation and missed cues. But Justin *was* that senator."

Onstage Justin seemed to be able to express things more freely than he could in real life. In *Scrooge,* Justin's character had legions of elves working for him. "Justin really liked the role because he got to be in charge," says a cast member. "Usually people picked on him and didn't listen to him. But in the show he was the boss, and he could yell at people." Similarly, in *Outrageous Fortune,* Justin played another adult who got to tell off the other characters.

Offstage Justin was less and less able to attract attention. "After a while I think people got used to him, and they just ignored him, which probably drove him even more crazy," says a classmate. "I guess it's more or less like a wart on your foot. First it bothers you, then you think it's gross, and then after a while you just don't notice it anymore."

At home Justin kept his problems hidden. Anne had taken a job as a dispatcher for the Putnam Valley Police Department and worked many evenings; Giles commuted to his job in Manhattan. Although their schedule of volunteer activities was busier than ever, they believe they spent as much time as they could with their children, as much as most parents. If Justin needed more, he didn't show it. "Very rarely would he approach us to talk about things or ask for help," says Giles. "Very rarely would he take the initiative." Adds Anne, "But it's not as if he was taking his problems to anyone else as far as we know. He just didn't express his problems, period." It was difficult to tell when Justin was upset. He rarely raised his voice and never threw tantrums; when angry, he grew quiet and disappeared into his room. Occasionally, however, Justin left a curious clue to his mood. Several times Giles came home to find a pile of wood shavings on the living room floor. When he asked Justin about it, he learned that Justin, exasperated over the failure of some scheme, had taken a knife and a stick and begun whittling.

As Justin grew older, Giles felt frustrated at not being closer to his son. "I would have liked to have more conversations with him about what was going on in his life," he says. "I remember going through a lot of turmoil in my own adolescence and not having anyone I could sit down and talk to. I never had heart-to-heart talks with my father, and I was looking forward to having them with my son. I was hoping that as he became interested in girls, we could talk about that. I had ideas that I wanted to share with him about what to say and what to do and what not to say and what not to do."

But Justin rarely talked about girls. "In a lot of ways he didn't know what he was yet," says Anne. "Sex almost didn't enter the picture yet. He was still in the 'girls are to throw rocks at' stage." Justin spoke admiringly of a young actress on "Buck Rogers," and once, chatting with his mother, he mentioned a girl he had known in seventh grade who was, he allowed, "pretty okay." But as far as Anne knows, Justin never mentioned his feelings to the girl. "He was very male-oriented," says Giles. "He did not seem to have much of an interest in girls. I was a little concerned about that." Girls were even less interested in Justin. When asked what his female classmates thought of him, one girl responds matter-of-factly, "Nothing." She explains: "No girl would go out with him because it would be so damaging to her reputation. I mean unless she were incredibly ugly or drugged out, she wouldn't be seen with him unless he totally changed."

Giles attempted to get closer to his son. "I tried to do it as naturally as possible," he says. "I didn't want to make a point of 'okay, now we're going to sit down and talk.' There were times that we would talk about things, and I was hoping that from general worldwide problems we could get down to specifics in his own life. But I was not very successful in getting him to open up." Though the issue of sex came up, it tended to come up as another dinner table topic, like world hunger or nuclear proliferation. "I can't remember having a 'man-to-man' talk with him or anything like that," says Giles. "It was always in a family context with his mother and me and sometimes even his sister there. We would talk about it in general, about young people getting involved sexually."

In November, Giles and Justin watched "The Day After," a made-for-TV movie depicting the aftermath of a nuclear holocaust. Justin, who tended to take the world's problems to heart, had often fretted over the disarmament issue. When the program was over, Giles could tell that Justin was upset. "I knew it had a strong impact on him because ordinarily he talked about these things, but this time he didn't. He seemed dispirited." Giles tried to draw him out but was unsuccessful. "It was as if he were in a state of shock and couldn't talk about it," he says. "He seemed to get the feeling that nuclear destruction was almost inevitable." That night Justin lay awake and wept, thinking about the movie and what could happen. The next day he wrote a letter to President Reagan saying that he had been so concerned about the threat of nuclear holocaust that he hadn't slept. Couldn't we find a better way of solving our problems? Justin never mailed the letter.

As the New Year began, Justin was brimming with plans. He intended to perform puppet shows at the library during February recess. He had started writing science fiction stories. He had arranged John Denver's song "Perhaps Love" as a solo with chorus backup and planned to audition with it for the spring musical. He was excited about returning to camp—this time he wanted to stay for two weeks. He was trying to persuade his parents to let him attend a summer Dungeons and Dragons convention in Minnesota. He was already talking about what kind of party he wanted for his fifteenth birthday the following October, and he was campaigning for a new archery bow as a Junior High School graduation present. "It's only $169, Mom," he'd plead as he danced around her. "I really need it if I'm going to be an Olympic archer in 1992."

In February his Honors English class read *Julius Caesar* aloud. Justin, who adored Shakespeare, lugged his massive two-volume edition of the complete plays into class each day, but the teacher, exasperated, told him he had to use the same edition as the other students. Justin won the role of Caesar, which he read with great feeling and flourish. Though he tended to show off a bit, the class was impressed.

On Sunday evening, February 12, there was a Youth Group meeting. Justin had pushed for the session, at which he unveiled an elaborate scheme to raise funds for scholarships to camp. He proposed a flea market and barbecue modeled on the church's annual barn sale. Reverend Cox didn't want to quash Justin's enthusiasm, but he said it didn't seem practical. He suggested a car wash or a bake sale. He promised to discuss Justin's plan at the next board meeting. The other boys and girls in the group agreed that Justin's project was too complicated. Although Justin quickly changed the subject and proposed that next week his parents talk to the group about their work in emergency services, Cox could tell that Justin felt deflated. That evening when Giles picked up his son, he asked him how the meeting had gone. "Well," said Justin, "they shot me down again." They talked about it a little on the way home, and Giles knew Justin was disappointed because he was so quiet.

Tuesday, February 14, was Valentine's Day. Justin was up in time to have a quick breakfast with his father before Giles left for work. Then he and Leah caught the bus for school. That morning Justin got a French test back. He had done very well and showed his paper to Mike LoPuzzo, to his guidance counselor, and to anyone else who would look. "This is the best I ever did," he exulted. After lunch Reverend Cox happened to be at the school discussing plans for the annual career day with the principal when Justin walked into the office. Cox, remembering Justin's defeat at Youth Group, asked him how he was doing. Justin said he was fine and told Cox about his success on the French test. In English class that afternoon Justin performed the role of Caesar with his customary panache.

At the end of class the teacher handed out Valentine's Day carnations. Each year the Student Council took orders for flowers at one dollar apiece, and at the end of the school day on February 14 they were distributed. Coaches bought them for members of their teams; friends bought them for friends; and some bought them for classmates they had crushes on. While popular students received several—one pretty ninth grader received eight—some people didn't get any. Justin, of course, was one of them. "I don't think it bothered him," says a classmate. "I'm sure he didn't send one, so I'm sure he didn't expect to receive any." Justin told Mike he would bring him another book of Doonesbury cartoons tomorrow.

When Anne returned from shopping at three, Justin and Leah were already home from school. She had bought Justin some jelly beans and a valentine but decided to save them until Giles got home so that he could sign the card too. Justin was out playing with a friend. Anne called him in and kissed him good-bye, then left for her four-to-midnight shift as police dispatcher. When Giles arrived home around 6:30, it was already cold and dark. Leah was inside playing with a friend. Giles asked her where her brother was. Leah said she had gone out for a while and when she'd returned, Justin was gone. Giles thought this was a little odd. On the living room floor there was a pile of wood shavings.

Giles went outside and called for Justin. When he chooses to use it, Giles has a booming voice that carries quite a distance; often when Justin was out playing or even when he was indoors at a friend's house, Giles would call to him and Justin would hear and come home. This time there was no answer. Giles grew concerned. He telephoned some of the neighbors and the parents of some of Justin's classmates. No one had seen him. Between calls Giles went to the door and shouted his son's name into the night.

Giles worried that Justin had fallen and hurt himself or that he might have made wisecracks to some older teenagers and they had ganged up on him and beaten him. Once before when Justin had disappeared, that is what Giles had feared. Justin, eleven at the time, had been with friends at Lake Oscawana, about a half-mile from home. By dusk Giles and Anne were worried and had called his friends, who said Justin had walked home alone hours before them. Giles recruited some neighbors, and they had fanned out and searched the neighborhood all the way to the lake, calling his name. They didn't find him. They called the police, who hurried over. While Giles and Anne were in the living room telling the police what they knew, in walked Justin, rubbing his eyes, wondering what all the fuss was about. He had been asleep for hours in the storage room and had just awakened.

By 10:30, Giles had tried everyone he could think of. He called Anne, who thought of some more people to call. At 11:15, Giles called Anne again and said he was really worried and wanted her to come home. Anne arranged for someone else to finish her shift. A friend at the station offered to help, and grabbing a couple of battery-powered searchlights, they drove quickly to Lookout Manor. When they got home, the three of them began searching the neighborhood, calling Justin's name. Giles looked around the rocks where Justin and his band liked to play war; Anne searched the yard. Then she and her friend crossed the road and walked into the woods, their flashlights cutting tunnels of light in the dark. About a hundred yards from the house Anne heard her friend cry out, "Oh my God." She started toward the sound of his voice, but he came crashing forward, shouting at her to stay put. He ran toward the house, yelling for Giles. But Anne couldn't be still. She turned on her light and saw her son, his eyes dilated, his tongue swollen and protruding, hanging from a tree.

———

The following morning one of Justin's teachers was driving to school when news of his death was broadcast on the radio. She was so shocked she nearly drove off the road. News travels fast in Putnam Valley, and by the time students arrived at school, many of them had heard. Students and teachers clustered in the halls crying, and as new arrivals were told, some of them burst into tears. The first reaction of a few students was, "Good—he's gone," but when the truth sank in, they were stunned into silence. Diana Wolf hadn't listened to the radio that morning, and when she arrived at school, she heard a girl spreading the news. "I went up to her and said, 'What are you talking about?' She said, 'Justin hung himself. My mother heard it on the radio.' I said, 'I don't believe you.' I went to my homeroom teacher and asked him if it was true. He had yelled at Justin for being late just the day before. He looked down and said, 'Yes.' In my first class everybody was talking about it. One kid said, 'Well, it's the only thing Justin ever did right. He finally did something right.' "

At his locker that morning Mike LoPuzzo heard the talk about Justin and prayed that it wasn't true. "I thought, 'Geez, I hope nothing happened to him because these people don't give a damn about him, they're gonna love it.' " First period he was alone in a classroom, minding computers for a teacher, when he looked out the window and saw several policemen talking to Justin's father. "I knew then that something had really happened." Mike thought of the Doonesbury book Justin had promised to bring him that day. "In a strange way I felt that he let me down," he says. He felt even more let down by the thought that his classmates had finally gotten to Justin. "I was mad at him. 'Why did you let them get to you?' I said to myself. 'That's just what they wanted. How could you let those idiots push you over the edge?' " Later that day a school counselor approached Mike. "I hear you were friends with Justin," he said. "Well, I really wasn't his friend, but I was friendly to him," Mike replied. After he said it he felt guilty and wondered why he had been defensive.

Early that morning Richard Brodow, the superintendent of Putnam Valley schools, was having his car fixed at a garage when he got a call from the school telling him what had happened. Brodow, who had known Justin enough to say hello to him by name, was stunned. The biggest problems he had faced as superintendent of the small, eleven-hundred-student district had been budget fights—just the day before he had steered a lengthy but productive budget meeting. The idea of a suicide seemed unbelievable. "As an administrator you may be trained in curriculum, you may be trained in personnel, you may be trained in supervision," he says, "but this is something that you're never trained for."

There had been suicides in Putnam Valley before, including those of teenagers, but they had been met with hushed silence, almost as if people agreed to pretend they hadn't occurred. However, even if Brodow had wanted to bury it, which he didn't, the notion of business as usual was absurd. When he arrived at the school during first period, students were still gathered in the halls, sobbing. His teachers were doing their best to cope, but many of them were as bewildered as the students. It was obvious that no lessons could be conducted—the entire school was essentially in shock. Brodow telephoned Peekskill High School and asked them to send over two counselors who, in addition to Putnam Valley's psychologist and guidance counselor, would visit each classroom to discuss Justin's suicide and answer questions. Students were told that counselors were also available in the guidance office to talk privately. The staff drew up a list of students who seemed particularly distressed, and a counselor met with each of them. Their parents were called and told that their children should be watched closely over the next several days. After-school activities were canceled; the flag was lowered to half-mast.

For many students Justin's suicide was their first experience with death. That the death was of someone their own age was frightening; that it was intentional was incomprehensible. Students who had teased Justin were terrified that they had driven him to suicide. "Why did I pick on him?" they would say. "Why did I tell him he smelled?" Others felt guilty for tolerating the teasing or for ignoring Justin. "I think he was just too good for us," one child told a counselor. Teachers wrestled with their own feelings of guilt. They worried that they had not treated Justin as well as they might have, that they had missed signs, that somehow they could have prevented his death.

The last class of the day was Honors English, in which Justin had played Julius Caesar with such intensity twenty-four hours earlier. Today, the guidance counselor spoke to the class about Justin's death. He had met with Justin the day before to discuss his schedule for his first year at high school. Justin had seemed cheerful and confident, said the counselor, but perhaps he had already made his decision to kill himself, and that had made him seem happy. Diana Wolf, who had kept control over herself all day, began to weep. At the end of the day when Brodow, over the public address system, asked the school to stand for a moment of silence in Justin's memory, Diana couldn't stop sobbing. When she got home, she went to her room, took out her journal, drew a fat black X instead of the day of the week, and wrote: "One of my classmates, Justin Spoonhour, hung himself last night. He's dead. Our class of 115 is now a class of 114. I'll never see him again. . . . Nothing like this has ever happened to me before. I can't handle it. Right now I'm crying uncontrollably. This is awful. I don't know what to do. I don't want to take a shower. I don't want to go for a walk or go to sleep. I haven't eaten all day, and I don't intend to because I might throw it up. I'm going to watch 'The Guiding Light' now. I better blow my nose first. Justin, underneath, we did love you. Why did you do it?"

Over the next few days the entire town struggled to answer that question. Certainly, many people were aware that Justin Spoonhour had been "a square peg in a round hole," as they said, and that he had been ostracized for it. But he had never complained or indicated that he was unhappy or depressed, and he had never spoken of death. He had endured the teasing for years—why had he killed himself now? Some were convinced it had been an accident, that Justin had been playing around and had gone too far. A few people murmured that Justin had become so involved in Dungeons and Dragons that he had been unable to distinguish fantasy from reality and had committed suicide as part of the game. Others felt that on Valentine's Day, when the whole world was supposed to be in love, the years of isolation had finally gotten to him. Still others suggested that Justin may have gotten the idea of killing himself from the newspaper. Ten days earlier thirteen-year-old Robbie DeLaValliere had been found hanging from a tree in the town park in Peekskill, ten miles south of Putnam Valley. His suicide had made headlines in the local papers. Justin had not known DeLaValliere, and no one had heard him mention the boy's death, but people wondered if he had read about it and decided that he had found a solution to his problems.

But there were no convincing answers. Justin himself had left no note, and although everyone kept expecting someone—a friend to whom he might have confided his plans, perhaps—to come forward with an explanation, no one did. There were rumors, of course. Some said that Justin had fought with his English teacher that afternoon; others claimed that he had been given a flower as a Valentine's Day joke. One student said that on the school bus a few weeks before his death Justin had showed him a noose he had fashioned from a piece of string. "See?" Justin had said. "This is a strong knot." But that was all he had said. It was just another stray clue that seemed significant only in retrospect, like the pile of wood shavings Giles had found on the living room floor that night. But while the clues were inconclusive, Justin, in the end, seemed resolute. The coroner determined that he had hanged himself about six o'clock, three hours after getting home from school, with a rope from the cellar.

Most of Justin's classmates came to the wake, including many of those who had harassed him. One boy with whom Justin had had a shoving match at a basketball game a few months earlier came several times, each time with different friends. Many of the children wept, and a few became hysterical as they approached the open casket where Justin lay in his size 20 collegiate jacket, his chorus sweater, and a burnt-orange turtleneck, borrowed from a friend of Anne's, to cover the rash where the rope had bitten into his neck.

Justin looked handsome and neat, but not too neat. Before the wake Anne's best friend had leaned over the casket and mussed his hair.

Friday at noon, several hundred people packed Grace United Methodist Church for Justin's funeral. More than half his class attended with their parents. Reverend Cox, who had stayed up until 2 A.M. writing the eulogy, spoke of his shock at Justin's death. He wondered why Justin hadn't come to him, why he hadn't recognized any signs of unhappiness, and he concluded that perhaps he had attributed an adult maturity to Justin that he did not have so early in his life. As for reasons, said Cox, we can speculate, but only God can know. Giles, one hand on Justin's coffin, spoke of the terrible irony of a father burying his son. "I had been looking forward to sharing so many things with him—school and college and career choices and helping him struggle with adolescent problems and dating and getting serious and choosing someone and raising a family. . . . I will miss him, and I'm convinced I will see him again." Giles nearly broke down several times. "I shaved this morning with the razor I was going to give to Justin," he said. "My God, my son wasn't even old enough to shave yet." When Anne sang a hymn to her son, the church was pierced with sobs. "There are no answers for what happened," she told Justin's classmates. "But if you want to honor my son, you will try to love and be more aware of each other." The organist played the "Ode to Joy" from Beethoven's Ninth Symphony, and Justin's drama teacher sang "Perhaps Love," the song Justin had hoped to sing in the spring concert:

> Perhaps love is like a resting place
> A shelter from the storm.
> It exists to give you comfort
> It is there to keep you warm.
> And in those times of trouble
> When you are most alone,
> The memory of love will bring you home.

On a gray, drizzly day Justin was buried a quarter-mile from the church at Rose Hills Memorial Park. Giles and Anne had placed several things in the casket with their son: the sheet music to "Perhaps Love," some Beethoven tapes including a recording of the Ninth Symphony, and the jelly beans and valentine that Justin never received.

II

THE SLOT MACHINE

ON THURSDAY EVENING, two days after Justin Spoonhour's death, a public meeting was held at Putnam Valley Junior High. The topic of the meeting, which had been called by school superintendent Richard Brodow, was "Adolescents in Crisis," but everyone knew it was really about suicide. Although 250 chairs had been set up in the auditorium, by the time the meeting started, people were standing in back. The audience consisted mostly of parents and teachers but included some teenagers. Diana Wolf and Mike LoPuzzo were there.

Kenneth Schonberg, a pediatrician from nearby Chappaqua whom Brodow had asked to speak, could feel the tension in the room. He had conducted meetings like this before. Nine months earlier in the town of North Salem, fifteen miles east of Putnam Valley, a high school girl had hanged herself in the restroom of a drive-in movie after a quarrel with her boyfriend. A month later the boy hanged himself in his family's home. Schonberg had spoken to the town's anxious parents. He sensed that tonight's crowd was even more tense because the suicide had occurred so recently. Although he knew he could give them no real answers, he wanted to ease their fears, to put Justin's death in some perspective. He gave a brief overview of adolescent suicide and talked about the complexities of parent-child relationships. He said that feelings of anger, guilt, fear, and sadness were natural responses to the tragedy. "What

36

you must understand and let your children know is that they are not to blame for what happened."

Although Justin was on everyone's mind, his name was rarely mentioned. Parents worried that what had happened to Justin could happen to their own children. A couple whose son had known Justin was concerned because their son didn't want to talk about Justin's death. A mother who had been taking notes asked, "What if a youngster denies feeling suicidal but he walks the floor all night?" Another mother wondered, "How do you make your child talk about it if he doesn't want to?" Schonberg suggested that parents not force the issue but ask gently whether something was on their child's mind, and be ready to listen. "Ninety-nine percent of this is not to prevent another suicide," he said, "but to make your kids feel comfortable talking about it." One woman voiced the fear shared by most parents at the meeting: "What happens if we go through all this, we talk about it, and we have another one?" Said Schonberg, "It's the same chance as lightning hitting twice in the same place. There's no reason for anyone to think that this is a contagion. Just because it happened to one child doesn't mean it will happen again."

Near the end of the meeting a gray-haired man stood and said, "I've been a resident of this community for a long time, and I can remember previous incidents of this kind. What disturbs me is that it takes an event like this to bring us together. Kids want to talk, but parents don't. We as parents should discuss these things." He sat down to applause.

By the end of the meeting there was a feeling of catharsis and a sense that the community was pulling together. As they drifted out, people greeted their friends and neighbors. Many of them stopped to thank Schonberg and to pick up a directory of crisis services available in the area and a list of "the warning signs of suicide." As couples drove home on the winding roads of Putnam Valley that night, they talked about their families. Some looked in on their sleeping children when they got home. One woman phoned each of her children around the country. "I want you to know I love you," she told them. "I want you to know you can talk to me."

That night, not long after the meeting ended, twenty-five miles south of Putnam Valley in a town called North Tarrytown, an eighteen-year-old boy named Jimmy Pellechi shot himself in the head.

Much of what Kenneth Schonberg told Putnam Valley parents about suicide that evening was new to them. Because they tend to avoid the subject until it hits close to home, most people are shocked when they find out how many people choose to end their own lives. Justin Spoonhour was one of 29,286 Americans to commit suicide in 1984. On an average day eighty Americans kill themselves, fourteen of them under twenty-five years of age, five, like Justin, under twenty. In a country with one of the highest murder rates in the world, half again as many people kill themselves as are killed by others.

Still, the government-certified statistics are believed to be far lower than the actual numbers, because families may cover up evidence, rearrange a death scene, or hide suicide notes in order to qualify for insurance benefits or avoid stigma and shame. Pressured by families to rule a death an accident, some coroners and medical examiners classify a death as suicide only when a note is found (about 15 to 20 percent of all cases); others report only hangings and overdoses, overlooking shooting, jumping, drowning, and a dozen other methods that can be interpreted as accidents. Many experts believe the true suicide rate may be two or three times the reported rate.

For many years suicide was associated with older white males. Three times as many males as females commit suicide, and the rate rises with age. Statistics show that older white males are at the highest risk. Over the last three decades, however, a dramatic change has taken place. While the overall suicide rate has remained stable, the rate for adolescents (fifteen to twenty-four, as defined by federal statisticians) nearly tripled, from 4.5 suicides per 100,000 in 1950 to 13.6 per 100,000 in 1977. That year, 5,565 young men and women took their lives. (Under-reporting may be particularly prevalent for adolescents, for whom accidents are the leading cause of death, accounting for 40 percent of all fatalities.) During the last thirty years advances in medicine have lowered the mortality rate for every age group in America except fifteen-to-twenty-four-year-olds, whose rate has risen, largely because of the increase in suicides. "The real importance of this is that it shows a real, fundamental change in the phenomenon of suicide in this country," Mark Rosenberg, an epidemiologist at the Centers for Disease Control, told reporters. "Whereas a few years ago it might have been your grandfather . . . now it's your son."

While most of the attention has focused on teenagers, there are twice as many suicides in the college-age group (twenty to twenty-four) as among high school students (fifteen to nineteen), although the rate has risen remarkably for both. (There has been a 300 percent increase in the rate for ten-to-fourteen-year-olds.) Suicide is now the third leading cause of death among teenagers, behind accidents and homicides, and the second leading cause of death for twenty-to-twenty-four-year-olds, behind accidents. The increase can be narrowed down still further. Five times as many males as females kill themselves in this age group, compared to a three-to-one ratio in the population at large. One of every seven suicides in 1984 was a male between the ages of fifteen and twenty-four. Blacks of both sexes, young and old, commit suicide less frequently than whites, but the suicide rate of young black males has more than doubled in the last twenty-five years. Native Americans may have the highest adolescent suicide rate of any group. But the increase in the adolescent suicide rate is largely accounted for by white males twenty to twenty-four.

Suicide deaths represent the extreme range of adolescent suicidal behavior. Official statistics on attempted suicide are not kept, but studies estimate that for every adult suicide there are ten attempts; for every adolescent suicide there may be twenty or more. Psychologist Kim Smith of the Menninger Foundation, assembling data from several studies, suggests that 2 percent of all high schoolers have made at least one suicide attempt, which would mean that 2 million high schoolers, at some point in their lives, have attempted suicide. Most of them are female. While five times as many adolescent males as females kill themselves, three times as many females make attempts.

While some psychologists believe that nobody goes through adolescence without thinking of suicide at some point, it's clear that many young people have suicide on their minds. One study found 50 percent of teenagers have "seriously considered" suicide by the time they graduate high school; another study found 20 percent claimed they were "empty, confused, and would rather die than live." In a third study, 58 percent said they knew someone who had attempted suicide, and 10 percent had themselves made an attempt. And in a survey of high school and college students that asked, "Do you think suicide among young people is ever justified?" 49 percent said yes. Michael Peck, a Los Angeles psychiatrist who has studied adolescent suicide for more than two decades, asserts that up to 10 percent of the youngsters in any high school classroom may be considered at some risk for suicide; he believes more than 1 million adolescents enter suicidal crises each year.

Although many clinicians have been aware of the rising rate of adolescent suicide for more than two decades, only recently has national attention recognized the problem. That recognition was spurred by the growing suspicion that adolescent suicides tend to come in bunches. In 1983 when eight teenagers in fourteen months killed themselves in the wealthy Dallas suburb of Plano, teenage suicide became a big story. Suddenly, suicide seemed to be snatching, according to the media, "the best and the brightest" who had "everything to live for"—the football captain and the cheerleader as well as the loner or the delinquent. Across the country the questions poured out: Why was the adolescent suicide rate increasing so rapidly? Why these bunches of young suicides? Why are young people so unhappy? Why are they killing themselves?

No one knows why people kill themselves. Trying to find the answer is like trying to pinpoint what causes us to fall in love or what causes war. There is no single answer. Suicide is not a disease like cancer or polio. It is a symptom. "The problem of suicide cuts across all diagnoses," says John Mack, a psychiatrist and coauthor of *Vivienne,* the story of a fourteen-year-old girl who hanged herself. "Some are mentally ill, most are not. Some are psychotic, most are not. Some are impulsive, most are not." Says psychologist Pamela Cantor, "People commit suicide for many reasons. Some people who are depressed will commit suicide, and some people who are schizophrenic will commit suicide, and some people who are fine but impulsive will commit suicide. We can't lump them all together." And just as there is no one explanation for the five thousand adolescent suicides each year, there is no one explanation for any particular suicide. While it is often said that suicide may be committed by twelve different people for twelve different reasons, it may be just as true to say that one person may choose death for twelve different reasons or one hundred different reasons—biological, sociological, and psychological factors that finally tighten around one place and time like a knot.

Although many adolescent suicides are said to have come "out of the blue," the majority of adolescents who kill themselves can be found, on closer inspection, to have had clearly discernible and often long-standing difficulties. Certainly, although Justin Spoonhour's suicide was unexpected, there were many possible contributing factors that might be emphasized by different experts according to their professional orientations. After his death some Putnam Valley townspeople said, "He killed himself because he wasn't given a flower on Valentine's Day." Although this is a simplistic response, a psychiatrist might point out that Justin's rejection on Valentine's Day mirrored rejections he had experienced throughout his life by his classmates. Others observed, "He killed himself because he was different, he was a loner—he liked Beethoven and everyone else listened to Michael Jackson." Although listening to Beethoven is not commonly known to cause suicide, it is one example of Justin's isolation and how that isolation led to ostracism. Even his few attempts to belong to the "mainstream"—joining the Cub Scouts, becoming the track manager—were met with scorn. Another psychiatrist might point to the high standards Justin set for himself, standards that were difficult for the rest of the world to live up to. His being "different" was encouraged by parents who themselves were somewhat different. A third psychiatrist might point to the lack of a stable family life. Although he was the child of an intact marriage, Justin was often alone at home, both because of his lack of friends and because his parents' activities often kept them away. Justin seemed, in fact, to be most at home in the fantasy worlds he created.

Other experts would highlight other influences. A sociologist might point out the effect of changing social mores and the difficulties faced by a child of sixties' parents growing up in the conservative eighties. And though much of Justin's isolation seemed to be self-imposed, another sociologist might stress that in rural towns like Putnam Valley making and keeping friends is especially difficult when they are all a car ride away. A philosopher might point to Justin's extreme sensitivity to the problems of the world, especially his apparent anxiety over the nuclear threat. A physician or a developmental psychologist would certainly observe that all of these influences were heightened by the traditional chaos of puberty, a time when biological changes were shaking up his world, and Justin was beginning to grapple with questions of sexuality.

All of these responses might be correct, but separately, no one of them would be the truth. Like the blind men who grab different parts of the elephant and misidentify the beast, suicide experts, exploring suicide from their own perspectives, end up supplying only part of the whole. "Suicide is a biological, sociocultural, interpersonal, dyadic, existential malaise," says Edwin Shneidman, a psychologist who has devoted his life to the study of suicide. Shneidman's definition is cumbersome, but it may be the most accurate we have.

What are some of these "biological, sociocultural, interpersonal, dyadic, existential" variables? In 1985 psychologist Lee Salk published the results of a research project on adolescent suicide. By comparing 52 teenagers who committed suicide with two control groups, he discovered that the teenagers who killed themselves were three to four times more likely to have mothers who had a chronic disease or condition during pregnancy, to have mothers who had no prenatal care in the first twenty weeks of pregnancy, or to suffer respiratory distress in the hours immediately after their birth. Released at the height of public concern about teenage suicide, the study made headlines. Many of the stories intimated that Salk had proved anemia or high blood pressure during pregnancy caused adolescent suicide. Salk explained that his research did not conclude this at all. "What it suggests," he said, "is that kids who have problems at birth or even before are more vulnerable to the stresses of life later on, to the point of taking their own life."

Salk's study and the reaction it provoked illustrate the hazards of interpreting the scant research on adolescent suicide. Most studies are retrospective—a researcher examines case histories of suicides hoping to find common characteristics. Finding commonalities, however, does not necessarily establish a causal relationship. Indeed, many clinicians say that, given certain circumstances, we are all vulnerable to suicide. Nevertheless, while there is no such thing as a typical suicide, research suggests that some adolescents may be more vulnerable than others.

Not surprisingly, suicidal adolescents are more apt to come from families where there have been problems: loss of a parent through divorce, death, or desertion; constant parental quarreling; physical or emotional abuse; poor communication; frequent moves. As early as 1938 psychiatrist Gregory Zilboorg noted the greater frequency of parental death in the history of suicidal people and suggested that the loss of a family member when a child was at the height of the Oedipus complex or in the transition to puberty led to a morbid identification with the dead person and rendered the child especially susceptible to suicide. "This is probably the most primordial cause of suicide in the human breast," he concluded. Since then many studies of suicide have found a high incidence of parental loss. In a study of fifty suicidal patients of all ages, psychiatrists Leonard Moss and Donald Hamilton identified what they called a "death trend"—95 percent of the patients had suffered the death or loss of a close relation. In 75 percent of the cases the deaths had occurred before the end of adolescence. A University of Washington study of 114 completed and 121 attempted suicides found that the death of a parent had occurred significantly more often in the childhood of the actual suicides than in that of the attempted suicides. They concluded that an inability to come to terms with a parent's death in childhood leads to an inability to cope with loss in later life. If that early parental loss is by suicide, it is even more difficult; studies have shown that people who have had a suicide in their family are eight times more likely to commit suicide themselves.

But death is not the only way in which adolescents may lose someone close to them. Comparing 505 children and adolescents who had attempted suicide with a control group, psychiatrist Barry Garfinkel found that the attempters came from families that showed more "disintegration." Families of attempters had higher rates of medical problems, psychiatric illness, alcohol and drug abuse, paternal unemployment, and a rate of suicide or suicide attempts eight times higher than normal. Both parents were present in fewer than half the families. Child psychiatrist Cynthia Pfeffer of Cornell University Medical College found that parents of suicidal children were subject to intense mood shifts, lacked the ability to delay gratification, and were extremely dependent and incapable of communicating with or guiding their children. In short, they were like children themselves. In a study of 159 adolescents who had attempted suicide, Harvard epidemiologist Eva Deykin found a frequent incidence of physical or sexual abuse. "Violence is a learned response to frustration and anger," she says. "An individual who has been exposed to child abuse might incorporate that response, turning aggression inward, as a means of coping with outside infringements. In addition, children who have been abused have very low self-esteem, a characteristic which has been identified as a central factor in suicide attempts." Psychiatrists at the Los Angeles Suicide Prevention Center found that over 40 percent of the suicidal youngsters they studied had had physical fights with family members.

In much of this research, science merely confirms common sense. A child who grows up in a troubled, dysfunctional household is more apt to have problems later on. But these "problems" may erupt in a variety of ways; no one has yet discovered which are more likely to lead to suicide and which to drug abuse, alcoholism, or other symptoms of unhappiness. And while many suicides come from broken, disturbed homes, many grow up in intact, loving families. What makes one child grow up liking himself and another child grow up hating himself?

Many psychiatrists believe that the seeds of self-esteem and the ability to cope with stress are planted in mother-infant bonding, the connective tissue of looks, touches, and words that forms between mother and child within the first year of the child's life. When a crying baby gets a gentle, loving response, he develops what psychoanalyst Erik Erikson calls "basic trust." He is more apt to grow up feeling loved and lovable, to develop a sense of self-worth and a belief that he is not powerless in the world. The English psychoanalyst John Bowlby, a pioneer in the study of bonding, demonstrated that young children are upset by even brief separations from their mothers. If the child's cries or tantrums are ignored, the child, he says, may adopt a permanent pose of detachment that may render him unable to form meaningful relationships for fear of being abandoned, as he felt he once was by his mother. "A baby repeatedly left to cry alone ultimately learns to give up and tune out the world," says Lee Salk. "This is learned helplessness and possibly the beginning of adult depression."

Orthodox Freudians trace the roots of adolescent suicide back to mother-infant bonding. "Nearly every suicidal child we've seen has suffered a break, a problem, in the mother-infant bond," write the authors of A Cry for Help, a book on adolescent suicide: "We must realize that the suicidal impulse can be ingrained within the first few months of life." But to blame suicide on bonding failure at one month is as myopic as tracing it to a mother's respiratory ailment during pregnancy. (And to blame mother-infant bonding, one would be obliged to trace that failure back to how that mother bonded with her mother, and so on.) The seeds of trust planted in infancy merely provide the base on which a sense of self-esteem is built. That sense is constantly reinforced or undermined by subsequent life experiences. In adolescence, however—an especially vulnerable stage in which a young person is beginning the process of breaking away from his parents and searching for his own identity—conflicts over separation and dependence are at their most intense. "The child who feels unloved in infancy or in early life, whether perceived or true, is more likely to grow up feeling unloved and unwanted, and unable to love and be loved," says psychologist Pamela Cantor. "This may cause difficulty in forming meaningful relationships and lead to frustration, anger, and depression."

For many years clinicians tended to link suicide almost exclusively to depression, as if there were a threshold—different for every person—that one could not bear to sink below. Suicide was seen as depression's last stop. Although in the last few decades clinicians have recognized that many people who are not depressed kill themselves, experts nevertheless estimate that 70 percent of all suicides are in some way associated with depression. According to the National Institute of Mental Health (NIMH), people who suffer from clinical depression have a rate of suicide twenty-five times higher than the general population. NIMH says that 15 percent of people with clinical depression will kill themselves. One in four Americans suffers from clinical depression at some point in his life.

Until twenty years ago, however, psychiatric dogma held that children and adolescents did not experience depression. This belief was based primarily on

Freud, who said that depression was anger turned inward by the superego. Children and adolescents, it was believed, did not have fully developed superegos and thus could not get depressed. They could be moody and sad, but such feelings were attributed to the vicissitudes of growing up. The refusal to recognize depression in younger people no doubt contributed to the belief that adolescent suicide was rare, and was another reason why so many young suicides were catalogued as accidents. Even today, despite evidence that indicates children as young as three have taken their own lives, the National Center for Health Statistics does not recognize suicides under the age of ten; they are classified as accidents.

Today, it is accepted that children and adolescents suffer from depression, although they may manifest different symptoms from those of adults. (Children and younger adolescents tend to camouflage depression with overt behavior, acting out their feelings through restlessness, temper tantrums, and fighting—so-called masked depression. Older adolescents may show signs of masked depression, such as promiscuity and excessive risk taking, but they display classic adult symptoms as well—disturbed sleeping habits, change in appetite, and inability to concentrate.) In fact, the psychiatric literature maintains that depression *peaks* in adolescence. NIMH estimates that one in five children suffers from depression. In a study of the health problems of fifty-six hundred adolescents, depression was second only to colds in frequency. "I think that depression, in a funny way, is an inevitable part of adolescence," says psychiatrist Paul Walters, director of health services at Stanford University. "In fact, if you *don't* get depressed, I think there's something wrong."

Most adolescent depression is caused by a reaction to an event—a poor grade, the loss of a relationship—rather than a biochemical imbalance. Most adolescent depressive episodes, however intense, are brief, and coming as they do at a stage of life in which an individual is groping for autonomy and identity, are developmentally normal. Feeling blue after not getting into one's first-choice college is as appropriate as feeling happy after scoring a winning touchdown. But many adolescents who experience depression for the first time don't realize that it won't last forever. They tend to keep their sadness to themselves. They may believe that depression is a sign of weakness. They may worry that they are going crazy.

"One kind of person most likely to kill himself is someone experiencing a depressive reaction for the first time," says Douglas Powell, a psychologist at Harvard University. "Young people who are depressed often think that one thing, one event will make it all better—a good grade, a boyfriend. It's important to help them realize that it's perfectly possible to have a date that isn't earth-shattering and that even if it's not such a great time, you're still the same person afterward and it's not the end of the world." Depressed adolescents are apt to blame themselves for feeling bad and to punish themselves for their imagined failures. "Kids who have never experienced failure go into a tailspin when they get a 23 on a biochemistry test," says Chicago psychiatrist Derek Miller. "One of the most important things we can do for our children is build some failure into their lives so they learn that it is possible to fail without being a failure." San Francisco psychiatrist Jerome Motto drew applause at a conference on adolescent suicide when he suggested: "Early on, we should give children puzzles they can't solve—and then give them love when they fail."

What distinguishes a "normal" depression from a "clinical" depression? They generate many of the same symptoms. The difference may just be a matter of duration—the persistence of symptoms for at least two weeks. No one knows what causes clinical depression. Certain forms of depression may have a genetic base; recent research has found a genetic marker for manic depression. Studies have found that parents of depressed and suicidal adolescents are more apt to suffer from depression. Others suggest there may be some sort of genetic susceptibility to certain types of stress. Some suicides may be traced to a biological cause. Researchers have found that the corpses of certain suicides show abnormally low levels of a brain chemical called serotonin. They propose that there is a link between low levels of serotonin and increased aggressiveness. The study samples have been small, however, and researchers continue to explore the link.

While depression and suicide are closely related, depression is not the only answer; for every teenage suicide there are one thousand depressed teenagers. Depression is twice as common in females as males, yet suicide is three times more common in males. Clinicians have tried to isolate the factors that separate suicidal depression from depression, but they tend to come up with descriptive abstractions like "loneliness," "isolation," "low self-esteem," and "a profound sense of worthlessness." Psychiatrist Aaron Beck, the founder of cognitive therapy, cites "hopelessness" as the key factor. Psychologist Calvin Frederick, of the Department of Psychiatry and Biobehavioral Sciences at UCLA, goes two h's further: "helplessness, hopelessness, and haplessness." (Again, science seems to confirm common sense—someone thinking of ending his life is not apt to feel hopeful about his future, and vice versa.)

Recent studies have found a significant relationship between hopelessness and what psychiatrists call "locus of control." People who believe that the outcomes of events are due to forces outside themselves, and whose sense of self-esteem is based on what others think of them, tend to feel more hopeless than those who feel that events are contingent on their own actions. Adolescents who depend on others for a sense of self-worth may find a reason to live in someone or something else. They put all their eggs in one basket—a sport, a grade, a person—which then becomes all-important. Often that reason may be a boyfriend or girlfriend. "If the adolescent has no other sources of self-esteem, the relationship becomes tremendously overvalued," says Samuel

Klagsbrun, a psychiatrist in Westchester County. "It becomes the foundation of the person's life. 'If the other person loves me, I'm okay.' But if that goes, it's as if everything goes—because there is nothing else to bank on."

Recent studies of completed suicides suggest that depression is less frequently associated with suicide in young people than in adults. While young female suicides are apt to suffer from depression, a number of adolescent suicides, male and female, do not fall under any psychiatric diagnosis but include socially inhibited adolescents who were likely to be perfectionists or prone to acute anxiety in the face of social or academic challenges. A large proportion of young male suicides have been found to have a combination of depression and antisocial or aggressive behaviors, often complicated by drug or alcohol use. Many of them had a history of disciplinary problems at school or with the law. In preliminary reports from a study of suicides age nineteen and under in the New York metropolitan area, psychiatrist David Shaffer found that a minority of suicides—mostly girls—showed a picture of uncomplicated depression, and the largest diagnostic group, about 25 percent—mostly boys—was comprised of adolescents with both aggressive and antisocial symptoms and depression. Such a description certainly fit Jimmy Pellechi, the eighteen-year-old who shot himself in North Tarrytown two days after Justin Spoonhour's death. A big, awkward adolescent, Jimmy dropped out of high school during senior year, drank heavily, never backed down from a fight, spent evenings racing friends on his motorcycle, and had what his best friend described as an "I don't give a fuck" attitude and what older townspeople called "a death wish." One night after drinking heavily, Jimmy telephoned the girl he had been seeing and told her that he had a gun and if she didn't promise to stop going out with other boys, he would kill himself. She refused; Jimmy put his father's shotgun to his head and pulled the trigger.

For the depressed and suicidal teenager, the breakup of a relationship may be what clinicians call the "precipitating" or "triggering" event. This event can be a bad grade, an argument, the death of a pet, or being the victim of an assault or rape. After such an incident the adolescent may feel he has failed and that his failure is unacceptable to his parents, peers, or himself. Teenagers arrested for the first time on charges of drunken driving and jailed overnight, for instance, are often overwhelmed by shame. Feeling they cannot face the outside world, they may take their own lives, often during the first few hours of confinement. (One young man, jailed on a minor charge, hanged himself while his parents were in the next room posting his bail.) Adolescents confused about their sexuality may commit suicide rather than admit to themselves or their parents that they might be gay. "In all the teenage suicides we see," says Judy Pollatsek, a counselor in Washington, D.C., "the kids always have some secret and are terrified that someone is about to find out." A few hours after learning that she was pregnant, a fourteen-year-old girl, fearing her parents' reaction, killed herself by kneeling in front of a train.

The "triggering event" need not be momentous. One often reads newspaper accounts of teenagers who kill themselves for seemingly trivial reasons: the fourteen-year-old boy who, according to his parents, shot himself because he was upset about getting braces for his teeth that afternoon; the girl who killed herself moments after her father refused to let her watch *Camelot* on television. For Justin Spoonhour, not receiving a flower on Valentine's Day or having his plans rejected by his church's Youth Group may have been the triggering event. Such incidents are often misinterpreted as the "reason" for a suicide, but they are usually the culmination of a long series of difficulties. "Interpersonal loss, perceived, actual, or anticipated, oftentimes is the last blow," says psychologist Alan Berman. "A relationship, a breakup, or a fight with one's parents may open wounds of deeper pain." The triggering event may seem to verify the lack of self-worth the teenager may have felt all along. "They are like a trivial border incident which triggers off a major war," wrote A. Alvarez in *The Savage God*.

The triggering event may seem inconsequential to adults, but it may be a matter of life and death to the teenager. "If youth is the season of hope, it is often so only in the sense that our elders are hopeful about us; for no age is so apt as youth to think its emotions, partings, and resolves are the last of their kind," wrote George Eliot in *Middlemarch*. "Each crisis seems final, simply because it is new." Says psychiatrist Samuel Klagsbrun, "For adolescents, the moment is everything. They think, 'I've got pain, and the pain is lasting for more than two minutes—that means the pain will last forever.'"

To an adolescent in pain, suicide can seem like an instant cure. This is "like treating a cold with a nuclear bomb," as one therapist puts it. "When young people are suicidal, they're not necessarily thinking about death being preferable, they're thinking about life being intolerable," says Sally Casper, former director of a suicide prevention agency in Lawrence, Massachusetts. "They're not thinking of where they're going, they're thinking of what they're escaping from. Recently, a fifteen-year-old girl came in here. In one pocket she had a bottle of sleeping pills, and in the other pocket she had a bottle of ipecac, a liquid that makes you vomit. She said, 'I want to kill myself, but I don't want to be dead. I mean, I want to be dead, but I don't want to be dead forever, I only want to be dead until my eighteenth birthday.'"

This girl was indulging in what clinicians call "magical thinking." Like Wordsworth, who observed, "Nothing was more difficult for me in childhood than to admit the notion of death as a state applicable to my own being," suicidal adolescents may not understand the permanence of death. They may describe it as a sanctuary, a womb, a long sleep, or a tranquil vacation. They may feel, in the words of the theme song from "M*A*S*H," that "suicide is painless" and what comes afterward is pleasant. They might agree with Peter Pan: "To die will be an awfully big adventure." But they may not understand that it is an adventure from which they cannot return. "I thought death would be the happiest place to be," a seventeen-year-old Texas girl who attempted suicide three times after breaking up with her boyfriend, told *Newsweek.* "I thought it would be like freedom, instantly. You'd be flying around happy and you wouldn't be tied down to earth."

"Suicidal teenagers may be grieving over some sort of loss in their lives, whether it be that of their self-esteem, a relationship, or a family problem," says psychiatrist Michael Peck. "But if you could say to them, 'Don't commit suicide because I can get you away from the pain without dying,' they'd likely be ready to do it." Unfortunately, when depression weighs heavily on them, suicidal adolescents are often unable to see other options. A study by psychologists Roni Cohen-Sandler and Alan Berman found that suicidal children have a black-and-white perspective. In solving problems they give up looking for alternative solutions and become frustrated and depressed. And the pain may become so great that death is seen as their only option. As one fourteen-year-old girl told Berman, "If I died, I wouldn't hurt as much as I do now."

"Suicidal adolescents suffer from tunnel vision," says psychologist Pamela Cantor. "They are looking down a long tunnel, and all they see is darkness. They don't know where they are in the tunnel; they think it goes on forever. They don't know that there is light at the other end." Perhaps more accurately, at a certain point the suicidal adolescent believes that there *is* light at the end of the tunnel and that light is suicide. This was expressed by a depressed fourteen-year-old girl who made repeated suicide attempts, one of which was fatal. About a year before she died, she wrote this poem:

> *I wandered the streets,*
> *I was lonely; I was cold.*
> *Weird music filled the air.*
> *It grew louder and louder.*
> *There was no other sound—*
> *Only weird, terrible music.*
>
> *I began to run as though I was being chased.*
> *Too terrified to look back,*
> *I ran on into the darkness,*
> *A light was shining very brightly, far away.*
>
> *I must get to it.*
> *When I reached the light,*
> *I saw myself,*
> *I was lying, on the ground.*
> *My skin was very white.*
> *I was dead.*

Such concepts as mother-infant bonding and locus of control may help us understand some of the factors that might lead a young person to suicide, but they do little to explain the 300 percent rise in the adolescent suicide rate over the last three decades. To account for this "epidemic" of youth suicide, a host of explanations has been proposed: the unraveling of America's moral fiber, the breakdown of the nuclear family, school pressure, peer pressure, parental pressure, parental lassitude, child abuse, drugs, alcohol, low blood sugar, TV, MTV, popular music (rock, punk, or Heavy Metal, depending on the decade), promiscuity, lagging church attendance, increased violence, racism, the Vietnam War, the threat of nuclear war, the media, rootlessness, increased affluence, unemployment, capitalism, excessive freedom, boredom, narcissism, Watergate, disillusionment with government, lack of heroes, movies about suicide, too much discussion of suicide, too little discussion of suicide. While none of these factors has been proved to have more than an incidental correlation with the rising rate of adolescent suicide, all of them represent very real reasons why, as one psychiatrist says, "it may be more difficult to be a kid today than at any other time in history."

According to psychologist Calvin Frederick, "The primary underlying cause of the rising suicide rate among American youth seems to be a breakdown in the nuclear family unit." While the disintegration of the nuclear family is an easy target—it has been blamed for everything from asthma to schizophrenia—there is evidence that at a developmental stage when they are most in need of it, adolescents have been receiving less support. The divorce rate tripled over the past twenty years, keeping pace with the adolescent suicide rate. More than half of American marriages now end in divorce—the highest rate in the world. A recent study found that only 38 percent of America's youth live with both natural parents. Although a causal relationship to suicide cannot be proved, of course, a correlation exists: While 50 percent of American couples eventually divorce, an estimated 70 percent of adolescents who attempt suicide come from divorced families.

Psychologists point out that holding on to a bad marriage can be more debilitating to a child than a divorce. "The quality of parenting, not the quantity of parents, counts most in raising children," observes the literature for Parents Without Partners, a self-help group for single parents. Even where there are two parents in the house, they are not likely to be home. Along with 91 percent of America's fathers, half the mothers of preschoolers and nearly two-thirds of all mothers with children over six now work outside the home. Parents increasingly subcontract child-raising duties to day care, babysitters, and, most of all, to the child himself. Cross-cultural studies show that parents in the United States spend less time with their children than parents in any other nation in the world. Working mothers have shouldered most of the blame; fathers have relied on tradition to excuse their absence from the house. Either way, the child suffers the consequences. Statistics show mothers spend between three and five minutes a day on educational activities with their children; fathers log in at zero to one minute. Cornell professor Urie Bronfenbrenner attached microphones to the shirts of small children and found that their fathers spent an average of thirty-seven seconds a day alone with them, less time than they would devote to cooking a soft-boiled egg.

An adolescent's diminishing support extends beyond the nuclear family. The pioneer spirit that once sent American families West in search of opportunity now sends them crisscrossing the country in pursuit of upward mobility, leaving behind the traditional support system of friends and extended family. Over a five-year period, one-quarter of the population moves. Both the executive blueprint for success and the blue-collar struggle to stay employed demand more movement than ever and result in less chance for a child to make a place for himself. There are new schools to attend, new cliques to break into, new identities to establish. When their sixteen-year-old son killed himself a year after the family moved for the fifth time, one Texas couple decided to have the body cremated. "Where would we bury him? Where is home?" said his mother. A sixteen-year-old whose family had moved from New Rochelle to Shaker Heights to Houston hanged himself from an oak tree in the backyard of their rented house, leaving a note: "This is the only thing around here that has any roots."

Over the last few decades there has also been a fundamental change in child-rearing philosophy: Parents have been encouraged to give their children "space." But with too much space, teenagers may feel as if they're growing up in a vacuum. "Once childhood is over there is a tendency for parents to stop parenting," says psychiatrist Michael Peck. "They just say, 'If that's the way you feel, do your own thing.' And so all the things that kids did twenty years ago at age seventeen or eighteen, when they are more physically mature and have better judgment, they're being given the freedom to do at twelve and thirteen. Many parents are afraid to teach their children, afraid to set rules and enforce them. But a feeling that they can do anything they want is terrifying to kids." Peck says many of the suicidal young people he sees in his practice get little clear-cut guidance, lack goals, and feel "a sense of floating along in time without direction." Left to their own devices, adolescents are turning to sex, drugs, and alcohol earlier than ever. By age fifteen an estimated one-third have had intercourse. By sixth grade one-third have tried beer or wine and one-tenth have tasted hard liquor. A *Weekly Reader* survey found 30 percent of fourth graders felt peer pressure to drink.

If adolescents are becoming premature adults, parents are increasingly willing to meet them halfway. They seek their child's friendship while fearing his rejection. A generation of parents raised on the idea that parents are parents and children are children began, in the 1960s, to blur that line. In the golden age of divorce the child has become confidant to the single parent. "To be sure, the good parent of the 1950s or 1960s also spent considerable time patiently explaining things to his child," wrote Marie Winn in a 1983 article called "The Loss of Childhood." "But it was the ways of the world the parent clarified— the world of nature, of politics, of social relations. A great many of today's laborious parental explanations, however, refer not to the causality of natural or social phenomena, but to the parents' own feelings, anxieties and insecurities." The result is the psychological equivalent of the old Clairol commercial in which the viewer can't guess which one is the mother and which one is the daughter. "People tell us we're more like sisters than parent and child," the mother of a sixteen-year-old Texas girl says proudly. "I never really *had* to be a mother to her. We were so close—there wasn't *anything* we didn't talk about." She still can't understand why her daughter didn't tell her how unhappy she was. Instead, her daughter came home from school one day, took an overdose of pills, and then slashed her wrists, though not fatally.

While adolescents today grow up with a frightening degree of freedom, they also feel tremendous pressure to succeed. "Many families have bought the message that we educators gave them in the last ten years, that to get a good job you need a good education, but they bought it to the nth degree," says George Cohen, a high school counselor in White Plains, New York. "A lot of parents I meet today think that the road to happiness goes only through Harvard, and unless their kid is on that road, he's doomed to misery." Joe Solanto, a Westchester County psychologist, says that many of the high schoolers he works with tell him that their parents don't care about who they really are, they care only about the image they can help them project to the rest of the world. Solanto recently attended a meeting at which some students admitted that they really didn't *want* to go to an Ivy League university, they wanted to go to a more low-key college. They were tired of being in a high-pressure academic environment. One parent stood up and said, "That's okay for you to say, but for the rest of the year we have to drive around with those City College stickers on our back windows. How is that going to look in town?"

Parents who struggled hard to get where they are today don't understand why their children are so unhappy. "I know two or three other people whose children have been suicidal, and the kids always blame the parents," says a St. Louis woman whose seventeen-year-old daughter recently took a nonfatal overdose. "I don't think it's all Mom and Dad's fault. I don't think these kids learn how to be responsible for themselves. They can't handle the slightest rejection, not only by parents but by boyfriends, and in school. My husband and I grew up in what is now the ghetto. When we went to school, you were lucky if your dad had a job. The stress you had was whether your father came home with a paycheck, whether you had enough for bus fare to school, whether there was food on the table. For kids today the stress is, 'Do I have an Izod shirt? What boy am I going with?' I've talked to more people who say, 'My son won't go to school today unless he has Nike sneakers' or 'My daughter won't go unless she has Jordache jeans.' I have a friend whose son had been going with a girl. When she tried to break off the relationship, he attempted suicide. So his mother bought him a car, thinking it would help.

"I think they've had it easy. We've overindulged them. We've given them material things, but we haven't made them responsible people. As long as you say yes, they're fine. The minute you say no, they're off the deep end. To this day my daughter never says, 'I attempted suicide,' she says, 'My parents *drove* me to it.' But you can't blame everything in the world on parents; you have to learn how to cope with those things. If it's the parents' fault, why didn't *I* turn out this way? I had a mom who never knew I was there and a father who beat me. But I never blamed them, I just figured that's the way it was. When we were young, we were so busy trying to survive, we didn't have *time* to think about committing suicide."

Whether from their peers, their parents, their schools, or from within, many adolescents feel pressure to achieve. But in a time of increased unemployment and fierce competition, they find themselves trapped between high expectations and low opportunity. "People are telling them these should be the best years of their life," says Solanto. "They look around and see their life-style and level of affluence, and they think, 'When I'm out of college, I'm going to be living in a two-room apartment making $18,000. I'm not going to have a brand-new car, a boat, fancy vacations. It's going to be years, if ever, before I can duplicate the kind of life-style my parents have created for me. I'm going backward, and what sense does that make? What am I going to do? How am I going to catch up to where I'm at?' "

In an increasingly Darwinian world, traditional support systems are often shed; relationships become contacts, sex is substituted for love, marriage is postponed in favor of a career. In a 1967 survey of college freshmen, the vast majority declared their most important goal was "developing a meaningful philosophy of life." In 1987, "being well off financially" was cited as a key goal by more than 70 percent. A recent study by the Stanford Research Institute illustrated the cost of these changing values. To the question "Do you believe success comes only at the expense of others?" nearly twice as many people age eighteen to thirty-four answered "yes" than did people over thirty-four. Fifty percent more of the younger group believed that success requires giving up some friends. Observes one high school guidance counselor, "Kids are taught to compete with their buddies, not make a connection to them."

With parents setting no rules and friends perceived as competition, where do adolescents learn how to cope in a crisis? "I've had more kids tell me, 'I don't know how people solve problems—I've never seen anybody do it in my life,' " says Dallas pediatrician John Edlin. "Adults of the current generation have great difficulty dealing with the pain in their lives. What do you do if you have a fight? You get a lawyer and get separated. What do you do if something goes wrong at work? You get a lawyer to see if you can sue the boss. There's no feeling that things can be worked at. Kids pick that up. Why work it out? I won't be going to this school tomorrow. My parents divorce each other. What are my role models for how to handle pain?"

While parents spend an average of two minutes a day communicating with their child, the television set spends an average of three and a half hours a day with their child. The average child will watch more TV by the time he is six than he will spend talking to his father for the rest of his life. (A study of 156 preschoolers found almost half preferred watching TV to being with their fathers.) By the time he graduates from high school, he will have logged twenty thousand hours in front of the TV, compared to eleven thousand in the classroom. Parted from this third parent, children may experience severe separation anxiety. Television doesn't cause suicide, of course, but adolescents often watch it to reduce loneliness and may thus become less likely to develop real relationships. A thirteen-year-old boy whose family had recently moved to northern California was reluctant to go to his new school because he was overweight. He stayed in his room and watched the television he had been given as a reward for earning good grades at his previous school. His father removed the TV from his room, telling him he would get it back when he returned to school. Hours later the boy shot himself, leaving a note that said, "I can't stand another day of school and especially another minute without television."

Real life may pale next to television. "TV bombards kids with the glamorous and the thrilling, and then they have to go out and live their lives, and their lives are not glamorous and thrilling," says high school counselor George Cohen. "TV doesn't help kids understand that life on a day-to-day level can be boring and mundane and upsetting. Being held up to that image when you have to face the realities of your life can be discouraging, if not depressing." And on TV no problem is so great that it can't be solved in half an hour.

Often the solution is achieved by violence. By the time he is graduated from high school, the average child will have witnessed eighteen thousand murders and eight hundred suicides on television. One study computed that murder is one hundred times more prevalent on television than it is in reality, and that television crime is twelve times more violent than crime in real life. "Television has brought about the virtual immersion in violence into which our children are born," George Gerbner, dean of the Annenberg School of Communications at the University of Pennsylvania, told a House subcommittee during 1981 hearings on "The Social/Behavioral Effects of Violence on Television." There is increasing evidence that children saturated in television violence are more apt to solve their own problems that way. A 1982 NIMH report concluded:

"Violence on television does lead to aggressive behavior by children and teenagers who watch the programs." At a 1985 conference on "Children and Television," Yale professor Victor Strasburger suggested, "Pediatricians need to take a 'TV history' just as they take a medical history, when they see a violent, troubled, or obese child."

Violence on television—or in movies, videos, and books—reflects violence in the outside world, and the chicken-or-the-egg question of precedence will continue to be debated. Whatever the cause, violence as a solution is used increasingly inside and outside the family. And a teenager ready to explode is more likely than ever to have the means at hand. The rate of gun ownership in the United States has risen steadily in the last two decades, as has the rate of youth suicide by firearms. Guns were used by 62 percent of all suicides who were fifteen to twenty-four years old in 1980, compared to 47 percent in 1970. "The increase in the use of guns accounts for almost all of the increase noted in youthful suicide," says psychologist Alan Berman.

Personal struggles can appear even more hopeless when the outside world seems no better off—when on any given day a teenager can pick up a newspaper or turn on a television and learn about war in the Middle East, starvation in Africa, and an abundance of murders, muggings, accidents, and natural disasters. At the breakfast table children pour milk from a carton that bears the faces of children their age who are missing and perhaps kidnapped; in coloring books they fill in a picture of a boy running from a stranger who has offered him a ride; at the mall they are fingerprinted so they will be more easily traced if they disappear. In a model child-abuse prevention program in Tacoma, Washington, children as young as four are taught to memorize the police phone number. A study comparing fears of fifth and sixth graders in 1939 and 1977 found that boys in 1939 worried mainly about finding a job and having enough money; in 1977 they were more fearful of robbers, kidnappers, rapists, and strange people following them.

Hovering over all of this is the threat of global suicide. "The fear of nuclear holocaust is ever-present for today's children," says Rabbi Earl Grollman, author of several books on death and suicide. "Kids today are actually living with a sword over their heads." Although psychiatrist Robert Coles argues that the children who worry about it are those whose parents worry about it, the fear is real regardless of its origin. "Many children feel they are living on the brink of annihilation and are afraid they won't grow up," says psychiatrist John Mack, who directed a study of one thousand elementary and high school students in the Boston area about their attitudes toward nuclear war. In 1984, Brown University students voted to urge the university to stockpile cyanide pills to be dispensed in the event of nuclear war. (The school refused the request.) Although their intent was to dramatize their outrage at the nuclear arms race by equating it with suicide, their fatalism is shared, therapists say, by many of the adolescents they see in their practices. The powerlessness of the outside world to solve its problems may match the powerlessness a teenager feels inside. Faced with an increasing sense of impotence, an adolescent may believe that the one thing he still owns is his life and suicide is the only way he can exercise control over his universe. *If I can't control my life, I can control my death.*

"What we're doing is looking at a rising suicide rate and trying to determine what is different now from twenty-five years ago," says psychologist Pamela Cantor. "You can point to the rising divorce rate. You can point to increased mobility. You can point to two-career families. And therefore that's what gets blamed. I think they are responsible, but maybe they're not. It may just be correlation because you can also point to the fact that the weather has gotten colder." She smiles wryly. "I'm not being facetious. We just don't know what the answers are."

In 1971, teaching a psychology course at Boston University, Cantor asked her class how many had seriously considered suicide. All but two students raised their hands. Cantor has been studying suicide ever since. Her private practice consists primarily of young women, many of whom have attempted or threatened suicide. In the past decade Cantor has traveled the country speaking to students, teachers, and professionals about adolescent suicide. A member of the Presidential Task Force on youth suicide prevention and president of the National Committee for Youth Suicide Prevention, she has been asked hundreds of times why the rate is rising, and in a voice filled with concern and urgency, she has tried to answer that question.

Cantor feels concern not only as a psychologist but as the parent and working mother of two children in a high-achieving, two-career family in a wealthy Boston suburb. She frets about her own parenting; as a psychologist she has vast knowledge of its hazards and, as a parent, of its rewards. She is keenly aware of how different her children's world is from the world she knew growing up on Long Island in the early fifties, with Debbie Reynolds and June Allyson for role models. "There's no safe place anymore," she says. "When I was young, our safe place used to be larger than just our home. I could gain mastery over my world by going to the village to get a loaf of bread, by going out for a tuna fish sandwich, by walking to and from school. I could take the train into New York City and stroll up and down Fifth Avenue. I had a great sense of freedom and autonomy without any threat of danger. Today, I will not even let my kids walk to the neighborhood school. I drive them every morning although it's less than a mile away, and I pick them up every afternoon. When we get out of the car, we lock it; when we get in the car, we look in the backseat. We look under the car before we get in. One Sunday I left the kitchen window open. My husband and children were at home. I went to see a friend, and when I came home, I found out that a man had climbed through the window and wandered through the house and nobody ever saw him. We keep the window locked now. It's ridiculous. And sad. And this is not only part of my life but part of theirs. Surely it affects their attitude and their well-being. Does it lead to suicide? I don't know.

"The suicide literature is very frustrating. I feel that frustration when I speak to parents because I will go through the list of things that have been pointed to as factors, and I always come up feeling empty because when you're all through, it really doesn't help you determine what to do and what not to do. Yet people want the answer, and I don't blame them—I want it, too. That is why this subject is so frightening to parents, because you can't say, 'If you do a, b, and c, you will protect your children from suicide, and if you do d, e, and f, you will lead them down the path of self-destruction.' The bottom line seems to me that if a person likes himself, he won't kill himself. But how do you get children to like themselves? What do you do? And even if you do everything you think you're supposed to do and you give them love and a sense of security and the feeling that you care, some kids still don't like themselves. And some kids who *do* like themselves go through periods when they *don't*. One evening my daughter told me she didn't like being herself because she wasn't popular. But she has *lots* of friends. How seriously do you take it? When do you listen? When don't you listen? When do you do something? You have to follow your instincts, and I guess all I'm saying is that the best you can do is give children two parents who genuinely love them." She sits back in her chair and shrugs.

In all of this speculation there is one theory that is quantifiable. Sociologists believe that the higher the percentage of a certain age group, or "cohort," within the population, the more stress there will be on members of that age group. Because of the postwar baby boom, in the past few decades there have been more adolescents in the United States than at any other time in history. At the same time the proportion of adolescents within the total population has also been larger. Psychiatrist Paul Holinger graphed the percentage of adolescents in the United States back to 1900 and compared it to the suicide rate for that age group. The two lines on the chart were nearly identical. Whenever the percentage of adolescents in the population soared, as it did around 1910 and again from 1950 to 1977, the suicide rate kept pace. Whenever the percentage dipped, as it did around 1950, the adolescent suicide rate fell proportionately. In 1977 when the number and percentage of adolescents in the population was highest, their suicide rate was the highest for that age group in history.

The "cohort effect" suggests a sort of adolescent overcrowding in which a greater number of young people are competing for the same number of jobs and college places, for spots on the football team and in the chess club. With bigger high school class sizes there is increased stress, isolation, and difficulty in establishing an identity. The cohort theory predicts that, just as laboratory rats forced to live in overcrowded cages turn on each other, in times of overcrowding for a certain cohort, one will find not only more suicide but other indices of pain as well—homicide, alcohol and drug abuse, teenage pregnancy, all of which have indeed risen for the fifteen-to-twenty-four-year-old cohort.

The cohort effect is further supported by statistics that show that as the baby boom generation moves into their thirties—and out of the fifteen-to-twenty-four statistical zone—the adolescent suicide rate has plateaued. After the peak of 1977, the fifteen-to-twenty-four suicide rate leveled off in the 1980s. Holinger and other demographers predict that the adolescent suicide rate will continue to decrease of its own accord—until the mid-1990s when the proportion of fifteen- to twenty-four-year-olds in the population will increase again, as will their suicide rate.

While the cohort effect can help explain why there is increased competition and stress, it cannot explain why some adolescents turn to suicide, some to drugs, some to alcohol, and some to hard work and future success. All of the factors mentioned as contributing to the increase in suicide—divorce, rootlessness, increased competition—cause stress and pain that may be expressed in a variety of self-destructive behaviors, all of which have increased over the last three decades and all of which are correlated with increased risk of suicide. They are connected to suicide like stars in a constellation. From 1960 to 1980, while the suicide rate for ages fifteen to twenty-four increased 136 percent, homicide deaths among the same age group increased by 164 percent. Arrests involving teenagers have doubled, and studies have found a high rate of previous suicide attempts among juvenile offenders. Studies of homeless and runaway youths have found an extraordinarily high instance of depression and attempted suicide. The pregnancy rate for Americans age fifteen to nineteen is 96 per thousand, more than double the rate of any other industrialized nation. More than 1 million adolescents become pregnant each year, and four out of five are unmarried. The suicide rate for teenage mothers is believed to be seven times greater than that for teenage girls without children.

It has been estimated from autopsies that one-third to one-half of teenage suicides are under the influence of alcohol or drugs shortly before they commit suicide, while 30 percent of teenage attempters are drunk or high shortly before their attempt. The Department of Health and Human Services estimates that 5 million adolescents, or three in every ten, have drinking problems. While drugs and alcohol don't cause suicide—after all, millions of teenagers drink or use drugs and do not kill themselves—under their influence, underlying rage is more readily translated into aggression. Alcohol is a depressant, which can make an already depressed person more depressed, and as "liquid courage" it can lower inhibitions and release suicidal impulses. Drugs and alcohol themselves offer a withdrawal, a step away from reality and a step toward suicide. Alcohol abuse is one of many self-destructive behaviors that have been called "slow suicide." Sometimes, however, it is not so slow. In January 1985 a fifteen-year-old boy from Longmont, Colorado, went to a party and drank nine cans of beer, a quart of bourbon, and half a bottle of whiskey. He died that night.

While these statistics have led some to jump to the conclusion that drugs, alcohol, and teenage pregnancy cause suicide, they indicate that adolescents are increasingly unhappy and are turning to drugs, alcohol, promiscuity, violence, crime, eating disorders, and risk-taking behavior to cope with their pain. These are all forms of communication; suicide is merely the most radical. And adolescents who use these other methods are more apt to turn to suicide if their communication is not answered. Says John Tiebout, a counselor at The Suicide and Crisis Center in Dallas, "Today, teenagers have to go to more and more extremes to get what they want. And maybe suicide fits into that dynamic. Being depressed or getting high is not a strong enough way to communicate to the world how miserable and fucked up you are."

None of this explains a single suicide, of course, but it gives the background against which young people choose to live or die. It is a paradoxical world in which the 350,000 commercials teenagers see tell them to be the fastest, strongest, brightest, best-looking, Be-All-That-You-Can-Be, Michelob-Light-for-the-Winner, while eighteen thousand TV murders, the morning paper, and the evening news tell them they might not be alive tomorrow. Adolescents are caught in the middle between these extremes, and the gap between who they are and who they are told they should be grows larger. "Winning isn't everything—it's the only thing," said Vince Lombardi, the legendary football coach. With our current definitions of success, not everyone can win, and an increasing number of adolescents are deciding that if they can't win, they won't play. If they can't be number one, they don't want to be in the game at all. Number two or two hundred or two thousand is not enough. And to that growing chorus of voices chanting "USA! USA! USA!" and "We're Number One! We're Number One!" which beats like a tom-tom on a teenager's brain, there is a flip side, expressed in the lone answering voice of the seventeen-year-old senior who, at his high school graduation in Massachusetts, stepped to the podium and announced, "This is the American way," pulled a gun from beneath his robe, and shot himself, though not fatally.

The vast majority of American teenagers maneuver through adolescence without killing themselves. In 1984, for instance, 39,995,000 of 40,000,000 adolescents chose not to commit suicide. Although suicide is the second leading cause of death among adolescents, young people have the lowest suicide rate of any age group. While most people wonder why so many people commit suicide, some clinicians suggest that we have the question backward. Why don't more adolescents kill themselves? And why do so many consider it and then back away? Robert Litman, a psychiatrist at the Los Angeles Suicide Prevention Center, talks about something he calls "the suicide zone." He believes that suicide-vulnerable individuals move in and out of periods of suicidal risk—sometimes for brief periods, sometimes for moderate or long periods—as their life circumstances fluctuate. But of all those people who enter that zone, very few actually kill themselves. "For every hundred people at high risk," he says, "only three or four will actually commit suicide over the next couple of years."

For that to happen, says Litman, a multitude of things must occur. "It's like a slot machine," he says. "You can win a million dollars on a slot machine in Las Vegas, but to do that, six sevens have to line up on your machine. That happens only once in a million times. In a sense it's the same with suicide." Those spinning sevens represent all the biological, sociological, psychological, and existential variables that are associated with suicide—broken family, locus of control, decreased serotonin, triggering event, and so on. "In order to commit suicide, a lot of things have to fall together at once, and a lot of other things have to *not* happen at once," says Litman. "There's a certain random element determining the specific time of any suicide and, often, whether it happens or not."

In Litman's slot machine metaphor, suicide is seen as an exceedingly rare event that requires everything to be in alignment for it to take place—a sort of perverse, malevolent music of the spheres. "It's as if you need to have six strikes against you," Litman says. "And we're all walking around with one or two or three strikes. Then you get into a big crisis and you have four strikes. But to get to all six really takes some bad luck."

III

BRIAN

BRIAN HART WAS the kind of young man who would have been prized by the classmates who scorned Justin Spoonhour. Handsome, athletic, and out-going, Brian was as much in the thick of things as Justin was isolated and alone. Brian grew up in a large, loving family in Bedford Hills, an upper-middle-class community halfway between Putnam Valley and New York City. As hard as Justin tried to be different, Brian tried hard to be one of the guys, but he could never succeed to his satisfaction. He grew up with one very large strike against him, one that ultimately set him apart every bit as much as Justin Spoonhour.

Family photographs seem to cover every surface of Patrick and Mary Hart's modest home: grade school portraits, graduation pictures, baptisms, first communions, birthdays, weddings, Thanksgivings, Christmases, and St. Patrick's Days. "The Rogues Gallery," Pat and Mary call it. When they come down-stairs in the morning or go up to bed at night, they are surrounded by the smiling faces of their family. Home and family are important to the Harts. Pat grew up less than a mile from this house, on the estate where his father was superintendent. When Pat was sixteen, his father died, and he was forced to support his mother and two younger siblings. Mary grew up on Long Island, but the family was broken up during the Depression when her father lost his job. After living with various aunts for two years, Mary was reunited with her family in Mount Kisco. Pat and Mary met in the eighth grade but didn't date until junior year. Pat played basketball and baseball; Mary was prom queen. In their graduation portraits, which hang side by side at the top of the stairs, they look serene, Mary ravishingly beautiful, Pat confident and strong. Their heads are cocked, gazing up and off to the right, looking, as the photographer no doubt intended, toward the future.

Four years after graduating, Pat and Mary were married. Four years after that, they had five children, the last two, twins. Pat got up long before dawn for his job as a milkman, then went to night school for his college degree. In 1962 he became an officer for the local Teamsters union, eventually becoming a federal labor mediator. Mary raised the family and did volunteer work. Seven years after the twins were born, agreeing that they had never had time to truly savor raising a child because they were always busy caring for the next, Pat and Mary decided to have one more child—"the last hurrah," as Mary says. "The gang" was thrilled with the news. When the Harts drove up to church on Easter Sunday in their nine-seater Pontiac, they leaned out of every window. "Guess what!" they yelled. "We're going to have another baby!" On November 27, 1964, Brian Hart was born.

As an infant, Brian was like an only child with seven doting parents. Each morning when Mary woke she never knew in whose room Brian would be: The first child to wake would lift Brian from his crib, take him to his or her own bed, and feed him his bottle. As soon as the children got home from school they would drop their books and run through the house looking for their baby brother. Brian was the little prince of the family. If he wanted anything, he was given it; if he was hurt in any way, there was hysteria; if there was an activity, he was included. But gradually his brothers and sisters went off to college or to jobs, and by the time he was twelve, Brian was the only child left at home.

One Saturday morning in October of his seventh grade year, Brian was playing with friends in the next-door neighbor's backyard. Though Brian had never been allowed to play with toy guns, they were using the friend's BB rifle. By accident one of the boys fired a shot that hit another in the eye. Brian was close enough to hear the splat. Pat, hearing screams, went to the door in time to see the other children, terrified, fleeing the scene, followed by Brian, one arm around the injured boy whose eye was streaming blood. When Brian returned from walking the boy home, he went into the backyard where the boy had been shot and gathered up the bloodstained leaves from the ground. At the brook behind his house he knelt and carefully washed the blood from each leaf.

Though Brian didn't talk about the incident, his parents could tell it bothered him. He began to have problems concentrating in school. His teachers said that while most of the time Brian was bright, eager, and responsive, at times he was withdrawn, almost "out of it." (In the elections at the end of the year, his classmates would vote Brian Most Popular and also Most Moody.) They suggested he get professional help. Although reluctant—Brian's therapy would be a family first—the Harts found a respected young psychiatrist named Eugene Kornhaber, who began seeing Brian once a week. Brian was initially resentful, but gradually he seemed reconciled to being in therapy and would joke to his family and friends about his "shrink."

Brian seemed to be getting along well until the following year when the Harts' beagle, Kelly, died. Kelly was kept tied to the clothesline on a running leash, and the Hart children had been told never to let her loose because the commuter railroad tracks ran in back of the house. But Brian occasionally took Kelly across the tracks to play on the hill. One day while Kelly was crossing the tracks, a train approached. Brian called her, but Kelly panicked and ran in front of the train. The train hit her, and Brian saw Kelly tossed between the cars. After the train passed, Brian heard a weak bark and ran to Kelly just as another train approached from the opposite direction. He darted in front of the engine, grabbed Kelly from the tracks, and jumped off the embankment. Brian rushed her to the house—he could hear her bones grind as she moved—but she died within the hour. Brian buried her in the backyard. That night Brian couldn't stop crying. He was sure that he had led Kelly to her death.

Though he rarely talked about them, these two incidents would haunt Brian throughout his life. Years later doctors would point to them as crucial traumas in his development. Because the injured boy, who had to get a glass eye, was on the Harts' property when he was hit by the BB, the Harts were involved in a lawsuit that wasn't settled until Brian was seventeen. And in eleventh grade Brian wrote an essay in which he described the guilt he felt over Kelly's death. Sometimes when he walked into the backyard, he could still hear Kelly howling in pain.

After Kelly's death, Brian's ups and downs became more pronounced. When Brian was up, his determination, exuberance, and sense of humor were infectious. He was extraordinarily handsome, with sandy hair, blue-green eyes, and a wide grin. Girls developed instant crushes on him, teachers were reminded of why they had gone into teaching, and friends' parents wondered why their sons couldn't be as charming as Brian Hart. "With Brian, nothing was halfway," says his mother. "He didn't do anything gradually, he'd jump right in, feet first." When Brian took up jogging, he immediately started running five miles a day—and won two medals for ten-kilometer races. When he became interested in cooking, he tested recipes on his parents and made plans to write a cookbook. When he became interested in girls in eighth grade, he fell in love at least once a week. When Brian was up, he believed anything was possible. Watching a TV show in which a New York Giants football player discussed the upcoming season with pessimism, Brian composed a four-page letter to the Giants' administration, telling them a player with that attitude shouldn't be on the team—a person should never give up.

At times, however, Brian was remote and morose. "Sometimes he was afraid to be alone. He'd walk out with me—not with me but behind me, like a puppy, afraid to let me out of his sight," says Mary, who had been elected town clerk. "Sometimes he would call the office and ask me to come home and talk to him. I'd drop everything and rush home, and then he wouldn't talk." When his parents asked him what was wrong, he would say, "I'm just low." At night when he went upstairs and his parents, sitting in the living room, looked up, Brian demanded, "What are you staring at?" After an eighth grade basketball game, Brian's father kidded him about a play in which the player he was guarding had cut around him to score a basket. Brian was silent for a moment, then said quietly, "Dad, you shouldn't criticize me." Pat was taken aback but realized that Brian just wasn't the type to be teased. When Brian asked his mother not to come to his games, she was saddened that he might be embarrassed by her presence—the Harts had always attended their children's activities—but she agreed. "If this was the only way he could function, without our being too close, that was all right," she says.

Finding a balance between showing their love for Brian and not putting pressure on him was frustrating. Pat and Mary fretted about Brian's grades, which fluctuated with his moods. They suspected that he smoked marijuana, and they knew he drank with his friends in the neighborhood. Liquor occasionally disappeared from their cabinet, and for a while they kept it locked in the basement. The Harts were especially concerned about alcohol because Pat had had a drinking problem years earlier. There were occasional arguments and fights, and once when Brian was in the eighth grade, his mother marched him down to the local Alcoholics Anonymous office, where a counselor gave Brian a talking-to. More often the Harts tried to give their son space. "At that point we were beginning to walk on eggs," says Mary. "We were hoping that everything was working and that the psychiatrist was able to help." Dr. Kornhaber told the Harts that their son's case was difficult to diagnose, and he was having a hard time pinpointing what should be done. But though he wasn't sure what was wrong, everyone agreed that things were not quite right.

The summer before tenth grade, the Harts sent Brian to a camp for teenagers in Maine. Brian's letters home described the swimming, boating, and hiking in exuberant detail. He seemed to be involved in everything. Although Brian had failed math that spring and would have to pass a special examination before returning to school, he solved the problem in typical Brian style: He found a pretty girl at the camp who also needed instruction, and they canoed daily across the river to the house of a math tutor. When the Harts picked him up at summer's end, Brian was euphoric. "We felt we had a different Brian back," says Mary. "He was happy and confident, he knew he was going to pass the test, and he was on top of the world." The day of the test Pat returned from a meeting to find a phone message from Brian: "Your stupid son managed to get an 86 in math and just wanted to let you know!"

Two months later, in mid-October, Brian took the Preliminary Scholastic Aptitude Test. When Mary picked him up at school that afternoon, she found him surrounded by five of his friends. "I don't know what's the matter with Brian," one of them said, "but he's just not with it." When Brian got in the car, Mary knew immediately that it was something serious. Brian's face was expressionless, and he could barely speak. "I couldn't do anything" was all he could say. "I couldn't do anything." Later, the Harts were told that Brian had checked off the same answer for almost every question on the test.

The next day, after examining Brian, Dr. Kornhaber told the Harts that Brian was having a psychotic episode and that he would have to be hospitalized. (The Harts would learn later that Brian had tried to kill himself that morning by pulling a plastic bag over his head and wrapping a phonograph cord around his neck.) Although they hardly understood what was happening themselves, Pat and Mary explained to Brian that something in him had snapped and needed to be fixed, and that he would have to go to the hospital. Brian seemed almost to welcome the news, and he packed an overnight bag with two pairs of pants and a sweater, enough clothes for a few days.

Brian would be in the hospital for nine months.

The Harts had been warned by Dr. Kornhaber that when someone enters a psychiatric hospital for the first time, his psychosis may initially increase, both because the doctors may experiment with various medications, which can take weeks or even months to evaluate, and because of the change of environment. Still the Harts were unprepared for their first visit with Brian, two days after they had driven him to Stony Lodge, a private hospital in Ossining. The Harts were escorted through two locked doors and into a stark common room in which several men gazed numbly at a television. Brian stood in the doorway on the far side of the room. He was neatly dressed in a white T-shirt and corduroy pants, but he looked pale and terrified. He didn't move. The Harts went to him and put their arms around him, and the three of them hugged and wept. In a tiny voice Brian said over and over, "I'm scared. I'm scared. I'm scared."

Brian thought his parents had abandoned him. "Why am I here?" he kept saying. His parents tried to reassure him that it was for the best, but they were unnerved. Heavily medicated with Thorazine, an antipsychotic drug commonly used to sedate patients, Brian had difficulty speaking and couldn't articulate his fears. He just squeezed their hands so hard he left marks. Driving home that afternoon, Pat and Mary were deeply shaken. "We wondered if we were doing the right thing," says Mary. "But people that know say you're doing the right thing. You're putting your whole life in the hands of strangers." Says Pat, "We wondered if we'd ever have him back. We wondered if we'd ever have him right." Wild ideas flashed through Mary's mind. She thought of fleeing with her son into the woods and taking care of him there.

The next months were agonizing. The BB gun lawsuit had recently gone to court, and Brian was terrified that his family would lose their house and all their possessions because of the incident. At the same time he insisted he wasn't as sick as the other patients, that he would be back in school soon. After a month or so he seemed to improve. He began to make friends with other young patients. He refinished chairs and tables in the woodworking shop, made pottery and paintings for family Christmas presents, and kept up his school-work with a tutor. Brian was anxious to go home, and his parents, telling him to try to live it day by day, continued to pay his tuition at his private school each month in the hope that he would soon be well enough to return. They visited him as often as they could; after Brian started improving, Mrs. Hart drove over almost every night. "I used to watch 'M*A*S*H' on TV, and a commercial would come on and say, 'Did you hug your child today?' And oh . . . I'd feel so awful. And I'd get in the car and take off to Ossining to see Brian."

Eventually, Brian was allowed home for weekends, when he did all the things he used to do—football games and skiing with his family, movies and pizza with his friends. But he didn't seem to be getting truly better, just having good days and bad days. At times he would be what his parents came to think of as "good Brian"—bubbling over with excitement and energy. Other times he was depressed. Brian and his father usually went to the Giants game on Sunday afternoon. Afterward, Brian went home for dinner; sometimes, though, he would ask to be driven straight back to the hospital, and the Harts knew he was feeling down. At one game in December, Patrick sensed that Brian was not really conscious of what was happening on the field, and he asked him if he wanted to leave. Brian said yes, and Pat drove him straight back to Stony Lodge. The following day Mary got a call from the psychiatrist in charge, who told her that Brian had disappeared.

With images of dragnets combing the roads and radio bulletins warning the public about "an escapee from the mental hospital," a frantic Mary Hart called the Bedford chief of police, whom she knew in her job as town clerk. They drove the streets between Ossining and Bedford Hills but saw no sign of Brian. Shortly after they got back to her house, Brian walked in the back door. "I'm home," he said. He had left the hospital after breakfast and walked seven miles through the woods. Mary was overjoyed that her son was safe, but as she hugged him she knew she had to tell him he had to go back. While Brian changed his clothes, she made him a chicken sandwich, then she drove him back to the hospital. Brian was quiet. "To this day," says Mary, "I'll never forget the look he gave me as I took him back to the hospital again: How could you do this to me? How could you do this to me?"

That spring the doctors, who still hadn't settled on a diagnosis, decided to try Brian on lithium, a drug used successfully to treat manic depression, an illness characterized by extreme mood swings and having a possible genetic base. At that time manic depression was thought to manifest itself most commonly in the mid to late twenties. Brian was believed to be too young for the diagnosis. And yet for Brian (whose illness would indeed eventually be diagnosed as manic depression), lithium seemed to be a miracle drug. He was no longer subject to drastic mood swings. Says Mary, "He was himself again."

In July, as he approached the day of his release, Brian wrote in his journal about his feelings on leaving the hospital after nine months:

Today I hit a landmark. Today for the first time since late February I was and am depressed. Not really heavily depressed like I used to be, but a kind of melancholy, silent mood. . . . I figured out why I was depressed. I'm going to leave this land of make-believe where everyone is nice and so much like you. No matter how much I cursed and damned this place, no matter how long I prayed, hoped, dreamed, and begged to get out of here, it still was a heavy big part of my life I'll never forget. I've made friends here. I've grown accustomed to this life. Being babied and looked after. I'm used to it but at the same time sick to death about it. I want my independence back! Give me Liberty or give me Death! I'm happy to say I'm alive enough to say that. You see, if I didn't come here I surely would of found some way and enough guts to end my life. Kill myself. Now I'm ok, I want life. I want, need challenge, excitement and a girlfriend. Not necessarily in that order.

What I'm saying is that I want and deserve to be let out. The question is, will I want to come back to the false security like I described in the last passage? Only time will tell.

Brian had his heart set on returning to Kennedy High School, but on the advice of his doctors and teachers the Harts decided he should go to a special school for a year, to phase him back gradually into the mainstream. That fall Brian entered the Anderson School in Staatsburg-on-Hudson, forty-five miles north of Bedford Hills; it was a small, coed, residential high school for students "whose behavior, emotional, and/or family problems are hindering their educational process." The school's fifty students take standard courses in math, English, and history but receive extra attention and counseling from a staff of special education teachers, mental health workers, nurses, and physicians. In the first weeks after he arrived Brian held himself aloof, trying hard to show that he was much less troubled than his classmates. He succeeded so well that some of the staff wondered whether there had been some mistake—one counselor referred to Brian as another "Jack Armstrong, all-American boy." But gradually Brian's polish began to wear off. One night during a fire drill he stayed in his bed staring at the ceiling. When staff members came to get him, they were shocked when he refused to move and began cursing at them.

With only three ninety-minute classes a day, academics at Anderson were designed not to push the student, but Brian pushed himself. He arrived early to class, sat in the front row, always did his homework, and given an option to rewrite a paper, usually took it. He loved to read—Tolkien, Dickens, and Stephen King were his favorites—and always seemed to have a stack of books under his arm. At a school where to be called "not a problem" was high praise, Brian was "an ideal student," according to Sandy Martin, his English teacher. "I remember one day when the kids had been giving me a rough time and I'd had it," she says. "After class Brian came up and said, 'I want you to know that I really appreciate your putting up with their BS. I get angry when people fool around when you're trying to teach something.' That made my day. I remember I wanted to hug him, but he was not a kid you could hug. He wanted to be hugged, but if you touched Brian, he would tense up."

While he was well liked by his teachers and classmates, Brian had no close friends at Anderson. "The other kids thought he was great, but Brian couldn't believe it," says Sandy Martin. "Inside he didn't think he was worthy. He'd say, 'Why would anyone want me?' " His lack of confidence was especially apparent with girls. Although he desperately wanted a girlfriend, and with his good looks and charm, girls flocked around him, Brian couldn't seem to make the right connection. He had a crush on a ninth grader, but she liked him as a friend, not as a boyfriend. Although with a four-to-one ratio of boys to girls, few of his classmates had girlfriends, Brian felt inadequate for not having one.

There was another reason why having a girlfriend was especially important to Brian. At about this time he began to talk to his mother about his fears that he might be gay. During eighth grade he had been propositioned by a man in the town park. Brian had fled. His psychiatrist suggested he tell the police, but Brian feared the police would assume he was homosexual. Brian didn't mention the incident again, but he told his mother that when they had put him in the hospital, he had been terrified that it was a whorehouse for men. Mary listened to her son, but Brian was so popular with girls, she didn't believe his fears were justified. "What's the difference?" she would say. "Stop beating yourself over it—you are what you are." Brian's counselor at Anderson also felt his fears were groundless, stemming from common adolescent panic at being unable to connect with the opposite sex. But Brian was troubled by it; talking with his mother he would hold his hands up and shake his head sadly. "These hands," he would say. "They're such feminine hands."

His worries about his sexuality made Brian feel even further from the normalcy he strove for. Brian didn't want to be a "special case," but it bugged him that in order to be "normal" he had to take pills twice a day and have his blood level measured once a month. And so part of trying to be normal was skipping his lithium, which he called a "weakness." "I refuse to take it anymore," Brian would announce to a friend. "I'm going to try to do it on my own." When he was feeling good, Brian would persuade himself that he could do without it, and he would stubbornly try to overcome his mood swings through sheer force of will. Other times he would get high and forget to take it. Without the lithium, however, he would sink into a deep depression. At meals, where he was usually at the center of a laughing group of students, he would sit alone, staring into space like a robot. If someone asked him to go for a walk or play a game, he would reply in a monotone, without looking up, that he didn't feel like it. "He would phase out and you couldn't get through to him," says one teacher. "It was as if there were a plastic shield around him that you couldn't penetrate. You'd want to take him by the shoulders and shake life back into him." The difference between Brian's highs and lows was so great that at staff meetings it was common to hear teachers say, "Which Brian are we talking about?"

Brian's two moods are strikingly juxtaposed in his journal. Four months after arriving at Anderson he described his feelings about the school, concluding:

It's kind of funny, but I'm due out of here in June, too. To go home, with Mom, Dad, and Vicky, good pup. That's kind of fun, no, sad. Because chances are I'll be due to leave there to college in a year after I get home, then on my own. It seems so unfair to me that two years of my life could have been taken away from me like that. I feel cheated, as surely my parents do too. The pain and guilt they must have felt signing their baby into a loony bin, to get him back for themselves two years later, only to send him away again. Oh Mom and Dad, I love you so much. Please forgive me.

Six weeks later Brian circled the entry and wrote below it in a scrawled, angry hand:

I read that now and all that seems like total BULLSHIT! It's like a script to a soap opera. Reading that is like cutting your way out from the bottom of a giant bowl of spaghetti with clam sauce. No matter how fast or how much you chop, you fall, sink deeper and deeper, gasping for air, almost drowning from a roomful of smoke, then fog, then finally rain of liquid lead.

Underneath he drew a picture of a man disappearing under a massive weight. Only the man's hands are visible as he struggles to stay alive.

One Friday afternoon in June near the end of his first year at Anderson, Brian's friends became concerned about him. The students at Anderson were a tight-knit group, bound together by their troubles. If a student played hooky for an evening or was involved in drinking or drugs, his friends typically covered for him, but when someone was in a deep depression, they alerted the staff. Suicide attempts at Anderson were frequent—almost one per week, according to one teacher. Most were not life-threatening—cuts from flip-top cans, razors, knives, or glass, or overdoses of medication. When Brian seemed to be withdrawing that weekend, his friends spoke to his teachers. On Saturday morning when Brian discussed suicide with some of his friends at breakfast, again those teachers were alerted. But it was too late. Sometime after breakfast Brian disappeared.

The next week was a blur of telephone calls and search posses. The school believed Brian might head out West to see one of his sisters. The Harts hired a private investigator who was convinced that Brian had not left the area. The students at Anderson were somber—almost all of them had considered or attempted suicide at some point, and they were fearful that they might come in one morning to learn that Brian had been found dead. "In all honesty people expected to find him hanging in the woods," says an Anderson teacher. The police searched the shores of the Hudson for Brian's corpse. The Harts never believed that Brian would kill himself but feared he might have a psychotic break, wander off someplace, and be hit by a train. As the days went by and the chances of Brian's being found alive grew slim, they were terrified that perhaps this time they had lost him forever. Friday morning at the breakfast table, six days after he had disappeared, they began to discuss where to bury Brian. That afternoon when Mary got home from work she heard a soft, apprehensive voice on the answering machine: "Mom, I'm all right. Can you come get me? I'll call back."

Fifteen minutes later the phone rang. It was Brian. He was calling from a pay phone in a park twelve miles from school. Mary sped up Route 9, furious at every red light, terrified that Brian wouldn't be there when she arrived. Though it was seven o'clock when she pulled into the park, it was still light out. Families ate at picnic tables and children's voices pierced the warm summer night. Then she saw Brian walking across the field toward her, his jeans and sweatshirt coarse with grime, his hair tangled, and his face with a week's growth of beard. People at the picnic tables eyed him nervously. Mary put her arms around him, but Brian, self-conscious, said, "Let's get in the car." Not long after they got on the road Brian asked his mother for a hug. Mary stopped the car and clutched her son tightly.

Brian had no idea how long he had been gone. All he remembered of that week was a few images: lying in a gutter in the rain, hearing people call his name but being unable to respond; finding a deserted hunter's cabin in the woods where he had eaten a jar of moldy peanut butter; sneaking down to the park at night to scavenge watermelon rinds and other scraps from the garbage pails; wading into the Hudson River with the intention of drowning but then walking out. When he talked about that week with his counselor at Anderson, his eyes widened with fear. "Jesus, what a thing to do," Brian would say. "How could I go through that?" For almost a year the terror of that week would return to Brian like a sudden chill, and he would relive it for a moment.

After going AWOL even Brian realized that returning to Kennedy for his senior year was out of the question. But once he was back on lithium his senior year at Anderson went smoothly. He earned an A in an expository writing course at a local community college. He was accepted at all four colleges he applied to and decided to attend the State University of New York at Brockport, a small liberal arts college near Rochester. When he came back to Anderson after a weekend at home and told people about his new girlfriend, he was so enthusiastic that one teacher thought he had invented her. Mary, a pretty, red-haired girl Brian had known at Kennedy, was devoted to Brian. She visited him as often as possible, drove him back on Sunday nights after weekends together, and wrote him long, encouraging letters almost every day. Brian's parents were so delighted that even when Mary's mother called to tell them that she and her husband had come home unexpectedly and found Brian and Mary in bed, they couldn't be too angry—Brian was so happy.

Brian felt closer to the mainstream than he had in years. In an essay for his class on "The Modern Age," he wrote:

Anderson is an escape. It is an escape from real life. It is more relaxed and less distressing. I am bored of this make-believe world, and I am anxious to graduate to the real world. I have become too comfortable in this safe, get-over world. But there have been times when I needed this escape like a man with a bullet wound cries for morphine. The realization of my departure is solidifying as my graduation day grows nearer each passing moment. But I jump for the chance of change! So I will take everything I have learned about myself and people, as well as everything else I have learned and move on. . . . I will move on, change, and weep later.

On June 28, 1983, Brian was graduated from Anderson, first in his class of eighteen, winner of the prize for Best Attitude, and valedictorian, as voted by the teachers. In his address Brian urged his classmates to make use of what they had learned at Anderson as they went on to face new challenges. He concluded:

On behalf of the graduating class of 1983 I thank each teacher, dorm parent, social worker, cook, kitchen worker, maintenance man, housekeeper, administrator, secretary, as well as our parents and our families for their support and guidance whether or not they knew they gave it. We must leave to be born again, to start fresh, to take our second chance with an understanding of why we had it: We are loved and we are believed in. Thank you.

That summer Brian dove back into the mainstream with a vengeance, as if trying to make up for lost time. He worked as a clerk in a department store by day and as a busboy in a White Plains restaurant at night. Then he would party with his old Kennedy friends. His parents would hear him come home as late as two or three in the morning. He occasionally skipped his lithium, and his mother grew tired of asking him whether he had taken it. He was going to be alone at college, and he would have to learn. Brian saw less of his girlfriend Mary. He wanted to "cool" the relationship before his freshman year at Brockport.

As late August approached Brian started to get apprehensive. At a precollege orientation seminar at a nearby hotel, the other young men and women had seemed so sure of themselves; they knew what they wanted to major in, and their careers seemed planned and focused. Brian's aspirations—forestry, social work, and the Peace Corps were among the possibilities he had mentioned—were as changeable as his moods. He fretted that although he had been a star at Anderson, an Anderson education was not as rigorous as that offered by public high schools. He worried that he might not be up to college. One night shortly before school started when his parents were out to dinner, there was a call from Brian asking if he could come and talk to them. He arrived at the restaurant in a panic. He had been talking to another college-bound Anderson friend whose nervousness had kindled Brian's fears. His parents tried to calm him, telling him he didn't *have* to go, but Brian's response was, "I'll go, I'll go." The night before they drove him to Brockport, Brian seemed dazed. He couldn't decide what to pack although he had been planning all summer. On the ride up, as he talked about the courses he wanted to take, Brian was clearly anxious. At registration Brian thought he saw someone from Bedford Hills. He was upset—it seemed that even as a college freshman hundreds of miles from home he couldn't start out with a fresh slate, he couldn't be like everyone else.

That fall Brian worked hard to be like everyone else. In early October when Pat drove up for Parents Weekend, he was impressed at how Brian seemed to be a part of everything, at how many people knew him. They went to a football game, to a play, and to church. But though it had all the earmarks of a typical college weekend, Pat could tell Brian was on edge, straining hard to have him think that things were under control.

One night not long after that weekend the Harts received a call from Brian, who was weeping and said he couldn't handle college. "Oh my God," Mary thought. "Why don't you come home," she said. "Everything will be okay." Brian told her he was calling from the phone booth in the school cafeteria, and he didn't want the other students to see him crying. Mary told him to stay there. She called Dr. Kornhaber, who called Brian. They had a long talk, and Brian managed to get through the night and remain in school.

Once again Brian was up and down. The Harts would receive a ten-page letter full of plans and projects, telling them he was going to stop fooling around and get down to work and that they shouldn't worry. Brian was taking his lithium, they could tell. Then there would be a phone call at two in the morning and a thin, lonely voice asking, "Are you okay? Is everything okay?" When Sandy Martin, his English teacher at Anderson, who had received many spirited, chatty letters from Brian, called in November, Brian was stoned. "I'm losing it," he told her. "I'm partying too much." His grades were sinking, and he had skipped several midterm exams. He said that he was hanging out with the drug crowd and didn't have enough self-control to break away from them. Searching for a spark of the old Brian, Sandy encouraged him to make a list of things he needed to do to get his act together. Brian said he would do it, but he sounded drained and sad.

"At Thanksgiving vacation when I picked up Brian at the train station, he was wearing blue jeans and a white cable-knit Irish sweater and he looked terrific," says Mary Hart. "He got in the car, but when I asked him if he wanted to drive, he said no. I knew something was off. He started talking about his girlfriend, Mary. 'She's been so good to me, and I've been so bad to her,' he kept saying. He cried and started pounding the seat with his fist. I had never seen him this disturbed, and I said, 'Brian, you're frightening me. I think we'd better go to the hospital.' He said, 'No, I'm all right. I am just really, really upset.' I held his hand, and he squeezed mine so tight I thought he might break it."

On Thanksgiving Day at a family reunion at their cousins', Brian's sister told her mother that something seemed wrong with Brian. Mary Hart went downstairs where Brian and his cousins were watching a football game. She saw immediately that Brian was "not right." He was gripping the chair tightly, and there was a dazed expression on his face. "We'll go home now, Brian," said Mary. "Good," Brian said in a remote, clipped voice. "Good. Yeah. I want to go home." As they walked into the house, Brian turned to his mother and waved both hands at her, as if shooing her away. "It was the oddest thing," she recalls. "He was looking at me, but he was seeing something that he didn't want to see and he kept waving his hands, as if to say, 'Please go away.' I realized afterward that he was hallucinating."

The next day Pat took Brian to Dr. Kornhaber, who told them that Brian's blood levels were unbalanced and would have to be stabilized. Brian later admitted that he hadn't been taking his lithium at school, and to compensate had gobbled a handful of tablets on the train home. Kornhaber recommended hospitalization. Brian said no. Kornhaber said if Brian refused, he could not take responsibility for him. Brian reluctantly agreed. That afternoon his parents drove him to Stony Lodge. As they pulled in the drive, Brian looked out the window. "I was in this place for my sixteenth birthday," he said quietly, "and it looks as if I'm going to be in it for my nineteenth birthday."

Once again Brian believed that he would be at the hospital for only a few days. But this time, instead of being edgy to get out, by the end of a month he stopped asking when he would be released. His parents grew concerned that he was becoming too comfortable there, that he might be giving up. Neverthe-less, when the doctors decided Brian was ready to go home, provided he found a job, Mary realized she wasn't sure she was ready: "I didn't know if I could take it, if he was going to get into drugs again," she says, shaking her head. "We had tried just about everything. We had tried Brian at home. We had tried freedom at college. Now home and work. I didn't think he was well enough to come home. I just felt things were not quite right." Meanwhile, the insur-ance for Brian's hospitalization was running out, and Brian's dropping out of college had cost them another $2,000. "Everything seemed to be going down the tubes, and Brian just didn't seem to be getting better," says Mary. Her frustration concerned the doctors, who suggested Pat and Mary begin family therapy with Brian. The Harts agreed. On January 10, 1984, after seven weeks in the hospital, Brian was discharged.

Brian found a job almost immediately. Jim Candon, a supervisor at the Margaret Chapman School in Hawthorne, says he will never forget his inter-view with Brian: "I asked him what made him think he was right for the job. Brian said, 'Because I have a lot of love to give.' I interpreted that to mean he needed a lot of love." The Margaret Chapman School is a school for profoundly retarded children, many of whom cannot perform even simple tasks for themselves. As a teacher's aide Brian dressed the children, toilet-trained them, brushed their teeth, washed their hands and faces, combed their hair, fed them, and assisted them in the classroom with their drawing and counting. Many new staff members are squeamish when asked to brush a child's teeth or wipe his bottom, but Brian showed no reluctance, even volun-teering for tasks that others refused to do. The staff realized that Brian had a gift for working with these children. Playing basketball with kids who could barely move, he would guide them around, encouraging them, getting them involved in the game. In class he persuaded a little girl who had always drawn with only one crayon to use four other colors. "There was an immediate bonding between Brian and the kids," says Jim Candon. "He had a gentleness about him, a way of being able to reach the kids without the necessity of verbal expression. These children were real human beings to Brian. He always treated them as normal, not retarded. I think he found in the children a reflection of his own brokenness, and thus, more than any of us, could empathize. He could see the human being beneath the mask, the real person struggling, aching, and reaching out for understanding."

Once again Brian was full of plans. He talked about his work at Chapman with his parents, overflowing with ideas for programs, passionate about the need for funding to help retarded children. He talked about returning to school for a degree in special education so he could make a career of this work. Reconciled to living at home for the time being, he began buying plants and hanging posters of rock groups on his bedroom wall. With his first paycheck from Chapman he bought a stereo. He worked double shifts to help save for a car. He enrolled in a sculpture course at Westchester Community College and talked about clearing a space in the cellar for a studio. He constructed a collage from magazine photographs of his favorite things—skiing, travel, wildlife, and women—and hung it on his bedroom wall. He jotted down lists of things he planned to do.

But just as it had at Anderson and at Brockport, Brian's period of normalcy began to fray. Once again the Harts could tell he wasn't taking his lithium. He grew a scraggly beard and dressed less neatly; at his grandmother's birthday dinner he was the only man without a tie. He hadn't talked to his girlfriend Mary since before Thanksgiving, and he spent most of his free time with Melinda, a sixteen-year-old girl he had met at the hospital who had been a member of the fast crowd. He had started smoking pot again, going to parties, and coming home late. He began to skip his sculpture class and to arrive late for work. Some days he didn't show up at all. Questioned by his parents, he would offer vague answers and half-truths. While the Harts were concerned, they agreed that they shouldn't hector Brian. Once again, they were walking the fine line between protecting and intruding.

One evening in January, Brian called his parents from a bar in the nearby town of Mahopac. He would hitchhike home, he said. It was a cold night, and several inches of snow lay on the ground. As the evening wore on and Brian hadn't returned, the Harts grew concerned. Pat drove to the bar. Brian wasn't there. Pat combed the roads between Mahopac and Bedford Hills, and finally saw Brian hitchhiking. When Brian got in, Pat could tell his son had been drinking heavily, and he questioned him about it. Suddenly Brian reached for the door handle and tried to jump from the moving car. His father grabbed his arm and tried to hold him as he slowed the car. When the car stopped, Brian jumped out. Pat got out of the car and chased him through the snow. Brian swore at his father. "Leave me alone," he screamed. "Leave me alone." Pat finally tackled his son and held him down. But as soon as he got up, Brian took off again. Pat caught up with him again, but Brian shook loose and rolled under a guard rail and down a ravine toward a two-lane parkway. Pat was terrified that Brian would be hit by a car, but he saw Brian get up and cross the road. Pat got back in his car and tried to follow. When he reached the exit ramp from the parkway, he saw Brian lying on the road. He stopped the car and pleaded with Brian to come home. "You don't want to miss work," he said. "Yeah, they love me, those kids," Brian kept saying. "I love those kids and they love me." But Brian broke loose again and ran off into the night. Pat finally drove home, feeling frightened and powerless.

Mary went out to look for Brian and found him downtown. She pulled up beside him, opened the door, and said, "Come on in, Brian." Brian lunged at the car and kicked one of the headlights. Mary drove farther down the road and parked where she thought he couldn't see her. She wanted to stay close to her son in case he fell or passed out in the snow. When Brian came up over the hill, he spotted the car, walked up, and spat at it. "Leave me alone," he shouted. "I'm not an alcoholic. Leave me alone." Then he stomped off. Mary went home.

Half an hour later, as Pat and Mary sat in the living room, they heard the back door open. Brian walked in. Nobody said a word as he went straight up to his room.

The following morning Brian showed up at his mother's office at the town hall and asked to borrow her car. He wouldn't say where he was going, he just insisted that it was important. Feeling uneasy but wanting to let him know she still trusted him, Mary gave him the keys. When he returned, he gave her the keys and a big hug and told her he had been to Alcoholics Anonymous. "This is the first of ninety meetings in ninety days," he said. But his enthusiasm for AA lasted only a few sessions. He continued to drink and to have his ups and downs, but now there were more downs than ups. Brian was verbally abusive to his parents, and they could tell he was doing drugs again. Brian's friends were away at college, and he had more or less pulled away from everybody except Melinda, with whom he now spent much of his free time. One day Mary called her and asked her to persuade Brian to go to work. That Tuesday night Mary arrived home to find Brian at the dining room table, sketching, and saying over and over again, "Fucking bitch. Fucking bitch. Fucking bitch." Mary, who had to prepare for a town board meeting that night, went to her room and closed the door. Brian stormed in, swearing at her. She lost her patience. "Get out of here," she shouted. "Just get out of this room." Brian stomped into his own room, which adjoined his parents', and banged on the wall.

On Thursday, boiling with anger at his parents, Brian announced to Dr. Kornhaber that he refused to attend any more family sessions. But by Friday morning he had changed his mind, and their therapy session was their best ever. Brian was more open and forthright than he had been in some time. He acknowledged that he'd been drinking and smoking pot, and even gave them a rundown of the drugs he'd tried at college—cocaine, acid, and angel dust. He admitted that he had been lax in his attendance at work, and he vowed to apologize to his boss. He talked about saving money for a car and about returning to school part-time. Though Pat and Mary couldn't help but think, "Here we go again, off on another roll," they were elated.

Brian got a haircut, shaved his beard, and even washed his clothes—every last shirt and sock. His apology was accepted at the Chapman School, and Brian worked Saturday and Sunday. Sunday afternoon he visited Melinda, but instead of staying out late as usual, he was home by supper time. Mary cooked veal parmigiana, Brian's favorite dish.

After dinner Brian and his parents sat in the living room and talked. They didn't discuss anything in particular, it was just a pleasant, relaxed conversation—about college, the New York Giants, Melinda, how he'd appreciated his mother making veal parmigiana, how he'd started smoking pot in the sixth grade, the rock concert he planned to attend the following Saturday night. "It was nothing spectacular," says Mary. "It was just a mother and a father and a son talking." But after all the troubles and frustrations, during which Brian and his parents had become almost adversarial, the evening was so relaxed and normal that Mary was almost overwhelmed with relief. She believed that this might be the beginning of a new level of honesty between them. Now, looking back, she thinks that her son was saying good-bye.

The following evening, when Mary and Pat got home, there was a note on the kitchen blackboard: "Gone for a walk. Going to stop at library. Don't worry. Love, Brian." An hour and a half later, as they sat in the living room, they heard a thump in the attic. They rushed upstairs. Brian was walking down the attic stairs. His mother asked him what he'd been doing in the attic, a rarely visited storage area. "Looking for books," he said. The Harts knew it was too dark to see much up there. Brian said he'd used matches. Pat, concerned about the fire hazard, started to get angry, but Mary gave him a look, and they didn't pursue the matter.

Later, Mary was sitting in her bedroom when Brian came in. He looked pale, and she noticed a red mark on his neck. Brian told her it was just a rash. She said it didn't look like a rash. Brian admitted that he had bought a rope that day and had been trying to hang himself in the attic. But his ears had started popping, the rope had slipped, and it hadn't worked. Mary was unnerved, but because Brian had been in such good spirits the past few days, she did not really believe him, and she remembered a counselor telling them years before that if someone has to tell you about a suicide attempt, it's not serious. "Come on, Brian," she said. "Wasn't that stupid." She even teased him a little—there wasn't even room enough to stand up straight in the attic. When she and her husband talked about it later, they agreed that if Brian had *really* wanted to kill himself, he would have done it. In any case, Brian was scheduled to see Dr. Kornhaber at noon the following day.

In the morning Brian talked with his mother in the kitchen before she left for work. He seemed a little shaky but not unusually so. "I don't know what I'm going to do, Mom," he said. "I just don't know." "Just try and take it day by day, Brian," his mother said. "Day by day." They talked about the previous evening, and she kidded him lightly. "Why did you pick the attic?" she asked him. "We wouldn't have found you for days." "Well, I wouldn't want to bother anybody," said Brian. She joked, "Sure, we would have smelled you in about three days." They talked briefly about Arnold Caputo, a nineteen-year-old college sophomore who had hanged himself in his parents' Mount Vernon home three weeks earlier. Mary said what a shock it must have been for his family to find him.

Brian seemed okay. He told her his plans for the day. He was borrowing her car to do some errands—to fill a prescription for lithium and buy some toothpaste—before meeting Dr. Kornhaber at noon. When Brian left at 8:30, he gave his mother a big hug and a kiss. "Good-bye, Ma," he said. "Good-bye, Brian," she said. "Drive carefully."

At eleven Pat called Dr. Kornhaber from his office, as he usually did before Brian's sessions, to tell him how things had been going since the last meeting. He described how pleasant and relaxed the weekend had been, but when he told him about Brian and the rope in the attic, the psychiatrist was immediately concerned. He told Pat to try to reach Brian. Pat called home, but Brian wasn't there. Mary hadn't heard from Brian either. Brian missed his noon appointment. At two Dr. Kornhaber called Mary and urged her to go to the police department and report Brian as missing and suicidal. Mary thought he was overreacting—Brian had been gone only a few hours—but the psychiatrist insisted. She thought the police would find him immediately because the whole town knew the license plate with the Harts' initials—MFH–PJH. But as the afternoon wore on she grew increasingly anxious. Yet even that night as she and her husband lay in bed unable to sleep, listening for Brian, they believed he would return. "I fully expected him to come in," says Mary, "because this wasn't the first time it had happened, and in the past he had always turned up."

Next morning at work, every time the phone rang Mary picked it up expecting it to be Brian saying, "I'm home." She couldn't concentrate. Shortly before noon she called her husband, who had stayed home that day, and asked him to come and get her. When she got home, she made some phone calls to members of the family. While she was telling her daughter in California about Brian's disappearance, she heard a knock on the front door. Mary hurried downstairs. The police lieutenant was telling her husband that the car had been found at the rear of Oakwood Cemetery in Mount Kisco, several miles from their house, the motor still running, vacuum hoses carrying exhaust from the tailpipes into the car. Brian might have been in the car as long as twenty-four hours. Pat and Mary Hart were amazed to find that mixed in with the shock and the sadness there was a feeling of relief. "It was over," says Pat. "He was in such a struggle within himself, and that struggle was finally over." Mary says, "Brian had found his peace at last."

The funeral was held on St. Patrick's Day. St. Matthias, a small Catholic church, was filled with more than two hundred people. Mary's brother, a monsignor who had baptized Brian, said the Mass. Brian's three brothers and three friends, two from Kennedy and one from Anderson, were pallbearers. At Mary's request the organist added some traditional Irish music to the recessional. "The funeral was quite impressive, actually," says Mary. "Brian would have been very uncomfortable about all the fuss, I'm sure. He didn't like to be fussed over."

In the following weeks Pat and Mary talked with their children, laughing and weeping as they shared memories of Brian's ups and downs. They talked with Dr. Kornhaber, who had been stunned by Brian's death. They looked everywhere for a note. They searched the house, scoured the car, checked the pockets of Brian's clothes, and even played through the tape on the tape recorder in case he had recorded a last message. Each day they checked the mail, thinking he might have written them a letter, but they found nothing. Although Mary recognized that even if they found one it could never fully explain Brian's death, she would have liked to find something.

They also read through Brian's journals and notebooks, hoping to gain some insight, some clues. They didn't find a single key that explained everything; they learned little that was new or surprising. But they realized his highs had been higher, his lows lower, and the change from one to the other more abrupt than they had known. His journals brimmed with bittersweet evidence of his determination: his hopes, schemes, pep talks, self-exhortations, and renewed vows to start afresh. Even in the last week of his life he had compiled lists of things he wanted to buy for his room—posters, plants, sketchbooks—as well as notes about goals for his artwork and ideas about where to market his work. The last thing Brian wrote was a note to himself on his clipboard Thursday night, four days before his death: "I'm going to stop the pot. I'm going to get it together. I'm going to clean up my act."

IV

SOMETHING IN THE AIR

A FEW HOURS AFTER Brian's body was found the media began calling. In the days that followed, as the Harts struggled with their shock over Brian's death, they also struggled with the flood of journalists who clogged the telephone lines at Mary's office and patrolled Bedford Hills in search of interviews. One afternoon Pat came home to find a television reporter waiting in his driveway. Pat politely refused to answer her questions, but when he opened the front door, the reporter began to follow him in. After she was finally persuaded to leave, she drove into Bedford Hills and found a teenager on the street to interview. That night the Harts watched the evening news as a boy who had never met Brian was asked why teenagers were killing themselves. "I guess these rich kids don't know what to do with their time," he replied.

Brian's death made the headlines in every newspaper the Harts saw: "Suicide Stuns W'chester," wrote the *New York Post,* and in the following edition, "Town Mourns Suicide Teen." *The New York Times* was more cautious: "Another Teen-Ager Is Believed a Suicide in Westchester Area." The *Gannett Westchester Reporter Dispatch* wondered, "Another Teen-age Suicide?"

Brian Hart's death brought the number of teenage suicides in the Putnam-Westchester area to five in less than six weeks. Ten days after the suicide of Robbie DeLaValliere on February 4, 1984, Justin Spoonhour had hanged himself. Two days later eighteen-year-old Jimmy Pellechi shot himself. Eight days later Arnold Caputo, nineteen, hanged himself in his parents' home in

Mount Vernon. And now Brian. With each death the press coverage and the pandemonium grew exponentially, and by now the "Westchester suicides," as they were called, were the top story on the nightly news, not only in New York but across the country. The suburbs north of New York City responded with a growing feeling of panic. At first many had believed that the series of suicides was a coincidence. None of the teenagers had known each other or attended the same school. But as the toll began to mount, the suspicion grew that these suicides were somehow connected. Had one suicide triggered another? Can reading about suicide in the newspaper or hearing about it on TV cause suicide? Is suicide contagious? When would it stop? *Would* it stop? Who was next?

Certainly the panic was contagious. Crisis hot lines, school officials, guidance counselors, and therapists were swamped by calls from anxious parents seeking reassurance. "My son's been withdrawn lately," they would say. "I don't want him to end up like those other boys." News programs publicized the warning signs of teenage suicide, and parents checked their children for symptoms of depression. "You get paranoid," said the Westchester mother of a thirteen-year-old at a workshop on adolescent suicide. "You look for red eyes to see if he hasn't been sleeping. You look to see if he's sleeping too much."

Therapists struggled to explain the situation. Suicide, said one Westchester psychiatrist, is "a contagious illness. It's not something that spreads from one person to another, like a cold. It's something that's in the air, in the culture, in the environment." In an article on the "Westchester suicides," Susan Blumenthal, head of the Suicide Research Unit at the National Institute of Mental Health, speculated that suicide could become "sort of like punk rock—something that catches on." Even Westchester County Mental Health Commissioner Eugene Aronowitz, who had from the start firmly insisted the suicides were unconnected, was ruffled. "They seem to be related to each other because one seems to be kicking off the other," he told Tom Brokaw on "NBC Nightly News," "so to that extent, until we put a stop to it in some way, we've got an epidemic here."

On April 7, three weeks after Brian Hart's death, eighteen-year-old Kelly Keagan of Carmel, a small town in Putnam County, hanged herself in her dormitory room at Mount St. Mary's College in Newburgh.

On Friday, May 25, seventeen-year-old Charles Castaldo, Jr., shot himself in the head in a bedroom of his father's home in Greenburgh, near Scarsdale.

The following Monday nineteen-year-old Kevin Harlan was found hanging in a stairwell outside a church in the tiny middle-class community of Sparkill across the Hudson River in Rockland County. His death brought the number of teenage suicides in the tri-county area north of New York City to eight in four months.

As horrifying as the "Westchester suicides" were, they were hardly unique. They merely added to the growing evidence that youth suicides tend to occur in bunches. Even as Justin Spoonhour and Brian Hart were taking their lives, in Arlington, Texas, a Dallas suburb, there were five youth suicides in the first four months of 1984. In Beverly Hills, California, there had been three between January and April. And before that, starting in February 1983, there had been eight in fourteen months in Plano, Texas. In Columbus, Ohio, there had been five in a single month, including three freshmen at the same high school in one weekend. In 1982 in Cheyenne, Wyoming, there had been three in seventeen days. In 1980 in Englewood, Colorado, three in five months at the same high school. In 1979 in West Milford, New Jersey, six in twenty months. Beginning in 1978 in the North Shore suburbs of Chicago, twenty-eight in seventeen months. In 1978 in Chappaqua, in Westchester County, two in three months at one high school, followed by five attempts in seven weeks.

Was there something in one suicide that acted as a "triggering incident" for another? Did each successive suicide lower the threshold for the next, as a firecracker, once lit, starts to detonate the rest of the string? Adding to the fear was the confusion of the experts who struggled to explain the phenomenon. Their bafflement was reflected in the variety of words they used to describe the various episodes: epidemic, rash, copycat syndrome, serial suicides, ripple effect, cascade, clump, contagion, fever, outbreak, chain, follow the leader, domino effect. Eventually, they would settle on the slightly more clinical-sounding "cluster."

While these terms seem to suggest that suicide might be catching, in the fashion of measles or the flu, experts believe that suicide doesn't pick its victims that randomly. Researchers have long suspected that when one suicide occurs, it may lower the threshold for vulnerable people in the same geographic vicinity. People with a previous suicide in the family, for instance, have an incidence of suicide eight times higher than the general population. Yale researchers Bruce Rounsaville and Myrna Weissman studied sixty-two patients who were seen in an emergency room following suicide attempts; four had made their attempt within four weeks after the suicide or suicide attempt of someone to whom they were close. In three of the four cases a similar method was used. They concluded that clustered suicidal behavior was not infrequent. In certain settings, often confined places in which there is a rigid social structure, one suicide seems to spur others. Clusters have occurred in prisons, boarding schools, colleges, army barracks, and mental hospitals. After a suicide most hospitals routinely place the rest of the patients under heightened security or "suicide watch."

Adolescents, at a developmental stage in which they are highly suggestible, may be especially prone to imitation in suicide. "When a suicide happens, even people who don't know the person are affected," says Harvard psychologist Douglas Powell, who has counseled students after campus suicides. "One always has the thought, 'This could happen to me. Is it *going* to happen to me? If it happened to *him* and *he* didn't seem troubled . . .' " One adolescent suicide will, in a sense, bring other suicidal adolescents to the surface, but experts agree that the suicide can influence only someone who is already vulnerable. "Reading about a suicide does not *make* someone suicidal," emphasizes Judie Smith, program director at The Suicide and Crisis Center in Dallas, who worked with Plano students, parents, and teachers after the 1983 cluster. "But if that person is already at risk of suicide, the media reports may inadvertently convey the message that it's okay to kill yourself, that suicide is an acceptable solution to your problems." Westchester psychiatrist Samuel Klagsbrun says, "When one kid actually goes ahead and does the unthinkable, it's almost as if it gives permission to others to also do the unthinkable."

The more attention a suicide provokes, the more a "permission" is apt to seem like an invitation. "The way we handle this frightens me," says psychologist Pamela Cantor. "There is often so much adulation after a teenage suicide—they name a school building after him, they have a ceremony, they dismiss school for the day. A kid who has felt lonely and out of it can suddenly go from being a nonentity to being a hero." A letter to columnist Ann Landers described a thirteen-year-old Cincinnati girl who had been unable to make the cheerleading squad or to get admitted into any campus club. When she won a raffle at a pizza parlor entitling her to a pizza dinner for fifteen, she turned down the prize, saying she didn't have fourteen friends. A few weeks later she killed herself. At her funeral more than two hundred schoolmates signed the guest book, wept, and placed flowers on her casket.

After Arnold Caputo was buried, front-page articles described the posthumous outpouring of grief and affection for the young rock musician, noting that according to his wishes he was buried with his guitar. "Is it important for us to know that?" wonders a Westchester high school counselor. "A troubled kid who reads that may say, 'Hey, I'll go out with my basketball or my hockey stick.' " Like Tom Sawyer, who enjoyed fantasizing about the effect of his death on the Widow Douglas, a vulnerable teenager may imagine the effect of his suicide on those left behind. "I've talked to lots of people, like over a hamburger at lunch, about who would be at our funerals if we died," says a Texas teenager. "If you're feeling depressed one day and you feel you don't have any friends, you think, 'If I died, whoever came to my funeral would be my friends.' " A suicidal teenager may have a magical belief that he'll be able to savor the reaction to his death. But unlike Tom Sawyer, he won't be around to attend his own funeral. A lonely, overweight thirteen-year-old California boy who shot himself wrote in his suicide note, "Please tell my classmates what happened and watch if they are sad or if they laugh."

If the notion of imitation seems understandable, there is disagreement on what constitutes a cluster. In 1983, Plano became embedded in the national consciousness as a prototype. A bedroom community twenty miles from Dallas, Plano sprouted during the seventies when a steady influx of professionals swelled its population from seventeen thousand in 1970 to ninety thousand in 1983 and dotted the landscape with sprawling developments of expensive homes with manicured lawns, automatic garage door openers, and six-foot "privacy" fences. Its $37,000 average family income was 50 percent higher than the national norm, and many of the town's teenagers were equipped with their own stereos, televisions, and sports cars. It was a town in which, as the media noted, an adolescent seemed to have "everything to live for."

The first suicide occurred on February 23, 1983. Four days after his best friend died in a freak drag racing accident, sixteen-year-old Bruce Carrio was found dead of carbon monoxide poisoning in his parents' garage. The tape he had been playing on his car stereo had wound down to Pink Floyd's "Goodbye Cruel World." Six days later eighteen-year-old Glenn Currey, also a student at Plano High School but not a friend of Carrio's, killed himself by carbon monoxide poisoning. Six weeks later Henri Doriot, fifteen, shot himself in the head with a .22-caliber rifle. Pinned to his bulletin board were clippings about Carrio's death. Within fifteen months of the first suicide there were seven more and at least sixteen attempts. Seven of the eight students who killed themselves were students at the same school; five belonged to the same social circle or had relatives who belonged to that group.

After the fourth suicide the national media descended on Plano. The town resented the attention, and many people blamed the press for the subsequent suicides. But the story was a natural: Plano fit a stereotype as the dark underside of the American dream. "Suicides in Paradise," headlined the *Los Angeles Herald Examiner.* "Teen-age Suicide in the Sun Belt—An Idyllic Dallas Suburb Is Discovering the Sorrows of Rootlessness and Isolation" was the headline in *Newsweek.* The *San Antonio Light:* "Plano: Where Suicide Is Preppy."

But tagging upwardly mobile boomtowns as incubators for adolescent suicide gave communities like Plano an undue share of notoriety. Over the past decade, clusters have taken place in cities, suburbs, rural farming communities, and on Indian reservations. In some instances subsequent suicides knew a previous victim; in others they may have heard of other suicides through word of mouth or the media. Some clusters drew a great deal of publicity; others were hardly mentioned. In some the adolescents used similar methods; in others they used a variety.

When the media began to focus on the teenage suicides occurring north of New York City, it treated Westchester and Plano as if they were virtually interchangeable. *Ladies' Home Journal,* for instance, portrayed Westchester County as "a sprawling bedroom suburb that could be the definition of upward mobility." Television news reports ran footage of gracious homes, rolling hills, and young girls show-jumping horses. The word "affluent" was used so often that it made wealth sound like a terminal illness. " 'Contagious' Teen Suicides Worry Town" was the headline for a story in the *Dallas Times Herald,* which like many other media accounts discussed the "affluent suburb" of New York as if the suicides had occurred in a single community, not in eight different towns in three different counties with a total population of more than a million. The eight teenagers, in fact, represented a broad range of socioeconomic backgrounds and lived in towns ranging from the prosperous bedroom community of Mount Vernon, to rural Putnam County, to the racially mixed, largely blue-collar towns of Peekskill and North Tarrytown. The majority came from families whose circumstances could be described as modest. Most of the victims' families had lived in their communities for many years. None of the victims knew one another or attended the same school. None of the suicides was directly linked to a previous suicide, although the teenagers may have read or heard about them. It would have been difficult not to because almost every day there seemed to be another newspaper article or television spot about the "Westchester suicides."

The press was prone to make the cluster larger than it actually was. When Christopher Ruggiero, the seventeen-year-old son of the fire chief in Pelham, was found hanged by his bathrobe sash in his bedroom closet on February 21, five days after Jimmy Pellechi's death, most newspapers assumed he had become the fourth suicide in the Westchester cluster. Several days later the county medical examiner said that Ruggiero's death was not a suicide. People were perplexed. Then an article appeared in *The New York Times* on auto-erotic asphyxiation (AEA). A practice familiar to medical examiners and coroners but little known to the public, AEA is a form of masturbation in which erotic sensation is enhanced by decreasing oxygen to the brain, usually by means of a noose around the neck. Although sexual pleasure, not death, is the goal, an estimated five hundred to one thousand practitioners a year— most of them young white males—go too far, become unconscious, and asphyxiate. Whether or not it results in death, the practice is clearly masochistic, risk-taking behavior. Yet deaths due to AEA are ruled accidents. Many, however, are mistakenly classified as suicides. In Christopher Ruggiero's case, although his death was lumped with the other suicides, swelling the Westchester cluster beyond its actual extent, the medical examiner ultimately ruled that the death was due to "undetermined circumstances."

What exactly is a cluster? Are some adolescents more vulnerable to suggestion than others? Are some towns more vulnerable than others? Do suicides cluster by method? In Plano four were by carbon monoxide, four were by gunshot; in Westchester five of eight were by hanging. What are the geographical boundaries of a cluster? If a teenager in New Jersey reads about a cluster in New York and kills himself, is he part of the New York cluster or the possible beginning of a New Jersey cluster? Do clusters spawn clusters? Did Plano beget Westchester? Do older people commit suicide in clusters? If there were a cluster in Harlem instead of an affluent suburb like Plano, would we hear about it? Have there always been clusters or is the media merely reporting them more fully? Does reporting contribute to clusters? Are certain kinds of coverage more lethal than others?

While the term "cluster" is new, the phenomenon it describes is almost as old as suicide itself. As Forbes Winslow, an English physician, observed in 1840: "The most singular feature connected with the subject of suicide is, that the disposition to sacrifice life has, at different periods, been known to prevail epidemically, from a perversion, as it has been supposed, of the natural instinct of imitation."

There are several ways in which "the natural instinct of imitation" can work. Throughout history, during times of religious persecution, political oppression, or social upheaval, there have been instances in which a town, a country, or a religious group has been swept by a collective impulse to suicide. Classical Greek and Roman history is filled with accounts of entire towns and armies that chose death over surrender. When Philip of Macedon besieged the city of Abydos, he triggered a frenzy of suicide among its inhabitants. Hoping to stanch the self-slaughter, he withdrew his army for three days. When he returned there was no one left alive. In A.D. 73, Jewish zealots defending the fortress of Masada in Israel chose death over surrender to the besieging Roman legions. Nine hundred and sixty men, women, and children died. In 1190, in York, England, more than five hundred Jews under siege by idle ex-crusaders killed one another to avoid persecution and torture; at Verdun in 1320, another five hundred did the same. In 1944, after surrendering to Allied troops, the entire Japanese population of Saipan committed suicide. Soldiers blew themselves up with grenades; civilians walked off cliffs or drowned themselves in the Pacific. These are but a small fraction of the instances in which groups have chosen death over surrender.

Collective suicide has also been occasioned by plague. "In the year of Grace 665," wrote Roger of Wendover, a thirteenth-century monk and historian, "there was such an excessive mortality in England, that the people crowded to the seaside, and threw themselves from the cliffs into the sea, choosing rather to be cut off by a speedy death than to die by the lingering torments of the pestilence." Seven centuries later the Black Death of 1348–50 spurred an even greater toll of suicides, including many Jews who, falsely accused of causing the plague by poisoning the wells, burned themselves to escape the Gentiles' fury. In *Journal of the Plague Years,* his imaginative reconstruction of London's Great Plague of 1665, Daniel Defoe wrote, "Some threw themselves out at windows or shot themselves, or otherwise made themselves away, and I saw several dismal objects of that kind." An outbreak of smallpox among American Indians on the Central Plains during the 1830s set off an equally virulent outbreak of suicide. As one observer noted, "Very few of those who were attacked recovered their health; but when they saw all their relations buried, and the pestilence still raging with unabated fury among the remainder of their countrymen, life became a burden to them, and they put an end to their wretched existence, either with their knives and muskets, or by precipitating themselves from the summit of the rock near their settlement. The prairie all around is a vast field of death, covered with unburied corpses."

Collective suicide often occurs in the face of an enemy less tangible than a disease or an army but no less real to its victims. In the mid-seventeenth century the Old Believers, a Russian Orthodox sect who believed that the Anti-Christ was to arrive in 1666, burned their villages around them. In less than a decade some twenty thousand had taken their own lives. In Tiraspol, Russia, in 1897 twenty-eight members of a religious sect buried themselves alive to escape the census, which they regarded as sinful. In May 1910, when it was widely believed that the earth was about to pass through the tail of Halley's comet, clusters of suicides were reported in Spain, France, and the United States. In 1978, under the spell of their charismatic leader, Jim Jones, who persuaded them that their way of life was threatened by a hostile outside world, 912 members of the Peoples Temple drank cyanide-laced Kool-Aid at Jonestown, Guyana. Collective suicide has even been occasioned by ecstasy. During the dancing manias in Italy and Germany during the fourteenth century, hundreds of men and women tarantellaed off the cliffs in a frenzy.

In these instances a collection of individual impulses seems to detonate simultaneously, often under the influence of a leader who acts as a sort of lethal pied piper. At other times a single suicide seems to set off a chain reaction in which the act of suicide is passed like a baton from despairing person to despairing person, often using the same method. In ancient Greece, Plutarch described such an episode:

A strange and terrible affliction once came upon the maidens of Miletos from some obscure cause—mostly it was conjectured that some poisonous and ecstatic temperament of the atmosphere produced in them a mental upset and frenzy. For there fell suddenly upon all of them a desire for death and a mad impulse towards hanging. Many hung themselves before they could be prevented. The words and tears of their parents and the persuasions of their friends had no effect. In spite of all the ingenuity and cleverness of those who watched them, they succeeded in making away with themselves.

The epidemic abated when city magistrates decreed that the corpses of suicides would henceforth be dragged naked through the marketplace, whereupon, as author A. Alvarez observed, "vanity, if not sanity, prevailed." Similar rashes of suicide among women are said to have occurred in Marseilles and Lyons during the Renaissance. In 1792, after a soldier hanged himself from a beam at Les Invalides hospital in Paris, five other wounded soldiers hanged themselves from the same beam within a fortnight, and a total of fifteen took their lives before the corridor was closed. After the suicides of two of his grenadiers at St. Cloud, Napoleon issued an order asserting that "to abandon oneself to grief without resisting, and to kill oneself in order to escape from it, is like abandoning the field of battle before being conquered." (Napoleon himself had contemplated suicide as a melancholy teenager and is said to have attempted it by overdosing on opium after the death of his mistress Josephine.) In 1928 in Budapest, after 150 drownings were recorded during the months of April and May, a "suicide flotilla" patrolled the Danube, saving nine of ten would-be suicides. Primitive tribes, recognizing the possibility of contagion, have devised more direct remedies. In his 1960 study, *African Homicide and Suicide,* anthropologist Paul Bohannan writes: "The East African societies all destroy the tree on which or the hut in which the suicide occurred, burning it and the rope expressly so that an epidemic of suicides will not occur."

Adolescents may be especially susceptible to imitation. "A child is more open to suggestion than an adult, in suicide as in all other matters," observed David Oppenheim in 1910. "In fact, the power of suggestion shows itself with horrifying clarity in many youthful suicides." Oppenheim, a professor of classical languages in Vienna, was speaking in Sigmund Freud's living room at a meeting of the Vienna Psychoanalytic Society. The meeting, perhaps the first interdisciplinary symposium on suicide, had been called in response to a crisis that bore remarkable similarity to the situation in the United States in 1984. An epidemic of adolescent suicide seemed to be sweeping Europe, Russia, and the United States around the turn of the century. In Moscow, to cite just one example, seventy children in a single school district took their lives between May 1908 and October 1910. The epidemic was widely reported in the press, and writers, doctors, and clergymen rounded up a familiar list of suspects: illegitimacy, divorce, excessive ambition, lack of discipline in the schools and in the home, and a general weakening of moral fiber. "To all this may be added the weakmindedness which springs from forced, hothouse education, begun too early and goaded on too fast . . ." wrote one American critic. "Boys and girls to-day are often men and women in the experience of life and its excitements, and *ennuyés* or *blasés* at an age when their grandparents were flying kites and dressing dolls."

Those words could have been written today, and the discussion that took place in Freud's living room in 1910 was not unlike those heard at dozens of youth suicide symposiums in the 1980s. Freud's distinguished panel discussed the social conditions that made suicide more likely, while noting that the focus must be on psychological vulnerability to stress rather than on the stress itself. They criticized journalists who oversimplified or sensationalized the problem, and raised concerns about the role of suggestibility and imitation. "The sensational fashion in which so many newspapers present such news [of a suicide]," observed Karl Molitor, "and the aura of martyrdom they delight in placing around these unfortunates, can all too easily induce another victim to follow the fatal example." They called for better research and for suicide prevention education.

One issue raised in Freud's living room that is increasingly debated today is the effect of music and literature on imitation. Certain books, videos, movies, and rock music are accused of acting as spurs to suicide. An oft-cited name on the list of rock musicians whose lyrics have been said to inspire suicide is Ozzy Osbourne. "Suicide is the only way out / Don't you know what it's really all about," sang the heavy-metal star in "Suicide Solution," from his album *Speak of the Devil*. The song was a favorite of John McCollum, a nineteen-year-old from Indio, California, who one night in October 1984 went to his bedroom, put *Speak of the Devil* on the stereo, put on the headphones, and shot himself with his father's pistol. His father filed suit against Osbourne and his record company, claiming that Osbourne's "violent, morbid, and inflammatory music . . . encouraged John McCollum to take his own life."

Each generation has its Ozzy Osbourne. Two hundred years ago it was Johann Wolfgang von Goethe. Goethe's novel *The Sorrows of Young Werther* (published in 1774, when the author was twenty-four) is perhaps the most famous prod to youthful suicide in history. The hero is an angst-ridden young man who shoots himself when his love for a married woman goes unrequited. The book touched a nerve. Like Werther, young men all over Europe dressed in blue tailcoats and yellow waistcoats. Like Werther, they talked and acted with exaggerated sensitivity. And, like Werther, some of them shot themselves. Romantic suicidal melancholy was dubbed Wertherism, and those whose suicides were linked to the book were said to have been suffering from Wertheritis. Goethe biographer Richard Friedenthal writes: "One 'new Werther' shot himself with particular *éclat:* having carefully shaved, plaited his pigtail, put on fresh clothes, opened *Werther* at page 218 and laid it on the table, he opened the door, revolver in hand, to attract an audience and, having looked round to make sure they were paying sufficient attention, raised the weapon to his right eye and pulled the trigger." The book was banned in Leipzig and Copenhagen; when an Italian translation appeared in Milan, the Catholic clergy bought up and destroyed the entire edition.

Goethe was not the only author whose works, according to many people, encouraged a preoccupation with death and suicide. In an 1805 sermon, "The Guilt, Folly, and Sources of Suicide," New York City minister Samuel Miller asserted that "the mischievous influence on popular opinions produced by many dramatic representations and by licentious novels, may probably be considered as leading to many cases of the crime before us." As the Romantic Age bloomed, Byron's *Manfred,* Chateaubriand's *René,* and Lamartine's *Raphael* were all accused of sparking suicides and were duly reviled by the clergy. Even Thomas Paine's 1796 treatise, *The Age of Reason,* was accused of sponsoring suicides by "weakening the moral principles."

In 1928, when thirteen boys and girls killed themselves in thirteen weeks in the town of Liesva in the Ural mountains, investigators from Moscow found they had been members of a suicide club formed in honor of Sergei Esenin, a Russian poet who had hanged himself in 1925. The students held meetings at which they discussed Esenin's poetry and debated "Is life worth living?" and "Is suicide justified?" In 1936 in Budapest the suicides of eighteen young people were linked to the popularity of a ballad called "Gloomy Sunday." The lyrics of "The Hungarian Suicide Song," as it came to be known, concluded with the words, "My heart and I have decided to end it all." (Thirty-two years later, Reszo Seress, the song's composer, jumped to his death from his apartment window.) In the late forties many adolescent suicides in the United States and Canada were attributed to the pernicious effects of horror comic books; in Montreal policemen initiated a campaign to ban them from the newsstands. In recent years several films have been accused of romanticizing suicide and triggering the deaths of young people. *The Deer Hunter,* a film about the Vietnam War that contains a graphic depiction of Russian roulette, has been linked by researchers to forty-three Russian roulette deaths since its release in 1978. After the death by hanging of Robbie DeLaValliere, the first of the Westchester cluster, many people blamed the film *An Officer and a Gentleman,* in which a charismatic young naval cadet hangs himself. DeLaValliere had seen the film and had talked of it frequently before his death by hanging.

As Goethe himself noted, however, artistic creations reflect rather than create the mood of a time. Robbie DeLaValliere was a troubled youngster long before he had ever seen *An Officer and a Gentleman.* And John McCollum, the heavy-metal fan who killed himself while listening to "Suicide Solution," had other problems besides Ozzy Osbourne. According to news reports, he had dropped out of school in the ninth grade and had "had some trouble with the law," including an arrest for drunken driving. (His father's suit against Osbourne was dismissed by a judge who commented, "Trash can be given First Amendment protection, too.") As one columnist observed: "We must grieve with Jack McCollum for the loss of his son. But there's no reason to blame the artist who may have been his son's only solace in a hostile and extremely unbearable world." At a recent conference on youth suicide, a young woman in the audience voiced a similar point of view: "Maybe we should look at rock music not as a cause of problems but as a symptom of our time. Instead of condemning our youth we should start listening to them. And instead of banning their music we should start listening to it."

Long before Plano and Westchester, media accounts of actual suicides were blamed for triggering further suicides. In 1828, English physician George Man Burrows wrote, "When the mind is beginning to aberrate, [it is] very essential to prevent persons affected by moral causes or inclined to suicide, from reading newspapers, lest the disposition and the mode be suggested by something similar." While Burrows recommended that vulnerable people be kept from newspapers, William Farr, director of vital statistics for the British Registrar-General's office, urged the press to control themselves. "No fact is better established in science than that suicide (and murder may perhaps be added) is often committed from imitation," he wrote in 1841. "A single paragraph may suggest suicide to twenty persons; some particular, chance, but apt expression, seizes the imagination, and the disposition to repeat the act, in a moment of morbid excitement, proves irresistible. Do the advantages of publicity counterbalance the evils attendant on one such death? Why should cases of suicide be recorded at length in the public papers, any more than cases of fever?"

The debate reached its climax at the turn of the century. After the *New York World* published the article "Is Suicide a Sin?" in 1894, *The New York Times* accused the *World* of provoking an unprecedented number of suicides. A rash of Cleveland, Ohio, suicides in 1910 was attributed to press coverage, and in 1911 the National Association of Retail Druggists protested newspaper reports publishing the dosages of poisons used in suicide attempts as "inducing morbid people and criminals to use these poisons." That same year at the annual meeting of the American Academy of Medicine, statistician Edward Bunnell Phelps denounced "the pernicious influence of neurotic books and newspapers" as "an accomplice in crimes against the person." He singled out morbid literature and plays, newspaper accounts of suicide, and lurid tales in the Sunday supplements—a "literary chamber of horrors" from which he culled a few examples: "The City of the Suicide Germ," "Chain of Suicides Strangely Arise from Love Match," and "That Pathetic Mystery of Suicide on the Eve of Marriage—What Secret Hides Behind the Recurring Tragedies of Self-Destruction at the Brink of Nuptial Union, Even Where Every Known Promise Is for a Happy Future."

Did morbid literature and sensational newspaper accounts of suicide really increase the number of suicides? Or were the suicides that were blamed on the printed word the deaths of troubled people who would have killed themselves anyway? The sociologist Émile Durkheim believed the latter. In his landmark 1897 study, *Le Suicide,* he reviewed the research linking suicide and suggestion, and concluded that the effect of imitation on the national level of suicides was minimal. Those few suicides that might be triggered by suggestion, he said, would have eventually occurred in any case; a book like *Werther* or a sensational newspaper report merely hastened the timing.

Seventy-seven years later David Phillips, a thirty-year-old Princeton-trained sociologist, disputed this conclusion. Checking the vital statistics of the United States against *The New York Times* index for front-page stories on suicide since World War II, he found that suicides increased significantly in the month after a highly publicized suicide story. The greater the publicity, the greater the increase. For instance, the suicide of Marilyn Monroe in 1962 spurred a 12 percent jump (197 more suicides than would have been expected in the month following her death). Phillips also found that the increase occurs primarily in the geographic area in which the story is published. Finding that there was no matching "dip" in the rate after the publicity had died down, Phillips concluded that these deaths were "extra" suicides, not inevitable suicides that would otherwise have taken place a little later. Phillips called this phenomenon "the Werther effect."

While his work offers compelling evidence linking suggestion and suicide, Phillips is careful to emphasize that the media story does not itself cause suicide. "The factors that drive a person to suicide may build up over many years," he says. "I've been investigating only one aspect of it. I'm studying the trigger and not what loaded the gun." Phillips goes on to speculate on how that trigger might be squeezed: "A suicide story in the newspaper may be a sort of natural advertisement. Just as, suppose, watching television, I have this strange vague feeling inside me, but I can't put a label on it. Then I see an ad for McDonald's, and I say to myself, 'Come to think of it, I think that strange vague feeling I have is hunger. And there are various ways to assuage my hunger, but now I've seen this option suggested. I think I'll go to McDonald's.'

"Now it's possible that unhappy people out there, who may or may not realize they're unhappy, read the story about Marilyn Monroe's suicide and become aware that they *are* unhappy and maybe also become aware of an option to end their unhappiness. They may feel they have been given permission because they see another person has done it. Maybe they say, 'Gee, if even Marilyn Monroe is feeling bad enough to do this, shouldn't I do it, too?' "

In 1986 two controversial and troubling studies on adolescent suicide and contagion were reported in *The New England Journal of Medicine.* Examining the effect of thirty-eight nationally televised news or feature stories about suicide from 1973 to 1979, Phillips and a colleague found a significant increase (7 percent) in teenage suicides during the week following the broadcasts. The more networks carrying the story, the bigger the increase. Girls were more susceptible to the influence than boys. (They did not find a significant increase in adult suicides following the programs.) In the second study Madelyn Gould and David Shaffer of Columbia University researched the effect of four made-for-TV movies about teenage suicide broadcast over a six-month period in late 1984 and early 1985. Teenage suicide rates in the Metropolitan New York area rose in the two weeks after three of the four movies were broadcast; six more teenagers than would have been expected took their lives. Attempted suicides rose by 40 percent. In an editorial accompanying the articles, psychiatrist Leon Eisenberg wrote, "It is timely to ask whether there are measures that should be undertaken to limit media coverage of suicide."

The studies were challenged by the television networks, which pointed out that there is no way of knowing whether the teenagers who killed themselves actually saw the television movies or news broadcasts. Sociologists employed by NBC extended Phillips's study through 1984 and found an increase for the 1977 to 1980 time period but no overall increase. In 1987, Phillips himself contradicted Gould and Shaffer's findings. Looking at the effect of the same movies on teenage suicide in California and Pennsylvania, he found no rise in the rate. Psychologist Alan Berman also questioned the data in the Gould-Shaffer study. Collecting statistics from nineteen medical examiners across the country, representing 20 percent of the U.S. population, he found no increase in youth suicides in the two weeks following three of the TV movies; in some areas there was a decrease. (He did find evidence that one of the broadcasts may have influenced the methods used by young people already predisposed to suicide.)

Despite these conflicting results the responsibility of the press in reporting suicides remains an issue. "If the mass media were to reduce the publicity of suicide stories, it's pretty clear that the number of suicides would go down," says Phillips, who nevertheless opposes censorship. "I grew up in South Africa where the press is controlled and individual freedom substantially limited," he says. "I think it would be extremely unfortunate if my studies were used as ammunition to pressure the media to change their coverage. If the media want to do this voluntarily, it's up to them." In the past several years, in fact, some newspapers have tempered their suicide coverage. Prevention centers and clinics have organized seminars to educate the media about suicide. "I don't suggest that the media stop reporting suicide, but they have a responsibility not to romanticize it," says Westchester high school counselor George Cohen. "The line between reporting and romanticizing suicide is easy to draw—whether it's splashed on the front page with a romantic headline or put on page four with the basic facts."

But in 1984 suicide and suicide clusters were a hot story. Ironically, however, the focus on clusters may allow us to overlook the extent of youth suicide generally. The *Los Angeles Times* pointed out that the number of suicides in clusters recently paled in comparison to the routine youth suicide toll in L.A. County. Reviewing coroners' records for a six-month period in late 1983 and early 1984, they found seventy-three cases of suicide by people age twenty-four and under, "a total significantly greater than all of the clusters elsewhere combined." While focusing on "affluent suburbs" like Plano, the Dallas papers virtually overlooked the fact that the teen suicide rate was far higher in their own city. The Centers for Disease Control concluded that suicide clusters may account for no more than 5 percent of all youth suicides.

Westchester, Putnam, and Rockland counties would have a total of twelve adolescent suicides in 1984. Westchester County alone would have a total of six teenage suicides in 1984, compared to an average of five over the previous eight years and fewer than the high of seven in 1979. In that case the 1984 suicides barely qualify as an "epidemic," which is defined as "more than would normally be expected," leading some to suggest that the "Westchester cluster" was a statistical mirage.

On February 16, 1985, seventeen-year-old David Balogh of Tarrytown was found in a car parked at a landfill, dead from carbon monoxide poisoning. In the following three weeks there were three more adolescent suicides in Westchester County, the same number as in 1984 when the suicides had ignited media and public hysteria. "Last year at this time it was chaos," says George Cohen. "This year there hasn't been a peep. No calls from the media. Nobody mentions the word 'cluster.' Says psychologist Joe Solanto, "I'd like to think it's because the media is more sensitive to the issue, but the more cynical side of me wonders if it isn't just old news."

With or without media attention, adolescent suicides continued in the tri-county area. But gradually the suicides became just a part of the overall rate of adolescent suicide in the United States. Some people say, in fact, that the attention showered on the Westchester suicides of 1984 was, in fact, ultimately beneficial because it focused attention on the problem of adolescent suicide after many years of silence. "I think the way the media dealt with that particular episode had some very positive results," says Westchester pediatrician Kenneth Schonberg. "Despite the fact that, in all honesty, that was not a very exceptional year. Unfortunately, adolescents are dying at a rather constant rate from suicide, and it wasn't restricted to the late winter and early spring of 1984. Eighty-four or '83 . . . which was it? I forget already."

V

DANA

"I USED TO LIE IN BED and imagine what my life could be like. I'd set up these great scenes in my mind. In my favorite I'd be driving down the road and there'd be a car accident, and I'd jump out and save the guy's life, and it would be in all the newspapers—'Hero Saves the Day.' Or I'd go to college, become a doctor, and every hospital in the country would want me because I'd pioneered some new operation. Or I'd win the Olympics in swimming— every distance, every stroke imaginable. Or I'd be out at a romantic dinner, the kind you see on TV, where the camera focuses on the couple staring into each other's eyes. The man would be tall, with a great body. Rugged good looks. Like Tom Selleck. And he couldn't live without me."

At 7:00 on a Tuesday morning in March, Dana Evans heard her mother leave for work. She rolled over and went back to sleep. It was a school day, but she didn't feel like going. When she woke again, it was 9:30. She turned on the television set at the foot of her bed. Then she got up, shuffled downstairs to the living room, and poured herself a mug of vodka—straight, as always. She knew that if she added tonic, she wouldn't get drunk as fast. Then she climbed back into bed and stared at the TV. Dana paid little attention to the game show. She sipped her vodka and thought about how miserable her life was.

Although Dana, a high school senior, had often been told she was smart, she rarely did her homework, skipped school at least once a week, and was failing several classes. Although she was a promising swimmer, she had quit the team at the end of her junior year. Although she had a cute face and brown curly hair, she was convinced she was ugly. She had never had a boyfriend and was certain she never would. She had no close friends. Her parents were divorced. Her father lived in Texas, and her mother, who worked two jobs, was rarely home. Her older sister was away at college. While her classmates were obsessed with boyfriends and college plans, Dana spent most of her time sleeping, watching television, drinking, or getting high.

Suddenly Dana slammed the mug of vodka down on her bedside table, pulled on some jeans and a T-shirt, and stomped angrily through the apartment, pausing occasionally to punch the wall. Her head rang with imagined insults:

Here you are again, hanging out, doing nothing.
Well, that's cuz no one wants to be with you.
That's cuz you're an asshole and you're ugly.
Well, so, what do you expect?
Well, you're stupid.
Well, you're ugly.
Well, you're a fucking asshole.
Well, then fuck it. *Today's the day.*

It was 11:30. Dana realized that she would have to hurry. Tammy, a classmate who was staying with Dana and her mother, was due home at 5:15. Dana had always imagined that she'd leave a note telling her mother, her sister, and Tammy that she still loved them. Now she decided against it—let them wonder, she told herself. She thought about where to do it. "I decided I'd better use the bathroom because from what I'd read, that's where everyone kills themselves," she says. "Plus if I got the bedroom rug dirty"—there is no trace of irony in her voice—"my mother would *kill* me."

At noon Dana went to her room and fished a razor blade from her purse. She walked into the bathroom, locked the door, and stood at the sink. "And then I just started," she says. "I cut my wrists. I watched the blood go into the sink, and because the sink was already wet, the blood spread out and I realized how neat it looked." She made vertical and horizontal slices on both wrists, lightly at first, and then, after taking a breath, deeply. "It hurt, but I didn't mind," she says. "It was almost as if I wanted it to hurt because I wanted to be tough." Every so often she paused. "Everything in the bathroom is white," she says. "White tile walls and white tile floors. I had to keep stopping and cleaning up because I didn't want to make a mess. I poured water in the sink so the blood would go down the drain. I'd rest my arms on my pants to soak up the blood so it wouldn't get on the floor." Dana felt herself grow weak, but she kept cutting. Then she stopped for a moment, looked at herself in the mirror over the sink, and said aloud, "Good-bye."

Dana Evans is one of an estimated 120,000 adolescents who attempt suicide each year. While attention to adolescent suicide has focused almost exclusively on what professionals in the field call "completed suicide," for every adolescent who dies there are at least twenty who make an attempt. Until recently people who attempted suicide and survived were called "unsuccessful" or "failed" suicides; those who died were called "successful." The suicide attempter was regarded as a double failure—not only at life but at death.

For many years attempted and completed suicide were regarded as psychologically similar acts, differing only in their outcome. Most suicide research, in fact, was based on attempters—who were available to be interviewed—and then generalized to include completers. Clinicians now suggest, however, that attempters and completers form two different though overlapping groups, each with its own goals and motivations. Completers tend to be male: Three times as many men as women kill themselves. Attempters tend to be female: Three times as many women as men attempt suicide. Completers tend to be older than attempters. Fifty percent of all attempters are under age thirty. As might be expected, completers use more lethal methods—guns, hanging, and jumping—while 70 to 90 percent of all attempters swallow pills and about 10 percent cut their wrists, methods that also allow more time for rescue. Attempts are often made in settings that make survival not only possible but probable. Ninety percent of adolescent suicide attempts take place at home, 70 percent while parents are in the house.

Given these figures it is tempting to assume that people who complete suicide truly want to die and people who attempt merely want attention. However, many people who commit suicide don't intend to die. Some lack knowledge of pharmacology and unintentionally overdose. Some mistakenly count on rescuers arriving in time to save them. On the other hand, some attempters survive who seem truly bent on dying. Many people have lived through six-story jumps or bullets in their heart. In *King Lear,* when blind Gloucester leaps from what he believes is a Dover cliff but is actually level ground, he is, in intent, making a serious suicide attempt. With adolescents, who are prone to risk-taking behavior, the line of intention is particularly difficult to draw. Suicide attempts range from swallowing a dozen aspirin in front of a family member to jumping off the Golden Gate Bridge. Clearly, one attempter has a greater determination to die than the other, but every suicide or suicide attempt has its own degree of ambivalence. "Most people who commit suicidal acts do not either want to die or to live," psychiatrist Erwin Stengel has written. "They want to do both at the same time, usually the one more, or much more, than the other."

While a suicide attempt is a move toward death, it may also be a way of moving toward other people. The person who threatens to jump from a building is an example. "The man up there is saying, 'Look at me. See how bad I feel,' " says psychologist Norman Farberow. "Sitting on the ledge of a building is a tremendous effort at communication." People use such an extreme form of expression—"a desperate version of holding their breath until turning blue," psychiatrist Mary Giffin calls it—because other forms have failed or because they have never learned more effective ways of asking for help. It may also be a last-ditch attempt to change a seemingly intolerable situation. In *A Cry for Help,* Giffin described a thirteen-year-old Illinois girl who, one week after her father moved out of the house, slashed her wrists in the bathtub shortly before she knew her mother would be bathing. "I didn't really want to die," she said later. "I just hoped and prayed that if Mom and Dad knew how upset and unhappy I was, Dad would move back in."

Clinicians use a variety of expressions to describe such low-lethality attempts: manipulative behavior, histrionic suicide attempts, abortive suicides, fake suicides, psychological blackmail, and gestures. Because death is clearly not the object, these attempts are often dismissed as not serious. But the line between serious and not serious is a fine one. *"Gesture?"* says Warren Wacker, former director of Harvard University Health Services. He smiles ironically. "If someone slashes her wrist lightly, it's a gesture. If she cuts deeper, it ain't." As Wacker suggests, making that distinction can be dangerous. "Clinicians use these terms pejoratively," says psychiatrist Douglas Jacobs, "but just because an attempt is minor does not mean a patient is not suicidal." A Michigan youth hospitalized after a suicide attempt was chided by the doctor, "This wasn't very serious, was it?" The young man says, "It's like if you're saved, it wasn't serious. If you succeed, they say they should have taken you seriously."

Clinicians and parents, dismissing an attempt as attention-getting, often refuse to give that attention—or give the wrong kind. Many doctors show anger toward attempters: A woman who had made numerous cuts on her wrists was told by her emergency room physician, "If you really want to do a good job, why don't you just take a knife and make a real good, deep cut." A sixteen-year-old Texas girl who slashed her wrist says, "The doctor told me he'd sew me up so I could see the scar and for the rest of my life I would never forget what I'd done. And he did, too." Parents may minimize or deny the attempt. One study found that only 38 percent of treatment referrals after an adolescent attempt were acted on. Another found only 41 percent of families came for further therapy following an initial session. "It's often difficult to get parents to acknowledge the problem because they *are* the problem," says Peter

Saltzman, a child psychiatrist at McLean Hospital in Belmont, Massachusetts. After making an attempt, one of Saltzman's patients was told by his father, "Next time, jump off the Bourne Bridge."

An adolescent whose suicide attempt is belittled or ignored may feel forced to take more drastic action. One young girl, after an argument with her parents, slashed her wrists lightly. For several mornings in a row she appeared at the breakfast table wearing short-sleeved shirts that clearly revealed her fresh scars. Nobody in her family noticed. When this attempt at communication failed, she slashed an artery.

If dealt with improperly, a "failed" suicide may lead to a face-saving "success." Ten percent of those who attempt suicide will eventually kill themselves, 2 percent within a year. An estimated 25 to 40 percent of those who complete suicide have made a previous attempt. A lonely sixteen-year-old Minneapolis boy felt distant from his father who, he believed, lavished most of his attention on his Cadillac. One night after leaving a note on his bulletin board saying that he was an outcast at school, he stole the keys to the Cadillac and smashed into an oak tree in the front yard. After spending several months in the hospital recuperating from his injuries, he was pronounced "straightened out." But he came home to find little had changed. Eight months after his first attempt, his mother found him behind the wheel of his father's brand-new Cadillac, dead from carbon monoxide poisoning.

———————

A bright, outgoing girl, Dana Evans received good grades in elementary school, played war with the neighborhood kids, and went home to a hot supper each evening in a split-level ranch house in a small town eighty miles north of Manhattan. "We had a dog, two kids, a two-car garage, and two cars," she says with a touch of sarcasm. "It was all so perfect." But all was not so perfect. At nine months she developed spinal meningitis, and not long afterward her mother noticed Dana had difficulty bending her right leg. Over the next eighteen years dozens of specialists would be unable to pinpoint the problem. As a child Dana did special exercises daily, had a slight limp, and wore a shoe with a built-up sole to compensate for her shorter left leg. At school she was called names like "pegleg" and "the polio kid." Although Dana tried to ignore the taunts, she was self-conscious about her leg and never wore a dress except on Thanksgiving and Christmas.

Dana was also affected by the friction between her parents. She felt intimidated by her father, a quiet, remote, engineer whom she desperately wanted to please. He often gave her the vague feeling that he would have preferred a son. When she was seven, he asked her if she wanted to be in a swim meet. She said yes. "When the gun went off, everybody dove in except me," Dana recalls. "I didn't know that was the signal. Eventually, I dove in. Halfway down the pool I started crying because everybody else had finished and I was still in the middle of the pool." But Dana was determined to please her father, and she doggedly went to swim practice. Swimming soon became an important part of her life.

When Dana was nine, her parents separated, and she and her mother and older sister moved into a massive apartment complex in a neighboring town. To support the family Mrs. Evans returned to work full time as a secretary and also took a weekend job as a waitress. To relieve her loneliness she went to singles bars with friends several nights a week. "Before, my mother had always been there when I came home from school," says Dana. "Now I had to carry a key because I was the first one home. At first I thought, 'Hey, this is great—no one around to tell me what to do.' " Dana learned to smoke, and she and her sister smuggled boys into the house when their mother was out. "But after a while it wasn't so much 'great, there's no mother around,' " says Dana, "as 'where's my mother?' "

Even when Dana's mother was home, there was little communication. A pragmatic woman, Mrs. Evans had her hands full trying to support her family and live a life of her own. She was reluctant to discipline her daughter because she felt Dana had suffered enough already from the leg problem. When Dana didn't do her chores, her mother overlooked it. When she caught Dana smoking, she let her off with a warning. When Dana got drunk for the first time, her mother said, "All kids try it—just don't make it a habit." Dana found herself wishing that she could get a stronger reaction from her mother. Dana never talked about her problems, and her mother rarely asked. "I don't think we ever sat and chatted about our feelings," says Mrs. Evans. "I think it's because parents in my generation did not. Adults were adults and children were children. There was no such thing as 'parent effectiveness training.' Today if the kid comes home and kicks the cat, you're supposed to say, 'Did you have a rotten day in school?' Back then you'd scold them for kicking the cat! My father and mother didn't deal on a feeling level with each other, let alone with their children." She shrugs. "So my children and I did not get into personal, emotional subjects. But I perceived that as being the way all parents were with their children."

Dana's father, who lived with his second wife and her two daughters, was even less of an influence. Dana dreaded their weekends together. Although he rarely criticized her, she believed that nothing she did ever pleased him. Yet she longed for his approval. One day when Dana was thirteen, after picking up Dana and her sister for the weekend, her father told them that his company was transferring him to Texas. Dana felt wounded. "I think I knew rationally that he was not moving to get away from us, but I didn't understand why he wanted to move so far away when his children lived here," she says. "I remember feeling, 'Jesus Christ, if they transferred you to the *moon,* you'd go.' "

Dana also had difficulty getting attention at school. Because of a series of operations on her knee, she missed fifty-three days of her seventh grade year and found it hard to make a place for herself in the huge new junior high. "At school there were the jocks and the nerds and the heads," she says. "I swam, but for a club team, not for the school, so I wasn't a jock. And I had a deep aversion to the nerds. That's not a group you become a member of by choice; you're born into it. So I never really fit in anywhere." But late in her seventh grade year, when Dana was twelve, she found a way of belonging. A classmate asked her if she wanted to buy a joint, and Dana said sure. "I took it home and hid it in the back of my desk, and one afternoon after school I sat on my bed and smoked it. It was great. I loved being high. It put me in such a different head than I had been in all my life. Everything looked so different. Everything looked okay."

Once Dana found an identity, she pursued it with a vengeance. Dana and the other druggies would meet at lunch in the woods in back of school and get high. She stopped wearing the corduroy slacks with color-coordinated blouses that her mother bought her and wore old jeans, T-shirts, and concert jerseys emblazoned with the names of favorite rock bands—Led Zeppelin, the Grateful Dead, The Police. She wore mirror sunglasses and a cloth cap pulled low over her eyes. A Walkman filled her ears with rock music. From her weightlifting and swimming she developed huge shoulders, arms, and biceps, which she liked to show off by rolling up her T-shirt sleeves. She cultivated a swagger and a glare that kept people at a distance. She became friends with a tough girl named Stacey. "We'd meet in the girls' bathroom and get high next to the open window so no one could smell anything," says Dana. "If anyone was there when we went in, it was like 'this is our office, get out.' And they would."

Dana also began to drink heavily. She had first tasted alcohol as a child when, fetching beers for her father, she was rewarded with the first sip. At age eleven, at a family dinner in an Italian restaurant, she and her cousins managed to sneak a carafe of wine down to the children's end of the table. Dana drank most of it and blacked out. By thirteen she was stealing from the liquor cabinet and pouring water into the bottles so her mother wouldn't suspect. "She kept one bottle of everything, so I'd take a little of each and have a mug with vodka, gin, and bourbon." By the end of eighth grade Dana was drinking or getting high almost every day.

As Dana began to get attention for the first time, her behavior became more and more extreme. "In trying to fit in somewhere and to get people to realize that I existed, I did some really weird things." In the hallways she was apt to push girls up against a wall and threaten them. In science class she stole her classmates' lab books, ripped out their homework if they were ahead of her, and poured hydrochloric acid on their experiments. She even intimidated some of the teachers. At the end of class when her science teacher asked the students to push in their chairs, Dana glared at her and kicked her chair out from behind her. "My general attitude toward the world was 'Don't mess with me or I'll kill you,' " says Dana. "I loved it when people were scared of me." Dana was proud of her new nickname: Tuffie. She liked the idea that she cared about nothing, and nothing could get to her.

For years swimming had been the one thing Dana truly cared about. She loved the feel of her body hitting the cold water and the grueling discipline of laps. During the day she might get high, mouth off to teachers, and wear sloppy clothes, but every weeknight she worked out rigorously with her local club team. "I *occasionally* went to school," she says. "I *always* went to practice." But the more she partied, the more practices she skipped. Sometimes she'd show up high. She kept a pint of J&B scotch in her gym bag, which she sipped on "trips to the bathroom." She quarreled with the coach, a gentle, earnest man who had gone out of his way for Dana ever since she had joined the team, picking her up for meets and staying late to help her develop a new racing start because her knee didn't bend enough for the standard position. After a race she would ignore his congratulations, leaving him standing there with his hand out. Sometimes she swore at him or gave him the finger. "I'd get kicked out of practice about once a week," she says. "Afterward I'd try to apologize, but it would come out all wrong. He'd say, 'You can't tell me to go fuck myself in front of the other kids,' and I'd *want* to say, 'I don't know why I swear at you because I really like you,' but I'd end up saying something stupid like, 'Well, you deserved it.' And he'd say, 'Don't talk to me like that.' And I'd say, 'Well, fuck you.' " Dana shrugs. "I wanted to be friends with him, but I was holding back so much from everything. I was like a snake keeping people away from me."

In March of Dana's junior year she and her coach argued over whether she would be allowed to miss part of an important meet to attend the junior prom. The coach excused her from a few events. Dana says, "If you don't go to the prom, the word is out, like 'she's a loser, she'd have to *pay* somebody to take her.' " Nobody had asked Dana, so, as time was running out, she invited a boy in her chemistry class whom she hardly knew. "It was a disaster," she says. "We were assigned to a table with people we didn't know. We hardly talked the whole night. Afterward we went with another couple to an Italian restaurant where I got smashed. My date didn't drink a drop. He thought we were all pretty stupid. So the rest of us drank and drank and drank, and then we all drove down by the tracks to watch the sunrise. I passed out in the car."

Four hours later Dana stood on the starting block for the hundred-yard freestyle. She was still drunk. "When the gun went off, I dove into the water and my stomach turned. I swam to the other end, did a flip turn, swam back, and did another flip, and when I came up and took a breath, I got some water in my mouth, which happens occasionally. But this time I just stood up and got out of the pool. It was the first time I had ever not finished a race."

Dana stayed on the team for two more months. One day in June she threw her sweatsuit at the coach. "I don't need your shit anymore," she said, walking out. "Swimming was my life," says Dana. "I spent ten years doing it, and in one day I just threw it all away."

Without swimming, Dana had little left but her identity as a druggie. "Senior year I just said, 'Screw it—I'm going the whole nine yards,' " she remembers. "I sort of said good-bye." She got high at school almost every day and began using hashish and mescaline as well as marijuana. She cut school at least once a week, forging excuses from her mother, and spent the day in bed sipping vodka and watching "Jeopardy," "I Love Lucy," and "The Brady Bunch." If she went to school, she would come home in the afternoon and drink and sleep until her mother arrived. Sometimes she would just put on a sad record and smoke pot. Without swim practice she usually spent nights in front of the TV, drinking. "I knew every single show from six o'clock until eleven," she says. "I was like a walking *TV Guide.*" At parties she got drunk or high as quickly as possible. "There was no such thing as stopping when I got a buzz on—it was *Go for it.* My big worry at parties was that other people would drink too much because the more they drank, the less there was for me." At the beginning of a party she would hide a few bottles of beer to make sure there would be enough for her to get drunk on. "At school on Monday morning, people would tell me what I'd done that weekend," she says. "Even good friends told me I drank too much. And I *knew* I drank too much. But I knew I had to. I had to take a break from life. I was depressed when I wasn't drinking, and I thought drinking would save me, I thought it was like my best friend. But the drunker I got, the less fun it was."

Although it seemed everyone around her had a boyfriend, Dana had never had one. Occasionally, a friend would include her in a double date, but Dana wasn't much interested. "I thought I must be a lesbian 'cause I didn't like guys. I didn't like girls either, though. I thought maybe I was asexual." She tried not to think about it. "I just hoped it would all go away, that I'd grow up and everything would be fine. But I figured that even if I ended up liking guys, there wasn't much hope since I wasn't pretty. Dating seemed like a big pain in the ass anyway. First you have to explain yourself to somebody and get to know him, and then you gotta get closer and then you fight and then you stop seeing each other, and you both get really hurt."

Dana talked to no one about her sexuality, her depression, her drinking, or about anything else personal, not even Tammy, a classmate who came to live with the Evanses when her own parents moved from the area. Dana and Tammy would gossip for hours, but Tammy did most of the talking, primarily about boys she was interested in. Anyway, thought Dana, with her silky hair, perfect figure, and steady boyfriend, how could Tammy understand what Dana was feeling? "We were like two different grades of people—she was like large Grade A, and I was . . . day-old bread, twenty-percent discount." Even if there had been someone to talk to, Dana wouldn't have talked. The last thing in the world she would admit was that she felt scared.

Dana knew she was depressed, but in the back of her mind she expected things to get better when she turned eighteen. "I thought that adults had it infinitely easier than kids and that the day I turned eighteen and became an adult my whole life was going to magically fall into place." On the night of her eighteenth birthday Dana had a party at her house. About twenty people came, most of them druggies. To celebrate the fact that Dana was of legal drinking age, Mrs. Evans bought the beer. Among her friends' presents were an enormous joint and a silver mug inscribed with Dana's nickname. Dana made full use of both gifts, and long before the party was over she passed out. "The next day I woke up hung over. Nothing had changed. It was just . . . Sunday morning. I thought, 'Well, here I am, I'm eighteen, but I still don't know what I want to do with my life. If anything."

Dana had long been fascinated by the subject of suicide. "I used to read everything about it I could get my hands on," she says. "I wrote a paper in eleventh grade English on suicide—the statistics, men versus women. I got a B plus." Dana had never consciously considered it as an option for herself, but about two months before her birthday she started carrying a razor blade in her wallet. She had found it in the family toolbox where it was kept for scraping expired registration stickers off the car windshield. At first it was a kind of toy she was fond of playing with, carving patterns on desks, but gradually she began to think of it as a means of escape. "It was my security blanket: 'Well, if it gets too bad, I'll just bail out.'"

About a month after her eighteenth birthday Dana knew she was going to kill herself. "I didn't know what it would be like to be dead, but I knew it would be better than this," she says. "I wasn't setting a date, but I knew it would be soon. I was walking around thinking, 'Hey, it doesn't matter what happens 'cause I ain't going to be here!' I was just waiting for the right time." Even now Dana is not sure why she chose March 16, 1982. Later she told people it was because she had an English test the following day, but "that was just to give them an answer they'd understand." By the time she used the razor blade she felt so angry at herself and at the world that even after she slumped to the white tile floor of the bathroom, she continued to hack away insistently at her wrists, her arms, and her legs until she slipped into unconsciousness.

When Dana woke, a blur of policemen and paramedics hovered above her, asking her name, wrapping gauze on her wrists, reaching for the razor blade in her hand. Dana said nothing but squeezed her fist tighter, as if the blade were a jewel they were trying to steal. When they carried her downstairs, she fought and kicked, breaking the dining room window. They tied her down on a stretcher and loaded her into the ambulance. On the ride to the hospital a medical technician tried to soothe her. "Everything is going to be okay," he said softly. Dana thought, "How the fuck would *you* know?"

In the emergency room Dana received seven stitches on each wrist. Afterward, as she lay tied to a cot, she dimly recognized Tammy, who had come home early from school to find Dana in a pool of blood on the bathroom floor, and her mother, who had arrived home from work just after the ambulance had left and raced to the hospital. Dana kept moaning that she wanted to go home, but the doctors had signed ninety-day commitment forms. The doctors suggested the state hospital, but Mrs. Evans refused to consider it and chose a private psychiatric hospital in Westchester County. Dana was put in a straitjacket, loaded into an ambulance, and driven to the hospital, where a nurse made her strip, gave her a hospital gown, and told her to get in bed. "These are going into the garbage," said the nurse, holding up Dana's bloody jeans. "Don't fuck with my pants," snarled Dana, frightened but determined to be tough. Her mother came in to say good-bye. "When she leaned over to kiss me," says Dana, "one of her tears dropped on my face. I said, 'You're dripping on me.' "

For the first few days in the hospital Dana refused to talk. Even after she gave in, she stared at the floor as the doctors administered a battery of psychological tests. Three times a week she met with a psychologist. "Therapy was a joke," says Dana. "He'd ask me how I felt and I'd talk about how I hated hospital food, and he'd tell me stories from his college days." The psychologist prescribed Mellaril, an antipsychotic, but when Dana gained weight she refused to take it. He recommended that she attend meetings of Alcoholics Anonymous in a nearby town. Escorted to her first session, Dana wore a Yukon Jack whiskey T-shirt—though when she realized the other people were serious about not drinking, she folded her arms across her chest so they couldn't read the logo. But she was skeptical. "I didn't think I had a drinking problem," she says. "I didn't think the problem was me—I thought that things *around* me had to get better. I thought if only my mother were happy, then I'd be happy. Or I'd think if I fell in love and got married, I'd be fine. Or if only I went to a good school. Or if only I found some friends." She shrugs. "I didn't think I belonged in the hospital because a hospital was for crazy people, and I wasn't crazy. I thought if someone would just fix my life, I could go home and everything would be fine."

Dana came to like the hospital. She made friends with three girls her age, and they smuggled alcohol, drugs, and boys into the girls' ward. In many respects her life was no different from the way it had been at home except that she didn't have to go to school, cook meals, or clean up. "All in all, once I learned the system and how to get around it, I had a ball." She even found her first boyfriend, a young patient from Pennsylvania. One night when they got permission to watch TV together, they turned out the lights and made love on the ward floor—Dana's first time. The boy was discharged not long afterward, however, and after a few brief phone conversations, he stopped calling.

As the months went by, however, Dana grew anxious to get out. She told the doctors what she thought they wanted to hear—that she was getting better, that she would stop drinking, that she didn't want to hurt herself anymore. In July, after four months at the hospital, Dana was discharged.

That fall, Dana enrolled as a freshman at a college on Long Island. "I was going to start all over again where no one knew me," she says. "I thought, 'This is it. I'm going to meet new people, maybe find a boyfriend, and live the good old college life. I'll just be somebody different this time.'" Her first night at school Dana unpacked, arranged her clothes in her bureau, tacked her Tom Selleck poster to the ceiling above her bed, and studied the school's catalogue. The second night she went to a beer party down the hall, played a drinking game called Pass Out, went back to her room, threw up, and passed out.

Dana had drunk very little during the month she had been at home, but once she had ruined her clean slate at the party, she figured, "Why not? I've already blown it." Soon she was drinking every day again. Her bottom desk drawer became her liquor cabinet. Of the $50 weekly food allowance her parents gave her, she spent all but $3 on liquor; with the rest she bought a packet of bouillon cubes and a can of powdered juice mix. She rarely went to class, and though she opened the books on her desk every night, she never got around to reading them. Her roommate moved out to live with friends down the hall, and the two girls with whom Dana shared a bathroom were seniors she rarely saw. While her classmates lived "the good old college life"—flinging Frisbees across the quad, shouting conversations from dorm to dorm, aiming their stereo speakers out the window and blasting music across the campus—Dana spent almost all of her time alone in her room, drinking and watching television.

One Friday night in early November, Dana was in the laundry room when she ran into a boy from down the hall with whom she occasionally talked about sports. They ended up in her room watching TV. Although the boy didn't drink, Dana did—"I don't mind drinking alone, I'm used to it," she assured him. Later that night she blacked out. When she woke up shortly before dawn, the boy was in bed next to her. "I assumed we'd had sex," she says. "I didn't ask. I didn't want to know." Promising that he would stop by and see her later that morning, he stumbled back to his room. Dana realized she didn't even know his last name.

Dana spent Saturday staring at her textbooks, hating herself, hating the boy, but wanting him to come back. Saturday night, as rock music from a dormitory dance floated through her window, Dana stayed in her room drinking, watching TV, falling asleep, waking, watching TV, drinking.

When Dana woke up Sunday there was a half bottle of rum on her bureau and the television was on. She spent the afternoon finishing the bottle and growing more depressed. "I had no friends. I wasn't doing any work. I knew that even if I finished the semester, I would flunk everything anyway. I was thinking, 'Here we are again. Everything's just the same, and I managed to do it in two months!' " That evening she decided she had had enough. She rummaged through the toolbox her mother had given her to help decorate her room and found a small knife with a two-inch blade. "This time I wanted to do it right," she says. "I knew I had all the time in the world because no one ever came to my room. I could sit in that apartment for days, and nobody would come looking for me." She sat down at her desk and began to cut her wrists, just as she had done nine months before. After making repeated cuts she decided to cut her jugular vein because she knew it would be quicker, but when she got up to use the bathroom mirror, drunk and weak from loss of blood, she fell back into her chair.

No one ever did come looking for her, but the dormitory's resident assistant, looking for Dana's roommate, knocked on the door, let himself in with his pass-key, and found Dana instead. Five minutes later the police came into her bedroom. This time they were not gentle; they twisted her arm until she dropped the knife, tied her wrists and ankles tight, and strapped her to a stretcher. At the busy hospital an orderly walked by and saw her cursing and struggling to free herself. "I wish you *had* died," he said.

The second time around at the hospital was no more effective than the first. Although her old buddies were gone, Dana found a new pack of friends to party with. But as the months passed and her friends were discharged, and new patients entered and were themselves discharged, Dana realized she didn't want to leave. "I wanted to live there," she says. "I didn't have to work, all my meals were made, and I had friends." She didn't tell anybody this—like the others, she badmouthed the hospital and submitted frequent requests for a discharge hearing, which she always ripped up before it was too late. When she was finally allowed to leave, she ran through the ward shouting, "I'm getting out of this jail! I'm free!" But inside she was terrified.

Dana was released on the Fourth of July weekend. Her mother was away with her boyfriend in Vermont. Dana and her best friend from the hospital spent the weekend cruising around Dutchess County. "I drove around all weekend with a beer in one hand and a joint in the other," Dana remembers. When her friend, out on a weekend pass, returned to the hospital on Sunday afternoon, Dana was restless and lonely. She decided to drive down to the hospital and see her friend. When she arrived, still drunk and high, the staff wouldn't let her leave. They didn't even bother readmitting her; they just tore up her discharge papers. She had been out only forty-eight hours.

When Dana called her mother that night and told her she was back at the hospital, she was surprised by her response. "Usually my mother came running down with clothes and cigarettes and money and sympathy." This time Mrs. Evans said that she and her boyfriend were going to California for a wedding, as planned, and they would see Dana when they got back in ten days. Dana was angry. The doctors were also less tolerant. They allowed Dana no visitors or phone calls, forbade her to talk to other patients, and plotted her daily schedule down to the last minute. Although this infuriated her, for the first time in a long while Dana had time to think. "I began to realize I was getting tired of it all," she says. "I knew I couldn't stay at the hospital for the rest of my life, but I also knew I couldn't handle it outside."

Dana's mother and her boyfriend came to see her the night they got back from California. The three of them sat outside in the warm summer evening. Mrs. Evans asked Dana if she thought she had a problem. Dana surprised herself by saying, "Yeah. I do." "Is it alcohol or drugs?" her mother asked. "Well, sort of both." "Do you want to stop?" her mother asked. "No," said Dana. "I like it." Dana was surprised. After so many months of automatically saying she was getting better, that things were going to be different, for the first time she felt she was telling the truth.

Dana admitted to her mother that if she had any hope of improving, she couldn't stay at this hospital—it made life too easy for her. Dana was discharged one day in August, and the following day her mother drove her to Four Winds, a psychiatric hospital in nearby Katonah.

From the very first day Dana realized that Four Winds was going to be different. At the other hospital there had been a few hours of therapy a week; at Four Winds there were more than twenty. At the other hospital it had been simple to smuggle in drugs and alcohol; at Four Winds the no-drugs-and-no-alcohol rule was enforced with urine tests and frequent hall checks. Transgressors were immediately asked to leave. At the other hospital Dana had controlled her therapy sessions; at her first Four Winds session, when Dana kept her eyes on the floor, the therapist, a young social worker named Terry, suddenly stopped talking and literally pulled her head up. Dana was scared. That night she called her mother in tears. "These people are weird," she cried. "You've got to get me out of here."

At the old hospital Dana felt it had always been the patients versus the staff. Here, she realized, people worked at getting well. "At the other hospital, if you showed any sign of being interested in treatment, it was like 'What's wrong with you?'" she says. "At Four Winds, if you *weren't* into treatment, you were on the outside." In group therapy the staff leader would ask, "All right, who wants to work today?" And the other patients raised their hands. Dana never did. She kept her arms crossed and her eyes on the floor. Sometimes she'd get dragged into the discussion, but she got out as soon as possible. "Dana, what do you think?" the leader would ask. "I don't think," she would say.

One day in therapy Terry criticized her for being cruel to the other patients. Dana felt herself begin to cry. She kept her head down until she was able to stop so that Terry couldn't see her tears. She was furious. "I couldn't believe that he'd gotten to me," she says. "*No one* was supposed to get to me. I was so pissed off at myself." When the session was over, Dana ran back to her room and made light cuts all over her arm. "I was at the point where I knew that killing myself was not going to help, but I needed to release the pressure. Out in the world or even at the other hospital you could drink or get high or talk. At Four Winds I couldn't drink or get high, and I wasn't talking to anybody, aside from saying, 'Fuck you.' So I found another way." About once a week, after she had verbally abused someone or when someone had penetrated her wall for a moment, she would feel guilty. "Whenever I felt upset about something, I always thought it was my fault. And because it was my fault, I felt I deserved to be hurt." She would come back to her room and scratch her arms with a metal triangle she had cut from a soda can and hid in her drawer. They were superficial scrapes; the nurse would clean and bandage them, and Dana would roll her sleeves down as if nothing had happened.

One night about three months after Dana had arrived at Four Winds, there was a meeting of the patients in her unit. Dana, as always, sat in sullen silence, arms folded across her chest. Suddenly everyone in the group turned on her. "We're sick and tired of you," they said. "You haven't done anything since you got here. If you didn't feel so damn sorry for yourself, maybe you could do something. But since you're not doing anything, why don't you leave?" Even her best friend, a patient named Lucy, joined the attack. Dana was stunned, but she kept her head down, saying nothing. After the meeting she spent the night shooting pool in a fury, sending balls flying off the table. "I felt betrayed," she says. Next morning her favorite nurse cornered her. "I hear they really gave it to you last night—it's about time," she said. "You know they're right." "No, I don't," said Dana. "Yes, you do," said the nurse. The following day in group therapy when the staff member asked, "Who wants to work today?" Dana raised her hand.

After so many years of carefully constructing defenses to keep the world at bay, opening up was slow, painful, and frightening. "How do I change what I think?" Dana would ask Terry. "Just change it," he would answer. "How?" "Just act as if you cared about yourself." "If it's fake, I'm not going to act it." "Just give yourself a break. Once in a while don't talk like that about yourself." "But that's acting." "It's a first step." They would end up shouting at each other, and Dana would stalk out of the room. Gradually, however, her armor began to chip away. Both staff and friends tried to support Dana's efforts. "I still had a sharp tongue from years of bad habit, but now every time I swore, even the most timid person would say, 'I don't like that.' If someone said 'hello' and I said, 'Hey, bitch,' they'd say, 'Don't call me bitch,' and I'd apologize."

After many arguments with Terry, Dana even put aside her jeans and T-shirt for corduroys and blouses. The first time she wore them, a young male patient called out, "Well, look at the young lady, don't she look pretty?" Dana ran to her room and climbed back into her jeans. She told Terry that if she were going to change, people couldn't tease her. "You can't program people," he said. "You have to risk it." Two days later she tried again. The same boy gave her a wolf whistle. Dana cringed but kept walking.

Dana had never let people get close to her. "I could be friends with someone, but there was always an unspoken agreement that *I* could get to know *them,* but *they* weren't allowed to get to know *me,*" she says. Before, when her friends saw that Dana was depressed and asked her what was wrong, she would say, "Nothing." If they persisted, she would swear at them. Now when they asked her what was wrong, Dana would start to say, "Nothing," but catch herself and say, "I don't know." "It was a start," admits Dana. "After a while they'd say, 'What's wrong?' and eventually I'd be able to tell them."

Dana soon had a true test of her progress. In December her father visited. Although he had often been in New York on business, he had never visited Dana during any of her hospitalizations. They had never talked about her suicide attempts or her therapy. He called her occasionally at Four Winds, but their conversations were so stilted she stopped accepting his phone calls. In the weeks before his visit Dana worked in therapy on being open with her father. In psychodrama the instructor made her and another patient, who played her father, sit back to back—"because you two never face each other." "Dana, how are your grades?" her "father" would say. "Fine," said Dana. The instructor would stop her, and they would try again. "Dana, how are your grades?" "I'm not doing well." "Why not?" " 'Cause I'm not studying much." Gradually, Dana was able to be more open about her treatment and her plans for the future. But as the day of her father's visit approached, she was terrified.

When her father and his wife arrived, Dana gave them a quick tour of Four Winds. "They'd already eaten dinner at the hotel, but they took me to a diner so I could have a hamburger," she says. "I was very nervous. I had never said a word to my father about my drinking, but I told him I was an alcoholic and I was going to AA five times a week. I told him about my treatment. I told him I had problems getting close to people. I told him about all the things Terry and I were working on, and when I finished he said, 'Well, that's good. I took you to dinner to tell you I'm moving to Japan.' " Dana was crushed, but she kept her composure while they had coffee. After they dropped her off back at Four Winds, she rushed down to the smoking room and wept.

The following day she and her father met with Terry for a therapy session. Terry told her father some of the reasons Dana felt she couldn't relate to him. Her father nodded thoughtfully, and when Terry had finished, he admitted that it was difficult for him to talk about feelings because he hadn't been brought up to do so. "But you two need to talk to each other," said Terry. "Do you think you could try?" "Sure, we can try," said Mr. Evans.

As she walked her father to his car, Dana said, "There's something else you don't know." She rolled up her sleeves and showed him her arms, crisscrossed with scars. "I used to cut myself," she said. "Oh," he said. "Well, thank you for telling me." There was an awkward silence, and Dana said she had better get back to the group. They said good-bye, and Dana went inside.

"It could have been worse," Dana says now. "I was worried he'd just say, 'I've had it with you.' And though he didn't say, 'Please get well,' he never said, 'I don't care about you.' For him that was something—that he said we'd try."

That spring Dana continued to open up. In therapy, as she and her mother began to talk about her mother's work, about her boyfriends, about Dana's leg, and about the divorce, they became more understanding of each other's struggles. At AA meetings Dana began to take an active role, making the coffee, setting up chairs, participating in discussions. "I was actually letting a few people get to know me a little bit," says Dana. "It was terrifying. I had never trusted anybody. I always thought if I told someone something, they'd print it in the local paper. Terry told me I had to risk it." Dana and Lucy became even closer. "I would tell her something that I thought would be embarrassing, and she would say, 'Oh, I did that, too.' " In April, Dana was scheduled to have major surgery to replace her kneecap. She was so afraid the operation would fail that she couldn't talk about it in group. But a few nights before the operation Dana went to Lucy and said, "I'm terrified." It was the first time she had ever admitted to anyone that she could be frightened. On the eve of the operation Lucy stayed up all night with her.

Dana spent three weeks in a hospital in Manhattan. She thought that while she was away they would forget about her at Four Winds, but Terry called her every day. A staff social worker who lived in Manhattan visited her three times a week. Every so often the unit nurse would call on the ward phone, and the patients would take turns talking to her. One day a friend from the ward walked into her room. "What are you doing here?" asked Dana. Then Nan, the head nurse, entered, followed by Lucy. They wheeled Dana down to the solarium. "There were fifteen people there!" says Dana. "Half the unit! I couldn't believe it. It was great! I figured I wouldn't see those people for three weeks. They didn't tell me they were coming down. They'd posted a sign-up sheet—'Sign up if you want to see Dana'—so no one *forced* them to go." She smiles. "More people wanted to go, but there wasn't enough room."

Dana was discharged from Four Winds in May 1984.

VI

"Use the Enclosed Order Form to Act Immediately. You Could Save a Life"

GEORGE COHEN WALKS INTO a social studies classroom at White Plains High School carrying a slide projector and a tape recorder. Setting them on a desk, he pulls a white screen down from the row of furled maps above the blackboard. The bell rings. While Cohen sets up his projector, a stream of tenth graders floods the room. He observes them for a moment before asking for quiet. Cohen, a middle-aged man, is dressed in a brown tweed jacket and striped tie, but his mop of dark curly hair, pudgy face, and ready grin give him a rumpled, informal look. "I've asked your teacher to let me come in and talk to you today," he says. "I'm here for two reasons. The first reason is that the problem of teenage suicide has grown tremendously. Three times as many kids kill themselves today as when I was in high school. The second reason is that everyone in this room can do something about it."

Cohen begins his program with a sixteen-minute slide show describing the extent of teenage suicide, the warning signs of depression, and how to help in a crisis. As the slides progress, some of the students watch intently. One girl takes notes as furiously as she chews her gum. Others are less attentive—a girl whispers to a friend at the next desk; a boy studies his history book; a girl fishes a compact from her purse and begins meticulously to apply eye shadow. Gradually, however, the whispering stops; the boy looks up from his homework, the girl abandons her makeup. Soon the only sound in the room is the voice of the narrator and the click of the slide projector.

111

The slide show offers some basic information about suicide and its prevention. Suicides rarely happen out of the blue; experts say four of five people who commit suicide leave clues to their plans. Some clues are behavioral—giving away prized possessions, for example. If someone gives his watch or record collection to a friend, he may be trying to say good-bye. Other clues are verbal. When someone says, "You won't be seeing me around anymore" or "The world would be better off without me," he may be thinking of suicide.

Although there are few precise indications of when a depressed adolescent will turn to suicide, there are signs that suggest when an adolescent is experiencing depression severe enough to warrant concern: sudden changes in behavior (for instance, when someone who takes great pride in his appearance suddenly neglects himself); dramatic changes in appetite; sudden weight gain or loss; sleeping difficulties (insomnia or a desire to sleep all the time); poor performance in school; trouble concentrating; unexplained lethargy or fatigue; loss of interest in friends, hobbies, or social activities; increased drug or alcohol use; constant feelings of worthlessness or self-hatred; excessive risk-taking; a philosophical preoccupation with death, dying, or suicide.

When the slide show is over, Cohen paces in front of the class. "After seeing this, what feelings are you left with?" he asks. "Sad," says a girl sitting in the front row. Cohen nods. "How many of you have known someone who has thought about or attempted suicide?" Eleven of twenty students raise their hands. "What was it like?" he asks. "It was scary," says another girl. "You'd worry about her every minute, wondering whether or not she would do it." Another girl adds, "It was confusing because it seemed like she had everything she wanted. I couldn't understand why she would want to do that." Cohen turns to the girl who had been putting on makeup. "Did you know her?" he asks. "What was it like for you?" The girl looks up. "I didn't believe her," she says. "Why?" asks Cohen. "Because she came right out and said she was going to do it." Heads nod agreement. "That's the toughest part—knowing whether they really mean it or not," says a boy in back who had seemed to sleep through the film. "They may just be trying to get attention," someone murmurs. Cohen looks up. "Sometimes people will joke about it—'Man, I'm gonna kill myself,' " he says. "But it's important to ask, 'Are you serious?' " Too often, he tells them, out of uneasiness or fear, a friend may laugh off a plea or ignore a clue. And one of the biggest myths about suicide is that people who talk about it won't do it. "It's very important to take them seriously."

Cohen has an easygoing, cheerful manner, and he quickly establishes a rapport with the students. He always asks a student his name; the next time that student raises his hand, Cohen remembers it. "What do you say to someone who has told you he's thinking of killing himself?" Cohen asks the class. "I'd say, 'Let's go get help,' " suggests one boy. "I'd ask why," says a girl. "That's good," says Cohen. "Depressed people feel hopeless, and one of the things they need most is someone to listen." A girl with hoop earrings says,

"I would tell her that I care about her." Cohen nods. "Yes, it's important to let them know that you care," he says. "And there's something else I'd like you to tell them. I'd like you to tell them: 'Don't do it.' Sometimes people have made their decision, but they need to hear someone who cares say no.

"What if a friend makes you promise to keep a secret, and then he tells you he's going to kill himself? What do you do?" After a moment of silence a young man speaks up. "I'd tell somebody and get help anyway," he says. "If that person is a true friend, you'd care enough to want to keep him around." Another boy nods. "It's someone's *life,*" he says. "You keep a secret when it's about a boyfriend or girlfriend, but not when it's someone's life." Some of the kids worry that breaking a promise might anger their friend, but they nod agreement when Cohen says, "It's better to have a live angry friend than a dead one."

Cohen asks the students to whom they would turn for help, and the students name the school nurse, counselor, and school social workers. Cohen mentions the two school psychologists; not one of the students has heard of them or knows where their offices are. When Cohen suggests parents, the kids chuckle and shake their heads. "They'd just get hysterical," says one girl. "What would they say?" asks Cohen. A girl sitting in back affects a high, shrill voice: "Oh, *my* baby wouldn't do that." The class bursts into laughter. "Yes, you may get a lot of denial," says Cohen, "but it's a good idea to talk to the parents because they have the responsibility." Cohen also suggests the local suicide hot line. He passes out a list of warning signs and resource numbers, and asks if there are any more questions. "Thank you for letting me talk to you," says Cohen. "If anyone wants to talk more, let me or your teacher know." The bell rings, chairs scrape on linoleum, and the students rush out to their next class.

Two or three times a week Cohen, who is a human relations specialist with the White Plains Public Schools, brings his projector to classrooms, auditoriums, church basements, and libraries throughout Westchester County, to talk to teenagers, teachers, social workers, and parents about suicide. His thirty-nine-minute program, designed to fit into a high school period, is sponsored by the Westchester County Mental Health Association Interagency Task Force on Adolescent Depression and Suicide, of which Cohen is chairperson. The group's imposing name belies the modesty of its operation. The group was formed in 1979 after two suicides and five attempts in five months at the same high school in Chappaqua left Westchester County health professionals realizing how little they knew about suicide. The Task Force, an unpaid volunteer group of teachers, counselors, and therapists, began meeting regularly to discuss the problem. Although Westchester had one of the largest mental health budgets per capita of any county in the nation, it had no specific suicide prevention program directed at adolescents. In the fall of 1982 the Task Force began offering this program, free of charge, to high schools in the county. While some schools welcomed the program, the Task Force met resistance from administrators who believed that talking about suicide would only encourage a youngster to commit it. Others felt that suicide prevention was not the school's responsibility; it was a family matter. Others feared that if students were exposed to the program, teachers and counselors would be overwhelmed with students wanting to talk about their troubles. Some said there was simply no need for the program; in *their* school, suicide was not a problem.

In 1984, as the "Westchester suicides" made headlines, demand for the program soared. Many of the schools that had been reluctant were suddenly eager. As far as Cohen knows, none of the students who have seen the program has committed suicide. "But even if a youngster went out and killed himself after seeing it," he says, "I wouldn't back away from the program because I know a lot of youngsters are getting help because of it." After almost every program, while he is putting away the projector, a student approaches Cohen to tell him about a friend she is worried about or about her own suicidal thoughts. "One night at ten I got a call from a girl who had seen the program in class. She said, 'I have a friend in the next room who wrote a note that says she's going to kill herself.' I told her to keep her friend there, and I was able to get over and talk to the kid and get her into the hospital. Today, I see that kid walking around the streets of White Plains, and I feel terrific. Without the program I'm not sure her friend would have known what to do."

While Cohen's presentation may seem tame, it would have been unthinkable even two decades ago. At that time, although there were three hundred suicide prevention centers across the country, there were no programs aimed at younger people. Prevention was geared toward adults, whose rate was highest. In a 1969 article on the prevention of adolescent suicide, recommendations made by suicide "experts" ranged from the suggestion that students be "encouraged to participate in extra-curricular activities" to increasing "the relevance of education to the modern world." No one broached the idea of actually educating teenagers about suicide—that, it was assumed, would be too dangerous. Many schools prohibited talking about suicide in any context; the only mention of it might occur in English class when the students read *Hamlet* or Hemingway. If a student committed suicide, teachers were expressly forbidden by school administrators to discuss it with students. It was simply not a school matter; these were "crazy kids"—they must be, or why would they kill themselves?

In 1974, a decade before the "Westchester suicides," eleven teenagers killed themselves in San Mateo County, a string of bedroom communities south of San Francisco. Today it would be called a cluster. At the time it wasn't called anything; as was the case elsewhere, schools generally hushed up the deaths. Charlotte Ross, director of the Suicide Prevention and Crisis Center of San Mateo County, found that all eleven teenagers had left clues recognizable to people with training in suicide prevention. Over a period of several days, for example, a sixteen-year-old asked his teacher, "Do you have to be crazy to kill yourself ?", wrote the word "Death" across the back of his hand, and one morning told a friend he was "going to heaven very soon." That day in class the boy slipped a revolver from a brown paper bag and killed himself.

That same year Ross attended a World Health Organization conference in Luxembourg which asserted that suicide among youth had reached "epidemic" proportions. Ross returned from that meeting determined to try a new approach to preventing adolescent suicide. Adapting the program she used to train her hot line volunteers, she went into the schools and trained teachers to recognize and respond to signs of depression and suicide. She found that students were crying out for help but not getting it. Teachers were dealing with suicide threats and attempts more and more frequently but had never been told what to do. They were terrified of responding to veiled suicidal messages for fear of putting the idea into a student's head. "We had cases where an English teacher would receive an essay on suicide and return it to the student corrected for grammar," said Ross, who taught the teachers not to be afraid to ask specifically about suicide.

The program worked. Teachers reported increased confidence in dealing with the subject, and there were more calls to the prevention center from adolescents as well as from teachers and administrators asking for advice. But training teachers didn't reach the heart of the problem. In a survey of 120 high school students asking to whom they would turn in a suicidal crisis, 109 said they would turn first to a friend. Parents were perceived as part of the problem, "unable to understand, but able to interfere," observed Ross, while guidance counselors were for "getting you into college." Ross decided to go into the classrooms to teach students themselves about warning signs, depression, and how to help one another.

Today, suicide prevention in the schools has reached epidemic proportions. All across the United States, social workers and counselors are going into health classes and assemblies, teaching students, teachers, administrators, and parents about suicide. A slew of pamphlets, films, slide shows, seminars, and curricula on adolescent suicide has been developed. Public service announcements on radio and television, featuring Bette Midler, Mariette Hartley, and Nancy Reagan urge teenagers to choose life ("If you have suicide on your mind, wait a minute. I'm Mariette Hartley . . ."). Largely through Ross's efforts, in 1983, California became the first state to mandate suicide prevention programs in the schools. New Jersey, Louisiana, and Florida have since followed suit. Two national committees on youth suicide prevention have been organized (one of which is directed by Ross), and a federal bill calling for programs throughout the country has been proposed. Mark Fisher, former director of The Suicide and Crisis Center in Dallas, could be describing most of these programs when he says, "Our goal is to help youngsters, sometime during junior high or high school, learn the warning signs of suicide in the same way they would learn the warning signs of an impending heart attack, and come up with sort of an emotional CPR: that when you know someone who's suicidal or you recognize suicidal things in yourself, you know exactly what to do—the people to contact and the resources available."

The programs range from free, one-shot presentations like George Cohen's to the "comprehensive" program offered by the South Bergen Mental Health Center, in which teachers and school personnel, then parents, and finally the students themselves, are trained over the course of several months. While most programs are aimed at high school students, curricula are available for younger students. The Wheeler Clinic in Plainville, Connecticut, trains high school students to teach and counsel students in grades five through twelve about suicide prevention. The Dayton, Ohio, Suicide Prevention Center runs a stress management program for junior high students, ten fifty-minute lessons with titles like ". . . But Everybody's Doing It" (peer relationships) and "2 Plus 2 = PANIC" (problem-solving techniques). They also perform puppet shows about death and dying for elementary school children, designed to help them develop a realistic concept of death. Though the puppet show does not deal specifically with suicide, the topic often comes up in discussion. "Children, with a clearer understanding of the nature of death, may be expected to choose suicide as a less attractive behavior during a time of depression or agitation in their lives," conclude two assistant professors at Wright State University in a monograph on the puppet show.

Some programs stress the importance of reaching teens on their own ground. On the north shore of Chicago, where twenty-eight teen suicides in seventeen months beginning in 1978 brought it the title "the Suicide Belt," young social workers are sent into school and community hangouts—school smoking lounges, gymnasiums, hamburger joints—to meet and talk to kids on their own turf. A prevention center in Ithaca, New York, sends its young counselors into four local high schools where they hang out in the gym, cafeteria, and carpentry shop, and are available to any students who want to talk. In one school, in fact, a potential "cluster" may have been averted by the intervention of the "drop-in counselors." A bright, popular student attempted suicide, and within days one of his friends took an overdose. Three others in their circle made threats or left clues suggesting possible suicide intent, but the drop-in counselor quickly met with each of the five students involved and, in some cases, made referrals to therapists. The chain of suicide threats and attempts stopped. In an even more direct attempt to speak to teenagers in their own language, a prevention group in California is developing video games for use in teaching suicide awareness.

An increasing number of programs focus on teenagers helping one another. Many high schools offer peer counseling; a few prevention centers sponsor telephone hot lines on which teenagers counsel teenagers. Several centers offer group therapy in which suicidal adolescents meet weekly with a therapist to discuss parents, school, friends, drugs, sex, and suicide. In Westchester County a group of teenagers who have attempted suicide perform skits about suicide at area high schools, then lead discussions. While these programs focus on the importance of getting suicidal adolescents to adult help, some experts worry that they may place too heavy a burden on young people who already have more than enough to cope with in their lives. Another prevention group helps students act out key scenes from *Romeo and Juliet*, encouraging them to identify and write alternative endings.

But these are only a few of the available programs. At a recent meeting of the American Association of Suicidology, a table near the registration desk was stacked with brochures hawking dozens of prevention curricula appealing to a range of budgets. For $6.60, William Steele offers *Preventing Teenage Suicide*—"A must for every parent and those who work with teenagers"—a workbook that includes "rating scales, assessment guides, guided discussions, actual situations, role playing scripts, methods of communicating and helping, quizzes about suicidal issues, situations and the suicidal person." At $48.95, a Denver psychologist markets *Youth in Crisis,* an "action manual" that "motivates the reader to become a community leader in youth suicide prevention" and is "presented in a durable, attractive three-ring binder allowing for reproduction of the various forms and instruments provided." For $150, Southwest Associates, Inc., Management Resources/Nexus Plans, an affiliate of Netcare Corporation, urges you to "Order Your Copy Today!" of its manual, which will help you develop and institute "a comprehensive school-based and community program for preventing the *Number Two Killer* of Our Teenagers today—SUICIDE." (In its excitement, Southwest Associates, Inc., miscalculated; suicide is the third leading cause of death for teenagers.) For $395, LexCom Productions of Columbia, South Carolina, offers "a sensitive, insightful two-part video series" with "vivid slice-of-life vignettes." The company urges people to "use the enclosed order form to act immediately. You could save a life."

While no doubt well intentioned, such mail-order suicide prevention kits are unsettling. They hold out the promise that a recipe exists for preventing suicide and that *they* know the best ingredients. As a culture we seem to have gone from a time when no one talked about suicide to a time when virtually any talk about it is seen to be good. Schools without programs are increasingly seen as "neolithic" and resistant. Westchester psychiatrist Samuel Klagsbrun has written, "Any school administrator that stands in the way of an intelligent adolescent suicide program, which includes a healthy discussion with teenagers, has to be able to live with death on his or her hands." But what is an intelligent program? In the field of suicide prevention mere good intentions are often taken as the litmus test of worth, but in fact few of these programs have been objectively evaluated, and the effectiveness of a program depends largely on who teaches it. And while most programs revolve around teaching the warning signs, there are other approaches, some of which seem to have more in common with the tactics used at Miletos in 500 B.C. than with those used in George Cohen's classroom.

Convinced that the rise in adolescent suicide was due in large part to a romanticized conception of death and suicide, Victor Victoroff, chief of psychiatry at Huron Road Hospital in Cleveland, decided to show teenagers what he calls "the real face of suicide." In his presentations to high schools, Victoroff shows graphic color slides of young people who have come to emergency rooms following suicide attempts: a girl whose stomach is being pumped; a girl with slit wrists; a boy whose face has been blown away by a gunshot. He displays the suture kits used to sew up wounds, the tracheotomy kits used to cut new air holes for breathing, the tubes used to pump stomachs. He hands out a "suicide packet" that contains a card bearing the phone number of the local suicide hot line and a cotton pad soaked in ipecac. "I ask them to smell the ipecac—it really stinks—and I tell them, 'This is what we pour down people's throats after an overdose,' " says Victoroff. "I make it clear that being treated for a suicide attempt is likely to be one of the more unpleasant experiences a person may have to endure. I explain how many attempters end up half-blind or paralyzed. I want them to know that playing around with suicide is a dangerous game."

At this point "an opportunity is provided for observers to leave if they wish," says Victoroff. "Few do." Slides are then shown of completed suicides on the autopsy table: examples of suicide by strangulation, stabbing, poisoning, electrocution, asphyxiation, and gunshot. Victoroff concludes by asking everyone in the audience to "kill themselves." "I get out a clock and say, 'Now we're all going to commit suicide. I want you to hold your breath for thirty seconds.' As they hold their breath, I tell them that they are lying in bed. They have taken pills, and the poison is beginning to work. Then I tell them they have four minutes left before they lose consciousness and die." Victoroff pauses. "The point is that I'll use any means I can to cut through the romantic haze that sometimes surrounds suicide. I want the students to know that suicide is not romantic at all. It's hard and dirty—and it involves a lot of heartache and agony."

The local suicide prevention center calls Victoroff's approach "shock treatment" and suggests that it may encourage suicidal teenagers to make sure they do the job completely. Victoroff, who calls his approach "confrontation and engagement," says that over the years he has received a stack of letters from would-be suicides thanking him for dissuading them from killing themselves. He estimates that he has made his presentation to ten or fifteen thousand adolescents. "And until somebody tells me what I'm doing is wrong," he says, "I'm going to continue."

A rising tide of opinion suggests that talking about suicide is the best prevention. Still, some psychiatrists fear that programs that promote openness about suicide may in fact encourage it by lowering the taboo on the act and making it seem less forbidden. (They point to the drug education programs of the early seventies, which did not markedly affect the drug abuse problem.) In one of the first rigorous evaluations of prevention efforts, psychiatrist David Shaffer studied the effect of three different programs in New Jersey high schools. While there was no evidence that the programs caused wide distress, he found no significant attitude change, and found that those who were already suicidal became even *more* distressed after being exposed to the program. Calculating that the number of students who might be saved by such programs is minuscule, Shaffer concluded that the possible benefits of such programs are outweighed by the possible harm. "I believe there should be a moratorium on suicide awareness programs directed at students," he told a stunned audience at the 1988 annual meeting of the American Association of Suicidology.

Meanwhile, George Cohen continues to lug his slide projector into schools and talk about the importance of breaking a promise and saving a friend. Although some principals continue to resist the program, it has now been given in more than half of Westchester's forty school districts. "My feeling is that there is no way we can just sit on our hands and say, 'Well, it might create a problem, so we won't do it.' Before the program was in the county, there were kids killing themselves. This isn't much, but it's better than nothing."

Because it is aimed at ninth to twelfth graders, Cohen's program did not reach Steven Perro's class at Albert Leonard Junior High School in New Rochelle. The thirteen-year-old eighth grader had been unhappy about living with his mother, stepfather, and three stepbrothers, and he wanted to move in with his grandmother in the Bronx. By November 13, 1984, he decided to do something about it. "On Monday, Steven walked up to me at lunchtime and said he wanted to kill himself," a classmate said later. "He gave me the combination to his locker in case I wanted to take anything. He was laughing. I didn't think he meant it, so I didn't do anything." That same day Perro told at least two other friends that he was going to kill himself. All of them assumed he was kidding. On Tuesday afternoon Perro asked a thirteen-year-old girl who lived near him for a knife. "I asked him why he wanted it, and he said he was going to kill himself," she said. "He was always saying things like that. I didn't think he meant it." That afternoon Perro wrote several good-bye notes to friends, went up to the attic, and hanged himself.

VII

Beginning to Close
the Door

TWO YEARS AFTER BEING discharged from Four Winds, Dana Evans was on the dean's list at Dutchess Community College. She hadn't taken a drink or used drugs since she entered Four Winds. She attended three AA meetings a week and had started a chapter at school. She had told several friends that she is an alcoholic; one or two friends that she was in a psychiatric hospital; and no one about her suicide attempts. She was living at home. She and her mother were getting along better. "We're not best friends or anything, but it's okay. We talk about work and school. Sometimes we even share makeup."

When I met Dana, she looked like a different person from the one she was in her drinking days. She was slim, pretty, and neatly dressed. Although she was witty and sharp, able to make others laugh easily, her own laughter came self-consciously, and her defensiveness and anger occasionally flared. Her biggest problem, she told me, was loneliness. She had few friends at college, and though she remained close to some of her Four Winds friends, she spent much of her time by herself. "I've still got a long way to go. It takes a long time to break an eighteen-year habit. At Four Winds, when Terry and I started working on how to relate to people, I was at ground zero. And in two and a half years you don't exactly become proficient at making bosom buddies. But it's only going to get better as my confidence grows and I get more used to doing things and not caring so much about what people think." Dana laughed.

" 'Cause I still care what Joe Schmo thinks, and who the hell is he? I don't even know him!' "

In the first few months after Brian's death, Mary Hart visited her son's grave several times a day. It helped her to stand there and talk to him. "I could say things to him, and he couldn't talk back." Sometimes she would shout at him: "Why did you do this, you dumb kid? Why?" For a long time she and her husband believed that if Brian had taken his medication regularly, he would still be alive. While her husband kept his feelings more to himself, Mary felt an endless, restless need to talk about Brian's death. The weight of his suicide threatened to crush her. "One day I found myself in the garage thinking all I have to do is to trip this button and close the garage door, and I'd be asleep too."

Mary and Pat began seeing a therapist, and gradually Mary's rage and frustration dissipated. "I had been looking for Brian around every corner. It was hard for me to say, 'This is the end,' but after a while I realized that this was his choosing and there was nothing more. The therapist helped me begin to close the door."

Nevertheless, there were unexpected reminders: going down to the cellar to fetch something and coming across Brian's skis; looking through her recipe file and finding a note in Brian's handwriting on the back of one: "Ma, I've gone to the mall to look for some Christmas gifts"; waking at four in the morning and feeling the need to pore over the roster of people at Brian's wake. She continued to visit Brian's grave several times a week, but when she spoke to him, she was more gentle. "I talk about the things we'll never know—what he would have looked like, what his children would have been like, what he might have done. And about the pain he must have gone through . . . and how much I wish we could have understood that pain more."

Two years after their son's death, Sandy Martin, Brian's English teacher at Anderson, sent the Harts some snapshots she had taken of Brian. As they looked at them the Harts realized that these were probably the last new photographs they would ever see of their son. Pat hung one of them in the Rogues Gallery, a picture of Brian in a bright red polo shirt, flashing a broad smile.

"Whatever caused Justin Spoonhour's death, we all had a part in it," Lora Porter, the Putnam Valley librarian, told me. "We failed him by not raising our children to be kinder to one another. Do you remember that line from *South Pacific*? 'You've got to be carefully taught to hate.' Well, the same thing applies to love. You've got to be taught to love and respect, and I don't think we do that enough."

With money donated by members of the library board, Porter ordered some special animal puppets and sewed labels on them that said "Justin's puppets." Having worked with hundreds of children over the years, Porter was surprised at the hold Justin's memory had on her. In her heart of hearts she still thought of his death as an accident, although her head told her it wasn't. If Justin could only have survived adolescence, Porter believed, he would have blossomed. "He was just marking his time through childhood. In another few years he would have graduated high school and been out on his own. I think he would have come into his own when he became an adult. And I would like so much to have known him when he grew up. I would have liked to have him as a friend. The world needs people like Justin. There are too many pedestrians. Justin could fly."

On the day after Justin's suicide his English class was due to read aloud the scene in which Julius Caesar is killed. As they began, the irony stunned the class for a moment, but no one said anything. The teacher took over the role of Caesar, and they finished the play as quickly as they could. In the first few days two dozen junior high school students saw guidance counselors; the second week, only a few sought help, and by the third week, recalled one administrator, things were "back to normal." "Nobody talked about it," said a student. "He was just crossed off the attendance list, everyone was careful not to mention his name, and it was like that was that."

There were a few official observances. At the spring concert the chorus director played Beethoven's "Ode to Joy" in his memory. Justin's class dedicated its yearbook, *Tiger '84,* to him: Under the lyrics of "Perhaps Love" there were four photographs of Justin, including curmudgeonly poses from *Scrooge* and *Outrageous Fortune,* as well as his formal graduation portrait. The caption read, "Putnam Valley Junior High deeply regrets the loss of Justin Spoonhour." At graduation Justin's name was not mentioned. On the first anniversary of his death teachers were reminded to be particularly alert in case students remembered the anniversary and were upset. But no one mentioned it or came to the counselors for help. And yet a visitor to the cemetery that day found that some children had left notes and flowers on Justin's grave.

"I'm not sure a school ever gets over something like this," Superintendent Richard Brodow says. "It's something you always remember, and you *should* always remember because it lets us know how vulnerable we are." Brodow's forthright handling of the tragedy was praised by parents and teachers, and over the following year, when other schools in the area experienced suicides, they turned to him for advice. Brodow wrote about Justin's suicide in a short essay, which begins with a quote from Jean Giraudoux: "Out of the heart of darkness comes the light." Brodow firmly believed that the school learned something from the tragedy. "Certainly there is more awareness and sensitivity on everyone's part for youngsters who have difficulty." But the next year, after Justin's classmates had moved on to high school, the new ninth graders found another outcast to pick on—teasing him, calling him names, urinating in his locker.

Mike LoPuzzo saved all the newspaper clippings about his friend's death. He attended all the town meetings on suicide, sitting near the front, listening attentively. Although at first he thought that Justin had killed himself because of the teasing, Mike realized that couldn't be the entire answer—Justin had endured it all his life. "He didn't leave us a note. He didn't want to make it easy for us. He didn't want to give us an answer. He wanted to leave us with questions. He wanted us to think about it. Maybe he was saying, 'Take a look at yourselves.'"

Two years after Justin's death Diana Wolf was surprised to find herself thinking of Justin once more. "I wear contact lenses, and sometimes I have problems with them and have to use glasses. And when I wear them, I don't like the way I look at all. One day at school I was wearing glasses and I was feeling bad. I didn't like the way my hair had come out, I wasn't wearing flattering clothes, and I was feeling fat and ugly. In English class some kids were being snotty to me, and in social studies my regular work partner wasn't there. Usually I'm pretty popular, but this time I couldn't find anyone to be my partner, and I felt terrible.

"After school I was walking home alone from the bus. It was a damp, drizzly day. I felt lonely and pretty miserable because I just hadn't fit in. It was the worst feeling, that not fitting in. I was really depressed. But I went home and took off those glasses. I showered, put on some different clothes, and managed to get my lenses back in. I felt so much better just because I accepted myself again. And then I suddenly thought, 'What I felt like for one day is what Justin must have felt like all the time.'"

Anne and Giles Spoonhour quickly tried to put their son's death behind them. Two days after the funeral they kept their appointment to speak at Justin's Youth Group about their emergency services work. They talked for almost two hours to the children about how to handle a crisis, what resources were available, and so on—without once breaking down. Early on, Anne made a conscious decision not to look back. "My thinking was, 'It can't be undone, no matter who did it or why. Now what are you going to do? Let's get on with it.'" She threw herself into her work as police dispatcher, became a member of the volunteer fire department, worked as steward chairman of the church, and wrote long letters to the local newspaper about community issues. But each night when she went to bed, the first thing she saw when she closed her eyes was the image of her son hanging from the tree.

While Anne struggled to look ahead, Giles seemed unable not to look back. Each morning at seven he would start into Justin's room to wake his son up for school, and then he'd remember. Each evening when he came home from work and heard the neighborhood children playing in the yard, he waited to hear his son's voice. Although he tried to keep control, he felt broken with pain and confusion. "I was angry at Justin for not feeling comfortable enough to talk with me or with Anne. I was a little angry at Leah and Anne for not noticing it. And I was angry at myself because as a counselor, as a professional, I'm supposed to be able to pick up on things like that." Occasionally his anger exploded. Conflicts that had existed in his marriage all along were brought to the surface by Justin's suicide. Three months after their son's death, Giles and Anne began seeing a counselor, who told them that 60 percent of the parents of an adolescent suicide eventually divorce.

Leah had sessions with the school psychologist and with Anne and Giles in their therapy. She didn't talk much to her parents about her brother's suicide, and they didn't force the issue. But Anne and Giles tried to watch her more closely without making their worry obvious. They went out of their way to chauffeur her to meetings and friends' houses whenever possible. They didn't like her to be alone at home, and since her brother's death, neither did she. Anne felt uncomfortable in the house, too. "When I got off work late at night or went out on a call at midnight, I didn't like seeing the damn trees in the dark. I guess I've sort of turned against trees. I've decided I like sky, a lot of sky." Within a year of Justin's death they moved to a house on the other side of Putnam Valley. "Anne and Leah didn't want to stay in the old house because the memories of Justin were so strong," says Giles. "I would have *preferred* to stay because the memories were so strong."

One of the ways Anne and Giles tried to work through their grief was by talking about it. The week after Justin's death Anne got a call from WCBS-TV in New York asking for an interview. She said yes. "I thought I may as well make out of it what I could. Nothing was going to change the fact in this instance, but it might alter future instances." Over the following year she and Giles told their story to *People, Ladies' Home Journal, The New York Times, USA Today,* the "Donahue" show, the BBC, and more than sixty local newspapers and radio and television stations. They spoke at suicide prevention centers, churches, and high schools. Anne became a member of the New York State Council on Youth Suicide Prevention. At one presentation Giles was asked what advice he would give to parents. "Many teens don't like to be held, to be touched. But I encourage parents to hold, to show love physically. Touch the head," he said, almost involuntarily reaching out with hands that had been still for nearly an hour. "Put an arm around the shoulders—whatever seems comfortable. And even if it doesn't feel comfortable, do it anyway. Because the more you practice, the easier it gets."

Anne and Giles's efforts in suicide prevention had a peculiar effect on the town of Putnam Valley. Despite the outpouring of concern immediately following Justin's suicide, the community seemed to put it quickly in the past. Two nights after the death, the meeting called by Richard Brodow at Putnam

Valley Junior High was attended by more than 250 people. Two months later, when Anne Spoonhour called for a meeting on adolescent suicide prevention, only about a dozen parents showed up. As Anne became increasingly involved in suicide prevention, some people in the community resented her efforts, which they felt reflected negatively on Putnam Valley. In conversations at the library or at the grocery store there was talk that "enough is enough" and "let's not call attention to ourselves." Some worried that the Spoonhours were making Putnam Valley "the suicide capital of the world." A friend of Anne's who had helped her with her prevention work was stopped on the steps of the church one day by a prominent local citizen. "What are you people trying to do?" he demanded. "Win an Academy Award for Justin Spoonhour?" Although the Putnam Valley Mental Health Department beefed up its programs for adolescents, two years after Justin's death Putnam Valley still had no suicide prevention program in its classrooms. "What are we waiting for?" asked one mother. "Are we just going to sit back and wait till the next suicide?"

But something curious took place at the same time. Several years before Justin's death there had been another teenage suicide in Putnam Valley. A high school junior had walked into the woods and shot herself. Like every other suicide in Putnam Valley before Justin's, the death had been hushed up. "Nothing was said in school although everybody knew," recalled Lora Porter, whose son was in the girl's class. "It was almost as if the entire town conspired to pretend it hadn't happened. Then when Anne and Giles chose to handle Justin's suicide by talking openly about it, I think they effected a catharsis for Colleen's group. As people began talking about Justin, Colleen's friends began talking about Colleen for the first time, saying that it was too bad she didn't have anyone to talk to, too bad no one saw what was happening to her. They had never had a chance to talk about it before. I don't know whether I would have had the courage to speak out the way Anne and Giles did, but I have often thought they did a very great service for this group of young people."

Two years after Justin's death the Spoonhours' house in Lookout Manor was empty. The grass was overgrown and the swing set was rusting in the backyard. An orange "Totfinder" sticker still clung to one window. On the mailbox the name "Spoonhour" was crossed out. Anne's father, who owned the house, was trying to sell it. He talked of going into the woods across the street and cutting down the tree from which Justin hung, but Anne and Giles said no. They did not want to destroy a living thing.

2
HISTORY

—◆—

I

PRIMITIVE ROOTS:
THE ROCK OF THE
FOREFATHERS

Lo, my name reeks
Lo, more than carrion smell
On summer days of burning sky . . .

Lo, my name reeks
Lo, more than that of a sturdy child
Who is said to belong to one who rejects him . . .

To whom shall I speak today?
Brothers are mean,
One goes to strangers for affection . . .

To whom shall I speak today?
I am burdened with grief
For lack of an intimate . . .

Death is before me today
[Like] a sick man's recovery,
Like going outdoors after confinement . . .

Death is before me today
Like a man's longing to see his home
When he has spent many years in captivity.

THESE LINES WERE WRITTEN four thousand years ago in the first inter-
mediate period of the Middle Kingdom in Egypt. They are part of the first
recorded reference to suicide. In *The Dispute Between a Man and His Ba,* a
man who is tired of life and buffeted by ill fortune considers killing himself.
Angered by his complaints, his soul, or *ba,* threatens to leave him. The man
implores his *ba* to remain, since to be abandoned by his soul would deprive
him of an afterlife. His *ba* urges him to enjoy life, to surrender himself to
hedonistic pleasures. These lines are taken from the man's final answer, four
poems in which he deplores the greed and injustice of the times, laments his
isolation, and speaks longingly of death. In the end his *ba* agrees to stay; it
is not clear whether the man goes on to kill himself.

The seven sheets of papyrus that make up *Dispute* describe an interior
landscape not unlike that of almost any lonely, despairing person considering
suicide in the 1990s. Just as Dana Evans invented insults to reinforce her
self-loathing, the anonymous Egyptian sings out his own curses: "Lo, my name
reeks / Lo, more than carrion smell." Just as Justin Spoonhour was overwhelmed by the cruelty of the world around him, the Egyptian is stung by the
indifference of society and swamped by loneliness: "I am burdened with grief /
For lack of an intimate." His final words to his *ba,* in fact, perfectly articulate
the interior journey of a suicidal person: from loss of self-esteem, to despair
of finding comfort in the outside world, to a conception of death as a refuge—
"Like a man's longing to see his home / When he has spent many years in
captivity." From these seven sheets we can trace an unbroken line of loneliness,
despair, and hopelessness that has been common to suicidal people for four
thousand years.

Yet if the inner world of the suicidal person has changed little over four
millennia, the way we view the act of suicide has varied widely. Today in the
Western world we think of suicide primarily as a psychiatric problem. We
study it, search for its causes, and struggle to prevent what we consider a tragic
and sometimes shameful act. It is an attitude the ancient Egyptian might have
found puzzling. In his time and place earthly existence was considered a mere
prelude to blissful afterlife. Death was not an end but a beginning. There were
no social or religious prohibitions against suicide, and the Egyptian would
certainly not have been considered mentally ill. For him suicide was not only
an acceptable escape from an intolerable life but a path to blessed immortality.
"Truly, he who is yonder will stand in the sun-bark," he tells his *ba,* "making
its bounty flow to the temples." During the turbulent period when *Dispute* was
written, suicide seems to have been a frequent occurrence. In *The Admonitions
of a Sage,* a popular story of the time, a wise man reveals that suicide is so

common the crocodiles are glutted with despairing people who have hurled themselves into the river.

Since the beginning of man in all times and in all places, there has been suicide, but the way a culture judges its suicides varies from place to place and time to time, largely depending on how that culture views death. Attitudes have ranged from fierce condemnation and hostility to mild disapproval and tolerance, to acceptance, encouragement, and incorporation into the socio-cultural system. If our ancient Egyptian had killed himself in pre-Christian Scandinavia, for example, he would have been guaranteed a place in Viking paradise. If he had taken his life during the Roman Empire, his death would have been honored as a glorious demonstration of his wisdom. If he had cut open his stomach in feudal Japan, he would have been praised as a man of principle. If he had killed himself in fifteenth-century Metz, however, his corpse would have been crammed into a barrel and floated down the Moselle, sending the tainted body beyond city limits. In seventeenth-century France his corpse would have been dragged through the streets, hanged upside down, then thrown on the public garbage heap. In seventeenth-century England his estate would have been forfeited to the crown and his body buried at a cross-roads with a stake through the heart.

According to Christianity suicide was a sin against God and a crime against the state, and such punishments were designed to deter despairing people from its evil. These penalties (often waived if the suicide was deemed insane) gradually disappeared during the eighteenth and nineteenth centuries. The last recorded crossroads burial of an English suicide took place in 1823, when a man named Griffiths was interred at the intersection of Eaton Street, Grosvenor Place, and King's Road, London. By that time the scientific study of suicide had begun, and the question became not whether suicide was a sin or a crime but why it occurred. Gradually, suicide was seen not as a moral issue but as an act of pathology. Still, the rationality of science hardly dispelled the opprobrium attached to the act: In England, confiscation of a suicide's property was not abolished until 1870, and as late as 1955 a man was sentenced to two years in prison for attempting suicide. Punishment for attempted suicide was finally abolished in 1961 when Parliament passed the Suicide Act. Even after that, moral outrage found legal approval. In 1969 an Isle of Man court ordered a teenager who had attempted suicide to be flogged.

Deep in central Africa, in what is now Uganda, live the Baganda. When English missionaries first traveled among them in the second half of the nineteenth century, they learned that the lives of the Baganda, like those of most primitive tribespeople, were circumscribed by an elaborate web of myths. "The Baganda were very superstitious about suicides," wrote the Reverend

John Roscoe in 1911. "They took innumerable precautions to remove the body and destroy the ghost, to prevent the latter from causing further trouble." Some of those precautions must have seemed familiar to Roscoe, an Englishman who lived among the Baganda for many years. After a suicide the body was taken "to a distant place where cross-roads met" and burned, in an attempt to destroy the ghost, using as fuel the tree or hut from which he had hanged himself. (People would not live in the hut in which a suicide had taken place for fear they might be tempted to follow suit.) When women passed the spot, they threw grass or twigs on the site to prevent the suicide's restless ghost from entering them and being reborn.

Twentieth-century historians suggest that Christian punishments of suicide echoed the purification rituals of primitive tribes. But the law that condemned Mr. Griffiths to burial at a London crossroads in 1823 was born of moral disgust, while the Baganda custom was born of fear that the suicide's ghost would return to impregnate young tribeswomen. (The same precautions were taken with the corpses of twins and of children born feet first.) In the former it was the act itself that provoked horror; in the latter it was the consequence of the act.

Primitive fear of the suicide's ghost stemmed in part from a general fear of the dead, especially of those who met a sudden or violent death. Their ghosts were considered particularly restless because of the desperate state of mind in which they left life. The soul had not made a smooth break; it was considered "unclean." Extensive purification rituals were performed to expiate the "blood guilt," to appease the ghost of the slain, and to dissuade it from haunting the living. Such precautions were crucial in the case of suicides, whose ghosts were notoriously malevolent. Not only had the suicide spilled blood, he had spilled family blood, which was even more "powerful." And while the ghost of a murdered man haunted only his murderer, the ghost of a suicide might seek revenge against an entire tribe, an entire world that had troubled him. In various cultures a suicide's ghost was believed to cause tempests, famine, hailstorms, or drought, or to make barren the earth that it touched.

Some tribes, therefore, like the Baganda, buried a suicide's corpse at a crossroads so that the ghost might not find its way home. In other tribes the corpse was mutilated or burned so that the suicide's spirit would be unable to "walk." In others the body was buried far from the graves of his kinsmen so that his soul might be quarantined from the souls of those who died from other causes. The Bannaus of Cambodia buried suicides in a corner of the forest; natives of Dahomey left the bodies of suicides in the fields to be devoured by wild beasts. The Alabama Indians threw them into the river. Among the Wajagga of East Africa, after a man hanged himself a goat was sacrificed with the same noose in hopes of mollifying the dead man's soul.

Such measures, it was hoped, would isolate the suicide's soul and render it unable to cause mischief. The Jakuts believed that the soul of a suicide never came to rest; the Omaha Indians believed that a self-murderer was excluded from the spirit world; the Paharis of India believed that the suicide's ghost hovered eternally between heaven and earth. Both the Iroquois and Hidatsa Indians maintained that the souls of suicides occupied a separate village in the land of the dead because their presence made other dead souls uneasy. The Dyaks of Borneo said that suicides went to a special place where those who had drowned themselves lived forever up to their waists in water and those who had poisoned themselves lived in houses built of poisonous wood, surrounded by plants that emitted noxious fumes. The Dakotas believed that a suicide's ghost was forever doomed to drag behind him the tree on which he had hanged himself—hence women hanged themselves from the smallest trees that would bear their weight.

The belief that a suicide's ghost might return to pester the living went hand in hand with the notion of revenge suicide. In some primitive societies suicide was committed as a direct act of vengeance, in the belief that as a ghost one was more easily able to persecute those who had wronged him. "Man has an enemy whom he cannot fight successfully," observed an ancient proverb. "He can successfully disgrace his enemy by hanging himself in his enemy's front yard." An ancient Chinese law placed responsibility for the death on the person who had supposedly caused it, and people frequently killed themselves in order to entangle an adversary in legal proceedings, to embarrass him, or to ensure his harassment by the suicide's angry ghost. The ghost was believed to haunt the place where the act had been committed, trying to persuade others to follow his example and attempting to strangle those who chose to live.

Some revenge suicides worked more directly. The Tshi-speaking peoples of Africa's Gold Coast believed that if, before committing suicide, a person blamed his act on another, that person was required by tribal law to kill himself using the same method unless the suicide's family was compensated with money. For many years India had several accepted forms of revenge suicide. In certain areas of southern India if a man tore out his eye or killed himself after a quarrel, his adversary was required to do the same either to himself or to a relative. An eye for an eye, a suicide for a suicide was the rule. A woman who had been insulted might smash her head against the door of the woman who insulted her, whereupon that woman had to do the same. If a woman poisoned herself, the woman who "drove her to her death" followed suit; if she refused, her house would be burned down and her cattle would disappear. Until recently a legal method of debt collection in India was to sit at the debtor's door and refuse food or drink until the charge was paid. If "sitting *dharna,*" as it was called, ended in starvation, the creditor believed that public opinion would avenge him upon his enemy. When one of the Rajput rajas levied a war tax on the Brahmans, a number of the wealthiest, having argued in vain, stabbed themselves with daggers in front of the raja while cursing him with their last breaths. Thus denounced, the raja was shunned even by his friends.

The notion of revenge suicide or "killing oneself upon the head of another" may seem archaic, but the primitive tribesman who hangs himself on his enemy's doorstep provides a literal illustration of Freud's theory that suicide is a sort of inverted murder in which anger meant for another is turned inward on the self. Today, revenge, conscious or unconscious, is still a powerful motive in many suicides although the punishment exacted is, of course, more psychological than physical. A particularly cruel example, pointed out by historian Henry Fedden, is that of the nineteenth-century Frenchman whose mistress was unfaithful. Before killing himself he told his servant that after his death a candle should be made of his fat and carried, lighted, to the woman. To accompany it he composed a note telling her that as he burned for her in life, so he did now in death.

Among most tribes, primitive fear of suicide was not based on moral judgment although precautions taken to assuage vengeful ghosts might eventually have given birth to the idea that the act of suicide was in itself, like murder, something "wrong." (And precautions may have evolved into punishments.) In fact, certain cultures tolerated and even encouraged suicide. The Goths believed that those who died naturally were doomed to languish eternally in caves full of venomous creatures; therefore, old men threw themselves off a precipice called the Rock of the Forefathers. The Iglulik are among several Eskimo tribes who believed that a violent death ensured a place in paradise, which they called the Land of Day; those who died by natural causes were confined to the Narrow Land. In some cultures elderly suicides were provoked by the belief that a man entered into the next world in the same condition as he left this one; consequently, it behooved him to take his own life before he grew feeble. The ancient Celts considered natural death shameful, and men who threw themselves from cliffs were celebrated with song. "They are a nation lavish of their blood and eager to face death," wrote Silvius Italicus of the Spanish Celts. "As soon as the Celt has passed the age of mature strength, he endures the flight of time impatiently and scorns to await old age; the term of his existence depends upon himself." Among the Chukchee of Siberia, those who died voluntarily were said to have the best abode in the afterlife: "They dwell on the red blaze of the aurora borealis and pass their time playing ball with a walrus-skull."

In pre-Christian Scandinavia only those Vikings who died a violent death were permitted to attain Valhalla, "the hall of those who died by violence," where they fought mock battles and then feasted, drinking from the skulls of their enemies. Vikings unlucky enough not to die in battle often slew themselves with swords or threw themselves from cliffs to gain entrance to Valhalla. Odin, the god of war, who presided over the "feast of heroes," was himself said to be a suicide. As death approached he assembled his warriors and stabbed himself in nine places, declaring that he would join the gods at their immortal feast, where he would welcome all those who died with weapons in their hands.

Recommending violent death as a passport to paradise was a way of promoting a properly bellicose spirit in warrior societies. Elsewhere, "economic suicide" by the elderly and infirm was encouraged during periods of hardship so that there would be sufficient rations for the tribe to survive. In other cultures sacrificial suicides were carried out to honor the gods or to ensure a good harvest. Among the Aztecs a young man was selected each year to impersonate the god Tezcatlipoca. He received the homage of his people for one year, at the end of which he offered himself up to death at the altar, and his living heart was cut out. In the mountains of Tien-tai in China each year several Buddhist monks sacrificed their lives, hoping to obtain Nirvana for themselves and protection from evil spirits for their community. On the appointed day the monk, observed by a crowd of spectators, entered a furnace and sat on a wooden seat. The door was shut and the furnace lighted. Afterward the ashes were collected, washed, and revered as the relics of a saint. A sixteenth-century traveler to the province of Quilacare in southern India learned that the king's reign was fixed at twelve years, at the end of which he hosted an extravagant feast in honor of the tribal idol.

> The king has a wooden scaffolding made, spread over with silken hangings: and on that day he goes to bathe at a tank with great ceremonies and sound of music, after that he comes to the idol and prays to it, and mounts on to the scaffolding, and there before all the people he takes some very sharp knives, and begins to cut off his nose, and then his ears, and his lips, and all his members, and as much flesh off himself as he can; and he throws it away very hurriedly until so much of his blood is spilled that he begins to faint, and then he cuts his throat himself.

Such suicides were ostensibly voluntary, but social custom rendered them all but compulsory. In India, when sacrificial suicides were, on occasion, rescued by the military, the victims escaped whenever possible and returned to embrace death. Similarly, according to an old custom in Malabar, people who were taken ill prayed to their idol for recovery. Once healthy they fattened themselves up for a year or more and then on a festival day gratefully cut off their heads before the idol who had saved their life.

Some contemporary suicides kill themselves in the hope that their death may reunite them with a lost loved one. In primitive societies such suicides were common, but the act was compelled less by grief than by cultural tradition. "There is another world, and they who kill themselves to accompany their friends thither will live with them there." This Druid maxim expresses the motivation behind a custom dating back to ancient Egypt, where wives and servants took poison and were buried with their pharaohs, along with weapons, furniture, perfumes, combs, the means of grinding corn, and anything else that would make life in the next world comfortable. As Egyptian civilization progressed, the corpses of wives and servants were replaced by symbolic figurines; in other societies, however, the practice persisted. In Siam, after the king's corpse was laid in his grave, his wives, concubines, and ministers of state drank poison and were placed alongside him along with six horses, twelve camels or elephants, and twenty hunting dogs, thus providing the king with means of diversion in the afterlife. In Scythia, Herodotus tells us, a king was buried with his cook, butler, groom, steward, chamberlain, and one of his concubines—all of them strangled—who were expected to wait on their master in the next world as they had in this. A year after the king's death fifty of his servants and fifty of his horses were strangled, stuffed with chaff, and mounted on scaffolds around his tomb, each dead servant riding a dead horse, ever prepared to fight for his dead master. At the burial of the king of Benin in Western Africa, the ruler's favorite lords and servants leaped into his tomb, vying for the honor of being buried alive with their master's corpse.

Just as these African servants competed for the privilege of accompanying their master in death, so too did the wives of the Crestonaeans of Thrace, according to Herodotus. Following the death of a Thracian man, a "keen competition" was held among his wives to determine which among them he had most loved. The winner was slain over the grave and buried with her husband. The custom of a widow or concubine taking her life on the death of her husband has been practiced in nearly every part of the world. After the death of an Inca leader, a number of favored attendants were cremated with him; women not chosen for this honor often killed themselves anyway. At Fijian funerals the wife who met death with the greatest devotion became the preferred wife in the abode of spirits; a widow who refused to let herself be killed was considered an adulteress. The gender reverse of this was seldom observed, although in one tribe on the Gold Coast a man of low rank who married a sister of the king was expected to kill himself on the death of his wife. "Should he outrage native custom and neglect to do so," noted one anthropologist, "a hint is conveyed to him that he will be put to death, which usually produces the desired effect."

The best-known example of wifely suicide is the Hindu practice of suttee, named after a heroine of Hindu mythology who threw herself onto her husband's funeral pyre to prove her devotion. The practice is a blend of choice and coercion. A Hindu wife is expected to dedicate herself to her husband—no matter how miserably he may treat her—even after his death. The *Padmapurana,* an eleventh-century religious text, outlined a virtuous woman's duties to her husband—"whatever his defects may be, a wife should always look upon him as her god"—and instructed her that when her husband dies, she should "allow herself to be burnt alive on the same funeral pyre; then everyone will praise her virtue." Hindu widows are bypassed by inheritance laws; they are forbidden to attend wedding or birthday celebrations or to wear jewelry, makeup, or bright clothing. The alternative is suttee, for which a widow is honored above all other women, bringing respect to her memory and to her family.

Suttee was already in vogue when Alexander the Great invaded India in 327 B.C., and when the English arrived two millennia later, they were horrified to find it still practiced widely; in 1821 there were 2,366 reported cases. Outraged by this "primitive act," the British declared it illegal in 1829—only six years after they abolished stake-and-crossroads burial in their own country. But the custom persisted, and even today the practice continues in remote areas. In 1987 in the village of Deorala, several days after her husband's death from a ruptured appendix, eighteen-year-old Roop Kanwar climbed onto her husband's funeral pyre of sandalwood and coconuts soaked with clarified butter and cradled his head in her lap. The pyre was set ablaze and she burned to death. Although Indian feminists protested the death and several family members were later arrested and charged with aiding and abetting a suicide, no one interrupted the ceremony. Twelve days later more than one hundred thousand Rajputs gathered in the village to honor Kanwar's memory. The town took on a carnival atmosphere; booths were set up to sell pictures of the dead couple, and a loudspeaker system was installed to help locate lost children.

Scholars of self-destruction classify such acts as "institutional" or "ritual" suicides—deaths that are all but demanded by cultural tradition—as if they were embarrassing anachronisms that had nothing in common with suicides in the "civilized" world. They are thus dismissed as the acts of primitives. Yet in Japan for thousands of years suicide has been an acceptable, often honorable, way out of intolerable situations. "The Japanese calendar of saints," wrote one nineteenth-century Western historian, "is not filled with reformers, alms-givers and founders of hospitals or orphanages, but is overcrowded with canonized suicides and committers of *hara-kiri*. Even today, no man more . . . surely draws homage to his tomb, securing even apotheosis, than the suicide, though he may have committed a crime."

The Buddhist tradition places less value on life in this world than on life in the next. Existence on earth is an ephemeral state, the body is merely a temporary lodging of the soul, and biological life is not only meaningless but filled with suffering. Death is the point at which a person makes contact with the eternal world. If a person acquits himself well at the moment of death, offenses committed during his earthly life are forgiven. In some cases suicide can be the most exquisite death of all.

Historically, suicide in Japan has enjoyed not only religious tolerance but state approval. The romantic aura that surrounds suicide grew out of the development of *seppuku,* a traditional form of suicide better known outside Japan as *harakiri,* or "belly-cutting." It was practiced by the samurai, or military class, who followed an ethical code known as *Bushido*—"the way of the knights." At the heart of *Bushido* was the creed of loyalty to one's lord or to any matter of principle. When a *bushi,* or knight, was forced to choose between two courses of action, one of which involved the sacrifice of principle and the other the sacrifice of life, he unhesitatingly chose the latter. At the same time a man raised in the samurai tradition was taught from an early age that a samurai's most important trait was to suppress outward displays of emotion, be it pleasure or pain. The supreme test of a samurai's self-discipline and devotion to principle was the act of *seppuku.*

Seppuku originated about a thousand years ago during the beginning of Japanese feudalism as an honorable way for a soldier to avoid the humiliation of capture. By the seventeenth century it was widely used as a death penalty for the samurai. While common criminals were hung in the town square, a member of the military class condemned to death by his lord might be allowed to expiate his crime by his own hand. Thus, obligatory *seppuku* was a privilege granted by the feudal lord, saving the samurai the shame of being handed over to the public executioner. Members of the military class were trained from an early age to prepare for the possibility of voluntary death by self-disembowelment, and it is said that warriors frequently rehearsed the *seppuku* ceremony, in which every step was prescribed by custom.

A noble suspected of misconduct or of disloyalty would receive a letter from the emperor politely hinting that he must die. The letter was often accompanied by a jeweled dagger. On the appointed day, clothed in ceremonial dress, the doomed man knelt on a red mat on a small platform built for the occasion in his baronial hall or in the temple. Officials and friends formed a silent semicircle around him. After prayer the emperor's envoy handed the dagger to the noble, who publicly confessed his wrongs. The noble stripped down to the traditional loincloth, plunged the dagger into the left side of his abdomen, drew it across to the right, then turned the blade and cut upward. As he fell forward, the *kaishaku,* a friend of the noble, severed the noble's head with a long sword. The bloodstained dagger was taken back to the lord as proof of his noble's obedience.

Often, a disloyal noble anticipated the wishes of his lord and committed *seppuku* without prompting. There was incentive for this: If death had been demanded by the lord, only half the samurai's property was forfeited to the state; if voluntary, his dishonor was erased, and his family inherited his full fortune. Over the years voluntary *seppuku* became common in a variety of circumstances: to follow one's dead lord into the next world; to avoid beheading by the enemy in a lost battle; to restore injured honor in a situation where revenge was impossible; to protest the conduct of a superior; to admit an error;

to keep a secret; to turn one's lord from a course of action that might injure his reputation. Whatever the motive, *seppuku* ensured the samurai an honorable burial and a respected memory.

Seppuku eventually extended beyond the military class and became the national form of honorable suicide. It is believed that during the feudal ages more than fifteen hundred cases of *seppuku* occurred each year, more than half of them voluntary. "The Japanese are an obstinate, capricious, resolute and whimsical people," observed Montesquieu. "They have a natural contempt of death, and rip open their bellies for the least fancy." In 1868 twenty samurai involved in the murder of a French officer were condemned to commit *seppuku* before the French ambassador. The latter found it difficult to appreciate this gesture, and after eleven of the soldiers had proved their remorse, he reprieved the remaining knights. While the practice appalled foreigners, it remained sacred to the Japanese; the following year a member of the Japanese parliament proclaimed *seppuku* "the very shrine of the Japanese national spirit and the embodiment in practice of devotion to principle."

Although obligatory suicide was prohibited by law in 1873 and the frequency of voluntary *seppuku* declined, it continued to be practiced—and acclaimed—as an honorable death. In 1891, protesting the failure of the government to take action against Russian encroachments on Japan's northern border, Lieutenant Ohara Takeyoshi became a national hero by disemboweling himself in front of the graves of his ancestors in Tokyo. After the Japanese-Chinese War, when Japan allowed Port Arthur to be occupied by the Russians, more than forty Japanese army officers committed *seppuku* in protest. But *seppuku* has often been chosen under less obviously heroic circumstances. In 1929, for instance, the almost 250 recorded cases of *seppuku* included rebels making political protests, railway watchmen atoning for accidents resulting from their negligence, and teenagers reprimanding their drunken fathers. That same year a Japanese naval captain at the Moscow embassy, taunted by his Russian teacher about his unflinching loyalty to the emperor, lost his temper and threw a chair at the woman, striking her on the hand. The mortified captain saw only one way to redeem his honor. He gave three thousand rubles to the teacher, wrote his will, and, kneeling in front of a photograph of the emperor, committed *seppuku*.

Seppuku is, of course, only one method of suicide used in Japan, but it is not the method that distinguishes Japanese suicide so much as its central role in the national tradition. There exists, in fact, a special vocabulary to describe various social genres of suicide. The naval captain who killed himself following the quarrel with his teacher was committing *kashitsu-shi*—suicide to admit failure or to atone for a mistake. Such suicides are a frequent occurrence in a country that places a premium on competition. In 1986, for example, 275 company directors killed themselves after business disappointments or corruption scandals. Studies have attributed the high rate of Japanese adolescent suicide to fierce competition in schools. Failure to pass the exam for entrance to a university—or failure to be admitted to a prestigious university—brings shame to both student and family and is often an occasion for suicide. The boys who committed *seppuku* to protest their fathers' drunkenness were committing *kangen-shi*—a way of communicating a criticism to a superior in a society where few modes of criticism are available. A well-known example of *gisei-shi*—sacrificial suicide—occurred at the end of the second century, when Ototachibana-Hime drowned herself to appease the sea god, in the hope that her husband's ship would be saved in the stormy sea. A modern secular equivalent exists in the *kamikaze* ("divine wind") pilots of World War II, about twenty-two hundred of whom plunged to their deaths shouting, *"Tenno Heika Banzai"*—"Long Live the Emperor!"

Although the compulsory suicide of wife, retainers, and slaves following a lord's death was outlawed in A.D. 659, *junshi*—suicide following a master's death—continued to flourish. In 1912 all of Japan was inspired when General Kiten Nogi, beloved hero of the 1904–5 war with Russia, and his wife committed *seppuku* following the death of Emperor Mutsuhito. "He mingles with the gods on high, my mighty sovereign lord," wrote Nogi, "and, with intensely yearning heart, I follow heavenward." On the morning of the emperor's funeral, when a gun fired on the palace grounds to announce that the body of the emperor had begun its journey to the grave, the sixty-three-year-old Nogi decapitated his wife as she plunged a dagger into her stomach, and then he disemboweled himself.

Suicide committed by more than one person is called *shinju* (literally "inside the heart"). *Jyoshi shinju*—love-pact suicide—became widespread toward the end of the seventeenth century, when increasingly rigid class stratification and strict codes of behavior forbade love between unmarried people. *Kabuki* and *bunraku* (puppet) drama is full of love-pact suicide, usually involving a commoner and a geisha. Their union forbidden in this world, they kill themselves, often by tying themselves together with a rope and drowning, to ensure their union in the next. With arranged marriages the rule until recently, *jyoshi shinju* continued to flourish. In 1954 there were almost one thousand cases, and a few years later, in a poll asking teenagers what to do about a love that parents opposed, 45 percent answered that the "most beautiful" solution was double suicide. In 1985 when their marriage plans were forbidden by their families because they were said to be too old, a seventy-year-old man and a sixty-nine-year-old woman, both widowed more than twenty-five years, committed *jyoshi shinju* by hanging themselves in a hotel room.

Oyako shinju—parent-child suicide—is still common. Plagued by poverty, unable to pay back loans, or humiliated by spouses, parents will kill their children and then kill themselves. In Japan being an orphan is considered a fate worse than death, and *oyako shinju* has been traditionally viewed as an act of devotion and caring. The majority of cases involve the mother, often under threat of impending divorce. In Japan, where women are trained to show obedience, divorcees have difficulty finding respectable jobs, and in some instances even their own families will not take them in. Some four hundred examples of *oyako shinju* are believed to occur each year. In some recent cases a mother, despondent because her sixteen-year-old son was depressed about his forthcoming school entrance exams, murdered her son and attempted to gas herself; a jobless man and a woman who suffered from heart disease strangled their eighteen-year-old daughter and then gassed themselves; a woman suffering from stomach trouble strangled her two daughters, aged eight and ten, who had slight cases of asthma, then attempted to gas herself. "My daughters and myself are so weak physically that we have caused you so much trouble," she wrote her husband. "Please allow us to go ahead of you."

Because of suicide's honored place in Japanese culture, it is often assumed that the Japanese suicide rate dwarfs that of Western countries. Yet despite Durkheim's contention that "the readiness of the Japanese to disembowel themselves for the slightest reason is well known," suicide in Japan is no more prevalent than in the Occident. In 1984 Japan's rate of about nineteen per hundred thousand was higher than that of the United States but lower than those of many northern or eastern European countries.

Since World War II, however, it is said that, like many other Japanese institutions, suicide has become "Westernized." *Seppuku* has all but disappeared; Japanese suicides now prefer pills, gas, or hanging. Newspaper and magazine descriptions of suicides are followed by familiar-sounding discussions of the breakdown of the nuclear family, economic strain, and psychological crisis. Suicide prevention organizations have multiplied; recently, the Japan Association for the Prevention of Parent-Child Suicide was formed. The Japanese, it is said, now kill themselves for the same reasons people kill themselves in the West. The military official who kills himself in shame over a security leak and the man who kills himself to protest a political action, although acting according to time-honored traditions, are now likely to be discussed as psychological misfits. This evolution in attitude was especially striking in the suicide of Yukio Mishima.

One of Japan's most celebrated twentieth-century writers, Mishima was born into an aristocratic samurai family. Mishima deplored what he saw as the materialistic decadence and moral decay of Japan's Westernization, and in both his writing and his life he urged a return to the purer values of Imperial Japan and the samurai tradition. Mishima took up bodybuilding at thirty and became an expert in karate and *kendo,* the ancient sword-fighting art practiced by samurai warriors. He organized the Shield Society, a private eighty-five-man army dedicated to restoring the samurai spirit. All his life he was infatuated with suicide. "If you want your beauty to endure," he wrote at age thirty-four, "you must commit suicide at the height of your beauty." In one of his most famous short stories, a young army officer and his wife commit *seppuku* after a night of passionate lovemaking. Mishima subsequently made the story into a film in which he played the lieutenant.

On November 25, 1970, at forty-five, after sending his publisher the final portion of *The Sea of Fertility*, a quartet of novels he had been working on for many years, Mishima and four members of the Shield Society raided the Tokyo headquarters of Japan's Self-Defense Forces. From a balcony overlooking a courtyard Mishima harangued a crowd of twelve hundred servicemen, accusing the Self-Defense Forces of impotence, denouncing Japan's United States–imposed constitution, and urging them to restore the prewar Japanese state based on rule by the emperor. The soldiers hooted and called Mishima a fool. Realizing the futility of continuing, Mishima walked inside, shouting, "*Tenno Heika Banzai,*" and then performed the ancient ritual of *seppuku.* His chief lieutenant served as *kaishaku,* severing Mishima's head with a sword before committing *seppuku* himself and being beheaded in turn.

Although a few right-wing groups called Mishima a hero, for the most part, both in Japan and abroad, his death was seen more as an example of histrionic posturing than of protest, a pathetic gesture rather than a noble act. (The Japanese prime minister suggested Mishima was mad.) The three young disciples who survived the raid were sentenced to four years in prison on charges that included "murder by request"—the first time in Japanese history that the venerable custom of beheading a friend as he committed *seppuku* was made the basis for criminal charges. In the many articles appraising Mishima's life and death, Japanese and Western writers alike focused on his domineering grandmother, his homosexuality, his narcissism, his obsession with death. A book reviewer for *The New York Times* described Mishima as "a sadomasochistic homosexual for whom death was the ultimate act of exhibitionism and self-gratification. It would not be too much to see Mr. Mishima's suicide as a fatal form of masturbation."

Mishima's suicide may have stemmed as much from his sexual psychoses as from his loyalty to the samurai principle; more accurately, the two were inextricably linked. But in the rush to psychoanalyze Mishima, we may lose sight of his death as being his own, as having meaning beyond the aberrant motives we assign to it. As after any suicide, Mishima's entire life was reinterpreted in light of his death. Even his literary output was reevaluated; reviewers found weaknesses they had apparently not noticed before, the psychosexual elements were highlighted with knowing remarks, and his stock as a writer dipped. Today, most Japanese regard Mishima with embarrassment. The postmortem seemed an ironic illustration of what Mishima's suicide was ostensibly protesting. The suicide of a man who had killed himself to protest Japan's Westernization was viewed from a distinctly Western perspective.

Despite the change illustrated by the aftermath of Mishima's suicide, however, it is important to recognize the age-old gulf between primitive and Eastern acceptance of suicide and its condemnation by the West. In his book *Suicide and Mass Suicide,* psychiatrist Joost Meerloo told the story of a sociologist and a psychologist who flew to the Orient to attend a conference on alienation and self-destruction. Out for a stroll one night, they saw a man hanging from a tree. They rushed to the spot, quickly cut him down, and tried to restore him to consciousness. As they worked feverishly over his prostrate body, a crowd gathered and began to murmur ominously. The air grew thick with tension. Although they had saved the life of the stranger, the sociologist and the psychiatrist were starting to fear for their own lives when a policeman appeared just in time to rescue them from a probable lynching.

Relieved at being saved from the mob, these good Samaritans were shocked when the policeman hauled them off to court, where the judge informed them that they had committed an outrageous offense—they had interfered with the plans of a holy man who wished to join his ancestors. They were ordered to pay a stiff fine, and since the holy man had given away all his earthly possessions in preparation for his suicide, the sociologist and psychologist were ordered to assume full responsibility for his material needs for the rest of his life.

II

GREECE AND ROME: "HE IS AT LIBERTY TO DIE WHO DOES NOT WISH TO LIVE"

WHERE DID CONTEMPORARY Western attitudes toward suicide come from? In ancient Greece, the birthplace of Western civilization, suicide was on the whole considered a respectable option. It is true that there were a few taboos surrounding the act; for instance, in Athens the corpse of a suicide was buried outside the city, the offending hand cut off and interred separately to prevent the suicide's ghost from attacking the living. But these were the products less of moral judgment than of the ancient Greeks' abhorrence of any violent or untimely death—murder, stillbirth, abortion—and their horror of shedding kindred blood. The Greek language hardly distinguishes between self-murder and murder of kin. Suicides from starvation, which were bloodless and slow, were rarely denied ordinary rites; there was no sudden wrenching of the soul from the body, which the Greeks most feared.

In fact, the histories and literature of ancient Greece brim with suicides, which are usually described without shock or blame. They seem to aspire to one quality: honor, whether originating from pride, patriotism, shame, or grief. The first Greek suicide on record is Jocasta, who, on discovering that she had married her son Oedipus, "steep down from a high rafter, throttled in her noose, she swung, carried away by pain." Homer recorded her suicide without comment, as a natural, even inevitable, response to an intolerable situation. Leukakas jumped from a rock into the sea to avoid being raped by Apollo. Dido preferred to stab herself on her husband's funeral pyre rather than remarry. Erigone hanged herself from a tree when she discovered the body of her murdered father, touching off an epidemic of suicide among Athenian women. Charondas, the lawgiver of Catana, a Greek colony in Sicily, set forth a law that no armed men should enter the assembly under pain of death. Returning to the assembly in haste one day, he forgot to remove his dagger, thus breaking his own law. He quickly drew his weapon and killed himself. When Theseus sailed for Crete to slay the Minotaur, he promised his father that if he were successful, he would hoist a white sail on the return voyage. Years later, in the excitement of victory, Theseus forgot the signal; Aegeus, seeing his son's ship with its usual black sail, flung himself into the sea, which forever after was called the Aegean.

Suicide to avoid capture was almost de rigueur among the ancient Greeks. At ninety the Athenian orator Isocrates starved himself to death rather than submit to Philip of Macedon. Demosthenes took poison to avoid falling into the hands of Antipater. Entire regiments or towns committed suicide rather than surrender. In 425 B.C. the oligarchs of Corcyra, trapped in a temple and condemned to death, took their own lives, according to Thucydides, "thrusting into their throats the arrows shot by the enemy, and hanging themselves with the cords taken from some beds that happened to be there, and with strips made from their clothing; adopting, in short, every possible means of self-destruction." It is perhaps not surprising then that Pantites, one of two survivors of the battle of Thermopylae, found hanging himself the only way to redeem his reputation on his return to Sparta.

Although Greek poets recorded numerous cases of insanity, only the most extravagant suicides were attributed to it. Herodotus informs us that in 490 B.C., Cleomenes, king of Sparta, "went quite mad," and "began to mutilate himself, beginning on his shins. He sliced his flesh into strips, working upwards to his thighs, and from them to his hips and sides, until he reached his belly, and while he was cutting that into strips he died." Cleomenes' suicidal delirium was blamed by some on the drinking of unmixed liquors, a nasty habit he had picked up from visiting Scythians.

However, in classical Greece suicide was not the province of physicians but of philosophers, who introduced most of the arguments that we use today. The Pythagoreans disapproved of suicide. They taught that man is a stranger in this world, and his immortal soul lies in the body as in a tomb. Imprisoned in the body, it undergoes a process of atonement and purification, the success of which dictates whether at death it will return to its divine origin or transmigrate into another body and start over from scratch. Suicide, therefore, interfered with that process, and the Pythagoreans forbade men "to depart from their guard or station in life without the order of their Commander—that is, of God." Reinforcing their antisuicide stance was Pythagoras' theory of numbers, which hypothesized that there were a fixed number of souls available for use in the world at any given moment. Suicide skewed the spiritual mathematics, for it was possible that no other soul was ready to fill the gap caused by such an abrupt exit from life.

In Plato's *Phaedo,* Socrates, condemned to death by the state, refined this theme. Mortals are the soldiers of the gods, he said, and a man's life is akin to a soldier's watch. Suicide, therefore, was desertion. We may leave our station only on orders from above. Furthermore, he said, man belongs to God, and suicide was therefore destruction of divine property. "If one of your own possessions, an ox or an ass, for example, took the liberty of putting himself out of the way when you had given no intimation of your wish that he should die, would you not be angry with him, and would you not punish him if you could? . . . Then, if we look at the matter thus, there may be reason in saying that a man should wait, and not take his own life until God summons him, as he is now summoning me." Socrates explained that in *his* case he had been called by God, and calmly swallowed the hemlock.

The *Phaedo* provoked disparate reactions. While the Greek orator Libanius claimed that the arguments in the *Phaedo* kept him from committing suicide after the death of the emperor Julian, the young Greek philosopher Cleombrotus was so fascinated by Socrates' description of the soul's immortality that he flung himself into the sea and drowned. Plato himself was somewhat divided on the subject. In the ninth book of his *Laws* he reiterated his general condemnation of suicide but admitted certain circumstances in which it may be justified—extraordinary sorrow, unavoidable misfortune, intolerable disgrace, or compulsion by the state. On one cause he was adamant: Those who commit suicide "in a spirit of slothful and abject cowardice" shall be buried "in deserted places that have no name."

Plato's student Aristotle borrowed the Pythagorean notion of responsibility beyond the self but asserted that we belong not to God but to the state. Suicide weakened the city economically by depriving it of a citizen. In a discussion of courage Aristotle sparked a debate that continues to this day: "To kill oneself to escape from poverty or love or anything else that is distressing is not courageous but rather the act of a coward, because it shows weakness of character to run away from hardships, and the suicide endures death not because it is a fine thing to do but in order to escape from suffering." Nevertheless, when Aristotle died in exile at sixty-two, there were persistent rumors that he had killed himself.

While Plato found suicide justifiable when external circumstances became intolerable, the Epicureans turned the argument inside out, making the choice of suicide an internal process. Plato's "objective" circumstances under which suicide was permissible became subjective. Suicide was no longer an involuntary act dictated by outward circumstances but a voluntary assertion of freedom. Epicureans held that pleasure should be the guiding principle in life: Whatever produced pleasure was good, and whatever produced pain was evil. Death, they believed, was neither good nor evil, and they professed to be as indifferent to it as to life. "The many at one moment shun death as the greatest of evils, at another yearn for it as a respite from the evils in life," said Epicurus. "But the wise man neither seeks to escape life nor fears the cessation of life, for neither does life offend him nor does the absence of life seem to be any evil." While pointing out the folly of killing oneself through fear of death, Epicurus urged men "to weigh carefully, whether they would prefer death to come to them, or would themselves go to death." Lucretius, the Roman poet and Epicurean who killed himself at forty-four, put it more seductively: "If one day, as well may happen, life grows wearisome, there only remains to pour a libation to death and oblivion. A drop of subtle poison will gently close your eyes to the sun, and waft you smiling into the eternal night whence everything comes and to which everything returns."

For the Stoics, "to live consistently with nature" was the ideal. When the conditions essential to that ideal no longer existed, suicide was a rational and reasonable choice. Zeno, founder of the Stoic school, lived to the age of ninety-eight without encountering a reason sufficient to depart life. Then one day, upon leaving his school of philosophy, he stumbled, put a toe out of joint, went home, and hanged himself. The suicide of his successor, Cleanthes, seems only slightly less arbitrary. Suffering from a gum boil, he was advised by his doctor to refrain from food for two days. The remedy was effective, and he was told he could resume his normal diet. Cleanthes declined, saying that "as he had advanced so far on his journey towards death, he would not retreat," and he starved to death. It is said that Timon of Athens grew a fig tree so that he might never lack a branch from which to hang himself.

At certain times in ancient Greece suicide even enjoyed official sanction. As early as 500 B.C. in the Greek colony of Ceos, citizens who were over the age of sixty or incapacitated by sickness were allowed, even encouraged, to take their own lives. After crowning their brows with floral garlands they drank state-provided hemlock or poppy juice. (Some say the custom was introduced during a time of famine.) At the Greek colony of Massilia (modern Marseilles) magistrates kept a supply of poison on hand for those who, pleading their case before the Senate, obtained permission to kill themselves. (Acceptable reasons included illness, sorrow, and disgrace.) The law was intended to prevent hasty, impulsive suicides and to make reasonable, state-approved suicides as rapid and painless as possible. "Such a discussion is tempered with a manly benevolence; which does not suffer any one to quit life rashly, but affords means of accelerating the end of him, who has wise reasons for his departure," wrote Valerius. "Any one for instance may thus make an approved and honourable exit, who experiences the extremes of good and bad fortune; either of which affords sufficient grounds to covet a termination of life—the former lest it should forsake us or the latter continue with us."

This type of rationality seemed irrational to Libanius. Referring to a similar state-sponsored suicide program briefly practiced in Athens, he wrote sarcastically of a man who pleaded permission to kill himself to escape from his garrulous wife; a man distressed because his neighbor's wealth had outstripped his; a man who preferred to part with his life rather than to part with a treasure he found.

In Alexandria in the third century B.C. the philosopher Hegesias taught that life was so fleeting and full of cares that death was man's happiest lot. He lectured so eloquently that, according to Cicero, many of his listeners committed suicide. Eventually, "the orator of death," as Hegesias was known, was banished from Alexandria. Two centuries later, during the reign of Cleopatra, herself a suicide, there seems to have existed in Alexandria a school that taught the best ways of committing suicide; some "students" were rumored to have killed themselves during sumptuous banquets.

Such excess anticipated the Roman Empire. For if the Greeks rationalized suicide, the Romans made it a fashion, even a sport. Like Greece, the Roman Republic had its share of suicides and for much the same reason—to avoid dishonor and disgrace. In the fourth century B.C., when an earthquake left a vast rift in the Forum, oracles declared that it would close only after receiving the gift of Rome's most precious possession. Marcus Curtius, declaring that there was nothing more precious than a brave citizen, leaped into the smoking gulf, which closed over him. During the civil war between Pompey and Caesar, the tribune Vulteius and his men were attempting to cross the Adriatic when they were surrounded by Pompey's fleet. After repelling attacks all day, Vulteius saw the situation was hopeless and called his men together. "Nobody need complain that he has only a few hours of life left; these are enough for suicide, and the glory of such a deed cannot be diminished by the thought that he would soon have been killed in any case," he told them. "The future is always unforeseeable; and though it is a noble act to cut short a long expectancy of life, it is no less noble to sacrifice one's last few hours deliberately." Inspired by Vulteius' lengthy exhortation—and by his example—his men hurled themselves upon one another's swords until no one was left alive. Impressed by the carnage, Pompey's generals gave the bodies an honorable cremation. "No ship's company had ever earned comparable praise," noted Lucan, who told the story, "yet even this glorious precedent has not taught cowardly nations how easy it is to escape servitude by self-immolation; because when tyrants impose their will by terror liberty shrivels, until nobody realizes that the purpose of the sword is to secure individual freedom. If death were only the exclusive reward of brave men, denied to cowards!"

The noblest Roman suicide of them all was Marcus Porcius Cato, whose death has been cited as a model of rational suicide throughout the ages. A just, scrupulous man, Cato dressed simply, never rode when he could walk, and "even from his infancy," wrote Plutarch, "in his speech, his countenance, and all his childish pastimes, he discovered an inflexible temper, unmoved by any passion, and firm in everything." Cato had placed his life at the service of the

Republic, and when Caesar crossed the Rubicon in 49 B.C., Cato followed
Pompey into Greece. After Pompey's defeat, Cato fled to Utica, where he tried
to rally the Republican party. But when several defeats put an end to his hopes
for the survival of the old virtues of liberty and republicanism, he decided to
die rather than live under Caesar. Cato spent the last evening of his life arguing
favorite philosophical questions with his friends, then retired to his chamber
to read Plato's *Phaedo.* Glancing up, he noticed that his sword was missing
from its usual place. His son, suspecting his plans, had removed it. Confronting
his friends, Cato accused them of forgetting their stoic ideals, asking them to
"show cause why we should now unlearn what we formerly were taught." His
friends wept. The sword was sent to him, carried by a child. "Now I am master
of myself," said Cato, who, after testing the sword's point, returned to the
Phaedo, reading it through twice before falling into a sleep so deep the men
outside could hear him snore. Near midnight he sent one of his men to the port
to make sure the transports had left safely. Plutarch wrote:

> Now the birds began to sing, and he again fell into a little slumber. At length
> Butas came back, and told him all was quiet in the port. Then Cato, laying
> himself down, as if he would sleep out the rest of the night, bade him shut
> the door after him. But as soon as Butas was gone out, he took his sword,
> and stabbed it into his breast.

When his friends heard Cato fall from his couch, they rushed in to find him
in a pool of blood, alive. As a physician began to sew up the wound, Cato
regained consciousness and, according to Plutarch, "thrust away the physician, plucked out his own bowels, and tearing open the wound, immediately
expired."

Cato was acclaimed as a hero. "The people of Utica flocked thither," wrote
Plutarch, "crying out with one voice, he was their benefactor and their saviour,
the only free and only undefeated man." His suicide impressed even Caesar,
who, on receiving the news, exclaimed, "Cato, I grudge you your death, as you
have grudged me the preservation of your life." Horace composed an ode in
his honor. His act also won the approval of antisuicide writers like Cicero, who
declared that death may sometimes be the least of evils, for "when God himself
shall give a just cause, as formerly to Socrates, lately to Cato, certainly every
man of sense would gladly exchange this darkness for that light." Valerius
Maximus called it "a noble lesson to mankind. How much superior in the
opinion of all honest men is dignity without life to life without dignity." Seneca
declared, "Jupiter himself could not have seen anything more beautiful on
earth."

Seneca was the most prominent teacher of the Roman Stoics, who would
raise suicide to an art form during the Roman Empire. For the Stoics suicide
was a final resource, an ultimate weapon against the vicissitudes of life.

Whether the complaint be incurable illness, insufferable pain, or *taedium vitae*—the boredom and purposelessness of life—the stoic attitude was *Mori licet cui vivere non placet:* "He is at liberty to die who does not wish to live." The Stoics did not condone irresponsibility, however. Suicide was not to be a rash, impulsive act but accepted or rejected after a careful weighing of pros and cons. Praising an ill friend's extensive deliberations, Pliny the Younger wrote, "A resolution this, in my estimation, truly arduous, and worthy of the highest applause. Instances are frequent enough in the world of rushing into the arms of death without reflection, and by a sort of blind impulse: but calmly and deliberately to weigh the motives for life or death, and to be determined in our choice as reason counsels, is the mark of an uncommon and great mind." Pliny the Elder maintained that the option of suicide was proof of man's superiority to the gods—man at least has the power of escaping to the grave. Conversely, he considered one of the greatest proofs of the bounty of Providence was that it had filled the world with herbs by which a sinner might procure a rapid, painless death. For the Stoics, suicide was the ultimate proof of man's freedom. The human spirit need never be broken, for, as Seneca observed, death was only a moment away:

Foolish man, what do you bemoan, and what do you fear? Wherever you look there is an end of evils. You see that yawning precipice? It leads to liberty. You see that flood, that river, that well? Liberty houses within them. You see that stunted, parched, and sorry tree? From every branch liberty hangs. Your neck, your throat, your heart are all so many ways of escape from slavery. . . . Do you enquire the road to freedom? You shall find it in every vein of your body.

Seneca clung to his right to suicide with passionate tenacity: "As I choose the ship in which I will sail, and the house I will inhabit, so I will choose the death by which I leave life," he said. ". . . In no matter more than in death should we act according to our desire." His own death was consistent with his teachings. When his friends wept upon being informed that Emperor Nero, his former pupil, desired his death, Seneca chided them. "Where had their philosophy gone, he asked, and that resolution against impending misfortunes which they had devised over so many years?" wrote the historian Tacitus. Seneca bade farewell to his wife, Paulina, but she insisted on sharing his death. "I will not grudge your setting so fine an example," he said. "We can die with equal fortitude. But yours will be the nobler end." They each cut their arms, but the aged Seneca bled slowly. A Stoic to the end, he had his wife carried into another room because "he was afraid of weakening his wife's endurance by betraying his agony—or of losing his own self-possession at the sight of her sufferings." Paulina survived; the emperor insisted on her rescue and treatment. Nero, who over the years demanded the suicides of dozens of his subjects, would himself commit suicide three years later, stabbing himself in the throat while fleeing a revolt.

The Romans' approach to suicide was reflected in their laws, which denied the *liber mori* only to criminals, soldiers, and slaves. A man accused of a crime committed another crime if he took his own life to avoid trial. Roman criminals often took their own lives because felony was usually punishable by death and the confiscation of property. Suicide *before* trial saved the suicide's goods for his family. Roman law also forbade the suicide of slaves because a Roman slave was his master's property—to kill himself, therefore, was to steal from his master. In fact, slaves came with a six-month antisuicide guarantee: Any slave who attempted to kill himself within a half year of purchase could be returned to his former master. A soldier's suicide was likened to desertion and regarded as a weakening of the Roman legions that, if unpunished, might spread and become a threat to Roman security. Suicide by a private citizen, according to Justinian's *Digest* of A.D. 533, was not punishable if caused by "impatience of pain or sickness, some grief" or by "weariness of life . . . lunacy, or fear of dishonor." Suicide was a crime only if it was "without cause"—an irrational suicide—the premise being that a man capable of killing himself for no reason might be just as apt to kill someone else instead.

In Imperial Rome, therefore, the only objections to suicide were not moral but economic; suicide was a crime only in proportion to its effect on state finances or security. Otherwise the morality of a "Roman death," as the poet Martial called it, was beyond dispute. The question was no longer *whether* but *how.* Suicide was a final test of character, to be carried out with dignity, courage, even bravado. When Caecina Paetus was condemned to death for his part in an unsuccessful conspiracy against Emperor Claudius, he knew that suicide was his only honorable option, but fear made him hesitate. His wife, Arria, seized his dagger and stabbed herself. Dying, she handed his weapon back to him, saying, "It does not hurt, my Paetus." The actual fact of death seemed almost irrelevant; the manner of death was the thing. Corellius Rufus, incurably ill, postponed committing suicide throughout the reign of Domitian, declaring that he did not wish to die under a tyrant. Following Domitian's assassination he took his own life with a clear conscience, a free Roman. Convinced that Nero sought his death, Petronius Arbiter, a celebrated voluptuary whose exquisite manners earned him his nickname "the Arbiter of Taste," determined to evade the emperor by taking his life. Calling his friends about him at his villa, he opened and closed his veins at will, prolonging his death as he arranged his affairs, took naps, or engaged in conversation. Unlike Cato, he spent his final hours not in contemplating philosophical questions but in cheerfully exchanging epigrams, songs, and gossip. Finally, he opened his veins for the last time, and in the middle of a sumptuous banquet Petronius Arbiter died as elegantly as he had lived.

For sheer exhibitionism the suicide of Peregrinus is unsurpassed. A wealthy native of Propontis, Greece, Peregrinus spent many years wandering through Palestine and Egypt, and after flirtations with Christianity and Eastern mysticism, found his niche in the doctrines of the Cynics. Preaching the vanity of pleasure and a contempt for death, he grew in reputation as he traveled along the Mediterranean coast. Expelled from Rome for insulting Emperor Antoninus Pius, he decided to solidify his position among the early Cynics by ending his life in a manner illustrating that school's disdain for death. He announced that he would die on a flaming pyre at the Olympic games in A.D. 165. Vast crowds gathered to witness the death. Telling them that he was about to bring "a golden life to a golden close," Peregrinus doffed his Cynic's robes, threw incense on the burning pyre, and, invoking the spirit of his ancestors, walked into the flames and disappeared as the moon rose. It is said that a brilliant phoenix flew upward from the fire.

One had to go to extremes to be noticed at a time when thirty thousand people a month were sacrificed for sport in the arenas and pet fish were fed the blood of slaves. The Stoic enthusiasm for suicide was a reflection of the general Roman attitude toward death, a nonchalance perhaps unrivaled in history. Scottish anthropologist Sir James Frazer reported that in Rome at the time of the Punic Wars, volunteers offering to be beheaded for public sport for five minae—payable to the dead man's heirs—were so plentiful that many people, to improve their chances of getting the job, offered to be beaten to death rather than beheaded because that was a slower, more painful death and hence more appealing to spectators. With the barbarousness of the arena, the casual cruelty of the emperors, and the turmoil into which the Empire was frequently thrown by intrigues and civil wars, indifference to death may have been an important survival skill. It is in the moral chaos of the later Roman Empire, however, that the roots of Christianity's fervent antisuicide sentiment can be found.

III

CHRISTIANITY: "A DETESTABLE CRIME AND A DAMNABLE SIN"

CONSIDERING CHRISTIANITY'S nearly two thousand years of intense opposition to suicide, it is surprising that neither the Old nor the New Testament directly prohibits the act. There are six suicides in the Old Testament. They earn neither blessing nor condemnation. Saul, wounded by the Philistines, fell on his sword to avoid capture, whereupon his armor-bearer did the same. Abimelech also killed himself to avoid dishonor. During his siege of the tower of Thebes, he was mortally wounded by a millstone thrown by a woman; he commanded his armor-bearer to kill him so that it could not be said that a woman had slain him. When Zimri realized that his siege of Tirzah was doomed, "he went into the citadel of the king's house, and burned the king's house over him with fire, and died." Praying, "Let me die with the Philistines," Samson pulled down the walls of the temple of Dagon, destroying both his enemy and himself. After deserting his master King David, Ahithophel, his advice rejected by Absalom, "saddled his ass, and went off home to his own city. And he set his house in order, and hanged himself." Even Ahithophel's suicide is recorded without criticism, and he was provided a ritual burial in his ancestral tomb. In the New Testament, Judas Iscariot's suicide after his betrayal of Jesus Christ is viewed as a natural gesture of repentance; it is simply observed that "he went and hanged himself."

In the succeeding two millennia, pro-suicide writers cited the Bible's matter-of-fact treatment of self-destruction as evidence of Christian tolerance of the act. Antisuicide forces interpreted it as an implied condemnation, suggesting that suicide is so atrocious as to make specific written prohibition unnecessary. "In the same manner," wrote one eighteenth-century minister, "I do not recollect in Scripture a single word against man-eating." More probably the scarcity of suicide resulted from the strong commitment to life felt by Jews of the Old Testament period. An oft-cited example is Job. Although his sheep, oxen, camels, servants, and children had been destroyed and his body afflicted "with loathsome sores from the sole of his foot to the crown of his head," Job refused to lose faith. When his wife suggested that he give up in the face of such adversity, bidding him "curse God, and die," Job was outraged. "You speak as one of the foolish women would speak," he told her. "Shall we receive good at the hand of God, and shall we not receive evil?" Ever since, Job has been employed as a role model for antisuicide moralists who find in his patient fortitude the proper attitude toward suffering. However, it was an example not often followed by early Christians.

In fact, by teaching that man's earthly existence was merely a grim prelude to the eternal afterlife, Christianity offered an unmistakable, if unintentional, incentive to suicide. The longer one's life, the more opportunity there was to sin and the less chance of eternal bliss. Suicide—in the form of martyrdom— became the quickest ticket to heaven. Baptism wiped the slate clean of original sin; martyrdom erased the transgressions of a lifetime. Not only was the martyr guaranteed redemption, but he earned posthumous glory, annual commemoration in the church calendar, and an income for his family from church funds.

Christians had ample opportunity to sate their appetite for martyrdom. Anti-Christian mobs roamed the streets, and each day the authorities fed hundreds of Christians to the lions. More often than not the Christians met the Romans halfway. Aedesius slapped the governor of Egypt; he was tortured and thrown into the sea. The centurion Marcellus threw down his arms in the middle of a parade and cried, "I am a soldier of Jesus Christ"; he was executed. The histories of the first three centuries A.D. overflow with what we now call "indirect" suicides but at the time were described as "the splendid martyrs of Christ" who "everywhere astounded the eyewitnesses of their courage."

The Christian martyrs received moral support from the church hierarchy. Even Clement, bishop of Alexandria, one of the few early Christian writers to attack voluntary death, condemned it not because suicide is sinful but because the martyr tempts the pagan to commit the sin of murder. Tertullian forbade his flock even to attempt to escape persecution. Like a football coach before a big game, he exhorted imprisoned Christians to die heroically, citing celebrated pagan suicides such as Lucretia, Dido, and Cleopatra as role models, and pointing out that Jesus Christ on the cross had given up his spirit voluntarily before crucifixion could kill him. Invoking the primitive notion of "killing oneself upon the head of another," Tertullian promised posthumous revenge: "No City escaped punishment, which had shed Christian blood."

And so the Christians rushed the pagan judges, confessing their faith and begging for martyrdom. Eusebius, bishop of Caesarea, described a woman who celebrated her death sentence by "rejoicing and exulting at her departure as if invited to a wedding supper, not thrown to the beasts." Once condemned, the Christians leaped into the flames, hugged the lions, and baited the pagans. Three young Christians who had destroyed pagan idols turned themselves in and were ordered to die on gridirons. As the execution began they called to the governor: "Amachus, give orders that our bodies may be turned on the fire if you do not desire to be served with meat cooked only on one side." Ignatius, bishop of Antioch, en route to Rome and a date with the lions in the arena, was giddy with anticipation: "Let fire and cross, encounters with wild animals, tearing apart of bones, hacking of limbs, crushing of the whole body, tortures of the devil come upon me," he wrote, "if only I may attain to Jesus Christ!"

In the face of such enthusiasm Roman authorities grew embarrassed. A perplexed Pliny the Younger wrote to Emperor Trajan for instructions. "When finally guilt is proved, Christians are still to be offered life and freedom," Trajan replied. "All that is asked is that they shall prove their good faith by a single sacrifice to the orthodox gods. The duty of the judges is not so much to punish as reclaim and only when every effort has failed are the punishments to be applied." This more lenient Roman policy was augmented by a liberal grace period between sentencing and execution that was tacitly understood to be a chance to flee. But Roman clemency was met with renewed provocation. Surrounded by a mob of insistent Christians who demanded their death sentences, a frustrated proconsul, Antoninus Pius, cried, "Unhappy men, unhappy men! If you are thus weary of your lives, is it so difficult for you to find ropes and precipices?"

Death by lion was the easy way out compared to the chosen fate of St. Simeon Stylites, who is said to have stood on a sixty-foot pillar near Antioch for thirty years, exposed to wind, rain, and snow. For one of those years he stood on one leg while the other was covered by hideous ulcers. His biographer was delegated to retrieve the worms that fell from St. Simeon's body and to replace them in his open sores, as the saint urged the worms, "Eat what God has given you." St. Simeon was one of many early Christian monks and hermits whose stupefying asceticism often led to madness, early death, and sainthood. One lived for thirty years on crusts of barley bread and muddy water; another carried 150 pounds of iron and lived in a dried-up well. To twentieth-century psychiatrists such "chronic suicide" would be traced to masochism, but to the early Christians it was a blessed ending, perhaps even more praiseworthy in the eyes of God than being killed in the arena. "Lo! for these thirty years and more I have been dwelling and groaning unceasingly in the desert!" boasts St. Anthony in Flaubert's *The Temptation of Saint Anthony.* ". . . [A]nd those who are decapitated, tortured with red hot pincers, or burned alive, are perhaps less meritorious than I, seeing that my whole life is but one prolonged martyrdom."

St. Anthony lived to the age of 104. More common, perhaps, was the fate of the nun who, as St. Jerome recounted approvingly, retired to a convent at age twenty and inflicted penances on herself that led to her premature death. Aspiring monks who despaired of winning the battle between celibacy and nature chose suicide by more direct means. The biographer of Pachomius, a young monk who applied asps to himself in an unsuccessful suicide attempt, wrote that in this struggle with the devil "many have destroyed themselves; some, bereft of their senses, have cast themselves from precipices; others laid open their bowels; others killed themselves in divers ways." Still others, as Gibbon put it, "judged it the most prudent to disarm the tempter." (Castration, the church eventually realized, was a partial suicide. A Church canon later declared, "He that gelds himselfe cannot be a Clerke, because he is an Homicide of himselfe, and an enemy to Gods creature.") Perhaps the most revered of all martyrs were the numerous Christian women who preferred death to defilement by heathens. Fifteen-year-old Pelagia, fearing for the loss of her chastity—"of all dreadful things the most unbearable," commented Eusebius—jumped from a roof to escape a Roman soldier and was canonized for her suicide. "God cannot be offended with this, when we use it but for a remedy," observed St. Ambrose.

It is not known how many martyrs died all told during the early years of Christianity. Contemporary estimates range from ten thousand to one hundred thousand. While there is no way to compute how many of these martyrs were voluntary, by all accounts the percentage was high. Martyrdom, after all, was the ultimate proof of faith. Believers calculated the virtue of their sect by the number of dead martyrs. By this measure the Donatists of North Africa were the most virtuous—so virtuous that the embarrassed Church would eventually declare them heretics. Gibbon wrote:

> The rage of the Donatists was inflamed by a frenzy of a very extraordinary kind; and which, if it really prevailed among them in so extravagant a degree, cannot surely be paralleled in any country or in any age. . . . Sometimes they rudely disturbed the festivals, and profaned the temples of Paganism, with the design of exciting the most zealous of the idolaters to revenge the insulted honour of their Gods. They sometimes forced their way into the courts of justice, and compelled the affrighted judge to give orders for their immediate execution. They frequently stopped travellers on the public highways, and obliged them to inflict the stroke of martyrdom, by the promise of a reward if they consented, and by the threat of instant death if they refused to grant so very singular a favor. When they were disappointed of every other resource, they announced the day on which, in the presence of their friends and brethren, they should cast themselves headlong from some lofty rock; and many precipices were shown which had acquired fame by the number of religious suicides.

Clearly, things were getting out of hand. There was evidence that some of the suicides were not religious zealots but impoverished Christians who found martyrdom the only way to secure food for their families. Others pursued martyrdom as far as prison in order to receive the alms and gifts that were often showered on prospective martyrs; then, well before their appointments with death, they recanted and were freed. In the fourth and fifth century, as the Roman Empire crumbled and the Church grew more powerful, ecclesiastical writers began to voice their disapproval. Gradually, suicide under persecution was no longer recognized as martyrdom, extreme asceticism was disparaged by the Church and by public opinion, and even suicide for chastity's sake was no longer unanimously praised. Tentative disapproval calcified to harsh denunciation. "If it is base to destroy others," declared St. John Chrysostom in the fourth century, "much more is it to destroy one's self." To St. Augustine, writing in the early fifth century, suicide was "monstrous."

In *City of God,* Augustine set forth the arguments that would become the cornerstones of the Christian view of suicide, a position which, on the whole, remains that of the Catholic Church today. Realizing that Christianity contained a logical dilemma—if paradise is achieved by avoiding sin, the most sensible step following baptism is suicide—Augustine tried to demonstrate that suicide itself was a sin greater than any that it could atone for. He took his arguments not from the Bible but from Plato's *Phaedo.* Life is a gift from God, explained Augustine, and suffering is sent by God to be endured. To bear suffering is a test of a soul's greatness; to evade it is an admission of weakness and an act against the will of God. To reject God's gift is to reject him—which is a sure path to eternal damnation. Furthermore, if a man kills himself to *atone* for his sins, he sins, for no private individual has the right to kill a guilty person; and if an innocent man kills himself to *avoid* sin, he has innocent blood on his hands—a sin worse than any he might have committed by living, for a suicide has no time to repent. Finally, he maintained, a man who takes his own life kills a man and thus breaks the Sixth Commandment. Suicide, according to Augustine, was murder.

Augustine's condemnation was unequivocal. A suicide under any name— martyrdom, asceticism, even preservation of chastity—was a sin. True purity, he reasoned, is in the mind. "Just as bodily chastity is lost when mental chastity has been violated, so bodily chastity is not lost, even when the body has been ravished, while the mind's chastity endures." A virgin suicide deserved compassion but not celebration, for she committed "certain murder while the offence, and another's offence at that, still remains uncertain." Augustine had some difficulty accounting for such suicides as Samson and Pelagia, who had already snared sainthood or churchly praise. They acted, he explained, under special orders from God. But Augustine warned that such cases are rare, and should the reader be tempted to follow suit, "only let him take care that there is no uncertainty about the divine command." If not sure, he had better think again, "for those guilty of their own death are not received after death into that better life."

Augustine's arguments against suicide, devised to restrain the mania of martyrdom, were based on a respect for life that contrasted sharply with the barbarity of the Roman Empire. Nevertheless, they triggered a severe reaction. Though Augustine himself did not recommend punishment for what he called "a detestable crime and a damnable sin," his pronouncements, combined with the growing tide of public opinion, resulted in the first Christian edicts against suicide. In A.D. 452 the Council of Arles, declaring suicide to be caused by diabolical possession, reaffirmed the Roman slave clauses prohibiting suicide by servants. In 533 the Council of Orleans denied funeral rites to anyone who killed himself while accused of a crime. "The oblations of those who were killed in the commission of any crime may be received," they wrote, "except of such who laid violent hands upon themselves." Not only was suicide a crime, they implied, it was the worst of crimes; ordinary criminals were still allowed Christian burial. In 563 the Council of Braga denied funeral rites to all suicides; and in 693 the Council of Toledo declared that even attempters of suicide would be excommunicated.

The Church could not have made itself clearer. Suicide was a mortal sin. In a few centuries it had gone from being a passport to paradise to being the shortest route to hell. When the Albigenses of southern France sought martyrdom in droves in the thirteenth century, they were following in the footsteps of the early Christian martyrs. Near Narbonne, 140 of the group's spiritual elders cheated the executioner by throwing themselves on a burning pyre; elsewhere, seventy-four knights chose hanging over recantation and freedom. While the early Christian martyrs had earned sainthood for such acts, the Albigensians had compounded their sins by suicide and thus, it was said, deserved the savagery with which some five thousand of them were put to death in 1218. Suicides were no longer martyrs for God; they were, according to the eleventh century's St. Bruno, "martyrs for Satan." In this ecclesiastic revisionism, Judas, theologians claimed, was more damned for killing himself than for betraying Christ. Rather than being the ultimate proof of faith, suicide was now conclusive proof of faithlessness; the suicide had despaired of God's grace. When Joan of Arc, imprisoned at Bouvreuil in 1431, threw herself from her cell window to avoid falling into the hands of the English, her suicide attempt was used by the bishops at her trial as further proof of her possession by the devil.

By then a curious transformation had taken place. The Church had reversed its position on suicide so forcefully, it seemed to jar loose the primitive superstitions surrounding suicide that had been submerged through the Classical Age. Unrestrained by the rationality prevailing in Greek and Roman civilizations, these instinctive fears came to the surface. In England custom dictated that a suicide must leave the room in which he died not by the door but through a hole bored under the threshold. In Danzig the corpse was lowered by pulleys from the window and the window frame subsequently burned. The corpse was then hanged from a gallows. Each town had its own variations; in some areas the bodies of suicides were burned, in others they were buried on the beach below the high water mark. In Zurich a suicide who had killed himself by jumping from a height was buried under a mountain whose weight would press upon his restive soul. While these customs had their origins in the primitive rituals designed to placate the suicide's ghost, the ghost was no longer the primary target; now the act itself was the object of punishment, and the rituals began to be defined by fury more than by fear.

What started at Arles as canonical legislation was soon reinforced by civil law. Feudal lords had an economic stake in seeing that their workers didn't kill themselves. In 967, England's King Edgar gave civil sanction to the ecclesiastical penalties. Gradually, the connection between suicide and murder that the Church had forged by its interpretation of the Sixth Commandment found secular approval. The suicide was a self-murderer, subject to similar punishment. In England the first civil mandate against suicide was probably imported by the Danes during their invasion in 1013: "Let him who hath murdered himself, be fined in all his goods to his lord: let him find a place of burial neither in the church nor church yard; unless ill health and madness drove him to the perpetration." The thirteenth-century legal authority Henry de Bracton recorded that the ordinary self-murderer forfeited his goods; the person who killed himself while awaiting trial forfeited both goods *and* land. There were exceptions: "The madman, or the idiot, or the infant, or the person under such acute pain as to produce a temporary distraction, who kills himself, shall forfeit neither lands nor chattels, because he is deprived of reason." Suicide was (self-) murder unless the perpetrator was insane—the loophole by which Catholic and Jewish suicides have been allowed burial to this day.

In *Summa Theologiae* (1267–73), a codification of ecclesiastical teachings, Thomas Aquinas, summing up the Church's position on suicide, reflected the changes since Augustine. Augustine had based his antisuicide stance on spiritual arguments; Aquinas reinforced the religious objections with secular rationale. He reiterated Plato's "life as a gift from God" argument as filtered through Augustine. "Life is a gift made to man by God," wrote Aquinas, "and it is subject to him who is *master of death and life.* Therefore a person who takes his own life sins against God, just as he who kills another's slave injures the slave's master, or just as he who usurps judgement in a matter outside his authority also commits a sin. And God alone has authority to decide about life and death." Aquinas went beyond this familiar reasoning to raise two secular objections to suicide. First, he maintained that suicide is unnatural; it goes against man's instinct for self-preservation and is contrary to the charity that a man ought to bear to himself. Second, borrowing from Aristotle, Aquinas said that by killing himself a person injures the community of which he is a part. Furthermore, he asserted that anyone who commits suicide to avoid punishment is a coward.

By combining secular and religious arguments Aquinas offered an intellectual justification for civil penalties against suicide. An act that had been a rational end to the Greeks, an honorable end to the Romans, and a means to heaven to the early Christians was now damned by God and despised by man. Suicide, concluded Aquinas, was "completely wrong."

In Canto XIII of the *Divine Comedy,* written at the start of the fourteenth century, Virgil leads Dante below the burning heretics, below the murderers in their river of blood, to a dark, pathless wood. Dante hears human voices weeping all about him; frightened, he reaches out and snaps off a twig. "Why dost thou rend me?" cries the trunk, turning dark with blood where the twig had been broken. "Men we were and now are turned to trees." Dante is in the forest of suicides where the souls of self-killers languish for eternity. Every tree and bush in the wood harbors the soul of a suicide. The tree whose twig he plucked holds the soul of Piero delle Vigne, once the chief counselor to Emperor Frederick II of Sicily. In 1249, unjustly accused of treason, imprisoned and blinded, he dashed his brains out against his cell walls. Now delle Vigne explains to Dante that when the soul tears itself from its own body, it is cast into the seventh circle of hell where it grows into a gnarled, thorny tree. The Harpies, winged creatures with human faces and sharp claws, nest in the trees and pick at its leaves, causing the branches to bleed and the souls to cry out in pain, thus repeating the violent action of suicide every moment for eternity. On the Day of Judgment, when most souls are reunited with their bodies, the bodies of suicides will hang from the branches of the trees as a lasting reminder of the life they chose to throw away.

IV

THE RENAISSANCE:
"IT IS HIS CASE,
IT MAY BE THINE"

LIKE A KNIFE THROWER'S TARGET, medieval man was circumscribed by Christian dogma, which taught him that life was hell, death was torture, and hell was worse. In this scheme of things suicide was unspeakable. Against this joyless landscape the Renaissance blew in like a cool breeze, bringing an awareness of the world's beauty and a renewed faith in man's possibilities. *"Memento mori,"* the somber slogan of the Middle Ages, became *"memento vivere."* Earthly life was once again valued for itself and not merely as a transition to the hereafter. With the rise of Humanism, Renaissance scholars rediscovered classical art, literature, and philosophy, and the Greek and Roman ideals of self-reliance and self-determination were reborn. In his *Oration on the Dignity of Man,* Pico della Mirandola imagines God addressing humanity: "Thou, constrained by no limits, in accordance with thine own free will, in whose hand We have placed thee, shalt ordain for thyself the limits of thy nature . . . as though the maker and molder of thyself, thou mayest fashion thyself in whatever shape thou shalt prefer." And if man's life was his own, so was his death. The decaying flesh, voracious worms, and eternal torment that filled the medieval vision of death gave way to a serene new view:

> *Death is a remedy against all evils:* It is a most assured haven, never to be feared, and often to be sought: All comes to one period, whether man make an end of himselfe, or whether he endure it; whether he run before his day,

161

or whether he expect it: whence soever it come, it is ever his owne, where ever the threed be broken, it is all there, it's the end of the web. The voluntariest death, is the fairest. *Life dependeth on the will of others, death on ours.* In nothing should we so much accommodate our selves to our humours, as in that.

In his essay "A Custome of the Ile of Cea" (referring to state-sponsored suicide in the ancient Greek colony of Ceos), Michel de Montaigne, whose skeptical essays questioned prevailing attitudes on almost any subject, based his defense of suicide, written in the 1570s, on classical notions of free will. Seneca, his favorite philosopher, is quoted approvingly, and even the "Orator of Death" is cited: *"Hegesias* was wont to say, that even as the condition of life, so should the quality of death depend on our election." But Montaigne was less interested in endorsing suicide than in demystifying death. "All the wisdom and reasoning in the world boils down finally to this point," he once wrote, "to teach us not to be afraid to die." And in the end Montaigne's stoicism was leavened with Renaissance optimism. He found suicide not immoral but a bit foolish. "The opinion which disdaineth our life, is ridiculous," he wrote, "for, in fine, it is our being. It is our all in all." He introduced a practical argument that would become a staple of twentieth-century suicide prevention: "Moreover, there being so many sudden changes, and violent alterations in humane things, it is hard to judge in what state or point we are justly at the end of our hope. . . . I have seene a hundred Hares save themselves even in the Greyhounds jawes."

"A Custome of the Ile of Cea" was the first significant discussion of suicide to question the Church's blanket prohibition. After eight centuries suicide was once more a topic for debate. Even those who argued against it, like the fourteenth-century humanist Petrarch, disdained religious terrorism in favor of balanced argument. In *The Funeral,* Erasmus explained that God meant death to be dreadful "lest men far and wide commit suicide. And since, even today, we see so many do violence to themselves, what do you suppose would happen if death weren't horrible? Whenever a servant or even a young son got a thrashing, whenever a wife fell out with her husband, whenever a man lost his money, or something else occurred that upset him, off they'd rush to noose, sword, river, cliff, poison." Yet in *The Praise of Folly,* Erasmus described those who killed themselves in disgust at the miserable world as "people who lived next door to wisdom." As early as 1516, Thomas More's *Utopia* offered what may have been the first Christian consideration of voluntary euthanasia. In More's ideal republic, although provided the best possible medical care, the terminally ill were permitted, even encouraged, to end their lives.

But yf the dysease be not onelye uncurable, but also full of contynuall payne and anguyshe, then the priestes and the magistrats exhort the man, seynge he ys not able to doo annye dewtye of lyffe, and by ouerlyuing hys owne deathe is noysome and yrkesome to other, and greuous to hymself; that he wyll determyne with hymselfe no longer to cheryshe that pestilent and peynefull dysease: and, seynge hys lyfe ys to hym but a tourmente, that he wyll nott bee unwyllynge too dye, but rather take a good hope to hym, and other dyspatche hymselfe owte of that paynfull lyffe, as owte of a pryson or a racke of tormente, or elles suffer hym selfe wyllynglye to be rydde owte of yt by other. And in so doynge they tell hym he shal doo wyselye, seynge by hys deathe he shall lyse no commodytye, but ende hys payne.

In Renaissance literature suicide was once more a conversation piece. Less than a century after Dante condemned suicides to the seventh circle of hell, Chaucer used Thisbe, Dido, Lucretia, and Cleopatra as models in his *Legende of Goode Women*; Lucretia became a heroine of Tudor and Elizabethan poetry and a popular model for Renaissance painters. In *The Faerie Queene,* Edmund Spenser presented the traditional arguments against self-destruction in a debate between the Red Cross Knight and Despair, whose cave is littered with the corpses of suicides. In one stanza Despair tempts the Knight:

> *What if some litle paine the passage have,*
> *That makes fraile flesh to feare the bitter wave?*
> *Is not short paine well borne, that brings long ease,*
> *And layes the soule to sleepe in quiet grave?*
> *Sleepe after toyle, port after stormie seas,*
> *Ease after warre, death after life does greatly please.*

The Knight responds with an argument borrowed from Plato:

> *The knight much wondred at his suddeine wit,*
> *And said, The terme of life is limited,*
> *Ne may a man prolong, nor shorten it;*
> *The souldier may not move from watchfull sted,*
> *Nor leave his stand, untill his Captaine bed.*

Despair, pointing out that the longer the Red Cross Knight lives, the more he'll sin, presses a dagger upon the Knight. Suddenly, cool argument gives way to the magnified heartbeat of a true suicidal crisis:

> *. . . his hand did quake,*
> *And tremble like a leafe of Aspin greene,*
> *And troubled bloud through his pale face was seene*
> *To come, and goe with tydings from the hart,*
> *As it a running messenger had beene.*

In the nick of time, however, Lady Una appears to snatch the knife from the Red Cross Knight. Despair, his plans foiled, attempts suicide—unsuccessfully.

The suicidal person's internal landscape was most fully explored by Shakespeare. In his eight tragedies there are fourteen suicides. Shakespeare examined what were known as honor suicides—to avoid capture, to rejoin a lost loved one, and so on—and saw them not as types but as individuals with complex motives. Cassius, for instance, who orders his servant to run him through with his sword, is not simply the traditional "suicide to avoid capture" but a proud man undone by his refusal to compromise his lofty self-concept. Othello, too, values his good name more than his life. He stabs himself not so much out of guilt for killing Desdemona but as a way of reviving his reputation. As M. D. Faber has pointed out in an essay on Shakespeare's suicides, Othello kills the bad part of himself (the jealous monster who killed innocent Desdemona) so that the good part (the just, noble warrior) may live on posthumously. Faber suggested that Romeo's suicide is less a romantic attempt to rejoin his lost loved one, Juliet, than an impulsive act of rage, spite, and frustration. " 'I defy you, stars,' cries Romeo just as he decides to die, and in that cry we have much of what is driving him," wrote Faber. ". . . his suicide is, in large part, an obscene gesture directed toward the world and the world's authorities." Hamlet, the melancholy Dane, unable to express his anger at his mother for marrying his uncle, turns his rage inward and contemplates suicide. In his famous soliloquy he moves from the religious prohibitions, his dismay that God had "fix'd his canon 'gainst self-slaughter," to a practical consideration of the pros and cons. Although he admits that exchanging "a sea of troubles" for the "sleep of death" is "a consummation devoutly to be wished," he hesitates, worried that what comes after death might be even worse than his troubled life.

In 1608, seven years after *Hamlet* was first produced and published, John Donne summed up the arguments for and against suicide in *Biathanatos*, subtitled: *A Declaration of that Paradoxe, or Thesis, that Self-homicide is not so Naturally Sinne, that it may never be otherwise. Wherein The Nature, and the extent of all those Lawes, which seeme to be violated by this Act, are diligently surveyed.* The first defense of suicide in the English language was as formidable as its title. Its three parts, devoted to demonstrating that suicide does not contradict the laws of nature, of reason, or of God, were a witty, erudite dismantling of the traditional arguments against what Donne called "the disease of head-long dying."

Donne concluded his vast and detailed survey of suicide by observing that "in all ages, in all places, upon all occasions, men of all conditions, have affected it, and inclin'd to doe it." Suicide is universal, as much a part of us as the instinct of self-preservation it seems to deny. Donne's conclusion rendered the moral question less absolute, affirming that "No law is so primary and simple . . . but that circumstances alter it. In which case a private man is Emperor of himselfe. . . . And he whose conscience well tempred and dispassion'd, assures him that the reason of selfe-preservation ceases in him, may also presume that the law ceases too."

Donne's insistence that each case must be judged individually was probably the result of his own "circumstance." In the preface to *Biathanatos* he explained his reasons for writing the book. After describing a man "eminent and illustrious, in the full glory and Noone of Learning" who was prevented from throwing himself off a Paris bridge, Donne confessed that he had considered suicide himself. "I have often such a sickely inclination," he wrote, although he could not explain exactly why. "Whensoever any affliction assailes me, mee thinks I have the keyes of my prison in mine owne hand, and no remedy presen's it selfe so soone to my heart, as mine own sword."

In *The Savage God,* A. Alvarez explored the reasons for Donne's "sickely inclination." Donne wrote *Biathanatos* at the age of thirty-six, when his brilliant career as poet and courtier was at low ebb. Having been dismissed from his post as private secretary to the Lord Keeper of the Privy Seal, Donne lived with his wife and children outside of London. Unable to write or to find a job, Donne thought of death. In a 1608 letter to a friend he wrote of the "thirst and inhiation after the next life" which often overtook him. But Donne admitted that his suicidal thoughts were not wholly due to his reduced circumstances "because I had the same desires when I went with the tyde, and enjoyed fairer hopes than now."

Whatever kept him from "head-long dying" is not known, but that same year Donne wrote *Biathanatos.* Alvarez has suggested that the book itself saved Donne. "I wonder if *Biathanatos* didn't begin as a prelude to self-destruction and finish as a substitute for it," he wrote. "That is, he set out to find precedents and reasons for killing himself while still remaining Christian—or, at least, without damning himself eternally. But the process of writing the book and marshaling his intricate learning and dialectical skill may have relieved the tension and helped to re-establish his sense of his self." Although Donne, who took vows to enter the Church in 1615, continued to be preoccupied by death in his sermons from the pulpit as dean of St. Paul's and in his divine poems, he forbade publication of *Biathanatos* "because it is upon a misinterpretable subject." Indeed, when it was finally published in 1646, fifteen years after his death, it created a storm of comment. But despite its learned discussion of the pros and cons of the right to suicide, the book's main contribution may have been in the simple confession of the preface. Suicide, Donne explained, may be neither a heroic, rational choice nor a sin and a crime, but "a sickely inclination" that can overwhelm a person.

Donne's "sickely inclination" sounds like depression. In the seventeenth century it was known as melancholy, a catchall term that described a variety of moods and symptoms. In the Middle Ages it existed as *accidie,* a sinful malaise born of despair of the grace of God. In "The Parson's Tale," Chaucer described how *accidie* made a man "hevy, thoghtful, and wrawe." A different sort of melancholy was found in the ballads of medieval troubadours, who sang of dying lovers and the supreme value of love on earth. That romantic seed bloomed in the Renaissance when melancholy stemmed not from the sinner's horror of death and eternity but from a realization of the brevity of life. In literature and drama, melancholy would become associated with sensitive, thoughtful, superior minds, even genius, and it threatened to become a fashionable affliction.

To Robert Burton melancholy was far too painful to consider glamorous. "If there be a hell upon earth, it is to be found in a melancholy man's heart," he wrote in 1621 in *The Anatomy of Melancholy,* a chatty, rambling guide to the varieties of the species. According to Burton, melancholy was near-ubiquitous, and the fact that his book went through seven editions in forty years may support his claim. A parson and Oxford don who lived, he admitted, "a silent, sedentary, solitary life," Burton himself suffered from persistent melancholy, which he could sometimes alleviate by going down to the Isis to listen to the shouts and curses of the bargemen. But many melancholics, he wrote, found relief only in death. (Burton was rumored to have hanged himself.)

Though the parson in Burton gave antisuicide arguments and quoted the laws and penalties against the act, the humanist in him seems to have realized that suicide, like the melancholy from which he suffered, may not be a matter of choice: "In extremity, they know not what they do, deprived of reason, judgment, all, as a ship that is void of a pilot, must needs impinge upon the next rock or sands, and suffer shipwreck." He questioned the Church's damnation of suicide and suggested that man himself is in no position to pass judgment. "What may happen to one may happen to another. Who knows how he may be tempted? It is his case, it may be thine."

If the Stoics, with their ultra-rational approach, had made suicide seem heroic, icy, and a little impersonal, Christianity, by damning and degrading it, had made it seem foul, distant, and inhuman. With the Renaissance, Donne, Shakespeare, and Burton managed to humanize suicide, showing it as an object of sympathy rather than of worship or horror. This change was even reflected in the work of several ecclesiastical writers, who, while condemning suicide, admitted to certain exceptions. "There be two sorts of voluntarie deathes," observed Reverend Tuke in *A Discourse on Death* in 1613, "the one lawful and honest, such as the death of Martyrs, the other dishonest and unlawful, when men have neyther lawfull calling, nor honest endes, as of Peregrinus, who burnt himselfe in a pile of wood, thinking thereby to live forever in mens remembrance." Saint Cyran's "Casus Regius" listed thirty-four situations in which the self-murderer was innocent, and theologians and philosophers of the school of Grotius and Pufendorf condoned suicide when committed to avoid dishonor or sin, to save oneself from death by torture, or to offer up one's own life to save that of a friend. In 1613, alarmed by a rash of suicides near Rothenburg ob der Tauber, Protestant minister Johannes Neser preached three sermons in which he reiterated that those who committed premeditated suicide when sane were damned. But men who were driven to suicide by intense vexations, chronic sickness, or extreme pain were not damned, he said, because they did not know what they were doing. When in doubt as to a suicide's sinfulness—as in cases of gout, bladder stone, and urinary gravel, where acute pain might cause temporary derangement—he concluded that the verdict must be left to God.

In 1637, concerned by an apparent increase in suicide, an English country clergyman named John Sym wrote *Lifes Preservative Against Self-Killing*. While agreeing with prevailing seventeenth-century opinion that suicide was the devil's work and "utterly unlawful," Sym compiled what may have been the first collection of warning signs: "gastly lookes, wilde frights and flaights, nestling and restlesse behaviour, a mindlessnesse and close dumpishnesse, both in company and in good imployments; a distracted countenance and cariage; speaking and talking to, and with themselves, in their solitary places and dumps; reasoning and resolving with themselves about that fact, and their motives to it, in a perplexed disturbed manner, with the like." If these signs were present, said Sym, the melancholy man must take precautions to keep the devil at bay: "shunning to go upon lawfull calling into solitary retired places; over waters, bridges, upon battlements of houses; or neere steepe downe places . . . shunning to be alone, or in dark places." Drawing on his experience counseling potential suicides Sym concluded, "Self-murder is prevented, not so much by arguments against the fact; which disswades from the conclusion; as by the discovery and removall of the motives and causes, whereupon they are tempted to do the same: as diseases are cured by removing of the causes, rather than of their symptoms."

Sym's conclusion—treat the causes and not the symptoms—was ahead of its time. Despite sympathetic consideration for the suicide in Renaissance philosophy and literature, there remained a vast gap between enlightened opinion and the law. Whether a man be pushed to suicide by melancholy, by fever, or by the devil, he risked a variety of punishments. Even the benevolence of More's *Utopia* extended only so far: Unauthorized suicides were to be "caste unburied into some stinkyng marrish." Their fate was mild compared to that of suicides in the real world. Facing what they believed to be a rising toll of suicides, courts invoked stiffer penalties in the hope that if fear of eternal damnation was not enough to deter the potential suicide, concern for his property, family, reputation, and corpse might be.

In fifteenth-century France the body of one Louis de Beaumont was to be dragged through the streets "as cruelly as possible, to set an example for others." An ordinance of 1670 reaffirmed that suicide was treason against God and king. The suicide's corpse was dragged through the streets of the city, hanged upside down, then thrown into a sewer or the town dump. His property was forfeited to the king. If the deceased was a nobleman, he was declared a commoner. His forests were razed, his castle demolished, his shield and coat of arms broken, and his memory defamed *ad perpetuam rei memoriam*—to the end of memory. If the corpse of a suicide could not be found, a sentence of defamation was brought in against his memory. In 1582 in Scotland, where according to the law "self-murder is as highly criminal as the killing of our neighbor," the Kirk Sessions of Perth refused to allow the corpse of a man who had committed suicide by drowning to be "brought through the town in daylight, neither yet to be buried among the Faithful—but in the little inch [island] within the water." In 1598 in Edinburgh the body of a woman who drowned herself was "harled through the town backwards, and thereafter hanged on the gallows." In Finland suicides judged insane were buried outside the churchyard without traditional ceremonies; if "of sound mind," the corpse was burned on a pyre in the forest. Those who attempted suicide were imprisoned with a diet of bread, water, and flogging. In Italy suicides were hanged; if the corpse could not be found, it was hanged in effigy. In Austria a person who attempted suicide was imprisoned "until he be persuaded by education that self-preservation is a duty to God, the State and to himself, show complete repentance and may be expected to mend his ways."

In 1601 the lawyer William Fulbecke matter-of-factly described the English punishment of the day: "The body is drawn out of the house, wherein the person killed himself, with ropes; not by the door, for of that he is unworthy, but through some hole or pit made under the threshold of the door; and is thence drawn by an horse to the place of punishment or shame, where it is hanged on a gibbet; and none may take it down, but by order of the magistrate." Suicides were tried posthumously in the coroner's court. The usual penalty for *felo de se*—property confiscation and burial at a crossroads with a wooden stake through the heart—could be avoided if the jury ruled the deceased had acted from insanity. To secure a proper burial friends and relatives of the dead man had to persuade the court that their loved one was a madman. If the deceased was a man of wealth or position, he was more apt to be found insane and allowed burial; less fortunate suicides were usually awarded the stake and crossroads. Thus, in Shakespeare's *Hamlet,* although Ophelia is allowed burial in sanctified ground, she is denied full rites; the priest explains to Laertes: "We should profane the service of the dead / To sing a requiem, and such rest to her / As to peace-parted souls."

The colonies seem to have been more lenient. In 1700, in his charter to Pennsylvania, William Penn recommended "that if any person, through temptation or melancholy, shall destroy himself, his estate, real and personal, shall, notwithstanding, descend to his wife, children, or relations, as if he had died a natural death." A vestige of legal punishment inherited from their English forebears was found in Massachusetts, where a 1660 law on "Self-Murther" proclaimed:

If any person Inhabitant or Stranger, shall at any time be found by any Jury to lay violent hands on themselves, or be willfully guilty of their own Death, every such person shall be denied the privilege of being Buried in the Common Burying place of Christians, but shall be buried in some Common High-way where the Selectmen of the Town where such person did inhabit shall appoint, and a Cart-load of Stones laid upon the Grave as a Brand of Infamy, and as a warning to others to beware of the like Damnable practices.

Thus, in the spring of 1707 one Abraham Harris of Boston, a young white-washer, having "felloniously and willfully Murthered himself, by Hanging himself with a Neckcloth—Contrary to the Peace of Our Soveraign Lady the Queen," was buried at a crossroads near the gallows on the Roxbury Highway, and a cartload of stones was laid on his grave. The burial cost the county sixteen shillings, including one shilling "for money lay'd out in drink" for the constable and six gravediggers.

"Wheresoever you finde many and severe Lawes against an offence," observed Donne in *Biathanatos,* "it is not safe from thence to conclude an extreame enormity or hainousnesse in the fault, but a propensnesse of that people, at that time, to that fault." Clergymen were convinced that a loosening of morals during the Renaissance inspired an increase in suicide. The act, wrote an anonymous observer in 1647, "is now growne so common, that selfe murther is scarce accounted any newes." But the evidence is not conclusive. The nature of suicide, however, seems to have changed. In the early years of the Renaissance numerous suicides aspired to the classical mode. In 1538 the Florentine patriot Philip Strozzi, accused in the assassination of Alessandro de Medici, was captured; fearing that under torture he might betray the names of fellow conspirators, he decided on suicide. After carving a line from Virgil— "Arise from my bones, avenger of these wrongs!"—on his cell wall, he stabbed himself, leaving behind a note in which he asked that he be permitted to have his place with Cato of Utica and other great suicides of antiquity. In the late seventeenth and early eighteenth centuries, the stage abounded with classical suicides. In France there were plays about Lucretia, Brutus, Cassius, and at least two on Cato. In England, Joseph Addison's *Cato* was a hit in 1713. Alexander Pope, who wrote the prologue, observed to a friend that "Cato was not so much the wonder of Rome in his days, as he is of Britain in ours." Twenty-four years later Addison's cousin and protégé Eustace Budgell loaded his pockets with stones and threw himself into the Thames, leaving behind a note: "What Cato did and Addison approved cannot be wrong."

But Budgell's suicide was hardly in the tradition of Cato. A writer and scholar, he had lost twenty-two thousand pounds in the South Sea Bubble speculation and died a failed, lonely man. If his death lacked the classical touch, it hinted at something more complex and more human. By the end of the Renaissance, suicides could no longer be seen simply as the result of honor, black bile, or the devil. They were the product of human struggle, of pride, loneliness, melancholy—and especially poverty. Between 1597 and 1644, of three hundred suicides in three English counties, more than half left no goods at all. The suicides included twenty-nine laborers, thirty-seven spinsters, and assorted shoemakers, tinkers, hostlers, bricklayers, and so on. Far more characteristic than the showy, heroic suicide of Philip Strozzi was that of Richard and Bridget Smith in 1732.

Smith was a bookbinder who had fallen into debt after a series of losses and disappointments. He and his wife, agreeing that a life of numbing poverty had little to offer, decided to commit suicide. After cutting their daughter's throat, they hanged themselves from the bedpost, leaving a note addressed to the public:

> These actions, considered in all their circumstances, being somewhat uncommon, it may not be improper to give some account of the cause; and that it was an inveterate hatred we conceived against poverty and rags, evils that through a train of unlucky accidents were become inevitable. For we appeal to all that ever knew us, whether we were idle or extravagant, whether or no we have not taken as much pains to get our living as our neighbours, although not attended with the same success. We apprehend the taking our child's life away to be a circumstance for which we shall be generally condemned; but for our own parts we are perfectly easy on that head. We are satisfied it is less cruelty to take the child with us, even supposing a state of annihilation as some dream of, than to leave her friendless in the world, exposed to ignorance and misery. . . . We are not ignorant of those laws made *in terrorem,* but leave the disposal of our bodies to the wisdom of the coroner and his jury, the thing being indifferent to us where our bodies are laid. . . .

Richard Smith
Bridget Smith

The Smiths were buried at the crossroads near the Turnpike at Newington.

V

THE ENLIGHTENMENT: "A CURE FOR GOUT, WHY NOT FOR LIFE?"

DURING THE ENLIGHTENMENT, discussion of suicide was more vigorous—and, on the whole, more sympathetic—than it had been since the Roman Empire. In an age that scorned anything hinting of medievalism and put a premium on the rights of the individual, suicide seemed an essential human liberty. "To be *happy* or not to be at all," wrote Jeremy Bentham, the founder of utilitarianism, reworking Hamlet. "Such is the option which nature has given to every human being." To Rationalists like Montesquieu, Rousseau, and Voltaire, Richard and Bridget Smith's decision to end their lives was reasonable, and to punish it with a stake through the heart was an outrage. Suicide, they insisted, was not a mortal sin or a crime against the state—to elevate an essentially private act into a cosmic blow against the universe seemed absurd.

"When I am overcome by anguish, poverty, or humiliation, why must I be prevented from putting an end to my troubles, and harshly deprived of the remedy which lies in my power?" wrote Montesquieu in 1721. In *Persian Letters* the Oriental traveler Usbek, writing from Paris to a friend in Smyrna, is astonished by the "ferocity" of the European laws against suicide. "They are put to death for a second time, so to speak; their bodies are dragged in disgrace through the streets and branded, to denote infamy, and their goods are confiscated." He argues that if life is a gift, if the gift ceases to give pleasure, why is one not free to part with it? The body is destined to perish in any case, he

171

concludes, and the soul to live on, so how is the order of Providence disturbed? In the vast scheme of things, the persistence of a person in bearing the agonies of a hopeless illness seems merely vain. "All such ideas, my dear Ibben, originate in our pride alone," he writes.

Fifty years later another letter discussing suicide stirred controversy. In Rousseau's novel, *La Nouvelle Héloïse,* Saint Preux, a young man disappointed in love, writes an impassioned letter to his English friend Lord Bomston, explaining that suicide is neither a crime nor inconsistent with belief in God. "Every man has a right by nature to pursue what he thinks is good, and avoid what he thinks evil, in all matters which are not injurious to others," he writes, echoing the Stoic argument. "When our life becomes a misery to ourselves, and is of advantage to no one, we are thus at liberty to put an end to our being." God gave man reason to enable him to choose between good and evil, says Saint Preux, and reason tells us that an unhappy life must be remedied as much as a diseased body: "If it is permitted to seek a cure for gout, why not for life?" He compares the man who does not know how to relieve an unhappy life by seeking death to the man who allows his wound to gangrene rather than summoning a surgeon. As for theologians who insist that suicide disqualifies us from Providence, Saint Preux maintains that in killing ourselves we merely destroy our bodies but bring our immortal souls, in death, closer to God. Saint Preux admits exceptions: People who have duties to others should not dispose of themselves. But, he concludes, since he is not a magistrate, has no family to support, and for friends has only Lord Bomston, nothing stands in his way.

"Young man, a blind ecstasy leads you astray," Lord Bomston begins his reply, in which he discusses the importance of remaining at one's post and stresses the cowardice of despair. He suggests that his friend might find relief in helping others. "Each time thou art tempted to quit life, say to thyself, let me at least do one good action before I die, then go in search for one indigent person, whom thou mayest relieve; for one under misfortune, whom thou mayest console; for one under oppression, whom thou mayest defend." While Rousseau followed this prescription in his own life, readers of *La Nouvelle Héloïse* felt that the passion of Saint Preux's arguments overwhelmed the elegance of Bomston's and indicated where Rousseau's sympathies lay. Preachers accused him of spawning suicides; Saint Preux would become a model for Goethe's *Werther,* which would in turn be blamed for a rash of self-killing. In a letter to Voltaire, Rousseau wrote that the wise man will sometimes give up his life when nature and bad fortune give a distinct order to depart. Rousseau's own unhappy life was increasingly haunted by madness, and after his death in 1778 there were rumors that he had killed himself.

Voltaire's position on suicide was not unlike that of many twentieth-century liberals. On one hand, as a passionate opponent of superstition and injustice, he opposed laws that degraded a suicide's corpse and deprived his innocent family. Calling confiscation of the suicide's property "brigandage," Voltaire, with characteristic acidity, noted that in practice "his goods are given to the King, who almost always grants half of them to the leading lady of the Opera, who prevails upon one of her lovers to ask for it; the other half by law belongs to the Inland Revenue." In his novels and plays Voltaire attacked dogmatism and oppression and proclaimed the individual's mastery over his own destiny. If "self-murder" was a wrong against society, he argued, are not the voluntary homicides committed in war and sanctioned by the laws of all countries far more harmful to the human race? Like Donne, he believed that circumstance, not dogma, must be our guide in judging suicide. Every case must be weighed on its own merits—"Each one has his reasons for his behavior." To Voltaire some reasons were better than others. He teased the hypersensitive melancholics and suggested that young girls who drown themselves for love should not be hasty—change is as common in love as it is in business. Voltaire complained that eighteenth-century suicides could learn a thing or two from the old masters: "We kill ourselves, too," he wrote, "but it is when we have lost our money or in the rare excess of a wild passion for an object which isn't worth it." As for himself, the antisuicide laws made his own suicide improbable, he jokingly confessed in a letter to his friend the Marquise du Deffand: "It is a decision that I shall not take, at least not yet, for the reason that I have got myself annuities from two sovereigns and I should be inconsolable if my death enriched two crowned heads."

The arguments of the eighteenth-century Rationalists were summed up by Scottish philosopher David Hume in his essay *On Suicide.* With the confidence of a sharpshooter he set up his targets—"If suicide be criminal, it must be a transgression of our duty either to God, our neighbour, or ourselves"—and then picked them off one by one.

Were the disposal of human life so much reserved as the peculiar province of the Almighty, that it were an encroachment on his right for men to dispose of their own lives, it would be equally criminal to act for the preservation of life as for its destruction. If I turn aside a stone which is falling upon my head, I disturb the course of nature; and I invade the peculiar province of the Almighty, by lengthening out my life beyond the period, which, by the general laws of matter and motion, he has assigned it.

A hair, a fly, an insect, is able to destroy this mighty being whose life is of such importance. Is it an absurdity to suppose that human prudence may lawfully dispose of what depends on such insignificant causes? It would be no crime in me to divert the Nile or Danube from its course, were I able to effect such purposes. Where then is the crime of turning a few ounces of blood from their natural channel?

If all events proceed from God, said Hume, then so too does suicide: "When I fall upon my own sword, therefore, I receive my death equally from the hands of the Deity as if it had proceeded from a lion, a precipice, or a fever." To those who insisted that suicide was a crime against nature, Hume pointed out that man alters nature in many acceptable ways: building houses, cultivating land, sailing upon the ocean. "In all these actions we employ our powers of mind and body to produce some innovation in the course of nature; and in none of them do we any more. They are all of them therefore equally innocent, or equally criminal."

Turning to the argument that suicide is a crime against society, Hume maintained that "a man who retires from life does no harm to society: he only ceases to do good; which, if it is an injury, is of the lowest kind." Furthermore, like Montesquieu, Hume believed that citizenship is a two-way responsibility; when man withdraws himself from society, is he still bound any longer? In any case, wrote Hume, "I am not obliged to do a small good to society at the expense of a great harm to myself: why then should I prolong a miserable existence because of some frivolous advantage which the public may perhaps receive from me?"

To Hume the flaw in the "crime against the self" argument seemed self-evident. "That suicide may often be consistent with interest and with our duty to ourselves, no one can question, who allows that age, sickness, or misfortune, may render life a burden, and make it worse even than annihilation." In any case, he wondered, why was the rest of the world so wounded by a suicide? "The life of a man is of no greater importance to the universe than that of an oyster."

Written at least twenty years before Hume's death, On Suicide was not published until 1777, the year after he died. It was promptly suppressed and was later published from the apparently more tolerant grounds of Basel. But Hume's "oyster" did not go down easily; he and his fellow eighteenth-century "apologists" for suicide, as their enemies referred to them, provoked a fresh torrent of rhetoric from antisuicide moralists. (One London minister, remarking that On Suicide had reportedly inspired a friend of Hume's to shoot himself, suggested that Hume should have practiced what he preached.) From pulpits and printing presses across Europe they redoubled the volume of hellfire and brimstone against what they variously described as "a pusillanimous escape," "that miserable insanity," "the foul offspring of vile progenitors," "The Certain Characteristic of a foolish, weak Mind," "An Atrocious Offense Against God and Man," "the offspring of hell," "a crime of the deepest dye," "the most sordid and unworthy selfishness," and "the act of cowards, poltroons, and deserters." As for the causes of this act, they compiled an impressive list of culprits: "gambling," "government," "vanity," "modern philosophy," "intemperate drinking," "licentious novels," "want of benevolence," "want of ambition," "Habits of Idleness," "the examples of profligates," "Indulgence of Criminal Love," "a criminal love of the world," "A Gloomy and Misguided Imagination," "a weakness and timidity of mind," "the difficulty of procuring a livelihood," "the great number of authorized lotteries," "a base, corrupt, loathsome sinful State of Mind," "the fatal insanity of commercial speculation and the irrational desire of becoming wealthy on a sudden," "the mistaken fashion in education which has latterly prevailed, [in which] The superficial shewy and frivolous accomplishments are almost universally preferred to solid science and modest virtue," and, above all, "want of submission to the Judge and Arbitrator of human affairs," or, as another preacher put it, "Godlessness."

To stem what they believed to be a growing tide of self-destruction, they called for increased church attendance, fewer insanity verdicts in coroners' courts, and stricter antisuicide penalties. "The carcass should have the Burial of an Ass, and the utmost Marks of Reproach cast upon it," suggested one writer, "in order to deter others from giving way to, or falling into the like Snares and Wiles of the Devil." Another proposed that these "sons of perdition" be hanged in chains head down and every minister required to preach against the crime once a year. Another suggested that the bodies of self-murderers be dissected publicly on stages in market places and the skeletons handed over to surgeons to "contribute somewhat to the advancement of *anatomical knowledge.*" One minister favored a combination of all of the above. "It might not only be refused all rites of burial, but be exposed naked to public view, be dragged on an hurdle in the most ignominious posture, and undergo every disgraceful mark of shame, contempt and abhorrence," he wrote. "The populace on these occasions might be harangued with energy on the foulness of the crime, and then the carcass delivered over (like that of the common murderer) for the purposes of public dissection; so that he, who had voluntarily withdrawn himself from being further useful to society in his life, might become so in his death."

Throughout the eighteenth century a steady flow of sermons, essays, and pamphlets invoked new rhetoric to cloak some of the traditional ideas of duty to God, state, fellow man, and self. The following voices offer a sampling:

The minister Samuel Miller on "The Guilt, Folly and Sources of Suicide," at the United Presbyterian Church in New York City, in February 1805:

Nor let anyone plead that his case is peculiar, and that society can lose but little by the destruction of a single life: for if *one* individual, because he feels the inclination, has a right to take away his own life, then every other individual who feels a similar inclination has the same right; and if every one were to think and act accordingly, into what a field of blood would our world be converted! What darkness and mourning would cover the face of society! What distrust, anxiety and consternation would reign in every family, and torture every bosom!

The British Reverend John Herries, in "An Address to the Public on the Frequent and Enormous Crime of Suicide: Recommended to the Perusal of all

who Are Distressed in Mind, in Body, or in Worldly Circumstances," available
to the public for one shilling in 1781. From the table of contents:

> The text illustrated—Frequency of Suicide—Instances of it in the Bible—
> that it is contrary to our natural love of life—that it proceeds from want of
> fortitude, ambition, benevolence, and gratitude—that it indicates a neglect
> of duty, a perverted imagination, and a disregard to the divine authority—
> Awful thoughts on futurity—Objections of the infidel—View of annihila-
> tion—An appeal to the wretched on their past happiness—Suicide as unjus-
> tifiable in the infidel as in the Christian—Refutation of the arguments in
> favor of suicide; from life being a burden, from pain, poverty, reproach,
> remorse, disappointments, loss of friends, etc.—Motives to acquiescence and
> fortitude—A concluding address to the audience, with arguments drawn
> from every situation in life to dissuade from the crime of suicide.

Buried in the bombast were important arguments—duty to the state, the
virtue of suffering, responsibility to family—but their shrillness obscured their
logic. "Many of those who have maintained the criminality of Suicide have
indulged an intemperance of zeal, a bitterness of expression, which are ill
suited both to the teacher and the investigator of moral science; and which tend
to cast unfavourable suspicions, as well upon the Reasoning as upon the
Reasoner," observed Richard Hey, a graduate student at Cambridge, whose
dissertation on suicide won a university prize in 1783. "It is time that we cease
to injure our cause by an injudicious defence of it." Hey noted that a softer
touch was also more effective with would-be suicides. "There is a singular
impropriety in using a severity of address to the persons whom we would retain
from the commission of Suicide," he wrote. "The state of mind in which this
crime is *usually* committed, requires gentleness of treatment; as far as may be
consistent with an open and full representation of the truth. Wherefore all
unnecessary harshness is to be studiously avoided, as tending in a peculiar
manner to defeat our principal purpose." While Hey's approach was sympathetic, his conclusion was familiar: "Suicide must stand *universally* condemned."

In *A Full Inquiry into the Subject of Suicide,* published in 1790, Charles
Moore, the rector of Cuxton and vicar of Bloughton-Blean, Kent, condemned
suicide as an affront to nature, God, society, and the individual's own interests
since it might deprive him of heaven. Moore's two-volume tome closed with
twelve precautions designed to help the reader "to resist temptations to suicide
should they attack us." He stressed advance planning. "It is probably too late
to begin reasoning against suicide when under actual temptation to commit,"
he wrote. "Wherefore it behooves us in the days of full health and strength,
of pleasure and enjoyment not to be backward in fortifying our minds against
any future temptation, by impressing on them . . . all the general, forcible

arguments that decide against its practice." He reminded his readers that "temperance and employment are the great bulwarks of health, contentment and happiness."

While preachers reiterated familiar theological arguments, the reasoning of antisuicide philosophers became increasingly secular. They focused their arguments on an idea first raised by Aquinas that suicide goes against human nature. In 1690, John Locke published his *Second Treatise on Government,* a manifesto based on the assumptions that life is an "inalienable right" and "life-preservation" a primary law of nature. To the pro-suicide Rationalists the option of suicide was a mark of man's freedom. To Locke freedom was based on self-preservation, which ruled out suicide: "Freedom, then, is not . . . for everyone to do . . . as he pleases. . . . Freedom . . . is so . . . closely joined with a man's preservation, that he cannot part with it. . . . Nobody can give more power than he has himself, and he that cannot take away his own life cannot give another power over it." Locke's work would influence several generations of antisuicide philosophers, including the early utilitarian Francis Hutcheson, and Denis Diderot, whose entry on suicide in *The Encyclopedia* began: "As for the morality of this act, it is necessary to say that it is absolutely against the law of nature." Immanuel Kant took the argument one step further. Kant, who believed that Hume's skepticism signaled the end of philosophy, proposed an absolute moral code in which "duty" occupied a central position. Man's first duty was self-preservation; suicide was therefore a vice. "The rule of morality does not admit of it under any condition because it degrades human nature below the level of animal nature and so destroys it." Although his argument was largely secular, Kant's "categorical imperative," which declared that individual behavior ought to serve as an example for all mankind, prohibited suicide no less rigidly than did religion.

It was Madame de Staël who summed up eighteenth-century objections to suicide. *Reflections on Suicide,* published in 1813, was as straightforward and sensible as Hume's essay; parts of it, suggests one twentieth-century historian, "might still serve as a model plea against the individual's right to commit suicide." Seventeen years earlier de Staël had written *On the Influence of the Passions,* an essay supporting suicide. "I have ever since repented of that inconsiderate expression," she wrote in a footnote to the 1813 work. Her later essay reflected the experience of one who had suffered, and in her dedication she admitted that she wrote it "at a time when misfortune rendered the solace of meditation necessary to sustain me." Like Donne she maintained that there could be no blanket judgment. "The causes of misery, and its intensity, vary equally with circumstances and individuals," she observed. "We might as well attempt to count the waves of the sea, as to analyze the combinations of destiny and character." She urged that "in forming an opinion of the happiness or unhappiness of those who are constituted differently from ourselves, a profound knowledge of the human heart is essential to the philosophical and just conclusion." Rather than arguing from the authority of the Sixth Commandment, "Thou shalt not kill," she based her case on the Beatitude "Blessed are they that mourn, for they shall be comforted."

De Staël's main quarrel was with the idea that suffering was an excuse for killing oneself: "The greatest faculties of the soul are developed only by suffering, and this purification of ourselves restores us, after a time, to happiness; for the circle closes up again, and carries us back to those days of innocence which preceded our faults," she wrote. "We then abandon virtue when we fly to suicide as a refuge from misfortune; we reject the enjoyments that virtue would bestow by enabling us to triumph over our distresses." In an argument reminiscent of Kant's categorical imperative, de Staël sketched the portrait of a virtuous man and suggested that the true measure of his dignity was his unselfishness. Any suicide that sprang from devotion to duty, such as Cato's, was commendable. But for the majority of suicides her attitude was one of sympathy: "We ought not to be offended with those who are so wretched as to be unable to support the burden of existence, nor should we applaud those who sink under its weight, since, to sustain it, would be a greater proof of their moral strength." This was a factor that writers on both sides of the debate had largely overlooked: Would-be suicides were unhappy and in pain. The discussion of suicide could not be limited to a moral debate of right or wrong, cowardice or bravery, sin or honor; the suffering that may lead to the act must be acknowledged. Indeed, at one point de Staël seemed to be overwhelmed by feeling. "Oh!" she wrote. "What despair is required for such an act! May pity, the most profound pity, be granted to him who is guilty of it!"

While opposing suicide on moral grounds, many writers argued against the antisuicide laws. The Italian jurist Cesare Beccaria pointed out that in economic terms the state was more wronged by the emigrant than the suicide since the former took his property with him, whereas the latter left his behind. Confiscations inflicted injustice on a man's family, and punishment of the corpse, he observed, was as futile as beating a statue. Only God, he concluded, could punish a suicide. Under attack by the eighteenth-century Rationalists, antisuicide laws gradually fell into disuse. In Geneva indignities to the corpse were abolished in 1770 after the body of an "innocent" man was dragged through the streets. In southern France armed citizens stormed a prison to seize the body of a suicide and prevent its being hauled through the town. The following year, in the same district, a crowd gathered to halt the execution of a sentence against a suicide's corpse; police called to the scene made numerous arrests. In 1770 degradation of the corpse was also officially abolished in France; legal action was to be taken only against the suicide's name. In 1790 the French National Assembly, on the motion of Dr. Joseph Guillotin, who would become famous for championing a swift mode of execution, repealed all sanctions against suicide. In the new penal code of 1791, it was not even mentioned. Suicide was legal.

In England, although there was no change in the law through the eighteenth century, coroners' juries made increasing use of the insanity loophole to spare the suicide's corpse and his innocent family. Between 1770 and 1778 coroners in the county of Kent investigated 580 possible suicides and returned only fifteen verdicts of *felo de se.* Such leniency dismayed legal purists. "The excuse of not being in his senses ought not to be strained to that length, to which our coroner's juries are apt to carry it," grumbled the celebrated jurist William Blackstone, "viz. that the very act of suicide is evidence of insanity; as if every man, who acted contrary to reason, had no reason at all: for the same argument would prove every other criminal non-compos, as well as the self-murderer." Lunacy, however, remained largely an upper-class prerogative; the verdict of *felo de se* was apt to be applied only to lower-class suicides. "A penniless poor dog, who has not left enough money to defray the funeral charges, may perhaps be excluded the churchyard," observed *The Connoisseur,* a satirical magazine, "but self-murder by pistol genteelly mounted, or the Paris-hilted sword, qualifies the polite owner for a sudden death, and entitles him to the pompous burial and a monument setting forth his virtues in Westminster-Abbey."

England's stubborn refusal to relax its official position on suicide may have been partly the result of its reputation. During the eighteenth century it became generally accepted—by everyone but the English—that as a people they were particularly prone to self-destruction. "We do not find in history that the Romans ever killed themselves without a cause; but the English are apt to commit suicide most unaccountably; they destroy themselves even in the bosom of happiness," wrote Montesquieu in *The Spirit of Laws* in 1748. "This action among the Romans was the effect of education, being connected with their principles and customs; among the English it is the consequence of a distemper." Other reasons put forth for "the English malady" ranged from religious decay, rationalism, licentiousness, and lack of exercise to the people's fondness for butcher's meat, rich foods, sea coal, gambling, and tea. The most frequently cited culprit was the weather. An anonymous eighteenth-century French novel begins, "In the gloomy Month of November, when the people of England hang and drown themselves . . ." In 1805, in a letter to a friend, Thomas Jefferson reflected that his country's clear skies would offer protection against any predilection for hanging that Americans might have inherited from their ancestors. In a satirical essay Boswell suggested that freezing might be a useful suicide prevention device. As November approached, "the English, instead of hanging or drowning themselves, will certainly prefer having themselves frozen up . . . and when it is fine weather, up they will spring like swallows to the enjoyment of happiness."

Some Englishmen were unamused. "Self-murder! Name it not; our island's shame; / That makes her the reproach of neighb'ring states . . ." lamented Robert Blair in his poem *The Grave.* "O Britain, infamous for suicide! / An island in thy manners! . . ." cried Edward Young in *Night Thoughts*. "It is a melancholy consideration, that there is no country in Europe, or perhaps in the habitable world, where the horrid crime of self-murder is so common as it is in England," thundered John Wesley, founder of Methodism, proposing that the tide of English suicide would turn if self-murderers were hanged upside down in chains. Others questioned whether England's notoriety was deserved. An entry on suicide in the 1797 *Encyclopaedia Britannica* attributed it to rigorous newspaper reporting of suicide—a point Voltaire had made when he remarked that if Paris newspapers kept statistics as accurately as England's, France's reputation for suicide would rival its neighbor's. In an 1804 travel book Thomas Holcroft wrote, "I doubt if as many suicides be committed through all Great Britain in a year as in Paris alone in a month."

The intercontinental competition raged throughout the eighteenth century. Although the numbers were debatable, the nature of suicide had unquestionably altered. A century that began with the suicides of Richard and Bridget Smith would conclude with the deaths of two French soldiers, twenty and twenty-four, who shot themselves out of ennui on Christmas Day, 1773. "No urgent motive has prompted us to intercept our career of life except the disgust of existing here a moment under the idea, that we must at one time or other cease to be," they explained in their note. "We leave our parts to be performed by those, who are silly enough to wish to act them a few hours longer." Accounts of such blasé suicides filled newspapers and drawing room conversations: the Englishman who hanged himself "in order to avoid the trouble of pulling off and on his clothes"; the Frenchman who, when asked to dine by a friend, replied, "With the greatest pleasure—yet, now I think of it, I am particularly engaged to shoot myself." Suicide had become decadent, trivial; one could not take it too seriously. "There are little domestic news," complained Horace Walpole, whose correspondence was spiced with world-weary references to self-destruction, in a letter to Richard Bentley. "If you insist upon some, why, I believe I could persuade somebody or other to hang themselves; but that is scarce an article uncommon enough to send cross the sea."

This nonchalance surrounding the subject of suicide would become even more flagrant in the Romantic Age. If eighteenth-century Enlightenment thinkers made suicide philosophically defensible, the Romantics of the early nineteenth century made it positively seductive. The Romantic movement began as a reaction to the rationalism of the Age of Reason. If a man's life was indeed of no more importance to the universe than that of an oyster, to the Romantics a man's death was everything. "Life exists for the sake of death," observed the eighteenth-century poet and philosopher who wrote under the name Novalis. "Death is at the same time the ending and the beginning." Death represented a reunion with nature and with God. "How wonderful is death," wrote Shelley. "A quiet of the heart," Byron called it. Keats longed to "cease upon the midnight with no pain." Taking the Renaissance combination of creativity and melancholy one step further, the Romantics coupled genius and premature death. The poetic sensibility was too good for this world; best to burn brightly and die young, like a shooting star. And some did. Keats died in 1821 at twenty-five, Shelley a year later at twenty-nine, and Byron two years after that, at thirty-six.

If dying young was glamorous, suicide was the ultimate thrill. The act showed an enviable, even heroic refusal to accept the banality of the world. In their preoccupation with suicide the Romantics had two early models. Thomas Chatterton, the precocious son of a schoolmaster, had begun publishing his brilliant poems at age sixteen. At nineteen, penniless, starving, and unappreciated, he swallowed arsenic in his lodging house garret. The details of Chatterton's suicide in 1770 were hardly romantic. What was distilled from them, however—a combination of genius and early death—was irresistible to the Romantics. "The marvelous Boy, the sleepless Soul that perished in his pride," as Wordsworth called him in his "Monody on the Death of Chatterton," became the model of the doomed poet for several generations of Romantic poets and would-be poets.

Four years after the death of Chatterton, Goethe's *The Sorrows of Young Werther* offered a second lethal symbol in the lovesick young hero who shoots himself. As a young man Goethe himself had longed for a glorious death. He had admired Emperor Otto's suicide by stabbing and decided that he would kill himself like Otto or not kill himself at all. "By this conviction, I saved myself from the purpose, or indeed, more properly speaking, from the whim, of suicide," he later wrote. "Among a considerable collection of arms, I possessed a costly, well-ground dagger. This I laid down nightly by my side; and, before extinguishing the light, I tried whether I could succeed in sending the sharp point an inch or two deep into my heart. But as I truly never could succeed, I at last took to laughing at myself, threw away all these hypochondriacal crotchets, and determined to live." Writing *Werther,* it has been suggested, kept Goethe from becoming Werther.

Like Goethe, most of the Romantic writers confined their intoxication with death to literature. Those who followed their own prescription hardly "cease[d] upon the midnight with no pain." Poor, lonely, rejected, and nearing fifty, the poet Thomas Beddoes took curare in Basel. German playwright Heinrich von Kleist, who had proposed suicide pacts to friends for a decade, finally found an accomplice in an incurably ill young woman. After shooting her, Kleist killed himself. Gérard de Nerval, tormented by insanity, used a frayed apron string to hang himself from a lamp post in Paris at age forty-six. More often, like Goethe, the Romantics merely toyed with suicide. The young Chateaubriand brought a shotgun to a lonely forest on his father's estate with the stated intention of killing himself, but his suicide was interrupted by the unexpected arrival of a gamekeeper. He died of old age at seventy-nine. The twenty-year-old de Musset, shown a beautiful view, cried, "Ah! It would be a beautiful place to kill oneself in!" Although de Musset asserts that twice he laid the point of a dagger against his heart, he never drew blood and eventually died at forty-six of a heart attack.

These celebrated writers stopped short of the act itself, but many young men who lacked the talent to express the Romantic ideal in prose expressed it with their deaths. Life imitated art: *Werther,* of course, was said to have inspired suicides all over Europe for decades, and numerous deaths were blamed on Byron's *Manfred,* Chateaubriand's *René,* and Lamartine's *Raphael.* Alfred-Victor de Vigny's play *Chatterton* was said to have doubled the annual rate of suicide in France between 1830 and 1840, when young men "practised it as one of the most elegant of sports," according to one historian. Suicide clubs flourished. In his letters, Flaubert, writing nostalgically of the friends with whom he spent his youth, captured the essential spirit of the Romantic flirtation with suicide: "We swung between madness and suicide; some of them killed themselves . . . another strangled himself with his tie, several died in debauchery in order to escape boredom; it was beautiful!"

VI

SCIENCE: MORAL
MEDICINE AND VITAL
STATISTICS

WHAT SEEMED BEAUTIFUL to Flaubert—and to other victims of what German poet Clemens Brentano called "hypertrophy of the poetic organ"— would soon be attributed to brain lesions, excess phosphorus, heredity, liver disease, madness, and masturbation. The assault of Enlightenment writers on the Church's condemnation of suicide had cleared the way for a secular approach to the subject, while the rapid growth of science and medicine in the seventeenth century laid the foundations for the scientific study of suicide. For the first time self-destruction was discussed not primarily as a philosophical or moral dilemma but as a medical and social problem. The question was not whether suicide was right or wrong but why it happened. The scientific study of suicide had two strands. The statistical model, which would provide the basis for a sociological approach, located the cause of suicide in society. The medical model, forerunner to the twentieth-century psychological approach, located the cause of suicide in the body.

Under the impression that suicide was primarily an English phenomenon, physicians explored the effects of climate on the body. Many believed that changes in temperature and precipitation affected the brain. In *The English Malady: or A Treatise of Nervous Diseases of All Kinds, as Spleen, Vapours, Lowness of Spirits, Hypochondriacal, and Hysterical Distempers, etc.,* published in 1733, George Cheyne found that the English had more "nervous distemper" leading to suicide because they ate too many rich foods, did not exercise, and lived in large cities choked with pollution. In 1758, in *A Treatise on Madness,* William Battie, physician to St. Luke's Hospital for Lunaticks, discussed weather and suicide: "Whatever may be the cause of Anxiety, it chiefly discovers itself by that agonising impatience observable in some men of black *November* days, of easterly winds, of heat, cold, damps, etc. . . . In which state of habitual diseases many drag on their wretched lives; whilst others, unequal to evils of which they see no remedy but death, rashly resolve to end them at any rate."

Like most eighteenth-century physicians who wrote on self-destruction, Cheyne and Battie seasoned their scientific theories with antisuicide bias. The first to separate completely the medical argument from the moral was a Frenchman named Merian who in 1763, in *Mémoire sur le Suicide,* stated that suicide was not a sin or a crime but a disease. All suicides are in some degree deranged, he said, otherwise they would not so completely contradict the law of nature. As for the cause of that derangement, each physician had his favorite culprit, according to his own theories of insanity: climate, the change of seasons, heredity, cerebral injuries, physical suffering, liver disease, melancholia, hypochondriasis, insanity, suppressed secretions, intoxication, gastritis, unnatural vices, and derangement of the *primae viae,* among others. Physicians conducted autopsies of suicides in search of physical clues. Some discovered lesions on the brains of suicides and suggested this was the cause. The French physiologist Pierre-Jean-Georges Cabanis believed suicide was caused by excess phosphorus in the brain. Franz Joseph Gall, the founder of phrenology, believed that the shape of the skull indicated specific characteristics: Composers had a special bulge around the ear; suicides, he asserted, had thick craniums. In 1818 his protégé, Johann Cristoph Spurzheim, concurred, claiming that suicide was a form of insanity produced by an abnormal thickening of the skull.

"Few, perhaps, are aware how frequently suicide results from the habit of indulging, in early youth, in a certain secret vice which, we are afraid, is practised to an enormous extent in our public schools," wrote one London physician. "A feeling of false delicacy has operated with medical men in inducing them to refrain from dwelling upon the destructive consequences of this habit, both to the moral and physical constitution, as openly and honestly as the importance of the subject imperatively demands." Perhaps suffering from a chronic case of false delicacy himself, the good doctor continued, "The physical disease, particularly that connected with the nervous system, engendered by the pernicious practice alluded to, frequently leads to the act of self-destruction. We have before us the cases of many suicides in whom the disposition may clearly be traced to this cause."

While most physicians searched for a specific physical cause of suicide, Jean-Étienne Esquirol, chief physician at the Royal Asylum at Charenton, maintained that suicide was not a disease *per se.* In his 1838 book, *Des*

Maladies Mentales, he wrote, "Suicide presents all the characteristics of insanity of which it is but a symptom. . . . There is no point in looking for a unique source of suicide, since one observes it in the most contradictory circumstances." Esquirol had reached a conclusion generally accepted by the medical profession today: Suicide is a symptom, not a disease. Accordingly, "The treatment of suicide belongs to the therapy of mental illness," he wrote, ". . . and one has to have recourse to treatment proper to each kind of insanity in order to treat an individual who is propelled toward his own destruction." In the early nineteenth century that might involve a variety of remedies. In his 1840 book, *The Anatomy of Suicide,* Forbes Winslow, a member of the Royal College of Surgeons in London, shared the following prescriptions:

A lady, shortly after her accouchement, expressed, with great determination, her intention to kill herself. Her bowels had not been properly attended to, and a brisk cathartic was given. This entirely removed the suicidal disposition.

The loss of a small quantity of blood has frequently been known to remove the propensity to self-destruction.

Disease of the stomach and liver frequently incite to suicide; hepatic affections notoriously disturb the equilibrium of the mind. Many a case exhibiting an inclination to suicide has been cured by a few doses of blue pill.

In certain diseases of the nervous system, particularly when associated with morbid conditions of the mind leading to suicide, the influence of music may be had recourse to with great advantage to the patient. . . . The monotony of the sound is supposed to have a soothing influence over the mind, similar to what is known to result from the gurgle of a mimic cataract of some mountain rill, or to a distant waterfall.

Every physician had his pet cure. Leopold Auenbrugger suggested drinking cold water: "A pint every hour; and if continuing pensive and taciturn, forehead, temples, and eyes sprinkled with it until more gay and communicative." While numerous physicians swore by this treatment—a Dr. Schonheyde even made his patients eat salt herrings to work up a thirst—others urged temperance. "Once in a while this was hard on the patient, particularly if he had tried to drown himself," noted Esquirol's pupil Jean-Pierre Falret. "But one patient who had been cured by the copious use of water continued to drink it both through gratefulness and habit to the point that at the age of eighty he was drinking twenty-four to thirty pounds of water a day!"

Some physicians found the plunge bath—sudden immersion into cold water—particularly effective in driving suicidal thoughts from the mind. (The plunge bath was discovered, according to Esquirol, when an insane carpenter threw himself into a pond; he was fished out half-drowned but fully sane.) Van Helmont advocated holding the patient under almost to the point of drowning, to ensure that self-destructive ideas were nipped at their root. Goethe's physician Hufeland cited the benefits of the douche—buckets of cold water thrown from a height onto the patient's head—in driving such thoughts from the mind. Johann Reil, known in Germany as the father of psychotherapy, suggested the insane and possibly suicidal patient be suspended by ropes from a considerable height "between heaven and earth," while hospital attendants discharged firearms beside him or threatened to scorch his body with flames. In his 1803 *Rhapsodies on the Application of Psychic Therapy Methods to Mental Disturbances,* Reil also outlined a sort of psychodrama in which asylum personnel would act as a celestial jury; the preview of life in the next world was intended to shock patients into their senses in this one.

Most suicidal patients, of course, received less dramatic treatment: bleeding, purging, and cupping, as well as drafts of mercury, bark, quinine, mineral waters, whey, and, occasionally, wine—"but its employment exacts much prudence," warned Joseph Guislain in 1826. Some doctors swore that large doses of opium would restrain self-destructive urges; others preferred morphia. What success these narcotics had with suicidal patients may have resulted from keeping them too drugged to act on their impulses. Tartrate of antimony, another popular remedy, kept them too nauseous. The rotary chair, a contraption in which the patient was whirled in circles as on an amusement park ride, led to copious vomiting and a submissive patient; the chair was recommended for those with "mental alienation with a suicidal propensity."

In order to restore the mind as well as the body, physical remedies were supplemented with "moral" treatment. Winslow suggested that "travelling, agreeable society, works of light literature, should be had recourse to, in order to dispel all gloomy apprehensions from the mind." Falret, however, cautioned that gay spectacles tend to dampen the spirits of the suicidal. Maintaining that suicidal people think too much, Esquirol said that it was necessary to hinder them from reflection or to force them to think otherwise than they do think. Reasoning, he said, is of no avail. A protégé of Philippe Pinel, whose unchaining of the inmates at Bicêtre marked the beginning of the modern asylum, Esquirol advocated the use of gentle remedies, preferring warm baths and drinks to bleeding and the plunge bath. Of the latter he remarked, "I should as soon think of recommending patients to be precipitated from the third story of a house, because some lunatics have been known to be cured by a fall on the head." He suggested that suicidal persons lodge on the ground floor in a cheerful setting where they could be watched by vigilant persons. He concluded that a little kindness goes a long way. "How many females have come to the Salpêtrière, whom misery or domestic grief has decided to end their days," he wrote, "and who are cured by affectionate attention, consolations, the hope of a better future, and by good nourishment!"

While the new view of suicide as a medical problem brought attention to the plight of suicidal people, it introduced several troubling themes. When the discipline of medical psychiatry emerged in the eighteenth century, it preserved the medieval assumption of a close relationship between insanity and suicide. The increased use of the insanity defense to avoid forfeiture and degradation of the corpse in suicide cases, however charitably intended, reinforced that link. Although Enlightenment writers had fought to establish the right to suicide as a moral, rational act, the argument in the nineteenth century was not whether suicide was moral but whether suicide could *ever* be rational. Physicians attempted to calculate what proportion of suicides were mentally ill. Estimates ranged from Brierre de Boismont's 14 percent to the 100 percent of Esquirol, Falret, and others. "As no rational being will voluntarily give himself pain, or deprive himself of life, which certainly, while human beings preserve their senses, must be acknowledged evils," wrote a Dr. Rowley, "it follows that every one who commits suicide is indubitably *non compos mentis.*" Thomas Chevalier, professor of anatomy and surgery at the Royal College of Surgeons in London, came to slightly less sweeping conclusions: "I am far from supposing that all suicides are lunatics; but I must contend that from the facts I have stated, the *onus probandi* lies on those who *deny* the existence of insanity in such a case." A suicide was a lunatic until proven rational.

Some disagreed. "The pathological and etiological history of suicide does not appertain entirely to the province of mental medicine," wrote German physician Wilhelm Griesinger in *Mental Pathology and Therapeutics.* "In fact, whatever certain scientific authorities may assert, we are not warranted in coming to the conclusion that suicide is always a symptom or a result of insanity. There is no insanity present where the feeling of disgust with life is in exact relation to the actual circumstances; where evident moral causes exist which sufficiently account for the act; where the resolution has been deliberately made, and might have been abandoned had the circumstances changed; and in which we discover no other symptom of mental derangement."

The insanity debate had dangerous implications. In nineteenth-century medicine many types of mental illness were believed to be inherited, and some physicians maintained that suicide was the most hereditary type of insanity. Medical texts and histories of the period are studded with examples of intergenerational suicide. "Two cases have occurred, one in Saxony, the other in the Tyrol, in each of which seven brothers hanged themselves one after another," reported one journal in 1891. The mere existence of such cases was accepted as proof that suicide was an inherited trait. "We know, as a fact, that there is no abnormal constitutional state more commonly transmitted from parent to child than this tendency to self-destruction," asserted Samuel Strahan, a respected physician and lawyer, in *Suicide and Insanity,* published in 1893, "and that the major part of the annual increase of suicide, as well as of other degenerate conditions of which we have spoken, is due directly to propagation is absolutely certain." Maintaining that self-preservation is the first law of nature, Strahan declared "the absence of this fundamental instinct . . . is *per se* irrefragable proof of unfitness to live." He cited eleven family trees (many from his own practice) "showing how the offspring of the suicide and his contemporary relatives often sink so low in the scale of vitality that the stock becomes extinct." Pursuing the thought to its ugly conclusion, he wrote, "The practical lesson to be drawn from these family histories is: that the unfit cannot be propagated indefinitely. If the experiment be persisted in, infantile death, sterile idiocy, barrenness and self-destruction will appear and extinguish the stock."

Although the medical profession eventually accepted that suicide is not genetically transmitted, over the course of the nineteenth century a new stigma emerged. "All the superstitious fear of the queer and the mad attached itself to suicide; the instinctive withdrawal of the sane from the tainted extended itself to cases of the calmest and most rational suicide," wrote Henry Fedden in *Suicide.* "Finally, these new medical ideas hardened family prejudice against suicide: a suicide in the family became tantamount to insanity in the family, a stigma not confined to one member, but attaching jointly to the whole group and its descendants." With the birth of the medical approach to suicide, the act of self-destruction was no longer viewed primarily as a sin and a crime but as something abnormal and sick.

While physicians searched for the cause of suicide by examining the body, social scientists searched for it by sifting through statistics. The state had begun keeping track of the number of suicides in the Middle Ages, when the king of England needed to account for his taxpaying citizens. In 1215 the Magna Carta charged "the guardian of the crown's pleas," or coroner, with keeping written records of births and deaths in his area. The coroner was, of course, particularly interested in deaths by murder or suicide, in which case the dead man's property was forfeited to the crown. The coroner's "rolls" were the sole source of such information until 1527, when Bills of Mortality, periodic lists of deaths and their causes, were published in London. Thus, the bill of August 27, 1573, in the parish of St. Botolph Without Aldgate, finds that "Agnis Miller wieff of Jacob Miller who killed selfe with kniff was putt in the ground." Common folk studied the bills for morbid tidbits of gossip, while the wealthy kept an eye on increases in death during times of plague to help decide whether or not it might be prudent to leave the city for a while.

The first attempt to use these bills for anything more scientific was in 1662, when John Graunt, a London tradesman, published his *Observations made upon the Bills of Mortality,* in which he sorted the information into various categories, including cause of death. Thus, Graunt told us that 1,306 died of apoplex, 998 of jaundice, 829 drowned, 279 grief, 243 dead in the streets, 158 of lunatique, 136 vomiting, 86 murthered, 74 of falling sickness, 67 of lethargy, 51 of head-ach, 51 starved, 26 smothered, 22 frighted, 14 poysoned, 7 shot, and 222 hanged themselves, among others. Graunt pointed out that while certain causes of death—plague, spotted fever, measles—claimed a varying toll from year to year, others—"consumption, dropsies, grief, men's making away themselves"—remained fairly constant. Like an oddsmaker he estimated the likelihood of a person dying from a particular cause. "I dare ensure any man at this present, well in his Wits, for one in the thousand, that he shall not die a *Lunatick* in *Bedlam* within these seven years, because I finde not above one in about one thousand five hundred have done so," he wrote. "The like use may be made of the Accompts of men, that made away themselves, who are another sort of Mad-men, that think to ease themselves of pain by leaping into Hell; or else are yet more Mad, so as to think there is no such place; or that men may go to rest by death, though they die in *self-murther,* the greatest Sin."

During the eighteenth century writers tabulated "moral statistics" in an attempt to measure social ills such as crime, divorce, illegitimacy, and suicide. In one of the most ambitious early studies, Brierre de Boismont gathered data on 4,595 French suicides between 1834 and 1842. He also interviewed 265 people who had planned or attempted suicide. While admitting that many suicides were caused by mental illness, de Boismont denied that all suicides were insane. In his list of causes he attributed 652 to mental illness, 530 to alcoholism, 405 to painful or incurable disease, 361 to domestic troubles, 311 to sorrow or disappointment, 306 to disappointed love, 282 to poverty and misery, 237 to ennui, 99 to indolence and want of occupation, and so on. Among the victims de Boismont noted a higher proportion of males, alcoholics, unmarried people, and the elderly. Like many investigators he remarked on the increasing suicide rate, which he attributed to the pressures of urban life. Suicide, he proposed, was a consequence of societal changes that led to disorder and alienation.

This conclusion was shared by the swarm of statistical studies that appeared over the following four decades in France, Germany, Italy, and England, examining the distribution of suicide in relation to age, sex, marital status, occupation, social class, place of residence, education, degree of culture, race, religion, height, skull size, skin color, disease, intemperance, topography, climate, and lunar cycle.

One of the first arguments these studies attempted to settle was that of nationality. Despite the assumption that suicide was "the English malady," the statistical microscope revealed that England had no more suicides than Belgium and far fewer than France. Paris, in fact, had one suicide for every 2,700 people in 1836, compared to London's one in 27,000 during 1834–42. (The purveyor of these statistics, it must be confessed, was an Englishman.) Berlin dwarfed both cities with one suicide for every 750 persons. At the opposite end of the scale, Palermo had only one in 180,000. Summarizing studies of suicide and nationality in his 1881 book, *Suicide and the Meaning of Civilization,* Thomas Masaryk concluded, "The evil frequently appears among the Danes, Germans, French, and Austrians, seldom among the Spaniards, Portuguese, Yugoslavians, Irish, and Scottish, moderately in England, Sweden, Norway, and the United States."

The effect of climate on suicide was a controversial subject. After analyzing dozens of studies, Italian professor of psychological medicine Henry Morselli posited the existence of a suicide belt between 47 and 57 degrees north latitude and between 20 and 40 degrees east longitude. "On this area of about 942,000 square kilomètres are found the people who of all others in the civilized world manifest the greatest inclination to suicide," he wrote. Morselli attributed this inclination to the temperate climate they shared. Another writer agreed, observing that "extremes of heat and cold lessen the prevalence of self-destruction." But others suggested that extremes of temperature increase suicide by adversely affecting the nervous system. Still others believed that the crucial factor was not the temperature but a sudden change in weather. Boudin believed that when the thermometer rises, so does the suicide rate. Fodéré and Duglas identified 22 degrees Réaumur (approx. 82°F) as the boiling point for suicidal despair. Other writers linked fluctuations in suicide to the phases of the moon or to the effect of the west wind—perhaps influenced by the popular superstition that strong winds rose whenever someone hanged himself. Villemair maintained that exactly nine-tenths of suicides occur on rainy or cloudy days; Cabanis asserted that a rainy autumn following a dry summer is particularly conducive to violent death. But the long-held belief that gloomy November was the month of suicide was debunked. Suicide was most frequent in the spring. "Suicide and madness are not influenced so much by the intense heat of the advanced summer season as by the early spring and summer," explained Morselli, "which seize upon the organism not yet acclimatised and still under the influence of the cold season."

The relationship between occupation and suicide was exhaustively scrutinized. "A very low suicide frequency appears among clergymen of all forms of worship; poets, artists, and men of genius are often seized by the tendency to suicide," asserted the author of an early German study. "Crowned heads commit suicide not infrequently; professional beggars almost never." In France, tanners and saddlers were apparently most prone to self-destruction, while a study of Viennese suicides found attorneys at the top of the list. Morselli's study of Italian rates from 1866 to 1876 determined men of science and art to be most suicidal, followed by soldiers, public administrators, and tradespeople; at the lower end of the scale were domestic servants, priests, and nuns. These findings led Morselli to conclude, "Certain it is that in the upper classes of society the act of suicide spreads daily, owing to the direct ratio it has with the increased over use of the brain power."

Nineteenth-century studies left few statistical stones unturned. They tabulated method: "Nationality has a noticeable effect on the choice of means," observed Masaryk. "The French and Romantic peoples, in general, often shoot themselves; the Scandinavians, Germans, and Slavs frequently hang themselves. The Parisians—men—choose drowning more often than shooting. In Italy, men shoot themselves most frequently; women drown themselves; but hanging is less frequent than in all other lands." They explored place of death: A study of Prussian suicides from 1872 to 1875 found that 918 ended their lives in the woods, 639 in rivers, 419 in the streets, 284 in gardens, 220 in jails, 144 in hotels, and 21 in trains, carriages, or ships. They examined height: "The frequency of suicide in the various parts of Italy generally is in a direct ratio with stature," wrote Morselli, "and the inclination to self-destruction increases from south to north as the stature of the Italians gradually increases." They explored time of day, day of the week, and weeks of the month: In 1833, M. A. Guerry reported that of 6,587 cases, suicide was committed most frequently on Monday, least frequently on Sunday, while de Boismont found that a majority of suicides occurred during the day and that the suicide rate was highest during the first ten days of the month. Morselli was at a loss to account for this finding. "From whence this fact proceeds is not clear," he commented, "unless it be that in the first days of each month debauchery, dissipation, orgies, especially in large cities, are more numerous."

While their exuberant statistical explorations were often scattershot, nineteenth-century social statisticians, or "sociologists," as they were now called, uncovered several patterns that remain true today. Although their statistics were admittedly inaccurate (de Boismont estimated that they represented about half the actual incidence), the studies concurred that males kill themselves about three times more frequently than females; that suicide rates rise with age; that single or divorced people are more apt to kill themselves than married people, urban dwellers more often than rural, Protestants more often than Catholics. They learned that suicide occurs more often in spring than in fall and winter, that it declines in time of war and rises in periods of rapid economic change, political crisis, and social instability. And no matter what variations were found from country to country, one thing on which all studies agreed was that the number of suicides was soaring. (At century's end a German priest calculated the total number of nineteenth-century suicides to be more than one and a half million.) Almost all agreed on the cause: "The certainty of the figures and the regularity of the progressive increase of suicide, from the time when statistics were first collected to now," wrote Morselli in 1881, "is such and so great even in respect to countries different in race, religion, and number of inhabitants, that it is not possible to explain it otherwise than as an effect of that universal and complex influence to which we give the name of *civilization.*"

It was clear that society played a role in suicide, but no one knew exactly how. For all the dogged statistical digging, no overarching social theory made sense of the confetti of numbers until the publication of Émile Durkheim's *Le Suicide* in 1897. Durkheim was not primarily concerned with suicide. He was interested in establishing the new discipline of sociology as a science. Like many of his peers, however, he had been struck by the fact that industrialization and economic progress seemed to be accompanied everywhere by a rise in suicide, and the trove of suicide statistics afforded him an ample data base from which to formulate and test his sociological theories.

In *Le Suicide,* Durkheim analyzed European suicide statistics for the last half of the nineteenth century and, like his predecessors, noticed that suicide occurs with varying frequency in different populations. Durkheim then examined the impact of race, heredity, imitation, humidity, and temperature on the suicide rate and concluded that they had little effect. To understand suicide, he said, it was necessary to examine social forces rather than isolated individual motives. Suicide was explicable only by the state of the society to which the individual belonged. While a certain number of suicides were inevitable in every society, some societies were more conducive to self-destruction than others. In societies where social ties were strong, there would be little suicide; where they were weak, there would be more. The more an individual was integrated into social groups—religion, family, community—the less likelihood of suicide.

Durkheim suggested that every suicide could be classified as one of three types—egoistic, altruistic, or anomic—according to its social context. Egoistic suicide occurs when an individual is left to his own resources instead of being well integrated into a social group, whether it be family, religion, or community. This, said Durkheim, helped explain why the rate of suicide by Protestants was higher than that of Catholics although both religions condemn the act. Protestantism, which encourages the spirit of free inquiry and emphasizes free will, may tend to encourage suicide while the traditional, strictly ordered belief system of the Catholic Church offers a more strongly integrated social community. Similarly, the traditional family life of grandparents, parents, and children living under one roof offered stability in a world in which divorce and transience were increasingly prevalent. Thus the suicide rate of unmarried people was higher than that of married people of a similar age. Children offered added protection; the more children in a family, the lower the rate of suicide for the parents. So, too, rural communities offered greater opportunity for social contact than did big, impersonal cities and therefore had lower suicide rates. The egoistic suicide is often the lonely, the unemployed, the single, the divorced person living alone who has no one or nothing to which to belong. One way of belonging, oddly enough, is war. Observing that suicide rates tend to dwindle during wars and other national emergencies, Durkheim reasoned that in times of crisis, society literally rallies round the flag, and personal problems are dwarfed by concern for family and country.

The opposite of egoistic suicide is altruistic suicide, in which an individual is *excessively* integrated into a social group. In some cases society's hold is too strong on certain individuals, who sacrifice their own identities and goals, and even their lives. Such suicides, says Durkheim, result from insufficient individuation. Many Greek and Roman suicides, Indian suttee, and Japanese *seppuku* are examples of altruistic suicides. Durkheim noted that altruistic suicides are more common in primitive societies where under certain circumstances suicide is encouraged (the aging Eskimo who walks off into the snow rather than burden his community), and in rigidly structured groups like the military, where certain suicides have a sacrificial element: the soldier who tosses himself on a grenade to save his platoon. As notions of suicide have changed over time, altruistic suicide is said to have become rare in the Western world, but each culture has its examples. The Eskimo is not unlike Captain Lawrence Oates, who wandered off to die in the Antarctic snow believing his weakness made him a hindrance to Scott's polar expedition; the Hindu woman who throws herself onto her husband's funeral pyre is not unlike the captain who goes down with his ship; the 967 Jews who killed themselves at Masada rather than surrender in A.D. 73 are not unlike the 912 who swallowed cyanide-laced Kool-Aid at Jonestown in 1978; the kamikaze pilots of World War II are not unlike the Palestinian terrorists who served as human bombs in the 1980s. Many people resist thinking of these sacrificial deaths as suicides. But in recent years psychiatrists have pointed out that many "altruistic" suicides are not entirely selfless but arise from a complex tangle of motives that may include the need to give one's death—and life—a higher meaning.

Anomic suicide, Durkheim's third category, occurs when a person's life changes so abruptly that he is unable to cope. Like a man in a dream who finds himself in a strange town, he feels lost, his accustomed way of life seems useless, his normal supports are gone. He is overwhelmed by anomie. The change might be triggered by a death in the family, a painful divorce, a sudden financial reverse, or even unexpected wealth. Or it might be provoked by a more general disturbance—a plague, a decline in religious beliefs, or a stock market crash—that jars a society's equilibrium. At these times an entire society may experience anomie. Thus, suicides increased when the Black Death disrupted the stability of the Middle Ages, just as centuries later the U.S. suicide rate peaked during the Great Depression. Durkheim demonstrated a correlation between the economy and suicide, which rises steeply during a depression—as well as during a boom. At these times the wealthy were more likely to turn to suicide than the poor. "Lack of power, compelling moderation, accustoms men to it. . . . Wealth, on the other hand, by the power it bestows, deceives us into believing that we depend on ourselves only. . . . The less limited one feels, the more intolerable all limitation appears."

Le Suicide was a landmark book not only for establishing the field of sociology but for marking the beginning of the modern study of suicide. It offered the first comprehensive sociological theory of suicidal behavior—that "suicide varies inversely with the degree of integration of the social groups of which the individual forms a part." Since its publication in 1897 (an English translation did not appear until 1951) *Le Suicide* has been analyzed, refined, and criticized. Subsequent sociologists have challenged Durkheim's conclusions as being based on unreliable data. They have pointed out exceptions to his general rules—Catholic Austria, for instance, has long had one of the highest suicide rates in the world. Studies using more advanced statistical techniques have found that suicide may be as common among the poor as among the rich. Other studies have found high rates of suicide in rural areas. Still other critics assert that Durkheim's typology is too broad and that the distinction between anomic and egoistic suicide is often blurred. (Durkheim admitted that egoism, anomie, and altruism "are very often combined with one another, giving rise to composite varieties; characteristics of several types will be united in a single suicide.") But no one has ever seriously challenged Durkheim's basic theory, and his work has served as the foundation for all subsequent sociological investigations.

While *Le Suicide* was a milestone in the study of suicide, it did not explain why some people who were Protestant, widowed, or divorced killed themselves when most did not. Durkheim's belief that "social facts must be studied as things, that is, as realities external to the individual," made the psychology of the individual suicide virtually irrelevant to his theory. Without a psychological understanding of suicide, however, the work of Durkheim and his predecessors was incomplete. "When we learn that the most densely populated parts of the world have the highest incidence of suicide, and that suicides cluster in certain months of the year, do we thereby learn a single adequate, explanatory motive?" asked psychoanalyst Alfred Adler in 1910. "No, we learn only that the phenomenon of suicide is also subject to the law of great numbers, and that it is related to other social phenomena. Suicide can be understood only individually, even if it has social preconditions and social consequences."

Adler was speaking at the Vienna Psychoanalytic Society's special session on suicide in children, thirteen years after the publication of Durkheim's masterpiece. The focus of the discussion in Freud's living room was light years away from the social determinism of Durkheim and his disciples. The talk was not of religious affiliation, marital status, or amount of annual rainfall but of revenge, inferiority, and sexual repression. Each analyst explained suicide according to his own theoretical perspective. Adler emphasized the strength of the aggressive drive and the desire of the suicidal person to inflict pain on surviving relatives. "Thus the unconscious creates a situation in which sickness, even death, is desired," he said, "partly in order to hurt the relatives, and partly to show them what they have lost in the one they have always slighted." Isidor Sadger asserted that "the decisive factor here is erotic. . . . The only person who puts an end to his life is one who has been compelled to give up all hope of love." The psychoanalyst Wilhelm Stekel emphasized the role of aggression and murderous impulses. "No one kills himself who has never wanted to kill another, or at least wished the death of another."

Freud's input that evening was limited to a few general remarks. Although his theories of depression and aggression would provide the framework for a psychoanalytic understanding of suicide, he never developed a comprehensive theory of suicide or wrote about it as a subject in itself. Freud brought the 1910 meeting to a close by urging, "Let us suspend our judgment till experience has solved this problem." And yet, as psychiatrist Robert Litman has pointed out in his paper *Sigmund Freud on Suicide,* the fifty-three-year-old Freud had had ample experience—both clinical and personal—with suicide. In 1883, Freud wrote his fiancée, Martha Bernays, about the suicide of a friend, a young doctor named Nathan Weiss, who hanged himself shortly after an ill-advised marriage. In 1885, a year before their stormy four-year courtship ended in marriage, Freud alluded to suicide in a letter to Martha: "I have long since resolved on a decision, the thought of which is in no way painful, in the event of my losing you. That we should lose each other by parting is quite out of the question. . . . You have no idea how fond I am of you, and I hope I shall never have to show it." The twenty-nine-year-old Freud, like some lovesick teenager, exemplified an observation he would make many years later in a discussion of melancholia: "In the two opposed situations of being most intensely in love and of suicide the ego is overwhelmed by the object, though in totally different ways." Although Freud suffered periods of depression throughout his life, this was the only time he is believed to have mentioned suicidal thoughts of his own.

Freud's case histories contain numerous descriptions of suicidal behavior. The only sister of the patient known as the Wolf Man committed suicide by poisoning. Plagued by hallucinations, the paranoid Dr. Schreber made frequent attempts to drown himself in his bath. The eighteen-year-old patient known as Dora forced her parents into obtaining treatment for her by leaving a letter threatening suicide in a place where they were sure to find it. Freud noted the attention-getting aspects of her act, and in analysis, when Dora spoke of her father's suicidal threats, Freud commented on the significance of the suicidal child's identification with the suicidal parent. In 1898 a patient of Freud's killed himself. "A patient over whom I had taken a great deal of trouble had put an end to his life on account of an incurable sexual disorder," he wrote in *The Psychopathology of Everyday Life,* in which he described his own unconscious efforts to repress the memory of the suicide.

In *Totem and Taboo* (1913), Freud returned to a consideration of the murderous component in suicide. "We find that impulses to suicide in a neurotic turn out regularly to be self-punishments for wishes for someone else's death," he wrote. In *Mourning and Melancholia* (1915), Freud restated his belief that murderous impulses turned inward could lead to suicide, but how did the mechanism work? Freud had based his work on his conviction that human behavior is ultimately shaped by instinctual drives. At the time of the meeting he believed that these drives were libido and self-preservation. How did suicide satisfy these drives? How could the ego consent to its own destruction?

Freud suggested that in both mourning and its pathological cousin, melancholia, when an object of love is lost, the ego re-creates an image of the loved one inside the self. Thus, the lost love object lives on in the ego in what Freud compared to a shadow. This identification or "shadow" is not fully integrated into the personality, thereby enabling part of the ego to "split off" and observe the rest. In this "ego splitting" a part of the ego may sit in judgment on the rest of the ego, criticizing it, attacking it, even condemning it to death. Suicide is the ultimate expression of this dynamic. In other words suicide originates in the wish to kill someone whom the suicide has loved or identified with; because he cannot kill this person, he "kills" him by destroying the internalized image of him. Psychologically, suicide is thus a kind of inverted murder or, as psychologist Edwin Shneidman has put it, "murder in the 180th degree."

At the time he wrote *Mourning and Melancholia,* Freud believed that all aggression had a sexual origin. In 1920 he proposed the existence of another basic instinct. "After long hesitancies and vacillations we have decided to assume the existence of only two basic instincts, *Eros* and *the destructive instinct,*" he later wrote. "The aim of the first of these basic instincts is to establish ever greater unities and to preserve them thus—in short, to bind together; the aim of the second is, on the contrary, to undo connections and so to destroy things. In the case of the destructive instinct we may suppose that its final aim is to lead what is living into an inorganic state. For this reason we also call it the *death instinct.*" Most aspects of human behavior, Freud believed, could be understood as the product of the struggle between the sexual drive and the death instinct, Eros and Thanatos, love and hate.

While Freud's primary purpose in proposing the death instinct was to explain the phenomenon of masochism, it also provided an explanation for suicide. While the death instinct exists in everybody, Freud said, in suicidal people it prevails over their instincts for love and life. "We find that the excessively strong super-ego which has obtained a hold upon consciousness rages against the ego with merciless violence," he wrote in *The Ego and the Id.* "What is now holding sway in the super-ego is, as it were, a pure culture of the death instinct, and in fact it often enough succeeds in driving the ego into death." Ten years after adjourning the Vienna Psychoanalytic Society's special session on suicide, Freud had devised a theory which, in part, suggested that every death is, to an extent, psychological self-murder.

VII

THE TWENTIETH
CENTURY: FAITH,
HOPELESSNESS,
AND 5HIAA

IN HIS 1895 ADDRESS to the Harvard Young Men's Christian Association on "Is Life Worth Living?" the philosopher William James concluded that suicide was a "religious disease," the antidote for which is "religious faith." In his lecture, which outlined the arguments one might use in reasoning "with a fellow-mortal who is on such terms with life that the only comfort left him is to brood on the assurance 'You may end it when you will,' " James emphasized the benefits of hard work and religion. "Too much questioning and too little active responsibility lead, almost as often as too much sensualism does, to the edge of the slope, at the bottom of which lie pessimism and the nightmare or suicidal view of life," he said. James, who had suffered from suicidal depression as a young man, concluded with the challenge, "Be not afraid of life. Believe that life *is* worth living, and your belief will help create the fact."

Eighty-seven years later, at the fifteenth annual meeting of the American Association of Suicidology, there was a workshop on "Suicide: The Challenge to the Clergy." The panel consisted of an articulate young rabbi, a middle-aged Catholic priest, and a quiet, white-haired Episcopal minister. Each gave a short presentation on how his faith had viewed suicide throughout history. Afterward, the question-and-answer session evolved into a discussion of whether suicide was a sin. "None of us is willing to label it a sin or a crime," said the rabbi, pointing out that in Jewish law only people who kill themselves "calmly and with clear resolve" are considered suicides, a diagnosis that allows all the others to be buried. The three clergymen agreed that if people who took their own lives were declared mentally ill, they were not suicides and therefore could be buried. "An enlightened point of view," murmured the minister.

Several people in the audience, however, questioned the necessity of declaring a person mentally ill in order to bury him. The priest responded that "the thinking is basically for someone to act *that* contrary to the drive of life, they must be crazy." There was a murmur of discomfort in the audience, which grew when he added, "Even with the terminally ill suicides, deep down you'll find disturbance in makeup of personality." A college chaplain in the audience maintained that some of the suicides he'd known had made calm, rational decisions. The priest replied quickly, "I don't think anybody who is perfectly normal will commit suicide." The Episcopal minister, sensing contention, pointed out that the presumption that a suicidal person is not in his right mind is born of compassion. But the debate continued for ten minutes. The priest became increasingly insistent. "I don't know of anybody who has committed suicide that wasn't a schizophrenic," he said. A voice from the back shouted, "I don't think it has anything to do with insanity." The priest's face reddened. "I'm making a judgment and you're making a judgment," he said, his voice digging in, "but my judgment is backed by empirical evidence." The voice in the back replied softly, "My judgment is backed by personal experience. It happened in my family."

The priest's insistence on describing suicide as proof of mental illness was unsettling; were he not wearing his clerical collar, he could have been mistaken for any of the psychiatrists presenting papers at the convention. But his stance was a reflection of how much the theological discussion of suicide has changed since William James described it as a "religious disease," and its cure "religious faith." In the twentieth century suicide has been seen not as a moral, ethical, or theological issue but almost entirely as a medical-psychological problem. "Have we a right to commit suicide? Is it selfish to kill one's self? Is suicide cowardly or courageous?" asked psychiatrist Gregory Zilboorg as early as 1937. "It is almost too obvious to say that whatever drawing-room or academic philosophical interest these questions may have, a scientific study of suicide must disregard them and their possible answers." Thirty years later an editorial in the *Journal of the American Medical Association* asserted, "The contemporary physician sees suicide as a manifestation of emotional illness. Rarely does he view it in a context other than that of psychiatry." The entry on suicide in the *Encyclopaedia of Religion and Ethics* notes, "Perhaps the greatest contribution of modern times to the rational treatment of the matter is the consideration . . . that many suicides are non-moral and entirely the affair of the specialist in mental diseases."

With this "rational treatment" antisuicide laws were finally erased. If suicide was the product of psychological disturbance, punishment was obviously inappropriate. In England, although a statute prohibiting burial of suicides in the highway was passed in 1823, confiscation of property was not abolished until 1870 and attempted suicide was punishable by up to two years in prison well into the twentieth century. When attempters regained consciousness in the hospital, they usually found a policeman at their bedside, waiting to interview them. Until World War I suicide attempters were often sent to prison, particularly after a second or third attempt. The sentence was considered to be, as one prosecutor observed, "in the interests of the defendant's health"—behind bars he might be prevented from trying again. By the 1950s prosecution and imprisonment were rare "unless there is some outstanding feature only a prosecution might cure, or if there have been repeated attempts at self-destruction," as Lilian Wyles explained in her 1952 book, *A Woman at Scotland Yard.* "A severe lecture on their stupidity is mostly delivered to the offenders by a senior officer." In 1955, of 5,220 attempted suicides known to the police, only 535 came to trial. Most of these were discharged, fined, or placed on probation. Forty-three were sentenced to prison, the majority for less than six months. In 1961, under pressure from doctors, lawyers, and clergymen, the Suicide Act was passed, abolishing the law that made suicide a crime and attempted suicide a misdemeanor. Shortly afterward London's Ministry of Health declared that attempted suicide was to be regarded as a medical and social problem, and cases were to be referred to a psychiatrist. In the United States only Texas and Oklahoma retain laws against attempted suicide, and these have not been enforced for many years.

With the "medicalization of suicide," as it has been called, other approaches have faded into the background. Like the priest on the AAS panel, many clergymen talk of suicide in terms of prevention, warning signs, and mental health. A few, however, have felt that the increasing attention to psychological factors has created too much sympathy toward suicide. "It is high time for the pulpit and religious press to emphasize strongly the wickedness of suicide," wrote Bishop Oldham in 1932. ". . . The warranted revolt from the barbarous practise of former centuries, whereby those who took their own lives were buried at a crossroads at midnight, and a stake driven through their bodies, has resulted in a weak sentimentality, and we have ceased to express and, perhaps, to feel the horror we ought." But the fierce moral debate that dominated the discussion of suicide for centuries has quieted. The handful of twentieth-century theologians who have written on suicide plow familiar ground—duty to God, state, and family—although most tend to emphasize the spiritual value of suffering rather than the sin of suicide. "At bottom, all the reasons leading to suicide can be reduced to one—namely suffering," wrote French philosopher Léon Meynard. "Disease, failure, misery, death are but some of the expressions, among many others, of the basic evil." Suicide, he said, represented a stubborn refusal to submit to suffering in the name of God. Meynard concluded, "The existence of God is the supreme argument against the legitimacy of suicide."

Suicide remains a sin in Roman Catholic canonical law. "Intentionally causing one's own death, or suicide, is therefore equally as wrong as murder; such an action on the part of a person is to be considered as a rejection of God's sovereignty and loving plan," reiterated the Vatican's 1980 Declaration on Euthanasia. "Furthermore, suicide is also often a refusal of love for self, the denial of the natural instinct to live, a flight from the duties of justice and charity owed to one's neighbour, to various communities or to the whole of society—although, as is generally recognized, at times there are psychological factors present that can diminish responsibility or even completely remove it." Except for the last phrase, the declaration essentially echoes the words of St. Augustine fifteen centuries earlier. But the verdict of insanity that is still invoked to ensure suicides a Christian burial now seems a firm belief rather than merely a tender mercy. And even that verdict is not always sufficient. A few members of the clergy still refuse to officiate at funeral services for a suicide, and as late as 1969 in Chicago a pregnant woman who killed herself was denied full religious rites.

The discussion of suicide as an ethical issue has been increasingly muted. "There is but one truly serious philosophical problem, and that is suicide," began Camus's *The Myth of Sisyphus,* published in 1940. "Judging whether life is or is not worth living amounts to answering the fundamental question of philosophy." Apparently, few agree. In a 2,100-item bibliography on suicide covering the years 1897 to 1957, only twenty-five entries were listed under the category "Religious–Philosophical." The rest were psychological, sociological, or medical titles.

But the sociological study of suicide has also been eclipsed by the medical perspective. Although hundreds of studies have been published since Durkheim's *Le Suicide,* the majority of them are reformulations of Durkheim's work. In a variation on his theme of anomie, for example, Andrew Henry and James Short examined fluctuations in rates and concluded that people who are deeply involved with others are at low risk for suicide while people who are isolated from meaningful relationships are at high risk. Sociologists Jack Gibbs and Walter Martin refined Durkheim's concept of "social integration" into what they called "status integration." Every individual, they said, belonged to several categories in which he played a clearly defined role. For instance, a man might belong to these statuses: male, black, plumber, married, and parent. The more frequently a person's combination of statuses conformed to the combination common in the population to which he belonged, the higher his "status integration"—and the lower his chances of suicide. Departing from Durkheim, Jack Douglas, in *The Social Meanings of Suicide,* questioned the accuracy of suicide statistics, pointing out that suicide has many different definitions and meanings, and insisted that rather than sift through statistics to find those meanings, we try to "determine the meanings to the people actually involved."

The main avenue of study has been psychological. After Freud's exploration of the unconscious, it was no longer possible to attribute suicide to simple causes such as poverty, loss of a job, or disappointment in love. The act of suicide was instead understood to be the end result of a complex variety of forces, conscious and unconscious. In *Man Against Himself* psychoanalyst Karl Menninger offered an illustration:

> A wealthy man is one day announced as having killed himself. It is discovered that his investments have failed, but that his death provides bountiful insurance for his otherwise destitute family. The problem and its solution, then, seem simple and obvious enough. A man has bravely faced ruin in a way that benefits his dependents.
>
> But why should we begin our interpretations only at this late point in such a man's life, the point at which he loses his wealth? Shall we not seek to discover how it came about that he lost it? And even more pertinently, shall we not inquire how he made it, why he was so driven to amass money and what means he used to gratify his compulsion, what unconscious and perhaps also conscious guilt feelings were associated with it and with the sacrifices and penalties its acquisition cost him and his family? And even those who have money and lose it do not in the vast majority of cases kill themselves, so we still do not know what this man's deeper motives were for this particular act. All we can really see from such a case is how difficult and complex the problem becomes as soon as we take more than a superficial glance at the circumstances.

As for the "deeper motives," different theorists have emphasized different components. In *Man Against Himself,* Menninger catalogued a multitude of self-destructive activities from "chronic" or "partial" suicides such as alcoholism, asceticism, and antisocial behavior, to "focal suicides"—self-mutilation and purposive accidents. He interpreted all of these as expressions of the death instinct described by Freud. Menninger believed that three elements must be present in order for someone to express the most extreme self-destructive behavior by committing suicide: the wish to kill, the wish to be killed, and the wish to die.

Freud's "death instinct" has not been widely accepted by psychiatrists, however, and as an explanation for suicide it is so broad as to be virtually useless. "To say that the death instinct gains the upper hand over the life instinct," observed Zilboorg, "is merely an elaborate way of stating that man does die or kill himself." Freud's formulation of depression, on the other hand, has become the basis for the psychoanalytic understanding of suicide, with the result that subsequent therapists—in the attempt to cast suicide as inverted murder—have underestimated other possible factors: grief, love, fear, hopelessness, rigid thinking, frustration, low self-esteem, magical belief in immortality, desire for reunion with a lost loved one. Even Zilboorg conceded that suicides combine a strong unconscious hostility with an unusual inability to love others.

Trying to reduce all suicides to a psychological common denominator has provided some farfetched results. Psychiatrist Maurice Farber concocted a mathematical formula describing the likelihood of suicide for a given person, in which DEC represents Demands for the Exercising of Competence, DIG represents Demands for Interpersonal Giving, TS is Tolerance of Suicide, Su is Availability of Succorance, and HFT is Degree of Hope in the Future Time Perspective of the Society:

$$S = f\left(\frac{DEC,\ DIG,\ TS}{Su,\ HFT}\right)$$

Despite such painstaking logic, suicide remains an enigma. At a conference in 1984 Karl Menninger, who spent his life studying the subject, confessed, "It's a durn mystery, you know, in spite of all we've written about it."

One of the newest and most promising directions in the study of suicide is the physiological. It has long been known that suicide tends to "run in families." During the past twenty-five years researchers have used adoption and twin studies in order to separate and analyze the contributions of nature and nurture to psychiatric illness. They have found genetic contributions to schizophrenia, alcoholism, and major mood disorders including manic depression, all of which are associated with increased suicide risk. (It is estimated that more than three-fourths of suicides are by people who suffer from affective disorders and/or alcoholism.)

Researchers are also looking for a unique biological component of suicidal behavior. By 1983 eighteen case studies had been reported on twin suicides. All the suicides were committed by identical twins; there were no fraternal-twin suicides. Extensive adoption studies in Denmark have shown a greater incidence of suicide in the biological relatives of suicides than in the adoptee relatives. They also found that these suicides were largely independent of the presence of psychiatric disorder, leading researchers to conclude that there may be a genetic factor in suicide independent of, or in addition to, the genetic transmission of a psychiatric disorder. Tentative support for this hypothesis came from a 1985 study of the Amish people of southeastern Pennsylvania. The Amish are ideal subjects for suicide research: Alcoholism, divorce, violence, and a solitary old age, all of which are factors that have been linked to suicide, are virtually unknown among a people who live in close-knit communities governed by a strict moral code. Suicide itself is still referred to as "that awful deed" or "the abominable sin." Janice Egeland, a medical sociologist from the University of Miami, found that there were twenty-six suicides among the Amish in the last one hundred years. Retrospective studies suggested that twenty-four of them would have been diagnosed with an affective disorder (depression or manic depression). All but seven of the suicides were distributed over four family lines. Again, however, it is not conclusive whether the genetic predisposition was for a psychiatric disorder or for suicidal behavior itself; those families with the most serious cases of depression were not necessarily those with the suicides.

Since the discovery in the 1950s of drugs that could alleviate certain symptoms of mental illness, many disorders that until recently were regarded as purely psychological are now thought to be caused by chemical imbalances. Extensive research has been done on the biochemistry of depression, much of it focused on neurotransmitters, molecules that carry chemical messages between neurons in the brain, affecting how people think and feel. When something goes wrong in this communication system, certain forms of depression may occur.

One of the leading researchers studying the biochemistry of depression is a Swedish psychiatrist named Marie Asberg. In the early 1970s Asberg and her associates at Karolinska Hospital in Stockholm were searching for chemical markers in the cerebrospinal fluid—the liquid that bathes the brain and spinal cord—of severely depressed patients. By identifying some of the markers they hoped to help describe some of the subgroups of depression. One thing they found was that about one-third of the sixty-eight patients in the study had especially low levels of a chemical called 5-hydroxyindoleacetic acid, or 5HIAA for short. This is a metabolite, or "breakdown product," of serotonin, one of the more than twenty kinds of neurotransmitters.

In June 1975, Asberg's research team learned that one of the depressed patients in the study had committed suicide by taking an overdose of his antidepressant medication. When told the news, one psychiatrist remarked, "All these low 5HIAA patients kill themselves." She explained that not only had this man had a low level of 5HIAA in his cerebrospinal fluid but so had another recent suicide, a woman who had drowned herself in a lake. When Asberg checked the case records, she found low 5HIAA among more than two-thirds of those who had attempted or committed suicide. Furthermore, many of the low 5HIAA suicides had chosen violent methods.

Asberg organized a study of forty-six suicide attempters, sixteen of whom suffered from severe depression, the rest from a variety of mental illnesses. Although some had normal levels of 5HIAA in their spinal fluid, the group as a whole had an abnormally low level—an average of 3.5 nanograms (a nanogram is one billionth of a gram) per milliliter less than the forty-five healthy volunteers in the control group. Within one year, six people in the study had committed suicide. All of them belonged to the low 5HIAA group.

The link between low 5HIAA and suicide has been confirmed by other studies. Whether patients suffered from depression, schizophrenia, alcoholism, or personality disorders, low 5HIAA seemed to be a common denominator in those who had made suicide attempts as well as in other forms of impulsive aggression and violence. Comparing the brains of suicides to the brains of those who died in homicides or violent accidents, researchers at Wayne State University and at NIMH independently found further evidence that some suicides may be influenced by a brain chemical abnormality. In both studies the suicides had been receiving imipramine, an antidepressant that, to be effective, must bind to certain chemical sites in the brain. The WSU study found that the brains of the suicides had 44 percent fewer imipramine binding sites than those of the control group. (The NIMH study found 30 to 40 percent fewer binding sites.) Imipramine binding activity, in turn, is believed to reflect the brain's ability to metabolize serotonin.

While a clear relationship between low serotonin and suicide exists, it is not known whether the low levels are a cause or an effect of depression or impulsiveness. Furthermore, the results may apply to only a small segment of the population at risk for suicide—those with histories of impulsive, aggressive behavior. The evidence is not clear regarding people who commit suicide deliberately using less violent means. A few studies have found no evidence linking serotonin levels and suicidal behavior of any sort.

However incomplete the evidence, "the biology of suicide" clearly holds great possibilities for prevention. Measuring levels of 5HIAA in the spinal fluid might indicate who is especially vulnerable to suicide. But suicide is a statistically rare event. Only about ten in ten thousand people try suicide, and the number who would have to be tested in order to screen out the few who might attempt it is enormous. In addition, the present method of measuring 5HIAA requires a painful, expensive, and time-consuming spinal tap. There is hope, however, that a drug might be developed to increase serotonin levels. At Wayne State University ten patients are taking fenfluramine, a chemical relative of amphetamine that affects serotonin activity. While researchers have found a preliminary decrease in self-destructive thoughts and behavior, conclusive evidence is a long way off.

Some suicide experts worry that the biologically oriented researchers slight the social, psychological, and philosophical elements of suicide. "Reducing suicide to a biological basis is to ignore the psychological pain which drives it," psychologist Edwin Shneidman has said. "There can be no pill that salves the human malaise that leads to suicide." The biologists reiterate that physiological characteristics do not *determine* suicidal behavior; they merely make some individuals more susceptible to impulsive, aggressive, and possibly suicidal behavior. Whether those impulses are acted on depends on a variety of social and psychological factors. "Suicide is a three-dimensional problem involving psychology, sociology, and biology," says Herman van Praag, chairman of the department of psychiatry at the Albert Einstein College of Medicine in New York City, who has conducted extensive research linking low

5HIAA to severe depression and suicidal behavior. "All three are important and continuously interacting. Biology is not the sole answer. Biochemistry, for instance, cannot explain why Rembrandt is a great artist. It might explain the colors and materials he uses. It's the same with suicide. To find out why someone is depressed it's very important to look at biology. But given a state of increased suicidality, the reasons why one picks up a gun, another takes a pill, and another suppresses the intention are very much caused by that person's personality and what kind of environment he lives in. The exploration of suicide must be three-dimensional."

Several years ago I attended a conference for suicidologists in San Francisco. Susan Blumenthal, a psychiatrist and then-director of the Suicide Research Unit at NIMH, was presenting a slide show to give "an overview of our knowledge base" about adolescent suicide. Because of time restrictions she had been asked to squeeze a presentation for which she usually allotted forty-five minutes into a fifteen-minute slot. Blumenthal spoke briskly about biochemical research—chemical markers, affective disorders, Marie Asberg's studies, low 5HIAA, as colorful slides crammed with data flashed across the screen, often so quickly that the audience was able to focus only briefly on a yellow bar here, a group of red dots there.

The slides flashed faster and faster until they seemed to blur like a kaleidoscope, while Blumenthal struggled to keep up, rattling off statistics as a baseball fan recites batting averages. I was able to decipher only scraps of her commentary: "Males would be the straight line . . . Six times greater incidence in the biological relatives of adopted young people . . . By no means would I suggest that all suicides are genetic. . . . People who have this finding are at twenty times greater risk of killing themselves . . . The squares are the violent suicides and the circles are the suicide attempts by poisoning . . ." As I watched this hectic *son et lumière,* I suddenly realized I had nearly forgotten that we were talking about human beings. And I thought of Justin Spoonhour and Brian Hart, of Cato and Hamlet, of Richard and Bridget Smith. I thought of the ancient Egyptian trying to convince his *ba* to accompany him into death, which lay before him "like the fragrance of myrrh / Like sitting under sail on breeze day." And I wondered with some discomfort at the possibility that their answers to the question of to be or not to be might all boil down to a matter of 3.5 nanograms of 5-hydroxyindoleacetic acid.

3

THE RANGE OF SELF-DESTRUCTIVE BEHAVIOR

—◆—

I

WINNER AND LOSER

Whenever Richard Cory went down town,
We people on the pavement looked at him:
He was a gentleman from sole to crown,
Clean favored, and imperially slim.

And he was always quietly arrayed,
And he was always human when he talked;
But still he fluttered pulses when he said,
'Good-morning,' and he glittered when he walked.

And he was rich—yes, richer than a king—
And admirably schooled in every grace:
In fine, we thought that he was everything
To make us wish that we were in his place.

So on we worked, and waited for the light,
And went without the meat, and cursed the bread;
And Richard Cory, one calm summer night,
Went home and put a bullet through his head.

LIKE RICHARD CORY, the subject of the Edwin Arlington Robinson
poem, Peter Newell seemed to lead an enviable life. At fifty-four he was a

handsome man with a full head of graying hair and a beard. He was a skier, golfer, and sailor. He held a well-paying job with a major corporation. He had two healthy and loving daughters and a two-year-old grandson. Amicably divorced for five years, he was living with an intelligent, attractive woman whom he planned to marry. One Sunday evening, however, Peter sat down in his favorite chair, placed a gun in his mouth, and pulled the trigger. On his desk he left a note, in his careful, boyish hand:

> The world is composed of winners and losers. The winners get stronger and the losers get weaker. As the winners get stronger, the losers just shine their shoes, load their dishwashers, and walk the dog for them. . . . It's innate, it's inborn. It'll never change, ever. Well, right on, winners, go ahead. But here's one loser you won't have to kick around anymore. I'm going to stop right now!

The disbelief that follows almost every suicide was especially pronounced after the death of Peter Newell. The word used most often to describe him was "gentleman." He had a firm moral sense—what a colleague at his funeral referred to as "the Quaker-like principles that dominated his life." Suicide seemed the antithesis of these principles. Peter was also a truly "gentle" man who could not bear to argue or fight. It was difficult to believe that such a meticulous and considerate person had chosen such a violent way to die. Several people close to him, in fact, insisted that his death must have been a murder and, even after they saw his suicide note, were convinced he had been forced to write it.

Peter had grown up in New Jersey and Connecticut, the second son of well-to-do parents who, he felt, considered him an unexciting "good little boy" as compared to his brilliant and difficult older brother. His father died when he was thirteen. Adolescence was an uncomfortable time for Peter. He was chubby and uncoordinated, and he often preferred to stay alone in his room at prep school, listening to music and thinking melancholy thoughts instead of socializing with his classmates. At Yale, he was on the verge of flunking out when he enlisted in the Navy. This, too, was a disappointment. It was the height of World War II, and Peter dreamed of being a fighter pilot, but he was such a fine aviator that the Navy felt he was more valuable as an instructor, and he was sent to Texas to teach cadets how to fly. What should have been a high compliment was a crushing blow.

Peter was still in the Navy when he married Barbara Spires, whom he had met on the beach in the Connecticut town where her family spent the summers. They had felt an immediate attraction, and Peter asked her out. She was a student at Smith College and he was in the service, so much of their courtship was carried out by letter. They married after Barbara's graduation in 1945 and lived in Texas until Peter was discharged from the service. He then returned to Yale on probation, where they lived with other married vets in Quonset huts close to campus. He graduated in 1948 with a degree in mechanical engineering. Like so many young postwar couples, they settled down to raise a family in the suburbs.

Outwardly, their early years in Darien, Connecticut, seemed an American idyll. They lived in a comfortable house with a half-acre yard in a quiet upper-middle-class neighborhood. Peter commuted to nearby Stamford where he worked as a graphic engineer for Time Inc., while Barbara settled into her role as housewife and mother. Peter was a playful, affectionate father to their two daughters. At the beach he splashed for hours in the water with his children and later was a patient swimming teacher. His younger daughter remembers how each time she washed her hair, her father would sniff her head and tell her how good she smelled. A gifted carpenter and handyman, Peter loved to work around the house, and as his daughters watched him painstakingly rebuilding a boat, remodeling the den, or taking apart the engine of his MG, they were proud of their father's skill.

Two years after the birth of their eldest child, Ruth, another daughter, Kathy, was born severely retarded and deaf. Peter was devastated. Once when Kathy was very sick and crying uncontrollably, Barbara sat in one room praying for her to live, and Peter sat in another room praying for her to die. When Sally was born, Peter and his wife felt that they could not handle all three children, so when Kathy was five, her father drove her to an institution near Hartford. Peter brought Kathy home for the holidays, but she would pull out all the pots and pans and books, and scream all night long. After a few years they no longer brought her home. Although Barbara continued to visit her occasionally, Peter refused. "Having a retarded child hit him fifty times harder than it did my mother," says Sally, "because he had this thing about failure—he just couldn't tolerate it—and I think he saw this as a failure on his part."

Although his daughter certainly needed help, institutionalizing her was consistent with Peter's character. He preferred things to be as neat and controlled as an engineering problem. "We were not an emotional family," says Sally. "There wasn't much hugging and kissing, and crying was done in private. My father never wanted to hear negative things. If I came to him upset by something at school, he'd never sympathize with me, he'd always wonder if it was my fault and say, 'Can't you stop complaining?' " Peter himself rarely complained; he seemed to assume that any mishap was his fault. Nevertheless, what mistakes he made, he preferred to hide. "He would never tell us about his failures," says Sally. "It would have been such a comfort if he had, especially when I started having problems at school. He was always on time, always prepared, always conscientious. He was the paragon, the brain, and we could *never* live up to him." Not until she was in her twenties did Sally find out from her mother that her father had had troubles in school himself, that he had, in fact, nearly flunked out of Yale.

One of the things Peter hid from his children was the growing tension in his marriage. He and Barbara had not known each other well before marrying. Gradually, they learned that they had little in common. Peter was active and athletic; his wife was uninterested in sports. On one of their first sailing trips, she got sick and asked to be taken ashore, and never went sailing again. He loved music of all kinds—jazz, classical, Broadway—and spent much of his time in the basement playing the harmonica or listening to records as he worked. She had little feeling for music. He loved to work outdoors; she spent much of her time indoors, reading. Their marriage roles divided along traditional lines. He handled the outdoor work; she handled the children. He handled the bills; she handled the cooking. He liked a clean house; she tended to be a little sloppy. He believed in disciplining the children; she was more permissive. He was acutely sensitive and occasionally depressed; she had little tolerance for his melancholic moods, and when she found him lying on the living-room floor, listening to sad music, just as he had as an adolescent, she would tell him with annoyance to get up.

This tension, however, was kept under wraps. "I never saw my parents fight," says Sally. "I always thought they deliberately postponed arguments until we were asleep." Although they presented a smooth facade to the outside world, their marriage deteriorated to the point where they were staying together only for the sake of their children. Although Ruth was a quiet, well-mannered girl, Sally was as wild and anarchic as her father was orderly and scrupulous. She had never done well in her studies, and in high school she was in danger of flunking out. She skipped classes and sneaked out of the house at night to go to parties, driving with her friends across the border to New York where the drinking age was lower. She also got heavily involved with drugs. At various times Sally was arrested for possession of marijuana, for shoplifting, and for criminal trespassing in a church.

At first her father set curfews, devised elaborate reward systems based on her grades, picked her up at the police station, and paid her fines. He sent her to a psychiatrist, but Sally was sullen and resistant, and after six months she stopped going. When Peter forbade her to drive his car, she took her mother's and immediately had an accident. He grounded her, but she would sneak out through her bedroom window. He lost his temper with her; she would scream right back. The more he tried to control her, the more out of control she became. It was the suburban parents' nightmare, and Peter felt he was a failure as a father. "I don't think he ever imagined something like this could happen," says Sally. "He had mapped out his life, and this didn't fit in." When Sally turned seventeen, Peter seemed to give up. From then on she came and went as she pleased. When she ate meals with her parents, the air was thick with tension. "Once, my father had to pick me up at the station after the police had brought me in, thinking I was a runaway," says Sally. "When he walked in, he looked like a beaten man." One evening Sally passed by her parents' bedroom and saw her father weeping, his head down on the dresser. It was the first time she had ever seen him cry. But communication between them had broken down long ago, and she just walked by.

Peter's younger daughter was not the only source of pain in his life. That year, Time Inc. closed its Connecticut lab. Although he was told the company would find a good position for him in its New York office, Peter was devastated. His wife remembers him coming home every night and crying. He became increasingly depressed, and this put even more strain on their marriage. Although Peter and Barbara had planned to stay together until Sally finished high school, even that now seemed ludicrous, since she had dropped out of school. In 1972, when Sally was eighteen, they divorced. In keeping with his lifelong feelings of guilt and responsibility, Peter asked for so little in the settlement that the lawyer they shared had to urge him to take more. Barbara kept the house and most of their possessions; Peter moved into a nondescript one-bedroom apartment in a modern high-rise in downtown Stamford.

The next few years were a period of change for Peter, in which he seemed to loosen up somewhat. He began to wear brightly striped shirts and jeans instead of white button-downs and tailored slacks. He bought a motorcycle and could be seen riding into town in his business suit with a pipe in his mouth. Once, when Sally gave him a joint, he even tried marijuana. Nevertheless, it was a lonely time. Since his departure Sally had become even more out of control. Although she kept him at a distance, Peter tried to be a dutiful father. When she broke both legs in a car accident, he visited her often during her two-week hospital stay. She got pregnant at age twenty by a boy she had met at a rock festival. "I told my mother right away, but it took me a long time to get up the nerve to tell my father. He took things so much to heart, I knew it would be a real blow. We talked for two hours, and he sort of begged me to get married for the baby's sake. He really put his heart and soul into that talk. He was so moving and caring that he persuaded me. It had been a long time since we talked that long." Though Peter had always dreamed of giving his daughter a traditional church wedding, he was one of the few witnesses when Sally and Bill were married by a justice of the peace. Four months later he rushed to the hospital in time for the birth of his grandson, Owen. And when Sally and her family moved to California, where they lived on welfare and food stamps, he wrote her faithfully, whether or not he got a reply.

After his divorce Peter joined Parents Without Partners, a group that sponsors parties and outings for people who are divorced or widowed. Through this group he met Anna, a woman with whom he began a passionate, stormy relationship. They fought, broke up, and made up many times. The breaking up was always painful for Peter, but the making up was so sweet that he stayed with her for nearly two years. But the relationship's downs seemed to throw him into despair; after a fight he would call Anna and beg her to come by. Alarmed at how depressed he sounded, she would relent and rush over to comfort him. In a four-page letter to his older brother, Gerald, Peter matter-of-factly described his job, his golf game, and his carpentry projects. Then he wrote:

> The next "event" on my calendar is the breakup of Anna and I in early November. All fall, at my suggestion, we had been seeing each other only every other weekend. I had suggested that we each do a little "outside" dating. She apparently did and I didn't, so finally she said she didn't think we ought to date each other any more, and we haven't. All this threw me into an absolute panic. I proposed. She refused. Pop's old revolver misfired. And I started dating another lady. All in the space of five days! Boy, do I need psychiatric help!

In the next paragraph he was back to news of mutual friends and a discussion of the weather. "Well, that's about all the news I have," he concluded. "My very best to you both." If the letter was a cry for help, it was characteristically well camouflaged, using offhand remarks and exclamation points to mask his deepest feelings. Gerald shrugged off the reference to "Pop's old revolver" as some unfamiliar figure of speech. In any case he did not reply to the letter for eleven months, and Peter did not seek "psychiatric help."

Peter's new "lady" was Jane Freund, a bright, vibrant woman who worked with problem learners in a Stamford elementary school. Eleven years younger than Peter, she had been divorced five years and had three teenage sons. They had met through Parents Without Partners, and a few days after breaking up with Anna, Peter asked her out. Before long they settled into a steady, intimate affair. After thirteen years of a strained marriage, Jane was surprised that a relationship could be so relaxed. Peter was gentle, with a good sense of humor and a miscellany of talents. Unlike Peter's ex-wife, Jane loved the outdoors, and they frequently skied, sailed, and hiked. On a week-long canoe trip in Minnesota, Jane remembers Peter playing chanteys, folk songs, and hymns on his harmonica in their tent during a rainstorm. She was impressed at how easily and naturally he made others happy. They also enjoyed simpler pleasures—movies, the theater, and long walks. "We'd have dinner at his apartment," recalls Jane. "He didn't know how to cook, so we'd put some food on to simmer and then go make love. One of our jokes was that we were going to write *The Lovers' Cookbook*—easy recipes that you could make quickly and then let simmer for an hour or two."

For Peter the relationship offered a real challenge. Jane was far more assertive, opinionated, and forceful than he. One night early in their affair Jane ran into a former lover at a party and kissed him warmly on the lips. Peter left the party deeply disturbed. The next day they had planned to go sailing. When the hour came and he had not come by to pick her up, Jane called him. "I'm not going," said Peter in a tight voice. "I can't see you. I can never see you again." Jane was confused. When she drove to his apartment, she found him in a terrible, agitated state. "I just can't talk to you now," he said, weeping. "I don't know what I'm going to do, but I just can't see you now."

Although they smoothed things over, Jane was alarmed by Peter's reaction. She found other aspects of his behavior similarly unsettling, if less extreme. "When we had people over, Peter was a wonderful host for the first ten minutes," says Jane. "He'd extend his hand, hang up coats, get people drinks, sit them by the fire, make small talk. But as the evening went along he sort of faded into the background." At one party Jane remembers hearing someone ask Peter if he was a commuter. "No," he replied. End of conversation. Later Jane explained to Peter that the woman wanted to know more about him, and asking whether he was a commuter was merely a conversational opening. At another party Peter remained silent during a spirited discussion of single-sex education at college. "Well, Peter, what do *you* think?" asked Jane. "I don't know," he said. "Come on," pressed Jane. "You must have formed some opinions about it." But Peter said no, he didn't have an opinion. Jane, who liked a good discussion, even an occasional argument, found this reluctance exasperating. "Peter was not a passive person," she says. "But in some ways he didn't know how to stand up for himself." Even discussing the relative merits of drip-dry and all-cotton sheets, or the best way to wrap meat for the freezer, Peter preferred to concede rather than to make waves. "Please tell me how to do it," he'd say, "then I'll just do it that way."

Annoyed by Peter's meekness in minor matters, Jane was troubled by the way he repressed truly important issues. When Peter mentioned that he had a third daughter, Kathy, who was in an institution, Jane asked him how she was. "I don't know," he said. He told her he hadn't seen her in many years. Jane, who worked with autistic children, was appalled. "He didn't want to be involved with anything that would tug at his heartstrings," she says. "He didn't like things that weren't clean and clear, that he couldn't solve. He seemed to block out really difficult and stressful things, just pulled the blinders down."

One night after making love they began talking about the worst times they had ever known. Peter said he had once felt so bad that he had put a bullet in a gun, spun the chamber, put the gun in his mouth, and fired. Jane was stunned. She asked how often he had done this, and he said, "More than once." Jane threatened to leave him if he didn't get help, so Peter went four times a week to a psychiatrist who put him on antidepressants.

They never talked about his suicide attempts again. Though Jane couldn't forget it, she dismissed it because they had happened before he met her and because things seemed to be going so well. "One thing that helped me put it out of my mind was that the sex was so beautiful and so loving. It was free and erotic with lots of laughing and tumbling around," she says. "So whenever this little worry came up, I would argue myself out of it by saying that anybody with whom lovemaking is this beautiful can't . . . you know . . ." Her voice trails off.

As Peter continued in therapy he seemed to be gaining confidence, toughening up. "He really didn't know how to stand up for himself," says Jane. "But he was learning." She smiles. "We had an argument once, it was something so stupid, it was about which material is warmer, down or Polarguard. We argued all evening long, and I kept thinking, 'Gee, he's not quitting.' Next morning I apologized, and he said, 'You know why I kept that argument going? I've never really been able to argue. Before this my stomach used to tie itself into knots, and this time my head kept sending messages down to my stomach saying, 'Everything all right down there?' and my stomach kept saying, 'I'm fine down here, keep it going up there!' "

When her youngest son went away to boarding school, leaving Jane alone in her four-bedroom house, Peter moved in. But as Thanksgiving approached, when Jane's children would be coming home for the holiday, Jane and Peter decided he'd better move back to his apartment until her children returned to school. Then they decided that if they loved each other, there was no need to be secretive. Peter stayed. Jane's children liked him, not only because he was pleasant and easygoing but because they saw how happy he made their mother. "He changed her a lot—she was not on edge so much," says her youngest son, Andy, who was fifteen at the time. "She seemed *much* happier with him than she'd ever been with anyone else." Peter grew especially close to Andy, a shy, introverted boy who had problems in school. Peter taught him how to sail and how to work the rotary mower. He took him on the back of his motorcycle on weekend errands into town or on Sunday night trips to get ice cream. Once, Andy asked Peter, "When are you and my mother going to get married? Because if you do, I'll like it that you're my stepfather." Moved, Peter had to turn away so Andy wouldn't see his tears.

Peter seemed to enjoy the new domestic arrangement. As always he loved doing yard work, rewiring electrical outlets, repairing old furniture. When Jane tried to teach him how to cook, Peter was initially resistant, but gradually he mastered omelettes, hamburgers, and chicken. During the summer he barbecued steaks on the hibachi and fixed elaborate salads. They soon settled into a period of domestic tranquility. Jane often thinks of lazy Sunday mornings in her backyard, trading sections of *The New York Times,* sipping coffee. Yet a part of Peter still held back; he continued to maintain his apartment even though he and Jane had begun to talk seriously about marriage.

Peter's work was a source of increasing unhappiness. In the past year he had been asked to join his company's paper purchasing group, an administrative post that used none of his technical skills. He ended up buying the paper for the subscription cards that fall out of magazines. He realized that he had been kicked upstairs, and he felt demeaned. "I think he worked not because he enjoyed it but because he had to earn people's respect," says Jane. "I think he was terrified of being without a job."

At that point Peter's relationship with his own family seemed to be improving. That summer Sally returned from California with two-year-old Owen. She moved in with her mother and got a job cleaning houses three days a week. Although life was still difficult—she and her husband were considering separation—she never told her father. "I would have lied rather than tell him how miserable my life really was," says Sally. "I guess I saw him as an innocent, and I didn't think he could take it." On the Fourth of July, Peter, Jane, Sally, and Owen watched the fireworks display at Fairfield Beach, Peter carrying his grandson on his shoulders. They swam at the pond near Jane's, and Peter held Owen on the surface of the water, just as he had held Sally when he taught her to swim so many years before. One night Peter, Sally, and Ruth, who had come east for a visit, went out to dinner. "I picked a little family-type place because my father always liked this Italian restaurant when we were young," says Sally. The evening was relaxed and pleasant, just the way they might have imagined it before all the troubled years. "He talked some about his personal life, and I felt really touched by that," says Sally. "I wanted to talk to him more like this. I felt I was finally getting to know him."

One night a few weeks later Sally had dinner with Peter and Jane. Her father drove her home. "We took the parkway and got off at Westport, and I said why this exit? He said he wanted to take the long way home. He said something about it being a prettier route, but it was unusual for him to go out of his way like that. We didn't talk about anything special, but later it occurred to me that he wanted to drag it out, that he may already have known what he was going to do."

Two weeks later Peter spent the weekend alone. He had told Jane that he missed having time to himself just to read or putter around the house. Jane was due to drive Andy up to his new prep school in New Hampshire and planned to return Sunday evening. Although she would have liked to have Peter's company, she suggested it might be a good opportunity for him to get some time alone.

That weekend Peter wrote an eight-page letter to Lizzie, a friend he had known since he was a teenager, to whom he had written often over the years. By Peter's standards the letter was extraordinarily frank. He told her of his doubts about his future with Jane; of his fear that because he was eleven years older he would end up being a burden to her; that one day he would be "old and tottering" while Jane was "still strong and healthy." He wrote of her intimidating strength. "Jane went through five years of psychoanalysis, which has left her overflowing with confidence. I'm just over a year into psychotherapy and, it seems to me, stalled out. The result sometimes is that I feel I am the one out of step." He wrote of how he sometimes found it difficult to be with Jane's children, fond as he was of them. "Those absolutely awful years with Sally have undoubtedly left a lot of scars on me. I would much prefer to stay completely out of the business of raising kids. . . . All of this makes me feel very old and very inflexible," he wrote. "Sometimes I think I'm best suited to be a hermit!" He wrote at length of his disappointment in his job:

> The work itself requires care and accuracy but absolutely none of my technical training and experience. In many respects it is clerk's work. For the first time in my years with Time, taking time off for vacations is a real problem and the load when I return is appalling. But I guess more than anything else, it is humiliating! I've been hanging on by my teeth until I can take early retirement at 56½, a whole year and seven months away. But sometimes even that seems an eternity. The early retirement benefits are very appreciable but I sometimes wonder if anything is worth it. It isn't so much that I want to be something else—I don't really know what I want to do—but I very much want to stop what I am doing.
>
> Enough of my troubles! The good news. Ruth continues to live in Boulder, Colorado, with her husband. She spent two days here in Connecticut this summer and . . .

Peter wrote of his daughters and his grandson—"a happy, fearless little boy in whom I take much delight." "Dearest friend," he concluded, "please forgive me for such a long lapse in writing. Please give my very best to your children and the rest of your family. Take care of yourself. Although I see no prospect of seeing each other, I do think of you often and hope you are well and happy. Love, Peter."

That afternoon Jane drove home in a storm from New Hampshire. She stopped off in Springfield to call Peter and tell him she would be home in a couple of hours. Peter sounded a little down—there were awkward pauses in the conversation—but Jane was impatient to get home and didn't press the issue. Rain beat down on the telephone booth. Cars roared past. Jane remembers feeling, "Oh, honey, I miss you, I can't wait to get home and snuggle up into your shoulder." But what she said to Peter was, "I can't wait to get home and have a drink."

When she got home, Peter wasn't there. She found a bowl of sliced peaches on the counter and thought perhaps Peter was making peach shortcake, one of his favorite desserts, and had gone to the store to get some whipping cream. Jane told herself he would be home in half an hour. He wasn't. She telephoned his apartment repeatedly, but there was no answer. In the back of her mind she thought of the possibility of suicide, but she couldn't believe it. "I was like a rabbit frozen in car headlights, paralyzed. I just sort of insisted on life as usual. I went to bed thinking, 'He'll come home at three in the morning and sit on the edge of the bed and tell me he's depressed.' "

At 6 A.M. she drove to his apartment and knocked on the door until her hand hurt. She called the police, who broke down the door. "At first I thought he was asleep. He was sitting with his legs crossed and his head tilted, and his hands were in his lap. And then I saw the gun in his hand. I saw that black metal and all the red, and I turned away and said to myself, 'Oh my God, he's done it.' I told everybody—his parents, my parents, his children, my children—that he looked sort of peaceful. But that wasn't true. His mouth was open, and there was a waterfall of blood."

Jane couldn't look anymore. She went into the kitchen. "A big policeman standing at Peter's desk called out that there was a note. I didn't want to go into that room again so I asked him to read it to me." At the morgue they gave her a brown envelope with the contents of Peter's pockets. "There was blood on the money and on his credit cards," she recalls. "I trimmed the edges of the bills where the blood was and washed the credit cards." She drove to New Hampshire to get Andy. She had told him on the phone that Peter had died but said she couldn't tell him how until she saw him. Andy guessed that Peter's commuter train had crashed or that he had been in an accident on his motorcycle. When he got in the car, she told him. Jane recalls: "He looked so sad that I pulled over at a gas station, and we took a walk into a field. We hugged, and he was crying so hard I thought his legs would buckle. I wondered how this man could have done something that would hurt a fifteen-year-old kid so much he's going to fall down if I don't hold him up."

The memorial service took place in the church that Peter and Jane had planned to marry in. "I was in charge of the arrangements, which was probably the most responsible thing I'd ever done," Sally says. "It made me feel like an adult." It was a simple service, as the family agreed Peter would have preferred. They sang the familiar Protestant hymns: "Eternal Father, Strong to Save" and "Abide with Me." The minister read from Ecclesiastes and from the Twenty-third Psalm. Jane spoke, as did Peter's daughters and a friend from work. One of Jane's sons remembers thinking how fragmented the group was. There were friends from different parts of Peter's life—his family, his friends from work, from the Navy, and from Parents Without Partners—but none of the different circles seemed to intersect.

In the week after the service Jane, Sally, and Ruth cleaned out Peter's apartment, looking for clues that might help them better understand his death. Jane found Peter's letters to his former girlfriend Anna in which he sounded pathetic and groveling. She was so upset by them that she burned them. Sally read a journal her father had kept one summer when Jane had gone to Alaska for a month; he had written of his feelings of rejection. She realized her father had been more insecure and unstable than she had imagined. "He must have been so unhappy all those years," she says, "and it gradually intensified until he couldn't stand it." Sally, who had herself toyed with the idea of suicide during her teenage years, had insomnia and nightmares. "I kept trying to imagine myself in his place, sitting in the chair with a gun in his hand. I just didn't know how he could do it." Andy noticed that there were fifty more miles on the speedometer of Peter's motorcycle than there were the night before he had left for school, when he and Peter had driven into town for ice cream. "On Saturday or Sunday," Jane says, "Peter must have taken a long ride somewhere, maybe to try to dissipate that sense of 'My God, it's coming over me again, that black cloud.' "

In their effort to find some answers, Sally and Ruth met with their father's psychiatrist. They talked for half an hour, but the psychiatrist, citing doctor-patient confidentiality, told them little. "We tried to work around that," says Sally, "by making statements like, "He was sensitive, insecure, had a poor self-image, and we wondered whether that might be the reason he committed suicide.' The doctor said yes, that was close. He said my father's death had taken him by surprise, too. But I was annoyed because he didn't seem very remorseful."

Jane, who was hounded for months by bloody nightmares, was bewildered. She knew Peter had been unhappy and depressed at times. She knew he had problems expressing his feelings. She knew that he had always had high standards and principles that perhaps at bottom he felt he could never live up to. She knew enough about psychiatry to realize that Peter had had lifelong feelings of inadequacy, and a part of him had seemed to need to be punished. She knew that he had attempted suicide before he met her. But why now? Why that weekend? Why just when it seemed everything was going so well? She wondered if perhaps he had been opening up so fast in therapy that it had scared him. Perhaps his melancholy had come over him at a time when he was vulnerable and no longer had enough defenses to cope. But at bottom there was something inexplicable, like the fifty extra miles on his speedometer.

When Jane met with Peter's psychiatrist, she found that the part of Peter she didn't know was larger than she had suspected. He told her that Peter had made three other suicide attempts before he met her. In fact, the psychiatrist had known about the gun and had told Peter that if he did not get rid of it, he would stop treatment. Instead, Peter had locked the gun in a metal case and put it in his cellar. "I think Peter thought he could always use it if he needed to," says Jane sharply, "and I wish the psychiatrist had stepped out of the traditional role and invited me in. It might have diffused the danger that lay in the secrecy of that gun. Peter was not an assertive person, and if he hadn't had access to a weapon, I don't think he would have done it. I think he would have just suffered through whatever black mood he was in.

"I feel I have to keep justifying him because I lived with him and I loved him, and if he came back, I would live with him again. But when I went back to the apartment, I found a velvet-lined case with another small gun and something that looked like a shotgun lying in pieces," she says slowly. "I don't know how to put that together with the man I knew. That's a mystery I'll never solve. There's no one who can tell me why because the person who knows is dead, and even he probably didn't know." Jane folds her hands. "But I know now what I hadn't known before, that it is possible for even the most deeply disturbed and desperately unbalanced among us to be a beautiful person."

II

UNDER THE SHADOW

FROM TIME TO TIME magazines print articles with titles like "Are You the Suicide Type?" They offer statistics on who is likely to commit suicide: three times more men than women kill themselves; whites commit suicide more than nonwhites; suicide rates rise with age, soaring after sixty; divorced men are three times more likely to kill themselves than married men; two of every three suicides are white males, and so on. Through these demographic factors a composite emerges, like a police artist's sketch, of an older, white, divorced, unemployed male who lives alone and is in poor health—the "suicide type" or "high-risk paradigm," as clinicians call it. As a white male who was divorced and approaching retirement, Peter Newell was in many ways the typical suicide.

Of course such articles usually conclude that there is no such thing as a suicide type. Suicide cuts across all sex lines, age groups, races, and diagnoses. Just as no two fingerprints are identical, no two lives are identical, and no two suicides are identical. While it may be impossible to pigeonhole suicides, it is important to be aware of the range of meanings and motivations. "No one ever lacks a good reason for suicide," observed the Italian author Cesare Pavese. But Peter Newell's reasons were different from Justin Spoonhour's. The man who responds to voices urging him to kill himself is different from the terminally ill man who decides he has had enough of life. The depressed woman who

222

builds up to the act over many years is different from the girl who, rejected by her lover, impulsively flings herself from a bridge.

"Suicide," says psychologist Edwin Shneidman, "is an attempt to solve a problem." That problem is rarely external pain or misery on a large scale, which seem to have little to do with suicide. In fact, adversity often seems to strengthen the desire to live. History is brimming with people who, in the face of prodigious bad fortune, poverty, illness, or torture, manage to survive, and with others who, despite being blessed with every possible advantage, like Peter Newell and Richard Cory, take their own lives. This is reflected on a macroscopic level by the higher rates of suicide in industrialized nations than in underdeveloped countries; in the upper classes than in the middle and lower; among whites than among blacks. It is also illustrated by the reported rarity of suicides and suicide attempts in the Nazi concentration camps. In *The Drowned and the Saved,* Primo Levi, noting the low incidence of suicide at Auschwitz, wrote, "The day was dense: one had to think about satisfying hunger, in some way elude fatigue and cold, avoid the blows. Precisely because of the constant imminence of death there was no time to concentrate on the idea of death." Yet many survivors seemed to have experienced a delayed reaction in which a built-up residue of depression found expression only after the immediate threat of death was gone. Levi was one of only three of his original convoy of 650 prisoners to return alive from Auschwitz. Forty-two years later, at age sixty-seven, suffering from periodic depression, the author threw himself down the stairwell of his fourth-floor apartment in Turin, one of numerous death camp survivors who ultimately took their lives.

The internal misery that leads to suicide often involves loss. "It is impossible to think that I shall never sit with you again and hear your laugh. *That every day for the rest of my life you will be away,*" wrote Bloomsbury painter Carrington in 1932, less than a month after her beloved Lytton Strachey died. One month later she killed herself. Three days after his bride died of asphyxiation when he had tried to smuggle her into the United States in a suitcase, a thirty-one-year-old Iranian émigré shot himself in the head with a pistol he had bought the day before after telling a friend, "I'm just dead. I lost everything." Such suicides often involve the conscious or unconscious fantasy that death will bring a reunion with the lost loved one. Not long after his beloved dog Boxer died, one elderly man fell ill, became despondent, and took a nonfatal overdose. When a psychiatrist examined him, the man spoke sadly of his life and physical infirmities. But when he was asked what he had imagined death would be like, he brightened up and said, "Well, I rather thought Boxer would be there."

Suicide is often occasioned by the loss or threatened loss of status, career, or power. People often kill themselves when they are on the verge of being exposed or captured, like Hitler and his lieutenants, who swallowed cyanide as the Allies closed in. One often reads of criminals who kill themselves even as the police are knocking on their door. "There is no refuge from confession but suicide; and suicide is confession," observed Daniel Webster, arguing a murder case in 1830. Newspapers often report the seemingly inexplicable suicides of powerful men. Only later does news of some scandal emerge. On January 10, 1986, in New York, for example, Donald Manes, the popular Queens borough president, was found at the wheel of his car, dazed and bleeding profusely from knife slashes on his left wrist and ankle. At first it was assumed he had been mugged—Manes insisted he had no recollection of the evening—but over the next few weeks, as a vast bribery and graft scheme unraveled around him, it became apparent that Manes had attempted suicide. His world continued to disintegrate. A close friend agreed to testify against him; the mayor of New York City, his political mentor, called him a crook. Then one night in March, while talking on the phone with his psychiatrist, Manes pulled a knife from his kitchen drawer, thrust it into his chest, and died. Months later a former friend and political ally, himself convicted of racketeering, described Manes as "one so corrupt that he chose suicide rather than face the consequences of his crimes."

Some people cannot face shame or loss of face. Paul Kammerer, the eminent Viennese biologist, spent most of his professional life attempting to prove the inheritance of certain acquired characteristics in a particular species of toad. In 1926 it was found that India ink had been injected into the paws of some of the toads, producing tainted results. Although it was never ascertained whether Kammerer or his assistant was responsible, his reputation was ruined. Six weeks after being accused he shot himself in the head in a forest outside Vienna.

The scandal can seem minor to the outside world. In 1956, when French bakers went on a nationwide strike, the mayor of a small town, scorned by citizens who felt he hadn't done enough to get bread supplies, climbed a power line and killed himself by touching a 100,000-volt high-tension wire. In 1980, Lady Isobel Barnett, a wealthy English widow, was convicted and fined the equivalent of $650 for shoplifting a tin of tuna and a carton of cream. "I have only myself to live with, and I can live with myself," she said after the trial. But four days later she electrocuted herself in her bath.

The suicide may involve the loss of a sense of self, as poignantly evidenced by the high rate of suicide in the Federal Witness Protection Program, in which government informants are literally provided with new identities—names, jobs, homes, and fingerprints. It may involve a threatened loss of image. A depressed psychoanalyst, urged by his therapist to enter the hospital, refused, saying it would hurt his image. When his therapist went on vacation, the psychoanalyst shot himself. Preserving his image was apparently more important than preserving his life. It may involve the loss of a way of life or of an idea of the self, as when a person fails to fulfill his early promise. Bruce

Gardner was voted the most valuable college baseball player in 1960, but after spending four years in the Los Angeles Dodgers farm system, he never achieved the greatness predicted for him. At thirty-two, a high school physical education instructor, he walked out to the pitching mound at his alma mater, the University of Southern California, and shot himself in the head. Clutched in his right hand was his diploma and next to his body lay a plaque commemorating his selection as an NCAA All-American a decade earlier.

Such deaths may be, paradoxically, an attempt to preserve that self-image. "I believe that suicide has a lot to do with the ideal—often unconscious—that one has of oneself based on early relationships," says psychiatrist Robert Litman. "Suicidal people tend to believe that if they do not live up to it, their lives must be a total failure. Often, then, they kill themselves in order to preserve that ideal, to save the flag, save the halo—in addition to punishing the failed self. You know that song Frank Sinatra sings: 'I did it my way.' Well, I think that the ideal of the hero who does it his way is suicidogenic—it's a breeding concept for suicide because many people think it's either my way or no way, and if it's no way, it's suicide."

For some, loss of sanity—or fear of its loss—may be a spur to suicide. In 1941, Virginia Woolf, plagued all her life by recurrent bouts of madness, stuffed her pockets with stones and walked into a river near her home. She left a note to her husband that began, "Dearest, I feel certain that I am going mad again. I feel we can't go through another of those terrible times. And I shan't recover this time. I begin to hear voices, and I can't concentrate. So I am doing what seems the best thing to do."

On the other hand suicide is often committed by people who are seemingly on the mend, like Peter Newell, who was making progress in therapy and on the verge of marriage to a woman he loved. "Paradoxical and tragic suicidal efforts may occur in a patient who is recovering from a psychosis out of a fear of 'getting well,' " wrote psychiatrist Lawrence Kubie, "when 'getting well' means to the patient that he must return to an unacceptable situation from which he can see no escape other than suicide." Kubie also describes the common phenomenon of "depressive response to success" in which people whose self-esteem is so low that they feel they do not deserve success or happiness may kill themselves shortly *after* something wonderful has happened or some long-sought goal has been attained.

Many suicides are aggressive acts directed at a particular person or group of people, motivated by conscious or unconscious rage or a desire for revenge and often accompanied by the fantasy of surviving to witness the enemy's suffering. In a graphic illustration of Freud's thesis that suicide is murder turned inward, a policeman under investigation during New York's corruption scandals of the 1930s arranged to meet his sergeant, who he believed had mistreated him, in a bar. While waiting he told several people there that he planned to kill the sergeant as soon as he saw him. The sergeant never showed up; after a long wait the policeman shot himself, leaving this note: "To whom concerned: Goodbye you old prick and when I mean prick you are a prick. Hope you fall with the rest of us, you yellow bastard."

Of course, the policeman may have planned all along to kill himself after killing the sergeant. Although no national statistics are kept on murder followed by suicide, one study in Philadelphia found that 8 percent of people who committed homicide also committed suicide, usually immediately following the murder. In the majority of cases a man killed himself after killing his lover or wife, often after a real or threatened separation. A Massachusetts man, upset when his girlfriend left him, doused her with gasoline and set her on fire, then did the same to himself. A 1969 literature review found that of eighty-eight women who had murdered a child, nearly half had also attempted or committed suicide. Murder and suicide are also combined in terrorist acts, from Samson to the Japanese kamikaze pilots to the contemporary Arab terrorists who smuggle bombs aboard planes.

Of course, many suicidal people unconsciously fantasize that they are killing others. They may even feel that by committing suicide they are not killing themselves but killing the entire world. This is a dynamic described in A. E. Housman's poem "I Counsel You Beware":

> *Good creatures, do you love your lives*
> *And have you ears for sense?*
> *Here is a knife like other knives,*
> *That cost me eighteen pence.*
>
> *I need but stick it in my heart*
> *And down will come the sky,*
> *And earth's foundations will depart*
> *And all you folk will die.*

While suicide is often motivated by loss, real or metaphorical, for many people it also represents, simultaneously and paradoxically, some form of psychic gain. The suicidal terrorist's religion tells him that earthly existence is but a prelude to an eternal afterlife in which he will be revered for his deed. The bereaved widow kills herself in the belief she may rejoin her lost love. Other gains are less conscious. The suicidal person described by Litman kills himself in the hope that his idealized image will live on; the speaker in the Housman poem perceives of suicide as a sort of trump card enabling him to triumph over a world that has rejected him. Like the drowsy person who pinches himself to see if he is awake, some suicides kill themselves to prove they are alive. Suicide may be the only way they know to assert order or control over a situation in which they feel trapped. "If I commit suicide, it will not be to destroy myself but to put myself back together again," wrote Antonin

Artaud, the avant-garde dramatist who spent much of his life in mental institutions. "Suicide will be for me only one means of violently reconquering myself, of brutally invading my being, of anticipating the unpredictable approaches of God. By suicide, I reintroduce my design in nature; I shall for the first time give things the shape of my will." (Artaud died of rectal cancer in 1948.)

"Suicide always seeks to achieve something, even if only peace or an end to pain," observes psychiatrist Robert Jay Lifton. In *The Broken Connection* he suggested, "Killing oneself may appear to be the only way to break out of the 'trap' or 'encirclement' and assert whatever it is one feels one wants to, or must, about one's life. One lacks the power to express that assertion in living, or even the power that certain forms of madness, or extreme psychological disorder, provide for alternative forms of assertion that at least keep one's life going." And so suicide seems the only way to survive. Lifton further wrote:

> Despair and hopelessness are associated with perceptions of the future. One's ultimate involvements are so impaired that one is simply unable to imagine a psychologically livable future. Whatever future one can imagine is no better, perhaps much worse, than the present ("However low a man has sunk, he can sink even lower, and this 'can' is the object of his dread," is the way Kierkegaard put the matter.) *More specifically, the suicide can create a future only by killing himself.* That is, he can reawaken psychic action and imagine vital events beyond the present only in deciding upon, and carrying through, his suicide. And for that period of time, however brief, he lives with an imagined future.

The search for self-knowledge is the essential motivation for suicide, according to James Hillman. In *Suicide and the Soul* the Jungian psychologist argued that we must experience death in order to understand and fully experience life. "The impulse to death need not be conceived as an anti-life movement; it may be a demand for an encounter with absolute reality, *a demand for a fuller life through the death experience*." The soul can experience death in ways short of suicide: depression, amnesia, intoxication, exaltation, failure, psychosis. Hillman, however, asserted that "for some, organic death through actual suicide may be the only mode through which the death experience is possible."

Although Hillman seems to have gone to an almost absurdist extreme, his basic premise—that suicide almost always involves an attempt at transformation—seems essentially true. Many people who survive a suicide attempt speak of its cathartic effects—a dynamic perhaps analogous to the truism that an alcoholic can begin to recover only after he "hits bottom." "The suicidal attempt may express a fantasy of returning to infancy for the purpose of living life over again," wrote Lawrence Kubie, one of whose patients, after making several attempts, told him, "I wanted to go right back to the very edge of obliteration *but not over the edge.* Then I could start afresh." It is also evident in the calm that many suicidal people feel after making the decision to kill themselves—what the Viennese psychiatrist Erwin Ringel calls an "ominous quiet." A twenty-five-year-old man who survived his suicide attempt recalls the triumph he felt when he decided to take his own life: "It was like being in class and everyone around you is giving the wrong answer, but the teacher isn't calling on you. But you know you have the answer. Blowing your head off is the answer. The answer to life, the answer to your identity, the answer to your self-preservation. That gun to your head is the most beautiful answer. And even as you are thinking of killing yourself, you can be full of passion, full of life. I think for many people it's that zest to live that makes them keep wrapping the noose around their neck. They're saying, 'I'll show you how much I want to live.' "

For some, suicide itself may be a kind of achievement. "Is it conceivable to murder someone in order to count for something in his life?" wrote Cesare Pavese. "Then it is conceivable to kill oneself so as to count for something in one's own life. Here's the difficulty about suicide: it is an act of ambition that can be committed only when one has passed beyond ambition." For whatever reasons—a father dead when he was six; a strict, demanding mother; the suicides of two close friends in adolescence—Pavese had a lifelong preoccupation with suicide. The idea of self-destruction—he called it his "syphilis"—runs like an underground stream through his diary, *The Burning Brand,* bubbling to the surface at moments of rejection, loneliness, and disappointment. "I know that I am forever condemned to think of suicide when faced with no matter what difficulty or grief," he wrote at age twenty-eight. "It terrifies me. My basic principle is suicide, never committed, never to be committed, but the thought of it caresses my sensibility." Although the "trigger" was a brief, unhappy affair with an American actress—the last of his many failed attempts to achieve a lasting relationship with a woman—his suicide had been percolating for his entire life. "Today I see clearly that from '28 until now I have always lived under this shadow," he wrote in 1950. Ten days later, only a month after winning Italy's top literary prize, he took a fatal overdose in a hotel room. In his last diary entry he wrote:

The thing most feared in secret always happens.
  I write: oh Thou, have mercy. And then?
  All it takes is a little courage.
  The more the pain grows clear and definite, the more the instinct for life asserts itself and the thought of suicide recedes.
  It seemed easy when I thought of it. Weak women have done it. It takes humility, not pride.
  All this is sickening.
  Not words. An act. I won't write any more.

Although its causes are infinite and unique, suicidal people share a common denominator of pain. "When I was nineteen, I had my first deep depression," says Anne-Grace Scheinin, a thirty-five-year-old author. "I was terrified. Everything—the way I walked, the way I talked—slowed to a crawl. I felt empty, like everything inside me had been cut up and pulled out. It was as if something had died inside me and was disintegrating. I couldn't concentrate. Reading a book, I'd find myself skimming the same passage over and over until I'd realize I had read the same paragraph sixteen times. After eight months I began to wonder whether my depression would ever lift. I envisioned spending my whole life like that. The feeling that it was never going to end is what made me think of suicide." Scheinin made six attempts in two years before being diagnosed manic depressive. Today, with lithium and periodic hospitalizations, she has not made an attempt in more than a decade.

Some describe that pain as a prison, a tunnel, a blizzard, a desert, the bottom of a well. In *The Bell Jar,* a fictionalized account of her breakdown and suicide attempt in 1953 at age twenty, Sylvia Plath, in the words of her heroine, Esther Greenwood, described her gathering depression as feeling "as if I were being stuffed farther and farther into a black, airless sack with no way out." After her suicide attempt, her patron financed her stay in a private psychiatric hospital. "I knew I should be grateful to Mrs. Guinea, only I couldn't feel a thing," commented Greenwood. "If Mrs. Guinea had given me a ticket to Europe, or a round-the-world cruise, it wouldn't have made one scrap of difference to me, because wherever I sat—on the deck of a ship or at a street café in Paris or Bangkok—I would be sitting under the same glass bell jar, stewing in my own sour air." Her mother suggested they pretend that her breakdown and suicide attempt had all been a bad dream, but as Greenwood observed, "To the person in the bell jar, blank and stopped as a dead baby, the world itself is the bad dream."

In that state the outside world gradually seems irrelevant; the person's focus narrows like the lens of a camera. Clinicians call this tunnel vision. Erwin Ringel called it the "presuicidal syndrome," a state characterized by constriction, inhibited aggression turned toward the self, and suicidal fantasies. He described it as "an experience of harassment, of being surrounded from all sides, and of being ever more intensely squeezed into a steadily tightening space." In Edwin Shneidman's *Voices of Death* a young woman recalls her feelings the moment before she jumped from a fifth-floor balcony: "Everything was like a terrible sort of whirlpool of confusion. And I thought to myself, 'There's only one thing I can do, I just have to lose consciousness. That's the only way to get away from it . . . everything just got very dark all of a sudden, and all I could see was this balcony. Everything around it just blacked out. It was just like a circle. That was all I could see, just the balcony . . . and I went over it."

A. Alvarez described this stifling state as a world apart, a foreign land with its own laws and "its own irresistible logic." That logic, he wrote, is not the kind employed by philosophers.

The logic of suicide is different. It is like the unanswerable logic of a nightmare, or like the science-fiction fantasy of being projected suddenly into another dimension: everything makes sense and follows its own strict rules; yet, at the same time, everything is also different, perverted, upside down. Once a man decides to take his own life he enters a shut-off, impregnable but wholly convincing world where every detail fits and each incident reinforces his decision. An argument with a stranger in a bar, an unexpected letter which doesn't arrive, the wrong voice on the telephone, the wrong knock at the door, even a change in the weather—all seem charged with special meaning; they all contribute.

Alvarez wrote from personal experience. In an epilogue to *The Savage God* he described his own suicide attempt at age thirty-one. He recalled the suicidal threats his parents made when he was a child, which imbedded the idea in his unconscious. Then one day, many years later, following "some standard domestic squabble," he realized that he wished he were dead. "After that," he wrote, "there was only one way out, although it took a long time—many months, in fact—to get there." Once he knew, it seemed an inevitability—"the last slide down the ice slope had begun and there was no way of stopping it." He described that slide: the marital fights, the drinking, the isolation. Inside, he experienced that "presuicidal syndrome." "My life felt so cluttered and obstructed that I could hardly breathe," he wrote. "I inhabited a closed, concentrated world, airless and without exits. I doubt if any of this was noticeable socially: I was simply more tense, more nervous than usual, and I drank more. But underneath I was going a bit mad."

Two months after deciding on suicide, following a Christmas spent drinking and quarreling with his wife, who finally walked out on him, Alvarez swallowed forty-five sleeping pills hoarded for this occasion. He went into a deep coma but recovered.

The constricted world described by Alvarez and the simultaneous urge for transformation described by Lifton and Hillman are both dramatically evident in the unpublished journals of Lisa Courtney, a talented twenty-three-year-old silversmith from Newburyport, Massachusetts. For Lisa, depression was a "fog" that settled over her each fall. One autumn a series of events made that fog even more dense: the end of a relationship, the breakdown of her car, anxiety over getting along with new roommates, concern with her work. In the journal she kept during this time she wrote on one hand about her art, family, and friends, and the possibility of new love, and on the other about her doubts, anxiety, and loss of confidence. In her journal entries one can trace her growing depression, her feeling of numbness—"as if I were encased in foam rubber packing," she wrote—and, at the same time, her need to change her life, "to be a different person."

October 2: . . . September just flew by. I want to slow things down; give me a break! This light fogginess around me prevails, I wish I could control it better. Even in trying to remember the week—there is a dimness about it. . . . God, I hope this mind fog will lift.

October 6: . . . Somehow I find a strength that makes it possible for me to smile for a little while. Then suddenly I feel paralyzed. I can't function. I can't do any of the little chores I want to get done. I started a letter [to an old friend], but too many letters to write and nothing to say (well, I couldn't gather my thoughts) made me stop. I just couldn't think at all to be able to start a sentence. . . . I have so many things to do—list after list, day after day, and they don't get shorter. . . . One thing at a time, I must get these things done. I can't work! I can't think! I have so much designing to do. I can't even begin because I am thinking of everything at once. I can't clear my mind to focus on one thing. . . . I have no physical desire. I feel empty. My body is shut off. I don't WANT. I want to cry. It hurts. . . . Everything just seems so pointless. Nothing is going anywhere. Nothing is *getting done*. Help me, Lisa. Don't lose your strength. Rest now, it's night.

October 16: . . . I fantasize about running away. Why does this fantasy always come to me? What am I running away from? What am I running towards? To change myself, be a different person. Why don't I like myself? I want to know so much more, experience so much more than I do now, force myself into situations that are very difficult that I will find my way out of, become a bit hardened and not so naive. I am so afraid, so cautious. I am in a larger box than I was before, but I still feel walls around me, the walls of fear and self-imposed confinement that I *must* break down. I keep thinking about external changes: dress differently, change my hair, but I know it is what is inside that I want to change. . . . I am afraid I am sick. My body feels weak sometimes. There's something wrong with my voice and my breathing. Sometimes I have to push out words. I am afraid and angry with myself. Almost embarrassed. Cigarettes oh shit. My vagina itches. I get sore from brief intercourse. I don't know what's wrong. I try not to think about this, but I'm afraid. Sometimes I think if I found out I were going to die then I might be able to break through the walls that limit me. Can't I do it now anyway?

November 13: . . . How can you tell people that you can't feel anything? They will hate you. You are no longer alive or worth knowing if you can't feel. HELP ME LISA help me.

Over the course of six weeks Lisa's handwriting gradually changed from small and neat to large and scribbled. On November 15 she wrote a chronology of her slide:

Fog is getting very deep.
Work is getting difficult. I don't want to design.
Having trouble concentrating on production. The new girl is learning so fast.
I am quiet at work. Have nothing to say.
Orders to do
car trouble again
don't want to work on new home—barely set up stuff—throw rest in cellar.
withdrawing from people. Can't think or communicate anything but confusion, panic, lost.
exhausted from work—just trying to keep from running out of the place and screaming help me God! I'm afraid.
I can't remember what day it is.
No relief except sleep.
morning: panic, can't get out of bed
work to do
car to fix
change addresses
make wedding presents
can't remember how to do things at work.
I feel nowhere
I have lost my place in time.
can't make decisions.
I can't design. I have two designs to work on but my hands aren't working right. I can't see how to make the heart symmetrical. I don't want to work. I have to get out of there. Everyone knows I am mixed up. I make bad vibrations. I am hoping they remember I am not always like this. I leave work.
Eat lunch slowly. Try to rest my mind.
I don't know where to go. I hate you Lisa. Come back to earth. I hurt. I hurt you Lisa.

That afternoon Lisa stabbed herself superficially in the stomach. She was able to drive herself to the hospital where she was stitched up and released. "I wasn't trying to die; I just wanted to cut through the fog," she told her parents. One month later the fog hadn't lifted. Lisa cut her wrists and throat with broken glass, then rolled off the roof of a six-story building to her death.

III

THE MANNER OF DYING

IN JAMES M. CAIN'S CLASSIC WHODUNIT *Double Indemnity,* whose plot hinges on a murder disguised as a suicide, a savvy insurance agent shows an associate a book of statistical tables on suicide. "Take a look at them," he says. "Here's suicide by race, by color, by occupation, by sex, by locality, by seasons of the year, by time of day when committed. Here's suicide by method of accomplishment. Here's method of accomplishment subdivided by poisons, by firearms, by gas, by drowning, by leaps. Here's suicide by poisons subdivided by sex, by race, by age, by time of day. Here's suicide by poisons subdivided by cyanide, by mercury, by strychnine, by thirty-eight other poisons, sixteen of them no longer procurable at prescription pharmacies. And here—here, Mr. Norton—are leaps subdivided by leaps from high places, under wheels of moving trains, under wheels of trucks, under the feet of horses, from steamboats. *But there's not one case here out of all these millions of cases of a leap from the rear end of a moving train.* That's just one way they don't do it."

Although Cain's insurance agent is wrong—people have killed themselves by jumping off the backs of moving trains—his basic point is correct. There are many ways to commit suicide. The National Center for Health Statistics has enumerated at least forty-four general categories. The method one chooses depends on race, sex, occupation, availability, psychology, and, to an extent, fashion. In ancient Greece death by hemlock was popular; in Rome

233

chic suicides fell on their swords or opened their veins in a warm bath. According to the scholar Servius, Roman suicides by hanging were "cast forth unburied." Such class snobbery persisted into the eighteenth century, when an Englishman, learning of a friend's suicide by hanging, remarked, "What a low-minded wretch to apply the halter! Had he shot himself like a gentleman I could have forgiven him." The lower classes usually chose the noose, of which a French author observed, "Hanging is a type of death of which the infamy is so well established that a man who would choose it in despair, unless he were the dregs of society, would be unpardonably dishonored among honest men. One must take poison, shoot oneself, or die by fire. Drowning is another vulgar death." Nevertheless, in Paris, where life centered around the Seine, drowning seems to have been à la mode in the nineteenth century. Downstream at St. Cloud, fishermen who found the bodies of suicides in their nets were paid a fee for each corpse they brought to La Morgue.

The introduction of domestic gas in the nineteenth century and the proliferation of drugs in the twentieth brought about a radical change in suicide methods. "Not only have they made suicide more or less painless, they have also made it seem magical," wrote Alvarez in *The Savage God.* "A man who takes a knife and slices deliberately across his throat is murdering himself. But when someone lies down in front of an unlit gas oven or swallows sleeping pills, he seems not so much to be dying as merely seeking oblivion for a while. . . . In suicide, as in most other areas of activity, there has been a technological break through which has made a cheap and relatively painless death democratically available to everyone."

In most countries firearms, hanging, and poison are the most popular methods of suicide, but their frequency varies from culture to culture. In the United States, where gun control restrictions are minimal, more than half of suicides are by firearms, followed in order of frequency by hanging and overdose. In 1986, 64 percent of male suicides chose firearms, as did 40 percent of all females. Women kill themselves more often by overdose, although in recent years the use of firearms by women has increased sharply. In England, where gun control laws are stiff, firearms rank fifth as a method of suicide, while domestic gas is first. In France and West Germany hanging is preferred. But the popularity of any given method is subject to change. In Sri Lanka, for instance, jumping into a well was the preferred way until the introduction of indoor plumbing rendered wells obsolete. Self-poisoning with pesticides now tops the list.

In Norway, 15 percent of suicides are by drowning, compared to one or two percent in most other countries. "Since many Norwegians live and work on the water, it is perhaps not surprising that some of them choose to die in the water as well," observed Herbert Hendin, who has made extensive studies of suicide in particular geographic or ethnic groups. Hendin pointed out that half of all black suicides in New York are by jumping, compared to about 25 percent in the city as a whole and less than 3 percent in the rest of the country. He suggested that just as life in Norway centers on the sea, life in Harlem centers on its rooftops. "Sexual experience, fighting, and drug usage frequently take place on the Harlem rooftops," he wrote. "In this context, it is not surprising that jumping from the top floors or roofs of such buildings is a very common method among black suicides." In the South, where guns are an accepted part of many households and children learn to handle them at an early age, firearms are used in suicide more frequently than in the rest of the country. In some cultures, of course, certain forms of suicide demand traditional methods: the belly-cutting of the Japanese samurai; the hurling onto her husband's funeral pyre of the Indian widow; the self-immolation of political protesters, beginning with Buddhist monks in the early years of the Vietnam War.

The popularity of suicide methods also varies according to profession. A study of physicians, who commit suicide at three times the rate of the general population, found that 55 percent of all physician suicides use drugs—to which they have easy access—while only 12 percent use guns. Dentists use anesthetic gas more frequently, merchant seamen have a higher rate of drowning, and more miners kill themselves with explosives than any other group. In a rash of ninety-three suicides by New York City policemen between 1934 and 1940, nine of ten killed themselves with their service revolvers. These examples suggest that people tend to use methods that relate to how they have lived their lives.

While the majority of suicides die by gunshot, hanging, poison, or drowning, less than one percent a year in the United States kill themselves by what the National Center for Health Statistics refers to as "unspecified means." This rubric covers a variety of methods that seems as infinite as the variety of causes for suicide. Over the past two centuries people have committed suicide by jumping into volcanos, vats of beer, crocks of vinegar, retorts of molten glass, white-hot coke ovens, or slaughterhouse tanks of blood; by throwing themselves upon buzz saws; by thrusting hot pokers down their throats; by suffocating in refrigerators or chimneys; by locking themselves into high-altitude test chambers; by crashing airplanes; by jumping from airplanes; by lying in front of steamrollers; by throwing themselves on the third rail; by touching high-tension wires; by placing their necks in vises and turning the handle; by hugging stoves; by freezing to death; by climbing into lions' cages; by blowing themselves up with cannons, hand grenades, or dynamite; by boring holes in their heads with power drills; by drinking hydrochloric acid or Drano; by walking in front of cars, trains, subways, and racehorses; by driving cars off cliffs or into trains; by swallowing poisonous spiders; by piercing their hearts with corkscrews or darning needles; by starving themselves; by swallowing firecrackers; by holding their heads in buckets of water; by beating their heads with hammers; by pounding nails or barbecue spits into their skulls; by strangling themselves with their hair; by walking into airplane propellers; by swimming over waterfalls; by hanging themselves with grapevines; by sawing tree limbs out from under themselves; by swallowing glass; by swallowing underwear; by stabbing themselves with spectacles sharpened to a point; by cutting their throats with handsaws, sheep shears, or barbed wire; by forcing teams of horses to tear their heads off; by decapitating themselves with homemade guillotines; by exposing themselves to swarms of bees; by injecting themselves with paraffin, cooking oil, peanut butter, mercury, deodorant, or mayonnaise; by crucifying themselves.

Such imaginative methods, which account for only a tiny fraction of suicides, receive wide publicity—they are often used as "humorous" filler items in newspapers—and may contribute to the idea that people who commit suicide are insane. On closer inspection they may seem unusual but not inexplicable. The man who jumped into a vat of beer was a Czechoslovakian brewer; the man in the high-altitude test chamber was an Air Force technician; the man who lay in front of the steamroller was a construction worker; the man who blew himself up with a cannon was a soldier; the man who constructed a guillotine and decapitated himself was an assistant executioner in Corsica.

In his 1920 paper "The Psychogenesis of a Case of Homosexuality in a Woman," Freud described his analysis of an eighteen-year-old Viennese girl who had attempted suicide. The girl had been strolling with an older woman with whom she was infatuated. They encountered her father, who disapproved of the liaison. He scowled at his daughter. The woman told the girl they must separate, and the girl immediately flung herself over an embankment onto a railway line. Freud, pointing out that the German word *niederkommen* means both "to fall" and "to be delivered of a child," believed that the girl's attempt expressed her desire to bear her father's child, and punishment for her murderous rage toward her mother. In a footnote to the paper he wrote, "That the various methods of suicide can represent sexual wish-fulfilments has long been known to all analysts. (To poison oneself = to become pregnant; to drown = to bear a child; to throw oneself from a height = to be delivered of a child.)"

Freud's tidy explication—one wonders, for instance, whether the girl would have run several miles in order to find a high place from which to jump had there been none at hand—has inspired numerous other attempts to invest suicide methods with universal symbolic meanings. "The choice of the manner of dying is in itself a significant tell-tale feature," wrote Freud's disciple Wilhelm Stekel. "Women who 'have fallen' or who struggle against temptations, throw themselves out of the window and into the street. The man who entertains secret thoughts of poisoning somebody, takes poison; one who yearns after the flames of love, sets fire to himself; he who believes himself surrounded by poisonous thoughts, turns on the gas." Stekel, who was in poor physical health, killed himself at age seventy-four by overdosing on aspirin. It is not known whom he secretly wished to poison other than himself. In *Man Against*

Himself, Menninger linked drowning to a desire to return to the womb; psychiatrist Joost Meerloo traced hanging to sexual frustrations and claimed that "jumping out of the window may quite paradoxically signify a wish to grow up." More recently, psychiatrists Sidney Furst and Mortimer Ostow suggested that suicidal male homosexuals stab or shoot themselves as an expression of their desire to be attacked by another man's penis. As for homosexuals who jump from heights, this was considered an expression of sexual guilt for "phallic erection under improper circumstances."

Of course, as farfetched as such interpretations seem, choice of method is rarely random, as Hendin demonstrated in his fascinating discussion of method and motive in *Suicide in America*. "Some suicides use their control over how they choose to die to express their feelings about why they want to die," he wrote. "A prisoner can hang himself because it is the only method of suicide available to him, but hanging is also used to express a variety of suicidal motivations. Some people hang themselves as punishment for their desire to choke others: one patient who did, used to 'playfully' choke his wife. For other suicidal individuals, hanging represented how choked and 'hung up' they felt. One such young man came from a family that blocked his every independent constructive effort, while constantly holding out hope of what they would do for him in time. No one could have more effectively 'hung up' anyone than this family 'hung up' their son, and his final retaliation was to hang himself." People whose anger, self-hatred, or need for punishment is especially intense may use particularly violent methods, according to Hendin. An enraged man who lost his job, fell into debt, and was deserted by his wife, killed himself by sealing off the kitchen, turning on the gas, stabbing himself in the chest, and then hanging himself. Hendin suggested that "the multiplicity of methods helped this man express the intense feeling that he was being attacked on all sides." It was no accident, in all senses, when a man depressed over his impotence blew himself up with a stick of dynamite; a lonely Massachusetts spinster suffocated by locking herself into her hope chest; a woman who felt abandoned by her family shut herself into an abandoned refrigerator in her basement; a talented young climber, despondent over breaking up with his girlfriend, leaped off the cliffs he had so often scaled, executing, as he fell, a perfect swan dive; an elderly opera buff in failing health jumped to his death from the top balcony of the Metropolitan Opera House.

Many suicidal people are impulsive and use whatever method is at hand. A man in traction transferred the pulleys and cords from his fractured leg to his neck and strangled himself. Prisoners hang themselves not necessarily because of sexual frustration, as Menninger implies, but because the only means at hand are their shoelaces, shirts, or bedsheets. One particularly desperate inmate chewed through the veins in his wrist. Mental hospital patients manage to procure a variety of tools: plastic bags, windows, broken glass, nails, coat hangers. Other suicidal people may plot their death for weeks, months, or even years, making lists of possible exits, sifting through the pros and cons, weighing the merits not of whether to live but how to die. "Suicides have a special language," wrote Anne Sexton in her poem "Wanting to Die." "Like carpenters they want to know *which tools. /* They never ask *why build*." Sexton thought and wrote about suicide for years before fatally overdosing in 1974. Some suicidal people are extremely choosy—their method must be in keeping with their personalities. Many women (and some men) reject shooting, jumping, or stabbing because they don't want to disfigure their faces or bodies. Hospitalized after many attempts with pills, one woman told her doctor, who was concerned at her being placed on a high floor of the hospital, not to worry. She could never jump, she said, because she was afraid of heights. (A young Chilean, slightly less acrophobic, tied a handkerchief over his eyes before leaping from a twelfth-floor ledge.) Some people go to great lengths to kill themselves by a certain method and will accept no substitute. "A man who has attempted to drown himself will not readily be induced to cut his throat, and *vice versa*," observed one nineteenth-century doctor. A study of six people who survived leaps from San Francisco's Golden Gate Bridge revealed that the bridge had assumed an almost mystical significance for them. All six said they had planned suicide only from the Golden Gate, and no other bridge—or method—would do. This type of insistence—conscious or unconscious—is illustrated by the story of the man on the window ledge. A policeman, drawing his revolver, cries, "Don't jump or I'll shoot!" The man obediently comes inside. This tale, of which several variations are told, may be apocryphal, but it is certainly psychologically accurate for some people.

"It takes a tremendous amount of energy to figure out how you're going to kill yourself," says a forty-seven-year-old woman who recently tried. "I wanted something that was final and wasn't going to be messy. I didn't want to jump off the roof; I might end up only half dead, and I wouldn't like that. I didn't want to blow my head off—I didn't happen to feel that physical disembodiment would be a particularly pleasant thing for everybody." She chuckles ruefully. "I kept thinking about what would be easiest for everyone else. Of course the easiest thing would have been if I'd lived." One night she drove to a nearby field, hooked up a vacuum cleaner hose to the exhaust pipe, zipped herself into a sleeping bag, and stuck the hose into her mouth. The police discovered her the next morning, curled in her sleeping bag, unconscious. She was revived at the hospital. No one could figure out how she had survived until a friend realized the car had a catalytic converter that filtered out carbon monoxide. She had taken the wrong car.

Like this woman, some suicides go to great lengths to avoid hurting loved ones by trying to make sure they won't find the body or that they won't find a disfigured corpse. Others, consciously or otherwise, design their suicides to punish, blame, or take revenge—a contemporary form of the Oriental practice of "killing oneself upon the head of another." A mother who disapproved of her daughter's fiancé killed herself at the wedding reception. A California woman lay across the tracks in front of the commuter train on which she knew her husband was returning home. One July 4 a thirty-year-old New York man, depressed over breaking up with his girlfriend, stuck a powerful firecracker in his mouth, lit it, and blew himself up on the front steps of her home. In 1939 a man wrapped himself in dynamite, wired it to the light socket, and tied the pull chain to his front door. Then he lay down and waited until his wife returned home from visiting a neighbor. When she opened the door, the bomb went off.

A decision related to choice of method is whether or not to leave some final word. Only one in five or six suicides actually leaves a note. Suicide notes have been written or typed on ordinary paper, hotel stationery, prescription slips, therapists' appointment cards, in books of poetry and prayer books. They have been etched in dirt, printed on a mirror with lipstick, written on a blackboard with chalk, scrawled in blood, and dictated onto audiotape and videotape. While they are usually addressed to spouses, family members, and friends, suicide notes have also been addressed to psychiatrists, police, coroners, the press, "to whom it may concern," or to the entire world. One man wrote to his dog: "Bow wow and good-bye, Pepper." Almost a third of those who leave notes leave more than one; one man left several notes in every room of his house. Most are left at or near the scene of the suicide, but some are mailed to friends and relatives. Suicide notes have been as long as dozens of pages and as short as a few words. One man simply wrote, "No comment." Another, "Good-bye, suckers."

For many years researchers believed that notes held a key to understanding motivation for suicide, but several dozen studies have revealed little more than that suicide notes reflect the range of emotions of suicidal people. In one early project, psychologists Edwin Shneidman and Norman Farberow categorized 900 notes according to socioeconomic level. They found that more advantaged writers spoke of being "tired of life" while lower-class suicides were apt to focus on physical illness and the press of details of living. A Philadelphia study of 165 notes found that slightly more than half displayed feelings of gratitude and affection while 24 percent were openly hostile and negative and 24 percent were "neutral." A British study of 136 notes found that people over sixty were more likely to complain of physical illness, refer to the hereafter, and leave instructions for management of their affairs, whereas those under sixty left notes that were reproachful and self-pitying. In a study by psychologist Calvin Frederick, five graphologists, five secretaries, and five policemen were shown forty-five sets of suicide notes, each consisting of a genuine note and three verbatim copies in the handwriting of a nonsuicidal person of the same sex and approximate age of the genuine note writer. Asked to select the genuine notes, the secretaries and detectives couldn't tell the difference. The handwriting experts selected the genuine notes more than 60 percent of the time. They found the penmanship of the suicidal individual to be "impulsive, spontaneous, aggressive, agitated, aimless, disorderly, and laden with anxiety." Investigation into why more than 75 percent of suicides do *not* leave some final written expression has turned up little. "Whether the writers of suicide notes differ in their attitudes from those who leave no notes behind it is impossible to say," observed psychiatrist Erwin Stengel. "Possibly, they differ from the majority only in being good correspondents."

Many note writers ask for absolution, like the minister who hanged himself in his church after scrawling on the paper wrapper that came around the rope, "God forgive me." Others go out of their way to insist that certain people are not to blame. But as Herbert Hendin observes, " 'You are not to blame,' written to a husband, wife, or parent, usually turns out to mean the opposite." Some attempt to provoke lingering guilt. After receiving a letter from his girlfriend telling him she was marrying another man, an Illinois man wrote, "Darling, I cannot live without you. I am going to the garage and use the car that is in there. Remember, I loved you so much I died for you." Others are more direct. "I hope this is what you want," wrote one man to his wife. Notes may be frank expressions of hatred and anger. A man who gassed himself after learning that his wife had run off with his brother wrote on the back of her photograph, "I present this picture of another woman—the girl I thought I married. May you always remember I loved you once but died hating you." One mother found her teenage son hanging behind the Christmas tree. A note pinned to him said, "Merry Christmas."

Notes may offer literal explanations for the suicide. Thomas Hardy's Jude, whose family had fallen upon hard times, found a haunting note underneath the hanged bodies of his three sons: "Done because we are too menny." Gay activist Michael Silverstein asphyxiated himself at thirty-six, writing, "Help isn't what I want now. I've decided it's alright to stop if I want to. *I'm tired.*" Rarely do notes offer philosophic defenses of suicide or treatises on the moral ramifications of the act. More often they are filled with practical instructions, outlining the disposition of property, guest lists for the funeral, reminders to "change the spark plugs on the Ford every ten thousand miles," to "please see that Tommy gets a Mickey Mouse watch for his birthday," or "Don't forget to put out the garbage on Thursdays." A thirty-year-old psychiatrist left this note: "Car to Helen or Ray. Needs a tuneup. Money to Max and Sylvia. Furniture to George plus $137 I owe him." A thirteen-year-old Los Angeles girl who shot herself shortly after actor Freddie Prinze's suicide left her parents an eight-page letter detailing which of her toys and clothes to give to whom, and advice on the care of her pets, plus repeated requests to "please let me be buried by Freddie." While such directives may be thoughtful ways to ease a family's burden, they can be subtle attempts to control a friend or relative after one's death. "I would like my sister Frances to have the piano that you have in your apartment," wrote a sailor to his girlfriend. "Do this or I will haunt you. Goodbye Sweets. Be seeing you soon. Love. Joe."

Some notes written after the overdose has been taken or the gas turned on may sound as if the writer is conducting a scientific experiment on the experience of dying. After swallowing a lethal overdose of sleeping pills, a sixty-eight-year-old man played solitaire, pausing occasionally to record his thoughts. At 9 P.M. he wrote, "No one's fault . . . no one to blame," and quoted Sydney Carton's last words from *A Tale of Two Cities:* "It is a far, far better thing that I do than I have ever done; it is a far, far better rest that I go to than I have ever known." Later he wrote, "Thirty-five minutes past nine. It works so slow." At the bottom of the page there was a final, plaintive entry: "I can't win."

On the other hand some people plan their suicides so carefully, so formally, that they choose to write their notes in verse. In 1774, John Upson, an English glover imprisoned for a felony, hanged himself with his garter after writing in a prayer book:

> *Farewell, vain world, I've had enough of thee,*
> *And now am careless what thou say'st of me;*
> *Thy smiles I court not, nor thy frowns I fear,*
> *My cares are past, my heart lies easy here.*
> *What faults they find in me take care to shun,*
> *And look home: enough is to be done.*

Two hundred years later a Dallas teenager left this poem behind:

> *When I look at myself*
> *in the mirror on the shelf,*
> *I see sadness all about*
> *I see solitude I despise.*
>
> *No one ever seems to care.*
> *No one is ever there*
> *To lift me when I'm down,*
> *Heal me when I hurt,*
> *Make me smile when I frown.*
>
> *Almost all my life I've been frightened and afraid*
> *I've been best friends with a razor blade*
> *With the fissure on my wrist*
> *I've felt the sharp edge of a knife*
> *Its bitter blade deep inside me.*
>
> *Sincerely,*
> *Joey*

Above all, notes reflect their authors' unhappiness. A twenty-year-old who gassed herself in a New York City rooming house on July 4, 1931, wrote, "This is my Independence Day—from life. Love and holidays are not for me. I'm tired and no one wants me." The celebrated young Brazilian cartoonist Péricles killed himself on New Year's Eve, 1962. After shaving and putting on his best white suit and silk tie, as if he were going to a party, he spread a blanket and pillow on the floor, turned on the gas jets of the stove, and lay down. He left this note for his mother:

I'm deeply sorry for you. I spent Christmas Eve alone in this apartment hearing the laughter and joy of neighbors. But it's impossible to go through it again. On a day like this everyone seeks the company of beloved ones. Here I am with nowhere to spend New Year's in anyone's company. It's simply my fault. Forgive me for such a vulgar note.

Fanny Imlay Godwin, the illegitimate daughter of the feminist writer Mary Wollstonecraft, suffered an unrequited love for her half-brother-in-law Percy Bysshe Shelley. In 1816, at age twenty-two, she poisoned herself at an English seaside inn, leaving this note:

I have long determined that the best thing I could do was to put an end to the existence of a being whose birth was unfortunate and whose life has only been a series of pains to those persons who have hurt their health in endeavoring to promote her welfare. Perhaps to hear of my death may give you pain, but you will soon have the blessing of forgetting that such a creature ever existed.

A fifty-year-old Massachusetts man simply wrote:

> *I'm done with life*
> *I'm no good*
> *I'm dead*

In the end the lengths to which suicidal people go to communicate their feelings are matched by the difficulty of writing something that can explain or mitigate such an act. David Kinnell was a depressed eighteen-year-old who had been known in his Massachusetts high school for his gifts as a poet and athlete before his parents started having marital difficulties and his life became centered increasingly around drugs and rock music. Many times he had asked his mother to listen to a particular record. "Can you hear it?" he would say. "Isn't it beautiful?"

Returning to live at home after graduation, following a brief attempt at working, David spent much of his time in the basement listening intently to his albums, copying down the lyrics as the songs played. One day he borrowed his mother's car, saying he had a job interview and wouldn't be home until after midnight. He drove five hundred miles to a park, where he had spent many happy times with his family. At an overlook called Inspiration Point he hanged himself from a tree. When the park ranger found him, the tape deck in his car, parked nearby, still blared music by his favorite group, the Grateful Dead.

In the week following his death David's family and friends began to receive packages from him in the mail. His psychologist received a stack of records and a note saying that killing himself was the right thing to do. The youth leader of his church received a book written by Jerry Garcia, the leader of the Grateful Dead, with a note asking him to pass it on to the psychologist after he had read it. A girlfriend received a record and a note saying, "Call my mother. Please come to it." (She did call his mother, and she did go to David's funeral.) David's thirteen-year-old sister received a $100 gift certificate from Laura Ashley for her birthday the following month. David's mother received a six-page letter that consisted largely of song lyrics by the Grateful Dead, Bob Dylan, Pink Floyd, and other groups, strung together, one song after another. "They were almost impossible to understand," says his mother. "But they seemed to say that he'd gone over the edge, and he couldn't come back. I think he felt so out of control, and finally he took control of his own life. . . . Toward the end of the letter there was a song that said, 'Carry on my wayward son / There'll be peace when you are done.' . . . It was a comfort to read that. I regarded it as an affirmative statement, that he was at peace."

David had labored over his farewell packages for several months. All those times his mother had seen him in the basement copying down lyrics from records, he had been composing his elaborate suicide notes. Then he had wrapped his gifts, put them in the trunk of his mother's car, and mailed them en route to the park where he had chosen to die. Yet while so much care, effort, and thought had gone into the packages, it seemed a tragic footnote that the boy who once expressed himself so well in poetry could only communicate through someone else's music. And even then he was unable to make himself understood. His mother took the note David sent her to a local youth counselor who identified some of the songs. "But I could research every single lyric, every single song, and I still don't think I'd understand," she says. She recalls all those times David asked her to listen to his music, how he had tried to explain, how she had tried to comprehend. " 'Isn't that beautiful?' he'd say, and I'd say, 'I can't understand it. Tell me why you think it's beautiful.' And he'd say, 'You just don't understand.' But now I think he meant much more than that—'you don't understand'—not just the lyrics, but the whole thing, everything."

IV

THE NUMBERS GAME

AT THE OPPOSITE END of the investigative spectrum from clinicians who look at suicide on an individual basis are the statisticians who churn out graphs and charts in pursuit of a broad, external perspective on suicide. What they tell us may at first seem sterile and esoteric; for instance, that from 1928 to 1932 males in Minneapolis were more apt to kill themselves on Tuesday, females on Thursday. But they are trying to answer the same question—why people kill themselves—not by examining case histories of individuals but by examining case histories of entire groups.

According to the World Health Organization, on an average day at least one thousand people take their own lives around the world. Although no countries or cultures are immune to suicide, some are more prone than others. In the nineteenth century, with the development of statistics, a country's suicide rate served as an index of national pride or embarrassment. In this century Sweden acquired an international reputation for suicide. In 1960, President Eisenhower provoked a fuss when he attributed Sweden's high rate to the country's liberal welfare policies, intimating that socialism had left Swedish citizens with nothing to struggle for. Eisenhower overlooked the fact that in the 1960s Sweden had about the same suicide rate as it had in 1910, long before its welfare policies were introduced. (Today, Sweden ranks ninth among the nations that report suicide statistics to the WHO.)

Scandinavia, however, presents an interesting paradox. While the suicide rates of Denmark and Sweden are among the highest in the world, Norway, also a welfare state, consistently ranks among the lowest. A six-year study recently undertaken by the four Scandinavian nations suggests that the reasons have little to do with politics. Focusing on Norway and Denmark, the Nordic Planning Group on Suicidology devised a complex system of measuring "social integration" and found that Norwegians had far stronger ties to family, neighborhood, social clubs, and church, bonds that Émile Durkheim and other sociologists have long believed reduce the likelihood of suicide. Why are Norwegians more apt than Danes—or Swedes or Finns—to form such bonds? Herbert Hendin, who spent two years studying suicide in Scandinavia, found that suicidal people were psychologically quite different in each of the three Scandinavian countries and that the difference reflected their cultural backgrounds. In Denmark, Hendin was struck by how often suicidal behavior was used to arouse guilt. Danish mothers often discipline their children by letting them know how hurt they are by their behavior, and the child learns how to use his own suffering to arouse guilt in others. Young Danes are also taught to suppress aggressive feelings. Dependence on the mother is encouraged far more than in America, Hendin said, making them especially vulnerable to what he calls "dependency-loss" suicides.

Swedes encourage their children to be independent, but they also foster an intense concern with performance, competition, and achievement. "Among the men, success or failure has a life-or-death meaning," wrote Hendin. "Expectations for performance are rigid and self-hatred for failure is great." At the same time Hendin found that Swedish children are taught not to express emotions; they deal with their anger by withdrawal and detachment. This response is exemplified in a common Swedish phrase, *tiga ijhal,* to kill someone by silence. Their psychological profile encourages what Hendin characterized as a "performance" type of suicide, triggered by a failure to live up to perceived expectations.

By contrast, Norwegian mothers tend to be warm and emotionally involved with their children without having rigid expectations. The child is encouraged to express his feelings, and as he grows he is less concerned with performance and more able to express his emotions. A common Norwegian phrase is *forurettet*—to be righteously indignant. Norwegians, said Hendin, are better able to express their anger and frustration in ways short of suicide.

According to Hendin, to understand suicide we must take a "psychosocial perspective"; that is, we must investigate its meaning within its cultural group, synthesizing psychological, social, and cultural factors. Suicide for a Japanese or for a Norwegian differs in meaning and motive from suicide for an American. Similarly, within America, suicide for an urban black differs from suicide for a suburban white or a Native American. "On some level all suicidal people are united by some common denominator of unhappiness," said Hendin. "But what makes them unhappy and why they want to die is a function of the time and place in which they live."

If the suicide rate is any barometer, Hungary, with a rate of 44.4 suicides per 100,000 people, is the unhappiest nation in the world. Although before the recent upheavals in Eastern Europe some Westerners blamed the failings of that country's communist system, Hungary's high rate actually predates her political conversion in the late forties. Others suggest it has more to do with an authoritarian family structure that allows little self-expression. Hungary is followed by Denmark (28.7), Austria (27.7), Finland (25.2), and Switzerland (25.0). Other nations with perennially high rates are West Germany, Japan, Czechoslovakia, and Sweden. While in the nineteenth century variations in suicide rates were attributed to climate, topography, and level of "civilization," rates today are more affected by a country's social, cultural, and religious attitudes, its economy, and its degree of urbanization. Prior to the fall of the Berlin Wall, West Berlin may have had the highest rate of any area in the world, more than twice that of West Germany as a whole. Alienated not only geographically but spiritually, culturally, and politically, the city was the embodiment of what Durkheim called "anomie."

At the opposite end of the spectrum are Italy (6.9 per 100,000), Spain (4.4), and Mexico (1.6). Although these low rates are usually attributed to the preponderance of Roman Catholics in these countries, Costa Rica and Northern Ireland, which are predominantly Protestant countries, have low rates while Catholic Austria has one of the highest rates in the world. (For centuries it has been traditional wisdom that Protestants have a higher suicide rate than Catholics and that Catholics have a higher rate than Jews. Actual figures are difficult to procure—death certificates in the United States do not record religious affiliation—but several European studies show that although the rates for all three groups have increased over the course of the twentieth century, the rate for Jews has risen more rapidly.) Of course, some of the disparity among countries is due to reporting techniques. Industrialized countries, which tend to have higher rates, also tend to have more sophisticated methods of gathering statistics and fewer taboos against doing so. Some countries may underreport for religious or political reasons. In 1985, for instance, a Nicaraguan newspaper reported that Sandinista censors objected to the publication of a story about a ninety-six-year-old woman who had killed herself. The story, said the Sandinistas, was "an attack on the psychic health of the people and, therefore, an attack against the security of the state." Although as of 1988 the U.S.S.R. did not report suicide statistics to the World Health Organization—suicide, party spokesmen asserted in pre-perestroika days, is a "bourgeois activity"—suicidologists suspect that its rate is high.

The United States ranks near the middle of the forty-three nations reporting to the WHO. Although its rate of 12.8 in 1986 was close to what it was at the turn of the century (10.2), it has fluctuated over time. During periods of economic depression there is more suicide; during times of war, when, as Durkheim pointed out, personal woes are overshadowed by the larger conflict, there is less suicide. During World War I the rate dipped from 16.2 in 1915 to 11.5 in 1919 before rising steadily in the twenties. The suicide rate rose during the Depression, reaching its apex in 1932 at 17.4. As the economy stabilized so did the suicide rate, and by 1936 it had dropped to 14.3. During World War II the rate sank to a low of 10.0. After the war it rose slightly, and ever since it has remained fairly constant, ranging from a low of 9.8 in 1957 to a high of 13.1 in 1977, when the youth suicide rate peaked. Although the rate of suicide among Vietnam veterans has been high, the war itself had little effect on the country's rate, perhaps because it was so controversial, fragmenting rather than uniting the citizens as did the more "popular" world wars.

Many studies have shown that suicide rates fluctuate according to the economy. When the United States rate is graphed against the economy over time, the two lines nearly mirror each other. A growing body of research links unemployment and ill health, suggesting that the stress of joblessness triggers problems in marriages, conflicts with children, and physical and mental difficulties among vulnerable people. Examining data from 1940 to 1970, sociologist M. Harvey Brenner of John Hopkins University estimated that when unemployment rises one percentage point, 4.1 percent more people commit suicide.

Within the United States itself the suicide rate varies widely. Nevada has long had the highest suicide rate of any state, consistently twice that of the nation as a whole. Its large cities of Las Vegas and Reno are a magnet for the transient, the divorced, and others hoping to reverse their fortunes. Other states with consistently high rates are Florida, Arizona, Colorado, Wyoming, Alaska, Montana, New Mexico, Oregon, and California, all of which are in the West with the exception of Florida, whose high rate can probably be accounted for by its unusually high proportion of the elderly. Some blame the high rate in the Western states on the stereotypical image of the Western male as tough, unemotional, and willing to use violence as a solution. Others advance an "end of the road" theory, suggesting that people often move West with the expectation of changing their lives, and when their problems persist, they may become disappointed, hopeless, and suicidal. Other explanations have also been proposed. In the 1930s, ever eager to blame suicide on the weather, some blamed San Diego's high rate on the effect of "too much sunshine," though in all likelihood the real culprit was, as in Florida, the concentration of older people. The lowest rates are generally found in the Northeast and the South. New England has had a consistently low rate, which some credit to a sort of "Yankee fortitude" (although recently this has been contradicted by Vermont's persistent appearance among the states with the highest rates).

Ever since statistics on suicide were first kept, statisticians have suggested that the rate of suicide is lower in the country than in the city, where, as one sociologist put it in 1905, "the struggle for existence is carried on with the greatest keenness, and . . . nervous tension reaches its highest pitch." Chief blame for the rising suicide rates of the nineteenth and twentieth centuries was placed on "urbanization." But in this country the difference between urban and rural rates has become less pronounced in recent decades. In 1929 urban areas recorded a rate of 17.4; rural, 11.0; in 1959 urban areas had a rate of 10.7; rural, 10.0. In recent years rural suicide rates may have been boosted by the rash of suicides among economically pressed farmers. (In Europe the disparity between urban and rural rates persists.)

Although for many years it was assumed that the larger the city, the higher the suicide rate, this is not always true. In Chicago and Philadelphia rates are moderate, and people are often surprised to learn that New York City has a rate no higher than that of the country as a whole, leading some to suggest that the grit of that city cultivates a survival mentality.

Rates vary not only from city to city but within cities themselves. Sociologists have demonstrated that rates are highest in two kinds of areas: neighborhoods with a shifting population and the most wealthy sections. A study of Minneapolis suicides from 1928 to 1932 found them concentrated in the center of the city, an area of rooming houses and cheap hotels that the researcher called "a land of transiency and anonymity." Studies of Seattle and Chicago yielded similar results. In his 1955 district-by-district survey of London, Peter Sainsbury found that social isolation was a more important factor than "indigenous poverty" in determining suicide areas. In the poor but close-knit working-class sections of London's East End, the rate was far lower than in prosperous suburbs like Bloomsbury, whose comfortable houses were interspersed with one-room flats, transient hotels, and boardinghouses. He also found high rates around railroad stations and areas settled by immigrants and the newly rich, both of whom, he suggested, faced problems of adjustment and "social isolation." Twenty-seven percent of London suicides had been living alone, while only 7 percent of the general population lived alone. One cannot, of course, conclude from these results whether suicidal people are drawn to living in lodging houses or whether living in lodging houses drives people to suicide.

Within cities, rates also vary according to ethnic group. Many studies have shown that first-generation immigrants have rates closer to those of their homelands than to those of their adopted country. For instance, German, Austrian, and Scandinavian immigrants to the United States have extraordinarily high rates, while Italian, Irish, and Greek immigrants have relatively low rates. Danish psychiatrists have pointed to the high rate of Norwegian emigration to the United States as the cause of Norway's low suicide rate compared to Denmark or Sweden. They have argued that depressed and suicidal Norwegians emigrated and became subsumed in American statistics.

Among Scandinavian immigrants, however, the Danish and Swedish rates remain two or three times that of the Norwegian rate.

The few studies of suicide by occupation find the highest rates among the medical profession. Rates for physicians are at least three times that of the general population, with an especially high rate among female physicians compared with the female population in general. Within the medical field, surgeons, who may often feel directly responsible for the life and death of their patients, tend to have high rates; obstetricians, pediatricians, and radiologists have lower ones. Psychiatrists have the highest rate of any medical specialty, six times that of the general population. To account for the rate of physician suicide, experts point to the high stress level of the work, the tendency of doctors to keep their feelings inside, and the pressure they feel to save their patients' lives. The type of personality often drawn to the field of medicine, they say, may be especially vulnerable. "It draws workaholics, overly conscientious people who take failure poorly, and idealists, who are frequently disappointed during their careers," psychiatrist Robert Litman has said. In addition, physician suicide is encouraged by the ready availability of lethal drugs and the knowledge of how to use them. (More than half of physician suicides overdose, while only 12 percent use guns—numbers that are nearly reversed in the general population.) Other professional groups with high rates include dentists, police officers, and lawyers.

Although Ishmael, in Herman Melville's *Moby Dick,* described suicidal depression as "a damp, drizzly November in my soul," T. S. Eliot was a more accurate emotional weatherman: For suicides, April *is* indeed the cruelest month. Its rate is some 12 percent above the average for the rest of the year. In November, in fact, the rate is near its lowest. The winter months generally have the lowest rate, and contrary to conventional wisdom, there is no increase around Christmas or New Year's or any other major holiday. Perhaps the rate rises in the spring because a person's depression is heightened by the regeneration around him. "A suicidal depression is a kind of spiritual winter, frozen, sterile, unmoving," wrote A. Alvarez. "The richer, softer and more delectable nature becomes, the deeper that internal winter seems, and the wider and more intolerable the abyss which separates the inner world from the outer. Thus suicide becomes a natural reaction to an unnatural condition." Statistics also tell us that Saturday is the least popular day for suicide and Monday the most popular, perhaps because people are back in the "real world" after the exhilaration of the weekend. However, the effect of these factors on a suicidal individual is considerably less than the effect of culture.

One of the most interesting examples of how culture influences suicide is in the black population. For many years it was believed that suicide was, as one researcher put it, "a white solution to white problems." Indeed, for many years the black suicide rate in this country has been about half that of the rate for whites. Attempts to explain this were derived from Freud's belief that suicide is the result of murderous impulses toward a lost love object turned inward. In dealing with frustration and aggression, social groups were said to turn either to homicide or to suicide, and rates varied inversely in a given community. Sociologists pointed to the high homicide and low suicide rates among American blacks as evidence (as well as the low homicide and high suicide rates in Sweden and Denmark). The generally held—if rarely expressed—opinion was that blacks killed other people while whites killed themselves.

A second explanation was also proposed, based on Durkheim's suggestion that the greater a person's status, the greater the potential fall and the greater the chance of suicide. Some said suicide was a luxury blacks couldn't afford because they were too busy trying to survive. "Black folks have so many problems they don't even have time to think about committing suicide," the saying went. Comedian Dick Gregory commented: "You can't kill yourself by jumping out of the basement."

Facts indicate otherwise. While the black homicide rate is high—seven to ten times higher than that of whites—suicide is also a significant and growing problem for blacks. This is largely due to the soaring rate of youthful black suicide. While the rate for young white males has nearly tripled in three decades, the rate for young black males has more than doubled. The age pattern of black suicide is different from that of whites. The rate peaks in youth (47 percent of black suicides occur among ages twenty to thirty-four, although this group comprises only 22 percent of the black population), then levels off after age thirty-five while the white rate rises. The black elderly rate is low, about one-third that of whites, for whom the elderly rate is highest. Why is the young black male rate so high? Why is the elderly black rate so low? Until recently these questions have gone unexplored.

Herbert Hendin's exploration of youth suicide in Harlem in the late sixties was one of the first studies of black suicide. He found that the rate for black New York males age twenty to twenty-five was higher—in some years twice as high—than that for white males of the same age. This had been true since 1910, when records began to be kept in New York City. (Since then, other studies have found this to be true in other areas of the country.) His findings contradicted conventional thinking on the relationship between suicide and violence. Interviewing young black men and women who had made serious suicide attempts, he found a direct relationship, not an inverse one, between suicide and homicide. Almost all had a history of violence in their childhoods—fathers who were physically violent or who died violent deaths, mothers who were abusive—and violence became a part of their lives. Hendin's subjects often thought of killing someone else—sometimes it didn't seem to matter whom—before they attempted to kill themselves. "Many of these subjects came to life only through acts or fantasies of violence," wrote Hendin. "In merely talking of past fights or brutality they became far more animated than usual. They see living itself as an act of violence, and regard death as the only way to control their rage."

For suicidal young blacks, parental rejection and abuse are compounded by rejection from society. Hendin believed blacks realize at an early age that because of discrimination and racism their opportunities for advancement are limited. "It does not seem surprising that suicide becomes a problem at such a relatively early age for the black person," he has written. "A sense of despair, a feeling that life will never be satisfying, confronts many blacks at a far younger age than it does most whites. For most discontented white people the young adult years contain the hope of a significant change for the better. The marked rise in white suicide after forty-five reflects, among other things, the decline in such hope that is bound to accompany age." A young black man who hanged himself in a juvenile detention center left this note: "I haven't got nothing. And I ain't never going to be nobody. Tell my mother good-bye, if you can find her."

As James Baldwin wrote, "To be a Negro in this country and to be relatively conscious is to be in a rage almost all of the time." Statistics can only begin to hint at the sources and consequences of that rage. Studies have shown that adolescents lacking a parent are more likely to attempt suicide, and today more than half of black children are born to unwed mothers. Half of all black children have no father at home. Divorce among blacks is twice as frequent as among whites. Unemployment among black men is at 16 percent, nearly three times as high as among white men; for black teens it is more than 40 percent. If, as Brenner believes, for every 1 percent unemployment there are 4.1 percent more suicides, it is remarkable that the black youth suicide rate is not even higher than it is now. Black family incomes average only 56 percent of white family incomes. The poverty rate for blacks is 31 percent compared to 11 percent for whites. Blacks also suffer from poor housing and education. Some 18 percent of black males drop out of high school, and many are turned away from college because of financial need. "Young urban black men are subjected to enormous stress," psychologist Richard Seiden concludes. "Indeed, if one wanted systematically to drive a significant portion of the population psychotic, one would be hard put to devise a more effective method than the one we've got."

It is perhaps not surprising, therefore, that many young blacks in the ghetto treat violence, including murder, with nonchalance. (The leading cause of death among black males age fifteen to twenty-four is homicide; in America today a white male has one chance in 186 of becoming a murder victim, a black male, one in 29.) "They believe they have nothing to lose," social worker James Evans, Jr., told *Time* magazine. "Even if they should lose their own lives, they feel they will not have lost very much. Besides, why should they be good, they ask. There is no reward for good behavior." Homicide or suicide may seem the only way of making a dent in a world that is repressive, contemptuous, or, at best, indifferent to their existence. In *Invisible Man,* Ralph Ellison described violence as a way for blacks to reassure themselves of their existence. "You ache with the need to convince yourself that you do exist in the real world, that you're a part of all the sound and anguish." Social worker Ruth Dennis, who has studied black suicide and homicide for two decades, points out that such violence has become an accepted cultural tradition for young ghetto blacks. "His group may demand that he prove his manhood by not 'backing down' from a life-threatening encounter even if it means his own destruction," she told the audience at a National Symposium on Black Suicide. "This behavior is demanded by the only group that accepts him." Dennis compared it to the behavior of eighteenth-century European gentlemen who felt obliged to challenge someone to a duel at the slightest insult.

Social scientists suggest that some young urban blacks express a combination of suicidal and homicidal impulses by provoking someone else into killing them. They may consider it a more acceptable form of death than suicide per se, which is seen as unmanly in the ghetto subculture. And so they engage, kamikaze-like, in shootouts with police against overwhelming odds, often triggering their own deaths. One young black man, for instance, brandished a pistol he knew to be unloaded at policemen and was shot. A few psychologists suggest that radical groups like the Black Panthers, one of whose slogans was "Revolutionary Suicide," have deliberately courted death at the hands of authorities. But others caution against easy psychologizing. "The problem with such speculations is that they often arise out of unconscious and sometimes conscious attempts to blame the victim for the brutal acts of another," writes psychiatrist Alvin Poussaint. "According to this rationalization, violence among blacks is suicidal behavior, a black who resists a white policeman is trying to commit suicide: so the policeman who murders is morally absolved of homicide. Such assumptions imply that blacks who rise up and rebel against an unjust system are crazy rather than courageous, insane rather than incensed. Many institutional authorities refuse to acknowledge the willingness of black youth to risk their lives because they want a better life."

Poussaint is one of several researchers to suggest that many black suicides are what Durkheim called "fatalistic." "There is a type of suicide the opposite of anomic suicide," wrote Durkheim. ". . . It is the suicide deriving from excessive regulation, that of persons with futures pitilessly blocked and passions violently choked by oppressive discipline." Durkheim felt that fatalistic suicide was rare, relegating it to a footnote in *Le Suicide* and citing as an example the suicide of very young (and presumably beleaguered) husbands. Nevertheless, he wrote, "Do not the suicides of slaves . . . belong to this type, or all suicides attributable to excessive physical or moral despotism?"

Durkheim's theory was supported by Warren Breed's 1970 study of suicide in New Orleans. He found that more than half of suicides by blacks occurred in the context of conflict with authorities—landlords, lawyers, tax officials, and police—compared to only 10 percent of white suicides. Many had a great (and perhaps justified) terror of the police, like the young man who had always expressed such a fear although he had never been arrested. One night during an argument he shot and wounded his girlfriend; when he heard police sirens, he turned the gun on himself. In many cases blacks committed suicide in the face of problems that could easily have been resolved had they had some basic knowledge of community resources—legal aid services, housing authorities, tax agencies, and so on. "The Negro is subject to the imperatives of two communities," wrote Breed, "and when his difficulties extend outside the Negro sphere, he is faced with authorities who are white—to him an alien force. He bears a double burden of social regulation. A white man can feel trapped, too, but the data demonstrate a much lower frequency of the 'authority' stress factor in white male suicide."

In 1938 psychoanalyst Charles Prudhomme predicted that as blacks in America entered the white-dominated mainstream, their suicide rate would approach the white rate. Some theorists say that this is now happening. They suggest that segregation acted as protection against suicide. "As racial discrimination decreases," writes Richard Seiden, "the stability of shared social relationships, the sense of community based upon discrimination by a common enemy, is likewise decreased." Just as women's suicide rates grew as they entered the mainstream of society, so too have black rates risen as their status—and their expectations—have risen. Some say the massive migration of black Americans from the South to the North, from rural to urban areas where they were exposed to new, unfamiliar stresses, is responsible for the rising rate. (Rates are higher for blacks in the North; in the South they are traditionally low.) Durkheim was the first to observe that poverty protects people from suicide because those who expect little are not disappointed when they receive little. Seiden writes: "Perhaps these unifying social ties are destroyed as personal aspirations are realized. Could increased suicide be the ticket of admission to the middle-class American dream?"

Ruth Dennis suggests there may be two forms of black suicide: the angry urban ghetto suicide Hendin describes and the suicide of those trying to assimilate, to succeed in a world dominated by whites. Success in the white-dominated world may be a double-edged sword. "The current increase in Black suicide can be attributed, at least in part, to young upwardly mobile Blacks who are isolated from their families, communities, and social institutions," wrote Robert Davis. "The Black community, in effect, does not function as a substitute society for these individuals." A 1976 study by Alton Kirk, an associate professor of psychology at Michigan State, found that blacks who attempted suicide had less racial pride and less sense of black identity than blacks who did not attempt suicide. Kirk feels that black consciousness, in giving one a more positive self-concept, offers a protective shield against suicide. Those who "try to become more assimilated into the contemporary white

American society," he says, will "find themselves in 'the ethnic twilight zone,' belonging to neither the white or the black world."

Elderly blacks, it is theorized, have made a certain peace with their lives in a racist society, perhaps scaling down their hopes to fit reality more closely. The suicide rate for white males over sixty is more than triple that for blacks. Elderly black women have the lowest rate of any age group in any ethnic group: 2.5 per 100,000. Why is the elderly black rate so low? Some psychologists suggest that because blacks are accustomed to adversity, they are better prepared to survive it. "Their expectations of life have been different from those of whites," suggests Alvin Poussaint. "Thus, tragedy that might drive a white man to self-murder might be accepted by a black man as one more incident in a life of hard times." One psychologist suggests that the majority of violent black males are removed from the population before they even reach old age, having killed themselves, been murdered, or been imprisoned. Another factor that might explain the reduced suicide rate among elderly black women may be the strong matriarchal tradition that extends over several generations. Black grandmothers play an important role in family life—caring for children, cooking, keeping house—which may give them a sense of purpose that many elderly whites say they lack.

Until recently there had been few studies of racial and ethnic minorities and suicide, and much of what existed had been done by whites. For several years, in fact, the American Association of Suicidology was unable to award its annual prize for research on minority suicide. Even today few prevention centers train volunteers, most of whom are white, in how to deal with callers whose ethnic and cultural backgrounds are different from their own. Minorities may avoid seeking help from the mental health system, which is hardly surprising given that the system is predominantly run by and geared toward whites. There are few symposiums or panels on black suicide, and those that do take place are sparsely attended. The 1985 NIMH Youth Suicide Conference drew more than four hundred clinicians, prevention experts, and educators, only sixteen of whom chose to attend the presentation on black youth suicide. "Blacks view suicide among blacks as a rare occurrence; whites see black suicide as a black problem," writes Alton Kirk. "Too many people, black and white, fail to see that black suicide is symptomatic of more general societal problems—societal problems which we must work together to solve before they destroy us all, both black and white."

One of the reasons that sophisticated research on black suicide has been scarce is that until 1964 all "nonwhites" were lumped together in a single statistical category by the National Center for Health Statistics. Since then, the office has subdivided this group into blacks (who make up 87 percent of nonwhites) and "all others," which still leaves Native Americans, Asians, and dozens of other groups in one category. Since Hispanic-Americans are buried within the "white" statistical category, research on Hispanic-American suicide is virtually nonexistent. One of the few large-scale studies surveyed five southwestern states (Arizona, California, Colorado, New Mexico, Texas) where more than 60 percent of all Hispanics in America live and where since 1975 death certificates have distinguished between Anglos and Hispanics. The study showed that the suicide rate of Hispanics (9.0) was less than the national rate for whites (12.7) and one-half that of Anglos living in that area (17.3). This was true for both males and females. And like black suicide, Hispanic suicide peaks in youth. Almost 70 percent of Hispanics who committed suicide were under age forty, and 33 percent were under twenty-five (compared to 17 percent of Anglos). For women the rate peaked early, then fell off sharply; for men the rates were highest in the twenties and after age sixty but still much lower than for Anglos. (It must be remembered, however, that this study was primarily of Mexican-Americans, and does not reflect vast cultural differences among various Hispanic groups.)

Research on Native American suicide is similarly sparse, a fact underscored during a six-week period in 1985 when nine young Native Americans (eight Arapaho and one Shoshone) killed themselves on the Wind River reservation in Wyoming. All were young men, all chose hanging—using rope, socks, baling twine, sweatpants, and the drawstring from a sweatshirt. In response to the suicides psychologists and counselors held weekly suicide prevention sessions in the reservation schools, discussing clues, warning signs, alcohol abuse, and so on. A task force delivered family counseling. A teen suicide hot line was established. But there was another, less clinically orthodox response. The community's young Arapaho took part in a sacred tribal ritual last performed in 1918 to ward off an outbreak of Spanish influenza. Four feathers, each decorated with a red ribbon and blessed with the Arapaho sacred pipe, were placed near the tribal sun dance ground to mark the points of the compass and purge the unhappiness that might have caused the suicides. Inside a tepee a tribal elder cleansed members of the tribe by tapping on the ground, painting their faces with scarlet paint, and having them step over a burning herb. Hundreds of young people waited their turn outside. There would not be another suicide for almost six months.

Although the two approaches may have combined effectively in this case, they demonstrate the cultural gap that many say led to the suicides. In pre-reservation days each Indian tribe developed its own attitude toward suicide. Chippewas, for instance, believed suicide was a foolish but not deplorable act; the Alabama tribes considered it cowardly; the Creeks were said to kill themselves "after the slightest disappointment." Many tribes released aggression and frustration in other ways. Among the Cheyenne, for instance, suicide was rare but not unknown. When a warrior grew depressed or lost face, a war party was often organized. In battle he would take some heroic risk that resulted either in a renewal of his self-esteem or in his death. Another outlet for masochistic aggression was the sun dance, in which warriors engaged in various kinds of self-mutilation.

"After they were confined to the reservation, the Indians were forbidden to hold their Sun Dance or carry out any other 'primitive and barbaric rituals,' " wrote Larry Dizmang in his study of suicide among the Cheyenne. "They could no longer hunt the nearly extinct buffalo, and of course fighting between tribes was outlawed. A Government program designed to improve health conditions forced the Indian men to cut their long hair, a prized symbol of their strength; and, because the Indian could no longer support himself or his family on the reservation, the Government was forced to set up welfare programs, which only added to the rapid downward spiral of increasing dependency and loss of self-esteem."

Today, the Cheyenne are one of many tribes to have found new ways to vent aggression: alcoholism, homicide, and suicide. The suicide rate for Native Americans is the highest of any racial or ethnic group in America. In 1975 the rate for all Native Americans was 21.6, 70 percent higher than the national rate. And it is rising. Between 1970 and 1975 the rate for all Native Americans increased 36 percent, in contrast to 9 percent for all races in that period. As with blacks the rate is highest for the young and lowest for the elderly. The rate for ages fifteen to twenty-four (27.9 from 1981 to 1983) is more than twice the rate for all fifteen- to twenty-four-year-olds. But while the suicide rate for American Indians as a whole is high, there is tremendous variation among the nation's four hundred tribal groups. The tribes with the highest rates are generally the ones with higher acculturation. Trying to fit into a dominant new culture while maintaining traditional values may result in what social scientists call "marginality"—the inability to form dual ethnic identification because of bicultural membership.

One of the world's highest suicide rates is found among the Eskimos of Alaska, Canada, and Greenland. Suicide has always played an important role in Eskimo culture, but it used to be the "economic" suicide of the elderly and ill who walked off to die during times of meager resources in order to perpetuate the survival of their tribe. Today, suicide among Eskimos is largely a problem of the young. Most researchers attribute the high rate of suicide to the rapidity with which the Eskimos have been dragged into the white man's culture. Young Eskimos who move to urban areas are isolated from their roots while even those who stay in their villages find the traditional way of life changing rapidly. Everything that once defined their culture—from language and family patterns to the subsistence hunting economy—is eroding. Snowmobiles have replaced dogsleds, and unemployment has replaced subsistence hunting and fishing (which have been greatly restricted by game regulations imposed by the white man's government). To counter this trend an Eskimo rights movement is currently organizing to restore the native languages, cultural traditions, and political autonomy. At present, however, many Eskimos are caught between two worlds. In 1978 there were a dozen suicides in Frobisher Bay, a town of twenty-six hundred people in the Northwest Territories, two hundred miles below the Arctic Circle. At a store there where Eskimo youths gather, one line of graffiti stood out: "I wish I kill myself like hell."

Just as ethnicity has an effect on suicide, so does sexuality. The history of homosexuality is strikingly similar to the history of suicide. Over the millennia both were viewed as a natural act, then as a sin and a crime, then as a disease. Just as suicides were dragged through the streets, hanged upside down, and burned, homosexuals were imprisoned, beaten, castrated, burned at the stake, and hanged in public squares. For centuries exposure in a homophobic society—and the attendant public humiliation, possible imprisonment, and loss of friends, family, and career—almost literally meant the end of one's life. Many homosexuals saw no option but to make that figurative end literal. Newspapers of the forties and fifties were filled with accounts of men who killed themselves after being arrested on a "morals charge." Many more went unreported: those who killed themselves after being blackmailed; those who killed themselves in shame as they acknowledged their feelings. "Prior to the development of the gay movement, public identification as a homosexual was, almost by definition, linked to scandal, social ostracism, blackmail and suicide," wrote Eric Rofes in *I Thought People Like That Killed Themselves—Lesbians, Gay Men and Suicide,* in which he discusses "the myth of the suicidal homosexual." As the title of Rofes's book suggests, for many years homosexuality and suicide were seen as synonymous. "I remember in the Fifties it was almost understood that you weren't really queer if you didn't feel the melancholia that would cause you to attempt self-destruction," observed Pat Norman, director of the San Francisco Gay/Lesbian Health Service, at the 1986 National Conference on Gay and Lesbian Suicide.

For many years the medical profession reinforced that myth. In the late nineteenth century homosexuality, like suicide, was reinterpreted as a disease to be "cured." As with suicide, homosexuality's evolution from a moral to a medical problem merely changed the nature of the stigma. Many mental health professionals, in fact, insisted that homosexuality in itself was a form of suicidal behavior. In 1962 the psychiatrist and suicide scholar Joost Meerloo wrote, "The homosexual act in itself may already represent a suicidal tendency, an inner fury against prolonging the race, or an unconscious need to merge with the stronger person of the same sex." The association of homosexuality and suicide was also reflected in novels, plays, and films in which homosexuals were frequently portrayed as miserable guilt-ridden individuals who ended up killing themselves. "Homosexuality used to be a sensational gimmick," Mart Crowley, author of the play *The Boys in the Band,* told *Time* in 1969. "The big revelation in the third act was that the guy was homosexual, and then he had to go offstage and blow his brains out. It was associated with sin, and there had to be retribution." In Lillian Hellman's 1934 play, *The Children's Hour,* a schoolteacher accused of lesbianism is driven to suicide by the homophobic citizens of a small southern town.

"Have lesbians and gay men internalized the myth of homosexuals as suicidal and engaged in massive self-destruction?" asks Rofes. Although accurate statistics are difficult to compile because sexual orientation is not listed on death certificates, various studies have found that gay men and lesbians attempt suicide two to seven times more often than heterosexuals. In *The Gay Report,* a 1979 questionnaire of over five thousand lesbians and gay men in the United States and Canada, 40 percent of the men and 39 percent of the women said they had attempted or seriously contemplated suicide. "There is no doubt that suicide and attempted suicide are frequent responses of gay people to the difficulties of the gay experience in a hostile society," concluded the authors. "It has been suggested that psychiatrists, clergy, and others who insist on characterizing gays as sick and sinful are responsible for driving many gay people to suicide."

Why is the suicide rate among blacks, who have also suffered centuries of persecution, lower than that of the general population while the gay rate is higher? Unlike blacks, gays often lack traditional supports that may act as a buffer against suicide. They are vulnerable to what Durkheim called "egoistic" suicide. Many have been rejected by their families, friends, and religions. In *Is the Homosexual My Neighbor,* a man comments, "Less than two months ago I was told by a sincere Christian counselor that it would be 'better' to 'repent and die,' even if I had to kill myself, than to go on living and relating to others as a homosexual." Homosexuality is no longer officially considered a mental illness; the American Psychiatric Association dropped it from the *Diagnostic and Statistical Manual of Mental Disorders* in 1973. But as Myron Mohr, director of the Baton Rouge Crisis Intervention Center, observes, "Regardless of what the APA has said, there are still therapists who believe that homosexuality is a disease they must try to cure." And though in the last few decades the gay rights movement has made it more acceptable to be openly gay, gay men and lesbians still face discrimination in employment, immigration, and the ministry. The National Gay Task Force found that more than 90 percent of two thousand gay males and lesbians surveyed had experienced abuse at some point in their lives because of their sexual orientation. In July 1981, Boston police raided a gay bar and arrested thirty-two men on charges of "open and gross lewdness." Two weeks later one of the men was found dead of an overdose.

Other factors in the high rate of gay and lesbian suicide are alcohol and drugs. For many years gay and lesbian socializing has revolved around bars, which are among the few places where they can comfortably gather. Some researchers suggest that gay men and lesbians turn to alcohol and drugs as a way of dealing with oppression and social stigma. Alcohol and drug abuse are two of the highest risk factors for suicide among any group, and the rate of abuse among gays and lesbians is estimated to be about three times higher than in the general population.

Suicide is a particular danger among gay and lesbian adolescents. "All of the problems that affect youth suicide in general affect gay youth suicide as well," says Paul Gibson, a social worker at Huckleberry House, a San Francisco shelter for runaways where approximately 25 percent of the clients are gay. "But gay young people have the doubly difficult task of not only trying to survive adolescence but of coming to terms with their sexuality and developing a positive identity." Several studies show that young gays and lesbians are two to three times more likely to attempt suicide than other adolescents. An estimated 20 to 35 percent of gay youth attempt suicide, while more than half experience suicidal feelings. In an Indiana University study of 979 homosexual men and women from the San Francisco area, 20 percent of gays had attempted suicide before age twenty. Despite these statistics, in the recent attention to adolescent suicide, gay and lesbian suicide has been all but ignored.

Although many adolescent suicide attempts are made in response to a stressful act, like the breakup of a romance, a 1987 study by the Los Angeles Suicide Prevention Center of suicidal behavior in fifty-two gay adolescents found that their attempts were more often the result of long-standing anxieties and fears surrounding their attempts to come to terms with their emerging homosexuality. In fact, some counselors believe that many of the seemingly inexplicable or so-called out-of-the-blue teenage suicides may be the acts of adolescents who are struggling with homosexual feelings, have no one they dare confide in, and decide suicide is the only solution.

Not surprisingly, the LASPC study found that young gays and lesbians often lacked the social supports generally available to heterosexual teens. "Gay and lesbian youth face total rejection from their family," says Gibson. "Many of the young people we work with at Huckleberry House were told to leave home when they came out to their parents. Gay and lesbian adolescents also face the prospect of not having any kind of peer group support. Many gay and lesbian young people lose close friends in coming out to them. Frequently they are harassed, ridiculed, and assaulted at school by their peers, either if they're open about who they are or if it's suspected. School becomes a scary place for them." Even when they seek help they may not have the support of counselors. Gibson says, "Helping professionals frequently worsen the problems of gay and lesbian youth by failing to accept their orientation." The one person who accepts the gay adolescent's sexual orientation may be his or her lover. In that case the relationship may take on a life-and-death intensity. "They put all the energy that's missing from the relationship with the family that doesn't want them and from the peer group that rejects them into their relationship with their lover," says Gibson. "When that relationship ends, they feel as if *everything* is over."

For gay men of all ages the problem of suicide has been immensely complicated by AIDS. "For persons at risk there is almost universal suicidal thinking," says Peter Goldblum of the Stanford Health AIDS Project. "This should
not be surprising. When you're dealing with AIDS, you're confronted with the
issue of death, and it is natural to think about having control over your own
death." A study of AIDS patients in New York City, one of the few systematic
studies of suicide and AIDS, found that AIDS patients are thirty-six times
more likely to kill themselves than other men aged twenty to fifty-nine, and
sixty-six times more likely than the general population. Right-to-die groups
that once catered primarily to the elderly report increased calls from young
men with AIDS and AIDS-related complex. Writes author Randy Shilts,
"Gay men facing AIDS now exchange formulas for suicide as casually as
housewives swap recipes for chocolate-chip cookies." Researchers point out
that the AIDS diagnosis may be more difficult to deal with than the diagnosis
of terminal cancer; if a gay man has seen someone die of AIDS—and many
gays can no longer count the number of friends they have lost to the disease—
and then is given an AIDS diagnosis himself, he may experience a total loss
of hope because he does not want to go through what he saw his friend suffer.
The suffering caused by AIDS is frequently exacerbated by lack of support.
AIDS patients may lose their jobs and their apartments; they may be abandoned by family and friends, even by lovers and hospital personnel. And
suicide is an issue not only for those actually diagnosed with AIDS but for
people at risk for AIDS, for those who have been exposed to the AIDS virus,
and for those with loved ones who have AIDS. One man who was given a
tentative diagnosis of AIDS hanged himself in a San Francisco park; it turned
out that the diagnosis had been inaccurate. The misinformation and hysteria
surrounding the subject only heighten the feeling of being out of control.
Psychologist Terry Gock says, "When we feel we are not in control anymore,
it is easy to look at ending it all as a way of gaining back some control."

In 1987, at a conference on suicide, a young San Francisco man who had
been diagnosed with AIDS spoke about how he tried to regain command of
his life. "I went from 145 to 102 pounds. I had to crawl on my hands and knees
to the bathroom, bleeding at times. I shook as if I had Parkinson's disease. I
was losing my hearing. I was losing my eyesight. I was doing nothing but going
to doctors and therapists. My quality of life went further down than I ever
imagined was possible. I had spent my life helping people. Now I couldn't even
help myself. I had already lost ten to twelve people in my life to AIDS. I
considered suicide. I saw a therapist. She said, 'Do you want to die?' I said,
'I can't see myself living.' I decided to kill myself. I had Tylenol, codeine,
Demerol. Each time I went to the pharmacy and got more, I would go home,
wrap it up, tie it with a ribbon, and put it away.

"I had made the decision. The day came. My therapist could have had me
committed, but she said, 'Jack, I hope I see you next week.' I'd bought flowers,

and I put candles around. I had spent most of the last six months writing letters to friends and relatives. It was the day of the gay parade. I put on my best drag, went out with some letters to mail, met two friends, and went to their car to drive to the parade. We were beaten and robbed by eight people. I had two ribs broken and had to go to San Francisco General Hospital.

"When I got out of the hospital, I began to laugh. I'm religious, and I thought maybe the mugging was God's way of saying, 'Jack, hold on.' I decided to volunteer at an AIDS hot line. It was the first step toward my rebirth and recovery. I deal with a lot of suicide calls, not only from AIDS people but from their friends, family, and lovers. The first six months were very difficult, and it's still hard. It still takes two hours to get up in the morning and I feel awful. But I have more purpose now. I still get depressed. I sure do. There isn't a day goes by that someone I know doesn't either slip into a coma or pass quietly on. I have a lot of talks with my doctors about suicide, and I know that the time may come when I lose control. It's a fact of life that I'm dying of AIDS. But it's a fact of life that I'm living with AIDS."

V

BACKING INTO THE GRAVE

———————

IN HIS SURVEY of the etymology of the word *suicide*, linguist David Daube traces the various phrases that reflect a particular culture's attitude toward the subject. The Old Testament has no specific expression for suicide; the act was merely described, as when "Saul took his own sword, and fell upon it." The ancient Greeks had numerous ways to denote self-destruction, most of which emphasized dying rather than killing: "to seize death," "to be delivered from life," "to leave the light," "to carry oneself off," "to consume oneself," "to dispose of oneself," and "to get oneself out of the way," among others. A noun for the act was not introduced until the second century A.D. when the Christian presbyter Clement of Alexandria observed that philosophers allow the excellent man "a sensible removal." Ancient Rome's vocabulary included the following phrases: "to seek death," "to procure one's own death," "to cause violence to oneself," "to fall by one's own hand." An unsuccessful suicide was "to wound oneself in order to die."

As "wounding oneself in order to die" became a sin and a crime, the vocabulary describing it became increasingly fierce. Someone who in Ancient Greece elected "to flee the light," in medieval England was said "to murder oneself," "to destroy oneself," or "to assassinate oneself." "Self-murder" became the most popular way to describe the act although the law favored the Latin *felo de se*. Others borrowed a term first used by Hamlet when he cried, "Oh that the Everlasting had not fixed his canon 'gainst self-slaughter."

Donne, says Daube, introduced the more clinical term, "self-homicide," in *Biathanatos*. In 1618, Edmund Bolton employed the term "self-killing." In his *Anatomy of Melancholy,* Robert Burton used a host of more sympathetic phrases: "to free themselves from grievances," "to put an end to themselves," "to dispatch themselves," "to precipitate themselves," "to fall by one's own hand," "to let himself free with his own hands," "to make away with themselves," and so on.

According to the *Oxford English Dictionary*, the word "suicide"—from the Latin *sui,* self, and *caedere,* to kill—was first used in 1651 by Walter Charleton, an English physician, when he said, "To vindicate oneself from extreme and otherwise inevitable calamity by *sui-cide* is not (certainly) a crime." A. Alvarez cites an earlier usage in Sir Thomas Browne's *Religio Medici,* published in 1642: "Herein are they in extremes, that can allow a man to be his own assassin, and so highly extol the end and suicide of Cato." In the 1662 edition of his dictionary, *A New World in Words,* Edward Phillips takes credit for the word: "One barbarous word I shall produce, which is *suicide,* a word which I had rather be derived from *sus,* a sow, than from the pronoun *sui,* unless there be some mystery in it; as if it were a swinish part for a man to kill himself." Today, although there are dozens of slang expressions like "offing oneself," "taking the pipe," and "hanging it up," and euphemisms like "to make away with oneself," the word suicide is widely used in English. Not surprisingly our vocabulary continues to reflect our attitude: While the act itself is no longer a crime, we still speak of "committing" a suicide, as we "commit" crimes, incest, perjury, or faux pas.

Although there is general agreement on the word, there is a great difference of opinion as to what it means. The definition of suicide would seem straightforward—"the act or instance of taking one's own life voluntarily and intentionally"—according to *Webster's Third New International Dictionary.* Yet even this description is imprecise. Everyone would agree, for instance, that a man who puts a gun in his mouth, pulls the trigger, and dies is a suicide. But what of the man who puts a gun in his mouth, not realizing that it is loaded? What of the man who loses at Russian roulette? Is he a suicide or merely unlucky? A strict interpretation of Webster's definition, in fact, might exclude many deaths that we classify as suicides but that are arguably "voluntary"— that of Socrates, for example, who was ordered to kill himself. And what of the Japanese samurai whose suicide is demanded by cultural tradition? The spy who takes his own life rather than divulge classified information? The terminally ill woman who asks her husband to put a fatal dose of pills on her tongue? The child who swallows poison from the medicine chest?

There is, in fact, little agreement on exactly what constitutes a suicide. Over the years dozens of definitions have been proposed, and entire books have been written on the problem of terminology. For medical examiners "suicide" is a medical-legal classification, one of five modes of death including accidental, natural, homicidal, and undetermined. Many deaths, however, fall through the cracks between these categories. Warned by his doctor that to drink again would kill him, an alcoholic with cirrhosis of the liver continued to drink heavily and soon died. His mode of death was certified as natural. A twenty-five-year-old laborer with a history of mental instability and suicide attempts drove his pickup truck into a wall at dawn, leaving no skid marks. His death was certified as undetermined. A woman took an overdose of barbiturates in the kitchen at 4:30 P.M. She knew that every working day for three years her husband had come home at 5 P.M. and his first act was to get a beer from the refrigerator. This afternoon, however, her husband was delayed and did not get home until 7:30. Her death was certified as a suicide.

In 1637, John Sym, the rural English clergyman who was considered something of a suicide prevention expert, pointed out in his book, *Life's Preservative Against Self-Killing,* that there were many ways of killing oneself, not all of them technically suicide. Sym divided suicide into "direct" and "indirect" categories. Indirect suicide included "*eating* to gluttony, and *drinking* to drunkennesse; using *labour* and *recreations* to surfeiting." The commission of a mortal sin, he said, was indirect suicide, as were duels, keeping company with "accursed persons," battle against a mightier adversary ("when *self-conceited, wilfull, foole-hardy men* will fight against their *enemies,* upon desperate *disadvantages;* and imminent perill of death"), and "when any doe out of a *bravery,* and gallantry of spirit, goe needlessly with a charge of money, or of men's persons, or errands; *either* in the night, through a place haunted and beset with murderous robbers; *or,* at any time through knowne *ambushments,* and strong *troupes* of enemies."

Sym's "indirect" suicide is the equivalent of Durkheim's "embryonic suicide." Durkheim observed that many people who had no conscious intention of killing themselves acted in ways that imperiled their lives. He suggested that "the daredevil who intentionally toys with death," "the man of apathetic temperament who, having no vital interest in anything, takes no care of health and so imperils it by neglect," and "the scholar who dies from excessive devotion to study" had much in common with the "true suicide." "They result from similar states of mind," wrote Durkheim, "since they also entail mortal risks not unknown to the agent, and the prospect of these is no deterrent; the sole difference is a lesser chance of death."

Freud, referring to such examples as "half-intentional self-destruction," said that people found many unconscious ways to express their death instinct. In *The Psychopathology of Everyday Life* he described an officer who, shortly after his mother's death, fell and was severely injured in a cavalry race, and a man who shot himself "accidentally" after being rejected by the army and by his girlfriend. Calling these "purposive accidents," Freud wrote, "I have now learnt and can prove from convincing examples that many apparently accidental injuries that happen to such patients are really instances of self-injury." This held true, apparently, even in the great psychiatrist's own household. "When a member of my family complains to me of having bitten his tongue, pinched a finger, or the like, he does not get the sympathy he hopes for, but instead the question: 'Why did you do that?' " In fact, when one of Freud's children fell ill and was ordered to spend the morning in bed, the boy threw a tantrum and vowed to kill himself, "a possibility that was familiar to him from the newspapers," noted Freud. In the evening his son showed him a chest bruise he'd gotten from bumping against a doorknob. "To my ironical question as to why he had done it and what he meant by it, the eleven-year-old child answered as though it had suddenly dawned on him: 'That was my attempt at suicide that I threatened this morning.' "

In *Man Against Himself,* Karl Menninger wrote that "in the end each man kills himself in his own selected way, fast or slow, soon or late." Menninger catalogued four hundred pages worth of self-destructive behavior, from nail biting to world war, and divided them into three types. In "focal" suicide, the self-destructive urge zeros in on a specific part of the body and results in malingering, "purposive accidents," impotence, frigidity, or self-mutilation. In "organic" suicide certain people lose the will to live and contrive their own illnesses and premature deaths via cancer, heart disease, diabetes, or emphysema. In "chronic" suicide a person kills himself slowly, through alcoholism, asceticism, martyrdom, neurotic invalidism, antisocial behavior, or psychosis. All of these, said Menninger, were expressions of the death instinct and represented "variant forms of suicide."

In the half-century since *Man Against Himself* was published, researchers have refined and added to Menninger's compendium of what is sometimes called "subintentioned death," "slow suicide," "suicide on the installment plan," or "suicide by inches." Some examples include smoking, drugs, reckless driving, obesity, high blood pressure, workaholism, procrastination, ulcers, overexercise, high-risk sports, eating disorders, running away from home, and delinquency. Then there are those people who don't take their medication; terminally ill patients who refuse life-saving operations; people who continue to eat fatty foods in spite of high cholesterol levels; women who avoid doctors when they find a lump in their breast; gays who continue to engage in high-risk sex, knowing that the odds of contracting AIDS are high. The French writer Henri Barbusse once remarked that two armies at war form one vast mass of humanity committing suicide. Well into his nineties Karl Menninger still traveled the country to decry what he called "the great and growing suicide club America seems to be caught in"—the nuclear arms race.

In his later work Menninger suggested that self-destructive behaviors are often, in fact, ways of postponing or averting true suicide. "The development of symptoms is a struggle for health, a struggle toward recovery, an effort to avert something which is even worse than that to which one must submit in order to escape it," he said. "The organism says, anything rather than suicide, anything rather than give up the most precious thing of all, namely my life. Sickness, even neurosis, even crime, but not that awful oblivion, that awful nothingness." Thus, according to Menninger, certain forms of self-destructive behavior may serve—paradoxically—as survival techniques. He warned that if substitutes fail, however, they often lead to the ultimate self-destruction of suicide.

The most dramatic use of self-destructive behavior as a way of staying alive is self-mutilation, the most common form of which is wrist-cutting. Primarily young females, some wrist-cutters are diagnosed as suffering from schizophrenia or borderline personality disorder while others have no diagnosable disorder but suffer from low self-esteem, intense guilt, and an inability to express themselves verbally. Their act is often precipitated by the threat of impending loss or abandonment—the hospitalization of a parent, being left by a lover. Their tension builds, their anger turns inward, and they punish themselves by repeatedly cutting their wrists—or arms, legs, neck, face, or abdomen. Despite such violence, most cutters say that they feel not pain but a catharsis. As one researcher characterized the meaning of the act, "I bleed; therefore I am alive."

This is the sort of affirmation described by Ellen Parker, a thirty-two-year-old hospital worker who has been periodically cutting her wrists ever since she was an adolescent. When Ellen was nine, her father died after a long illness. Her mother, who had spent many years caring for her husband, was also sickly, and Ellen felt ignored. A shy, reclusive teenager, Ellen often felt so much she thought she might explode, and at the same time she was terrified that she felt nothing at all, as if she had no relationship to the real world. "At times I would get so frustrated that I would pound the pillow or go outside and throw rocks. Sometimes I'd even bang my head against the wall—but I couldn't do that when my mom was in the house so I had to find quieter ways to relieve the pressure." The way she found was to cut her wrists, deep enough to bleed but not deep enough to require medical attention. Two decades later, despite years of therapy, Ellen still keeps a lot of her feelings inside. About once a month, when she feels especially depressed, she goes home and makes four or five cuts on her arm, from her wrist toward her elbow, about three or four inches long. After washing and bandaging the cuts, she usually has a glass of wine and listens to music before it's time for bed. Ellen doesn't think of these incidents—her "ritual" as she calls it—as suicide attempts. She has no intention of dying, and she knows the cuts are superficial. "It's a way of relieving the pressure," says Ellen. "It's kind of like letting out a sigh. I get a peaceful feeling and a kind of self-satisfaction at having hurt myself."

The form of "slow suicide" most likely to lead to the fast kind is alcoholism. Studies have found that as many as 30 percent of all suicides are alcoholic, and approximately 23 percent of attempted suicides are alcoholic. Looking at it from another angle, an estimated 5 percent of Americans are alcoholic; about 15 percent of them will die of suicide.

While there is agreement that suicide and alcoholism are closely related, there is little agreement on exactly how they interact. Some researchers believe alcoholism and suicide are different consequences of the same underlying causes. They agree with Menninger, who says that alcoholism is "a form of self-destruction used to avert a greater self-destruction." Alcohol may be used as an escape, and when this is not enough, the ultimate escape of suicide may be chosen. Other investigators dispute Menninger's hypothesis, given that so many alcoholics eventually kill themselves outright. They suggest the opposite progression—that alcoholism leads to social difficulties that lead to suicide. In a 1972 study of 147 suicidal male alcoholics, three-fourths of the sample reported that prolonged drinking led to rejection by friends, disruption in social relationships, and job difficulties, which precipitated suicidal thinking. Another study found that nearly one-third of alcoholic suicides had experienced the loss of a close relationship within six weeks of their death. Certainly, no matter what the sequence, increased drinking may lead to loss of control, and suicide is a way of reasserting control. Alcoholism, like depression, can be a way of stopping one's life at a certain point; suicide can be a way of stopping time permanently. For some, alcoholism may be suicide in a more acceptable guise. According to his first wife, the writer Jack Kerouac maintained that because he was Catholic, he couldn't commit suicide; he therefore planned to drink himself to death. He died in 1969 of a massive abdominal hemorrhage brought on in large measure by his acute alcoholism.

Excessive drinking is one way to kill oneself; insufficent eating is another. An estimated five hundred thousand people in this country, most of them young, white women, suffer from anorexia nervosa. In a misguided attempt to conform to cultural norms of attractiveness, they may literally starve themselves into illness and even death. The underlying causes of anorexia—low self-esteem, feelings of self-hatred—are not dissimilar to the roots of suicide, and the disorder is often accompanied by traditional suicide attempts. "I didn't think I was worth anything," said one young girl, who dropped from 120 to 80 pounds. "I had no friends, no one to talk to. I was really depressed. I wanted to kill myself. I had thought of taking a knife or pills, but I couldn't. That was suicide, and I knew suicide was a sin. So I just stopped eating." Another young anorexic who was close to death says, "I would rather have died than eaten." Many do. Fifteen percent of acute anorexics will die of what one psychiatrist calls "intestinal suicide."

An even greater number of people in this country suffer from bulimia. Bulimics, who tend to be middle- or upper-middle-class women with high intelligence and high standards, endure recurrent episodes of compulsive eating followed by self-induced vomiting, fasting, or the abuse of laxatives or diuretics. Some bulimics vomit as many as six times a day or take as many as three hundred laxatives a week. Although the ostensible purpose is to develop a more beautiful figure, the effect is a litany of self-destruction not unlike that achieved by early Christian martyrs. Bulimics may suffer from rotten teeth and receding gums (the result of being bathed in stomach acid each time they vomit), swollen salivary glands, sore throats, abrasions on the esophagus walls, numb or curling fingers and lips (from low potassium levels), and broken blood vessels in the eyes. In her attempts to vomit, one young woman repeatedly jammed her fingers down her throat so forcefully that years later she still has teeth marks on the back of her hand. Occasionally, bulimics die from a severe electrolyte imbalance or from rupture of the stomach or esophagus during a binge. But their self-destructive urges often take a more direct form; in one study one-third of bulimics had made at least one suicide attempt.

Experts suspect that many single-passenger auto deaths may well be suicides in disguise. Some, like Willy Loman in *Death of a Salesman,* who kills himself by driving into a tree, are unequivocal suicides. For Loman "autocide" seemed to be a way of ending his life without forfeiting his insurance premium. Others are somewhat less obvious about their intentions, such as the man who, after an argument with his wife, wrote a note saying, "You'll be sorry when I'm dead," jumped into his car, and sped off down the highway. Two minutes later he had a fatal crash. The police report concluded, "It looked as if he pointed it into the tree." But suicidal intent is difficult to prove, and such deaths are usually classified as accidents unless a suicide note is found. When a young Massachusetts woman drove on the wrong side of the highway with her headlights off and was killed in a head-on collision, her death was ruled an accident. Researchers estimate, however, that as many as 15 percent of single-car crashes are suicides, and auto accidents have been linked to suicidal behavior in several studies. Psychiatrist Melvin Selzer has demonstrated that suicidal people have more than twice as many auto accidents as nonsuicidal people. In a subsequent study Selzer compared ninety-six drivers responsible for fatal crashes with a control group of drivers. Almost half of the fatal-crash drivers had exhibited depression, violent behavior, and suicidal thinking, compared to 16 percent of the control group. Drivers in crashes were at least four times more likely to have been under severe stress from alcoholism, job problems, or financial troubles. "I don't think there are many overt suicides by auto," Selzer has said, "but the driver may be increasingly depressed, angry and frustrated until he reaches a state at which it is a matter of indifference to him whether he lives or dies." Young men in particular may drive in careless, risk-taking ways, speeding, racing, driving with their eyes closed, or engaging in games of "chicken" like that played by James Dean in *Rebel Without a Cause.* Reckless driving is often combined with alcohol; in one study more than 50 percent of a group of accident-prone drivers were alcoholics.

The connection between suicide and risk-taking behavior is most dramatically apparent in Russian roulette deaths, which coroners usually classify as accidents. A recent study of twenty victims, all but one of them men, found that they were young (many were students) and in good physical health. Half of them were known to have been depressed, however, and nearly 60 percent had a history of drug or alcohol abuse or psychiatric disturbances. "They use risk-taking behavior as a form of self-treatment for depression," observed Dr. David Fishbain, the study's main author. Although the researchers were unable to conclude whether the victims were "true suicides" or not, the urge for death was clearly evident; more than half of the victims had fired the gun more than once, and 16 percent had loaded more than one bullet in the gun. All had played the "game" with other people present.

The person who plays Russian roulette has a one in six chance of dying; the person who climbs Mount Everest has a one in ten chance of dying. Is it suicidal to attempt that climb? The odds are not good for war correspondents, soldiers of fortune, sky divers, motorcycle racers, daredevils, glacier skiers, climbers who spurn ropes and protective hardware, and others who spend their lives in pursuit of extreme physical risk. Some call them adrenaline junkies and suggest that such people need a high concentration of the stress hormones that are released by fear or excitement. University of Wisconsin psychologist Frank Farley believes that certain people have a physical predisposition for risk-taking. These "Type T" (for thrill-seeking) personalities are, he says, driven by temperament and perhaps by biology to a life of living on the edge. Edge-livers themselves dismiss the suggestion that they might harbor a "death wish." "I would describe myself as having a life wish," Himalayan mountaineer Gordon Wiltsie has said. "When you do adventurous things, you get a real sense of being alive and enjoying being alive. Life gains value when you realize that it could be extinguished." Freud said as much in a discussion of war: "Life is impoverished, it loses in interest, when the highest stake in the game of living, life itself, may not be risked. It becomes as shallow and empty as, let us say, an American flirtation."

Some people commit suicide by getting someone else to kill them, becoming what Aldous Huxley called a "murderee." Like the Christian martyrs who goaded the Romans into executing them, they provoke someone or something else into striking the final blow. Sometimes this strategy is invoked because of the stigma of suicide. Among the Malays, for whom suicide is a sin, if a man wished to die, he ran amok, killing people randomly until he himself was killed. In certain aboriginal tribes of Australia, if a native wanted to die but couldn't get someone to kill him, he might expose himself to a venomous snake. In order to evade the divine decree against suicide, eighteenth-century Irish Catholic convicts facing torture in Australian prisons chose to draw straws. The man holding the longest straw was killed, thus avoiding endless torture; the man who drew the second straw did the killing—whereupon he was executed by the authorities. In war, suicide may be disguised as heroism. "Many soldiers have the fantasy of throwing themselves into the turmoil of battle in order to die," wrote psychiatrist Joost Meerloo. "One of them, who was very courageous indeed, became very depressive after the war because God had not understood his magic gesture and had not used the enemy to kill him." Some would call such men heroes; sociologist Marvin Wolfgang might call them examples of "victim-precipitated homicide." In his 1950s study of murder in Philadelphia, Wolfgang stated that 150 of 588 consecutive homicides were cases of victim-precipitated homicide, many of them husbands who attacked their wives, provoking their wives into murdering them. One drunken man, for instance, beat his wife, then handed her a kitchen knife and dared her to use it on him. She said that if he hit her once more, she would. He slapped her in the face; she stabbed him to death.

Many of these people may be unaware of their desire to die, or they may prefer to leave their fate to chance. They may have some magical belief that they cannot take their own life, or they may feel an intense need to be punished by others or to be killed by a symbolic parent. Psychiatrists believe that some people actually commit murder in the hope of invoking the death penalty. (Some, in fact, oppose capital punishment partly because it may encourage violent, suicidal persons to murder.) A twenty-two-year-old babysitter who murdered two small children in her care told police that although she had loved them, she killed them in the belief that if her crime were sufficiently odious, the death penalty would be invoked. She had attempted suicide many times and believed she was incapable of killing herself. (She did not get her wish.) Many death row inmates have tried to insist on their right to the death penalty. In 1977 convicted murderer Gary Gilmore, who demanded to be shot by a firing squad, fought several stays of execution and made two suicide attempts before being executed.

Some forms of suicide are metaphorical. Beset by rumors of marital infidelity, 1988 presidential candidate Gary Hart challenged the press to "put a tail" on him. That very weekend he canceled his campaign appearances to dally with a young model. In the ensuing scandal he resigned from the race, the latest in a long line of politicians to have committed "political suicide." Such an unconscious need to fail had been recognized by Freud, who said that men who sabotaged their own success were commonly seen in psychoanalysis. In what has been called "pseudocide," some people fake their own suicide, disappear, and start over again somewhere else under a new identity. This is one of many forms of social suicide in which one withdraws from contact with the outside world, essentially declaring the rest of the world dead. In Melville's *Moby Dick,* Ishmael settles for temporary withdrawal; rather than giving in to "pistol and ball," he ships out for two years on the *Pequod.* Some suggest that various forms of nonaction are essentially suicidal, as in the renunciation of ambition or creativity. The poet Arthur Rimbaud stopped writing at nineteen although he lived almost two decades more. A long-term study of gifted young people found that some had been conspicuous failures in their adult lives, accepting what one psychologist called a sort of "partial death" in lieu of overt suicide. Joost Meerloo believed that such resignation is widespread:

"Most people are no longer alive after their entrance into maturity," he wrote. "They commit a partial and token suicide by stopping their growth and stopping the pleasure of expansion. They bury themselves in old accepted habits and customs, drowning their sense of curiosity regarding new inner and outer experiences. Contented apathy and the ending of inquisitive curiosity may be looked at as the early intrusion of death." Ernest Hemingway referred to such behavior as "backing into the grave." Hemingway himself went head-first, shooting himself when he felt his creative powers had deserted him.

Some theorists seem to believe that almost every action we take—or don't take—may represent some form of self-destructive behavior. In *How to Stop Killing Yourself,* a sort of layman's version of *Man Against Himself* published in 1950, Dr. Peter Steincrohn found examples of self-destruction almost everywhere—"exercisitis" (exercising after age thirty), "vacationitis" (being too relaxed on vacation), and even "disbelief in the philosophy of self-destruction" (a refusal to recognize that we are all suicidal in some way). But not all behavior having possible self-destructive consequences is necessarily motivated by a desire for punishment or death. Merely getting into a car could be considered suicidal behavior, given current accident rates. Some psychiatrists call entering a convent a form of suicide; others call it enlightenment. "One must be careful and not fall into the trap that Menninger did," writes French sociologist Jean Baechler. "Biting one's nails is a form of self-mutilation so removed from total suicide that there is something arbitrary about keeping it in a study of suicide. As ever, it is a question of degree."

Exploring the extent and variety of self-destructive behavior, however, may help us understand that within each of us there is the capacity for self-destruction that may emerge in various forms at various times. "There is a little murder and a little suicide dwelling in everybody's heart," wrote Menninger. "Give them a powerful weapon like a car, inflame their inhibitions or irritations or frustrations, and diminish their suppressive control by means of alcohol or fatigue, and the murder or suicide may get committed." Although few of us pick up the gun, much less pull the trigger, we all engage in activities that have within them a germ of self-destruction.

Several writers on suicide propose that suicidal behavior is best conceptualized as a continuum of behavior ranging over a broad spectrum. On one end there is the person who puts a bullet through his brain, the completed suicide. On the other, the person who lives a full, healthy, loving, creative, positive life. Ranging along that continuum are various forms of self-destructive behavior, from suicide attempts to alcoholism to reckless driving to cigarette smoking to the tiny acts of self-sabotage we engage in daily. We all lie on that continuum somewhere between those two extremes, moving along the scale in either direction as circumstances change. In *The Winter Name of God* author and priest James Carroll wrote:

A thousand people are "officially" dead of suicide every day, but they are not the only ones who are faced with the constant choice between life and death. We all are. . . . We might lack the nerve to commit the final act, and we may not recognize our "sinful" tendencies for what they are, but day in and day out we confront the problem of our innate attraction to self-destruction. We live in a world that encourages the small daily acts of negation that prepare us for the great one. There are meanings of suicide that neither the courts nor the dictionaries admit, but that make it impossible for us to regard those thousand people a day who do themselves in as very different from us. They are not necessarily "sick" or "sinners," but simply our sisters and brothers. And who are we? We are the resigned housewives, the compulsive playboys, the despairing priests, the addicted teenagers, the reckless drivers, the bored bureaucrats, the lonely salesmen, the smiling stewardesses, the restless drifters, the walking wounded. . . . It may be nothing more than the steadfast commitment to sameness. The simplest form of suicide is the act of refusing the adventures and challenges that offer themselves to us every-day. "No thanks," we say. "I prefer not to," we murmur, like Melville's Bartleby, preferring to stare at the wall outside the window. Preferring, as I do on especially bad days, to stay in bed.

4

PREVENTION

———◆———

I

CONNECTIONS

THE PHONE RINGS IN A small room in a one-story building in Los Angeles. Pat, a trim, forty-three-year-old woman wearing sneakers, jeans, and a sweatshirt, picks up the receiver and in a warm, gentle voice says, "Hello, may I help you?" As she listens to the answer, she becomes still. "Nine Percodans? I don't know," she says. "I'm not a doctor. . . . Did you take nine Percodans? Did someone you know take them?" After each question Pat listens intently before asking the next. "How old is your friend? . . . Nineteen? . . . Is she there with you? . . . No? . . . How frightening." Pat speaks slowly, her voice comforting but firm. "Your friend should get some help. Do you have anyone to call who can help you with this? . . . Maybe you should call the paramedics. Did you call her house? . . . She has roommates? . . . Might they know where she is? . . . Might she call you back? . . . No? . . . She just called you to say good-bye?"

Pat puts on her glasses as if it might help her focus even more closely on the caller. If she feels any tension, her voice doesn't betray it. "Do you have any idea where she might be, places she might go? . . . Does she have a car? . . . Does she have any family? . . . Have you called them? . . . They're looking for her? . . . What's your friend's name?" Pat's voice softens. "Is it that you don't want to give her last name? . . . If she calls us, can we call you?" Pat pauses a moment. "Are you frightened? . . . What of? . . . We're not the police. And even if we were, it's not against the law to kill yourself. . . . Is there anything I can do to help *you*?" Pat's head bows over the desk. "If you *are* Susan or if you have taken the Percodan, you need to get to the hospital immediately." There is a brief silence and then the sound of weeping spills from the phone. "What has happened?" says Pat with infinite tenderness. "Why do you want to die?"

It is 10 P.M. on a Tuesday night in April. Pat is sitting on the edge of a plastic swivel chair, leaning over a desk in a corner of the "telephone room" at the Institute for Studies of Destructive Behaviors and the Suicide Prevention Center, commonly known as the Los Angeles Suicide Prevention Center. The LASPC is one of the oldest and most famous of this country's suicide prevention centers. Pat is a volunteer on its twenty-four-hour crisis line. She is alone in the room, but two other counselors are handling calls in nearby offices. Otherwise, the building is empty. On the desk in front of Pat are the tools of her trade: a telephone with four incoming lines, an array of directories, and two Rolodexes with nearly three hundred referral options organized by category: Alcohol, Battered/Rape, Bereavement, Child Care, Employment, Food, Free Clinics, Incest, Pregnancy, and so on. Next to the telephone lies a pack of cigarettes. Pat never smokes during a call, but her hand sometimes closes over the pack during stressful moments. To the left of the desk two file cabinets are filled with folders, one for each person who has called the center in the last two months. The folders are stuffed with "contact sheets" marked with demographic data and a description of each call. Above the desk, a bulletin board is covered with schedules, newspaper clippings on suicide, notices of workshops on adolescent suicide, and a half-dozen messages: "Steve, Ruth called back to say she now has a volunteer job and is feeling much better," and "Erica called to thank us; she's feeling real good now," and "Vivien called to thank everyone for helping her son Rick. She said he'd called here a lot over the past 18 months."

The other half of the room has the look of a college lounge. A television set and a sheaf of magazines sit on a round wooden table. In the far corner are two brown couches where volunteers on the 1-to-7 A.M. shift catnap during lulls. A large map of Los Angeles County hangs on one wall. The room has one window whose venetian blinds are closed. The sound of traffic seeps into the room. The LASPC's one-story building, a former convalescent home, is in an ethnically mixed neighborhood on the edge of downtown Los Angeles. To the east the neon of bars and fast-food joints gives way to the lights of houses lying against the Hollywood Hills. To the west, beyond the downtown area, lies the Pacific Ocean. Somewhere in between is a nineteen-year-old girl who sits in her bedroom sobbing, telling the woman in this room that she wants to die.

As Pat tries to comfort the girl, she gathers information, trying to assess how lethal the situation is and what supports the girl might have to help her through this crisis. Like a climber struggling for a foothold on a steep rock face, she searches for a way to establish a connection with this girl. Though the girl sounds timid, despair makes her stubborn: She keeps coming back to her first question—will the nine Percodans kill her or leave her a cripple?

"*Any* medication could kill you; I don't have that information," Pat says. "Where is your pain coming from? Is it physical? . . . Have you spoken to anyone about it? . . . Does your therapist know how you're feeling? . . . You called her? She's away? . . ." Pat shakes her head. "I don't know. I don't have that kind of training—and even a doctor won't give you that information over the phone. . . . Do you live with your family? . . . Are you close to your father? . . . How about your mother? . . . Have you talked to her about this? . . . Why not? . . . What would she say if you told her? . . ." Pat twists slightly in her chair. "It must be hard when those you love are so far away from how you're feeling." She is silent for a moment, listening to the girl's quick anxious breaths. "You don't trust me at all, do you?" says Pat kindly. "I won't hurt you—I promise that."

This is the eleventh call Pat has taken since beginning her six-hour shift at 6:30. The Crisis Line at the LASPC receives an average of sixty to seventy calls a day from people who are lonely, depressed, angry, and perhaps suicidal. The lines are open twenty-four hours a day, 365 days a year. The LASPC is the only suicide prevention center or twenty-four-hour general-purpose crisis line in Los Angeles County. When other hot lines and therapists close up shop for the day, many of them leave the LASPC number on their answering machines for callers in crisis after office hours. Although the LASPC has four incoming lines, the phone company has told the center that during its busiest hours, 7 P.M. to 1 A.M.—the time when most suicides occur—callers must sometimes dial five or six times before they can get through.

The LASPC keeps careful records of who calls and why. They have learned that calls come from as wide a range of people and problems as seem to exist. More than 60 percent are from the troubled person himself. The rest are from third-party callers—concerned relatives and friends, or therapists seeking advice on how to handle a suicidal client. Two-thirds of the calls are from women. While the majority of calls come from the Los Angeles area, calls have come from as far away as Iowa, Florida, and France. Ten percent of their calls are from people under the age of twenty. Once, an eight-year-old boy called. He was lonely, he told the counselor. His mother traveled a lot on business, and he worried that he was the reason she was never home. Later, the counselor called the boy's mother. She was initially outraged at the intrusion, but when she realized that her son had been upset enough to call a suicide prevention center, she listened.

Although the notion of a suicide prevention center may conjure images of heroic volunteers talking desperate people into putting down a loaded gun, the majority of calls are much less dramatic. Most callers to the LASPC or to any of the over two hundred suicide prevention centers in the United States are not in immediate danger of killing themselves. This has led some critics to suggest that most people who call a prevention center don't really want to die. The LASPC agrees. They believe that even the most desperately suicidal people are ambivalent—a part of them wants to live, and a part of them wants to die. By calling the center they have issued a "cry for help." Nevertheless, many of those who call the center are at risk for suicide. A previous attempt is the most accurate predictor for subsequent suicide, and half of the people who call the LASPC have made previous attempts. Twelve percent of callers are considered to be at high risk; that is, they are so distressed that the LASPC believes they would have made an attempt within forty-eight hours if they had not called. Three percent of callers have already swallowed pills or cut their wrists when they call the center and may die unless the LASPC gets them immediate help.

Although contemplating suicide is not a prerequisite for calling the crisis line, counselors are trained to ask specifically about suicide on every call. "And we don't ask whether they're 'thinking of hurting themselves' or 'thinking of doing something to themselves,' " says Karl Harris, the burly ex-policeman who directs the crisis line. "We ask, 'Are you thinking of killing yourself?' " It can be a difficult question to get used to asking. Recently, Harris trained thirteen streetwise hostage negotiators, who manned the LASPC lines as part of their course. Harris couldn't get them to ask the question without pussyfooting around—they were afraid of putting the idea in the caller's mind. But it won't, says Harris. "People will lie about everything else on the phone, then you'll ask, 'Are you thinking of killing yourself?' Instant truth. If they're not, you'll hear, 'Good God, no way.' If they are, you'll hear a sigh of relief: 'Yes. I am.' "

About one-third of the calls to the LASPC are suicide-related. The rest are crisis-intervention inquiries not necessarily related to a suicide threat. The calls Pat has taken thus far tonight include an elderly widow who lives alone and says she wants to kill herself: "What is life if you have no friends and your children don't give a shit about you?" she sobs; a woman worried that her teenage son, who is terrified that he may be gay, is thinking of killing himself; an alcoholic who is drunk and says he wants to die; a gay man who wants and doesn't want to take the Valium he says he has, who has tried thirteen other hot lines tonight, all of which were busy or shut down for the night; a seventy-three-year-old man who is drinking and "thinking of doing himself in," a brain-damaged middle-aged "chronic" caller who telephones almost daily for an emotional boost; a forty-six-year-old woman who has just swallowed seven sleeping pills; a psychotic twenty-three-year-old man who is brilliant, incoherent, and angry. The callers seem to have little in common except that they feel the world is closing in on them and they have no alternative but to depend on the kindness of strangers.

Karl Harris likes to compare the crisis lines to a hospital emergency room.

"We're an ER for people with emotional problems," he says. "They come to us, and like an ER, we do triage; some just need aspirin or a Band-Aid, some need to be seen again, and others need extensive patching and follow-up." With each caller Pat is trained to assess the immediate risk of suicide, listen to the person's story, focus on the problem, and discuss possible options. Each caller has a different need. It is up to Pat to help the caller decide what might best fill that need. To the infirm, elderly widow Pat suggests she call her doctor in the morning, get some physical therapy, and become involved in a seniors group, for which Pat gives her several names and numbers. "Tomorrow, *call* the seniors group, and go to the doctor and get some answers about your physical condition," she says gently but firmly. "If you need to call us before you go to the doctor, please do. Now get yourself a Coke and a book and try to relax tonight. . . . Good luck to you. Thanks for calling us. I'll be thinking of you." To the mother of the gay youth she intersperses her sympathetic remarks with urgent suggestions; the boy needs professional help, she says, recommending that he come to the LASPC's clinic. She gives her the number of a gay community service and urges her to persuade her son to call the crisis line. "Put a card with our number on it by his bed," she says. To the elderly alcoholic she gives a referral to the nearest Alcoholics Anonymous group and some reassurance: "We're here," Pat says kindly when he frets she has left the line. "We're not going anywhere." To a lonely, middle-aged woman she describes the counseling available at the LASPC and patiently gives her directions to the center. "Sally, are you going to be okay tonight?" she says. "If you feel worse, will you give us a call back? . . . I'll be thinking about you. Okay, Sally, bye-bye."

Pat changes her approach to fit each caller's needs. With the older woman she is motherly; with the psychotic young man she patiently absorbs his anger; with the chronic caller who, like certain other "chronic" callers, has a time limit on his calls, she is gentle but firm. "Well, my friend, I'm going to have to hang up now," she says when his ten minutes are up. With the young gay man she is supportive but forceful: "You don't sound like you mean it," she says after he agrees to call back if he needs to. "You sound as if you're saying it because you think that's what I want to hear." Pat's voice inspires trust and confidence; even when the risk seems high, she never seems anxious or edgy herself, although in an extreme she may sigh and say, "Oh, mercy." Every caller is taken seriously, even one who apologizes for dialing the wrong number, to whom Pat says warmly, "I'm glad you did"—in case he had the right number and was too scared to talk. Pat takes nothing for granted; each caller is unique, each call its own world. And although she seems so relaxed and sure, at one point after a difficult call she turns to me and admits, "The longer I'm here, the more questions I have—and the less I know."

The girl is no longer crying, but her breathing is heavy. Slowly, Pat has established a thin ledge of trust. "Did something happen tonight?" she asks.

"Can you tell me what that was? . . . Was it something someone said? . . . Who?" After each question Pat lets the girl's answer settle for a moment before continuing. "What did he say? . . . Have you talked to him about it? What kind of compromises? . . . Sexual things? . . . Is this the person you want to spend your life with? . . . You care too much for him to leave him, but you have a hard time staying with him?" Pat pauses. "You know, suicide is a permanent solution to a temporary problem. . . . Is your fiancé in counseling? . . . Do you think you're ready to share your life with someone who thinks he's perfect? . . . Would it be so terrible to end your relationship with him rather than end your life? . . . Why? . . . How do you know you can't live without him? . . . You tried? . . . Maybe a month isn't enough. . . . Everything changes. Nothing stays the same." Pat hunches over, her elbows on her knees. "Have you ever told him you were thinking of killing yourself? . . . What does he say? . . . He doesn't believe you? . . . Have you talked to him tonight? . . . How did you end the conversation?" Pat listens to the answer, then repeats it softly to herself, nodding. "Sweet dreams."

Pat, who makes a living raising orchids, has worked on the crisis lines for ten years. Like many of the center's sixty-five volunteers, she became involved after suicide touched her own life when her nephew killed himself. A friend told her about the Los Angeles Suicide Prevention Center. "I'd never heard of it," Pat remembers. But eventually she called the center and enrolled in their support group for family and friends left behind after a suicide. When she finished the program, she decided she wanted to work on the telephone lines. Like many of the volunteers, Pat thought she would be getting into the business of saving lives. At her first interview she was asked why she wanted to work on the lines. "Because I want to help people," she said. Pat laughs now, remembering. "I wanted to be the Band-Aid queen," she says. "I thought I'd save the world. Of course I found out it wasn't quite like that."

Although some of the crisis line volunteers are graduate students in psychology or social work, most, like Pat, have full-time jobs and work at the LASPC in their spare time; among the center's volunteers are a stockbroker, a baker, an architect, several actors, and a zoologist. Training for the lines is rigorous. If the volunteer passes the initial interview with two staff members, she (two of three volunteers are female) attends twelve four-hour sessions over the course of six weeks. About half the training is devoted to lectures and discussions by the LASPC staff and guests from Alcoholics Anonymous, the Los Angeles Rape and Battery Hotline, the Gay and Lesbian Community Services Center, and Impact House, a drug treatment center. There are also sessions on the adolescent caller, the chronic caller, the depressed caller, the mentally ill caller, the alcoholic caller, and the survivor of suicide. The other half of training is spent role-playing in small groups where the trainee handles simulated calls from a variety of clients: gay callers, abusive or obscene callers, alcoholic callers, help-rejecting callers. The prospective volunteer must also put in at least ten hours of "observation," listening in while an experienced counselor handles actual calls. "We look for volunteers who care for people, who are good listeners, whose lives are pretty much in order, and who have shown they can handle crises in their own lives," says Chuck Gubera, a senior consultant on the lines. Applicants who have been suicidal or made an attempt are not rejected but must show evidence that they are strong enough to handle the work now. Of every one hundred applicants, about fifty complete training, of whom about thirty-five will be invited to work on the lines. Once accepted, volunteers agree to work one six-hour shift a week for a minimum of six months.

Most suicide prevention lines base their work on "active listening," a technique generally attributed to the psychologist Carl Rogers, founder of "client-centered therapy." In "active listening" the listener affirms what the caller is feeling. If the caller says, "I feel really awful," the listener might say, "It sounds as though you're feeling pretty awful." As the caller vents his feelings, the volunteer listens actively until the crisis has passed, then perhaps offers a referral. In fact, the LASPC's active listening has become a little more active in recent years. The staff has found that an increasing number of their callers are chronic, and counselors are urged to make sure that repeat callers have followed through on previous recommendations. At other centers volunteers are "workers," "listeners," or "befrienders"; at the LASPC they are "counselors." The LASPC counselor is trained not merely to listen but to probe, to ask questions, to solicit information, and to sort through options with the caller. But counselors must not make decisions for the caller, give answers, or pass judgment. Above all they are forbidden to play God or therapist. Recently, one counselor was dropped from the line. "He wanted so badly to help the callers that he almost wanted to change their lives," says crisis line coordinator Beverly Kalasardo, who came to the lines as a volunteer in 1973. "He heard someone needing help and thought, 'Quick, we have to fix it!' When he couldn't, he sometimes got angry." Kalasardo pauses. "Most of our callers would *like* us to fix their lives, they'd like to drop their problems in our lap. They tell us there's nowhere to turn, but there usually is. And we have to help them find that person or place. I think if we had a motto, it would be to help the callers help themselves."

Occasionally, a caller is in a crisis in which he cannot be helped to help himself, and more direct intervention is needed. While a few prevention centers do not trace calls or intervene with third-party callers to preserve confidentiality, the LASPC traces calls and often intervenes in third-party situations. About once a week an LASPC counselor must send the police or an ambulance to a caller's home. In keeping with their philosophy of helping the clients to help themselves, the counselor will first try to get the caller or someone else in the home to take such action or at least agree to let the counselor do so. If the caller refuses to give his address, the counselor will try to keep him on the line long enough to trace the call (which can take several hours) and dispatch emergency help.

More often, however, a counselor will maneuver behind the scenes. Recently, Kalasardo was on the line when a fifteen-year-old girl called in tears. Her boyfriend had just received his grades and realized he was going to fail. Making her promise not to tell anyone, he told the girl he had a shotgun and was going to kill himself. Kalasardo calmed the girl as they tried to find a solution. They couldn't talk to the boy's parents; his father was an abusive alcoholic, and his mother wouldn't have cared. They couldn't talk to her parents; they didn't like the boy either. Kalasardo asked the girl if she would feel comfortable talking to the school counselor. The girl said no. "I asked her if I could, and she said yes," recalls Kalasardo. "So I called the counselor and explained the problem. Meanwhile, the girl talked to their friends, who walked the boy from class to class. The counselor called the boy in, and without letting him know he knew about his plans for suicide, told him he had been looking at his grades, and while it was a shame they were low, he could go to summer school and pull them up without hurting his record. The boy hadn't thought of this option and was relieved. He told the girl. She called me. Later, she wrote me a nice thank-you letter."

Endings are not always so happy. The LASPC estimates that from 1 to 2 percent of its callers eventually commit suicide. Although they don't make a point of reading the obituaries, the staff occasionally learns of the suicide of a caller or former caller. When this happens, the staff meets to share their grief and to talk about how the caller had been handled, what might have been done differently, and what might be done in the future. One of the most troubling deaths occurred several years ago when a shy, young, unemployed accountant who had worked as an LASPC volunteer became depressed and suicidal. One day he called and told a volunteer he was going to kill himself. He asked the volunteer to call the police because he was terrified that his body might lie undiscovered for a long time. Keeping the young man on the line, the volunteer had another volunteer call the police. While the volunteer was still on the phone, the man shot himself the moment he heard the police knock on the door.

Such incidents explain why the LASPC staff stresses the importance of recognizing one's limits. "A lot of you came here thinking, 'I'm going to give these people something magic,'" Kalasardo told a recent class of trainees. "I know I did. And it was a rude awakening to realize I couldn't. Please understand your limitations. You're going to want to take them by the hand and lead them to a new life. But you can't. There is no special magic that will give a caller a new life or that will keep a caller from committing suicide if he really wants to. All you can do is listen, really listen. That's what people need when they're hurting." She pauses. "You may think that listening's not very much, but you may be the first person to ever listen to them. And you may be the last."

It is past eleven. As the city of Los Angeles begins to fall asleep, the volunteers at the LASPC are trying to put people to bed, like air traffic controllers trying to talk pilots down through heavy storms for a safe landing. But some do not want to come down and end up circling, circling. As the call continues, Pat leans still lower over the desk and holds the phone even tighter against her ear, as if by sheer will she might be able to squeeze into the telephone cord and travel through the wires across Los Angeles to some unknown room and sit beside this nineteen-year-old girl. They have been talking for more than an hour. Pat can feel the girl, like a fish on a line, pull away, then come closer, then pull away again. Pat is trying different approaches, her voice now a little softer, now probing, nudging, but never losing its concern. She asks fewer questions now and offers more suggestions. Although the girl has opened up a little, her voice is still a small, thin monotone, and she keeps coming back to the Percodan and whether nine will be enough.

"Are you determined to take those nine Percodan?" Pat asks. "I can't stop you. I hope you don't do that. . . . I think you're making a mistake. . . . It's going to take a little more strength to choose a different option." Her voice becomes firmer. "No, you haven't. You have *not* tried everything. . . . I suspect you're stronger than you sound. . . . I think you deny your strength." Pat senses the girl retreating. "I can't give you anything you don't already have," says Pat. "But I don't want you to hurt yourself. I don't want you to kill yourself. . . . Do you think you can get through tonight?" She pauses. "You may be moving into a place where you are going to have to grow, and that may feel very threatening to you. But you need to share this with your therapist. Will you call her tomorrow? . . . Would you let *me* call your therapist tomorrow? . . . Have you thought about changing your therapist? . . . Why don't you ask your psychology teacher to suggest a therapist? . . . Why would it embarrass you? . . . But you're *not* crazy." Pat is silent for a moment. "Go to that teacher and ask for a therapist." Pat listens. "One more thing: If you're thinking of killing yourself at any point again, will you call us first? . . . Will you? . . ." As the girl apologizes for taking up so much of her time and thanks her for listening, Pat imperceptibly shakes her head, then says softly, "Thank you for calling."

After the girl hangs up, Pat holds the phone in midair, staring at it as if more words or tears might still pour out. Then she gently sets it in its cradle. She lets out a deep sigh. "Oh, mercy," she says. It is 11:20, and she has been on the phone for eighty minutes. "I think she's going to kill herself," she says, "or at least make an attempt," and for the first time since she took the call Pat sounds tense, tired, and a bit defeated. "I told her I can't keep her from killing herself, but also you have to remember you can't make her kill herself."

She shrugs. "You have to hold on to that, working here." Pat shakes her head slowly, sadly. "She hung up crying, and when I picked up the call, she was crying."

Another counselor who has also just finished a call walks in and plops down on the couch. The LASPC staff stresses the importance of talking over each call afterward to give oneself time to recover before the next and to help forestall burnout. (The average LASPC volunteer works on the lines for about two years.) "I really felt I took it as far as I could," Pat says to her colleague, "that if we went any further, we'd get redundant." She begins to fill out a contact sheet, then looks up. "She was the most fragile caller I've ever had," she says. "It was like trying to hold water in your hands. It just keeps slipping through." Pat is quiet. For eighty minutes she has been aware only of the girl, of the sound of their voices meeting in the phone. Now the world begins to come back. The sound of traffic spilling through the venetian blinds is softer now, soothing. It is 11:30. The phone rings. Pat puts on her glasses, picks up the receiver, and in a warm, gentle voice says, "Hello, can I help you?"

II

"THERE IS NO LIFE SO MISERABLE BUT IT MAY BE WORTHY OF OUR ENDEAVOURS TO SAVE IT"

SUICIDE PREVENTION IS NOT a new idea, but the use of kindness, care, and patience, as demonstrated by Pat and the LASPC, is by and large a twentieth-century development. The first recorded instance of suicide prevention occurred in 600 B.C. when Roman soldiers, forced to cut drains and sewers, considered the work beneath a warrior's dignity and threw themselves off the Capitoline Rock. The epidemic abated only when the king, Tarquinius Priscus, ruled that soldiers who killed themselves would be crucified in public and abandoned to the birds and beasts of prey. For the next two millennia desecration of the corpse, confiscation of property, exorcism, and sermons enumerating the tortures of hell were what passed for suicide prevention. Although an occasional clergyman or physician earned a reputation for his ability to rid suicidal people of their demons, it was not until the twentieth century that prevention efforts focused on helping suicidal people rather than terrorizing them.

There were a few exceptions. During the Enlightenment, when there was great interest in using scientific advances to extend the human life span, societies were formed in which physicians, clergy, and laymen essentially acted as eighteenth-century paramedics. The members of one such group, London's Royal Humane Society, founded in 1774, were trained to restore life "to the drowned, those suspended by the cord, or otherwise suffocated: likewise in cases of intense cold; the aweful and tremendous stroke of lightning; and other premature, accidental or sudden deaths." Members were paid four guineas for each successful revival; unsuccessful attempts earned two. While preventing suicide was not its primary goal, the society came in contact with many attempted suicides. "By the Annual Reports of this society it appears, that since its first institution not fewer than five hundred cases of suicide have fallen under its cognizance," observed Reverend G. Gregory in 1797, "in about three hundred and fifty of which its interposition has been providential enough to restore the despairing culprit to himself, to his friends, and to society; and to rescue the soul of the sinner from the overwhelming pressure of despondency, and, perhaps from the danger of everlasting condemnation." The society's annual reports describe some of these cases:

B. Maxey, on the 12th instant, hanged himself, and, when cut down, was to all appearance lifeless: Mr. Dearns assisted in the inflation of the lungs, frictions &c. for a quarter of an hour, which produced pulsation; and the pupil shewed a tendency to contract: In about an hour the natural breathing took place; and in half an hour more his senses returned. The man must have been suspended half an hour, from the joint account of his wife and several neighbours. This desponding man has expressed the utmost sorrow for his horrid crime, and the greatest gratitude to us who were providentially instrumental in restoring him to his wife and family.

Although the society considered suicide a "horrid crime," its members were among the first to realize that suicidal people can and should be helped. They also recognized a characteristic of suicidal people that would be crucial to subsequent prevention efforts: ambivalence. After describing the rescue and rehabilitation of a homeless woman who attempted suicide in 1778, one member wrote, "This happy issue must give pleasure to every reflecting mind. It proves that there is no life so miserable but it may be worthy of our endeavours to save it; and it is an additional argument, to the many others Our Society has afforded, against a prevailing sentiment, that all attempts to save a suicide are in vain; for, they will repeat the act. A sentiment this, neither founded in the knowledge of human nature, nor justified by experience."

In the nineteenth century, despite the fascination with the medical and scientific aspects of suicide, few people took steps to prevent it. Durkheim and Freud both had principally a theoretical interest in suicide, although Durkheim did suggest that alliances of corporations, in the manner of medieval guilds, might give individuals a sense of belonging to the social structure, reduce their anomie, and decrease the suicide rate. At the turn of the century many physicians, in fact, refused to treat suicidal people, who were believed to be insane or doomed to suicide by heredity; suicide was a crime and a sin, and the medical profession did not wish to contaminate itself with such cases. Suicidal people were scorned, ignored, or locked up in asylums. The idea that they should be helped wasn't raised until 1906 when Harry Marsh Warren founded the National Save-A-Life League.

Warren was a thirty-nine-year-old Baptist minister who left his New Hampshire parish to go to New York City, where he became pastor at the Central Park Baptist Church. He also held regular services in hotel lobbies around the city for what he called "The Parish of All Strangers." One evening a twenty-year-old girl staying at a Broadway hotel called the night manager and asked to speak to a minister. The manager was unable to reach Warren that night. The following morning a maid found the woman unconscious, an empty bottle marked "Poison" near her bed. She was rushed to Bellevue Hospital, where Warren went to her bedside. The girl told Warren she was from a small West Coast town, had been jilted by her boyfriend, and had come to New York, where nobody knew her, to kill herself. She had wanted to talk to a minister first, she said, but had been too miserable to wait. "I think maybe if I had talked to someone like you," she told Warren, "I wouldn't have done it." Not long afterward she died.

If in its many retellings over the years the story of the young woman and the minister has gained a suspiciously smooth veneer, the result of their meeting is indisputable. In his next sermon to "The Parish of All Strangers," the shaken Warren described the girl and cried, "I wish that all who believed that death is the only solution to their problems would give me a chance to prove them wrong." He placed an ad in the newspaper urging anyone considering suicide to call on him. In the following week eleven people appeared. All of them admitted they had decided to kill themselves, yet all were eager to pour out their despair. Warren listened. All eleven eventually abandoned their plans for suicide. Warren gave up his pastorate, set up an office in his home on Washington Square, and devoted himself to what he called the National Save-A-Life League.

The idea that someone might *welcome* dealing with suicidal people was a novel one, and ministers, doctors, and social workers were delighted to send these troublesome people to the league. Newspaper stories and word of mouth drew others, and soon about eight people a day were arriving at the league's offices where they were treated with what Warren described as "human sympathy and understanding," by himself or one of several volunteers. While one-third of the cases required more than that and were referred to psychiatrists, Warren found that merely by giving troubled people a chance to talk confidentially to a stranger, he could help them get over a crisis. Although Warren believed "the one sure remedy lies in Paul's message to his Philippian jailer, 'Believe in the Lord Jesus Christ and thou shalt be saved,'" he did not proselytize and in a pinch was quick to offer more earthly aid: money to tide them over, a square meal, a train ticket home, or an invitation to rest at his twenty-one-room home in Hastings-on-Hudson, ten miles north of the city.

Warren didn't wait for would-be suicides to come to him. He arranged with churches, hospitals, and the police to interview attempted suicides and scanned the newspapers for stories about suicide and suicide attempts. Local attempters were visited by a league field worker. Out-of-towners received letters advising them against the futility of their act and, where possible, referring them to a league volunteer in their city. (Eventually, the league had representatives in thirty-five cities and received two thousand letters a year asking for help.) Families of New York City suicides were visited as soon after the death as possible, to be comforted, counseled, and, if necessary, helped financially. Children of suicides were sent to summer camp for a week at the league's expense, to help them "forget." At one time the league, which did not charge for its services and was funded by private donations, sponsored its own Saturday morning radio show in which it presented dramatizations of its cases and invited public support. In 1932 league volunteers interviewed 2,816 would-be suicides or their friends at its offices and visited 1,084 families where suicides had occurred and 2,168 homes where suicide had been attempted. According to Warren, the National Save-A-Life League more than lived up to its name; he claimed the league saved one thousand lives a year. By 1940, when Warren died and his son Harry Warren, Jr., took over the operation, the league, by its own estimation, had saved thirty-four thousand lives.

By then several other suicide prevention organizations were in operation. In 1906, the same year in which the league began, the Salvation Army founded the London Anti-Suicide Bureau, offering free consultation, sympathy, and advice. During their first year, 1,125 men and 90 women applied to the London Bureau, more than half of whom, according to Salvation Army founder General William Booth, had been driven to the brink of suicide by financial problems. Branches were established in Berlin, New York, Chicago, and Melbourne. Elsewhere, Zurich established its Anti-Suicide League, and Berlin a Suicides' Aid Society. In Budapest, after a wave of 150 suicides by drowning in April and May 1928, a "suicide flotilla" patrolled the Danube and managed to save nine of ten would-be suicides. In Odessa an antisuicide museum displayed firearms, knives, and poison bottles left by people who had killed themselves, as well as grateful letters from those dissuaded from their plans.

Vienna offered the would-be suicide a smorgasbord of services. All suicide attempts that came to police attention were reported to the welfare department. A written summons was issued to the attempter, and if it was ignored, a social worker made a house call. The social workers helped the attempters find housing, employment, and financial assistance. The Ethical Society Agency for Suicidal Persons, founded in 1927, tried to reach the despairing *before* they made an attempt. From six to eight each evening, lay volunteers and social workers were available to listen and provide advice, referrals, and occasionally financial aid to troubled people. Trained workers interviewed relatives, friends, and employers, and acted as mediators in family disputes and housing squabbles. To promote an *esprit de corps* among its clients, the center organized an annual banquet at which leading Viennese stage performers provided entertainment. To help prevent adolescent suicide, Vienna opened a youth counseling service in 1928 in which about thirty lawyers, teachers, physicians, social workers, and priests offered advice in their own homes. Unfortunately, these organizations disbanded when their leaders were forced to flee during the Nazi occupation. In 1947 the Lebensmuedenfuersorge (Society for the Care of People Who Are Tired of Life), a consortium of lawyers, psychiatrists, social workers, and clergy, was founded by psychiatrist Erwin Ringel. It is still in existence today.

Another suicide prevention agency still going strong traces its roots to 1935, when a recently ordained twenty-four-year-old Anglican minister named Chad Varah officiated at the funeral of a thirteen-year-old girl who, menstruating for the first time, didn't understand, had no one to ask, and killed herself. Her death made a deep impression on Varah, who had always been more interested in counseling than in other kinds of parochial work. In 1953, in response to a magazine article he had written on "the new morality," he received fourteen letters from people who said their problems had driven them to the verge of suicide. "They didn't need professional help," Varah recalls. "They needed someone to talk to, someone to listen. They needed a friend." Varah read that there were three suicides a day in London. He imagined them "dying miserably in lonely hotel rooms." Varah took out a newspaper ad that invited people contemplating suicide to telephone or visit him, and on November 2, 1953, he set up shop in the crypt of his church, St. Stephen, Walbrook, in London's business district. A newspaper article later gave Varah's service its name—the Samaritans.

In the beginning Varah and his secretary manned the telephone, but there were soon so many people calling and coming in to talk to him that volunteers were recruited to make tea for the troubled as they waited in line. By the time they reached Varah, many didn't need to see him—they already felt better after talking to the volunteers. Varah decided to use the volunteers to talk to the clients and found that caring contact between two people reduced the client's loneliness and despair. The concept of "befriending," as Varah called it, had been born. Befriending might mean a volunteer and a client talking on the phone, meeting for tea, or visiting at the Samaritan office or in the client's home. Befriending was not counseling or therapy; volunteer and client met on equal grounds. The recruiting slogan for volunteers was "Are you ordinary enough to be a Samaritan?"

Befriending was not intended to obviate professional help, but Varah's hunch that fear kept many people from seeking that help was justified. The Samaritans befriended one hundred clients that first year; today, there are 180 Samaritan branches in Britain (including 15 in London), staffed by twenty-two thousand volunteers who receive 2 million calls each year. Troubled people can call Samaritans in forty-four countries, including Thailand, New Zealand,

Pakistan, Bolivia, Botswana, the United States, and Zimbabwe. Despite their extraordinary expansion—they have become a veritable McDonald's of suicide prevention centers—the Samaritans have retained their intimacy and efficacy by clinging to their original formula. Over the years there have been many attempts by erudite researchers to analyze the essence of befriending, but as one Samaritan volunteer put it: "In its purest form, befriending is love."

For many years the National Save-A-Life League was the only prevention group in the United States. Other organized efforts to help the suicidal disappeared almost as quickly as they began. In 1936, for example, Robert Rehkugel, a sixty-four-year-old Methodist pastor in Oakland, announced plans for the Suicide Prevention Society of America, in which retired pastors would counsel potential suicides. Rehkugel planned a Suicide Prevention Sunday, a Suicide Prevention Week, and a Suicide Prevention Patrol of men and women to intercept would-be suicides and restore them to their families. The society's motto, he said, was "Prevent, Seek, and Save"; its goal, a 50 percent decrease in suicide by 1940. Beyond the fact that this goal was not met, it is not known what became of the project. Fifteen years later Julia A. Shelhamer, a seventy-year-old minister's widow distressed by reading of the suicide of a prominent Washington, D.C., man, placed a classified ad in the newspaper: "Discouraged? Call DI0614." Her phone rang steadily—one Sunday she received 110 calls. Her remedy was to listen to callers' problems, then ask them to pray with her. But her service seems to have quickly dissolved. In 1935 department store tycoon Marshall Field financed the Committee for the Study of Suicide. Under the direction of prominent psychiatrist Gregory Zilboorg, it collected in-depth data on more than fifteen hundred suicides, but work was suspended shortly after the United States entered World War II.

Beyond these isolated examples, the field of suicide and suicide prevention was primitive and taboo in the first half of this century. Indeed, there was no "field." "Prior to the 1950s, except for the efforts of a few courageous practitioners, suicide went untreated as a mental health problem and was hardly ever discussed," psychologist Calvin Frederick has written. "It was rarely a point of focus in the media, or in professional literature, though suicide has claimed consistently more victims than homicide." Although an occasional sociologist flung a statistical net at suicide, the subject was not considered a respectable research topic. The word itself seemed distasteful to professionals. (As late as 1955 a Veterans Administration project on suicide was tactfully named "The Central Research Unit for the Study of Unpredicted Deaths.") The few papers to be found in the professional literature consisted of several case histories or brief vignettes. No one had attempted to systematically examine the psychological characteristics of suicide and to use that research in prevention. Then in November 1949 a thirty-one-year-old psychologist found himself alone in a room with hundreds of suicide notes.

Edwin Shneidman was a precocious young man who entered the University of California at Los Angeles at the age of sixteen. He earned his master's degree in psychology before serving as a captain in the Army Air Force. After the war he received his Ph.D. from the University of Southern California and began work at the Brentwood Veterans Administration Hospital. In November 1949 he was asked to draft letters of condolence to the widows of two former VA patients who had committed suicide. To find out more about the men, he visited the Los Angeles County coroner's office one rainy afternoon. In a basement vault lined with dusty folders, Shneidman found the folder for one of the men, which contained copies of the man's suicide note. He looked in another folder and another, and realized that the coroner's office had been filing suicide notes in this room for decades. Shneidman spent the afternoon rummaging through the folders. Though Shneidman's interest in suicide until then had been tangential, he realized that the study of suicide was "a virgin field." "I felt," he says, "like a Texas millionaire coming home and stumbling into a pool of oil."

Shneidman called Norman Farberow, a VA psychologist who had written his doctoral dissertation on attempted suicide, and told him about the notes. Like Shneidman, Farberow was thirty-one, had attended UCLA, and had been a captain in the Army Air Force. Following the war he and Shneidman were fellow trainees in the new VA clinical training program, where they became friends. Yet while their backgrounds were similar, the two men were vastly different in appearance and temperament. While Shneidman, a short, compact man, sizzled with energy like water on a frying pan, Farberow was a slim, neat, almost elegant man with the manners and bearing of a diplomat. Shneidman's feisty, restless drive could be abrasive; the word used most often to describe Farberow is "gentleman." Shneidman's wild brilliance was complemented by Farberow's organization and attention to detail. For many years the two of them would make ideal collaborators.

With their cache of 721 notes, Shneidman and Farberow believed they might discover the key to suicidal motivation in the last words of people who kill themselves. They decided to compare the notes with a control group of simulated suicide notes—"pseudocide notes," as Shneidman dubbed them—composed by nonsuicidal people. Visiting labor unions and fraternities, they asked members to write the note they would write if they were about to take their own lives. While some of the longshoremen were skeptical—"you could see them smirking, thinking to themselves, 'What are these crazy people doing?' " Farberow remembers—they complied. The genuine and simulated notes were typed on index cards, numbered, and shuffled. Then Shneidman and Farberow analyzed them blindly. When they broke the key, they found that the pseudocide notes showed no particular personality patterns; the real notes betrayed various but recognizable characteristics. Fifteen percent, for instance, were written by what they called "surcease suicides"—older people seeking a release from pain. Many notes reflected a marked ambivalence—it seemed that part of the writer wanted to live, part to die. One note succinctly illustrated this: "Dear Mary: I hate you. Love, George."

The suicide note study was just the beginning. Working out of a cramped basement room in the Brentwood VA hospital, Shneidman and Farberow began a massive study of attempted, threatened, completed, and nonsuicidal people. From the coroner's office they collected the names of eight thousand people who had killed themselves over a ten-year period. Then they combed through two hundred thousand files at hospitals and clinics for the names, collecting suicide notes, case histories, psychological test results, diaries, and therapy records of these suicides. From physicians they gathered data on 501 attempted suicides. They wandered the wards of Los Angeles County General Hospital interviewing people who had attempted or threatened suicide. And from the local VA hospital they gathered a sample of nonsuicidal patients.

Their findings contradicted several widely held beliefs. Though it had long been assumed that people who threatened suicide never committed it, they found that three-fourths of suicides followed previous threats or attempts. Though it had long been assumed that "you have to be insane to commit suicide," they found that only 15 percent of suicides were psychotic. The vast majority were depressed. They discovered that almost half of those who killed themselves did so within ninety days after an emotional crisis, and at a time when they seemed to be recovering; one-third had seen a physician within six months of their death; most suicides were neither crazy people hell-bent on death nor people whose suicide came "out of the blue." These depressed people didn't really want to die; they left clues to their plans, and if family and friends had been alert to those clues, they might have been able to prevent the suicide. As Shneidman put it, it was possible for a person "to cut his throat and cry for help at the same time."

Shneidman and Farberow intended to confine their efforts to research, but as they prowled hospital wards gathering data, they developed a reputation among the staff as experts on suicide. Nurses began asking them to speak with patients who had been admitted following an attempt. The two psychologists politely refused; they were doing research, not therapy. "They'd say, 'This man came in last night; he drank some cleaning fluid. Would you talk to him?' or 'This man cut his throat. Would you speak with him?' But we said, 'We can't talk to him, we're here on research,' " recalls Shneidman. "Our access to patients dried up. Then someone advised us to buy candy for the nurse, and when she asked us to see a patient, say yes. 'But we know nothing about suicide,' I told him. He said, 'You know more than she does.' " Shneidman chuckles. "And willy-nilly we were in the treatment business."

That Shneidman and Farberow were accepted as clinical experts on suicide merely because of their interest in the topic is not surprising. If the subject of suicide was ignored by researchers, it was anathema to clinicians. "There wasn't much known or written about the suicidal patient—treatment was very hit or miss," recalls a social worker. "Most professionals did not want to deal with them. They were afraid of the responsibility. Social workers and psychologists referred—or deferred—to psychiatrists because they were able to hospitalize." Psychiatrists were no better equipped. "I was taught *nothing* about suicide in medical school and virtually nothing in my residencies," says one psychiatrist. "It was just something that you prayed wouldn't happen, and if you had a suicidal patient, you put him in the hospital." The hospital was equally unenlightened. "There was very little specific treatment of the suicide problem and very little understanding of why a person might be suicidal," says a social worker. "The standard procedure was to put all suicidal patients on one ward and just watch them a little more closely." Fear and ignorance were compounded by the anger many doctors felt at the suicidal patient, especially at those who were rushed to the hospital after an attempt. "Medical staffs were overworked, and many doctors resented spending their time and talents on the suicidal," says a social worker. "Some doctors while sewing up someone's wrists would say, 'You didn't do that right—next time you have to cut *this* way to do the job.' " Follow-up care was rare. "The idea was to pump them out, patch them up, and get them home as soon as possible," says Shneidman. "Nobody wanted the responsibility."

Eventually, Shneidman and Farberow began to discuss combining clinical and research activities in a service for suicide attempters. "We thought of it as a suicide prevention referral service," says Farberow. "The idea was to evaluate and help suicidal people while they were in the hospital, then make sure they got to some kind of resource in the community." They called Robert Litman, director of the psychiatric unit at Cedars-Sinai Hospital, a bright young clinician who had written a paper on how to deal with suicide on a hospital ward. "They had been working with notes and charts, and now they wanted to work with people," recalls Litman, whose interest in the subject of suicide had been sparked when his former college classmate, Thomas Higgen, author of *Mr. Roberts,* had taken an overdose and drowned in a bathtub. "They took me to a restaurant in Beverly Hills and literally plied me with liquor. Then they said, 'What do you think about the idea of a suicide prevention center?' I said, 'You're kidding.' They said, 'We'll put an ad in the telephone book saying suicide prevention, and suicidal people will get in touch with us. You'll take care of them, and we'll study them.' " Litman chuckles, remembering. "I thought it was crazy," he says. "I thought we would attract all the crazy people in town, and we wouldn't be able to handle them."

With the help of Harold Hildreth, a psychologist at the National Institute of Mental Health who believed that NIMH should be exploring taboo areas, Shneidman and Farberow were awarded a five-year, $377,000 demonstration grant, an extraordinary sum considering the time and the subject matter. Meanwhile, Shneidman, Farberow, and Litman discussed names for their service. They agreed that the title should include the word suicide. "It was time for the taboo problem and its attendant stigma to be brought out into the open where it could be acknowledged and dealt with openly and constructively," they wrote. "We were also aware that what we were planning to do was not *pre*vention, it was *inter*vention," recalls Litman. "But Suicide *Inter*vention Center?" He shrugs. "Didn't have a ring to it. Sounded lofty. So we decided to call it Suicide Prevention Center as a challenge rather than hide behind a less provocative title." On September 1, 1958, the Los Angeles Suicide Prevention Center opened with one phone line and a staff of five.

From its earliest days the LASPC had an improvised, informal quality. The center was located in an abandoned and condemned tuberculosis ward on the grounds of the Los Angeles County General Hospital. The dilapidated, eight-story red brick building, ringed with creaky wooden porches where TB patients had taken the sun, had a rococo appeal; television crews filming a story on the center would inevitably drift off to examine the architecture. The center was on the fourth floor, accessible by a clanging, wheezing, often out-of-order elevator. The rooms were high-ceilinged and dimly lit; some were tiled and held bathtubs twice the size of humans. Although a fresh coat of paint and shipments of secondhand desks and chairs from the VA made their corner of the building livable, the setting was bleak. Even as they moved in, the structure was being vandalized by community agencies for plumbing and electricity. One morning a Hollywood film crew arrived; the LASPC's home, it seemed, made an ideal bombed-out building for their latest World War II film. "We were concerned that the building would make our clients even more depressed," says Sam Heilig, a social worker who joined the center in 1960, "but when we'd ask patients if it depressed them, they said no, it sort of fit their mood." The hospital used a system of colored lines painted on the floor to guide patients to various departments from the guard station at the street. It seems fitting that the line leading to the LASPC offices was painted blue.

In its first year the LASPC worked with fifty patients. Each Monday morning Litman would walk over to the county hospital and scout the wards for people who had been admitted over the weekend for a suicide attempt. Usually, there would be at least a half-dozen, from which one would be selected as the center's "case of the week." Litman conducted a full psychiatric interview, a psychologist gathered test information, and a social worker interviewed the patient's family and friends. At Friday morning staff meetings the case was discussed in detail, and treatment recommendations and referrals to appropriate agencies were made. The goal was to examine each case intensively, to learn as much as possible about why that person had tried to kill himself. "None of us knew anything at that time, so we went very slowly," recalls Farberow.

"That was our intention," says Litman. "But what happened was that these people told their friends and their friends told their friends, and pretty soon people were calling us and literally saying, 'I'm just about to make a suicide attempt—do I have to take these pills or jump off a building before I can talk to you? Or could I shortcut it and come in directly?' " The LASPC became a magnet for suicidal people. Calls came from distressed people, concerned friends and relatives, and therapists happy to refer their difficult cases. One early call came from a teacher who walked into her classroom during recess and found a student hiding behind the blackboard with a plastic bag over his head. When she yanked the bag off and brought the boy around, his first words were, "That's all right. I have a knife at home." The boy was seven. He was referred to a psychiatric service. Another call came from a frantic psychiatrist. His patient was in the next room behind a locked door with a gun. What should he do? The staff member on duty calmed the psychiatrist, then talked him through the crisis, telling him not to call the police but to take his time, talk to the man, and bring in his friends and family. The psychiatrist followed the advice. Eventually the door opened, and his patient emerged and surrendered the gun.

Because no rules or guidelines existed for dealing with suicidal people, the LASPC improvised techniques as they went along. Though most of the staff had been trained in Rogerian or Freudian models, these strategies seemed impotent in a suicidal crisis. When a person was out on a ledge, metaphorically or otherwise, it seemed feckless merely to say back to him what he was saying and too time-consuming to take five years on the couch to find out why he was up there. "Both of those have given way to better clinical common sense," Shneidman wrote. "That is, we became directive, assertive, straightforward, even authoritarian—anything that it takes to keep a person from becoming a case in the coroner's office." To fulfill its mission the LASPC went to lengths unheard of in traditional therapeutic circles: The staff made house calls, met clients in restaurants, escorted suicidal people to the hospital, brought in family and friends, phoned across country to get one man's estranged wife to come and see him, dispatched ambulances or police, and traced calls. One day a client ran out of the offices onto the roof with several LASPC staff members in hot pursuit; they managed to grab her and wrestle her back inside before she could jump. Another time a suicidal young woman was brought in by her family; halfway through the consultation she ran out of the building. An LASPC staffer tackled her, put her in the car, and told her brother to sit on her while he drove her to the hospital.

Like polar explorers the LASPC staff probed the boundaries of the vast, uncharted territory of suicide and its prevention. Shneidman skittered out on the edge, mapping and naming the new field, inventing its vocabulary, sparking ideas, giving speeches, and writing papers. His wild, often abrasive brilliance was complemented by Farberow's meticulous organization, dependable scholarship, and attention to detail. As clinical director, Litman was the glue that held the center together, seeing his own patients, overseeing everyone else's caseload, assuming the responsibility for medication and hospitalization. On the rare occasions when a client committed suicide (of the center's first three hundred patients, there were two), Litman led the painful meeting at which the case was discussed; the staff tried to comprehend what had led to the person's decision and what else might have been done to prevent it. Litman had some of the brilliance of Shneidman and the affability of Farberow, and worked well with both of them. His genial, quirky manner and enthusiasm helped give the staff the feeling of a team. Suicide prevention, in fact, tended to scramble the mental health pecking order that placed psychiatrists at the top, followed by psychologists and then social workers. At the LASPC *everyone* was involved, and there were few rules about who did what. One of the most adept at handling desperate callers, in fact, was the receptionist, Alice Arnold, an outgoing woman who had never worked in the mental health field before. "She was supposed to take business calls, but when none of us was available, she had to take a lot of suicide calls," remembers Litman. "And she was great on the telephone. . . . When all else fails, you can fall back on being motherly and probably be right."

For many years suicide had been a subject no one talked about. On the fourth floor of the old TB building people talked of little else. "People used to ask us wasn't it depressing, but it was very lively," says Sam Heilig. "We had a great camaraderie, and we had a lot of laughs." And because no one had ever made this kind of intensive effort to study suicide, there was a feeling among the staff that they might solve the enigma. "I really thought that within a few years we would unravel some of the mysteries of why a person takes his life," says David Klugman, a psychiatric social worker who joined the staff in 1960. "I believed that by analyzing each event in depth as it happened, we'd find some key or clue that would explain it. Maybe I was a little naive, but I thought we were going to find the answer."

While they did not find the answer, they developed many of the concepts and techniques that are now standard in the field. (And published them. Between 1956 and 1966, Shneidman, Farberow, and Litman alone authored, coauthored, or edited four books and more than eighty papers on suicide, ranging from "Suicide Among General Medical and Surgical Hospital Patients with Malignant Neoplasms" to "Sex and Suicide.") They developed the concept of clues. They developed the concept of lethality, described by Shneidman as "the probability of an individual killing himself in the immediate future." Previously, a person was thought to be suicidal, or he wasn't. The LASPC proposed that some suicidal people are at higher risk than others, and for each person the degree of risk or "lethality" fluctuates over time. They devised a "Suicide Potential Rating Scale," based on demographic and psychological factors, to measure that risk. They developed the idea of "the suicidal crisis"—that most people are acutely suicidal for a relatively short time, and if helped through that time, will survive. During that crisis the LASPC stressed the importance of active intervention, constant contact with the patient, calling in the family, and breaking confidentiality if necessary. They described suicide as a "dyadic" event and suggested involving a person's "significant other" in treatment whenever possible. And for those who work with suicidal people, they stressed the importance of frequent consultations, sharing the burden, and working as a team.

The LASPC also invented the "psychological autopsy." In 1958, after giving a speech at the VA hospital, Shneidman and Farberow were approached by Theodore Curphey, chief medical examiner–coroner for Los Angeles County, whose office was responsible for determining the cause (heart attack, gunshot, and so forth) and mode (natural, accident, homicide, or suicide) of all deaths in the county. Each year some one hundred deaths were regarded as equivocal—the coroner was unable to determine whether the death was accident or suicide. Curphey suggested that the LASPC might be able to help. Just as pathologists and toxicologists ascertained the cause of death by examining physical evidence, the LASPC staff might collect psychological evidence, interviewing relatives and friends of the victim to reconstruct his state of mind preceding his death. LASPC staff members were made deputy coroners, and the "Death Investigation Team" annually performed more than one hundred "psychological autopsies," as Shneidman named them. Their best-known autopsy was case number 435, Marilyn Monroe. When she died of an overdose of barbiturates on August 4, 1962, Curphey asked Farberow and Litman to investigate. In the course of interviewing Monroe's friends and associates they learned that she had tried to commit suicide twice before and that she had been deeply depressed before her death. Their recommendation was for "probable suicide."

In the media glare following Monroe's death the "professional suicide workers" of the center's "suicide team" received nationwide attention, and the LASPC caseload grew exponentially. "By this time we knew that we needed to expand our services," says Farberow. "We had been conducting ourselves like a clinic, with regular office hours, eight to five. But people were calling us after hours. We knew that because the lines continued to ring whenever one of us was working late. It was usually somebody looking for help." Before they knew it they were in what Litman calls "the telephone business." They started by hiring a telephone exchange to transfer calls to staff members' homes. But the staff was small, and after a few weeks they realized that they were losing too much sleep. So they trained preprofessionals—psychiatric interns, graduate students in psychology or social work—and paid them $10 a night to take the calls at home. With the "Night Watch" program, help was now available twenty-four hours a day.

But the volume of calls continued to mount, and in 1964 the center decided to use trained nonprofessionals on the telephone. Although at the time the National Save-A-Life League and England's Samaritans used lay volunteers, the LASPC prided itself on its professional approach. "I had a lot of reservations," admits Klugman. "By 1960 I had a master's in social work and seven years of field experience, yet I felt ill-prepared and inadequate to handle some of the situations I was dealing with on the phone. So how were we going to train middle-aged housewives to do this?" Once they started, however, the LASPC learned the lesson the Samaritans had learned—that trained laypersons can do as well as professionals, even better in some ways. "They didn't let their professional guard get in the way," says Farberow. "They were able to interact on a very direct, personal basis with the suicidal person." The volunteers even began to see an occasional patient in the office and to provide counseling in selected cases. The LASPC caseload continued to grow. In 1966 the center was contacted by nearly seven thousand people.

Not only was the center's caseload expanding, but their single-minded devotion to suicide lured other professionals out of the woodwork. In 1963, having received a major increase and extension of its NIMH grant, the center moved out of the old TB ward and into a two-story building near downtown Los Angeles. Their new home on Pico Boulevard became a hub for the study of suicide and its prevention. Requests for advice, consultations, reprints, and speeches poured in from around the country and eventually from around the world. Staff members traveled the nation, teaching evaluation and treatment techniques to physicians, nurses, police, clergy, and mental health professionals. The center produced training films for police and for physicians on how to handle suicidal people. Twice a year the center offered three-to-five-day training institutes for people from all over the country interested in starting a suicide prevention center in their own community.

The center's diversity gave it the atmosphere of a small university. Clergy, sociologists, and psychologists visited the center to study suicide or to study how the LASPC studied suicide. Graduate students and interns spent semesters training at the center. Visiting professors gave speeches on suicide and self-destruction. Friday morning "case of the week" seminars were renowned for their spirited intellectual discourse. Shneidman organized a program in which distinguished scholars, including sociologist Erving Goffman, philosopher Stephen Pepper, and psychologist Elsa Whalley, spent several months at the center "to contemplate suicide and to think about death." Farberow, who spent 1964 abroad studying prevention organizations in London, Berlin, Paris, and Vienna, became active in the fledgling International Association for Suicide Prevention, and the LASPC's stream of visitors gained a global flavor. Ten years earlier no one had talked about suicide in the professional community; now the LASPC had become a sort of international think tank devoted solely to the study of suicide and its prevention.

Although their work had begun as a research effort and had only by serendipity come to include clinical work and the use of trained volunteers, Shneidman and Farberow now felt that the most important task was to disseminate the knowledge they had gathered. Comparing the suicide prevention center to "a lifeguard station on a dangerous beach," they believed that every city of any size across the country should have its own center. "Shneidman had no doubt in his mind that suicide prevention should be a movement," says a colleague. "When we talked about a suicide prevention center in every community, he carried it to the extreme—that *every* person should be a one-man suicide prevention center, should know the signs and be able to help in a suicidal crisis."

On October 14, 1965, Stanley Yolles, the director of NIMH, announced the establishment of a national center for research and dissemination of information on suicide. He asked Shneidman to head the project. Shneidman was ready to move on. He had become restless at the LASPC. For more than a decade he and Farberow had been partners and coauthors; one name was rarely seen in print without the other. In the public mind they were linked together as Shneidman and Farberow, suicide's Siamese twins. Shneidman was anxious to be on his own. The Center for Studies of Suicide Prevention, as it would be called, was an opportunity to advance both his own career and the growing suicide prevention movement. The following year he moved to Washington.

If suicide was still a taboo subject, suicide prevention had taken a giant step forward with the formation of the CSSP. The fifties and early sixties were a time of government largesse toward mental health, and in their 1966 reorganization NIMH designated five high-priority areas: alcoholism, drug abuse, child and family mental health, crime and delinquency, and suicide. For suicide, which only ten years before could not even be mentioned as a problem, it was an achievement of sorts. Now it had official recognition as a federal target, a social ill to be attacked, like poverty and crime, with good old American know-how and money. The CSSP could dispense grants for research, training, and demonstration projects, but the bottom line was clear. As Shneidman wrote not long after his arrival in Washington, "The goal of the NIMH Center for Studies of Suicide Prevention is to effect a reduction in the suicide rate in this country."

Suicidology—a word coined by Shneidman to describe the study of suicide and its prevention—had been born, and the movement's peripatetic ringmaster was everywhere, preaching prevention, inventing concepts, and fizzing with ideas. Identifying the dissemination of clues as "the most important single item for effective suicide prevention," Shneidman, who became known as "Mr. Suicide," called for a program in "massive public education"—and carried it out almost single-handedly by writing pamphlets, organizing symposia, and giving hundreds of interviews. "The 'early signs' of suicide must be made known to each physician, clergyman, policeman, and educator in the land— and to each spouse, parent, neighbor, and friend," he declared. Toward this end the CSSP funded the "First Training Record in Suicidology," in which actors dramatized calls to a prevention center; it commissioned *Quiet Cries,* a play highlighting the ambivalence and clues shown by people experiencing suicidal crises; it assembled a "basic library on suicidology" of ten books and twelve pamphlets, available for $40 a set; it published a journal, the *Bulletin of Suicidology,* that kept people abreast of developments in the field. It promoted the First National Conference on Suicidology, at which Shneidman was voted founding president of the American Association of Suicidology, an alliance of mental health professionals, sociologists, clergy, and prevention center volunteers. It sponsored a postgraduate fellowship program in suicidology at Johns Hopkins University, in which social workers, sociologists, and psychologists took courses in crisis intervention, the psychology of suicide, biostatistics, suicide and the law, and the epidemiology of mental illness; worked in acute treatment clinics; performed psychological autopsies; did field work in prevention centers; and acted as expert witnesses in moot trials involving suicide. Suicide prevention now had not only federal sanction but academic credentials as well.

The most visible evidence of CSSP's work was the proliferation of prevention centers. "Just as there are fire stations throughout our country, there ought to be suicide prevention centers in every part of the land," wrote Shneidman. There were fifteen when he arrived in Washington. A year later there were forty-seven, and by the time he left the CSSP in 1969 there were more than one hundred, with names like We Care, Rescue, Inc., Dial A Friend, Learn Baby Learn, Life Line, and Help. The suicide prevention movement coincided with the spirit of altruism and activism that marked the sixties, and saving lives seemed like the ultimate in caring. Magazines offered histrionic accounts of tearful calls and heroic rescues; movies like *The Slender Thread,* starring Sidney Poitier and Anne Bancroft, and *Dial Hotline,* with Vince Edwards and Kim Hunter, dramatized the risks and rewards of volunteering at a prevention center. Would-be lifesavers learned the ropes in articles that promised to teach them "How to Set Up a Suicide Prevention Center."

While the LASPC served as the prototype—many center directors trained there or used its manual—there were wide variations. Some centers were autonomous, others were affiliated with hospitals or community mental health centers. Some were organized by the clergy, others by physicians, social workers, psychologists, or nurses. While the common denominator was a twenty-four-hour phone line staffed by nonprofessional, trained volunteers, some centers offered face-to-face contact as well. A few offered group therapy. Some had outreach teams for emergencies; at one center volunteers accompanied policemen to the homes of attempters. San Francisco Suicide Prevention placed an ad in the newspaper inviting those too shy to call to write; a Gainesville, Florida, center encouraged suicidal pen pals. A prevention center in Buffalo hosted a weekly television and radio show on which the agency director interviewed people who had once attempted suicide and were now leading productive lives. One center served as an alternative service placement for conscientious objectors.

The CSSP did not fund centers for direct service, and most programs were dependent on community support. Budgets ranged from $500,000 yearly at the Buffalo center to $26.25 per month (the cost of a telephone and a listing) reported by a center in Bismarck, North Dakota. Centers raised funds with walkathons, dances, plays, dinners, rock concerts, house tours, and bingo. When donations fell short, volunteers often passed the hat among themselves. They publicized their services through interviews, telephone directories, brochures, bumper stickers, bookmarks, and newspaper, radio, and television ads. They posted flyers in banks, bars, barber shops, beauty parlors, bus stations, airports, motels, libraries, schools, factories, emergency rooms, police stations, and trailer parks. Some centers enclosed brochures with bank statements, industry paychecks, phone bills. The message was clear: Suicide prevention was everyone's business. Shneidman even pointed out that suicide was cost effective; he calculated that every averted suicide saved as much as $1 million in lost wages and taxes as well as ambulance and coroners' costs.

But the growth of knowledge about suicide wasn't keeping pace with the zeal to prevent it. The movement's accomplishments were measured in quantity: the proliferation of centers, the number of articles written. In a bibliography covering 1897 to 1970, Farberow noted that more papers and books on suicide had been published in the last thirteen years (2,542) than in the previous sixty-one. But a review of these publications reveals few rigorous studies, more groping than exploration, and little of practical use. A sample of journal articles includes "Lunar Association with Suicide," in which the authors found a slight increase during the new moon, which they were at a loss to explain, and "Suicide in the Subway," which discovered "important differences" between those who lay in the train's path ("traumatic death") and those who touched the third rail ("nontraumatic death"). "One of the problems in the study of those who kill themselves is that the subject of the study is deceased and hence not available for study," began an article, "Spiritualism and Suicide," which therefore suggested that mediums be used to contact suicides for research purposes. "If communication is established with a deceased suicide, it seems mundane to administer an MMPI or a Rorschach," observed the author, referring to two of the most common psychological tests. "However, a psychoanalyst, for example, might well be able to conduct an interview that would illuminate the psychodynamics behind the act. Occasionally, though, spirits have their own agenda for communicating and object to questions."

The author had a point: Research in suicide *is* limited by the fact that studies are ex post facto. "Individuals correctly determined to be suicides are not available for study," notes one psychologist. "They are at the morgue." Other methodological problems have frustrated suicidologists. Because suicide is a statistically rare event, it can take many years to accumulate a significant sample. There have been few long-term studies using sizable control groups. Much of the research is based on as few as two or three subjects, and the same case studies are trotted out again and again like prize pupils, often to illustrate different points. A 1972 summary of research findings since 1882 concluded that the vast majority of suicide research was monotonous, uninspired, and scientifically inept.

Meanwhile, there were mounting concerns about suicide prevention centers. By 1972 there were more than 300, but the feverish growth had been haphazard, and there were no accepted standards for service or training. The authors of a survey of 253 centers were "struck by the wide variability in training, efficiency, and effectiveness of the services." Callers to some centers had problems just getting through. In one study psychologist Richard McGee placed seventy-six calls to nineteen agencies in the Southeast. He was confronted by eight different types of answering and referral services—message machines, patch systems, callbacks, and so forth—and often experienced long delays before reaching a human being. A 1970 CSSP-sponsored task force, calling for the establishment of minimum standards for centers, admitted, "The establishment of suicide prevention programs was entered into by many who were serious and dedicated but, also, by others who were capricious and ill-advised. The result is a mixture of services which as a whole lack purpose, direction, commitment, and involvement."

Even more distressing was the growing evidence that suicide prevention centers were not preventing suicide. While centers often publicized their efforts by claiming their work "saved lives"—the National Save-A-Life League, for example, asserted that since 1906 they had saved one thousand lives per year—they offered no real proof. Few centers evaluated their services, and their assumption that the application of care and support prevented suicide was based on letters and calls from grateful clients. When a 1968 study found that the suicide rate in fifteen English towns with a Samaritan branch had fallen, the declining English suicide rate was credited to the Samaritans. But a subsequent, more carefully controlled study found no difference in the rates of comparable communities that had a Samaritan branch and those that did not. In the United States psychologist David Lester compared eight cities that had prevention centers in 1967, eight with centers in 1969 (but not in 1967), and eight without centers during those years, and found that the centers made no significant difference in the suicide rate. While centers provided a "needed and useful service" in counseling the distressed, Lester concluded that suicide was "relatively immune" to prevention programs. Other statistics seemed to support this. Between 1960 and 1970 the number of centers in California grew from one to nearly thirty; the suicide rate grew from 15.9 to 18.8. In Los Angeles, site of the movement's flagship prevention center, the rate jumped from 17.5 to 21.3. And in the United States as a whole it rose from 10.6 to 11.6.

The exaggerated hopes kindled by prevention programs underscored their apparent failure. The centers were discredited as quickly as they had been embraced. By 1969, Shneidman had left the CSSP for academia. Citing surveys that claimed only 12 to 15 percent of the calls to centers dealt with suicide, his successor, psychiatrist Harvey Resnik, advised centers to change their names to "Suicide Prevention and Crisis Intervention Center" in order to reach a broader base. The shift at CSSP reflected not only disappointment with the centers' failure to subdue the suicide rate but also the changing agenda of the federal government. During the late 1960s there was increasing pressure on the government to do something about runaways, teenage pregnancy, and "the drug epidemic." When Bertram Brown became NIMH director in 1970, he designated child mental health as the institute's top priority. Child mental health was in, drug abuse was in, minority groups were in. Suicide was on its way out. The government, which in ten years had spent more than $10 million on suicide research, decided it was a bad investment. In 1972 the CSSP was disbanded, and the concept that had launched the Los Angeles Suicide Prevention Center more than a decade earlier—that suicide was a proper and necessary research topic, that suicidal people could and should be helped—had been diluted. Fifteen years after Shneidman, Farberow, and Litman insisted that the word "suicide" be a part of their new center's title, a sign on the bulletin board at the UCLA meditation center printed the LASPC's telephone number above this all-purpose encomium: "Need a place for a good rap? Call the Los Angeles Suicide Prevention Center."

Why didn't all this time, money, and sheer good intentions have a measurable effect? Studies show that most calls to prevention centers are not from the severely suicidal. In a 1970 study of ten centers, 33 percent of their callers had been considering suicide, and the percentage of seriously suicidal callers was far smaller. More than half of the four thousand calls received monthly at the Suicide Prevention and Crisis Center in Buffalo, for example, were from crank callers, pranksters, or people who hung up immediately. The majority of suicides are older white males; the majority of prevention center callers are young white females. Although some suggest that most people are simply not aware that prevention centers exist, a study by San Francisco psychiatrist Jerome Motto found that while 80 percent of a group of depressed and suicidal persons had heard of the local prevention center, only 11 percent had used it. Suicidal people, reasons sociologist Ronald Maris, are simply too isolated to call a stranger.

Yet prevention centers clearly get many high-risk callers. At the LASPC, several follow-up studies have shown that about 1 percent of callers kill themselves within two years. Although these figures may be interpreted several ways, they indicate that prevention centers work with a high-risk group: Callers represent about one hundred times as great a risk of suicide as the general population.

Some say prevention centers do not offer enough. "They don't take responsibility for the patients," says psychiatrist Douglas Jacobs. "People call up and get referred, but research shows that follow-through is at best 50 percent. Many patients may never make it—they may feel they've already *made* a connection." Centers may be better suited to helping the "situational suicide," a caller whose stability has been upset by specific events, than the chronic suicidal caller. In his follow-up studies of LASPC clients Litman found that most subsequent suicides were by high-risk patients who were suicidal over a long period of time; they need more than just a patient ear and a referral. However, when the LASPC experimented with an eighteen-month follow-up program of callbacks and home visits to high-risk cases, there were seven suicides in the group that got extra care and only two in the control group. The specially trained volunteers felt "overwhelmed" by the demands of continued contact and wanted to turn over more difficult cases to the professional staff. The continuing relationship offered by the volunteers was "too little too late," concluded Litman.

Concerned by the unsupervised growth of centers in the late sixties and early seventies, the American Association of Suicidology is belatedly trying to impose minimum standards for prevention centers. But the AAS is a modest, relatively powerless group; with thirteen hundred members it is, as former AAS president Alan Berman noted at the 1985 annual meeting, larger than the American Tiddlywinks Society but considerably smaller than the International Barbed Wire Collectors Historical Association. Whether because of cost, excessive standards, or simply because it's not necessary, only ninety of the over six hundred suicide prevention and crisis intervention centers listed in the AAS handbook have been certified. This reinforces the skepticism felt by some mental health professionals about the centers' efficacy. Although attitudes have come a long way since 1965, when the San Francisco coroner referred to the staff of the local center as "a bunch of clowns," many psychiatrists disparage the "amateurism" of the volunteers and dismiss their work as "handholding." Others worry about the danger to callers who get busy signals

or an answering machine, or who are put on hold. (While such annoyances may further depress a caller, one suicidal woman who called a center and got an answering machine burst out laughing at the absurdity of the situation. The tension of her despair was pricked, and she survived the night.) A few analyze the motives of the volunteers; several studies have suggested that suicide prevention work may attract emotionally troubled people seeking to work out their own problems while attempting to help others. Nevertheless, therapists often refer their patients to prevention centers when they don't want to be disturbed. Centers report a boom of calls in August from people whose therapists have gone on vacation, leaving the local prevention center's number in their place.

At the same time, while admitting that they are no substitute for professional help, many prevention center volunteers harbor distrust and resentment of mental health professionals. (At one point, in fact, the rift between professionals and volunteers threatened to split the AAS in two.) "It's nothing but doctors figuring out how to protect themselves from suicidal patients," scoffs the head of one center, walking out of an AAS seminar. Hearing that a suicidal patient shows "strong cathexis of the self with superego aggressive energy and inadequate cathexis with narcissistic libido," a volunteer wants to know how to use that "on the firing line." As a result of such mutual antipathy the possible benefits of therapist-volunteer cooperation remain largely unexplored.

Meanwhile, prevention centers continue to refine their services. In an attempt to reach a greater number of high-risk callers, prevention centers have developed programs for specific target groups. Some centers operate special lines for AIDS, child abuse, rape, the homeless, gays, and lesbians. Some offer group therapy for the suicidal or support groups for bereaved family and friends left behind after a suicide. Others run training and education programs for the police, the military, or high school and college students. San Francisco Suicide Prevention runs a special twenty-four-hour hot line for the elderly, including regular callbacks and home visits. The Samaritans of Boston helped organize a suicide prevention program at the Charles Street Jail in which inmates befriend other inmates.

Although prevention centers no longer make exaggerated claims of efficacy, recent evidence confirms that suicide prevention centers do, in fact, help prevent suicide. A 1984 University of Alabama study comparing suicide rates in Alabama counties that had a center with those that did not, found that the centers were associated with a reduction of suicides by young white females— the demographic group to which most callers belong. Extrapolating their calculations to include the entire nation, they estimate that suicide prevention centers save the lives of 637 young white females each year.

With or without statistical reinforcement, the value of prevention centers should not be assessed solely by the suicide rate. While the word suicide is prominent in their advertising and an estimated one-third of their callers are

suicidal, suicidality is not a prerequisite for calling the LASPC or any other suicide prevention center. But if what keeps people alive is connection, centers may provide a small dose of caring that may prevent someone's loneliness from spiraling into suicide months or years down the line. "Most callers are lonely, frightened, desperate people who don't know where to turn, and when they call the center, at least they get some sort of answering voice," says Robert Litman. "That's not necessarily suicide prevention, but it does play a part in stabilizing society. It is a little bit of society's answer to the chaos that society creates." Just as Nietzsche said the thought of suicide "helps one through many a dreadful night," the thought of a suicide prevention center has gotten many thousands of people through their own dreadful nights. David Klugman remembers one of the first calls he handled at the LASPC. When he picked up the phone and said, "Hello, may I help you?", there was a silence. Then a timid voice on the other end said, "I can't talk now. . . . I just needed to know someone's there."

III

TREATMENT

THE VAST MAJORITY of people who attempt or complete suicide never come in contact with a prevention center, and even for those who do, the prevention center is only a first step. There are two steps to suicide prevention—identifying the person at risk and deciding how to help him. Most of the work of the prevention movement has focused on finding the suicidal person. Shneidman is one of many suicidologists who believe that suicidal people communicate their intentions through the kinds of "clues" described in Chapter I—giving away prized possessions, making statements like "You'll be sorry when I'm gone"—but that most people don't know how to listen. "Education is the single most important item in lowering the suicide rate," he says. "I don't mean suicide prevention classes. I mean a general heightening of awareness, so that if I give you my watch, you won't simply take it and thank me. You ought to say, 'Ed, sit down, tell me what's happening.' " Shneidman advocates mass media campaigns like the one that helped 40 million Americans give up smoking in the past twenty-five years.

Yet, even to trained suicidologists, clues are often recognizable only in retrospect—and in hindsight almost anything can look like a clue. "I'm sure if you or I went out the window right now, somebody might say, 'I knew that was going to happen someday,' " says Douglas Powell, a psychologist at Harvard University Health Services. In 1975, Powell did counseling work with the friends of a Harvard junior who had run through a dormitory window to his death shortly before final exams. For weeks afterward the boy's friends wondered why, agreeing there had been no apparent reason, no clues. Then his roommate recalled one detail: Nick had always set ashtrays, mugs, and postcards on his window sill. For several weeks before his death, each time Nick sat in front of that window, he had removed another object. "People say, 'Well, how can these things happen to your children and you not notice them?' " the father of a sixteen-year-old boy who attempted suicide told a reporter in 1981. "Well, all I can say is you can sit in a house and the sun goes down and you never see it go down, and the next thing you know it's dark."

People often recognize clues but fail to respond through fear, ignorance, denial, or even indifference or hostility. Psychiatrist Leon Eisenberg describes a college student having a turbulent affair with a classmate. "He said, 'If you don't go steady with me, I'll jump off this building.' She said, 'You don't have the guts.' He did. He ran right up the steps to the eighth floor, out on the roof, and jumped off," says Eisenberg. "And I might add that the young lady showed no remorse at all." It is not known what proportion of people who leave clues go on to kill themselves. "All the students come in at some point and talk about suicide," says one high school social worker. "I can't put them *all* in the hospital."

How should one respond to a cry for help? The most important thing, say experts, is to listen, to show empathy, and to take the problem seriously. Too often, because of uneasiness or fear, a friend may laugh off a plea or ignore a clue. "Anybody who talks about suicide is serious," says psychiatrist Michael Peck. "It's not up to us to make a judgment about whether he or she will do it or not." Although you may suspect the person is talking of suicide just to get attention, it is vital to take the person at his or her word. One of the biggest myths about suicide, as the LASPC learned, is that people who talk about it won't do it. While there are no statistics on how many of those who threaten suicide go on to attempt it, it's far better to overreact than to underreact. Avoid being judgmental. Telling the person to "snap out of it" is like telling someone with two broken legs to get up and walk. And the common response, "But you have everything to live for," may just deepen the person's feelings of guilt and inadequacy. Questions like "Are you feeling very unhappy?" and "How long have you felt this way?" are nonjudgmental and give a person the chance to vent his feelings and perhaps reduce his distress. Although people often worry that asking about suicide will put the idea into the depressed person's head, this is not true. Asking about suicide demonstrates concern and shows a willingness to discuss anything he or she might be feeling. Experts suggest asking directly, "Are you thinking of suicide?" If the answer is yes, ask if he has planned how he'll do it. If he has a plan, this indicates imminent danger and the need for immediate professional help.

But even when the signs are recognized and the person is brought into treatment, it is only the beginning. Every day in hospitals, emergency rooms, outpatient clinics, private offices, and prevention centers, clinicians must make quick decisions about the risk of suicide, sifting the highly suicidal from the suicidal from the nonsuicidal. Test chestnuts like the Rorschach, TAT, and MMPI have been of little help. Over the last two decades researchers have devised dozens of scales and questionnaires in an attempt to give clinicians an "objective" tool to quantify suicide risk.

Perhaps the first was the LASPC "Suicide Potential Rating Scale," used in both telephone screening and clinical interviews. Reviewing the records of twenty-six thousand clients, the staff devised fifteen questions based on demographic, situational, and behavioral signs. The degree of lethality is rated from nonrisk to high. Psychiatrist Jerome Motto, in a follow-up study of 2,753 depressed or suicidal patients, found that 136 had killed themselves. He identified fifteen variables—depression, suicidal thoughts, emotional disorder in the family, prior psychiatric hospitalizations, and so on—as significant predictors of suicidal outcome and developed "The California Risk Estimator," a one-to-ten scale that estimates the probability of suicide within two years. Psychiatrist Aaron Beck, the founder of cognitive therapy, has developed a host of scales, including the "Beck Depression Inventory," a "Hopelessness Scale," and a "Suicide Intent Scale" for attempters. His "Scale for Suicide Ideation" measures the intentions of people who are thinking of suicide, with nineteen questions beginning with "Wish to Live" (scored "moderate to strong," "weak," or "none") and "Wish to Die" (same scoring options). A ten-year test of the Beck Depression Inventory found that hopelessness is the strongest predictor of subsequent suicide. Two hundred and seven patients hospitalized for suicide ideation (suicidal thoughts or behavior) were rated on the scale and followed for five to seven years. Of the fourteen who committed suicide during that time, thirteen had high hopelessness scores.

Psychologists at the University of Washington decided to focus on why people *don't* kill themselves. Their "Reasons for Living Scale" scores forty-eight factors connecting to a patient's "survival and coping beliefs, fear of suicide, fear of social disapproval, consequences for family, moral objections, and child-related concerns." A group of California therapists believe that the patient is the best judge. In their paper "Patient Monitoring of Suicidal Risk," they suggest that the therapist simply ask his depressed patient how long and under what circumstances he will stay alive. The patient is then asked to make a pledge: "No matter what happens, I will not kill myself accidentally or on purpose at any time." The authors write, "If the patient reports a feeling of confidence in this statement, with no direct or indirect qualifications and with no incongruous voice tones or body motions, the evaluator may dismiss suicide as a management problem." The authors, who say that in five years none of the six hundred patients who have made "no-suicide" decisions have broken their pledge, declare that their technique is "suitable for use by inexperienced nonprofessionals as well as by experienced professionals."

Most scales are intended for those who may be thinking about suicide; some measure the seriousness of an actual attempt. Using psychiatrist Avery Weisman and psychologist William Worden's "Risk-Rescue Rating," a therapist may compute the lethality of an attempt by assigning points from the five risk factors (which include actual damage inflicted, and method—pills get one point, jumping and shooting, three) and the five rescue factors, which revolve around the chances of being found in time to survive. The rating is computed by dividing risk score by risk plus rescue scores and multiplying by one hundred. Thus, it is demonstrated that a thirty-eight-year-old unmarried waitress who ingested sedatives, then went to a movie theater where she was found in a coma and subsequently died, received an eighty-three, the highest possible score.

While these scales provide useful checklists for clinicians, playing "the numbers game," says psychiatrist Douglas Jacobs, can be dangerous. "You have to be careful. On a percentage basis young people are less likely to kill themselves, but if one of them does, for that person it's a hundred percent." The risk categories used in most scales may fluctuate. Suicide has increased dramatically among the young; the rate for the elderly has gone down. Some researchers suggest that different scales must be developed for specific populations: for young females, for middle-aged alcoholics, for patients in psychiatric hospitals. But no matter how specific the scale, there will be exceptions to the rule. In 1983, University of Alabama researchers, declaring that most existing scales are "too complex or cumbersome for practical and routine use," devised the "SAD PERSONS" Scale, an acronym for ten risk factors. Scoring one point for each, the patient's probability of making an attempt is rated from one to ten. Suggested treatment is based on score, ranging from "send home with follow-up" (0–2) to "hospitalize or commit" (7–10). The researchers admit that some people may slip through the statistical net. "For example, a four-teen-year-old girl who attempted to hang herself 'because the devil came and told me to' might score only three points on the scale."

What these scales prove most convincingly, in fact, is that our ability to predict suicide is negligible. "Although we may reconstruct causal chains and motives after the fact, we do not possess the tools to predict particular suicides before the fact," concluded Alex Pokorny after his scale for suicide risk proved unsuccessful in a prospective study of forty-eight hundred inpatients at a Texas VA hospital. Says Robert Litman, "Even for someone in a high-risk category the chances of suicide within a year are much less than the chance that he will *not* have committed suicide within that time. In twenty-five years I can remember perhaps three cases where I felt the chance of a certain person committing suicide within the next year was more than 10 percent."

Of course, while many of these scales are intended as research tools, even those designed for clinical use stress that they are a supplement to clinical judgment, not a substitute for it. "You can know all the statistics and scales but still not have any ability to assess a patient," says one psychiatrist. But if the scales have not proved their worth, neither has clinical intuition. In a 1973 study a computer proved more accurate than experienced clinicians in predicting suicide attempters. In addition, half the patients preferred the computer to a doctor as interviewer.

It is for some of these reasons that a number of mental health professionals scoff at the "clues" approach to suicide prevention. "We've reached the point of no return in defining vulnerable populations," says psychiatrist Herbert Hendin. "It amounts to looking for the proverbial needle in a haystack." Hendin knocks Shneidman's proposed educational blitz. "I don't follow the logic of putting millions into educating the lay public in something that psychiatrists haven't proven *they* can identify. It makes more sense to do something for the people you *do* find. A lot of seriously suicidal people present themselves to us in ways nobody can miss—they jump from five-story buildings—and nobody does anything for them." A previous attempt is the highest predictor of suicide risk; between 30 and 40 percent of suicides have tried before, and 1 percent of those who attempt will complete within one year, 10 percent within ten years. Yet most attempters are returned to the community after brief hospitalization, without provision for follow-up treatment. "If you could identify 20 percent of the seriously suicidal from those who make attempts and cure 10 percent," declares Hendin, "you could literally change the suicide rate."

Can clinicians "cure" suicidal people? The question is rarely asked. The bottom line at most prevention centers and in most prevention literature is to get the suicidal person to professional help. Although getting the person to that help can be difficult—reluctance by the person or his family to admit there is a problem, the stigma of being in treatment, and the high cost of quality care are a few of the obstacles—it is often assumed that once we do, the problem is solved. Yet professional help is no guarantee against suicide. One in three suicides has been in some kind of psychiatric treatment, ranging from a single consultation to many years of intensive therapy. Patients who have made attempts and entered into treatment have the highest suicide rate of any patient group. The focus of suicide prevention has been on assessment and prediction of suicide risk; treatment has been largely ignored.

How do clinicians treat suicidal people? A therapist's first task, of course, is to address the crisis, to decrease the risk of suicide, just as counselors are trained to do on the LASPC crisis lines. "The immediate goal of a therapist, counselor, or anyone else dealing with highly suicidal people should be to reduce the pain in every way possible," writes Shneidman. "Help them by intervening with whoever or whatever is causing their distress—lovers, parents, college deans, employers, or social service agencies. I have found that if you reduce these pressures and lower the level of suffering, even just a little, suicidal people will choose to live." In his book *Definition of Suicide,* Shneidman described a counseling session with a suicidal college student. Pregnant, single, highly religious, and overwhelmed by shame and guilt, the girl had decided to kill herself. Shneidman's initial task was to help her to realize that alternative solutions existed.

> I did several things. For one, I took out a single sheet of paper and began to "widen her blinders." Our conversation went something on these general lines: "Now, let's see: You could have an abortion here locally." ("I couldn't do that.") . . . "You could go away and have an abortion." ("I couldn't do that.") "You could bring the baby to term and keep the baby." ("I couldn't do that.") "You could have the baby and adopt it out." ("I couldn't do that.") "We could get in touch with the young man involved." ("I couldn't do that.") "We could involve the help of your parents." ("I couldn't do that.") "You can always commit suicide, but there is obviously no need to do that today." (No response.) "Now, let's look at this list and rank them in order of your preference, keeping in mind that none of them is perfect."
>
> The very making of this list, my non-hortatory and non-judgmental approach, had already had a calming influence on her. Within a few minutes her lethality had begun to de-escalate. She actually ranked the list, commenting negatively on each item. What was of critical importance was that suicide was now no longer first or second. We were then simply "haggling" about life—a perfectly viable solution.

Once the immediate danger has passed, how does a therapist treat a suicidal patient? Ask almost any therapist, and he or she is likely to answer, "Suicide is a symptom, not a diagnosis." Suicide is not listed in the *Diagnostic and Statistical Manual of Mental Disorders*. Nor is suicide dependent on a specific illness. "Suicidal behaviors may be generated in the presence of practically any diagnostic entity, and at times in the absence of pathological states," says psychiatrist Jerome Motto. Because a clinician can't "treat" suicide he must treat the underlying illness—the patient's closest diagnosable ailment, which is, more often than not, some form of depression. Many clinicians believe that if they successfully do so, they've treated the suicidal patient, as if suicidality were simply a nasty side effect of the underlying illness. Yet some suicidal patients have no diagnosable underlying illness, and patients often kill themselves shortly after coming out of a depression—or long after a depression has lifted. "Suicide proneness is primarily a psychodynamic matter; the formal elements of mental illness only secondarily intensify it, release it, or immobilize it," psychiatrists Dan Buie and John Maltsberger have written. "The urge to suicide is largely independent of the observable mental state, and it can be intense despite the clearing of symptoms of mental illness."

How is the "underlying illness" of the suicidal patient treated? There is little agreement on how to treat any mental illness. A person suffering from depression may be treated with antidepressant drugs, shock treatment, cognitive therapy, Yoga, or any of more than 250 types of psychotherapy practiced today. Of them, only psychoanalysis is agreed to be inappropriate for suicidal patients: "Most are either too anxious, too depressed, or just not well enough put together to stand it," says Herbert Hendin, himself a psychoanalyst. Although suicidal patients come in different diagnoses with different needs, they are likely to get whatever the therapist practices. "One would hope that clinicians had a number of strings to their therapeutic bow and would change depending on the nature of the problem," says psychiatrist Leon Eisenberg. "Unfortunately, this field is characterized by people who do the same type of treatment for every customer that comes along." A therapy that works with suicidal patients will be ignored by most clinicians if it is not their modus operandi. Beck's cognitive therapy, which helps depressed patients to reinterpret their negative, distorted thoughts in a more realistic, positive light, seems to reduce the feelings of hopelessness that may be at the core of suicide. Family therapy has been effective; some therapists, in fact, refuse to see a suicidal patient without also involving the family. But many more worry about overstepping patient-therapist confidentiality.

Group therapy with suicide attempters has been valuable in reducing stigma and isolation. "The person realizes she's not alone—that everyone else in the room has had suicidal thoughts so there's no need to maintain secrecy and isolation," says Chrisula Asimos, a San Francisco psychologist who has worked with groups of suicidal people since 1971. The group, in fact, tends to reduce the focus on suicide. "The issue of suicide loses its impact," says Asimos. "We talk openly about suicide, but we focus on other options. In a group people can see how other people who have been there longer have moved away from suicidal behavior and explored healthier alternatives." Bonding between group members (who are encouraged to be in individual therapy as well) extends beyond meetings; they organize group dinners and birthday parties, and like members of Alcoholics Anonymous who call each other when they have the urge to take a drink, they share home telephone numbers to be available to each other at times of crisis. When one group member who was acutely suicidal worried about jumping from her apartment window, the entire group helped her move from her lonely twentieth-floor rooms to a cheerful residence club on the ground floor.

But while group therapy seems to make suicidal patients more comfortable, few therapists are at ease leading groups of any kind, and the thought of working with a room full of high-risk patients can be daunting. "Group therapy for suicidal patients hasn't caught on because therapists are afraid of it, and I can well understand why," says Norman Farberow, who pioneered therapy groups for suicidal people at the LASPC. "Most suicidal people are insatiable in their need for care and support, and when you get a half-dozen depressed and severely suicidal people together, it's very draining." There has been no conclusive research on the efficacy of groups for the suicidal, but of the hundreds of high-risk patients who have been in Farberow's LASPC groups, none committed suicide while in the group, although two former members took their lives after they had left the group against staff advice. In Chrisula Asimos's sixteen years of running groups, no member has committed suicide. At one meeting, however, an older member suffered a fatal heart attack while in the bathroom. It was a traumatic experience for the group, but, says Asimos, "I'm convinced he came there to die—that we were his family."

In some therapeutic approaches the therapist himself seems to serve as a substitute family. In their work with suicidal patients over two decades, Boston psychiatrists John Maltsberger and Dan Buie have evolved what they call the "psychodynamic formulation" of suicide. "This approach looks at suicide in terms of developmental failures that make it impossible to maintain a sense of self-worth," says Maltsberger. "Many people who grow up suicide-vulnerable have failed to get the love they ought to have had from their mothers. Others have received good mothering but for little-understood reasons cannot make use of it." In normal development, he explains, capacity for autonomy increases with age, enabling one to endure degrees of loneliness, depression, and anxiety. Suicide-vulnerable people fail to develop sustaining inner resources; they must depend on external supports. When those supports fail, suicide is a danger.

Though Maltsberger's theoretical approach to suicide is heavily influenced by Freud, in practice the psychodynamic formulation is quite practical. "It boils down to finding out what a person has to live for," says Maltsberger. "Most people live for all sorts of things—friends, a special person, work—and if they lose something on one front, they pick it up on another. But suicidal people are quite deficient in any capacity to keep themselves afloat on the basis of inner resources. Once somebody threatens suicide, you start looking at what resources the person has."

Maltsberger and Buie specify three areas people live for: other people, work, and their own bodies. "Obviously, when someone who is dependent and depressive loses a girlfriend or a husband, it can precipitate a suicidal crisis," says Maltsberger. "Then there are people who never have relationships, who lock themselves in the library and devote themselves to scholarship. But when they retire or can't work anymore, they may kill themselves. A surgeon may live only to operate; if he loses the use of his hands, he may do away with himself. And there are people who may be very dependent and depressive, but as long as they can jog and look in the mirror and say, 'Gee, I'm in great shape,' they can go on.

"So if someone has relied all his life on some capacity to work at Sanskrit, and he goes blind, the task becomes to find what this person can substitute as a life-saving activity." Just as Shneidman worked to "widen the blinders" of the pregnant young woman on a short-term basis, Maltsberger, in the "psychodynamic formulation," tries to help the patient expand his long-term reasons for living. "It isn't always possible. Many people are quite indifferent to the love of others, for instance. Others may be indifferent to success at work. Suicidal people are very specialized in what they will accept as a reason for living." At first, says Maltsberger, the therapist himself may have to constitute that reason "until the patient can regain his balance and stand up again."

The psychodynamic formulation offers therapists a practical way to help decide *when* someone is suicidal, what to do for treatment, and whether hospitalization is indicated. It also requires a therapist to know a patient's history thoroughly and to spot events in a patient's daily calendar that might heighten suicide risk. "Treating suicidal people means being available—intensively—from time to time while they're between supporting figures or research projects," says Maltsberger. "I might call them on the telephone every day or even go to their house. You have to be there waiting like a net, hoping that as time goes on the person can widen his repertoire and make room for other sustaining influences."

Even the psychodynamic formulation, however, offers only temporary relief. Can vulnerability to suicide be altered? Maltsberger sighs, like the Wizard of Oz after giving out heart, brains, and courage only to find that Dorothy is still in search of a way to get back to Kansas. "That's most ambitious," he says slowly. "That means helping the patient restructure his mind, which is very, very difficult and, in some cases, impossible." He pauses. "Often, psychiatrists don't want to try."

Although there is no pill for suicide, there are scores for schizophrenia and depression. What is now referred to as the "drug revolution" had its beginnings in the late 1940s when French neurosurgeon Henri Laborit was looking for something to calm his patients prior to administering anesthesia. He found that chlorpromazine, a sedating antihistamine, produced a "euphoric quietude" in them. He recommended the drug to his psychiatrist colleagues, who tested it on a variety of mentally ill patients and found it effective in the treatment of manic depression and schizophrenia. In 1954 it was introduced to the United States: Thorazine, the brand name by which chlorpromazine would be known, achieved extraordinary results. Patients who had been unruly and assaultive were suddenly docile. In some hospitals the use of straitjackets, wet packs, and seclusion was cut in half. Many patients were able to return to the community.

At first many therapists believed drug therapy would be a panacea for suicidal patients. But the drugs offered control, not cure. In 1954, the year tranquilizers were introduced at Metropolitan State Hospital in Norwalk, California, the suicide rate more than doubled. Investigators suspected that the staff may have relaxed their vigilance because of the drugs' efficacy in controlling symptoms. While lithium has been highly successful in treating manic depression and the antidepressants have been effective and often lifesaving in correcting chemical imbalances that cause certain depressions—studies have shown that they relieve about 65 to 75 percent of biochemical depressions in adults—they can be a red herring in the treatment of suicidal patients. "Gratifying results with depressive patients, who may have been suicidal, prompt some therapists to overgeneralize the results to the point of believing that most suicidal patients can be successfully treated by such intervention," Harvey Resnik and Calvin Frederick have written. Says Herbert Hendin, "There has been very little evidence that the antidepressant drugs which have been known to alleviate depression have any effect on suicide." Says Maltsberger, "They do nothing to alter the underlying vulnerability to suicide."

The same drug that relieves depression may give a patient both sufficient energy to act on his impulses and the means to do it. "It's a Catch-22. You can't prescribe antidepressants without risk of the patient using them to kill himself, but it's very hard to treat depression without prescribing antidepressants," says one coroner. "It's a complicated issue," says Alan Pollack, a psychiatrist at McLean Hospital in Belmont, Massachusetts. "You have to judge whether patients can manage medication, how reliable they are in taking it, and how big a supply you can give them without their overdosing on it." Commenting on a 1970 study that showed that of two hundred people who committed suicide with barbiturates prescribed by physicians, over two-thirds had a history of previous attempts, psychiatrist Ronald Mintz observed, "One might indeed ponder what kind of a nonverbal communication the suicidal person must feel he is receiving when he is handed a prescription for a potentially lethal quantity of drugs."

While most psychopharmacologically-oriented therapists supplement drug therapy with psychotherapy, drugs are the *only* treatment method for some. "In state hospitals, community mental health centers, and as practiced by welfare doctors, it is often the sole therapy," observed Jonas Robitscher in *The Powers of Psychiatry,* "and the only contact the doctor may have with the patient is to inquire if the dose of drugs needs regulating." On the other hand, some therapists have neither the training nor the inclination to use psychopharmacology when appropriate. "Drugs are an essential part of medical management of suicidal patients," writes Norman Farberow. "However, drugs alone cannot be counted on to prevent suicide. The most important elements are human relations, psychologic support, and constructive action."

Partly because they are the only mental health professionals allowed to prescribe medication or to hospitalize, psychiatrists are generally regarded as the last word for suicidal patients. "We all use psychiatrists as backups for these cases," says a Boston social worker. "The psychiatrist is the bottom line." One would therefore expect psychiatrists to know a good deal about suicide. They don't, says sociologist Donald Light, who bases his belief on two years of observation at the Massachusetts Mental Health Center, one of the most highly regarded psychiatric training programs in the country. Like most residency programs the center did not offer specific instruction in treatment of suicidal patients. "Residents are trained as they get cases, by supervisors who were treated in the same haphazard way," says Light. "So a lot of homemade ideas about suicide care are perpetuated from one generation of psychiatrists to the next. In short, the blind lead the blind."

It is part of psychiatry's folklore that one is not a full-fledged therapist until one has had a patient who commited suicide. Once past this blooding ceremony a therapist may avoid the subject in the future or learn more about it, almost in self-defense. He will get no instruction except at his own initiative. "Experience is the best teacher," says one psychiatrist, expressing a widespread conviction. (Residents *are* likely to acquire experience; a majority of patients on training wards are there because of a suicide attempt or severe ideation.) Light disagrees. He has recommended a specific training module to the American Psychiatric Association in which each residency would have an in-house expert through whom all suicidal cases would be routed. Residents would be required to work with a crisis phone service and to attend regular seminars on suicide care, stressing availability, the need to relax confidentiality, the necessity of working with the patient's friends and family, and the importance of working in clinical teams. The APA's response has been "polite," says Light, but he remains insistent. "Psychiatrists have moved from a period when they refused to treat suicidal patients to a time when they're seen as the final resource," he says. "So if they're being fed suicidal cases, they simply have a professional and moral responsibility to be explicitly trained in that area."

Light's is not the only voice in the wilderness, although, as a sociologist among psychiatrists, his may be the most strident. "Suicidal behavior is the most frequently encountered of all mental health emergencies," says psychiatrist Alan Berman, whose 1983 survey of over three hundred training institutions found, on average, no more than half a day's formal education devoted to suicidology by any of the mental health disciplines. "It should be axiomatic, then, that those charged with assessing and treating these suicidal individuals would, at a minimum, be knowledgeable of risk factors and skilled in techniques designed to reduce assessed risk. Yet this simply is not the case." Psychiatrists, in fact, score no better than radiologists on tests determining their knowledge of risk factors; other mental health professionals score only slightly higher than college students and the clergy. After a rash of suicides at McLean Hospital, one of the most highly regarded psychiatric institutions in the country, Alan Stone, then director of residency training, concluded, "During the course of that epidemic it became painfully apparent that many psychiatrists possess no systematic or comprehensive approach for dealing with suicidal patients." In a series of papers Stone and the late Harvey Shein, his successor and former student, proposed that "suicidal risk must be *monitored* in a way that is analogous to the current hospital management of acute coronary artery disease." They suggested that suicidality be made an explicit focus of treatment and that the patient's family be brought in and told. "Once the patient's suicidal thoughts are shared, the therapist must take pains to make clear to the patient that he, the therapist, considers suicide to be a maladaptive action irreversibly counter to the patient's sane interests and goals; that he, the therapist, will do everything he can to prevent it."

Many therapists share with laymen simple misconceptions about suicide— for instance, the myth that if you ask a person about suicide, you'll be planting a seed in his mind and the person will do it, or conversely, that if a person talks about suicide, he won't do it. Or that if a patient really wants to kill himself, you can't stop him. "These false axioms derive primarily from fear of intense involvement with suicidal patients often arising from the residents' and staff's own social scotomata, professional concerns, and neurotic disabilities," Shein told the APA in 1974. The most common fallacy is the supposed distinction between serious and nonserious attempters. While it is tempting to assume, for example, that wrist cutters are "manipulators," Light insists that they should always be taken seriously. Writes Maltsberger, "Some patients almost ready for suicide but as yet undecided may betray their ambivalence through a minor attempt. . . . We know of one young schizophrenic woman who ingested six Stelazine tablets, an event misunderstood at the time as a negativistic gesture of little significance. A few days later, her indecision resolved, the patient fired her father's pistol through her head."

Sometimes, specific types of therapy may be harmful. One such approach involves what children call "reverse psychology"; while most therapy concentrates on the part of the patient that wants to live, "paradoxical technique" plays the flip side. The patient says life isn't worth living; the therapist agrees. Light remembers a psychiatrist who claimed never to have lost a patient with this risky technique. He came close. "One girl had a blade at her wrist and he kept saying, 'Go ahead, go ahead.' He was pushing her down the hallway, and she went screaming out of the hospital." She made a small cut but recovered.

Such brinkmanship requires an experienced therapist. Impressed with the jocular, Jewish-mother approach his supervisor used, a young resident tried it himself. "So already you should die" came out sounding like "you should die." Two months into treatment his twenty-two-year-old patient put the plastic slip of a record jacket over his head and suffocated.

Another therapist took the opposite tack. On learning that one of his patients, a businessman, had slashed his wrists, he rushed to the emergency room where the patient was being sewn up and gave him a right hook to the jaw. "How dare you do anything so stupid?" he yelled. "If you ever do anything like that again, I'll kill you." Perhaps encouraged by his therapist's concern—or stunned by his Sunday punch—the patient did in fact get better.

When Maltsberger was a resident he had a chronic suicidal patient who repeatedly slashed her wrists. "I was getting fed up," he recalls, "and one day

I said, 'If you're not interested in changing, we can arrange for you to be someplace else.' I think that remark was motivated by hate. My basic message was 'We're tired of you; get off your ass or get out of here.' " On the next attempt the patient nearly killed herself. It was the first time Maltsberger had confronted countertransference hate—an emotional response therapists may have to certain patients. Such reactions can be particularly intense with suicidal patients. Extraordinarily demanding, they may attack the therapist, verbally or physically; they may shadow him or make anonymous phone calls. (Maltsberger knows of two instances in which patients telephoned suicide threats at the moment they correctly guessed their doctors were eating Christmas dinner.) The mere passivity—"almost a sucking quality," says Alan Stone—of some suicidal patients is likely to inspire boredom, malice, even hatred in a therapist. "When you deal with suicidal people day after day after day, you just get plain tired," says James Chu, a psychiatrist at McLean Hospital. "You get to the point of feeling 'All right, get it over with.' "

In one of the few papers on the subject, Maltsberger and Buie describe how therapists may repress such feelings. A therapist may glance often at his watch, feel drowsy, daydream—or rationalize referral, premature termination, or hospitalization just to be rid of the patient. Sometimes in frustration a therapist will issue an ultimatum. Maltsberger recalls one therapist who, treating a chronic wrist cutter, "just couldn't stand it, and finally she said, 'If you don't stop that, I'll stop treatment.' The patient did it again. She stopped treatment, and the patient killed herself." Many studies have detailed similar unintentional abandonment of suicidal patients. In a 1967 study of six suicides at a clinic, psychiatrist Victor Bloom found that in each case the suicide was preceded by rejecting behavior on the part of the therapist. Reviewing the treatment of thirty men and women who had killed themselves as inpatients or within six months of discharge, William Wheat isolated several patterns that he believes contributed to the suicides: the therapist's refusal to tolerate a patient's immature, dependent behavior, the therapist's pessimism about treatment progress, and an event or crisis of overwhelming importance to the patient that went unrecognized by the therapist. "All of these processes," wrote Wheat, "can lead to a breakdown in the therapeutic communication resulting in the patient's feeling abandoned or helpless, thus setting the stage for the disastrous result of suicide."

Light contends that only certain psychiatrists are able to withstand the demands of suicidal patients. "We should be candid about the fact that most psychiatrists are not built for suicide care. Let's select about 10 percent who have the stomach for it, who can handle the high anxiety, who might even *like* it, who have a kind of Green Beret outlook, and give them special training and then make it clear to other psychiatrists that when they get a suicidal case, they refer it to this person."

Light has in mind people like Bruce Danto, a psychiatrist whose resume reads like that of an entire SWAT team. Danto, a former president of AAS and the author of numerous books on suicide, has given workshops on hostage negotiation and terrorism, lectured on stress to the FBI and the Royal Canadian Mounted Police, and trained police in psychological techniques for dealing with violent and suicidal persons. Danto, who lives and works in Orange County, California, receives many referrals for suicidal patients. "I think we need to change the role of therapist from passive listener to active intervener," he says. "With these problems you can't simply sit back in your chair, stroke your beard, and say, 'All the work is done right here in my office with my magical ears and tongue.' There has to be a time when you shift gears and become an activist. The psychiatric suicidologist must have skills over and above those of psychiatrists in general." The "psychiatric suicidologist," in Danto's view, is part social worker, part psychologist, and part cop. (With degrees in sociology, social work, and medicine, and a deputy sheriff's badge, Danto is all of the above.) Support may involve helping a patient get a job, attending a graduation, play, or wedding, visiting the hospital, even making house calls. "I would *never* send somebody to a therapist who has an unlisted phone number," he says. "If therapists feel that being available for telephone contact is an imposition, then they're in the wrong field or they're treating the wrong patient. They should treat only *well* people." The "psychiatric suicidologist" must also pay attention to "the tools of self-destruction." Danto has a collection of guns and knives belonging to suicidal patients, who hold receipts. "Once you decide to help somebody," he says, "you have to take responsibility down the line."

While many psychiatrists find such suggestions too aggressive, they admit that not all psychiatrists are equally fit to deal with suicidal cases. "There are many psychiatrists who don't necessarily have great experience in treating people who have made suicide attempts," Ari Kiev, a Manhattan psychiatrist, has said. "I would much rather have my social worker or even the receptionist deal with some suicide-prone patients than just any psychiatrist." Herbert Hendin gets many referrals from uncomfortable colleagues. "A lot of people who do reasonably well with other patients cannot deal with suicidal patients," he says. "The bigger tragedy is if somebody is *not* comfortable, you shouldn't spend ten years trying to analyze his discomfort—let him treat someone else." Robert Litman interviewed more than two hundred therapists shortly after the suicide of a patient. They expressed fears of being vilified in the press, of being sued, of being investigated, of losing professional standing, and of inadequacy. Litman points out that therapists must understand that no treatment—psychotherapy, drugs, electroshock, hospitalization—can guarantee that suicide will not occur. When he lectures residents about suicide, he tells them it is important to realize that they will undoubtedly have a suicide at some point in their practice. But potential psychiatrists, according to Donald Light, find death more threatening than do other medical specialists.

"Why are psychiatrists so scared of suicide?" asks Light. "It's an anthropological question—why is this event so disruptive to the emotional balance of the tribe? It's almost like a moment of black magic." He pauses. "One possibility is that suicide is the ultimate rejection of therapeutic effectiveness. The patient is committing suicide for other reasons, but in the process, since he's your patient, he's rejecting what you do. It's as if someone on the operating table decided to die."

"These doctors who get so anxious when a patient threatens suicide haven't settled in their own lives the question of who's responsible," says Maltsberger. "If there's any blame to be assigned, it would be on the person who brought the patient into that plight in the first place. That might be the patient, the patient's parents, or it might be God. Who knows? But it isn't the poor doctor!" In thirty years of practice Maltsberger has never had a suicide. Doesn't that make him nervous? "All the time," he says quickly. "But at this stage of the game if a patient of mine did away with himself, I would be very sad, but any self-reproach would have to do with how well I applied my art. It's like surgery. If you operate on somebody and you don't make any mistakes and you tie off all the bleeders and the patient doesn't make it, it's sad, but that's probably the way the ball bounces."

"I had a patient a couple of years ago who had dropped out of treatment to go back to school, but he continued to come in periodically," says Ari Kiev. "One night I got a message that he'd called at nine. I called back at ten, and whoever answered said he was asleep." Kiev speaks slowly. "Next day his girlfriend called me and said she hadn't been able to locate him. She'd tried at home and nobody had answered. I put two and two together and called 911. They went up there and he was dead. He'd gotten drunk and taken an overdose. So I was having second thoughts—since it wasn't like him to call me, maybe I should have acted on the call and insisted that whoever answered the phone wake him up, which is when I would have found he *couldn't* be wakened and called the police." He riffles through his appointment calendar. "I don't think I'm responsible, but you feel responsible." He pauses. "I can answer these things from the point of view of the psychiatrist's way of BS-ing the world and BS-ing himself—'it's the patient's responsibility'—but you're caught up with people, and it's not as easy as all that."

Certainly, some suicides may be resistant to any intervention. In a study of schizophrenic hospital patients, Shneidman and Farberow describe a man who received psychotherapy but remained acutely suicidal. He was given a steady barrage of shock treatments for several years, but he repeatedly tried to hang himself. He was given a lobotomy. He was calmer but remained suicidal. One day, despite the vigilance of hospital staff, he finally succeeded in hanging himself.

Yet amid a glossary of treatment techniques, clinicians sometimes overlook simpler treatment methods. "I had a slasher my first year in the hospital," recalls one psychiatrist. "She kept cutting herself to ribbons—with glass, wire, anything she could get her hands on. Nobody could stop her. The nurses were very angry. They hate these patients, and they get very angry at the resident whose patient it is. I didn't know what to do, but I was getting very upset. So I went to the director and in my best Harvard Medical School manner began in a very intellectual way to describe the case. To my horror I couldn't go on but began to weep. I couldn't stop. He said, 'I think if you showed the patient what you showed me, I think she'd know you cared.' So I did. I told her that I cared, that it was distressing to me. She stopped. It was a very important lesson."

One of the most difficult decisions for a psychiatrist is whether to hospitalize when a patient is, as Kiev puts it, "hot." Increasing attention to patients' civil rights has barb-wired the issue; a psychiatrist may be sued for putting a patient into the hospital or for keeping a patient out. "People often send people to hospitals not because they think they'll do better there but because they're afraid there will be a suicide for which they'll be held responsible," says Hendin. Such buck passing is based on the belief that a hospital is the safest place for suicidal patients. "We tend to think we've solved the problem by getting the person into the hospital," says Norman Farberow, "but psychiatric hospitals have a suicide rate more than five times greater than in the community." While admitting that hospitalization may be the only answer to a severe suicidal crisis, Farberow calls it "an expensive, frequently crippling, stultifying experience." In the opinion of some psychiatrists the hospital may literally be the last resort. "I rarely put suicidal patients in the hospital anymore," says Maltsberger. "People need the hospital when they have nothing else to sustain them. If they can get a good therapist without going in, they're better off. The hospital is the absolute end of the line."

Certainly, even at the finest hospitals and despite the most stringent controls, patients find ways to kill themselves. David Reynolds, an anthropologist who entered a California VA hospital under an assumed name and condition, found "hundreds of ways"—nails, windows, razors, plastic bags, broken glass, high places, coat hangers, tonguing and accumulating medication, stuffing toilet paper down one's throat, even clogging a sink, filling it with water, then banging one's head against a faucet until, unconscious, one drowns. Paradoxically, some in-hospital suicides may be a sign of a healthy environment. Studies indicate that if there is a very low rate of suicide in a hospital, restrictive measures may be excessive. "Very often hospitals are dominated by the same mentality that may have brought the patient there in the first place," says Hendin. "They don't want to be blamed for a suicide, so they devote their efforts to monitoring the patient—preventing and controlling." There is no evidence that seclusion rooms, surveillance cameras, twenty-four-hour observation, removal of "sharps" and other ingredients of "suicide watch" are effective. Half of all suicides at Metropolitan State Hospital in Norwalk, California, over a period of forty-two years took place in seclusion rooms. In fact, a study attributing a decline in suicides at Baltimore's Sheppard Pratt Hospital in the 1930s to a decrease in such measures concluded that protective restrictions may increase suicide by calling attention to it. Says a former mental hospital patient after two years of unshaven legs and cardboard spoons, "People started thinking about committing suicide because the hospital makes such a big deal about *keeping* people from committing suicide." Hendin snorts: "That's what the problem is! Suicidal people are into control, the hospitals are into control, and it becomes a power struggle in which no therapy can take place."

Therapy is a luxury few hospitals can afford. Among those few is McLean Hospital in Belmont, Massachusetts. "One of the so-called Ivy League of mental hospitals," I am told by a former staff member, McLean is nestled among 240 acres of wooded, rolling countryside designed by Frederick Law Olmsted (who designed New York's Central Park) on a location he believed would be "tranquilizing for mental patients." At McLean, each patient is assigned a four-person "treatment team," consisting of a psychologist (or psychiatrist), a nurse, a social worker, and a rehabilitation counselor. Each patient receives individual therapy three or four times a week, and group therapy every few days. Then there is "milieu therapy"—pioneered at McLean—the notion that merely mingling with other patients in the hospital environment can be therapeutic. The biggest problem regarding suicide at McLean, I was told, was being able to keep the patient long enough to effect proper treatment. Many insurance policies cover only thirty days of inpatient care, hardly long enough to evaluate a course of medication, let alone accomplish a course of in-depth therapy. Like hospitals across the country, McLean is under increasing pressure from insurance companies to make patient stays shorter, and under pressure from all sides to get patients "cured," or at least functioning, before their insurance runs out. At McLean prices—$729 a day for adults, $898 for children, excluding therapy—extended care is available only to a very select group.

The alternative is a state hospital, where, as one McLean psychiatrist explains with a sigh, "there are questions of maintenance and management." At state hospitals there are one-third as many nurses, one-third as many psychiatrists, and one-third the amount of money per patient as at private hospitals. "State hospital patients, who as a group need the highest level of psychiatric care, are thus forced to settle for the lowest," writes psychiatrist Robert Okin. "The understaffing of the state hospital is so profound, the training of staff so inadequate, the professional leadership in such short supply, the ward environment so deprived, the physical character of the ward so sterile, and the organization of the institution so inimical to genuine rehabilitative efforts that it is extremely difficult for state hospital staff to provide a true rehabilitative program to their patients. Moreover, these conditions lead staff to conclude that they are neither expected nor required to do much more than provide a safe place for patients to spend their time."

Today, even a "safe place" for patients to spend their time is difficult to obtain. When growing reliance on drug therapy, press exposés of state hospital "snake pits," and the Community Mental Health Centers Act of 1963 led to deinstitutionalization in the late sixties, the move was applauded as a reform in the tradition of Pinel striking the chains of Salpêtrière almost two centuries earlier. Beyond the great expectations, however, there was little planning. Thousands of patients were discharged annually to community facilities that were inadequate or nonexistent. The state hospital population plummeted from 559,000 in 1955 to 119,000 in 1984, setting adrift a flood of chronically mentally ill people to fend for themselves amid a patchwork quilt of mental health services that had neither the time, training, nor funds to cope with them. Many of the deinstitutionalized ended up wandering the city streets. Experts estimate the number of America's homeless to be as high as 3 million—as many as half of whom suffer from chronic mental illness, which goes untreated.

There has been no research on the effect of deinstitutionalization on suicide, but while state hospitals are crying out for qualified therapists (who can make three times more money in private practice), patients are crying to get in. In most states a person must be judged to be at risk of doing "serious harm to himself or to others"—homicidal or suicidal. But admission is often made on the basis of bed availability rather than need. "They take only the most violent, the most psychotic," fumes a community mental health center director in New York City who admits he has coached suicidal patients on how to act sufficiently disturbed when they present at a hospital. Suicide ideation no longer guarantees admission; people commonly *attempt* suicide to get in. Even then they may be refused. Investigating the suicide of a Los Angeles woman, an LASPC social worker learned that on the last day of her life she had tried to commit herself into three large hospitals with psychiatric units. She was turned away at all three. That night she killed herself. "In the old days the state hospitals provided sanctuary," says one psychiatrist. "They'd take you in for a month, you'd cool down, and you weren't all by yourself. Is it possible there's some connection between shutting the doors of state hospitals and the rising suicide rate?"

Even if a person manages to get into a public psychiatric hospital, stringent admission standards have changed the hospital milieu. "Ten or fifteen years ago you could send a depressed patient to the hospital for R and R," says an Oakland therapist. "Now people in the hospital are *very* crazy, and if you are able to get hospitalized, you're surrounded by psychotic patients, and it can be very scary." If a patient is not "crazy" enough, the hospital isn't apt to let him remain. Today, the average stay in New York state hospitals is seventeen days. "You get into unfortunate situations because the state hospitals often don't keep people who are suicidal unless they're incredibly suicidal," says McLean psychiatrist Alan Schatzberg. "It becomes a kind of dangerous game of chicken." The patient is usually the loser. Repeated studies have shown that the suicide rate jumps in the period after patients leave the hospital, often without a job, without follow-up contact, and without any discussion of outpatient treatment.

With treatment decisions increasingly based on legal or financial considerations rather than on treatment needs, the suicidal person is caught in the middle. At a time when the percentage of mentally ill people in this country has swollen, according to NIMH estimates, it is increasingly difficult for them to get care. The inability of the mental health system to cope with the demand has led to a practice that seems an unsettling symptom, as it were, of an underlying illness in the system. In the past few years more than a few overcrowded clinics and hospitals, frustrated by a particularly troublesome patient, have bought him a ticket and put him on a bus bound for a distant city, where he arrived homeless, friendless, and alone. "Greyhound Therapy," as it has been dubbed, seems a chilling end point to the humanism that, in part, inspired deinstitutionalization. It makes one wonder how far, despite our 250 different therapies, we have come since the medieval days when people loaded irksome madmen onto a boat and shipped them downriver in what became known as a "ship of fools."

While mental health professionals are seen as the bottom line in suicide prevention, many other groups come in contact with suicidal people. General practitioners, perhaps best positioned to help, are perhaps least prepared. An estimated 75 percent of all suicides see a doctor within four months of taking their lives. As many as 10 percent see a physician on the day of or immediately prior to committing suicide and are provided with the means for it by the unsuspecting doctor. NIMH data suggests that as many as 30 percent of people who walk into a general practitioner's office use physical complaints as a smokescreen for depression and other mental health problems and that GPs miss 90 percent of those cases. "Many people go to physicians hoping to be asked about suicide," says psychiatrist Alan Stone. They're not likely to be. Most physicians have never heard a single lecture on suicide; medical education is dominated by illnesses of the body, and the mind is relegated to a required course in psychology plus a four-to-six-week psychiatric rotation. Psychiatry is traditionally one of the worst-taught specialties in medical school. In a 1967 survey of five Philadelphia medical schools, half the students believed that if a person talks about suicide, he will not commit it. (Half also believed masturbation frequently causes mental illness. It is not clear whether this was the same half.) In a poll reported in the *Journal of the American Medical Association,* 91 percent of physicians felt their knowledge of suicide was inadequate. Yet there is a reluctance to introduce suicide into the curriculum. "We don't pay enough attention to psychiatric aspects of medical education, so I welcome anything in that direction," says psychiatrist Leon Eisenberg. "But specifically for suicide?" He shrugs. "We don't even teach our medical students how to deal with stress in themselves."

Modern suicide prevention programs were originated by religious groups, but with the medicalization of mental illness, suicide has been secularized and the clergy's role is ambiguous. "Studies say that 50 to 80 percent of people with mental health problems come first to the clergy," says Monsignor James Cassidy. "Often, the clergy are not aware of the problem and pass it off. Most clergymen don't realize their limitations and the importance of getting professional help." Earl Grollman, a rabbi in Belmont, Massachusetts, says, "I have to laugh when I read Ann Landers telling suicidal people to 'speak to your clergy person.' There might be three people in all of Greater Boston that I consider to be knowledgeable in this field. Clergypeople feel they have to give a religious orientation, not understanding that prevention consists of listening, caring, and touching." Grollman pauses. "There's a story told about Martin Buber. He is praying when someone knocks on the door and says, 'Can I see you?' Martin Buber says, 'I'm busy. Come back later.' The person never comes back—he commits suicide. And Martin Buber says, 'Here I had a chance to be with God, but I lost God in prayer.'"

"I don't think doctors appreciate the role of the pastor in counseling," says the Reverend Robert Utter of the Church of the Nazarene in Cambridge. "But that may be changing. They've come to realize we're available every hour of the night or day, and we don't charge a fee." For the parishioner in crisis Utter prescribes a list of scriptures, extra prayer, perhaps an outing with the church singles group, and in emergencies the counseling center at Eastern Nazarene College in Wollaston, Massachusetts. Utter has never had a suicide in the ten years he has been pastor at the small gray church. "We believe in hell, so our people would think twice before taking their life." He grips the armrests of his chair as if he is in a plane taking off. "There is an expression I use when counseling people who talk about suicide. I tell them, 'You think you have problems now; wait until you end up in hell. You'll just be out of the frying pan and into the fire.'"

Prescribing the Bible rather than antidepressants has become a risky therapeutic approach. In 1980 a southern California church and its pastor were sued for "clergy malpractice" by the parents of a twenty-four-year-old man. After a previous suicide attempt, Kenneth Nally had been in counseling with Reverend John MacArthur, Jr., of the Grace Community Church, who referred to suicide as "one of the ways that the Lord takes home a disobedient believer."

Nally nevertheless shot himself. His parents claimed that MacArthur and his staff had failed to refer their son to a psychiatrist and that they had made his condition worse by telling him that his depression was the result of his sinning. The $1 million suit was thrown out of court in 1985; two years later it was reinstated by the state appellate court, which commented, "Established principles of California law impose a duty of due care on those who undertake a counseling relationship with suicidal individuals." The California Supreme Court finally dismissed the suit in 1988, ruling that as "non-therapist counselors," the clergy had no legal duty to save lives.

In its response to suicide the clergy is often torn between viewing the person as patient or parishioner. Religion and psychiatry work in an uneasy truce, as if psychological and spiritual dimensions inhabited different halves of the person. While counseling in the emergency room of the Cambridge Hospital, psychologist Nancy Kehoe, who also happens to be a nun, realized that the subject of religion never came up in patient assessments. Kehoe sent a questionnaire to local clinics and found that out of fourteen hundred suicidal cases, religion was broached in fewer than three hundred, more often than not by the patient. "In the face of suicide, which is a person's ultimate statement about life and death, why do we separate mental health and belief?" asks Kehoe. Clinicians found many reasons to do so. "Many of them were taught that science and psychology should be separate from religion," says Kehoe. "Some are very uncomfortable with the subject. Others don't know what to ask beyond 'Are you Protestant, Jewish, or Catholic?'" Kehoe's definition goes beyond "God talk"; it means thinking about a person's spiritual life as part of a total picture. "Then when a person is talking about suicide, it's natural to say, "What do you think you're going toward? What kind of spiritual things keep you going?" Clinicians in Kehoe's study who did bring up religion found it useful. Says Kehoe, "Some even felt that if a person had lost faith, it was an indicator of suicidal risk." (One wrote, "Highly religious people do not commit suicide.") She sighs. "All I'm asking is whether we'd learn something about a person if we brought up his spiritual beliefs, without judging whether or not it's going to save lives."

Kehoe's findings are troubling. If suicide is purely a biological and psychological problem, then treatment is clearly the undisputed province of the mental health professionals. But the strands that combine to prevent a suicide are as numerous as those that combine to push someone to suicide. In the twentieth-century view of suicide from the medical model, we risk excluding not only the religious or spiritual dimension of suicide, as Kehoe points out, but the social and existential dimensions as well. "Suicide can best be understood in terms of concepts from several points of view," wrote Edwin Shneidman in *Definition of Suicide*. "It follows that treatment of a suicidal individual should reflect the learnings from these same several disciplines." Shneidman suggested that optimum treatment might be effected by a "Therapeutic Council." "Such a council would be concerned with the biological, sociological, developmental, philosophical, and cognitive aspects of its patients. It might include a biologically oriented psychiatrist, a psychoanalytically oriented therapist, a sociologist, a logician-philosopher, a marriage and family counselor, and an existential social worker." While Shneidman's proposal is, of course, impractical, the concept is sound. If suicide is caused by a variety of factors, suicide prevention must address each of those elements.

Even further, true suicide prevention might address the problem *before* people reach the point of crisis, before they call the hot line or appear in the emergency room. While not thought of primarily as suicide prevention measures, there are many steps that might help reduce the suicide rate: further developing our understanding of alcoholism, depression, and schizophrenia; tackling such social ills as unemployment, divorce, homelessness, unwanted children, neglect of the elderly, inadequate medical and social services, violence, loss of spiritual values, and the threat of nuclear war. In short, one might reduce the suicide rate by giving people more reasons to stay alive. Several years ago psychologist Pamela Cantor appeared on ABC's "Nightline" to discuss the causes of suicide. At the end of the show host Ted Koppel said, "All right, we have half a minute left. You've described the litany of ills that exist. Is there anything that can be done about it short of changing our society inside out?" "Well, I don't think you should say 'short of,' " answered Cantor. "I think that's what's necessary."

IV

SOCIAL STUDIES

ONE AUGUST DAY in 1937, H. B. Wobber, a forty-nine-year-old barge-man, took a bus to the Golden Gate Bridge, paid his way through the pedestrian turnstile, and began to walk across the mile-long span. He was accompanied by a tourist he had met on the bus, Professor Lewis Neylor of Trinity College in Connecticut. They had strolled across the bridge, which stretches in a single arch from San Francisco to the hills of Marin County, and were on their way back when Wobber tossed his coat and vest to Professor Neylor. "This is where I get off," he said quietly. "I'm going to jump." As Wobber climbed over the four-foot railing, the professor managed to grab his belt, but Wobber pulled free and leaped to his death.

Less than three months after the Golden Gate Bridge had opened to great fanfare, Wobber became its first known suicide. Since then more than eight hundred others have jumped, making it, as one researcher observes, "the number one location for suicide in the entire Western world." Excepting mass suicides like Masada and Jonestown, more people have chosen to end their lives at the Golden Gate Bridge than at any other location outside of Japan. As with most suicide statistics, the numbers are conservative. Only those who have been seen jumping or whose bodies are recovered are counted as bridge suicides. One expert suggests that more than two hundred others may have leaped unseen, in darkness, rain, or fog, been swept out to sea, and their bodies never found. A leap from the bridge is easy, quick, and lethal; one merely steps over a chest-high railing. At 70 to 85 miles per hour, the 240-foot fall lasts four seconds. If the force of the fall doesn't kill the jumper instantly, the fierce current will sweep him out to sea, to drown or be devoured by sharks. Of more than eight hundred people known to have fallen or jumped from the bridge since it opened, only nineteen have survived.

The Golden Gate Bridge is not the first location to exert a particular fascination for suicidal people. Throughout history certain cliffs, churches, and skyscrapers have earned reputations as suicide landmarks: Niagara Falls, the Cathedral at Milan, St. Peter's, the Eiffel Tower, the Empire State Building, and Giotto's Campanile on the Duomo in Florence are among them. Not all settings are so grand. In 1813 in a French village a woman hanged herself from a large tree; within a short time several other women followed her example, using the same branch. In New York's Bowery there was a saloon in whose back room so many vagrants killed themselves, it became known as "Suicide Hall." And, of course, most towns have their "lover's leap." In Japan, where self-destruction has enjoyed institutional acceptance, many suicides choose spectacular natural settings for their deaths—"almost any place in Japan that is famous for its scenery is also famous for its suicides," observed an American visitor in 1930. Today, the country's leading suicide spot is Aokigahara-jukai, a dense forest at the foot of Mount Fuji, where about thirty people a year take their lives, usually by hanging or overdose, many of them coming from far away. A study of 116 people who attempted suicide in Jukai found that many believed the forest to be "a sanctuary where suicide was allowed," a setting that would "purify" or "beautify" their death.

Japan is also the setting for the most powerful suicide magnet of all time, Mihara-Yama, a volcano on the island of Oshima, about sixty miles from Tokyo. On January 7, 1933, Mieko Ueki, twenty-four, and Masako Tomita, twenty-one, classmates at an exclusive Tokyo school, bought tickets on the small steamship that made three trips weekly to the island. After the six-hour passage the young women scaled the three-thousand-foot peak. When they reached the crater, which boiled and sputtered with sulfur clouds, Mieko told Masako that she had visited Mount Mihara the previous year and had been enchanted by the legend decreeing that the bodies of those who jumped into the crater were instantly cremated and sent to heaven in the form of smoke. This was a beautiful, poetic form of death, said Mieko, and she intended to jump. Masako protested but eventually agreed not to intervene. The two girls bowed to each other. Then Mieko leapt into the smoking crater.

The story of the maiden and the volcano quickly became legend. Japan was in the midst of an economic depression, and the volcano became a national attraction for both tourists and suicides. In the remaining months of 1933, 143 people followed Mieko's example; on one April day there were six suicides, while twenty-five more were forcibly prevented. The deaths kindled a mixture of fascination and horror. The steamship company bought two new ships and made daily trips to accommodate the tourist flow; company shareholders made a profit on their investment for the first time in four years. Along the harbor fourteen hotels, twenty restaurants, and five taxicab companies opened within two years; the number of island photographers increased from two to forty-seven; a post office was built at the crater's edge; three camels were imported to carry tourists across the mile-wide strip of volcanic desert that surrounded the crater; horses ferried them to the summit. And a twelve-hundred-foot "shoot the chute" was built to spice up the return trip down the slope for those who chose to make it. Suicide had become a spectator sport; on a day when several hours had passed without a death, a tourist laughingly shouted, "I dare someone to jump!" A man ran forward and threw himself into the crater.

Eventually, the embarrassed government intervened. It was made a criminal offense to purchase a one-way ticket to Oshima, and plainclothes detectives were instructed to mingle with passengers on the boat, arresting anyone who looked bent on self-destruction—their criteria are not known. Tokyo police patrolled the crater; by the end of 1934 policemen and civilian onlookers had restrained 1,208 people from jumping. A barbed-wire fence was erected and a twenty-four-hour watch was posted. The hastily formed Mount Mihara Anti-Suicide League even devised an elaborate arrangement of mirrors to give would-be suicides a terrifying view of the volcano's interior. Despite these efforts at least 167 more men and women leaped to their death in 1934, and 29 who had been restrained dove off the steamship returning them to Tokyo. By the time access to the mountain was closed in 1935, an estimated 804 males and 140 females had found their death in the volcano.

Although the authorities acted tardily in the case of Mount Mihara, else-where, when certain locations seem to beckon the suicidal, steps have been taken to discourage them. In 1850 an American physician traveling in Europe wrote: "At one time there seemed to be a growing propensity to jump from the Leaning Tower at Pisa; three persons—as I learnt from my guide while on a visit to it—having thus put a period to their existence; on which account visitors could no longer ascend it without an authorized attendant." In 1881 the column in Paris's Place Vendôme was closed following a wave of suicides. In the early twentieth century a lake near Kobe, Japan, was drained because of the number of people who drowned themselves in its waters. Fences and barriers have greatly reduced the number of suicides at St. Peter's, the Eiffel Tower, and the Arroyo Seco Bridge in Pasadena. In the first sixteen years after the Empire State Building opened in 1931, sixteen people jumped to their deaths; not until 1947, when a man landed on a woman in the street below, critically injuring her, was a seven-foot spiked fence installed around the eighty-sixth-floor observation tower. In the next four decades only fourteen others jumped. In many other instances in which barriers, window stops, or emergency phones have been installed, suicides have been eliminated or greatly reduced. Nevertheless, despite more than eight hundred deaths and five decades of debate, no barrier has been erected at the Golden Gate Bridge.

Even before H. B. Wobber leaped to his death, there was concern about the Golden Gate's potential for suicides. Although the bridge was designed to accommodate benches for pedestrians, the bridge's board of directors feared they might be used as stiles, making it even easier for people to climb over the rail. The benches were never installed. Over the years, as the death toll mounted, various measures were considered: electric fences, barbed wire, safety nets, a twenty-four-hour motorcycle patrol, signs advising "Think Before You Leap," and legislation prohibiting jumping from the bridge. As early as 1953 a barrier was proposed. An engineer told the bridge board that the existing railing could be raised to seven feet for $200,000. All of these proposals were rejected as being either too expensive, too dangerous to workers on the bridge, too foolish, or merely ineffective.

In the face of increased publicity and rising public concern, a few precautions were taken. In 1960 the bridge board ordered pedestrian sidewalks closed between sunset and sunrise. By 1970 a closed circuit television system had been installed in the toll office, enabling workers to scan the pedestrian walkway and dispatch officers to restrain possible jumpers. A two-man tow truck roved the bridge. Patrolmen were taught to be on the lookout for women without purses, people edging away from their tourist group, or people staring intently at the surface of the water. Bridge personnel were trained in suicide prevention by a local prevention center. Over the years bridge workers, patrolmen, toll officers, passing motorists, and pedestrians have talked down or pulled back hundreds of would-be jumpers, often at risk to their own lives. One state highway patrolman assigned to the bridge claimed to have prevented 217 suicides in nine years on the job. Indeed, it is estimated that for every suicide from the bridge, two others are prevented.

During the suicide prevention movement of the late sixties and early seventies, the debate over an antisuicide fence came to a head. A committee was formed to lobby for a barrier, and a debate raged in editorials and letters to the editor. The bridge battle was a microcosm of debates about personal freedom and the value of life that have taken place around the country wherever antisuicide barriers have been proposed. How far should we go to prevent suicide? Bridge directors received hundreds of letters, about two-thirds opposing the barrier. Some argued that it would spoil the view: Why destroy the view for so many for the sake of so few? Others felt it was a waste of money: Why spend money on someone who wants to die? Others felt the money would be better spent on free mental health care. Many defended a person's right to suicide. "If and when I decide to die I would prefer the bridge as an exit point and I don't want to be kept from it by a high, jail-like railing," one woman wrote to the *San Francisco Chronicle.* "There are worse things than death and one should be able to make that personal choice if necessary." A few even argued that an unfettered bridge saved lives by acting as a magnet to which disturbed people were drawn and could be more easily intercepted and delivered to treatment. The most popular argument against a barrier was that it simply wouldn't work; common sense said that suicidal people would simply go kill themselves somewhere else.

Arguing in favor of the barrier, suicidologists pointed out that suicide is often an impulsive act, and the impulse, once thwarted, is frequently abandoned. They cited studies showing that only 10 percent of those who attempt suicide go on to kill themselves. They pointed to the fact that 90 percent of bridge suicides jump from the side of the bridge facing San Francisco—facing what they're leaving behind—as an indication of their ambivalence. They explained that suicidal people are apt to choose a highly personal method, and if that method is unavailable they may abandon their plans rather than switch to another. In a suicidal crisis, people often lack the flexibility to generate alternatives when foiled. The suicidologists pointed to other locales in which barriers had decreased the number of suicides without spoiling the view. They indicated that the lethality of the bridge and the impulsiveness of many suicides made the bridge an especially deadly combination. "The bridge is like having a loaded gun around," said psychiatrist Jerome Motto at a 1971 hearing. "I think it is the responsibility of those in control to unload the gun." Although the bridge board authorized a $20,000 preliminary study and a sample of the winning design was constructed, the debate dragged on and the barrier went unbuilt.

Then Richard Seiden, a pro-barrier Berkeley psychologist, gathered the names of 515 people who had been restrained from jumping from the bridge dating back to its opening day. Checking their names against death certificates he learned that only twenty-five had gone on to take their own lives. Although his research proved that people did not inexorably go on to commit suicide using another method, critics argued that people restrained from jumping were not truly bent on death. What about those who had jumped and lived? In 1975 psychiatrist David Rosen interviewed six of the eight people known to have survived leaps from the Golden Gate Bridge. None of the eight survivors had gone on to kill themselves; the six he interviewed all favored the construction of an antisuicide fence. They all said that had there been a barrier, they would not have tried to kill themselves some other way. Their plans had involved only the Golden Gate Bridge; like those who attempted suicide in the forest of Jukai, they spoke of an association between its beauty and death. For them, Rosen said, the bridge was a "suicide shrine."

A second study by Seiden supported the notion that the Golden Gate Bridge had a "fatal mystique." Comparing Golden Gate suicides to San Francisco–Oakland Bay Bridge suicides, he found that although the two spans were completed within a few months of each other and are about the same height, five times as many people had committed suicide from the Golden Gate Bridge as from the Bay Bridge. Unlike the Golden Gate, the Bay Bridge does not allow pedestrian traffic. Yet even when pedestrian suicides were omitted, the Golden Gate still spawned three times as many suicides. The Golden Gate Bridge, said Seiden, had become "a suicide mecca"; while its suicides usually made the front page, Bay Bridge suicides were rarely publicized. Seiden found "a commonly held attitude that often romanticizes suicide from the Golden Gate Bridge in such terms as 'aesthetically pleasing,' and 'beautiful,' while regarding Bay Bridge suicide as 'tacky' and 'déclassé.' " His statistics supported this: Half of the bridge suicides who lived east of San Francisco had chosen to drive over the Bay Bridge and across the city to the Golden Gate Bridge to end their lives.

Although Seiden's and Rosen's research seemed to put to rest the notion that if people were kept from killing themselves at the bridge, they would simply "go someplace else," the campaign for a barrier became a moot political issue. "The bottom line is money," says Seiden. "If it costs money, the bridge directors don't want to do it." (Today, a barrier would cost several million dollars.) Seiden also believes that San Franciscans like to think of their city as a tough-living, hard-drinking town and may take a perverse pride in the bridge's reputation. Gray Line tour bus drivers recite the bridge's suicide statistics in their tourist litany; guidebooks describe its fatal allure. The city's newspapers keep a kind of running box score in which news of each new jumper concludes with the observation that it is the bridge's nth suicide. In 1981 there was even a lottery in which players bet on the day of the week when the next Golden Gate suicide would take place.

Meanwhile, the suicides quietly continue. When Seiden sends out his research papers, he pencils in the updated statistics—from six hundred to seven hundred to "more than eight hundred." By 1990 there had been 885 confirmed deaths, including a depressed man who wrote in his suicide note, before stepping over the railing and leaping to his death, "Why do you make it so easy?"

One breezy autumn morning Seiden and I drove from downtown San Francisco toward the Golden Gate Bridge. Just before the toll booths on the bridge's south side he directed me onto a narrow road on the right marked "Restricted Access." About fifty yards down the road there was a deserted, weedy lot littered with ladders, broken window casings, and confusions of chicken wire. In the midst of this, like an abandoned sculpture, stood a curious metal structure, an eighteen-foot section of steel fence painted the same russet red as the Golden Gate Bridge. Its pencil-thin spires rose about eight feet into the air. On one half of the fence the spires pointed toward the sky; on the other half they curved gently inward at the top, like the fingers of a cupped hand. Though the graceful spires there was a stunning view of the Golden Gate Bridge as it leaped more than a mile over the bay into the soft green hills of

Marin County. "Winning design number sixteen," said Seiden quietly. "It's been sitting here for years."

Bridge barriers, nets on observation decks, signs and emergency telephones on bridges, windows that don't open wide—these are only some of the ways in which "environmental risk reduction," as Seiden calls it, might help prevent suicide. "There is more than one approach to suicide prevention," says Seiden. "You can try to get inside people's heads and work with their self-esteem. You can work with parenting and with early recognition of depression, but you can also try to do something about the lethal agents of suicide—the guns, the pills, the bridges. It's the same as automobile safety. You can do driver training and you can make the car safer. You can change the environment as well as change the individual." With suicide seen almost exclusively from the medical model, however, the possibilities of environmental and social change have been all but ignored. Critics say that these are superficial measures, that Seiden is treating symptoms, not causes. "Sometimes that's all you can treat," says Seiden. "Frankly, we haven't had a good record in treating suicidal patients from the inside out."

For many years the most popular method of suicide in Great Britain was asphyxiation—sticking one's head in the oven and turning on the gas. After the discovery of oil and natural gas deposits in the North Sea in the fifties and sixties, most English homes converted from coke gas, whose high carbon monoxide content made it highly lethal, to less toxic natural gas. From 1963 to 1978 the number of English suicides by gas dropped from 2,368 to eleven, and the country's overall suicide rate decreased by one-third. Despite England's increasing unemployment and deteriorating race relations, it has remained at that lower level ever since. "If you could prescribe a situation that is tailor-made for suicide, England would be it," says Seiden. "Yet their rate is down 33 percent. Why? Because a highly lethal method has been taken away."

One area Seiden and other suicidologists are exploring is the link between the misuse of prescription drugs and suicide. British and Australian studies show that restrictions on prescribing barbiturates reduced the number of actual or attempted barbiturate suicides without increasing the number of suicides by other methods. Suicidologists have called for tighter regulation of potentially lethal medication and for training of physicians and pharmacists in clues to depression and suicide. They propose the use of blister packs, which require single capsules to be punched out individually, allowing more time for emotions to cool or rescuers to intervene.

"Much could be gained if we tried to make suicide more difficult for the potential candidate. . . . Opportunity makes the suicide as well as the thief," observed David Oppenheim at the 1910 meeting of the Vienna Psychoanalytic Society devoted to suicide. "An opportunity for self-destruction is offered to anyone who is in the position to bring about his death by some swift and easy action that is painless and avoids revolting mutilations and disfigurement. A loaded pistol complies so well with all these conditions that its possession positively urges the idea of suicide on its owner." Far more urging takes place now than in Oppenheim's day. There are an estimated 200 million civilian-owned guns in the United States, including some 60 million handguns. In the late 1960s a new handgun was sold every twenty-four seconds; in 1984 a new handgun was sold every twelve seconds. While numerous studies have linked increased gun ownership to increased rates of crime, armed robbery, and homicide, few have examined its effect on suicide.

Among all the countries in the world, only in the United States are guns the primary means of suicide. In a 1983 study, NIMH researcher Jeffrey Boyd scrutinized suicide rates for 1953 to 1978 and found that the firearm suicide rate had risen steadily while the rate by all other methods had declined. In 1953 firearm suicides accounted for 45.7 percent of all suicides; in 1978 they constituted 56 percent. The jump in firearm suicides accounted for an overall increase in the suicide rate from 12.4 in 1953 to 13.3 in 1978. Suggesting that the increase in suicide by firearms was related to the increase in gun sales and noting that handguns account for 83 percent of all suicides by firearms, Boyd concluded, "It is conceivable that the rise in the suicide rate might be controlled by restricting the sale of handguns."

Other research supports this hypothesis. A 1980 study found that the strictness of state gun-control laws was significantly correlated with suicide rates; in general, states with the toughest gun control laws had the lowest suicide rates. The rates in the ten states with the weakest handgun laws were more than twice as high as rates in the ten states with the strongest laws. A study of Los Angeles and California suicides during a three-year period in the mid-seventies found that citywide, countywide, and statewide the suicide rate by firearms rose and fell in near-perfect harmony with the volume of gun sales. "If guns are outlawed, only outlaws will have guns," a favorite National Rifle Association homily, implies that ordinary citizens need guns to protect themselves. Yet a handgun around the house is six times more likely to kill a family member than a burglar. In a study of eighty-two consecutive suicides in Cuyahoga County, Ohio, thirty-five were by gunshot. Only three of the guns had been purchased for the purpose of self-destruction; the majority had been acquired to protect the family. In a 1986 study of firearm deaths in the home in King County, Washington, there were thirty-seven suicides for every self-protection homicide. The use of a gun makes any suicide attempt five times more likely to be fatal. "If some persons would use slower methods of self-destruction, some lives might be saved," concluded a National Violence Commission report. "The possibility that the presence [of firearms] is in some instances part of the causal chain that leads to an attempted suicide cannot be dismissed. With a depressed person, the knowledge of having a quick and effective way of ending his life might precipitate a suicide attempt on impulse."

Despite these studies, while therapists commonly advise families of suicidal patients to "get the guns out of the house," little has been done on a broad scale to reduce firearm suicides. At the least, suicidologists recommend an enforced waiting period between purchase of a gun and the right to possess it since the suicidal impulse might fade during that time. Twenty-two states have laws requiring such a waiting period. Nevertheless, while more Americans kill themselves with guns than are murdered with them every year, suicide is rarely mentioned by either side in the gun control debate. In an editorial accompanying Jeffrey Boyd's research in *The New England Journal of Medicine,* Dr. Richard Hudgens admitted, "It is unlikely that the suicidal use of guns will be an important factor in any eventual decision to limit their availability, for suicide is not high on the list of America's political concerns." When approached with the idea that the soaring firearm suicide rate justified a call for tighter gun control, a National Rifle Association spokesman responded, "The NRA is not for gearing laws to the weakest element of society."

This Darwinian reflection seems to speak to the heart of the question of how far we should go to help prevent suicide. Clearly, we cannot and should not make the world "suicide proof" nor our lives a twenty-four-hour suicide watch. Even if we could, suicides would of course still occur. But even if bridge barriers and gun control legislation were to have no effect on the suicide rate, there may be compelling reasons why such measures should nevertheless be taken. To put up or not put up a barrier says something about the way we feel about suicide and the suicidal.

I remember discussing the proposed Golden Gate Bridge barrier with a San Francisco friend. "Ninety-nine percent of us don't need it," she said. "Is it fair to ruin the view for the sake of a few? If they want to die so much, why not let them?" I found this attitude shared by many people. Their view often seemed based less on respect for individual freedom than on ignorance of the psychodynamics of self-destruction and discomfort with the subject of suicide in general. Whatever their reasons, it troubled me that so many otherwise kindhearted people should object to preventive measures. For how far is it from this passive condoning to the chorus one sometimes hears when a crowd has gathered at the base of a tall building, to watch the weeping man on the ledge high above, shouting, "Jump, jump, jump"?

Fortunately, in answer to the voices who cry "Jump," there are many other voices that cry "Live"—not just the voices of family, friends, therapists, and prevention center volunteers but the voices of strangers. When the twenty-year-old manager of a Brooklyn clothing store began receiving telephone calls for a now-defunct suicide prevention hot line, he took time to listen to their problems. "They just start talking," he said. "I tell them they have the wrong number, but I ask them if I can help. . . . I believe in helping people out." When a twenty-six-year-old Austrian threatened to jump from the 446-foot steeple of St. Stephen's in Vienna, a thirty-four-year-old priest whose hobby is mountain climbing scaled the steeple and persuaded the man to descend. When an eighteen-year-old girl stood on the ledge of a seven-story building in Mexico City, threatening to jump, Ignacio Canedo, an eighteen-year-old Red Cross male nurse, inched out toward her. Canedo was tied to a long rope, held on the other end by a squad of firemen. "Don't come any nearer!" shouted the girl. "Don't, or I'll jump!" Canedo grabbed for her and missed. The girl screamed and jumped. Canedo jumped after her, caught her in midair, and locked his arms around her waist. They fell four floors before the rope snapped taut. Canedo's grip held, and he and the girl were hauled back to the roof. "I knew the rope would save me," said Canedo. "I prayed that it would be strong enough to support both of us." There are dozens of similar stories of potential suicides saved by strangers who instinctively reached out.

As a term project for "The Psychology of Death," a course taught by Edwin Shneidman at Harvard, one student placed an ad in the personals section of a local underground newspaper: "M 21 student gives self 3 weeks before popping pills for suicide. If you know any good reasons why I shouldn't, please write Box D-673." Within a month he had received 169 letters. While the majority were from the Boston area, others came from as far away as New York, Wisconsin, Kentucky, even Rio de Janeiro. They offered many reasons why he should stay alive. Some wrote of music, smiles, movies, sunny days, sandy beaches. Some quoted Rod McKuen, e. e. cummings, or Dylan Thomas. They suggested he spend time with others less fortunate than he; implored him to think of those he would leave behind; called him a coward and dared him to struggle and survive. Some referred him to a therapist. Others offered friendship, enclosing their phone number or their address. A few enclosed gifts: two joints of marijuana; an advanced calculus equation; a Linus doll; magazine clippings on the subject of kindness; a photo of apple blossoms with the message, "We're celebrating Apple Blossom Time." Some simply broke down in the middle of their letters and pleaded, "Don't," or "You just can't."

The student was not actually contemplating suicide, but the answers he received were real. Whether they might have persuaded someone truly suicidal to stay alive or not is impossible to say. But if the forces that lead someone to suicide are numerous, those forces that combine to prevent someone from killing himself may be equally complex; whether they be tricyclic antidepressants, a prevention center volunteer, a barrier on a bridge, a Linus doll, or the voice of a stranger saying, "I care." "There is no magic bullet that goes right to the heart of suicidality," says Robert Litman. "Many, many things together bring a person to suicide, and many, many things together prevent a suicide. But if you have, say, twenty suicidal things and you can relieve just one, leaving only nineteen, you're probably going to get a sense of improvement and a little more hopefulness. And if you can maybe relieve parts of two or three others and get it down to seventeen, to sixteen, you're going to get another little increment of hopefulness, and you're on your way."

Harry Warren, Jr., the second director of the National Save-A-Life League, used to tell the story of a young reporter who, after several years of success on small-town newspapers, went to New York, hoping to make it as a writer in the big city. Things went poorly. He was unable to get work. Alone and friendless, without money, convinced he was a failure, his thoughts turned to suicide. One rainy day he went to a bridge and leaned over, tempted to jump to his death.

"By a heroic effort he turned away," said Warren, "but still struggling with the thought, journeyed back downtown by an express subway train. The man next to him turned abruptly and asked, 'Does this train stop at Chambers Street?' Though a New Yorker of recent standing himself, the reporter knew that much about the city. 'Yes,' he said with a sudden, strange ardor, 'it does.'

"So trivial a thing as that—an ability to direct someone when he himself was a comparative stranger in town—served to re-establish his self-assurance at a critical time. He went to his room, changed into dry clothing, and went to work gathering material for a feature story he had started on a few days earlier and abandoned. This fellow turned out all right."

V

LIFE OR LIBERTY

MOST SUICIDOLOGISTS are governed by a simple rule: When a life is in danger, one does whatever one can to save it. There are some people who disagree. "Suicide is a fundamental human right," Thomas Szasz has written. "This does not mean that it is morally desirable. It only means that society does not have the moral right to interfere, by force, with a person's decision to commit this act." In numerous books, articles, and speeches, Szasz, a professor of psychiatry at the State University of New York in Syracuse, has articulated his belief that mental illness is a fiction invented by psychiatrists to justify coercive interventions and, in the process, trample on the rights of individuals. Not surprisingly he is vehemently opposed to such staples of suicide prevention as third-party intervention, physical restraint, call tracing, and, above all, involuntary commitment. The relationship between suicide preventer and suicidal person, which suicidologists liken to that of parent and child, Szasz views as something far less benign: "If the psychiatrist is to prevent a person intent on killing himself from doing so, he clearly cannot, and cannot be expected to, accomplish that task unless he can exercise complete control over the capacity of the suicidal person to act. But it is either impossible to do this or it may require reducing the patient to a social state beneath that of a slave; for the slave is compelled only to labor against his will, whereas the suicidal person is compelled to live against his will."

Szasz does not believe that society should support or encourage suicidal people in their desire to kill themselves; he considers counseling, therapy, or any other voluntary measures desirable. In his own practice Szasz—who says that none of his patients has ever committed suicide—readily offers help when and if requested. "In fact, I firmly believe that psychiatric help, including help concerning suicide, can be given more effectively if there is no threat of coercion overhanging it," he observed in a spirited debate with Edwin Shneidman in 1972. "I think I can be more effective in my work with persons who are suicidal because they know that they can talk as freely about suicide as they can talk about the stock market or divorce, and I will not intervene in the one any more than the other. I do not get uptight about it. And the ultimate decision remains in their hands."

Suicidologists insist that the opposition of Szasz and other civil libertarians to suicide prevention is based on a misunderstanding of suicidal thinking. They note that right-to-suicide advocates ignore the ambivalence and impulsiveness of most suicide attempts. They point to the many people who have attempted or contemplated suicide, and survived to live productive lives, including such well-known figures as the pianist Arthur Rubinstein, who tried to hang himself with his belt at age nineteen (the belt broke); the philosopher Bertrand Russell, who considered suicide as a teenager; and Abraham Lincoln, who was suicidally depressed after breaking off his engagement to Mary Todd. "The 'right' to suicide is a 'right' desired only temporarily," writes psychiatrist George Murphy. "Every physician should feel the obligation to support the desire for life, which will return even in a patient who cannot believe that such a change can occur." Over the past thirty years Herbert Hendin has interviewed four people who survived six-story jumps. Two changed their minds in midair, two did not, and only one attempted suicide again. In another instance a depressed twenty-eight-year-old who survived a leap from the Golden Gate Bridge in 1985 recalled the moment he left the rail: "I instantly realized I had made a mistake. I can't tell you how frightening that was."

In any case, say suicidologists, someone prevented from killing himself can always try again. Research shows that 10 percent of attempters will kill themselves within ten years. Most suicidologists believe that if someone is truly determined to kill himself, he will. "The right to kill oneself can be exercised quietly, without involving society, by anyone sufficiently determined to do so," writes Hendin. "Someone on the window ledge of a tall building threatening to jump or someone who is found unconscious after swallowing sleeping pills has forced society to notice him, whether or not he is hoping to be saved or helped. Surely confinement for a limited period for the purpose of evaluation with a view to providing help is indicated." Edwin Shneidman puts it more pungently: "Suicide is not a 'right' any more than is the 'right to belch.' If the individual feels forced to do it, he will do it."

Additionally, suicidologists point out that in exercising the "right to suicide," one may violate the rights of others. People who jump from high places occasionally land on innocent passers-by, injuring or even killing them. Carbon monoxide may seep from garages into adjoining houses or apartments, poisoning family or neighbors. People who use an automobile to commit suicide often injure or kill passengers in other cars. Suicide also inflicts psychological injury, most deeply on surviving relatives and friends but also on bystanders. "Although such cases have not been studied, individuals have been severely traumatized by seeing another person kill himself or herself," writes sociologist Samuel Wallace. "Do people in public places, in train stations, or on sidewalks beside tall buildings have a right to be free of the grotesque spectacle of public suicide?"

Although most right-to-suicide arguments describe suicide as a voluntary expression of free will and "rational" choice, most suicidologists insist that suicide is not an act of free will at all. "Suicidal persons are succumbing to what they experience as an overpowering and unrelenting coercion in their environment to cease living," writes sociologist Menno Boldt. "This sense of coercion takes many familiar forms: fear, isolation, abuse, uselessness, and so on." If we accept that suicide is not voluntary, says Boldt, "the ethical question of the right to suicide becomes largely academic." Because the suicidal person is psychologically coerced, he implies, physical coercion is justified as a protective measure taken on behalf of someone incapable of protecting himself—the same reasoning by which parents assume responsibility for their children.

At the bottom of such arguments is the widespread opinion that, as the medical historian Ilza Veith has put it, "the act [of suicide] clearly represents an illness." Finding suicidal people mentally ill has practical implications. Although standards vary from state to state, most involuntary commitment statutes specify that the individual must be considered dangerous to himself or to others and also mentally ill—criteria to be determined by the admitting psychiatrist. Although in recent years efforts by civil libertarians to abolish involuntary commitment have made it more difficult, suicidal persons are the only people who may be held against their will for weeks, months, or even years on the sole basis of what they "might" do in the future rather than what they have done in the past—and not to others but to themselves. One Arizona woman spent fifty-eight years without comprehensive review in a state mental hospital after a suicide attempt. "If a sociologist predicted that a person was 80 percent likely to commit a felonious act, no law would permit his confinement," comment the authors of an article on "Civil Commitment of the Mentally Ill: Theories and Procedures" in the *Harvard Law Review*. "On the other hand if a psychiatrist testified that a person was mentally ill and 80 percent likely to commit a dangerous act, the patient would be committed." Szasz offers another analogy: "If a middle-aged lady goes to the doctor with a terrible gall bladder and says, 'I really don't know what to do. Should I have it out or shouldn't I have it out?', and the doctor can't stand it, restrains the patient, takes her to the hospital, and has the gall bladder out, you know what will happen to the doctor!"

To Szasz the logic of suicide prevention is flawed from the start; he believes that mental illness is a myth invented by the mental health professions to consolidate their power and to justify coercive interventions. But even if one accepts the existence of mental illness, the difficulty of drawing the line between sickness and health is strikingly illustrated by the "expert" testimony of opposing psychiatrists in court trials. While one attests to the defendant's sanity, the other may just as persuasively insist that the defendant is insane. "If everyone who evinces some abnormality is to be regarded as mentally ill, there would hardly be a normal person left among the educated; all of us carry a secret fragment of a neurosis (and perhaps even the makings of a psychosis)," wrote psychiatrist Wilhelm Stekel in 1910. "I think it is the lazy way out to say, in order to relieve our consciences, that all suicides are ill, psychologically inferior persons who are no great loss anyway."

Calling suicidal behavior "sick" may help distance us from an act that strikes a disturbing chord. "I remember dealing with my first suicidal patient. I found it very difficult to understand that a person could really choose this," says psychologist Nancy Kehoe. "I had to go out for a long walk and try to take in how much pain that person must feel to want to take his own life." Now, dealing with suicidal patients, "I let myself get in touch with the times I've felt pretty desperate, the fleeting moments of driving down the turnpike and wishing a truck would hit you. We've all had those moments where we say, 'Enough—I can't take it anymore.' "

The diagnosis of mental illness is especially suspect when it comes to self-destruction. "The argument connecting suicide and mental illness is tautologically based upon our cultural bias against suicide," Zigfrids Stelmachers, director of a Minneapolis prevention center, has said. "We say, in essence, 'All people who attempt suicide are mentally ill.' If someone asks, 'How do you know they are mentally ill?', the implied answer is, 'Because only mentally ill persons would try to commit suicide.' " The Los Angeles Suicide Prevention Center reflects this bias, listing one of the symptoms of mental illness as "functional changes in which there is less achievement than usual of life-preserving and other valuable goals." A Harvard University study found that the highest estimate of mental illness when a sample had been diagnosed *before* suicide was 22 percent. Afterward the highest estimate was 90 percent.

"Suicide is pre-judged by the medical model of thought," wrote Jungian analyst James Hillman in *Suicide and the Soul.* "It can be understood medically only as a symptom, an aberration, an alienation, to be approached with the point of view of prevention." The analyst's goal, he stated, was not to be for or against suicide but to explore "what it means in the psyche." Believing suicide to be an attempt at transformation, Hillman observed that the analyst who tries to prevent suicide with tranquilizing drugs or confinement might be depriving the person of what might be the most significant experience of his or her life. "The analyst cannot deny this need to die. He will have to go with it. His job is to help the soul on its way. He dare not resist the urge in the name of prevention, because *resistance only makes the urge more compelling and concrete death more fascinating.*" This emphasis on the soul rather than on the body, on the spiritual rather than on the medical, on exploration rather than on prevention, "may release the transformation the soul has been seeking. It may come only at the last minute. It may never come at all. But there is no other way." Paradoxically, implied Hillman, *not* preventing suicide is the most effective form of suicide prevention. "By preventing nowhere, the analyst is nevertheless doing the most that can be done to prevent the actual death. By his having entered the other's position so fully, the other is no longer isolated. He, too, is no longer able to break freely the secret league and take a step alone."

The notion that a "death experience" or even death itself may provide a necessary "transformation" for the patient, fascinates a few therapists, disgusts others, and, in either case, is dismissed as irrelevant in the clinical situation, an attitude expressed by one therapist who, dismissing the right to suicide, points out, "No therapy can work with a corpse." In a review of Hillman's book, Robert Litman maintained that if philosophical and ethical theory are to have any relevance to the clinician, they cannot be developed apart from the clinical setting. Yet can clinical practice be developed apart from philosophical and ethical issues? Szasz writes:

> In regarding the desire to live, but not the desire to die, as a legitimate human aspiration, the suicidologist stands Patrick Henry's famous exclamation, "Give me liberty, or give me death!" on its head. In effect, he says, "*Give him* commitment, *give him* electroshock, *give him* lobotomy, *give him* lifelong slavery, but *do not let him choose* death!" By so radically illegitimizing another person's (but not his own) wish to die, the suicide-preventer redefines the aspiration of the Other as not an aspiration at all: the wish to die becomes something an irrational, mentally diseased being *displays* or something that *happens* to a lower form of life. The result is a far-reaching infantilization and dehumanization of the suicidal person.

Perhaps in an ideal world people would not want to die, but as Stelmachers says, "Some of the things that happen in these people's lives give them pretty rational reasons for ending their lives." If the cry for help can be translated "help me live," it can also be translated "help me die." "A totally open therapeutic relationship must make room for everything, including suicide," writes philosopher Peter Koestenbaum. "Only in such a way can the freedom of the patient be recognized and nurtured." Making room for suicide does not mean a clinician must set up suicide facilitation services in a prevention center or refuse treatment to a ten-year-old who has tried to hang himself, but that he must respect the possibility of suicide at least as much as he fears it. "If the person says, 'I'm going to kill myself,' " says Stelmachers, "one way to respond is to say, 'Well, maybe suicide *is* the best way out for you, but let's talk about it first.' This says many things to the person. . . . It says, 'I really am interested in you and your problems. Even more than in preventing suicides!' It also negates a sneaking suspicion he might have had about himself that he must be crazy to even consider such an act." Psychiatrist Herbert Brown, commenting on the physician's responsibility to the suicidal patient, says, "Our responsibility might be seen as an obligation to genuinely engage the patient and then to help to open him or her to a truly free choice as a whole and separate person, a choice that may be suicide."

At a conference on suicide sponsored by Harvard Medical School and the Cambridge Hospital, the ethics of prevention came up: "Do we have the right to say no?" wondered an audience member. There were appreciative chuckles; it is the oldest and, by clinicians, least seriously discussed topic in suicide. "Tough question," commented psychiatrist John Mack. "Shall we refer that one to God?" More chuckles. "We have a right to take a different position," continued Mack. "Our responsibility as clinicians is to choose life." Another panel member spoke up: "I think the philosophical answer is different from the clinical one." Until they are part of the same answer, the study of suicide and its prevention may never be complete.

VI

THE UNANSWERED
QUESTION

IT WAS THE LAST DAY of the fifteenth annual meeting of the American Association of Suicidology. More than five hundred suicidologists from dozens of states and countries had gathered at the Vista International Hotel in New York City for a four-day smorgasbord of workshops on "Suicide: Problems in the Big City," "Demographic Factors in Suicidal Behavior," "Fundraising: Effective Strategies and Methods for Suicide and Crisis Centers," and fifty-five other topics.

A Who's Who of suicide had assembled. Norman Farberow was there. So were Herbert Hendin, Ari Kiev, Bruce Danto, and Nancy Allen, the public-health worker who was instrumental in organizing the first "National Suicide Prevention Week" in 1974. And everywhere you looked there was Edwin Shneidman, speechifying, kibitzing, or just standing in the back of the room watching the proceedings like a proud father. Heady company; at one point twelve past presidents of the AAS sat at the dais. Their combined efforts represented more than a hundred books, a thousand articles, and two hundred years of experience in the study of suicide and its prevention.

Now, while volunteers took down posters in the lobby (a photograph of a blank brick wall—"suicide is a dead end"), and the silver-haired proprietor of the Thanatology Book Club closed up shop, the day's first meeting was getting under way downstairs in the Nieuw Amsterdam Ballroom. It was nine o'clock. Fewer than a third of the registrants were in attendance. Some were recovering from a "Backstage on Broadway" tour arranged by the entertainment committee while others opted for last-minute sightseeing or for confirming flights home, rather than this session on "Borderline Personality Disorders and Suicidal Behavior."

Grisly fare for a Sunday morning. Several people in back slept through presentations by mildly eminent psychiatrists. (My notes are hieroglyphs: "central organizing fantasy of narcissistic union" and "objective scrutiny of object relations.") As Otto Kernberg, who pioneered the study of the borderline patient, read a dense theoretical paper, a group of psychiatrists in front gazed up with adoration and a prevention center volunteer in back joked about marketing the speech as a sedative.

When Kernberg finished, the moderator, a young psychiatrist who had been alternating pensive nods with glances at his watch—it was his job to herd everyone upstairs in time for "Is There Room for Self-Help in Suicide Prevention?"—invited questions. Hands shot up in front, and their owners raised progressively complex issues. But a hand in back, belonging to a shabby fellow in a ponytail, persisted. And the moderator finally gave in.

The man stood. His jeans and flannel shirt were worn but not dirty. His ruddy face couldn't decide on a beard or a shave, and his eyes were as cloudy as his question, a stammering ramble proposing meditation as a panacea for suicide. Eyes started to roll in the audience, and there were tolerant chuckles. The moderator flashed the panel an embarrassed collegial smile. When the ponytailed man slowed for a moment, the moderator broke in: "That's an interesting question, but let's move on. We have time for one more." He looked for another hand; the man remained standing. The moderator began his thank-you-very-much-I'm-sure-we-all-learned-a-lot speech, and the man was beginning to sit, bewildered, when Kernberg reached for the microphone and said, "I'd like to answer that question," and in his textbook Viennese accent began responding with care and respect.

5

THE RIGHT TO DIE

I

A FATE WORSE THAN DEATH

AFTER MOST SUICIDES friends and family may feel guilt because they could not prevent the death. Billie Press feels guilty that she could not help her father kill himself. After most suicides friends and family grieve because their loved one chose to die. Billie grieves because her father wanted to end his life but couldn't. After most suicides friends and family believe their loved one died too soon. Billie believes her father died too late. In most suicides the tragedy is that someone died an "unnatural" death; for Billie the tragedy is that her father died a "natural" death.

When Billie's father, Bill, retired as head proofreader of *The New York Times* at eighty, he could look back on a full life. He had worked on newspapers for more than fifty years. A well-read man, he was fond of quoting Shakespeare and had an old-fashioned, courtly manner of speaking. He loved to sing—in the shower, in the car, or with the barbershop quartet of *Times* employees he had organized. After his retirement he moved in with his eldest daughter, Billie, a child development specialist, and her family in a Boston suburb. He read books, watched television, and worked in the garden. He joined a Golden Age club and went on excursions to museums and the theater. "He was so gallant," recalls Billie, who was named for her father. "He was one of the only men in the club, and on trips he always allowed all the women onto the bus first. By the time he got on, the only seats left were in the back, and his guts would get jounced up until his stomach hurt."

Although Bill had had a heart attack when he was fifty-eight, at a checkup at age seventy-five his doctor had marveled at what excellent shape he was in. But now his eyesight, hearing, and memory grew weaker. Cooking on the gas stove, he couldn't see well enough to tell when the flame was low; bending over for a closer look, he often singed his eyebrows. Scissors and tape would disappear, and when his daughter asked him where they were, Bill could never remember where he had left them. "His physical condition declined," says Billie, "but he still had a wonderful brain and a marvelous sense of humor." Although he was often lonely, Bill worked to keep up his spirits. One day his teenage granddaughter asked, "Poppy, isn't it terrible to be old?" Bill shook his head. "Oh, no," he said. "Not when you live with people you love."

At the age of eighty-five, the night before his granddaughter's wedding, Bill had a stroke and a heart attack. After six months of rehabilitation he was hopeful of a complete recovery when a second stroke left him paralyzed on his right side, unable to walk, and incontinent. Although he wanted to come home to live, his daughter and son-in-law could not afford round-the-clock nursing care. After much discussion and with great reluctance, Bill was moved from a cozy bedroom in his daughter's house to a cramped, drab room in a local nursing home.

Although the nursing home had a good reputation, it proved to be a torment. Unable to shift position or to move in any way, Bill was wholly dependent on the staff. But the staff rarely attended to his needs, and he soon developed bedsores. "I'd come over every day after work, and my father would be lying in his own feces," recalls Billie. "I'd clean his bottom, wiping off the shit they'd left." But things were no better at either of the two nursing homes they tried next. "What really makes me angry is that when my father went into a nursing home at age eighty-five, he had every tooth in his head," says Billie. "But they never brushed his teeth. In two years his teeth rotted and fell out one by one. Finally, he could eat nothing but gruel—my father, with teeth like a horse, who at age eighty could eat McIntosh apples." Billie shakes her head angrily. "You know that line from Shakespeare—'sans teeth, sans eyes, sans everything'? My father got like that."

Finally they found a home that provided acceptable care, but a series of small strokes left Bill increasingly immobile. He had no control over the left side of his face, and saliva dripped from a corner of his mouth. "Am I leaking?" he would ask nervously. Bill also suffered excruciating pain from osteoarthritis. "They gave him only three aspirin every four hours, and for three hours he'd be okay, but the last hour he was in agony," says Billie. "He kept telling me that they didn't control the pain." Perhaps even more harrowing was the lack of stimulation, the sheer numb routine of his days. Roused from bed each morning, Bill was strapped into a wheelchair and left on his own, face to the wall. When his position grew painful, he was unable to shift himself, and unless he shouted, aides checked on him only once every four hours. Most of the other nursing home residents were mentally as well as physically impaired, so although Bill's mind was sharp, there was no one to communicate with. It was all the more frustrating for him to be aware of his situation, yet powerless to change it. "My dad kept saying, 'I must have done something very bad in my life to deserve this,' " recalls Billie.

One day Bill, ever the scholar, said to his son-in-law with a sad smile, "Why can't I shuffle off this mortal coil?" He had occasionally joked about suicide; now he told Billie that he was serious about wanting to end his life but he had no access to pills, no gun, no rope, and he could hardly jump out the window or walk off the roof when he couldn't even shift position in his wheelchair. He fantasized about ripping his bedsheet into strips, knotting them into a rope, and hanging himself from the door. When he told Billie of his plan, she nervously tried to change the subject. But in the following weeks Bill continued to bring up suicide. "I would hold his hand, and we would weep when he talked about it," says Billie. One day he looked up at his daughter. "Sweetheart, can't you bring me the means for my demise?" he begged her in his characteristic, elegant manner of speech. Each night Billie lay in bed unable to sleep. "All I thought about was Dad," she says. "I loved him so much, and I hated to see him miserable. I felt he was entitled to end his life, and I knew that if I were in his position, I would want to die, too. I was determined that somehow I would help him. But how would I get the pills? How would I give them to him?" She discussed it with her husband, who feared that she would be arrested for aiding and abetting a suicide, and pointed out that even if she were acquitted, she almost certainly would lose her teaching license. When she told her father that if she helped him she might lose her job, he was adamant. "Sweetheart, you mustn't do it then," he said. "I must suffer to the end."

As his condition steadily declined, her father continued to say wistfully that he wished he could end his life although he knew it was impossible. The nursing home staff did little more than keep him alive. "They never put on his glasses or his hearing aid," says Billie. "I bought him a radio, but they wouldn't tune it for him, so he just sat there with static crackling, unable to see or hear." Gradually, he lost even his ability to talk. Says Billie, "Like an autistic child, he could just repeat the sounds he heard—my brilliant father, who had been head proofreader at *The New York Times*—he'd just rock and babble." When she visited, it took a great effort to get him to recognize her: "I'd get in front of him and take his hands and say, 'Daddy, Daddy, it's me. It's me.' "

Each time she saw her father, he was worse. "In the last year there was some mercy," says Billie, "because with each small stroke he was more out of it, and eventually he was no longer aware of what he was going through." When Billie visited she would wheel her father outside, and they would sit in the sun. "I'd always bring him bananas," she says. "He loved bananas, which were one of the few things he could eat by himself. I'd peel the banana, and he was just able to hold it in his one good hand." She talked to her father, but only rarely was she able to understand a word he said. "He looked terrible," she says, "so shrunken and wasted." One day Billie wheeled her father into town. She left him for a moment outside a variety store while she ran across the street to run an errand. Her father sat in his wheelchair, silent, impassive. When Billie came back a few minutes later, the owner of the store was standing angrily over her father. "How could you leave him here, lady?" he said. "He's scaring all the customers away."

One month before his ninetieth birthday Bill got pneumonia, slipped into a coma, and died. "It was such a relief," says Billie. "My father had been suffering so much, and now he'd finally escaped." It was almost three years after he'd first asked his daughter to help him commit suicide. More than a decade later, she continues to wrestle with her frustration at not having been able to help him die, and she finds it difficult to talk about his death without bursting into tears.

Her father's prolonged death also made Billie think hard about her own future. She is now in her sixties. Although she is healthy and active, she worries that one day, like her father, she might be hopelessly debilitated and want to die but be unable to do anything about it. "I am scared of going my father's route," she says firmly. "I don't want to repeat what my father went through." In the last few years Billie has read books and attended conferences on the right to die with dignity. She has joined the Hemlock Society, a national organization that explores the subject of voluntary euthanasia. "I think the worst thing that could happen in life would be to lose the ability to take one's own life," she says. "I can't imagine killing myself—ever—but it is such a comfort just to know that I have that option." She folds her hands. "For me the bottom line is that people should have choices. And when the quality of life is gone—whether because of terminal illness or extreme age—one of the choices should be the option of leaving this life. And if, like my father, one wants to but is unable to carry it out himself, one should be allowed to have help. To die a less painful death is a human right." She raps the table with her knuckles for emphasis. "Why did my father have to go on suffering for two and a half more years when he wanted so much to end it?"

In those cultures in which death is accepted as a natural part of life, the image of Bill strapped into his wheelchair, face to the wall, wanting to end his life but unable to, might seem absurd. They would consider his daughter's desire to help him end his suffering not as a sin or a crime but as a sign of respect. In many primitive societies, including some in which the act is otherwise taboo, suicide is common in extreme age or incurable illness. Anthropologist Paul Bohannan's 1960 study of six tribes in Nigeria, Kenya, and Uganda found that all of them considered suicide evil except in the case of hopeless illness. "Among the Karens of Burma," wrote anthropologist Edward Westermarck, "if a man has some incurable or painful disease, he says in a matter-of-fact way that he will hang himself, and he does as he says." Although their religion forbids suicide, it was common in India for Hindus suffering from leprosy or other incurable ailments to bury or drown themselves with appropriate religious rites. When an elderly Aymara Indian of Bolivia is terminally ill, friends and relatives keep a death vigil by her side. The invalid may ask for help, in which case the family withholds food and drink until she succumbs. Studies suggest that such deaths are caused not by starvation but by the will to die.

In Western civilization the concept of a "right to die" and of "death with dignity" are also venerable ones. The word euthanasia, in fact, is derived from the Greek words *eu,* meaning "well," and *thanatos,* meaning "death." In ancient Greece it meant just that: a good or easy death. "Thus was he blessed with an easy death and such a one as he had always longed for," wrote Suetonius of Caesar Augustus. "For almost always on hearing that any one had died swiftly and painlessly, he prayed that he and his might have a like *euthanasia,* for that was the term he was wont to use." For the Greeks, of course, a good death was often achieved by suicide. Even philosophers who generally frowned on suicide felt that killing oneself to escape intractable pain or hopeless illness was not only excusable but honorable. Plato, who condemned suicide when committed from sloth or cowardice, admitted that "if any man labour of an incurable disease, he may dispatch himself, if it be to his good." Pliny the Elder believed suicide was justifiable when one suffered from gallstones, stomach pains, or "diseases of the head." The Stoic Musonius said, "Just as a landlord who has not received his rent, pulls down the doors, removes the rafters, and fills up the well, so I seem to be driven out of this little body when nature, which has let it to me, takes away, one by one, eyes and ears, hands and feet. I will not, therefore, delay longer, but will cheerfully depart as from a banquet." The most eloquent spokesman on the subject was Seneca:

I will not relinquish old age if it leaves my better part intact. But if it begins to shake my mind, if it tears out its faculties one by one, if it leaves me not life but breath, I will depart from the putrid or tottering edifice. I will not escape by death from disease as long as it may be healed, and leaves my mind unimpaired. I will not raise my hand against myself on account of pain, for so to die is to be conquered. But if I know that I will suffer for ever, I will depart, not through fear of the pain itself, but because it prevents all for which I would live.

Such sentiments were met with sympathy by classical physicians. In his essay "The Arts," Hippocrates, the father of modern medicine, wrote that the physician was required to "do away with the sufferings of the sick, to lessen the violence of their diseases, and to refuse to treat those who are overwhelmed by their diseases, realizing that in such cases medicine is powerless." Physicians who believed a case was hopeless routinely suggested suicide, and often supplied the lethal drugs with which to accomplish it.

During the Middle Ages and the Renaissance, when suicide was perceived as the worst of sins, terminal illness was often accepted as a mitigating factor. Charles Moore, the eighteenth-century English clergyman who penned a six-hundred-page attack on suicide, conceded that "the most excusable cause seems to be an emaciated body; when a man labours under the tortures of an incurable disorder, and seems to live only to be a burden to himself and his friends." In More's *Utopia* priests and magistrates helped end the lives of terminally ill citizens who wished to die. What More fantasized in sixteenth-century Britain actually took place in seventeenth-century Brittany, where a person suffering from an incurable disease might apply to the parish priest for the Holy Stone. If the priest agreed, the family gathered, prayers were said, and the Stone was brought down upon the person's head, often by the oldest person in the village.

More often, ailing elderly were restrained from suicide by doctors, by relatives, or by religious beliefs. In his last years Jonathan Swift, who suffered from Ménière's disease and cerebral atrophy, may have longed for something like the Holy Stone. Partially paralyzed, his brain decaying, suffering from buzzing in his ears, and liable to attacks of giddiness, deafness, and memory loss, Swift spent eight years waiting to die. "I have been very miserable all night, and to-day extremely deaf and full of pain," he wrote to his niece in 1740 at the age of seventy-three. "I am so stupid and confounded that I cannot express the mortification I am under both of body and soul." Swift refused to commit suicide because he believed it was a sin. Nevertheless, knives and poisons were kept from his reach, and the pain in his eye was so great that it took five men to keep him from tearing it out. Finally, in 1745, after a series of convulsions lasting thirty-six hours, "he exchanged the sleep of idiocy for the sleep of death," as investigating physicians described it.

As medical treatment became increasingly sophisticated, scientists and philosophers debated the responsibility of doctors to hopelessly ill patients. "I esteem it the office of a physician not only to restore health, but to mitigate pain and dolors," wrote Francis Bacon, "and not only when such mitigation may conduce to recovery, but when it may serve to make a fair and easy passage." Benjamin Franklin, like Bacon, was fascinated by life-prolonging technology but deplored painful, extended deaths. "We have very great pity for an animal if we see it in agonies and death throes," he observed. "We put it out of its misery no matter how noble the animal." In 1798 in *Medical Histories and Reflections,* British physician John Ferriar cautioned against overweening devotion to duty. The physician, he wrote, "should not torment his patient with unavailing attempts to stimulate the dissolving system, from the idle vanity of prolonging the flutter of the pulse for a few more vibrations. . . . When things come to the last and the act of dissolution is imminent . . . he should be left undisturbed."

By the end of the nineteenth century there were appeals for more radical measures. In an essay entitled "Euthanasia," published in England in 1872, S. D. Williams claimed that "in cases of incurable and painful illness the doctors should be allowed, with the patient's consent, and after taking all necessary safeguards, to administer so strong an anaesthetic as to render all future anaesthetics superfluous; in short, there should be a sort of legalized suicide by proxy." In 1906 a bill proposing legalization of euthanasia for incurable sufferers who wished to die was introduced into the Ohio legislature. Though the bill was rejected, it triggered intense debate. Many protested that such a law would be an invitation to people who wanted to get rid of burdensome relatives, to fortune hunters who wished to hasten an inheritance, and to physicians who wished to disguise their mistakes. A *New York Times* editorial compared the practice of euthanasia to "practices of savages in all parts of the world." In 1935 such savages as H. G. Wells, George Bernard Shaw, Julian Huxley, and A. A. Milne became founding members of the Voluntary Euthanasia Society in London. "Vast numbers of human beings are doomed to end their earthly existence by a lingering, painful, and often agonising form of death," said founding president C. Killick Millard, a physician. "Voluntary euthanasia should be legalised for adults suffering from an incurable, fatal, painful disease." In 1936 a bill sponsored by the society that would allow terminally ill people to apply for euthanasia was defeated in Parliament. In 1937, as the debate reached a crescendo, G. K. Chesterton wrote, "Some are proposing what is called euthanasia; at present only a proposal for killing those who are a nuisance to themselves; but soon to be applied to those who are a nuisance to other people."

Chesterton's acerbic prophecy was already being fulfilled in Germany, where discussions of humanitarian euthanasia similar to those in Great Britain and the United States had been raised earlier in the century. In 1920, in their book *The Permission to Destroy Life Unworthy of Life,* psychiatrist Alfred Hoche and jurist Karl Binding introduced the concept of *lebensunwertes Leben*—"life unworthy of life." These distinguished professors argued that there were situations in which killing was consistent with medical ethics. Those who suffered from brain damage, retardation, and certain psychiatric illnesses were already "mentally dead," and ending their lives was not murder but "an allowable, useful act." This line of reasoning was adapted and twisted by the Nazis. When they took power in 1933, one of the first laws they enacted was compulsory sterilization of people with hereditary illnesses. This was only the beginning. What the Nazis called "euthanasia" was mass murder, decreed by Hitler and carried out by prominent German physicians and psychiatrists.

None of the victims were voluntary; none, in fact, were aware of what awaited them as they were shipped to one of six "liquidation institutions." From September 1939, when the program began, to August 1941, when it ended in response to public criticism by German clergymen, approximately one hundred thousand mentally and physically handicapped German men, women, and children were put to death. Not long afterward, of course, the Nazis began applying their mass murder techniques to millions of Jews.

Gradually, the meaning of the word euthanasia had changed. In ancient Greece it simply referred to a good death, whatever the cause. By the end of the nineteenth century it referred to the manner of death, the taking of life in order to end suffering. By the end of World War II it had come to mean the taking of life without permission. Since then the word has been avoided by many right-to-die advocates who prefer phrases like "self-deliverance," "accelerated death," "death by design," "self-termination," "elective death," and "the final freedom."

Whatever terminology is used, however, the last two decades have seen renewed debate on euthanasia and the right to die. This is in large part because the nature of old age and illness has dramatically changed. In 1900 average life expectancy in America was forty-seven. By 1986 it was seventy-five. In 1900 the three leading causes of death were pneumonia and influenza, tuberculosis, and diarrhea, for all of which cures have since been found. (Pneumonia, once known as "the old man's friend" for bringing a peaceful death to many elderly sufferers, is now routinely treated with antibiotics.) Today, half of all deaths are due to heart disease while one-fifth are caused by cancer. Respirators, heart-lung machines, intravenous feeding systems, heart transplants, pacemakers, and sophisticated antibiotics have enabled many to live longer, more productive lives, but these technological advances have been a mixed blessing. "For every illness, there is some procedure that can delay the moment of death," physician Morris Abram, former chairman of a presidential panel on medical ethics, has observed. "The question is: for how long, at what cost, at what pain, at what suffering?" Fifty years ago most Americans died at home; four of five now die in hospitals or nursing homes. "The classical deathbed scene, with its loving partings and solemn last words, is practically a thing of the past," ethicist Joseph Fletcher has written. "In its stead is a sedated, comatose, betubed object, manipulated and subconscious, if not subhuman." He asks, "Where can we draw the line between prolonging a patient's life and prolonging his dying?"

Fletcher worries that physicians may be ill-equipped to draw that line. Doctors are trained to regard preservation of life as their highest goal. The Hippocratic oath, once a staple of medical school graduation ceremonies, says in part, "I will give no deadly medicine to anyone if asked nor suggest any such counsel." Although the oath is rarely pledged these days, it decorates the wall of many a physician's office, and doctors are still conditioned to preserve life with unquestioning allegiance. One oncologist vows: "I'll treat my patients as long as they're still wiggling; that's my job." Some people worry that doctors' dedication to life at any and all cost—reinforced by fear of malpractice suits— may blind them to considerations of the quality of that life. At a hearing of the Senate Special Committee on Aging, Warren Reich of the Kennedy Institute of Ethics at Georgetown University said, "The terminal patient may desperately want rest, peace, and dignity, yet he may receive only infusions, transfusions, a machine, and a team of experts busily occupied with his pulmonary functions but not with him as a person." Such myopia often leads to miraculous recoveries—but sometimes to unintentionally sadistic scenes: A man suffering from terminal cancer, down to sixty pounds, was resuscitated fifty-two times in one month though he repeatedly begged, "For God's sake, please just let me go."

An increasing number of people are realizing that they don't want their lives to end this way, that there indeed may be fates worse than death. They propose that the quality of a life may be as important as its quantity. "The dignity starts with . . . choice," says a character in *Whose Life Is It Anyway?*, a play by Brian Clark about an artist paralyzed from the neck down who asks to be released from the hospital and allowed to die. "Without it, it is degrading because technology has taken over from human will. My Lord, if I cannot be a man, I do not wish to be a medical achievement." Joseph Fletcher has written, "We are discovering that saving life is not always saving people. And that death may not always be an enemy to be fought off, but sometimes a friend to be helped and invited." Some people suggest that in their use of life-support systems doctors may not be prolonging life but prolonging death. It is commonplace to hear elderly people say, "I don't fear death, but I fear dying." One terminally ill seventy-eight-year-old, who was intubated and connected to life-support systems despite repeated requests to be left alone to die, switched off his own ventilator during the night. He left a final message for his attending physician: "Death is not the enemy, doctor. Inhumanity is."

Right-to-die activists suggest that such scenes would be unnecessary were doctors permitted to practice passive euthanasia—a concept best described by nineteenth-century poet Arthur Hugh Clough, who wrote, "Thou shalt not kill; but need'st not strive / Officiously to keep alive." Many doctors admit to quietly practicing passive euthanasia for years, often by ordering the withdrawal of life-support systems at the patient's request. Or a doctor might call for a "No Code" or "Do Not Resuscitate" order, in which case a dying patient will not be given "heroic measures" of resuscitation. A doctor might hasten the death of a terminally ill patient by not treating an infection or by failing to prescribe antibiotics for pneumonia. Some doctors go further, into an even more hazy legal area. They may prescribe painkilling drugs, knowing that they will also hasten death. They may put a bottle of pills on the table of a terminally ill patient who has asked to die. "Take two if you can't sleep," they might say. "But don't take them all, or they will kill you." Christiaan Barnard, the South African surgeon who in 1967 performed the world's first successful heart transplant, admits that he has practiced passive euthanasia for many years. "I have learned from my life in medicine that death is not always an enemy," he wrote in *Good Life/Good Death,* a book about euthanasia. "Often it is good medical treatment. Often it achieves what medicine cannot achieve—it stops suffering." Many patients, however, do not have the kind of intimate relationship with their doctor that allows the issue of passive euthanasia to be raised. The "family doctor" has been replaced by a team of specialists, often strangers to the patient. But most doctors, it seems, are in favor of passive euthanasia. A 1988 poll of the American Medical Association found that eight of ten members favored withdrawal of life-support systems from hopelessly ill or irreversibly comatose patients if the patients or their families requested it. Many doctors who practice passive euthanasia, however, do not favor changing the laws; they believe they are handling things well enough on the sly.

Some right-to-die advocates claim that passive euthanasia merely means allowing people to die the way they did one hundred years ago, before the advent of what Barnard calls "rampant technology." They believe that in some cases more direct action is necessary. They contend that it should be legal for doctors to bring about death in terminally ill patients, at the patient's request, using injections or barbiturate overdoses. As an example of "active voluntary euthanasia" they cite the case of Sigmund Freud, who suffered from cancer of the mouth for the last sixteen years of his life. Refusing painkillers so that he could continue to work with his mind unclouded, Freud made a pact with his physician, Max Schur, that when his condition became unbearable, Schur would help him die. In 1939, when the pain became so great that he was unable to read or write and necrosis of the bone gave off an odor so foul that even his beloved chow kept his distance, Freud asked his physician to keep his promise. Schur gave him two injections of morphine, and Freud died quietly, at the age of eighty-three.

Few doctors admit to having practiced active euthanasia. At a 1984 conference of the World Federation of Right-to-Die Societies, in Nice, five French doctors signed a declaration admitting that they had "helped terminally ill patients to finish their lives under the least bad conditions possible." In some cases they had administered lethal drugs. German oncologist Julius Hackethal has admitted giving a lethal dose of cyanide to a woman whose face had been eaten away by cancer and who begged to die. "When my patient wants to live—and thank God most of them do—then I fight for his life as much as I can," says Hackethal. "But if he wants to die and I can't talk him out of it, then I help him to die in dignity and without torment." The vast majority of doctors, however, reject active euthanasia as a violation of medical ethics and an abuse of the doctor-patient relationship. Says one oncologist, "How could my patients' trust in me survive if they could never quite be sure whenever I approached their bed that I hadn't come to deliver the coup de grace?"

"What, morally, is the difference between doing nothing to keep the patient alive and giving a fatal dose of a pain-killing or other lethal drug?" Joseph Fletcher has asked. "The intention is the same, either way. A decision *not* to keep a patient alive is as morally deliberate as a decision to *end* a life." Legally, however, there is a vast difference. While in many states it is legal in some instances to withdraw life support systems, active euthanasia is considered murder. (As is mercy killing. Although suicide is legal, aiding and abetting a suicide is a felony in most states.) But laws vary from state to state, and the distinction among these acts is often murky. Who has the right to die? If a person is terminally ill, does he or she have the right to end his life? Who has the right to decide? The patient? What if the patient is swayed by depression? What if the patient suffers from Alzheimer's disease? Should a family member be permitted to make decisions about death for the patient? Should a doctor be permitted to help a patient die? These are questions that increasingly are being decided in court.

In 1975 the case of Karen Ann Quinlan put the issue of euthanasia before the nation. A few weeks after turning twenty-one, Quinlan swallowed a number of tranquilizers before drinking several gin and tonics with some friends at a local tavern, whereupon she fell to the floor, unconscious. Rushed to the hospital, she was given oxygen and put on a respirator, but she went into a coma and never regained consciousness.

Her parents, devout Catholics, kept constant vigil over their daughter. Every examining doctor agreed that Karen had suffered irreversible brain damage and had no hope of recovery. After three months the Quinlans, with the support of their parish priest, asked the doctors to disconnect the respirator and let their daughter "pass into the hands of the Lord." When the doctors refused, the Quinlans went to court, seeking permission to withdraw the respirator and allow their daughter to die "with grace and dignity." No American court had ever authorized the withdrawal of life-support equipment. The Quinlans' lawyer argued that Karen had a constitutional right to die and that keeping her alive "after the dignity, beauty, promise, and meaning of earthly life have vanished" constituted cruel and unusual punishment. A court-appointed guardian for Karen insisted that removal of the respirator would be an act of homicide and a violation of both the law and the medical code of ethics. A lawyer for the doctors claimed that no court could determine whether or not Karen might still recover.

The superior court judge ruled against the Quinlans, but the New Jersey Supreme Court reversed the decision on appeal, observing that "ultimately, there comes a point at which the individual's rights overcome the state's interests." On May 17, 1976, Karen's respirator was turned off. However, she did not die. She lived in a "persistent vegetative state" in a New Jersey nursing home. Fed a combination of high-calorie nutrients and antibiotics through a nasogastric tube, her 70-pound body (she weighed 120 before her coma) lay curled in a fetal position. Nurses turned her every two hours to prevent bedsores. Her father visited Karen each morning on his way to work; her mother visited several times a week, and a radio in her room played twenty-four hours a day. On her birthdays her family held a bedside mass, and cards arrived from all over the world. But Karen remained completely unaware of the outside world. She died of pneumonia in 1985, ten years after she had lapsed into the coma. Her father said, "She died with dignity."

The Quinlan case brought the right-to-die issue into sharp focus, personalizing questions that were easy to ignore in the abstract. The image of her in an irreversible coma imprinted itself onto the national consciousness. Many people realized that they didn't want to "end up like Karen Quinlan." Since 1969 an estimated one in five adults have signed Living Wills, which allow them to specify the conditions under which they would not wish to be kept alive by life-sustaining technology. In addition, millions have signed a Durable Power of Attorney for Health Care, in which they assign to another person the power to make their health care decisions in the event of incompetency. Although these documents are helpful as evidence of a patient's wishes, they may be ignored in the hubbub of emergency rooms. In one survey 70 percent of physicians said they would like to leave a Living Will for their own doctors, while 65 percent said they would *not* obey a Living Will with which they disagreed. "I've talked to physicians who say that if they are working in the emergency room and in the pocket of a patient who comes in they find a duly executed Living Will, they will take it out and throw it in the wastebasket," says a philosophy professor who leads hospital discussion groups on medical ethics.

Since the Quinlan decision there have been indications of increasing public acceptance of passive euthanasia. In a 1950 Gallup Poll, 36 percent believed doctors should be permitted to stop treatment at the request of a dying patient. By 1984 the figure had grown to 73 percent. According to a study reported in the *Journal of the American Medical Association* in 1985, doctors issue DNR (Do Not Resuscitate) orders three times as often as they did ten or twenty years ago. In 1983 a presidential commission on ethical problems in medicine urged that "competent patients' decisions regarding medical treatment should almost always be honored even when they lead to an earlier death." The commission also said that family members acting on behalf of incompetent patients should be allowed to make similar decisions. The following year, in an article in *The New England Journal of Medicine,* a group of prominent doctors suggested guidelines for physicians in the treatment of hopelessly ill patients. "Basic to our considerations are two important precepts: the patient's role in decision making is paramount, and a decrease in aggressive treatment of the hopelessly ill patient is advisable when such treatment would only prolong a difficult and uncomfortable process of dying." As regards patients who, like Quinlan, are in a persistent vegetative state, they wrote, "It is morally justifiable to withhold antibiotics and artificial nutrition and hydration, as well as other forms of life-sustaining treatment, allowing the patient to die." Even Pope John Paul II, while condemning euthanasia in a 1980 Vatican declaration, said, "When inevitable death is imminent in spite of the means used, it is permitted in conscience to take the decision to refuse forms of treatment that would only secure a precarious and burdensome prolongation of life."

This gradual acceptance of passive euthanasia has been reflected in a series of court decisions since the Quinlan case. In January, 1985, five months before Quinlan's death, the New Jersey Supreme Court expanded the Quinlan decision by ruling that feeding tubes, like respirators, could be withdrawn from a terminally ill patient when requested by the patient or the patient's guardian. Laws vary from state to state, however, and court rulings have been contradictory. In 1981, at the request of the patient's family, two California doctors disconnected the respirator of a comatose patient named Clarence Herbert. (In the past he had told his wife he did not want to become "another Karen Ann Quinlan.") When he did not die, they discontinued his intravenous feeding as well. When Herbert died six days later, the Los Angeles District Attorney charged the doctors with murder. Although the case was eventually dismissed, it was the first time doctors had ever been charged for removing life-support equipment, and it sent shock waves through the medical community. But doctors can also be sued for *not* following a request to cease life-sustaining measures. William Bartling was a seventy-year-old retired dental supply salesman suffering from emphysema, arteriosclerosis, chronic respiratory failure, an abdominal aneurysm, and a malignant lung tumor. In 1984, kept alive by a respirator, feeding and drainage tubes, and a device that vacuumed his throat every two hours, he requested to be disconnected from life-support systems and allowed to die. His doctors refused—and, for a time, tied his hands down so he could not pull out the tubes himself. After the state superior court ruled in favor of the doctors, a California appellate court overturned the decision, ruling that the hospital had violated Bartling's right to "self-determination as to his own medical treatment." Bartling, however, died twenty-three hours before the appellate court could hear his plea and two months before the courts affirmed his right to die.

With no clear guidance from the law, it is hardly surprising that doctors are apprehensive about making the life-and-death decisions they are confronted with daily. Many hospitals now have ethics committees that act as sounding boards and help review treatment decisions; a few employ full-time staff philosophers. Other medical centers have hired staff lawyers to give legal counsel on right-to-die cases. Often, doctors, lawyers, patients, and patients' families will try to work out a solution in private, before a case reaches the courts. In these "negotiated deaths" doctors and hospital administrators meet with the patient's family to discuss a comatose or terminally ill patient and whether, when, and how to withdraw life-support equipment. If an agreement is made, the plug is quietly pulled. Often, however, decisions must be made in emergency settings where extended consultation or philosophical deliberation is impossible, and many hospitals lack defined procedures for recording the wishes of dying patients. Dr. S. David Pomrinse, former president of the Greater New York Hospital Association, told *Time* magazine, "In hospitals that have no rules, in the middle of the night you have a poor twenty-one-year-old nurse trying to decide whether or not to call in the resuscitation team." In 1987 the Joint Commission on Accreditation of Hospitals announced that it would require hospitals to have formal policies specifying when doctors may refrain from trying to resuscitate terminally ill patients.

In 1920, Frank Roberts was convicted of murder and sentenced to life imprisonment with hard labor for supplying poison to his wife, who suffered from multiple sclerosis and had begged to die. In 1983, Betty Rollin helped her seventy-six-year-old mother, terminally ill and often in agony from ovarian cancer, obtain a lethal dosage of barbiturates, then sat with her while she died. A television journalist and author, Rollin described her mother's death in *Last Wish,* which became a best-seller and generated thousands of letters, the vast majority of them praising her act.

Despite such a change in reception, passive euthanasia remains a risky enterprise that usually comes under the legal rubric of aiding and abetting a suicide. Our increasing ability to keep people alive with technology may force more people to such extreme acts, some of them outside the law. One right-to-die advocacy group, studying newspaper clippings, estimates that the incidence of double suicides and assisted suicides involving the terminally ill has increased forty times since 1920. These admittedly unscientific findings probably represent a small part of the actual number of cases since only a fraction of cases ever come to court or surface in newspapers or books. The vast majority are carried out in secret. Says a woman who obtained a lethal dose of barbiturates for her terminally ill mother, then sat with her while she swallowed it, "What makes me sad and a little angry is that because what I did is against the law, for the rest of my life I will have to keep secret something that I feel so good about."

Although active voluntary euthanasia—actively causing a person's death at his or her request—is still against the law throughout the world, there is one country in which it has been tacitly accepted. Article 293 of the Dutch criminal code calls for twelve years' imprisonment for anyone who "takes the life of another at his or her explicit and serious request." Yet a series of court cases has established conditions under which doctors may practice active euthanasia without fear of prosecution. The patient must be suffering unbearably with no treatment possible. The patient's request must be voluntary. "Aid-in-dying," as it is called, must be performed by a physician with the approval of at least one other doctor. The patient's family must be consulted at each step although it is always the patient who makes the decisions. Within these guidelines Dutch doctors quietly help more than five thousand terminally ill patients to end their lives each year, either by providing drugs to be taken orally or by an injection, usually of a barbiturate and curare.

"Every patient, every human being, has the right to see his suffering as unbearable and has the right to ask a doctor for euthanasia," says Pieter Admiraal, a Dutch anesthesiologist and author of *Justifiable Euthanasia: A Manual for the Medical Profession,* a booklet published in 1980. "Every doctor has the right to do euthanasia. And every doctor has the right to refuse to do euthanasia." At a 1986 conference in Washington, D.C., on the right to die, Admiraal, who has been practicing euthanasia for more than a decade, described one of the hundreds of patients he has helped to die at his hospital in Delft. "She was twenty-four years old and she was in a nursing home," said Admiraal, a portly, bearded, genial man in his late fifties. "I had a phone call from her doctor that she wanted to speak to me about euthanasia. I said that she wanted to speak to me. That's not true. She couldn't. She hadn't been able to speak for a long time because she had cancer of the tongue. She couldn't swallow, and they had put a tube in her stomach, through her skin, to feed her. That also means that she couldn't swallow her saliva. People produce between one and two liters of saliva each day. She was a very, very nice and handsome girl, and she was sitting there, in one hand a tissue to remove continuously her saliva, and with her other hand to write down what she wanted to say to me. But I knew already what her problem was because that tumor was growing, very slowly but growing. The next step was a tracheotomy to open her trachea, to enable her to breathe if it closed. And that's what she refused. So she wrote down that she refused this kind of tube. And she asked me to assure her that I would give her euthanasia just before she should suffocate. And I agreed, of course.

"After a few weeks she came to our hospital because the tumor was bleeding. We all thought that she would bleed to death, but she didn't. She remained in our hospital for the next two days, and we discussed when we should do the euthanasia. It was, of course, always a group decision, never a decision on my own. We talked long with the priest, nurse, and doctor on the case. And she was writing to us or knocking her head when it was time to do it. And we agreed we should wait until the last moment because we were all there so we could do it immediately if something went wrong.

"And then two days later it proved that it was necessary to do so. First she saw her parents. Although usually the family are in the room at the moment of giving euthanasia, they refused to be there. In this case, then, the nurse, the priest, her doctor, and myself were there.

"She wrote on her paper a farewell. I kissed her and said, 'Have a very good journey.' And I gave her an injection and she died.

"I have two simple questions for you. I am always with my patients when they are dying, whatever the cause of their death, and if they have tongue cancer or cancer of that sort, then should not the doctor be there available to assist?

"And the second question is, if a doctor is there and he's standing in the back of the room with his hand on his bag and watches this patient suffocate, should not *this* doctor be liable to prosecution?"

II

"YOUR GOOD END IN LIFE IS OUR CONCERN!"

EACH WEEKDAY MORNING shortly after 8:00, Derek Humphry walks out the door of his rustic wooden house in the hills of western Oregon, gets into his Volvo, and heads off to work. The pleasant, eighteen-mile drive takes him through woodlands, small dairy farms, apple orchards, and Christmas tree nurseries. Arriving at his offices, a nine-room converted house in downtown Eugene, he banters with his coworkers in the brisk cadence of his native England before settling in at his desk and opening the morning mail. His neighbors in the other office buildings on Country Club Road include lawyers, dentists, insurance agents, and advertising salesmen. Humphry's job is somewhat more difficult to pigeonhole. Because of his work he has been called a savior, a godsend, and an angel of mercy. He has also been called a murderer and a Nazi, has been compared to Jim Jones and Adolf Hitler, and has been assured that he will burn in hell.

Humphry is executive director and co-founder of the Hemlock Society, a group dedicated, as its letterhead says, to "supporting the option of active voluntary euthanasia for the terminally ill." The society has two goals: to educate the public about right-to-die issues and to change U.S. laws to make it legal to assist the terminally ill to take their own lives. To this end Humphry has given hundreds of speeches and written dozens of articles and several books on the subject, including *Let Me Die Before I Wake,* a book that explains how to take one's own life.

Like many who become involved in right-to-die activism, Humphry was drawn to it by personal experience. In 1972, while they were living in London during Humphry's years as home affairs correspondent for the *Sunday Times,* his forty-year-old wife Jean discovered a lump in her left breast. Tests proved it to be malignant. Despite a mastectomy, chemotherapy, and radiation treatments, the cancer spread to her lymph glands, spine, and bones. In late May 1974 the doctors predicted she would die by the end of the year. Although Jean struggled to maintain a semblance of normal life, she was often in pain so excruciating that she had to be rushed to the hospital. After a particularly harrowing episode she asked her husband to make her a promise: When the pain became too great and she decided that she had had enough, he would simply supply her with the means to end her life. Derek promised.

Although her wits were as sharp as ever, Jean's physical condition steadily deteriorated. Eventually, she was forced to stay in bed, drugged into near-unconsciousness with medication, and using a wheelchair to get around the house on the rare occasions she was up to it. A doctor told Derek that the bones in Jean's legs were so brittle that they might snap if she tried to walk. One morning she broke a rib when she bent over too rapidly. When there was another outbreak of cancer at the top of her spine, the doctors at the hospital admitted that little could be done beyond making Jean comfortable. She would probably die within a few weeks. The morning after she returned from the hospital, when her husband brought her medication and her breakfast, Jean asked him if he had been able to procure a drug. Derek, who had obtained a lethal dose of Seconal and codeine from a sympathetic physician, said that he had. She told him that she would die at one o'clock.

Derek broke down and wept. He and his wife spent their remaining hours talking about their twenty-two years of married life. Shortly before one o'clock Derek prepared a cup of coffee for Jean, into which he stirred the lethal mixture. Returning to her room he placed the mug on the bedstand. They hugged each other and said good-bye. Jean drank the contents, leaned back on the pillow, closed her eyes, and fell into a deep sleep. Derek sat by her side until, fifty minutes later, she died.

Humphry let few people beyond the immediate family know the circumstances of Jean's death. One of those he eventually told was his second wife, Ann Wickett, who encouraged Humphry to write about his experience. Three years later, in 1978, *Jean's Way,* an account of his wife's last years and how Humphry had helped her die, was published. The book's first printing sold out within a week. The rights were sold for translation into French, Spanish, Japanese, and Norwegian. Humphry received three offers for the movie rights. (Columbia Pictures, which bought the rights, eventually dropped the project in 1980.) Humphry also received scores of letters from all over the world, some from terminally ill people asking for help in killing themselves, others from people who wanted to be prepared in case they ever became hopelessly ill.

Some revealed that, like Humphry, they had helped a family member die but had never told anyone. Others wrote that they had wanted to help a terminally ill loved one who begged to die but, fearing prosecution and stigma, had been unable to carry out what Humphry called "an act of love."

What Humphry considered an act of love could legally be considered an act of manslaughter. In 1961, when Britain's Suicide Act decriminalized suicide and attempted suicide, it added a law that made aiding and abetting a suicide a felony, punishable by up to fourteen years in prison (thus making it a crime to help someone commit an act that was itself not a crime). When a journalist asked the police what they intended to do about Humphry, who in the book and in television and newspaper interviews freely admitted he had helped his wife kill herself, an investigation was launched. Eventually, the public prosecutor dropped the case for "lack of evidence." Privately, he admitted that he had been moved by the book and thought Jean had been extremely brave.

In 1979, when *Jean's Way* was published in the United States, where Humphry and Wickett had moved, there was an even greater furor. Humphry told his story on "Donahue," "60 Minutes," and "Good Morning America," among others. Hundreds of letters poured in, many from people who wanted to know what kind of drugs Jean had taken and how to procure them. Humphry was struck by how many people faced situations similar to the one he and Jean had faced and who had nowhere else to turn. He combed through news clippings at the library of the *Los Angeles Times*, where he now worked. "I saw case after case just as compassionate and loving as mine, where people had been prosecuted for aiding and abetting a suicide," he recalls. Humphry felt there should be some sort of organization to help these people. He resigned from his job and organized a meeting of twenty experts in the field of death and dying: professors, lawyers, doctors, social workers, and nurses. He described his goal of a society dedicated to legalizing active voluntary euthanasia for the terminally ill and asked who would be willing to join. "They were all in favor in principle, but they said they couldn't get involved," recalls Humphry. "They were afraid of how it would reflect on their professional practices." Some feared for their safety. "My God, they firebomb the houses of pro-abortion people," said one attorney. "What do you think they'll do to us?" Nevertheless, on August 21, 1980, Humphry held a press conference to announce the formation of the Hemlock Society, named for the poison that Socrates used to commit suicide. There were four members: Humphry, his wife Ann Wickett, lawyer Richard Scott, and Gerald Larue, a professor of religion at USC.

Ten years later the Hemlock Society has more than thirty-seven thousand members, with an average of eight hundred more joining each month. There are local chapters in New York, Chicago, San Francisco, Nashville, Rochester, Palm Springs, and sixty-two other cities. From a modest office in Eugene, a staff of eight generates a surprisingly hefty amount of activity. Hemlock has published nine books, including *Jean's Way; Euthanasia and Religion,* by Hemlock president Larue; *Common-Sense Suicide,* a book advocating the right to suicide for the elderly, by Hemlock member Doris Portwood; *Double Exit,* Ann Wickett's study of double suicides; and *Let Me Die Before I Wake,* Hemlock's "book of self-deliverance for the dying." Hemlock also edits *The Euthanasia Review,* a scholarly journal, and the *Hemlock Quarterly,* a newsletter keeping members abreast of the movement. It has sponsored a thirty-minute educational video on euthanasia, available for sale or rent to colleges as well as to Hemlock members "for home use." It has organized four national conferences and has distributed more than one million copies of the Living Will and Durable Power of Attorney for Health Care. And it issues a canary-yellow plastic wallet-sized card on which members can specify their medical wishes in case of an accident.

Each day Hemlock receives some two hundred thirty letters and phone calls, most of which are requests for membership applications, Living Wills, and books. Hemlock also receives desperate appeals from people in harrowing circumstances: A man whose wife is dying of cancer wants the name of a pharmacist who will supply him with a lethal dose; a woman who has just been told she is terminally ill with pancreatic cancer says she must know where to get drugs immediately; a caller who has hoarded a supply of barbiturates wonders whether such-and-such an amount is enough to kill her. "People often offer us money to help them die," says Humphry. "I've been offered as much as ten thousand dollars to go into their home and sit with them while they die. One woman offered me her Cadillac if I would help her. It's a measure of their desperation. They say, 'Jean had you, I've got nobody, you *must* help me.' "

When such help is requested, no matter how acute or deserving the situation may seem, Humphry never actively intervenes or provides specific information about dosages. (He may suggest they read *Let Me Die Before I Wake.*) Not only is he mindful of the legal danger—in giving such information he could be charged with aiding and abetting a suicide—but it goes against his moral grain. "I never tell anybody what to do or what not to do, but I will discuss with them the pros and cons of their situation," he says. "How serious is their illness? Does their spouse know? Have they told their doctor of their plans? How long do they think they can hang on? Are they willing to go into the hospital again? Most people appreciate being able to talk this over with somebody. But it is for the individuals and their associates to make their decisions and carry out whatever actions they choose."

Humphry doesn't encourage these calls because of the legal danger, but he doesn't forbid them because he knows that the callers may have nowhere else to turn. In helping callers Humphry often provides information on other options. Hemlock has a list of sympathetic attorneys to whom callers can be referred for advice on natural death acts, informed consent, and other legal matters. Hemlock often refers callers to local hospices. Occasionally, people Humphry believes may be emotionally disturbed call or write. "We tell them we can't help them, and they would be wrong to join this society," says Humphry, a member of the American Association of Suicidology. "We suggest they seek help from a therapist or a crisis intervention center because mental illness can be curable. In addition, a mentally ill person can go and kill himself whereas a terminally ill person is often physically incapable of taking his own life."

Much of Humphry's time is spent trying to educate the public about euthanasia. Hemlock has advertised its work in such diverse publications as *The New York Times Book Review, Science Digest, Lancet,* and *Hustler.* (Only two publications, the Gray Panther newsletter and *Modern Maturity,* have refused to run Hemlock ads.) Lugging a briefcase crammed with Hemlock books, brochures, and membership applications, Humphry speaks wherever he is invited: high school and college classes, retirement communities, hospices, nurses' training courses, and professional conferences. He has hired a Hollywood public relations consultant to book him on radio and television shows. "We're probably the only euthanasia group in the world to employ a publicity agent," says Humphry with a laugh. "Colleagues accuse me of having 'gone Hollywood.' " As a former journalist Humphry knows the power of the press and how to court it: He has published a collection of news clippings on right-to-die cases and sends journalists yellow Rolodex cards labeled "Death/ Dying" on the tab, with a list of topics, from "Pulling the Plug" to "Double Suicide," on which he is prepared to give "background and quotes." Humphry admits that his efforts may appear overly gung-ho. "I'm a street fighter, not a philosopher," he says. "I'm trying to change public opinion." And when the laws have been changed to permit doctors to help terminally ill people take their lives, he says, "Hemlock will commit corporate suicide." Until then he vows to continue spreading the word. As he addressed Hemlock members in a recent fund-raising letter, "Your good end in life is our concern! Please help us to help you achieve it."

Many people assume that Hemlock members must be radical leftists, lonely depressives, or morbid weirdos. But according to a membership survey, Hemlock members, who pay annual dues of $20 ($25 for couples; $15 for senior citizens), represent an average cross-section of Americans except that they are apt to be older, wealthier, and better educated. Hemlock members range in age from nineteen to eighty-eight, with an average age of sixty. Two of three members are women—not surprising, given that in the United States there are four times as many widows as widowers. The membership includes more than two hundred doctors. Ninety-nine percent of members are white. Only one in twenty Hemlock members is terminally ill. Some join because of a philosophical belief in the right to die. Others join to obtain practical information about euthanasia in the event that they become terminally ill. "Hemlock is my insurance policy against pain, senile old age, and loneliness," writes one member. The majority join because they have seen someone close to them die in extreme pain and suffering, and are determined not to let it happen to them.

Hemlock members also join because the society acts as a support group. In 1985, 240 people came to Los Angeles from as far away as New York, Chicago, and Fort Lauderdale to Hemlock's Second National Voluntary Euthanasia Conference. In the Starlight Room of the Miramar Sheraton Hotel, a ballroom-sized space accustomed to hosting bridal shows and car dealers' conventions, they sat at long tables draped with gold tablecloths, listening attentively (some taking notes in Hemlock-provided notebooks) to two days of speeches and workshops on topics like "Memorial Societies and Funeral Prearrangement," "How Euthanasia Was Legalized in Holland," "The Law and Euthanasia," and "The Sexual Needs of the Terminally Ill Person." Anyone expecting Hemlock to behave like a typical special-interest group with an axe to grind would have been surprised by the roster of speakers, which included several opposed to suicide. Edwin Shneidman pushed suicide prevention in the keynote address. Stephen Levine, a Buddhist therapist, meditated before the audience in the lotus position before urging them to "meet pain with love instead of fear" and resist the temptation to leave their bodies in an angry, self-hating manner." At the pro-suicide end of the spectrum, German surgeon Julius Hackethal screened a videotape that showed him giving cyanide to a 69-year-old woman suffering from terminal cancer. And in his presentation on "Medical Questions in Euthanasia," Colin Brewer, a young English physician, said, "I want to urge upon you the values of the humble plastic bag. People seem to feel it has certain aesthetic objections. But in combination with even a smallish dose of sedative drugs, it does in fact form a very effective method of ending life because it's essentially a belt-and-braces policy."

As Brewer's advice suggests, the emphasis at Hemlock conferences is not on the philosophical but the pragmatic. During coffee breaks members were apt to be discussing the shelf life of certain drugs, the optimal wording of Living Wills, the names of medical textbooks containing tables of lethal dosages, and the ingredients of what some call the "recipe"—what drugs to take for a swift, painless death. Although there was also talk of active, happy lives—it was not uncommon to see people proudly showing photos of their grandchildren or discussing upcoming vacations—each person had come to the conference with a story and the need to tell it.

"I have lymphoma of the bones," said a man in a wheel chair. "I'm forty-four. The average age of the patients in my nursing home is seventy. There are people dealing with me that have no training. People are allowed to be in pain. They are put in positions that are painful, and their pleas for medication are often ignored. I came here because I was thinking of ending my life, and I don't know how to do it."

Despite popular belief to the contrary, suicide is not easy—particularly if one is old, infirm, or terminally ill. Under current laws those without access to lethal drugs are often driven by desperation to more secretive, violent, and lonely deaths. One terminally ill cancer patient, immobilized in a Stryker frame and partially paralyzed, doused his chest with lighter fluid and set himself afire. Even worse, without knowledge of proper dosages and methods, suicide attempts are often bungled, leaving the victim worse off than before. Many intended suicides by gunshot leave the person alive but brain-damaged; drug overdoses that are not fatal may have the same effect. One eighty-three-year-old woman obtained an insufficient number of pills and lost consciousness but did not die; her daughter ended up smothering her with a plastic bag.

"There is only one prospect worse than being chained to an intolerable existence: the nightmare of a botched attempt to end it," observed Arthur Koestler. In 1983, two years after writing these words, the seventy-seven-year-old author, suffering from Parkinson's disease and leukemia, made sure he did not botch it: He took a fatal overdose of barbiturates. His wife of eighteen years, Cynthia, although in good health at the age of fifty-five, decided she could not endure life without him and took an overdose at the same time. Their maid arrived one morning to find a note pinned to the door: "Please do not go upstairs. Ring the police and tell them to come to the house." Police found Koestler sitting in his armchair, his wife on a nearby sofa. On the coffee table in front of them were a glass of whiskey and two wineglasses with a residue of white powder. Koestler's suicide note, written ten months earlier and addressed "To Whom It May Concern," said, among other things, "After a more or less steady physical decline over the last years, the process has now reached an acute state with added complications which make it advisable to seek self-deliverance now, before I become incapable of making the necessary arrangements." In a footnote appended to her husband's farewell, Cynthia concluded, "I cannot live without Arthur, despite certain inner resources."

In an effort to ensure their members a death more like that of Arthur Koestler than that of the cancer patient who set himself on fire, several right-to-die societies have published books or pamphlets that provide instructions on how to take one's own life. Although the groups would prefer that doctors be allowed to supply the information and, if necessary, assist in the death, since that is currently illegal, they believe that people who take the matter into their own hands are in need of some guidance. Those who oppose these so-called suicide manuals—including other right-to-die-groups—fear that the information will be misused by depressed, suicidal people who are not terminally ill and that they communicate a toxic message of despair.

The first manual was announced in 1979 by the Voluntary Euthanasia

Society. After decades of quiet respectability, the British society had been invigorated by a recent influx of younger members, including general secretary Nicholas Reed, a brilliant, energetic Oxford graduate. One of the steps taken under his leadership was to change the society's name to Exit, a name more in tune with its new image. With increased visibility Exit received a growing number of letters and calls from desperate people seeking information on pain-free suicide methods. Under the Suicide Act of 1961, Exit could not advise these people without risk of prosecution for aiding and abetting a suicide. Although many right-to-die advocates were aware that information on lethal dosages had long been available in certain medical textbooks, no one had ever written a book on how to commit suicide. In October 1979, Exit announced plans for a ten-thousand-word *Guide to Self-Deliverance.* Stressing that the booklet was intended only for the terminally ill and not for the depressed, impulsive suicide, Exit said that to avoid possible abuse the booklet would be available only to members of three months' standing. Within several months of this announcement, membership—a matter of three pounds' dues annually, ten for foreigners—jumped from two thousand to nine thousand. But these anxious new members were forced to wait for their manuals. Fearing prosecution, Exit postponed release of the booklet. Meanwhile, in Scotland, where laws against assisted suicide are more lenient, a branch of Exit seceded and published its own guide, *How to Die with Dignity,* in September 1980. It was quickly followed by Hemlock's *Let Me Die Before I Wake.* Since then, manuals have been published in France, the Netherlands, and West Germany.

The guides constitute an intriguing cross-cultural study. Exit's *A Guide to Self-Deliverance,* a thirty-one-page booklet to which Koestler, a vice-president of the society, wrote the introduction, was finally published in June 1981. Like all the manuals it is intended for the terminally ill and not for the merely depressed. "Before considering Self-Deliverance," the book's inside cover cautions, "HAVE YOU RUNG THE SAMARITANS?" It urges the reader to explore alternatives—hospice care, second opinions, pain clinics, other methods of treatment—to make sure the distress is not temporary, and to consider the effect of the death on family and friends. Suicide, it stresses, is not a decision to be taken lightly but a matter to be pondered over a period of months, time permitting. This said, the manual recommends how *not* to commit suicide. It advises against shooting, jumping, wrist cutting ("ineffective as well as very messy"), and hanging, methods that are especially traumatic for friends and relatives and may leave the victim alive and brain-damaged rather than dead. The manual advocates peaceful, nonviolent methods, suggesting that "the body when found should look simply dead and not disgusting."

To achieve this end the guide outlines five bloodless methods, most of which combine drugs with a supplementary method—car exhaust, alcohol, drowning in a bathtub, plastic bags—to ensure lethality. "A combination of sedative drugs and a plastic bag should both shorten the process of dying and minimise unpleasant sensations," advises the manual. Written by a committee of Exit members, including several doctors, the guide is disarmingly matter-of-fact, as when it counsels the reader, "You need two plastic bags approximately three feet (one metre) in length and 18 inches (50 cm) in width. Bags smaller or very much larger than this should not be used. Kitchen bin liners are an obvious possibility." A "postscript" written by psychiatrist Eliot Slater strikes a lone lyrical note: "It is the sovereign right of the individual, absolute and inalienable, to say, 'I have thought well what my duties are to all those who love me, and to all others. I have thought also of the rights I owe to myself. Fate has called to me, and I say to you, Farewell.' "

Dedicated "To the memory of those many millions who lived for a while in agony and eventually died in torment because of cruel laws and the prejudices of bigots," the forty-four-page Scottish manual, *How to Die with Dignity,* is even more pragmatic. "I think that already-distressed people can do without long-winded paragraphs," George Mair, a retired surgeon, chairman of Scottish Exit, and author of the manual, told a reporter. "My book is more like a recipe for scones—you add a pinch of this and half a pinch of that." Mair's "recipe" stresses dignity and courtesy. The book is printed in thirteen-point type for the convenience of readers with failing eyesight, and in a section on "Methods of Self-Deliverance Which Should Not Be Used," the author advises that jumping off a ship is "highly inconvenient for the ship's crew and passengers," while jumping onto a live train rail is "not in any way dignified and is a great offence to witnesses." Those intending to die by dropping an electric cable in their bathtubs are advised to leave behind "a large notice instructing no one to touch 'anything' without first switching off the mains current." Dr. Mair adds, "It is a matter of personal choice as to whether or not some form of bathing suit is worn." The plastic bag, a method (in combination with drugs) advocated by English Exit, is dismissed with the comment, "This is not dignified." Mair outlines the recommended procedure—a lethal dose of barbiturates—in a seventeen-step list of instructions that concludes: "Take soda and spirits and drugs to bedside. Swallow the drugs as rapidly as may be convenient and sip both soda and spirits while doing so." Mair adds that if the place of "deliverance" is a hotel, it is advisable to ask the front desk to hold all calls, to hang the "Do Not Disturb" sign outside the door, and to leave a short letter "to thank the manager and apologise for abusing hospitality."

According to Derek Humphry, the Scottish and English manuals concentrate on technical "how-to" details at the expense of love and sharing. In *Let Me Die Before I Wake,* a one-hundred-page "book of self-deliverance," the specific drug dosages are buried within the stories of seven terminally ill people who committed suicide. This, Humphry believes, forces a person to read the book and partake of Hemlock's message of nonviolence, advance planning, and sharing. It also lessens the likelihood of legal problems. "We feel that the difficulties of decision-making, the timing of one's death, sharing the decision with one's family, and coping with the myriad of emotions during this time need to be explored, and wherever possible, solved," Humphry wrote in the *Hemlock Quarterly.* "These issues are, in our view, even more complex and difficult than the practical matter of how to actually practice self-deliverance when in an advanced state of terminal or incurable illness." Like the other manuals, *Let Me Die* is addressed to terminally ill people. Those contemplating suicide for other reasons are urged to speak to their family, friends, physician, counselor, minister, or suicide prevention center.

In April 1982, nine months after *Let Me Die* was published, another "how-to" guide appeared that made the manuals of the right-to-die societies seem relatively innocuous. *Suicide, Mode d'Emploi* ("Suicide: Operating Instructions"), the work of two young Parisian journalists, proposes suicide as a revolutionary act—not merely for the terminally ill but for anyone and everyone. The book contains a section listing fifty recipes for "cocktails" that will ensure a "gentle" death, giving precise lethal dosages and advice on how to forge prescriptions. Within five months of its publication *Suicide* sold fifty thousand copies. It had also been linked to ten suicides—none of them terminally ill, most of them young and unemployed. "I feel no remorse," said Alain Moreau, the book's publisher. "This is a book that pleads for life. But it also recognizes that the right to suicide is an inalienable right, like the right to work, the right to like certain things, the right to publish. What use is a right without the means to execute it?"

Suicide, Mode d'Emploi provoked the outrage of French psychiatrists, clergy, politicians, suicide prevention agencies, and the Association pour le Droit de Mourir dans la Dignité (a French right-to-die society). Although efforts to ban the book failed, a number of bookstores declined to stock it, and several newspapers, magazines, and radio stations refused to carry advertisements. By 1987 the book had sold almost two hundred thousand copies in France, had been translated into seven languages, had been the subject of eighty criminal complaints and four court cases, and had served as a blueprint for at least fifteen suicides. In one case a depressed, unemployed young woman from Nice killed her eight-year-old son, then killed herself. An annotated copy of *Suicide* was found on her bedroom table.

Though right-to-die societies around the world denounced the book, pointing out that *Suicide* had been aimed not at terminally ill people but at everyone, even some of the more responsible manuals have encountered difficulties. Among the more than twenty suicides linked to England's *Guide to Self-Deliverance* was a physically healthy twenty-two-year-old music student with a history of psychological problems who was found dead in a London hotel with the book at his bedside table. Although the pamphlet was ostensibly available only to members over the age of twenty-five, the boy had simply lied about his birth date. In 1983, *Guide* was withdrawn.

By that time Exit had run into even more serious trouble. In 1980, following the suicide of an elderly Exit member, police raided Exit's cramped basement offices in Kensington and arrested general secretary Nicholas Reed. Soon afterward sixty-eight-year-old Mark Lyons was also arrested; both were charged with various counts of aiding and abetting suicide. Over the following months an extraordinary and unsettling story emerged in court. Moved by heartrending calls from dying people who begged for help, Reed, without the knowledge of anyone else at Exit, had dispatched Lyons to their homes. Lyons, a bearded, shabbily dressed retired taxi driver, worked as an Exit volunteer. Carrying a bag containing brandy, barbiturates, and plastic bags, and pretending to be a doctor, he supplied his "patients" with the means for suicide, then sat with them while they died.

Most of the victims were tragic cases: a woman suffering from terminal cancer who had only a short time to live; a multiple sclerosis patient; a victim of spinal osteoarthritis; a man who had been an invalid for three years and who for the last six months had worn an oxygen mask twenty-four hours a day. In each case the victim had repeatedly begged to die. But Reed and Lyons had intervened in less extreme situations. In one, Lyons helped a physically healthy middle-aged agoraphobic to die. In another, a twenty-five-year-old ex-Army man told the court that he suffered from depression, drank heavily, and had attempted suicide several times. He had called Exit, met with Reed, and described his miseries. Reed notified Lyons. When Lyons telephoned and demanded thirty pounds for traveling expenses, the man grew suspicious and dropped the matter. And a bedridden woman suffering from severe spinal injuries testified that Lyons was "furious" when she changed her mind about wanting to die. She said that Lyons told her, "You are the only person to disobey me."

After a two-week trial Lyons was found guilty of five charges of aiding and abetting suicide, and one of conspiring to aid and abet suicide. Taking into consideration the 325 days Lyons spent in jail awaiting trial, the judge gave him a two-year suspended sentence and the admonition, "No more meddling with pills and plastic bags." Reed, found guilty of two charges of aiding and abetting suicide and one of conspiring to aid and abet, was sentenced to two and a half years (later reduced on appeal to eighteen months). As he was led from the dock of London's Old Bailey Criminal Court to begin his sentence, Reed shouted, "That shows the idiocy of the present law!"

The image of the erudite Reed and the eccentric Lyons with his "suicide kit" taking matters into their own hands was chilling. Although a few of the most radical right-to-die advocates maintained that the ends justified such means, the majority of euthanasia groups were appalled. Asked to comment on Reed's conviction, Exit chairman Barbara Smoker replied, "His compassion got the better of his discretion." Exit, which knew nothing of Reed's and Lyons's extracurricular activities until their arrest, was dubbed a "suicide club" by the tabloids, and its credibility was severely tarnished. Exit subsequently expelled Reed, changed its name back to the Voluntary Euthanasia Society, and assumed a decidedly lower profile for the next several years.

The Reed-Lyons affair was a cautionary lesson for the right-to-die movement. Thus far, Hemlock has managed to avoid such legal troubles, despite its growing visibility. In its tenth printing, *Let Me Die Before I Wake,* described by "60 Minutes" as "the bible of the euthanasia movement," has sold one hundred thirty thousand copies. Doctors and hospice administrators call Hemlock to request copies for patients who ask about euthanasia, and the book is a popular item at libraries. "Los Angeles City Library tells me it's their most stolen book," says Humphry proudly. "Now they keep it under lock and key."

When *Let Me Die* was first published in 1981, its sale was limited to Hemlock members of three months' standing. In 1982, spurred by appeals from people who said they needed the book immediately and knowing there had been no evidence of misuse, Hemlock decided to make the book available to the public in stores and libraries. "The biggest complaint about the book comes from little old ladies who don't want to dig through all the words to find the information," says Humphry. "They skim the book and say, 'It's too difficult—all I want is the little pill.' I tell them there is no such thing as The Pill. I tell them to read the book again, take notes, underline the important bits. Or I'll say, 'Page 60 is what you want.' I don't say what's on the page, I just say read page 60." Prodded by such complaints, Hemlock finally printed a brief, easily understandable toxicity chart in the *Hemlock Quarterly* with lethal dosages listed for seventeen drugs. "Only for the information of terminally ill, mature adults," it warns. "Keep this document in a secure, private place."

Humphry guards against criticism by operating as openly as possible without compromising confidentiality. "We're not ashamed," he says. "If we're doing anything wrong, we're doing wrong openly." When one woman asked him to send the book in a plain brown wrapper, Humphry refused. He is also aware of the risks. "A young man twenty-seven years old asked us to send him all of our books, and so we did. A week later he called and said he hadn't received them yet. The next day his mother called. She was furious. 'You sold my son books on how to kill himself,' she yelled. 'He's an alcoholic, he has problems.' I asked if she had known that her son was suicidal. She said no, and I said, 'Well, perhaps we've done you a favor.' And in the end she calmed down.' " Humphry, who never found out what happened to the young man, is well aware, however, that Hemlock walks a fine line. "If our book ever fell into the hands of a suicidal person (and we ask our members to cooperate in seeing that it does not) and this was the information which someone used to end his or her existence, we would of course regret it," Humphry wrote in the *Hemlock Quarterly.* "But we feel it important not to be deterred from heeding the genuine cry for help from that bona fide minority that is facing death and is therefore interested in the option of voluntary euthanasia."

Despite increased accessibility, thus far there has been no evidence of the book or list being used by emotionally disturbed, depressed people who are not terminally ill. There is no way of knowing exactly how many people have used *Let Me Die* for its intended purpose although Humphry estimates the number to be many hundreds. He has received numerous letters of thanks from survivors of those who have taken their lives with the aid of the book. In March 1986 an elderly Miami couple was found dead with a "well-thumbed" copy of the book beside them. The man, a doctor, suffered from leukemia. His wife, a retired psychiatrist, was not known to be in ill health. Police said the suicide was well planned; the couple had made their final dispositions and left a suicide note. In another instance an elderly Florida gentleman with a brain tumor ended his life after several months of keeping the book under his pillow.

III

"The Limits Are Obscure . . . and Every Errour Deadly"

Derek Humphry killed his wife;
Now he wants your granny's life.
If your granny's old don't keep her;
They say euthanasia's cheaper.
Hemlock Society you can't hide,
We still hang Nazis for genocide.
Euthanasia is a crime.
At least it was in Hitler's time.
Take 'em to Nuremberg and hang 'em high.
There's no such thing as the right to die.

AS HEMLOCK'S Second National Voluntary Euthanasia Conference continued in the Miramar Sheraton in Santa Monica, California, a dozen chanting protesters marched in a tight circle at the entrance to the hotel driveway. They carried placards that read, "This hotel loves Nazis" and "Pull the Plug on the Hemlock Society," and passed out leaflets urging passers-by to help halt the "international celebrations of Hemlock's death cult." On the sidewalk a folding table was adorned with a plastic milk bottle marked "Jonestown Kool-Aid." To guests entering the hotel the protesters shouted, "Don't go in—the water is laced with cyanide." Occasionally, a protester called out a new rhyming couplet; the others hooted with delight, then took up the chant. One man faked a German accent, drawing laughter from the others.

The protesters were members of the Club of Life, a radical right-wing organization under the aegis of Lyndon LaRouche. Over the years they have staged numerous demonstrations against Hemlock. On the first morning of the conference in Santa Monica, as Hemlock members settled back into their seats at the end of a coffee break for a panel discussion of "Ethical Dilemmas in Euthanasia," a young man walked up to the podium and announced, "I'm here to indict Derek Humphry and Gerald Larue for murder." There was a moment of stunned silence before Humphry and Larue wrested the microphone from the man and escorted him gently but firmly from the podium. At that moment a dozen other Club of Life members who had sneaked in during the coffee break to sit in the back of the room began to chant, "Let him speak! Let him speak!"

It was a curious scene: the protesters, mostly young, well-scrubbed, clean-cut men and women, chanting stolidly, staring straight ahead, while an angry flock of neatly dressed gray-haired women circled around them, half-shouting, half-pleading, "Get out, get out." "Did you pay?" an elderly lady in a red sweater asked one of the protesters, who ignored her. The elderly lady began to beg, "Please let us have our conference." A young woman in a raincoat the color of a robin's egg, her face pinched with passion, whirled around and shouted, "Why don't you commit voluntary euthanasia? It's what you're all about!" It soon became a rhetorical free-for-all, the demonstrators hurling slogans, Hemlock members trying to reason with them. "Never again!" shouted a balding young man with glasses at a white-haired woman who implored, "Please leave. Just please leave." Some Hemlock members wept in frustration because the protesters refused to budge or even to discuss their beliefs. A middle-aged man with a trim brown beard tried to talk quietly to a young man about the dignity of choice, but the young man refused to meet his gaze. "You're killing your grandmother," he suddenly shouted at the bearded man, who replied earnestly, "I *love* my grandmother." Meanwhile, reporters waded into the crowd to ask the protesters sensible questions about their philosophical beliefs. ("We're against euthanasia and genocide" was their standard response.) Hotel security men finally escorted the protesters out, still shouting, leaving behind a ring of dazed, angry, elderly people.

Whether a suicide is committed by an elderly person in failing health or by a terminally ill person with or without assistance, a wealth of passionate arguments condemn the act. Christian fundamentalists say that suicide is a sin, a violation, as Augustine maintained, of the Sixth Commandment, "Thou shalt not kill." Right-to-die advocates point out that exceptions have been made for self-defense and capital punishment and that the Church itself has often supported killing in battle. John Donne wondered "whether it was logical to conscript a young man and subject him to risk of torture and mutilation in war and probable death, and refuse an old man escape from an agonizing end." According to Albert Schweitzer, even Mahatma Gandhi, who literally wouldn't hurt a flea, saw fit to go beyond the law against killing. Moved by the prolonged agony of a dying calf, Gandhi gave it poison to end its suffering. (His act is doubly significant because cows are held in special veneration by the Hindu religion.) Ethicist Joseph Fletcher, who told the story in *Morals and Medicine,* commented, "It seems unimaginable that either Schweitzer or Gandhi would deny to a human being what they would render, with however heavy a heart, to a calf."

Right-to-die advocates also contend that suicide is not murder because one's body belongs to oneself. "Their argument turns on the proposition that since my life is my own, I can take it without committing murder in the same way that I can take my own money without being a thief," wrote the Russian émigré philosopher Nicholas Berdyaev in his 1962 "Essay on Suicide." "But this argument is false and superficial. My life is not solely my own, it does not belong to me absolutely, it belongs to God first. He is the absolute owner; my life also belongs to my friends, to my family, to society, and finally to the entire world which has need of me."

Berdyaev has summarized what some ethicists call the "property" arguments. Those who believe we are God's property insist that in performing suicide or euthanasia we are "playing God." Right-to-die advocates argue that if shortening our lives interferes with God's will, so too does lengthening them with life-support equipment. "If it is for God alone to decide when we shall live and when we shall die," wrote philosopher James Rachels, paraphrasing David Hume, "then we 'play God' just as much when we cure people as when we kill them." As one elderly woman says, "When I can't digest my food, when I can't breathe on my own, when my heart can't beat on its own, it could just be that God is trying to tell me something."

In response to those who, like Aristotle, hold that our lives belong to society as a whole, right-to-die advocates question how useful to the state a terminally ill person can be. "Human life consists in mutual service," wrote the author and socialist Charlotte Perkins Gilman in her 1935 suicide note. "No grief, no pain, no misfortune or 'broken heart' is excuse for cutting off one's life while any power of service remains. But when all usefulness is over, when one is assured of an imminent and unavoidable death, it is the simplest of human rights to choose a quick and easy death in place of a slow and horrible one." Gilman worked in the labor and women's suffrage movements until the age of seventy-five when, suffering from cancer, she ended her life. Even her death was intended as an act of public service. "The time is approaching when we shall consider it abhorrent to our civilization to allow a human being to lie in prolonged agony which we should mercifully end in any other creature," she wrote. "Believing this choice to be of social service in promoting wider views on this question, I have preferred chloroform to cancer." The following morning the headline in *The New York Times* read, "Charlotte Gilman Dies to Avoid Pain."

Many antisuicide authors have argued that to shorten or avoid suffering is cowardly. In 1642, Sir Thomas Browne observed, "When life is more terrible than death, it is the truest valor to live." According to Christian teaching there is intrinsic value in suffering—especially during the last moments of life—because in doing so one emulates the suffering of Christ on the cross. Terminal illness is thus an opportunity for spiritual enrichment. "The final stage of an incurable illness can be a wasteland, but it need not be," wrote British lawyer Norman St. John-Stevas, a longtime foe of euthanasia. "It can be a vital period in a person's life, reconciling him to life and to death and giving him an interior peace." Fletcher, however, pointed out that if suffering were truly ennobling, we would be bound to withhold *all* anesthetics and medical relief. While some may find the last stages of terminal illness spiritually rewarding, ethicists question whether it is a person's duty to stay alive because others insist that pain is good for him.

Many maintain that to choose death is wrong because a cure might be "just around the corner." While there is life, they say, there's hope. Responding to this argument, Seneca wrote, "Even if this is true, life is not to be bought at all costs." With the biomedical advances of the twentieth century, however, the odds of that hope being rewarded have improved. In 1921, physician George R. Minot was told that he had severe diabetes, for which there was no cure. For two years Minot fought a losing battle against the disease. In 1923 insulin was discovered, and he was saved. Eleven years later Minot won the 1934 Nobel Prize for Medicine for research that led to a cure for pernicious anemia. And there are numerous instances in which apparently "hopeless" cases have recovered. In the spring of 1986, for instance, a forty-four-year-old Maryland woman suffered a cerebral hemorrhage and fell into what doctors called "a persistent vegetative state." She had often told her husband that if she ever became comatose, she wanted him to pull the plug. After forty-one days her husband, a Presbyterian minister, went to court to stop treatment. The judge refused. Six days later the woman woke up, smiled, and kissed her husband. Three months later she was able to walk with the help of a walker, and her memory was returning. "Miracles can and do occur," said her husband. "I guess we've muddied the waters surrounding the question of a person's right to die."

One of the main justifications for suicide prevention among the young is that their problems are usually temporary and their judgment of them often skewed by depression. For the older person considering suicide, however, depression may be temporary, but loss of movement, vision, hearing, of friends and career is often irreversible. In 1919, German psychiatrist Alfred Hoche introduced the notion of *Bilanz-Selbstmord,* or balance-sheet suicide. He suggested that it was possible for clear-thinking, competent individuals to weigh the pros and cons of living and to decide in favor of death. More recently, philosopher Richard Brandt compared the choice of rational suicide to the decision of a firm's board of directors to declare bankruptcy.

But at the 1983 annual conference of the American Association of Suicidology, during a panel discussion of suicide manuals, a Minnesota counselor and stepmother of a girl who killed herself stood up. "Rational suicide is a contradiction in terms," she said. "I don't care how paternalistic it is, I think suicide ought to be against the law for everyone. I think life is all there is." The woman was expressing a common belief that suicide, even in terminal illness, is *per se* irrational. "There's a tendency in the medical profession to think that anyone who doesn't want to prolong life even a tiny bit longer must be incompetent and therefore cannot refuse treatment," says Curt Garbesi, Hemlock's legal counsel. Some believe that terminal illness itself makes people irrational; as one doctor was heard to comment in bioethics rounds, "No dying patient is sane." On the other hand, some right-to-die advocates believe that when faced with terminal illness, people see things more clearly.

Right-to-die groups often hold up Greek heroes or terminally ill patients as examples when arguing their case. Prevention experts usually cite the depressed, impulsive teenage suicide when rejecting the right to die. The majority of suicides, however, lie somewhere between these extremes. "Some writers opposed to suicide in general would have us believe that all euthanetic suicides are . . . acts of cowardice and fear," philosopher Margaret Pabst Battin has written. "I think this is false, but I think it is equally wrong to assume that all suicide in the face of terminal illness is a rational, composed, self-dignifying affirmation of one's own highest life-ideal."

More accurately, they are two different groups with some overlap. Older people are also capable of impulsiveness and flawed judgment: Many so-called right-to-die cases are complicated by depression, anger, and hostility. One recent study held that those who prefer suicide tend to be not only elderly and terminally ill, but also depressed. Some psychiatrists suggest that some so-called rational suicides may be death-oriented people waiting for an excuse to take their lives. Lending credence to this notion is a study which found that more people take their own lives because they wrongly believe themselves to be suffering from cancer than do those who actually have cancer. In fact, the suicide rate among terminally ill cancer patients is low: "They tend to cling to what life they have left," says psychologist Calvin Frederick. Certainly a plea for "rational suicide" cannot always be taken at face value. In one of the few articles on the subject, David Jackson and Stuart Youngner described six cases in which right-to-die issues masked feelings of depression and abandonment.

Mental health professionals point out that motives in mercy killings are often mixed—showing "mercy" as much for the killer, who may find caring for an incapacitated person an oppressive responsibility, as for the victim—and that suicide pacts are rarely as mutual as they seem. A study of uncompleted suicide pacts found that one partner—apt to be the male—is usually the aggressor, conceiving the idea and then pressuring the other to go along. After the double suicide of Arthur and Cynthia Koestler, several writers pointed out that the eerie decorousness of the death scene camouflaged a more complex psychological scenario. They suggested that Cynthia had been emotionally coerced into joining her husband in death. ("I'm going to kill myself, aren't we?" is how Edwin Shneidman mocked Koestler's message.) Cynthia had been dominated by Koestler since the beginning of their relationship, when she was a shy young secretary and he a famous author twice her age. She called herself his "slavey." "She was his appendix," wrote a Koestler friend. "That was her role in life. She was content with that role." Her suicide was an obvious and perhaps inevitable extension of their thirty-three-year relationship. "It is hardly an exaggeration to say that his life became hers, that she *lived* his life," wrote Harold Harris, editor of *Stranger on the Square,* the Koestlers' joint autobiography. "And when the time came for him to leave it, her life too was at an end."

Many mental health professionals and suicide prevention experts are sympathetic to the idea of suicide in the face of terminal illness on an individual basis—especially for themselves—but refuse to condone right-to-die groups and legislative changes for fear that they will invite abuse and encourage people to minimize the importance of life. "From an intellectual standpoint I can appreciate the importance of liberty and freedom in a truly democratic society," writes Richard Seiden. "On a deeper emotional level . . . I wonder whether the advocacy of suicidal deliverance does not act as an end of hope for those depressed persons fighting a psychological battle of life and death, a struggle to be or not to be." At Hemlock conferences each member has a compelling personal story that seems to clinch the case for legalized voluntary euthanasia, yet many seem unaware that the changes they propose have implications beyond their own circumstances. They are, in fact, seeking to change sanctions that have existed for four thousand years. "You are pioneers in the modern advocacy of suicide," Joseph Piccione, a policy analyst at The Child and Family Protection Institute, reminded his audience at Hemlock's 1986 national conference. "You are sociologically important. And I ask you to consider the risks in the possible and unintended outcomes of your work. Suicide is one of the last taboos. Will the destruction of that taboo open it up to other persons who are not terminally ill but are liable to persuasion? I feel that it is the maintenance of the taboo that may be one way to protect them."

In *Biathanatos,* John Donne argued in defense of voluntary euthanasia as a form of suicide. Nevertheless, he refrained from proposing guidelines or laws because "the limits are obscure, and steepy, and slippery, and narrow, and every errour deadly." Donne was articulating an argument known as the "slippery slope," which cautions against taking a certain action—even if the act is morally permissible in itself—for fear that it will lead to other actions that are impermissible. (This argument is also called the "thin edge of the wedge," the "domino" theory, or, more colorfully, the "camel's nose under the tent.") Opponents of euthanasia believe that to permit any instance of euthanasia will inevitably lead us down a slippery slope of abuse, at the bottom of which lies Nazi-style mass murder. In his oft-quoted 1949 essay, "Medical Science Under Dictatorship," psychiatrist Leo Alexander, an American consultant at the Nuremberg trials, traced Nazi atrocities committed under the banner of "euthanasia" on the rapid journey down that slope. It started with a campaign to promote a utilitarian attitude toward the chronically ill. Propaganda included films such as *I Accuse,* in which a woman suffering from multiple sclerosis was killed by her doctor husband "to the accompaniment of soft piano music rendered by a sympathetic colleague in an adjoining room." A popular high school mathematics textbook included problems detailing the cost of caring for the disabled and chronically ill. One question asked students to calculate how many housing units could be built and how many loans could be made to newlyweds with the amount of money spent by the state on "the crippled, the criminal and the insane." Alexander wrote:

> The beginnings at first were merely a subtle shift in emphasis in the basic attitude of the physicians. It started with the acceptance of the attitude, basic in the euthanasia movement, that there is such a thing as life not worthy to be lived. This attitude in its early stages concerned itself merely with the severely and chronically sick. Gradually the sphere of those to be included in this category was enlarged to encompass the socially unproductive, the ideologically unwanted, the racially unwanted and finally all non-Germans. But it is important to realize that the infinitely small wedged-in lever from which this entire trend of mind received its impetus was the attitude toward the non-rehabilitable sick.

Although few suggest that right-to-die advocates have a hidden agenda of Nazi-style euthanasia, for many people the specter of the Third Reich is sufficient to justify opposing any change. They point to recent polls and court decisions in favor of active and passive euthanasia as the preliminary signs of a slide down the slippery slope. "I think there is no way in which the right to die isn't going to very soon become the duty to die," warned Dame Cicely Saunders, founder of the hospice movement, in a discussion of right-to-die

groups on "60 Minutes." "If you had an illness which made you fairly dependent upon other people, and somebody gave you the possibility to have a quick
way out, would you really feel you could go on asking for that care? Human
nature being what it is, euthanasia wouldn't be voluntary for very long." In
The Right to Live, the Right to Die, former surgeon-general C. Everett Koop
warned that acceptance of euthanasia will invite deception and abuse; people
will use it as a loophole to hasten the death of burdensome elderly relatives
or to get at a legacy more quickly. "Once any group of human beings is
considered fair game in the arena of the right to life," wrote Koop, "where does
it stop?" Yale Kamisar, a professor of law at the University of Michigan,
opposes changes in the law because the benefit to a few might be outweighed
by the danger to many. "Miss Voluntary Euthanasia is not likely to be going
it alone for very long," he has written. "Many of her admirers . . . would be
neither surprised nor distressed to see her joined by Miss Euthanatize the
Congenital Idiots and Miss Euthanatize the Permanently Insane and Miss
Euthanatize the Senile Dementia." The German physician Auer has said, "I
have seen the true wish for death among my patients. . . . One must be able
to say to them, 'I have listened—but the consequences for humanity are such
that though I could open the door and let you out, others may then be thrown
out.' "

Derek Humphry admits that the slippery slope hypothesis is the strongest
argument against euthanasia. He insists, however, that safeguards protecting
against abuse can be written into legislation. "What happened in Nazi Germany was a lesson to mankind, but that was in a brutal, murderous dictatorship, whereas we live in a democracy under the rule of law," he says. "I believe
we can design laws that draw the line at mature, competent terminally ill
people." In any case Humphry maintains that the possibility of abuse is not
sufficient reason to abridge the rights of suffering individuals. "Where is the
sense . . . in telling a person dying of throat cancer that euthanasia cannot be
made available because Nazi Germany murdered thousands of people in the
1940s using a method labeled 'euthanasia'?" he asks in *The Right to Die.* "The
lessons of history are there to be learned, and the Nazi experience has taught
society how not to let government slip into the hands of an irresponsible
minority."

Despite Humphry's confidence in our ability to avoid the slippery slope, one
doesn't have to look far for slippage. Nicholas Reed and Mark Lyons are not
the only members of right-to-die societies to have taken the law into their own
hands. In 1981, the head of Holland's Society for Voluntary Euthanasia admitted supplying the means for suicide to six terminally ill people. And in 1986,
the secretary of the Voluntary Euthanasia Society in Auckland, New Zealand,
was acquitted on charges of counselling and inciting a sixty-four-year-old
woman to commit suicide, although she did not take her life. Hemlock itself
has undergone a rapid evolution in its attitude toward divulging information

on lethal drugs, from restricting the purchase of *Let Me Die Before I Wake* to members, to making it available to the public, to printing up a handy one-page list of lethal dosages.

Historically, right-to-die groups have attracted members with a variety of agendas. When the Euthanasia Society of America was born in 1938, its first president, the Reverend Charles Francis Potter, said that members "subscribed to the belief that, with adequate safeguards, it should be made legal to allow incurable sufferers to choose immediate death rather than await it in agony." In its early years, however, the society reflected a range of more radical beliefs. Its second president, Dr. Foster Kennedy, advocated the legalization of euthanasia for "creatures born defective, whose present condition is miserable and whose future . . . hopeless." Another supporter, Dr. Alexis Carrel, went still further: "Sentimental prejudice should not obstruct the quiet and painless disposition of incurables, criminals, and hopeless lunatics." The society settled down to a more moderate philosophy, eventually evolving into two groups, Concern for Dying and the Society for the Right to Die, both of which limit their agendas to passive euthanasia.

Although contemporary right-to-die societies insist that their focus is limited to the terminally ill, there has been no shortage of similarly unsettling statements by movement activists. Testifying in favor of a euthanasia bill in the Florida State Legislature, Walter Sackett, a physician who claimed he had assisted "hundreds" of patients to their deaths, pointed out that the state could save $5 billion over the next fifty years if "mongoloids" were permitted to succumb to the pneumonia they frequently contract. Psychiatrist Eliot Slater of the Voluntary Euthanasia Society has argued that the right to voluntary euthanasia should extend to the incurably mentally ill: "If a chronically sick man dies, he ceases to be a burden on himself, on his family, on the health services and on the community." Lawyer Mary Rose Barrington, a past chairman of the same society, is concerned that if people don't have the option of suicide, "there can be no possibility of an older person, who is a burden to a younger person, feeling a sense of obligation to release the captive attendant from willing or unwilling bondage." At the 1986 Hemlock conference an elderly woman asked, "With 20 million elderly Americans, shouldn't the Hemlock Society take more liberal action for the elderly nonterminally ill who have lost their zest for life? Shouldn't they at least get physicians to give some nonlethal dosages that the elderly can accumulate and use to end this life?"

The woman was raising the issue around which the "popularization" of suicide is most vulnerable: economics. In primitive tribes elderly suicide has often been accepted, even encouraged, when a person outlived his or her usefulness to the tribe or during times of extreme hardship and food shortage. The ancient Scythians, for instance, considered it an honor to take their own lives when they became too feeble to keep up with the nomadic life-style, saving the tribe the guilt and trouble of killing them. Sociologists call this "economic suicide" or "thrift suicide." Such deaths, however, were often a blend of suicide and murder, in which the elderly had to make a choice between killing themselves or being killed. Of the Massagetae, Herodotus observed, "They have one way only of determining the appropriate time to die, namely this: when a man is very old, all his relatives give a party and include him in a general sacrifice of cattle; then they boil the flesh and eat it. This they consider to be the best sort of death." The Tschuktschi of northern Siberia designated a relative or friend to strangle or stab an old man whose usefulness was over (elderly women remained valuable as midwives or menials); the nomadic Kalmuck Tartars abandoned their sick and lame with provisions in small huts on the banks of rivers; aged Hottentots were served lavish feasts before being abandoned in the wilderness; feeble Ethiopians allowed themselves to be tied to wild bulls and trampled to death; the Congolese jumped up and down on their elderly until they were dead; the Amboyna ate their failing relatives. Until recently in many Eskimo tribes, in times of famine and hardship, the elderly might walk off and freeze to death, hang themselves, or allow themselves to be walled up in an igloo and abandoned.

Such suicides, a sort of self-regulating mechanism for tribal survival in which the population was kept within the limits of the food supply, were often misunderstood by Westerners. The perhaps apocryphal story is told of some missionaries among an Eskimo tribe who discovered this practice and condemned it harshly as a sin against God. The Eskimos were impressed by this argument, and the missionaries departed, promising to come back in a few years to see whether their potential converts were keeping the faith. When they returned, there were no Eskimos left. The obedient tribe had died out, gradually killed off by the imbalance of too many people and too little food.

Some ethicists and demographers believe that the ingredients for such a scenario will soon exist in the United States. And although they do not suggest that we abandon our elderly in igloos, tie them to bulls, or jump up and down on them, they have suggested that they may have a similar "duty" to move on. In 1984, Colorado governor Richard Lamm, referring to the financial and ethical implications of this country's growing medical technology, said, "Like leaves which fall off a tree, forming the humus in which other plants can grow, we've got a duty to die and get out of the way with all of our machines and artificial hearts, so that our kids can build a reasonable life."

Lamm's comment, delivered to a meeting of Colorado health lawyers, triggered an uproar. ("Aged Are Told to Drop Dead," screamed the headline in the New York *Daily News.*) Many people were outraged, some called for Lamm's resignation, and one sixty-eight-year-old lobbyist who represents elderly interests likened the forty-eight-year-old Lamm to Hitler. Of the nearly three thousand letters Lamm received, however, the majority praised him for confronting the issue. Meanwhile, Lamm sought to clarify his remarks. "The time is not far off when there will be a direct conflict between the health of the individual and the health of the society," he wrote in *The New Republic.* "We cannot afford all the medical miracles that the profession stands ready to give, and choices will have to be made about the distribution of limited medical resources. Technological immortality is running into fiscal reality."

Financial considerations are undeniably a factor in many right-to-die decisions. "I don't want to be a burden on my children or my spouse" and "Please don't let my life savings be spent on keeping me alive for a few extra weeks" are common refrains among ailing elderly. The high cost of health care affects not only the individual, as Lamm pointed out, but the entire country. In 1985, 28 percent of America's $75 billion Medicare budget was spent on maintaining people over sixty-five during their last year of life. Eight percent was spent on their last thirty days. Today, one-third of the nation's total health costs are spent on the elderly. By 2020, when the baby boomers reach retirement age, an estimated 17 percent of Americans will be sixty-five or older, and many economic forecasters fear that we'll go broke. (Projections show that Medicare may be insolvent by the late 1990s.) If scientists continue to find cures for diseases, the financial strain will be even worse. A Washington research group estimates that it would have cost the federal government an extra $15 billion if Americans who died prematurely of heart disease in 1978 had lived to their full life expectancy. "The postponement of an individual's death is becoming a Federal affair," concluded the report, "and one whose implications we cannot ignore."

A growing number of economic analysts believe that the rationing of health care is inevitable. In Britain it is rare for people over fifty-five with kidney disease to be given dialysis, while patients over seventy are seldom admitted to intensive care. Although rationing may seem unthinkable in a nation accustomed to the idea that its citizens are entitled to unlimited medical resources, nearly half of all Americans believe that dialysis and chemotherapy should be rationed at the discretion of a board of doctors and the patient's physician. In his book *Setting Limits,* Daniel Callahan, director of the Hastings Center, a think tank for biomedical ethics, outlined the coming health care crisis and suggested a long-term strategy. His recommendations included restricted Medicare payments for such procedures as organ transplants, kidney dialysis, and coronary bypasses for the aged, and limited use of feeding tubes and costly antibiotics by the elderly. Although he firmly opposes active euthanasia, Callahan believes the elderly should be "creatively and honorably accepting aging and death, not struggling to overcome them," and suggests that Americans learn to accept a "natural life-span" that might last until the late seventies or early eighties. "How many years do we need to have a reasonably decent life, to raise a family, to work, to love?"

Some say that rationing already exists on an unofficial basis. "Any sophisticated doctor would acknowledge privately that rationing on demographic characteristics when resources are tight goes on already," Robert Binstock, a Brandeis University gerontologist, told the *Los Angeles Times*. This informal rationing can be found in any big city hospital emergency room, said Binstock, "where you have to make a choice of treating a . . . baby or . . . old man and you have only so many people and so much equipment." With increasing pressure on hospitals to control costs, such triage, he warned, could become official policy. Studies show that emergency room personnel tend to devote less time and effort to resuscitating elderly heart attack victims than they do to younger ones, and that older women with breast cancer often get less treatment than they need because of their age. According to one study, Diagnostic Related Group (DRG), the Medicare payment system in which hospitals are reimbursed a set amount for each specific ailment regardless of its severity, has led hospitals to discharge elderly patients "sicker and quicker" than younger patients. The American Association of Retired Persons has received hundreds of letters from older people who claim they were discharged from hospitals prematurely.

While acknowledging the importance of the economic issue, Derek Humphry doesn't want the right-to-die movement supported for the wrong reasons. "This is a very rich country, and it ought to be able to provide proper medical care for everybody," he says. "It would be deeply repugnant to us to say that people need to take their lives because there isn't enough money to take care of them. I would fight that tooth and nail." He shakes his head. "Voluntary euthanasia is an intimate, personal, libertarian decision." Nevertheless, a few rank and file right-to-die advocates believe that the ends justify the means. "I believe in triage," says a Hemlock member in his sixties. "It's a question of national priorities. Since there's not enough money to accommodate everyone's needs, I don't think the public has an obligation to keep me alive once I start becoming a drain on society." In *Common-Sense Suicide*, Doris Portwood concluded a discussion of costs, "Today, the needs of the individual and those of the social community appear to merge, in an economic sense, on the question of old-age suicide. A planned departure that serves oneself, one's family and also the state surely is worthy of decent consideration. . . . There are going to be more than thirty million American senior citizens by the year 2000. More than two million of them will be in nursing homes— perhaps double the current number. Those who have the will to opt out may not (yet) get a public vote of thanks. But who can dare say that they will be missed?"

Such comments are deeply troubling. The right to comprehensive medical treatment must be as fiercely protected as the right to refuse that treatment. Some people suggest that if we spent as much money and energy on giving the elderly reasons to stay alive as we do on developing technology to *keep* them alive, the euthanasia option might be less appealing. (The high cost of technology is one of the main factors cited by health care analysts for the decline in health care funds for the elderly.) Others propose that the energy spent on figuring out how to help elderly, terminally ill people to an easier death might be better spent helping them to a better life. Says psychologist Richard Seiden, "It is realistic to be concerned that sanctioning suicide or self-deliverance may deter society and government from making the difficult and expensive structural changes necessary to improve the life of the sick and elderly." At Hemlock's 1985 conference, in a panel discussion of "Medical Questions in Euthanasia," oncologist Matthew Conolly concluded an eloquent attack on active euthanasia by saying, "My plea to the Hemlock Society is give up this goal of self-destruction. Instead, lend us your energy, your anger, your indignation, and your creativity to work with us to build up such a system of hospice care that death, however it comes, need not be feared. Is this not a nobler cause? And is this not a better way?"

In many cultures—including most of those that encourage "thrift" suicide—the wisdom and experience of the elderly earn them respect and veneration. In America, although we strive at all costs to keep them alive, the elderly are more likely to face indifference, impatience, or scorn. "At best, the living old are treated as if they were already half dead," wrote Robert Butler in his Pulitzer Prize–winning book *Why Survive? Being Old in America.* "Many elders suffer a social death in which they are removed from the mainstream of life," observed sociologists Jack Levin and Arnold Arluke. "They are forced by law or custom to retire, give up leadership positions in their communities and become virtual prisoners in their own homes for fear of muggers and other criminals. Increasing numbers of elders are living in age-segregated housing or nursing homes where many are drugged into dependent states." Within a month after being robbed and assaulted in their Bronx apartment, one couple in their late seventies slashed their wrists and hanged themselves from their bedroom door. In a note they explained that they had lived in the neighborhood for many years and didn't want to move, but "we don't want to live in fear anymore."

Although suicide among adolescents has received an enormous amount of attention over the past decade, the suicide rate of elderly Americans (over sixty-five) is nearly twice as high as that of adolescents. In fact, the elderly have accounted for the highest suicide rate for as long as such statistics have been kept. The elderly comprise 12 percent of the population and commit 19 percent of the suicides. As in all age groups, men account for the majority of deaths. Almost three-quarters of suicides among people over fifty are by men, and 96 percent of those are by white men. The elderly are also less ambivalent about suicide. While for every adolescent suicide there may be as many as one hundred attempts, among those over sixty-five there are four or less. "When an old person attempts suicide," concludes an American Psychiatric Association report, "he almost fully intends to die."

It is often said that youth suicide is especially tragic because teenagers have "everything to live for." The elderly, it is implied, have "nothing to live for." Certainly the suffering of the elderly may be more readily apparent. If loss— and one's response to loss—is the root of depression and suicide, the high rate of elderly suicide is not surprising. For most people old age is characterized by an inexorable accumulation of losses. They face the loss of their jobs, willingly or unwillingly, to retirement. (A disproportionate number of male suicides occur immediately following the retirement age of sixty-five.) Retirement means loss not only of livelihood but of income. In 1987 more than one in ten elderly Americans had incomes below the poverty line. The elderly also face loss of connection. Illness and death claim an increasing number of their family and friends. About 31 percent of Americans over age sixty-five live alone. In part this reflects a decrease in the strength of family ties. Twenty-five years ago one in three Americans over sixty-five lived with their children; today, one in ten do. (In contrast, 70 percent of elderly Japanese live with a younger relative.) The rest live with their elderly spouses, alone, or in nursing homes. Not surprisingly, studies show that the elderly are more at risk for suicide if they live alone, have lost their spouse, and no longer work. But the factor that puts them at especially high risk for suicide is loss of health. Eighty percent of Americans over sixty-five suffer from at least one chronic illness.

There are numerous changes that might decrease the rate of elderly suicide. Butler's *Why Survive?* is a veritable encyclopedia of the ways we neglect and mistreat the elderly and of the steps we might take to improve their lot. The abolition of compulsory retirement ages, increased social security and pension benefits, safer housing, better public transportation, and improved senior citizens' programs are a few of the suggestions. Improved nursing home care is another; in a 1987 study more than one-third of federally certified nursing homes were found deficient. Better methods of pain control would reduce the need for euthanasia. "You don't have to kill the patient to kill the pain," Dame Cicely Saunders reminds us. A commission studying the case for euthanasia in England concluded, "If all the care were up to the standards of the best, there would be few cases in which there was even a *prima facie* argument for euthanasia; better alternative means of alleviating distress would almost always be available if modern techniques and human understanding and care of the patient were universally practiced."

Of America's half-million practicing physicians only about seven hundred consider themselves trained in geriatrics. Mental health care is especially deficient. Although depression remains the most common medical complaint of the elderly, a presidential commission found that most depressed older Americans go untreated. Most mental health professionals are poorly trained to deal with elderly patients. "Since the elderly depressed don't cause much trouble, their plight has been ignored," UCLA psychologist Gary Emery told the *Los Angeles Times.* "Their depressed state is often misdiagnosed by health professionals, family members, and the elderly themselves, and the symptoms dismissed as an inevitable result of the aging process. Yet severe depression can be effectively dealt with when recognized in time, and potential suicides can be averted." A study of 136 elderly nursing home patients found that one in four of the patients who were said to be suffering from senile dementia had severe but potentially reversible behavioral problems. "Too often the old are written off as treatable with pharmacology while younger patients get psychotherapy," said Herbert Hendin, addressing a sparse crowd on "Suicide Among the Elderly" at an AAS conference, while across the hall a discussion of adolescent suicide was standing room only. "The heart of suicide prevention has always been and remains suicide among older people." Nevertheless, while people over age sixty-five account for 19 percent of suicides, they account for less than 3 percent of calls to suicide prevention centers. Few centers train volunteers how to work with elderly callers, and fewer still have programs to encourage elderly clients. (An exception is San Francisco Suicide Prevention, which operates the Friendship Line, a twenty-four-hour hot line for the elderly, as well as a program of house calls to depressed, elderly clients.) Psychologist Robert Kastenbaum worries that talk of "respect" and "rights" is often used to camouflage our own unwillingness to respond to elderly people in need. "In general, where the 'geriatric case' is allowed to slip away to proper and timely death," he says, "a younger person with similar problems would receive keen attention."

At bottom, perhaps our most important task is to change our attitudes toward the elderly, to celebrate them as valued, integral members of our culture. Although we shrink from the idea of elderly suicide and euthanasia, we encourage it by our neglect and indifference. (Cross-cultural studies demonstrate that societies in which old age brings with it respect and veneration have low rates of elderly suicide.) And if we don't allow them the right to exit this life, we have a responsibility to make this life better for them. "Often people ask whether a human being has a *right* to end his life," says Nico Speijer, a Dutch psychiatrist. "This question is incorrect. We should say rather that everyone has a right to live and *we* have the obligation to make it possible for everyone to live in such a way that he can be a socially integrated member of society to the maximum of his abilities."

In *Common-Sense Suicide*, Doris Portwood compared the decision of an elderly woman to end her life with the decision to leave a party before it's over. "When an older woman leaves a social gathering—perhaps an hour after dinner and when younger guests are settling down to a game or a fresh drink—no one urges her to linger on. Someone may call a cab or offer a lift. She will receive thoughtful words during the process of departure, but no insistence on her staying. There is the assumption that she has, in fact, some good reason for going." This seems a sad, if understandable, equation. Certainly, she must be allowed to leave, but her hosts have a responsibility to make the party more enjoyable so she'll want to stay a little longer. If she were made more welcome, she might not want to leave so soon. The right to live with dignity may be as neglected as the right to die with dignity; if the first were looked into, the second might not seem so pressing.

As early as 500 B.C. on the Greek island of Ceos, the law encouraged all inhabitants over the age of sixty to drink hemlock in order to make room for the next generation. (Average life expectancy at the time was less than thirty years.) Since then, except for the Holy Stone of seventeenth-century Brittany, organized suicide facilitation has been confined to fiction. In *Utopia,* Thomas More wrote of a system of voluntary euthanasia in which incurably ill citizens who chose death were considered godly and virtuous while those who refused were to be provided with continuing medical care. In "The Suicide Club," a short story published in 1878, Robert Louis Stevenson described a leather and mahogany club where for an entry fee of forty pounds dissolute young men draw lots for the right to die. One member wins the right to die; another is obliged to kill him. "The trouble of suicide is removed in that way," explains a club member. In "The Putter-to-Sleep," a short story by Guy de Maupassant, the narrator, scanning a newspaper's suicide statistics, thinks of all the gruesome deaths the numbers hide. He dreams of an "Institute of Voluntary Death" where people might chat and gamble before they meet an "easy death." In 1892, several years after writing the story, de Maupassant cut his throat in an unsuccessful suicide attempt. He died in an insane asylum a year and a half later of paresis, the result of syphilis. In Kurt Vonnegut's short story, "Welcome to the Monkey House," suicide is encouraged as a solution to overpopulation. The "World Government" establishes a network of Federal Ethical Suicide Parlors staffed by six-foot virgin hostesses; people go there voluntarily to be killed painlessly while lying on a Barcalounger, listening to Muzak. Next door to each parlor is a Howard Johnson's where one is entitled to order a last meal. In the film *Soylent Green,* would-be suicides go to a government building where they can watch movies of idyllic pastoral settings, listen to Beethoven's Ninth, and be painlessly put to sleep.

What these writers proposed in literature, some people have proposed in all seriousness. "What we want, what our grandsons, or great-grandsons will probably have, is a commodious and scientific lethal chamber, which shall reduce to a minimum the physical terrors and inconveniences of suicide, both for the patient and for his family and friends," wrote William Archer, the British drama critic, in 1893. Alfred Nobel, inventor of dynamite and patron of the Nobel Prizes, envisioned a "suicide institute" on the Riviera where sufferers could be put to sleep with a view of the Mediterranean, to the strains of beautiful music played by a first-class orchestra. In 1919, Binet-Sanglé, a Sorbonne physician, proposed the establishment of public euthanasia parlors where one could choose from electrocution, poison, gases, narcotics, and other lethal methods, to attain an "individually styled" death. Jo Roman, a New York artist stricken with breast cancer who took a fatal overdose at age sixty-two, drew the blueprints for an "Exit House," which would assure nonintervention, or assistance if necessary, in a "gentle" suicide for anyone over forty. Roman's imagination placed Exit House next to the United Nations in New York, and equipped it with library, lounge, roof garden, swimming pool, public relations department, and well-tended gardens where "small safe animals such as chipmunks and squirrels go about their business of living and dying."

While perhaps based on good intentions, such proposals are nevertheless very much to be feared. For though these fantasies may sound far-fetched, with increasing economic pressure the "bureaucratization" of suicide, as philosopher Margaret Pabst Battin calls it, might conceivably be proposed. "The risk is not Nazism," says Battin, "but individual manipulation, which is coercive in effect." Suicide, according to Battin, can be manipulated in two ways. In "circumstantial manipulation" a person may be given shoddy care, inadequate pain medication, and so forth, so that suicide becomes an obvious choice. In "ideological manipulation" a social group's way of thinking is slowly altered so that suicide seems preferable. Battin suggests there are signs of ideological manipulation even now: increasing emphasis on self-reliance and autonomy, increasing discussion of the right to die, and an increasing number of sympathetic cases of assisted suicide. "At bottom, I think the fear we should all think about is that we may become a society in which the normal, ordinary, expected thing is to do your dying relatively early and easily rather than prolong it and impose a burden on family and on medical personnel." She compares this to the kind of expectation we have that people will marry, usually in their early twenties. "How easy is it to not marry?" she asks. "How easy would it be to resist this expectation about dying? . . . I can envision an elderly person's family and friends gathering round her and saying, 'It's time to think about how to bring this to a close, Granny. But don't be frightened, we'll be supportive.' How easy would it be to resist this?" Despite such troubling scenarios, Battin believes that the individual's right to die must be protected. "Even if the kind of choice it favors might calcify into an expectation," she says, "it still is not a reason to abridge the rights of those who choose to exercise that choice in the first place."

Basically, it is a question of how simple it should be to commit suicide. In de Maupassant's story the secretary of the "Institute of Voluntary Death" explains what he calls the "annihilations." "Why should death be gloomy?" he asks his bewildered visitor. "It should be indifferent. We have lightened death, we have made it blossom, we have perfumed it, we have made it easy." William Archer suggested that one day there would be machines by which a man could kill himself for a penny. "In a rational state of civilization," he said, "self-effacement should cost us no more physical screwing up of courage than a visit to the barber's, and much less than a visit to the dentist's."

But even those who advocate the right to die under certain circumstances warn that suicide should not be made too simple. "Robert Lowell once remarked that if there were some little switch in the arm which one could press in order to die immediately and without pain, then everyone would sooner or later commit suicide," wrote A. Alvarez. "People are going to help each other die," observes A. J. Levinson, director of Concern for Dying. "But there are risks—legal, moral, psychological. And I think those risks should stay there." John Arras, philosopher-in-residence at Montefiore Medical Center in New York City, frequently advises doctors on ethical dilemmas in medicine. "I believe that the classical philosophical argument for suicide or assisted suicide is very strong," he says. "But I'm wary of the popularization of suicide. It's one thing to stake out the abstract right to die, another thing to parade this before depressed people who may take advantage of it. . . . These are decisions that should be made in fear and trembling." Battin concludes her essay *Manipulated Suicide* by stating, "I myself believe that on moral grounds we must accept, not reject, the notion of rational suicide. But I think we must do so with a clear-sighted view of the moral quicksand into which this notion threatens to lead us; perhaps then we may discover a path around."

IV

A MODEL HEMLOCK COUPLE

I FIRST MET FRED AND HOLLY ISHAM in 1985 at the Second National Voluntary Euthanasia conference in Los Angeles. They were introduced to me by a friend who had described them as a model Hemlock couple: Articulate and attractive people in their eighties, they were planning a double suicide. When the time came, my friend said, they planned to take a fatal overdose on a mountaintop at sunset.

I liked the Ishams immediately; they were the kind of people one might choose for grandparents. Holly was charming, talkative, and as alert as a squirrel. A beautiful woman with neat gray hair and a luminous smile, she had turned eighty-three the day before I met her, but she looked much younger. Fred, a youthful eighty-four, was a small, balding, handsome man with a neat mustache, a shy, almost deferential manner, and a sheepish, endearing grin. Married fifty-nine years, they still looked into each other's eyes, they still touched each other with affection, they still seemed very much in love.

Six years earlier, Fred had learned he had cancer of the prostate. Although a bilateral orchiectomy—the removal of both testicles—slowed the growth of the cancer, two years ago a subsequent bone scan found bone cancer. "Fred had the option of radiation and chemotherapy, but he was told that his quality of life would be greatly impaired, so he refused it," Holly, who did most of the talking, told me. "So for the last two years we've been living it up. But we know there will come a time when the pain will be too great, and we want to be ready." Fred nodded assent. "We've seen so many of our friends and family go the hard way, and we don't want to go through that ourselves," he said. "I don't fear death, but I do fear dying." Holly shook her head. "As long as we have some control over that, I have a comfortable feeling," she said. "We've lived a long and happy life, and we do not want to be dependent on our children. After eighty-three years we feel it doesn't matter when it happens— we've already surpassed the average life span, so *que sera, sera.*" She gave a gay laugh. "I don't see why death has to be a fearful thing. I don't see why it can't be as happy and euphoric as our wedding day."

Fred and Holly were married in 1926, two years after they graduated from college. In the sixty years since, they experienced a full share of highs and lows: the Depression; the house they designed and built in 1931 and still occupied; their three children; their trips around the world. While Fred worked as a commercial artist until his retirement, much of Holly's adult life was devoted to caring for the youngest of their three daughters, Louisa, whose life was spent in and out of hospitals. At the age of seventeen, surgery to remove a malignant tumor of the spinal cord left her a paraplegic. But in her late twenties the cancer spread, and her life became a nightmare of radiation, medication, and surgery until her death at age thirty.

Seeing their daughter's harrowing end encouraged the Ishams to be more in control of their own deaths. When I met them, however, Holly and Fred seemed far from the end. They talked with excitement of tours they had taken to Nova Scotia, Tahiti, and Europe, of traveling around the United States to visit their two children, five grandchildren, and two great-grandchildren, of hiking near the cabin they had built in the mountains. They went to movies, concerts, and dinner parties. ("For twenty-two years we've spent New Year's Eve with the same group of friends," said Holly. "But we're dying off. Our group started with fourteen. Now we're down to seven.") Holly's datebook was crammed with lectures, bridge parties, community service meetings, and garden club get-togethers, most of them sponsored by the local women's club. Fred often drove her to meetings and helped her make place cards and posters for club functions. "I don't have a social life of my own, really," said Fred. "My activities are mostly related to Hol's." Fred seemed content to be somewhat in his wife's shadow; he was proud of her, and his quiet strength complemented her high-strung energy. Her devotion to him was evident even when she teased him about his passivity. "I've lived with him fifty-nine years, and I still don't know what he thinks about some things," she said. "He's so agreeable. He'll agree with you, he'll agree with me, he'll agree with everybody." She laughed and gazed at Fred with affection. "And it would take a man like that to put up with me."

As in most of their activities, Holly was the impetus behind their interest in Hemlock. They had joined two years earlier after she saw Derek Humphry interviewed on television. "I'm the aggressor in these things," she admitted. "Fred goes to these meetings to satisfy me." Holly had read *Let Me Die Before I Wake* and *Common-Sense Suicide,* and she studied the *Hemlock Quarterly.* "I talk to friends at the club about it if I feel they're ripe," she said. "I've circulated Hemlock books and membership applications, and I think I've gotten at least six members." At the Hemlock conference Holly was quite active, introducing herself to other members, exchanging stories and phone numbers, asking questions about insurance and death certificates, jotting down ideas in her brown Hemlock notebook. Fred, who hadn't read the Hemlock books, agreed in principle with much of the Hemlock philosophy but was uncomfortable contemplating its practice. "I think that self-deliverance, in connection with the two of us . . ." His voice trailed off. "I haven't sorted it out enough to definitely put me in the position or her in the position, but as an idea, I accept it." Said Holly, "He shares my interest but not my enthusiasm, I would say." Fred nodded: "That's probably it."

As we talked I realized that the mountaintop-at-sunset suicide scenario was Holly's, and her enthusiasm had made it seem as if it were shared by her husband. Holly had clearly thought a great deal about contingency plans. "If we don't have a pact to go together, if Fred died and I were the survivor, I would just weed out the house, get my affairs in shape, get the pills by some means or other, and have a kind of indefinite date as to when I'd use them," she said. "And if I felt deterioration in the quality of life or became dependent on others to the point that I wanted out, I would take my own life." Holly didn't have the pills yet and was anxious to find a source. "The only fear I have is of not being successful," she said. "And if I woke up and found I was unsuccessful, I hope I'd have a plastic bag handy and be able to finish it off with that." Despite her extensive planning for death, Holly talked with as much excitement about their upcoming sixtieth anniversary as she did about the possibility of a double suicide. "I'm not going to give up any sooner than I have to," she said. "We've had such a good life for fifty-nine years."

Fred, when pressed, said he didn't think about what he'd do without Holly because he was sure he'd die before her. If he didn't? "For the foreseeable future I would go on living here in this home," he said slowly. "Even though I'm sure our daughters would invite Hol or me to live with them, we don't want to be a burden. But I don't know what my life would be because so much of my life concerns her activities." Fred admitted that the Hemlock conference intrigued him. "Those meetings were so thought-provoking that I do want to read some of those books now." Holly beamed. "You can start reading *Jean's Way* this evening to me," she said. They looked at each other fondly.

Over the following year I received several notes from the Ishams written by Holly, who had signed both their names. In December I received a Christmas card, a Chinese watercolor titled *Flight* in which two people were hiking through mountains. "We have a few more aches and pains as the years rush by," Holly wrote in her neat, energetic hand, "but we try to ignore them and are keeping *very* busy with family, friends, and club activities. Who says eighty-four and eighty-five is old? Old is a state of mind."

When I saw Holly at the next Hemlock conference, in Washington, D.C., she was with her elder daughter, a nurse. Fred had stayed home. "It's not good," said Holly anxiously. "Things have deteriorated." Fred had undergone radiation treatments in February and again in August. "It's made him quieter and depressed," she said. "He just agrees with everyone—he always has—and he takes every treatment and every medication the doctors recommend." Over the summer he was hospitalized for congestive heart failure; his lungs filled with fluid. Holly and Fred asked the doctors to issue a no-code order. He recovered. "The doctors say he probably won't die of the cancer but of heart or kidney failure." As Holly talked, frustration and bitterness seeped into her voice. Although she cared deeply for Fred, she was clearly exhausted by the demands of caring for him. She said that there had been few conversations about suicide; she didn't want to push it. "But at one point I reminded him about the idea of going out together," she said. "I told him that I'd go to Mexico, get the drugs, and we could have a cocktail hour and go out together. He didn't say anything." Holly looked down. "I feel terribly guilty, but sometimes I feel as if I'm just waiting for him to die. He's so down about things. . . . I think he will hang on as long as he can. . . . So I guess my dreams of going out together are . . ." Holly raised her hands in a gesture of despair.

Two months later in Los Angeles, I arranged to see Fred and Holly. On the phone Holly told me the doctors had estimated that Fred had between six months and a year to live. For several months Fred had been confined to the house except for trips to the hospital. He slept up to sixteen hours a day and spent most of the rest of the time staring at the television set. The last time he and Holly had visited their cabin was many months earlier, and their last golf game was almost a year ago. Although her doctor and her daughters had urged her not to worry so much about Fred and to maintain her own activities, Holly, who spent most of her time caring for her husband, clearly felt hampered by the restrictions Fred's condition imposed on her life. And yet her voice had little of the anxiety that had been so evident in Washington.

When I arrived at their house, Fred was sitting in an armchair in a corner of their bedroom, in pale blue pajamas, watching television. He looked much older and more frail than when I had last seen him almost two years before. His face had sagged, and rather than promising a smile as it once did, the corners of his mouth turned down as if in fear. His voice was even softer and slower than before, and his hand shook as he sipped from a glass of water. His mind was still sharp. I was delighted to see him. He told me about his chemotherapy. "I've been lucky," he said. "It hasn't given me any discomfort." But he couldn't move around as much as he used to, he said, and he suffered from diarrhea. His right leg had been bothering him, and he worried that the cancer had spread there. When I asked him how his spirits were holding up, he gave a rueful smile. "I take it a day at a time," he said. "Sometimes I feel down, sometimes I feel okay."

One reason why Holly seemed less anxious emerged when Fred got up and walked slowly to the bathroom. Holly leaned forward and spoke even more urgently than usual. "I have a source where I can get drugs," she said. "Fred knows I have a source, but he doesn't know where. One night we were having a cocktail, and he asked if I was stockpiling drugs. I said yes. And he said, 'Well, get enough for me, too.' " Holly was pleased. "I told him that even though I was in good health and would probably live a long time, I don't want to. When he's gone, I'm sure I could *live* without him, I'm sure I could learn to adjust, but I would feel that my function in life was gone. I wouldn't be needed. So I'd just like to put my things in order and go. Or I'd like to go with him—if I'm lucky enough to get all we need, I'd just like to have a nice little cocktail party for the two of us."

Fred returned. "I've been telling George about how I feel about self-deliverance and about the talk we had," Holly said. Fred was silent for a moment. "I think we understand each other," he said as he walked to the couch. "I think we do," said Holly. Although they had discussed the relative merits of hospital, hospice, and home care for Fred, they hadn't talked about suicide since their brief conversation over cocktails. Holly would have liked to, but she didn't want to appear pushy. The presence of a third person seemed to make it easier. Holly talked about it with intensity; Fred was still a bit frightened and embarrassed by the subject. "I think our feelings on this will change from day to day," he said. "I know mine do. Some days I feel okay, and sometimes I feel I'd like to just get it over with. I'm uncomfortable with the idea [of suicide], but it's a matter of deciding whether life is worth living at that time. I wish it were legal and you could have a doctor give a shot."

Holly brought out the photograph album from their sixtieth anniversary celebration, which had brought Fred and Holly, their two daughters, five grandchildren, and two great-grandchildren together for two days. As Holly turned the pages, proudly pointing out her grandchildren, Fred stood behind the couch, smiling. They proudly and happily surveyed their work. "She's just a ball of fire . . . so energetic," said Holly of a grandchild. "I love her." Fred chuckled with pleasure. "Oh yes, oh yes," he said slowly, softly, and his hands moved from the couch to his wife's shoulders.

When it was time to say good-bye, I kissed Holly, shook Fred's hand, and squeezed his bony shoulder. Then I realized it might be the last time I would see them, and our bodies came closer in an awkward hug. "I hope to be back in L.A. soon," I said, then suddenly realized I meant, "I hope I'll be back in L.A. before one or both of you die." I was filled with sadness. I wanted to say, "Live, please live," to both of them. But I didn't. As I drove across the city, I wondered how I would react to the very real possibility of one or both of them committing suicide—or self-deliverance, as Holly called it. After the sadness, would I think it had been a "right" or "good" or "rational" choice?

In December I received a letter from Holly.

> . . . It became necessary for us to place Fred in a hospice. Our two daughters concurred with the decision, because I could no longer handle 24-hour nursing duty. Naturally it was a painful and tearful decision to make. He updated his Living Will with Durable Power of Attorney. Now his desires are: 1) No resuscitation 2) No intravenous 3) No intubation 4) No injections except for pain or sleep. Simply put, no life supports. Just let nature take its course. . . . I have just talked to Fred's doctor and to him. He called me. He has improved so much. He wheels himself around the hospital and is alert instead of sleeping 16 out of 24 hours. His doctor said there is some lung involvement now, but he may linger quite a while. C'est la vie! . . . Warmest wishes from

> Fred and Holly

The following June I received a letter from Holly that began "I thought that you would like to know that my gentle husband of 61 years died peacefully in his sleep at two a.m., May 1st."

Fred, I learned later, had prospered his first few months in the hospice. He played bingo, was elected president of the council, and was crowned King of Hearts on Valentine's Day. But as his health declined he lost interest in the organized activities, and he wept whenever Holly visited. One day he asked Holly about Hemlock. "He wanted to know how to do it, where to get it, how much to take," Holly recalled in a telephone conversation with me. "I said, 'Fred, if you had read all the material I'd put in front of you over the years, you'd know.' But I told him, 'I have enough pills saved up for us both, and we can take them and die a peaceful death, but you have to come home to do it. So you just tell me when you want to come home and we'll do it.' But Fred never gave me the high sign."

In April, Fred was bedridden for three weeks. "Finally, at the end, when he was having a very bad time, he said he guessed it was too late for Hemlock now. I said, 'Yes, because I couldn't get you out of the hospital now.' " Holly paused. "Fred was miserable because he was so weak, and he had trouble breathing. But the doctors provided enough painkillers so I think he was pain-free." At the end of April, Fred slipped into unconsciousness. He died three days later. "I saw him the night before," said Holly. "I couldn't rouse him, so I went home. At two in the morning they called and told me he had died peacefully. It was a blessing. He was at peace. The anxiety and suffering were over. It was the first day of May, one month shy of our sixty-first wedding anniversary."

In the months following Fred's death, Holly sorted through his belongings and talked with her family and to a counselor, trying to forgive herself for the resentment and anger she had felt during her husband's last years. "I'm doing very well," she told me. "I'm not lonely. My philosophy is that grief is a selfish thing so I've gotten right back into my activities and club life." When I asked about her own future, she said, "I know quite positively when I want to make my exit, so I'm making plans. I feel a burden to the kids. I was prepared for a double suicide. I had my notes all written out. Now all I have to do is change the we to I." I encouraged her to use her vast energy to stay alive. I told her I loved her and would be sorry if she were no longer on this earth. But she sounded certain. I made her promise that she would at least say good-bye.

Several months later I came home one Friday night to find a letter from Holly, saying good-bye, and a copy of her suicide note that she planned to leave next to her when she made her "exit." The letter had been written on Monday, and she intended to take an overdose on Thursday night, she said. The note, she wrote in her neat, elegant hand, "will capsulize my reasons for wishing to live no longer." It said:

To whom it may concern
"The right to die is as sacred as the right to live."
I am ending my life in a planned and deliberate manner. I have a loving and devoted family and friends who know that this act may be a possibility without knowing when it might occur.
I have lived a full and fruitful life, 61 years of which were shared with my devoted husband. He died May 1, 1987. Now I have become dependent on others because of increasing incurable loss of vision and painful, crippling arthritis.
All who know me know that I am fiercely independent. I feel that my family and friends deserve freedom from the anxiety which my declining years have caused them.

I will be 86 years old soon. I do not want to overstay my time. I am not depressed, I am sure that this is the right thing for me to do.

Now I choose to die in a peaceful and dignified way.

I have taken 30 vesparex which should be fatal.

Please respect my right to die.

Holly G. Isham

Fred's and Holly's ashes were scattered near the mountain cabin they had loved and shared for fifty years.

6

SURVIVORS

———◆———

I

MERRYL AND CARL

FOR MANY YEARS suicide was known as "the victimless crime." But whether the act of an impulsive teenager, a depressed businessman, or a terminally ill cancer patient, a suicide leaves behind a great many victims— wife, husband, parents, children, friends—for whom the pain is just beginning. "There are always two parties to a death; the person who dies and the survivors who are bereaved," wrote historian Arnold Toynbee. "There are two parties to the suffering that death inflicts; and, in the apportionment of this suffering, the survivor takes the brunt." The suffering of survivors is acute after any death, but the grief inflicted by suicide may be the hardest of all to bear. In addition to shock, denial, anger, and sorrow, the suicide survivor often faces an added burden of guilt and shame. Although the pain is over for the one who died, and his problems, in their way, answered, the survivor is left only with questions. "Suicide is the cruelest death of all for those who remain," says a counselor. "Each day the survivors face the gut-wrenching struggle of asking themselves 'why, why, why?' " What makes a suicide so difficult to resolve is that there may be no answers. "I'll never know why," says a man whose seventeen-year-old son hanged himself. "There's only one person who can tell me, and he's dead." After her husband, Carl, killed himself in 1982 at the age of thirty-three, Merryl Maleska's life was ripped open just when she believed it was most secure. It was the beginning of a long, excruciating journey in which she was forced to reexamine every moment of her life since she had first seen Carl sixteen years before.

———————

On a September evening in 1966, Merryl Maleska lay on a bed in her dorm room, flipping through the "pigbook," a thin yellow volume containing pictures of everyone in her freshman class at Tufts University in Medford, Massachusetts. It was her third night of school and there were hundreds of faces to scrutinize, but when Merryl got to the seventh photograph, she stopped. Something in the boy's eyes—a faraway, intense look—drew her in. She studied his picture. His name was Carl, and he was from a small town in Pennsylvania. She looked at the picture next to his: That boy was a standard-issue matinee idol, but she had passed right over him. Carl was handsome, too; even in a photo not much larger than a postage stamp, she was drawn to his smooth face and his thick brown hair, neatly parted on one side and a little windswept on the other in a way that reminded her of the Kennedys. But it was those eyes, looking straight at her yet keeping their distance, that stayed with Merryl. She called to her roommate, pointed at Carl, and said, "I'm going to marry him." They laughed, and then they laughed again because her roommate realized Merryl wasn't kidding.

In the following weeks Merryl often saw Carl walking across campus in a green high school football jacket with cream-colored sleeves. She was thrilled to discover they took the same biology class (he was a pre-medical student), and she sneaked peeks at him during lectures. In the cafeteria his name came up often. By the end of his sophomore year Carl had accrued four years' worth of honors—President of the Sword and Shield Honor Society, President of the Biology Club, the Biology Prize, highest GPA in his class. At the most prominent frat on campus, Carl was known as "the Golden Tongue" because, although he was quiet, almost shy, he was a riveting speaker. To Merryl he seemed everything his picture promised. When friends teased her about having a crush on a man she had never met, Merryl laughed. But she kept her eyes peeled for that green jacket, and when she saw it coming across campus, her stomach knotted. And before she went to sleep she often found herself pulling out the "pigbook" and turning to the seventh photograph. It seemed inevitable that someday she and Carl would meet.

They did, sort of, during sophomore year when Merryl's lab partner invited her to the annual Sword and Shield Dance. Merryl accepted, half because she knew Carl would be there. When they arrived, Carl, as club president, was greeting guests at the door. Next day Merryl swore to her roommate that when Carl shook her hand, he had given her a meaningful smile. Her roommate, reminding Merryl that she had always needed glasses, kidded that her perception had been blurred by myopia, not romance. But all evening as she danced with her lab partner to the Beatles, the Rolling Stones, and the Turtles, Merryl was aware of Carl and of his date, who Merryl felt wasn't nearly good-looking enough for him. For the evening's last dance the disc jockey put on "Light My Fire" by the Doors—and as they danced, people mouthed the words. As the song went on, Merryl found that she and her date were dancing in a corner next to Carl and his date, on the fringe of the vibrating crowd. As Merryl danced, sometimes it seemed to her that she was dancing with Carl and then sometimes with her date and then again with Carl, and she was exhilarated, and sometimes she knew Carl was watching her and it seemed he knew she knew he was watching, and yet he kept watching, and though the song lasted only 6 minutes and 50 seconds, to Merryl it seemed to go on forever.

Merryl spent her junior year abroad, studying English literature in London. Carl studied political science in Sweden. When Merryl returned to Tufts, she decided to write an article for the school newspaper about students who had lived abroad. One day in the cafeteria, with five of her girlfriends watching and praying, Merryl walked over to Carl and asked him for an interview. They agreed to meet Friday evening. Friday afternoon in front of her mirror, Merryl tried on every outfit she owned, finally settling on a gray wool dress that was prim yet flatteringly tight. That night they went to dinner and talked for hours. Carl was everything Merryl had imagined: intense, strong, and sensitive, with a gentle voice that inspired confidence. Merryl didn't bother taking notes—she never even wrote the article—they just talked and talked. Afterward, she asked Carl back to her room. When they arrived at her dorm, she made him wait on the stairs. She ran to her room, spent fifteen minutes stuffing everything under the bed—she had never expected him to come back and had left the place a mess—then ran back downstairs and invited him up. They spent the night together, and next morning they took a bus down to her family's summer house on Cape Cod, broke in through the bathroom window, and spent the weekend huddled in her parents' double bed. Merryl told Carl about her crush. He was surprised. He didn't remember her from the Sword and Shield dance, and he was sure he hadn't given her a meaningful smile. But now he did, and the next day, on the bus back to Boston, he asked her to move in with him.

Merryl threw herself into the relationship and was happily overwhelmed. Although Carl was shy and retiring by nature, his intellectual curiosity was fierce, and he cared passionately about certain things; he had dropped his pre-med program, in fact, to devote more attention to the antiwar movement, politics, economics. Merryl, warm and gregarious, had always felt a little diffuse and frivolous, and Carl's intensity lent her a focus she had not yet found. Carl was the teacher and Merryl his willing student. This imbalance kept their relationship somewhat tilted, and Merryl was often fearful that Carl would leave her. A year after their graduation, at Carl's insistence, they did break up and were apart for two years. But they got back together at the age of twenty-five and, two years later, they were married at Merryl's parents' house on Cape Cod. The bride and groom recited vows they had written in secret. Standing in a gazebo built for the wedding, Merryl expressed her belief that "our lives together will be infinitely richer than our lives apart." Carl's voice broke as he vowed, "I will be as open and honest with my emotions as I can possibly be."

After a honeymoon in Sweden they set up married life in a cozy carriage house in Evanston, Illinois, a short commute to the University of Chicago where Carl was a graduate student in developmental psychology. Merryl embarked on a seven-month job search that landed her an entry-level editorial position at Rand McNally. Carl was deeply involved in university life but managed to read widely, tend an indoor garden, and bake bread. It was a happy time. Merryl felt secure in Carl's love, and Carl, who had entered therapy, seemed at peace with himself. One Christmas he surprised her with a pillow he had stitched with a favorite scene: Merryl sitting at a picnic table in their backyard, looking up from her writing in delight as Carl serves her iced tea from a tray. Carl had worked on the pillow for months when Merryl was at work, carefully noting where the markers were on the sewing machine, stitching for hours, then adjusting the measurements to their original position before she came home.

Gradually, however, Carl's frustration with his work began to show. The University of Chicago had not been his first choice. Chicago didn't offer clinical psychology, only developmental psychology, which led to an academic career. But because the academic market was so tight, the only route assuring an eventual job in psychology was the clinical one. Carl felt cornered. Furthermore, Chicago emphasized adult and geriatric psychology; the sole faculty member who specialized in child psychology was two years younger than Carl, and he didn't feel she was the mentor he needed. In any case Carl was a perfectionist who hated to ask for help, and rather than admit uncertainty, he preferred to wait until a piece of work was flawless before turning it in. Carl was especially demanding about his dissertation, an analysis of toddlers' cognitive responses. Carl loved children, and he spent five hours a day on his hands and knees performing puppet shows for two-year-olds, taping their reactions, then recording the results in the dozens of spiral notebooks that lined his study. He made the puppets himself from dolls, proudly showing Merryl each painstaking creation: an elephant, a pilot, a truck. But the project seemed to take forever; there was always another paper to read, another reaction to research, another departmental requirement to fulfill. Friends began to joke about whether he would ever finish. At night Merryl would watch him work at his desk. Though Carl was doggedly trying to fulfill his marriage vow and be more open with his feelings, Merryl could sense the tension building inside him, and when she probed, it would often turn out that something had been irking him for days.

Meanwhile, after six years of graduate school, Carl was anxious to start earning money. But the resumes he sent out drew no response. He felt inadequate when he compared his stalled career to the smooth successes of the people around him. His brother had landed a job in a psychology lab at Harvard; his sister was winning awards at Harvard Medical School; Merryl was being given increasing responsibility at Rand McNally. Nevertheless, Merryl was prepared to move when Carl found work; she had given him a list of twenty-five states she'd live in. She preferred New England but would live almost anywhere east of the Mississippi. Texas and the Far West were out. Carl applied to schools in those twenty-five states, but he received no offers. As his dissertation dragged on, he typed and retyped his resume, changing only the date he expected his Ph.D. to be completed. The time was postponed so often that eventually he just used Wite-out to change the date.

In August 1980 they moved back to Boston. Merryl had landed a job as an editor at Houghton Mifflin, and Carl had been promised a job at a think tank. But Carl's position didn't come through, and though he seemed to make the best of it, for the next two years his life was a series of progressively more galling disappointments. The job search became numbing. Carl followed up every lead, every newspaper ad, every cocktail party conversation, but the only positions available, it seemed, were at junior colleges for sums so low that people apologized as they offered them. Merryl, who was delighted with her work at Houghton Mifflin, watched Carl get more and more depressed. But she still had great faith in him. She *knew* he would get a job, she told him, and someday he would teach in a university. So what if it happened at forty instead of thirty? For Carl's thirty-second birthday Merryl had his portrait painted. Important people had their portraits painted, she reasoned, and she wanted to let Carl know that he was an important person. Carl was pleased with the idea of the gift but was anxious about having an artist capture a time of his life when he felt so fragile. In the portrait Carl, in his green suit, looks young and terribly handsome. Whenever Merryl passed through the living room where it hung, she found herself looking up at him and marveling at how well the artist had captured that faraway look in his eyes.

Merryl's faith in Carl was so absolute that she was stunned when one January morning she was on her way out the door to work and Carl, lying in bed, said, "If I have to go through another job search like this, I'll kill myself." Unnerved, Merryl said, "Well, I don't want to come in this house and find you hanging." Carl's statement was so out of character that she put it from her mind. In any case, a month later Carl got a job. Merryl baked him a cake in celebration.

The job was as a research assistant on a study of the effect of a new drug on learning disabilities in children. Carl was the junior member of a three-person team. He did the paperwork and ferried the youngsters to and from the hospital where a clinical psychologist ran the experiments. But it was a job, and though it paid poorly, Carl drew a salary for the first time in years. His confidence was renewed. At night he worked on his dissertation; his proposal, two years in the writing, was accepted in June 1981, and Carl planned to finish by the following summer. Meanwhile, he and Merryl talked about having children of their own. They filled their bedroom shelves with books on pregnancy and parenting, and discussed buying a house. Although they tried for six months, Merryl did not get pregnant.

One night in late October, Merryl and Carl were filling each other in on their workdays. Merryl had chaired an important meeting and was feeling proud. Carl had always helped celebrate her triumphs, but Merryl sensed her success was making Carl's own dreams seem further from him. Later, when they were preparing for bed, Carl suddenly went into a tense, agitated tirade; he was worthless, he said. He hated his job and he hated himself. It disgusted him to be ferrying vials for someone whose job he would have had if only he'd stayed pre-med in college. As Merryl watched, horrified, he repeatedly punched himself in the temple with his fist. When Carl had calmed down, Merryl tried to persuade him to get help from a therapist. Carl refused, saying he didn't want anyone to see him like this.

Although there were no more violent outbursts, things got steadily worse. Carl's job was due to terminate in June, and he had to start looking all over again. He had several promising interviews, only to be told later that he was overqualified or the position had been eliminated. In the middle of May, Carl's brother called to say that he had just accepted a good position in the research department of a large company in New Jersey. Carl congratulated him but within half an hour of hanging up he was in a panic of self-loathing, muttering, "I'm worthless, I'm worthless," over and over. His face was drained of color, and his skin looked drawn and taut. Merryl was terrified; she hardly recognized him. This time when she insisted he get help, Carl agreed. Next day, Carl met with a psychiatrist who said he couldn't take on new patients until the end of the summer, but if Carl was ever in crisis, he would fit him in.

Each evening Merryl never knew what kind of mood to expect when she came home from work. Night after night they lingered at the table, dishes undone, trying to unravel what was happening. Carl ruthlessly criticized decisions he had made over the years. Merryl had had no idea how deeply Carl's self-hatred ran. She told him that she still felt he was the greatest. As far as this job search was concerned, she said, he was a square peg where there were only round holes. But one day there would be a square hole. Carl seemed to take heart. One night he got a call from Temple University. He had been recommended for a good job. "It's finally working," said Carl, hugging Merryl. "It's all going to pay off." On June 2, Merryl's thirty-third birthday, Carl flew to Philadelphia for his interview at Temple. He left a card for Merryl on the dining room table. To Merryl the printed words seemed absolutely perfect:

Everyone needs someone
to understand and care
Someone to depend on
and count on to be there . . .
Everyone needs someone
to make a dream come true
And I'm so glad my someone
is someone special—you!

Underneath the ornately scripted "Happy Birthday," Carl had written: "Dearest Merryl, You've been so supportive and so tender to me. I'll always love you for it. Happy Birthday! I'll hurry home to help celebrate it. Love, Your Carl."

And Carl seemed buoyed. He had an interview at Manhattanville College the following week, there was a possible job at a Boston VA hospital, and he was one of the top two candidates for the position at Temple. The chances of getting the kind of job he wanted seemed better than they'd ever been.

Then one day in early June, Carl announced that a problem in his dissertation was more serious than he had thought. He believed he had asked the children a question in which the pronoun had not been clarified. If this were true, he said, the research was contaminated. Merryl assured him it didn't sound as drastic as he thought, and Carl seemed soothed. But over the following week his doubts escalated, and on June 10 he told her he was certain his dissertation was ruined. Merryl reasoned with him: Even if one question was flawed, he could still salvage most of the project. She persuaded him to call his dissertation advisor in Chicago, who told him it didn't sound like a major problem. But Carl spent every spare moment in his study, chair pulled tight against the desk, flipping through his vast files.

On Sunday, June 13, Merryl woke to find Carl in a white-faced panic. "My life is over," he kept saying in a thin voice, staring straight ahead. "My life is over." Merryl reached for him, but he shrugged her off, saying, "Don't touch me—the pain is too great." All day Merryl sat with him, coaxing, cajoling, reasoning. She reminded him of his triumphs at Tufts: the biology prize, Sword and Shield, the highest GPA. Carl snorted; he wasn't smart, he said—if he'd been smart, he would have stayed pre-med, but he hadn't because he was a loser, he was worthless. Merryl reminded him of all the people who'd looked up to him, but Carl dismissed her. He'd always been the manager, not the player, always the odd man out, the second class citizen, the chump ferrying vials for the people he should *be.* No matter how she tried, Merryl couldn't seem to reach him—it was like trying to penetrate a plastic shield—and even if she made some headway, he'd soon fade further into his own world. "How do people do it?" he said at one point. "How do they kill themselves?" He shook his head. "Maybe it's a good sign that I'm talking about it. Isn't it true that when people talk about suicide, they don't do it?" Merryl told him she didn't think that was true.

On Monday night when Carl was no better, Merryl pleaded with him to let her call the psychiatrist. Carl said no, and Merryl couldn't bear the thought of going against his will, of treating him like a child. At 11 P.M. she finally coaxed Carl into letting her call. The therapist wasn't home; Merryl left her name with his answering service. By the time the psychiatrist called back the next day, Carl seemed stronger. Merryl, who stayed home from work to be with him, heard him tell the doctor that he was okay, and they made an appointment for Thursday. But Merryl couldn't get the previous day out of her mind. For a moment she wanted to grab the phone and tell the psychiatrist he didn't understand how serious this was. But she didn't; it wasn't right, she thought, and Carl did sound better. That afternoon he took a long nap. Merryl looked in on him from time to time and was relieved to see him sleeping like a baby. It was going to be okay. The worst had passed.

But Carl was up and down all week. One moment he'd be in his white-faced panic, calling himself "worthless." He wasn't eating right; he would push away his plate halfway through the meal. Sometimes he would get up suddenly and go for long walks. Merryl, worried, would ask to go along, but he always said no. One night she asked him whether he was going to come back, and a look flickered over his face as if she'd recognized his deepest fear, but then it disappeared and he said of course he was coming back. Carl spoke often of death. Once, he came in from a walk and said he'd seen a hearse going by and imagined he was in it. Another time when Merryl killed an ant, he grimaced and said he felt that life was squashing him, like that ant. Merryl told him that if he ever killed himself, he'd be killing her too. Once, in desperation, she suggested they simply walk off into the woods together. "Do you really mean it?" Carl said. Then he reflected on her suggestion and seemed disappointed. "People can live for forty days in the woods without food." Merryl talked to him about hospitalization, and he said no, it would gall him that the people taking care of him would be the doctors he should have been. At times Carl seemed like a stranger to Merryl—he had night sweats and even smelled different to her. But at other times she'd walk into the house and the Carl she knew was cooking dinner, or he'd be able to comment on some event in the outside world, like the recent British invasion of the Falklands. Merryl fought to keep in touch with that Carl, but he always ebbed away. Merryl began to have a recurring dream: She was standing on a dock while a vast steamship was pulling away in a dense, dense fog, leaving her alone. It seemed as if Carl was on the ship. The night was too foggy to be certain. But in the dream and after she woke, Merryl felt utterly abandoned.

On Thursday Merryl picked up her parents for dinner. Merryl's mother, who had cancer, had just learned that it had spread. As Merryl drove, the whole world seemed on edge; the traffic loomed dangerously, and shapes that seemed to be people were shadows. Halfway home she nearly hit a bicyclist, and the rest of the way home she squeezed the wheel tightly. When they walked into the house, Carl was in the kitchen making salad. He looked up, and Merryl could see he was in that white state, but it was concealed by a polite mask because her parents were there. When Merryl and Carl had a moment alone, she asked him if he was all right. As he stirred the salad dressing, he looked up at her slowly and in that thin voice that chilled her to the bone, said, "No." Her mother came into the room, and Carl went back to his stirring.

After dinner Carl said he was going for a walk. Merryl hurried into the kitchen after him and asked if he was sure he was okay. He was sure, he said. He just had to get out. After he left, Merryl's parents asked her what was wrong, and she told them Carl had been under a lot of strain lately. She didn't go into details—she felt it was her and Carl's business. They talked about her mother's illness, and Merryl felt pinned between the two problems. She felt guilty she hadn't had time to comfort her mother; at the same time she was anxious to find out what had happened at Carl's appointment with his therapist that day. Merryl herself had spoken with her gynecologist that morning about her difficulties getting pregnant, and with her own therapist that afternoon all she had talked about was Carl's depression. Yet life spun crazily through these tragedies—her mother, ever practical, pruning the philodendron that Carl, the gardener in the house, had neglected for months; her father noticing that the rug had been cleaned. When Carl came back after half an hour, he went straight into his study and shut the door.

After her parents left, Merryl asked Carl about his appointment with the therapist that day. Had he talked to the therapist about suicide? Yes, said Carl, he had. But he had said he didn't have the courage to do it, and the doctor had replied that he wasn't worried. Merryl felt a breeze of relief. But it was short-lived. That night Carl talked wildly. He spoke of giving up the dissertation; he was sure it would be exposed as a failure. He had to finish it, he said, but he couldn't. "If I give up the dissertation, I'm giving up my life." His life was much more than the dissertation, Merryl assured him. Carl looked up from his work and said, "What would happen if I didn't finish it? What would you do?" Merryl assured him she would still love him, that she would never leave him. Carl managed a tight smile and for a second seemed calmed, but then he was back inside himself, going back and forth in that small, thin voice about whether he could finish it. "This is the living out of my worst nightmare," he said. "I always knew I'd be a failure, and now I am." Eight or ten times he got up from his chair to pace, then sat back down, pulling his chair right up to the desk, his face scouring the quilt of papers; then he would push his chair back abruptly, wood screeching on wood, and pace once more. Once he looked up at Merryl and said, "You know, today I looked at that portrait of me that you say has such sensitive eyes." Merryl broke in and said, "They *are,* Carl." Carl leaped up, went into the living room, came back, and said, "They're not the eyes of a sensitive person, they're the eyes of a weak person." He stared at her. "I'm frightened of life."

When Merryl woke on Friday morning, Carl was already at his desk poring over his dissertation. Merryl went off to work carrying a pamphlet on infertility. At noon Carl called to say that he had been offered the VA job. Merryl was flooded with relief. Carl had to tell the man that afternoon whether he would take it, and Merryl suggested he ask for more time to decide because if his dissertation was okay, he would probably get the Temple job, which was a plum. The VA job could be his ace in the hole. Carl agreed. Ten minutes later he called back to say that they had given him a week to decide. He and Merryl talked about his sudden change of luck, and Carl said that he would pick her up at work at six. When they said good-bye, Merryl's last word was "Congratulations!"

That afternoon Merryl felt as if she and Carl had been pulled back from a precipice. She was able to free her mind from worry for the first time in weeks. She could also devote some thought to the upcoming weekend. Carl's brother's son had been born the week before. The baby had been named Carl, and the christening was to be that Sunday. Afterward Merryl and Carl were going to host a small party. Merryl knew Carl wasn't looking forward to it, but it had been planned months in advance, and maybe now that he had a job offer he would be less edgy about it. A woman at work had baked a cake in the shape of baby blocks, with the name *Carl* written across the top. The cake sat on Merryl's desk that evening as she waited for Carl to arrive.

At six o'clock there was no sign of Carl. At 6:15 Merryl called home. No answer. Maybe he was on his way. She waited ten minutes and called again. No answer. Her stomach began to knot. She called their landlord, who said his son had seen Carl leave at six. Carl had seemed agitated. By seven Merryl was frantic. At 7:20 she left a note on her desk: "Where are you, Carl? What happened?" With the cake melting in her arms she went outside and hailed a cab.

When she got home, she left the cake on the porch and ran inside. The first thing she noticed was a clothes hanger on their bed. She ran to the closet. One of Carl's suits was missing. For a moment she hoped maybe Carl was going to surprise her with a dress-up dinner out because he'd gotten the job. But then she saw that a second suit was missing, and her stomach went sour. She ran into the bathroom; his toothbrush was gone. She ran to the front closet; the suitcases were gone. Carl was gone; something had gone bad. Merryl fell sobbing to the floor.

She called her parents. They called her brother, who hurried over. She called Carl's therapist, and when Merryl told him Carl had packed suitcases, he said that didn't sound like a man who was going to kill himself. Merryl and her brother explored every possibility. Maybe he was in a hotel in Boston thinking it through, said Merryl. Maybe he was in his car, parked somewhere in confusion, said her brother; maybe he was even on some nearby street.

Merryl half-hoped he'd gone to Atlanta or to the Sun Belt, places he'd talked about where there might be jobs. She and her brother got out maps and traced possible routes to possible destinations. She waited for the phone to ring, and she imagined Carl's familiar voice saying he was in Atlanta, he'd been looking for a job, but he was on his way home. Or maybe she'd get a letter with a Texas postmark telling her he'd gotten a job in Dallas. That night while her brother slept on a mattress in Carl's study, Merryl sat up on her bed with the light on. Every five or ten minutes she'd hear a scratch or a whirr and run to the back door, thinking it might be Carl. But it was always a branch creaking or the wind blowing or a car driving by on another street. She pressed herself against the door so hard that months later marks from her forehead and fingers still lingered on the glass.

When the sun came up and the rest of the world started to unfold, the fullness of the fact hit her: It was Saturday morning and Carl wasn't there. Merryl ran to the mirror and screamed, "Where are you? Where are you?"

At noon Merryl called the police to report that Carl was missing. When a patrolman arrived, he told her that everything was going to be okay, that it happened all the time, that her husband was probably sitting in the car somewhere, just thinking things through. But as he stood in her living room filling out a Missing Persons Report, and she told him Carl's height, weight, and date of birth, Merryl realized that the world she had tried to contain was yawning wide.

On Saturday night Carl's parents arrived from New Hampshire. They had been packing to drive down for their grandson Carl's christening when Merryl called. They drove to Merryl and Carl's apartment instead. Saturday night became Sunday, and there was still no word. Merryl and her in-laws scoured the house for notes but found no hints. Carl had left everything neat. He'd taken out the garbage. He'd opened the windows so the breeze could come through.

At nine on Sunday night there was a knock on the door. Merryl sprang up to open it. A Brookline policeman wearing sunglasses handed her a slip of paper with a number on it and said, "Somebody's been trying to reach you all day." Merryl's mother-in-law told him they'd been in the house all day. "I don't know," said the policeman. "All I know is just call this number." He turned and left.

Merryl went into the kitchen, followed by her in-laws, and dialed the number, which had a New York area code. It rang once. A deep, heavy voice answered, "Medical." In the back of her mind Merryl knew from some TV show that this meant "Medical Examiner," but still hoping she said, "Is this a hospital?" There was a pause and the voice said, "Lady, this is the morgue."

Merryl dropped the phone and screamed. She ran through the kitchen, out of the house, and leaped off the back porch to the gravel driveway, a six-foot drop. She threw herself repeatedly onto the space in the driveway where Carl's car should have been. Then she crawled under her landlord's car and lay there screaming, wedged between the carburetor and the gravel.

Merryl could see her mother-in-law's face trying to tell her something as she knelt by the car. She could see legs and feet multiplying. She could hear her name occasionally surface from the thick blur of voices. And still she screamed. Her head felt as if it were on fire. Her face, her arms, and her legs were scratched and bloody. Her shirt was torn. She'd lost her glasses. She felt she couldn't be in a normal space; the world suddenly seemed so unnatural and misshapen and wrong and dangerous that the only place she could be comfortable was between the car and the gravel. If she had had her way, she would have stayed there forever, screaming.

II

THE MARK OF CAIN

IN AN EIGHTEENTH-CENTURY French engraving called *The Desecration of the Corpse,* the naked body of a young man is dragged through the streets of Paris by a spirited white horse. He lies facedown on a wooden sledge, his ankles roped together, his arms outstretched behind him, his fingers clawing the cobblestones. A crowd surrounds the body. One woman shrinks from the scene in horror, covering her face with her hand. A curly-haired child on hands and knees watches in open-mouthed terror. A bearded man, his fingers in his mouth, cringes in disbelief, and a dog gingerly sniffs the corpse. Even the horse seems to rear back in shock at his load, but a hand at his bridle pulls him on.

The young man has been "convicted" of suicide. We do not know why he took his life, but we know some of the consequences of his act. After he is dragged by his heels through the streets of the city, he will be hanged head down in the public square as an example to all who might contemplate such a crime. His body will be thrown into the common sewer or tossed in the town dump. If he had been a nobleman, he will be declared a commoner. His forests will be razed, his castle demolished, his goods and property forfeited to the king.

In the foreground of the engraving there is a young woman. She is the only member of the crowd who moves toward the body rather than recoiling from it. The bearded man has put his hand on her back as if to draw her away, and a part of her seems to respond to his touch. But her sorrow is stronger than her dread, and her left leg bends toward the sledge as if she were about to kneel. She is the dead man's wife. Behind her, on a balcony overlooking the street, two small children reach for their father with outstretched arms. We do not know what will become of this woman and her children. They own nothing but the clothes they wear. And although they cannot afford to leave the town, they cannot afford to stay because they would be forever shamed by the suicide in their family. Most likely the woman will wander until she finds a town where news of the suicide has not spread, where she and her children may live cautiously, telling people her husband died of a disease, praying no one will ever discover her secret.

Like Merryl Maleska two centuries later, the woman in the engraving is a survivor of suicide. Although survivors of other kinds of death can depend on the rituals civilization has developed to support them in their grief, for thousands of years survivors of suicide have suffered alone and in silence. Today, although suicides are no longer dragged through the streets and their property is no longer confiscated, survivors still face a legacy of antisuicide attitudes that have evolved over centuries.

***

In ancient Greece a stigma was a mark burned into the skin to identify a slave or criminal. Since then the definition of "stigma" has expanded to mean a mark of shame or disgrace whether visible or not. No subject has been more stained by stigma than suicide. In various centuries in various countries in Europe, Asia, and Africa, the corpse of a suicide might by law or custom be "decapitated . . . to render it harmless," "buried outside the city, its hand cut off and buried separately," "hastily removed and dumped outside tribal territories," "burned so it cannot walk among and wreak vengeance upon the living," "beaten with chains," "thrown out into the fields to be devoured by wild beasts," "buried in a corner of the forest far from the graves of his brethren," "lowered by pulleys from the window, and the window frame subsequently burned," "put in a barrel and floated down the Moselle," "buried at a crossroads by night with a stake driven through the heart," or "buried under a mountain whose whole weight shall . . . press down upon his restive soul." Though such special treatment was intended to prevent the suicide's ghost from wandering, one can easily imagine its effect on survivors.

When primitive taboos were adopted into organized religion and the attitudes of the Church buttressed by civil law, survivors were more directly penalized. In effect they were treated as an accessory to what was now a crime. In England the suicide's goods were forfeited to his feudal lord. (It was sometimes possible for an heir to buy back a suicide's confiscated goods. In

1289, it is recorded, the widow of one Aubrey of Wystelesburg redeemed her husband's property for three hundred pounds.) In France, according to a law of 1270, not only were the suicide's goods confiscated, but his widow was forced to surrender her possessions. In some areas the suicide's family paid a fine to the victim's in-laws for the shame the suicide had brought upon them. Such punishments were intended as a crude sort of suicide prevention in which survivors became innocent hostages. "What punishment can human laws inflict on one who has withdrawn himself from their reach?" asked the eighteenth-century jurist Sir William Blackstone in his *Commentaries on the Laws of England.* "They can only act upon what he has left behind him, his reputation and fortune; on the former by an ignominious burial in the highway, with a stake driven through his body; in the latter by a forfeiture of all his goods and chattels to the king, hoping that his care for either his own reputation or the welfare of his family would be some motive to restrain him from so desperate and wicked an act."

In order to evade these penalties, survivors learned to disguise suicides by destroying notes, hiding weapons, and securing premature burials. To soften the blow of forfeiture they smuggled valuables out of the house. In France, to counter this "abuse" of the law, a royal edict of 1712 empowered judges to investigate all cases in which the cause of death was doubtful, calling in medical evidence when necessary—an early version of the "psychological autopsy" developed by the Los Angeles Suicide Prevention Center more than two centuries later. In 1736 a second edict ordered that in cases of doubtful death no burial was permitted without license from the authorities. Since the Crown was the beneficiary of a suicide's fortune—and the prosecutor was entitled to a percentage of the take—questionable cases tended to be declared suicides. In the following year appeal by the family and heirs was made obligatory.

In England, where suicides were tried posthumously in Coroner's Court, the penalty for suicide was waived if it was ruled that the dead man had been insane. Juries had to decide whether a self-killer was an innocent madman or a sinful criminal. While the Crown usually argued that the deceased had formulated a deliberate suicide plan, survivors tried to prove either that the death had been an accident or that their loved one was a lunatic. In the case of Lancelot Johnson, a London merchant whose body was fished from the Thames in the early seventeenth century, the Crown claimed the defendant had been "observed to walk in a very sad, deep, melancholy and discontented manner along the river's side, there where he had no other occasion to be, but only to execute his said ungodly resolution" and that a note "containing the reasons and causes of his discontentment and purpose to destroy himself" had been destroyed by his wife. The widow Johnson, however, argued that her husband's death must have been an accident because he was too pious to have committed suicide: "He lived in good repute and esteem amongst his neighbours and acquaintances and also carried himself in an exceeding honest, upright, godly fashion." The jury's verdict is not known.

Survivors with powerful friends were able to evade such awkward courtroom scenes. On two occasions the diarist Samuel Pepys intervened to save the property of friends who had committed suicide. In 1667 his cousin Kate Joyce's husband, attempting to drown himself, was rescued but died shortly afterward, probably of pneumonia. Though the coroner's jury reached a verdict of death from fever and permitted a regular burial, the widow was threatened with confiscation of the estate because it was suspected her husband's attempt had been provoked by financial difficulties. By petitioning his friend King Charles II, Pepys was able to salvage her property.

During the Enlightenment, as philosophers began to speak out against the antisuicide laws, even those who opposed suicide on moral grounds argued against punishing survivors. Though he believed suicide to be "a theft from society and a crime against nature," Delisle de Sales reproduced *The Desecration of the Corpse* in his 1769 book *Philosophy of Nature.* He included an eight-page "Memorandum Addressed to the Legislators by the Widow of a Citizen Punished for the Crime of Suicide" in which he imagined the dead man's widow imploring the court for justice: "They have run through his body with a stake, they have dragged it through the dirt in the streets of the capitol, and they have refused to give his bloody remains the funeral services that one gives to the dead to ease the grief of their surviving loved ones." In 1790, Charles Moore, while denouncing suicide as "horrid and unnatural," nevertheless urged that "our tenderness and compassion should change its object and be solely employed in alleviating the distress of those whose affections and interests he has thus cruelly deserted."

Over the course of the eighteenth century many of the laws punishing suicide were erased, but the stigma they had helped create for survivors remained. In 1761, Marc-Antoine Calas, a French law student, hanged himself in his father's shop in Toulouse. When his parents discovered his body, they removed the rope from his neck and hid it in an attempt to conceal the cause of death. Their subterfuge backfired: A wave of religious fanaticism was sweeping the town, and when the boy's death became known, his father, a devout Protestant, was accused of murdering his son to prevent him from reverting to Catholicism. Found guilty and condemned to be broken on the wheel, the old man died protesting his innocence. The matter would have ended but for Voltaire, who took up Jean Calas's cause. Four years later the decision was reversed. In the retrial it was learned that the parents had concealed the true cause of death because they dreaded the scandal that news of the suicide would provoke.

The self-murderer's legacy of shame was often invoked by preachers in their attempts to seduce the would-be suicide from the path of damnation. "He plants a dagger not merely in his own breast, but in that of his dearest, his tenderest connexions," observed minister G. Gregory at St. Botolph's Bishopsgate in London in 1797. "He wantonly sports with the pangs of sensibility, and covers with the blush of shame the cheeks of innocence. With a degree of ingratitude which excites our abhorrence, he clouds with sorrow the future existence of those by whom he was most tenderly beloved; and (as is alleged by some concerning the first of murderers) he affixes a mark of ignominy on his unfortunate descendants." Eight years later, in New York City, Presbyterian pastor Samuel Miller was even more blunt: "Stay then, guilty man! Stay thy murderous hand! Extinguish not the happiness and the hopes of a family, it may be, of many families! Forbear, O forbear to inflict wounds which no time can heal, and which may tempt survivors to wish that thou hadst never been born!"

A more temperate argument was offered by Richard Hey, a fellow of Magdalen College, whose 1783 dissertation on suicide describes with surpassing empathy the singular effect of a suicide on a survivor:

The *Sorrow* which arises upon the Loss of a Friend, is heightened to the most pungent distress, if he has perished by his own hand. The most calm and gentle death, attended with every alleviation to the dying person, and even to his friends, is yet to these usually no small shock. Minds of the firmest contexture, and retained in the best discipline, if not void of common sensibility, cannot at once reconcile themselves to the change. Add but the circumstance of *Violence*, either accidental or by the lawless attack of the assassin; and the shock is redoubled upon the survivors: even the robust constitution may long experience its effects; weaker and more delicate frames are sometimes thrown into a state of disorder from which they never perfectly recover. But, if the violence proceed from the hand of him who falls by it, a certain amazement is superadded to the more common sensations: and while sorrow, commiseration, apprehension, abhorrence, contend for possession of the mind, they spread devastation over the scene of their mutual conflict.

In the nineteenth century, as suicide began to be interpreted as an illness rather than as a sin and a crime, there was a change in the nature of its stigma. While permitted to bury their dead in consecrated ground and to retain their property and possessions, survivors were now the targets of all the superstition and prejudice associated with insanity. Most physicians maintained that insanity was hereditary, and suicide was the most hereditary form of insanity. The English physician Forbes Winslow wrote in 1840:

With reference to suicide, there is no fact that has been more clearly established than that of its hereditary character. . . . It is not necessary that the disposition to suicide should manifest itself in every generation; it often passes over one, and appears in the next, like insanity unattended with this propensity. But if the members of the family so predisposed are carefully examined, it will be found that the various shades and gradations of the malady will be easily perceptible. Some are distinguished for their flightiness of manner, others for their strange eccentricity, likings and dislikings, irregularity of their passions, capricious and excitable temperament, hypochondriasis and melancholia. These are often but the minute shades and variations of an hereditary disposition to suicidal madness.

Suddenly, viewing them as potential suicides themselves, the medical profession took a keen interest in survivors. Winslow was one of many medical scholars who traced "singular" cases of suicidal reverberations within families in which relatives and descendants killed themselves, sometimes in the same place, sometimes by the same method, sometimes on the anniversary of a previous family suicide. In 1901 at the Annual Meeting of the Medico-Psychological Association in Cork, Ireland, J. M. S. Wood and A. R. Urquhart presented a family tree that in four generations had spawned six suicides, four people with suicidal tendencies, and six with "obvious" insanity. Several years later a certain George P. Mudge constructed a Mendelian pedigree for two English families, evidently attempting to demonstrate that suicides could be bred like prize-winning peonies. "There exists a tradition in the village in which they live that death by means of self-shooting belonged primarily to the B family, and death by self-drowning to the A family," he wrote in *The Mendel Journal.* "The two families have intermarried, and among their descendants three forms of suicide are manifested, namely, the two original forms, by shooting and drowning, and a new form, by taking poison." In what may be the most appalling toll ever recorded, the *Medical Record* of October 26, 1901, noted:

A man named Edgar Jay Briggs, who hanged himself on his farm, near Danbury, Connecticut, a few days ago, was almost the last surviving member of a family which has practically been wiped out of existence by suicide. The history of self-destruction in this family extends over a period of more than fifty years, and in that time, so it is stated, at least twenty-one of the descendants and collaterals of the original Briggs suicide have taken their own lives. . . . Many of the suicides were effected in an unusual way. One man drowned himself by holding his face in a shallow brook, another attached a weight to a collar about his neck and then waded into a pond. Others shot or hanged themselves in a way evidencing fixed determination to end their lives. All of the suicides were not blood relations, some being women who had married into the family. If the newspaper accounts, from which we have quoted, are correct, this is certainly a remarkable instance of contagion of the suicidal impulse which deserves accurate study and record.

Rarely did these instances, in fact, receive accurate study. Physicians merely recorded them with the precision of accountants and the gusto of barkers at a carnival freak show. The message to survivors was unmistakable: They were doomed to suicide themselves—or at the very least to insanity, alcoholism, or feeblemindedness. It is little wonder that many survivors began to regard suicide as an inevitable family fate. "Many are induced to think of suicide from the circumstance of their being conscious that they labour under an hereditary disposition to insanity," wrote Dr. Winslow. ". . . A gentleman, in full possession of his reasoning faculties, and a man of considerable powers of intellect, said to us one day, in a conversation we had with him on the subject of suicide, 'You may probably smile when I tell you that, happy and contented as I appear to be in my mind at this moment, I feel assured I shall fall by my own hands.' Upon our asking him why he thought so, he replied, that a relation of his had killed himself some years previously, and that he laboured under an hereditary predisposition which nothing would subdue."

These hereditary "theories" were especially terrifying for survivors when they intersected with the rise of the eugenics movement at the turn of the century. In his 1893 book, *Suicide and Insanity,* Samuel Strahan presented eleven family trees—the majority traced from his medical practice—as proof that suicides inevitably spawn imbeciles, murderers, epileptics, drunkards, lunatics, and more suicides. "The suicide by his last act places the bar sinister upon the escutcheon of his family," wrote Strahan, "and the man or woman who marries into such a family runs a terrible risk. Just as the appearance of idiocy, epilepsy, or insanity in a family shows that the stock is deteriorating, so suicide points to the fact that the family has wandered from the path of health." Strahan offered his findings to the public "in the hope that people may be induced to use intelligently, in the propagation of the human race some of the knowledge, care, and forethought so successfully exercised in the breeding of the lower animals."

It was not until the early 1950s that the medical profession generally accepted that suicide is not genetically transmitted. But the popular view of suicide as a social disgrace, fanned by the Victorian emphasis on family respectability, brought a new kind of stigma. A passage from James Joyce's *Ulysses* in which Leopold Bloom and two friends are en route to a funeral is characteristic:

"But the worst of all," Mr. Power said, "is the man who takes his own life."

Martin Cunningham drew out his watch briskly, coughed and put it back.

"The greatest disgrace to have in the family," Mr. Power added.

"Temporary insanity, of course," Martin Cunningham said decisively. "We must take a charitable view of it."

Bloom is silent; Cunningham, aware that Bloom's father committed suicide, discreetly attempts to change the subject. But Mr. Power's remarks reflect the modern notion that suicide was no longer primarily a personal failure but a family failure. A suicide was a black mark that polluted a family's marriage stock and lowered property values. The word itself, with its evil-sounding sibilance, was poisonous—a taunt hurled by neighborhood children, a secret whispered by their parents. Suicide became an explanation for a widow's quirks, for a young man's "madness," for a haunted house. "Nothing lowered the prestige of a family as much as the 'talk' that a suicide involved," wrote Henry Fedden in *Suicide*. "It broke the facade presented to the world; the suicide therefore was primarily culpable in relation to his family. He indeed created a *disgrace in the family*, for suicide, instead of chiefly bringing on a soul the wrath of God and the law, now brought to the ears of the family the twitter of malicious tongues." There was a kernel of truth in Cyril Connolly's sardonic observation that some people are afraid to commit suicide for fear of what the neighbors will say.

Whereas in the eighteenth century survivors had camouflaged the cause of death primarily to avoid losing money or property, now they dissembled in order to avoid losing face. Funerals were hasty and hushed up; servants were discharged "because they knew"; friends and relatives were avoided; and suicides were transformed in family myths into hunting accidents and heart attacks. Children were told the truth years later if they were told at all. Families entered unspoken agreements to avoid mentioning the name of the departed. Suicide was a family secret to be kept at all costs, a skeleton in the closet. Neighbors sifted evidence and assigned blame; phrases like "he drove her to it" echoed in gossip. Shunned by neighbors, families moved out of the house, out of the neighborhood, out of the state, where people "wouldn't know" and they could start life over. But just as in primitive cultures the suicide's wandering ghost was believed to haunt the living, so too did memories of the suicide pursue twentieth-century survivors. Whether to unhappiness, madness, or suicide, the survivor felt in some way doomed. Reaching back to the Old Testament to describe his feelings of being stigmatized, one man referred to his father's suicide by drowning as the time when "he placed the mark of Cain upon me."

And so survivors went underground, keeping their grief, guilt, and anger locked inside. Even when interest in the subject of suicide and suicide prevention grew in mid-century, survivors were overlooked by the mental health profession. In the traditional psychiatric model, the case was closed when the patient died. The therapist—if the suicide had been in therapy—tended to focus on his own feelings of guilt and grief instead of reaching out to the surviving family. Most survivors were too ashamed to seek professional help themselves. Some survivors eventually developed severe disturbances that forced them into treatment; only after months of therapy did they reveal that there had been a family suicide buried in their past.

Interest in survivors emerged in roundabout ways. When the Los Angeles Suicide Prevention Center began to perform psychological autopsies in 1958, researchers found widespread resistance, suppression of evidence, and mental trauma among suicide survivors. But they found something else as well. Although they had been apprehensive about approaching distraught relatives, they quickly discovered that survivors had a great need to talk—about their grief, their guilt, their anger, and often their own suicidal feelings. It was usually the first time the survivors had been given an opportunity to talk about the suicide, and they frequently found the interviews therapeutic. "I believe that the person who commits suicide puts his psychological skeleton in the survivor's emotional closet," wrote LASPC co-founder Edwin Shneidman. "He sentences the survivor to deal with many negative feelings and, more, to become obsessed with thoughts regarding his own actual or possible role in having precipitated the suicidal act or having failed to abort it. It can be a heavy load." Shneidman urged that suicide prevention programs address the psychological needs of survivors by offering counseling and support he called "postvention."

Like the LASPC, other suicide prevention centers soon realized that survivors were a high-risk group in need of their services. A 1967 study of a St. Louis center showed that one in three callers had had a previous suicide in the family. If, as one study shows, 25 percent of seriously suicidal people have a suicide in their background, helping survivors clearly constituted effective suicide prevention. "Given the present stage of our knowledge about suicide," wrote Harvey Resnik, Shneidman's successor as director of the Center for Studies of Suicide Prevention, "proper postvention seems the most promising avenue toward reducing the large number of suicides that occur annually." For centuries survivors had been penalized in the name of suicide prevention; now they were counseled in the name of suicide prevention.

Gradually, research on suicide widened its focus to include those left behind. In *Survivors of Suicide,* the first book to explore the problems of survivors, published in 1972, psychologist Albert Cain categorized a range of reactions: reality distortion, tortured object-relations, overwhelming guilt, disturbed self-concept, impotent rage, identification with the suicide, depression and self-destructiveness, search for meaning, and incomplete mourning. Other studies found that survivors inherit a legacy of guilt, anger, and frustration that may surface as depression or in stress-related medical problems such as exhaustion, migraines, ulcers, colitis. A bibliography on suicide from 1897 to 1970 lists only fifteen articles relating to survivors; a 1986 bibliography lists almost two hundred books and articles that scrutinize survivor issues from anniversary reactions to the impact of suicide on children to the effect of denial on grief.

As mental health professionals were busy studying them, survivors began to reach out to each other, forming self-help groups and organizing conferences. In 1980, two hundred survivors from more than thirty states and Canada attended a National Survivors Conference in Iowa City. Since then there have been frequent survivor seminars and panels on suicide and grief. In 1983 the LASPC was unable to get a celebrity survivor to speak at their twenty-fifth anniversary banquet; since then actress Mariette Hartley, whose father shot himself when she was twenty-two, actor Peter Fonda, whose mother cut her throat when he was ten, and comedienne Joan Rivers, whose husband took an overdose in 1987, have spoken out about their experience as survivors. At many schools and colleges suicidologists now counsel distraught students and faculty after a suicide on campus. Certain prevention centers and suicidologists also provide training to physicians, coroners, funeral directors, policemen, and the media on how to handle families after a suicide.

Most important, such openness has begun to diminish the isolation that centuries of stigma have encouraged. "When my brother killed himself, I knew *nothing* about suicide," says one woman. "For some reason I thought maybe this happened to three hundred people a year. I don't know where I got that figure, but it made me feel as if I was the only person it had ever happened to." Indeed, there are millions of survivors of suicide in this country. Even using a conservative estimate of 50,000 suicides annually, the ranks of survivors are swelled by 250,000 more survivors each year—a figure that leaves out the extended family, friends, and therapists, all of whom may be devastated by a suicide. Like the Japanese soldiers who emerged from their jungle hideouts to find World War II had ended decades before, some survivors are finding they no longer have to hide. One thirty-two-year-old Minneapolis woman who was four years old when her mother shot herself began only recently to speak about the suicide: "For twenty-eight years my pain was like a rock I carried wherever I went," she says. "When I finally began to grieve, it was as if my tears dissolved that rock."

But while suicides are no longer buried beneath mountains to trap their restive souls, their survivors are still struggling against the weight of centuries of stigma. More than a hundred years after confiscation of property was abolished, many life insurance companies continue to deny benefits to families of people who commit suicide within two years after buying a policy. More than two hundred years after Jean Calas hid the noose that had squeezed the life out of his son, survivors still conceal notes, suppress evidence, and pressure coroners to rule a death an "accident." Some have even submitted petitions signed by an entire neighborhood attesting to a dead man's sterling character as proof he could not have committed suicide. More than fourteen hundred years after the Council of Braga refused burial to self-killers, suicides are still technically denied burial rites by the Roman

Catholic Church; priests employ the traditional insanity loophole to justify burial in consecrated ground.

Long after most ministers ceased preaching about suicide's "mark of ignominy," many survivors still feel branded. "I used to drive down the street thinking I had a sign on my car that said MY SON KILLED HIMSELF," says Iris Bolton, an Atlanta counselor who travels the country to speak on survivor issues. "Another car would pass me and I would think, 'Now they know.' " The fact of the suicide can become an identity. "You're no longer yourself, you're the widow of the man who killed himself," says a woman whose husband took a fatal overdose. Although some of the stigma may be more imagined than real, research indicates that the families of suicides are usually perceived negatively by others and are offered less support. A 1980 study compared the reactions of 119 adults to two newspaper accounts: one of a child's death by suicide and one of a child's death by illness. The child's parents were liked less and blamed more for the child's death when that death was by suicide. Several years after the suicide of her sixteen-year-old son, a woman says, "Losing my son was painful enough, but the whispers, feeling like a leper, being avoided, having people not look me in the eye or acting like nothing happened, never mentioning the death, changing the subject, people being afraid it's contagious, as if it may happen to them if they touch me or reach out to me—is almost worse."

And so many survivors still feel they have something to hide. Twelve years after his brother's suicide one young man stubbornly insists his brother was murdered although he offers no suspects and no evidence. His only reason is that it can't be. Other survivors selectively edit their revelations. "I tell everyone my husband died of a cerebral hemorrhage," says one woman. "What I don't say is that it was from a self-inflicted gunshot wound." It is all too easy for survivors to find people who will corroborate their sense of shame. In a memoir about the suicide of his son, journalist James Wechsler described how the police offered to suppress the circumstances of the death. "Even in the numbness of those hours we were astonished at the prevalence of the view that suicide was a dishonorable or at least disreputable matter, to be charitably covered up to protect Michael's good name and the sensibilities of his family."

Even the people closest to the survivor are often eager to pretend the suicide never happened. Families may shut down; friends may keep their distance. The night after they found their nineteen-year-old son's body hanging in their vacation house, one couple had dinner with their closest friends. They had accepted the invitation weeks before, and despite the shock of their son's death, they decided it might be comforting to be with the people who knew them best. When they arrived at their friends' home, their hosts said, "Hi, how are you, how have you been?" They took their coats, poured them cocktails, served them dinner, chatted about the weather, sports, and politics, served them dessert, got their coats for them, wished them good night, and shut the door.

The entire evening had passed without a single mention of the boy's death. The friends were afraid to bring it up; the survivors didn't bring it up because they were waiting for their friends to bring it up. Neither couple thought of anything but the suicide.

III

MERRYL: THE TORTURE CHAMBER

UNDERNEATH THE CAR Merryl Maleska continued to scream. Neighbors, thinking someone was being raped, called the police, and within minutes two squad cars, sirens wailing, pulled up to the house. Merryl could hear the gruff voices of the policemen as they approached the car. Assuming she was on drugs, they shouted that they would arrest her if she didn't calm down and tell them what was wrong. When Merryl's mother-in-law mumbled something in one policeman's ear, they softened their approach. Five minutes later Merryl crawled out from under the car.

Supported by her in-laws, Merryl staggered into the house. She couldn't stop writhing. She clawed at her shirt and ripped strands of dark brown hair from her scalp. She was dimly aware that this should hurt, but she felt no pain. She howled that she was going to kill herself. The police, whose presence seemed to Merryl to turn the whole living room blue, said they'd have to take her to the hospital. Merryl screamed that she'd wait three months and then kill herself when no one was watching. The police said they'd lock her in the hospital anyway. Merryl stopped screaming and stared at them stonily.

After the police left, Merryl continued to pace, numbly pulling and scratching at herself. She felt unable to move or speak in customary ways; she hunched over, squatted in corners, and twisted her limbs; she felt her body had been turned inside out. "The world was completely wrong now," she remembers. "How could I stand up and talk and be normal?" When Carl's brother and sister-in-law arrived, Merryl's sadness and anger focused on them. "I hated the sight of them instantly. I didn't want to see them. I had loved Laurie, but now I resented her. She represented everything I didn't have—the baby, the doctorate, the home, the husband." When they touched her, Merryl turned away. She knew she was being unfair, but she couldn't help it. Sometime after midnight they left, and Merryl was alone with Carl's parents.

Carl's parents were, like Carl, quiet, contained, and responsible. They sat on either side of Merryl on the couch and the three of them held one another, swaying and moaning, sometimes just sighing, lulling. Occasionally her in-laws moved about the room as if in a slow-motion dream. Once, Merryl saw them hug and heard her father-in-law murmur "our firstborn." She was flooded with the sudden understanding that Carl was their son as well as her husband. For the first time they were realizing that their son had been deeply depressed. They gently asked Merryl questions about Carl. He had kept so many of his painful feelings from them; until that night they had never known he'd been in therapy. At one point Carl's father turned to Merryl and asked, "When was he last happy?" Merryl couldn't respond; the question made her unbearably sad, and she didn't know the answer.

From time to time one of Carl's parents would lie down in the bedroom, but no one slept that night. The sun rose shortly after four. It was June 21, the first day of summer, the longest day of the year. To Merryl the world outside her window seemed strangely garish: "I'll never forget that dawn. The painful light. Monday morning. People getting into their cars, starting their engines, going to their normal lives."

The moment she dropped the phone Merryl had known in her bones that Carl had killed himself. Later, Carl's father, who had retrieved the dangling receiver and finished talking to the man at the morgue, told Merryl that yes, it was suicide. Now it bothered Merryl that she didn't know more. That afternoon in the living room where Carl's and Merryl's families gathered, she wanted to know exactly how Carl had died. Her father-in-law got upset; why did she have to know every detail? Merryl's anger flared. "I knew everything about the way Carl lived," she said. "And I have to know everything about the way he died." Her father-in-law walked to the window and stared out. "He hanged himself," he said quietly.

Wanting to "protect" her, people tried to keep the details of Carl's death from Merryl, but over the next few days she pieced the story together. Carl had driven to the Greyhound station and taken a bus to New York City. He'd gone to the YMCA, probably looking for a room with exposed pipes, but when he found none, he walked down 34th Street and checked into a seedy single-room occupancy hotel near Pennsylvania Station. Sometime Saturday night or

Sunday morning Carl hanged himself from the steam pipe in his sparsely furnished room. The chambermaid found him Sunday morning at 10:30, at almost the same moment his nephew, Carl, had been christened in Cambridge, 220 miles away. When the police arrived at the hotel, they found pieces of paper with the telephone numbers of New York gun stores.

Three months earlier Merryl had noticed an article in *Redbook* on mourning called "Would You Be Prepared?" She skipped over it. She had always avoided anything to do with dying. She was terrified of cemeteries. But now she was the eye of a storm of activity focused on death. Funeral arrangements were made, ministers consulted, relatives notified, and through it all Merryl was treated like an invalid by the two families who had last all gathered together to celebrate Merryl and Carl's wedding. It was decided that Merryl would be moved to her parents' house on Cape Cod, where she and Carl had spent that first glorious weekend together twelve years before. Merryl's best friend helped her pack. Her three-year-old son had drowned two years earlier, and she seemed to know how to soothe Merryl. But inside, Merryl was frantic. How would Carl's body arrive? When would she see him? What would he be wearing? That night Merryl and her mother slept on the mattress in Carl's study. They had never been physically close, and Merryl was moved and comforted by their silent intimacy.

On Tuesday morning Merryl was driven to her parents' house. That same day Carl's body was shipped from New York City. The following afternoon Merryl visited the funeral home with her mother and two aunts. They stood in the waiting room while final preparations were made. When she heard the case being cranked to tilt the casket into viewing position, Merryl fell to the floor, sobbing. Her mother and her aunts knelt to help her to her feet. Then the door opened and a middle-aged man with a kindly but formal expression beckoned and said, "This way, please." On a platform at the far end of the next room lay a glistening red metal coffin. Merryl kept telling herself it held some stranger's body, that it couldn't be Carl, but as soon as she saw the wavy brown hair, she knew it was Carl. Her mother and her aunts left, and suddenly she was alone with him.

She studied his face. "I made myself aware of every tiny cell and inch of his body that was visible." There was a spot of dried blood behind his ear that Merryl assumed must have been left from the autopsy. There were red marks on his hands as if they'd been clenched. She touched his forehead. His skin was as cold as marble. She noticed the small scar near his right eye where a mole had been removed two years earlier. "He was incredibly well preserved, intact and normal looking. But he looked different. His jaw was set, and it gave him a determined, angry expression. But his eyebrows looked just the same. I had always loved his eyebrows. They were blond and soft and thick, and they looked exactly the way they'd looked when he was alive. And that made me so sad. I was overwhelmed with the terrible feeling that a week ago this person had been so filled with living, and now there were just the eyebrows. As I looked at him I could remember exactly what he was saying the week before at that exact time. I would go over and over the events of the week and be astonished and horrified that it had come out this way, that it ended in this permanent fixture in this coffin."

Merryl spent two hours with Carl that afternoon and four hours the next. Sitting on a chair by his coffin, she told him all the things she hadn't had a chance to say. She reminded him of moments in their married life. She told him what was happening now, about all the pain she was feeling. They'd been together almost every day for eight years, and so much of what she felt only Carl could understand. Sometimes she was angry at him, but gently. "Why did you have to do it? Didn't you remember *us?*" she asked. "Why, Carl, why?"

At the funeral Carl lay in a closed casket a few feet from where Merryl sat. Merryl had been very involved in organizing the service: discussing what should be said, deciding where Carl should be buried, talking to the minister about the eulogy. She even changed a few lines in a poem her father had written for Carl and planned to read at the funeral. She wanted to be part of anything that concerned Carl. But Merryl remembers little of the service: A flautist played something she recalls only as haunting; the minister's words were a blur. She sobbed hysterically through most of the service. From the back of the church the cries of Carl's two-week-old nephew seemed to pierce through her own cries into her heart and made her cry even harder. When Merryl stood at the end of the service, her legs shook uncontrollably. A friend, driving away from the church, told her husband that she doubted Merryl was going to make it. Back at her parents' house, while mourners quietly sipped coffee and ate cold cuts, Merryl lay in bed. A psychiatrist friend of Carl's spoke to her gently, expressing his concern and saying he'd had no idea anything was amiss with Carl. During the entire hour he talked to her, Merryl held pillows over her head.

In the following days Merryl began to attend to the loose ends Carl's death had unwound. While her brother searched parking lots across Boston for the Chevy Citation that Carl and Merryl had bought two years earlier, Merryl called the police in New York City, where Carl's belongings had been stored in a vault. In order to claim them she had to go over a list of what he had with him when he died: car keys, watch, wallet, glasses, wedding ring. Merryl called her friends, many of whom she hadn't spoken to for months, preoccupied with Carl's depression. "Hi! Where ya been?" they'd exclaim. "You don't understand," Merryl would say. "Carl committed suicide." There was never a question in Merryl's mind whether or not to tell people Carl's death was a suicide. "Nobody had ever been ashamed of Carl when he was alive, and there was nothing to be ashamed of when he was dead," she says. "It was just sad and tragic." At one point her brother said he was going to tell his tenants Carl died of a heart attack. "If you want to do that, okay," Merryl said, "but if you're doing it to protect me, forget it."

By Saturday, Merryl and her parents were alone. It was Carl and Merryl's sixth wedding anniversary. In the afternoon her father drove her to the cemetery. For over an hour while Mr. Maleska sat in the car, parked a little ways off, watching with tears in his eyes, Merryl lay on Carl's flower-strewn grave, weeping into the newly turned-up earth.

Sunday evening Merryl read from a book of poetry by Emily Dickinson. Her parents were pleased. They thought maybe she was getting better.

Monday, Merryl woke up and remembered: Carl was gone, and her life would never be the same. "I felt as if I had been pulled off the track," she says. "It was the busiest time of year at work, and everything was on a schedule. That very morning I was supposed to send certain books I'd edited to the typesetter. I thought of my colleagues at the office working so hard, and here I was lying in bed. The office seemed a million miles away. It seemed part of another life. Two weeks before, my work had consumed me, and now I didn't care if those books ever saw the light of day. And it hit me that this was the way it would be. I would never be interested in work again. I would never be interested in anything again. Nothing mattered and nothing ever would. I would never get out of this bed."

The bed she lay in was a rollaway sofa in her father's study. Designed for privacy, the study was an ideal haven for grieving. Merryl would spend most of the next four months in this room, which she had always loved but which she now came to think of as her "torture chamber." She would become intimate with its every detail, staring at her father's books on the shelves until she had memorized a dozen titles without realizing it. Most of her time was spent lying in bed, crying. She cried so much that her mother quickly learned Kleenex wouldn't suffice. It just wasn't strong enough. Instead, Mrs. Maleska made sure a fresh roll of paper towels lay on the floor near Merryl's bed. When Merryl wasn't crying, she screamed, sometimes for as long as an hour, until she was sure her head would burst. At first, when Merryl's parents heard her screams, they came running. Sometimes her mother brought Merryl a cup of tea to soothe her ragged throat. But it soon became clear that the screams were a necessary part of Merryl's life, and with the television on and the door shut—which Merryl insisted on—her parents could sit in the living room on the far side of the house and hear only muffled sounds. "They knew I was screaming, and I knew that they knew," says Merryl. "And I knew it hurt them. But I didn't want them sitting in the next room, waiting for me to stop."

For months Merryl kept the blinds drawn in her room. She couldn't stand seeing the sun. And if she opened the blinds, she would see the gazebo where she and Carl had exchanged their wedding vows six years before and the water where they had sailed and swum so often. At night, fearing the dark, Merryl slept with the light on. Soon, day seemed like night and night like day. In her dim cocoon, time became one vast, formless mass to Merryl, unchanging save one thing: Night or day, the digital clock on a corner of the bookshelf across the room seemed to print its luminous numbers in her head.

Merryl left the house only for frequent visits to Carl's grave, driven by her father. Sometimes she sat at the kitchen table while her parents ate dinner. Merryl rarely ate although her mother kept fixing her meals, just in case. After dinner she and her mother lingered at the kitchen table for hours, talking about Carl. Merryl went over every detail of that last week; everything she had done seemed to Merryl to be a reason why Carl had killed himself. Every second of that week held a missed opportunity, a moment she could have stepped in and done something to keep him alive. Why hadn't she called fifteen minutes earlier that last day? If she had stayed home from work that day, would Carl be alive now? Why hadn't she stayed at home all week? Why hadn't she grabbed the phone when Carl's therapist called? Why hadn't she made him understand how desperate Carl was? Why hadn't she understood when Carl had talked about suicide? How could she have been so blind? Why hadn't she hospitalized Carl? Why had she argued with him? Why hadn't she been more supportive? Why hadn't she loved him more?

Her mother listened, patiently pointing out the many ways Merryl had supported Carl. Mrs. Maleska was a quiet, thoughtful woman—Merryl had always joked that she had married someone like her mother. The Maleskas had loved Carl like a son and had been shattered by his suicide. Mrs. Maleska did not know whether her cancer would let her live five months or five years, but she listened to her daughter, comforting, questioning, persistently offering evidence of Merryl's love for Carl. They would dissect a single moment for hours before Merryl was convinced she had acted responsibly, but then Merryl would dredge up some fresh evidence and they would go over it again, then settle it again—and then reexamine it from yet another angle. Mother and daughter sat at the kitchen table into the night, Merryl's fingers tying and untying the frayed strands on the belt of her pink chenille bathrobe.

Merryl's father often listened from the next room, and occasionally joined them. He said little, though what he said was always helpful. But he didn't understand why Merryl needed to talk it through so many times. Eighteen months later when his wife died, he told Merryl that now he understood why she had been unable to let her grief rest.

Every night after talking with her parents, Merryl swallowed a capsule of Xanax, a mild tranquilizer, to help her sleep. But every night at four she would wake up and find herself thinking about Carl. She tried to imagine what he must have felt like in those last days, starting with the six hours between the time she had said "Congratulations" to him on the phone and the time the landlord had seen him drive away. When had he made his decision? When had he gotten up from his desk? Her imagination traced him from their house in

Brookline to the Greyhound bus station, on the bus to New York, and watched him walking the streets looking for a hotel with exposed pipes. And she pictured that final, sad, unfamiliar room. What had he been thinking of? What had he looked like when he was hanging? Merryl replayed that journey hundreds of times and found hundreds of ways to change the ending: She got home before Carl left and was able to soothe him; she raced to the Greyhound station and intercepted him; she ran down Broadway, saw his silhouette in the hotel window, and rushed inside to cut the rope just in time. And for an hour in the middle of the night Carl was alive again, and everything was all right. But by dawn the real story came back to her, and it always had the same ending— Carl hanging from a pipe in New York and Merryl in bed on Cape Cod, alone.

Gradually, Merryl's thoughts moved back in time from that final week, poring over her relationship with Carl like a piece of fine cloth, holding it up to the light and looking for frayed seams and holes in the fabric. She examined every job interview Carl had; if only he had gotten *this* one; why hadn't he tried for *that* one? Had she pushed him too hard? Had she been too soft? Why had they moved to Boston? Why hadn't they stayed in Chicago? Every second of their shared life was suddenly reflected through the fact of Carl's suicide. Merryl could spend an entire day in bed mulling over something she had said or done two, four, six years ago, a remark or a touch she had all but forgotten but now seemed critical: the time she yelled at him one Thanksgiving morning when he had brought home the wrong bread crumbs; the time she blamed him for having their apartment exterminated while the kitchenware was uncovered. Maybe if she had been gentler or kinder to him at that distant moment, he would still be alive. "I haunted myself with how I had not been a good enough wife for six years," she said. "I haunted myself with the feeling that maybe at bottom I just wasn't right for him, that maybe I had just reinforced the failure in him." Eventually, she wondered whether anything in their relationship had been real and good and true.

For every reason Merryl found to hate herself, for every clue she uncovered to reinforce her guilt over Carl's death, her parents, Carl's parents, her friends, and her therapist constantly reassured her that it wasn't her fault, that she had done everything possible. The head of Merryl's bed was lined with cards that friends and relatives had sent, which she read and reread as evidence that she wasn't all bad. She also kept all the cards she had given Carl by her bed. "I couldn't bear reading the cards he'd written me that told me how much he loved me," she says. "They made me feel guilty that maybe I hadn't done enough, that I didn't love him enough back. So I would read the cards I'd given him that said how much I loved *him,* and that would comfort me." She kept only one card from Carl at her fingertips, the one he had written on her birthday; she read it over and over to herself, often on her daily trips to his grave. Carl had left no suicide note, and Merryl felt that this card was a kind of good-bye. But she still found reasons to disbelieve its grateful message. And even if she managed to let herself off the hook for a second, it didn't matter—Carl was still dead.

Though Merryl raked herself over the coals in her conscious life, her unconscious was less ruthless. She never had nightmares about Carl though she dreamed of him often. In her dreams he was gentle and comforting. "He was always telling me in a loving sort of way, 'I had to do it, it was the only way.' " One night Merryl dreamed that because suicide survivors go through such torment, their loved ones were permitted to come back to life for two months each year, and the survivor could pick the dates. Merryl chose to have Carl returned to her every weekend so the joy of his presence would be spread out.

But each morning she felt back at square one. "Mornings were the worst," says Merryl. "When I woke up it would all come right back. And I would go into thought whirls about why and how and who he was and what I'd done. Each morning I was brought up against the fact that nothing would change." At ten or eleven Merryl's mother would bring her coffee, and they would start going over it again. "I wanted to talk endlessly about Carl, about what had happened, about the events, about why, why, why," says Merryl. "If I wasn't doing it out loud, I was doing it in my head. I was never *not* doing it. I thought if I just talked enough, I'd find the reason and get rid of the pain." About three weeks after the funeral Merryl decided the answer was to check into a hospital. "All I thought was that I have to keep talking this through, and at the hospital I'll get round-the-clock therapy. I had this dream that the hospital would be my salvation—I'd check in, do intensive therapy for six months, and it would be over."

On a hot, sticky, Fourth of July weekend Merryl and her mother drove to Boston to visit several hospitals her therapist had recommended. It was the first time Merryl had ventured farther than Carl's grave. Merryl had never been inside a psychiatric hospital, and she was shaken. "All I saw were men in pajamas, vacant-looking people watching TV in the afternoon." Her guide at the first hospital, a pleasant young man, told her she would spend her first month on a locked ward like this one. When Merryl asked about therapy, he told her that each patient received three hours a week. The rest of the time constituted "milieu therapy"; merely mixing with these people was considered therapeutic. And there was basket weaving. Merryl was not too numb to be appalled.

At the next hospital the admissions officer advised against hospitalization, telling Merryl she was in a state of grief, which is not necessarily depression, though they may feel the same. "If you check in," he said, "they'll treat you like a patient and you may start feeling like a patient, and then you may *become* a patient." He talked about grief cycles, anniversary reactions, and other things Merryl had never heard of. "I know it will be tough," she told him, "but I just want to do it and get it over with."

At the third hospital Merryl fell apart. "The interviewer was younger than

I was, and she was sunburned and smiling and had clearly come back from a happy holiday weekend," recalls Merryl. "She kept asking questions—'Now, how did he die?' 'What did you do after you got the news?'—as if she were reading from a checklist. I kept thinking, 'This is a nightmare. Why should this girl be doing it? Carl should be having this kind of job.' And I couldn't speak a word." Finally, unable to make herself talk, Merryl called her therapist, who calmed her down enough to enable her to get back to Cape Cod to her own bed where she could scream as much as she wanted.

Merryl thought constantly about killing herself or, more accurately, about wanting to die. She had always loved the ocean, but now she thought of it only as a place to drown herself. She even picked out a particular rock, near the marsh behind the house, that she could tie around her neck so she would sink to the bottom. In bed Merryl held a pillow over her face until she felt light-headed, trying to feel the way Carl must have felt when he was hanging. But she always came up gasping for air. She took fistfuls of the Percodan pills prescribed for her mother's cancer and spread them on her pillow. "I sort of taunted myself. I thought, 'What would it take to make me take them?' I would try to make myself feel as desperate as he was. I put them near my mouth, but I never swallowed any. I wanted to be dead, but I couldn't kill myself."

One month after Carl's death Merryl returned to work at Houghton Mifflin, two half-days a week. She was put on "short-term disability," a modified work schedule for employees who have had a serious accident or illness. Merryl didn't do much at work. She stared at the galleys that awaited editing on her desk. "I just sort of punched things through," she says. "I couldn't concentrate for more than fifteen minutes at a time without a break or a breakdown." Almost anything set her off: a conversation across the hall about a movie she and Carl had planned to see; a casual reference to self-confidence or assertiveness; a passage in a book she was editing that mentioned children; a colleague's conversations with an author named Carl; the sight of the woman who had baked the baby blocks cake. Once, her supervisor, referring to an author from Idaho, joked, "God, the places good people have to wind up these days." Merryl burst into tears. Idaho had been on the list of states she had been unwilling to move to.

Merryl spent much of her time crying at her desk. She never smiled or laughed. She avoided people's eyes as she shuffled down the halls so she wouldn't have to say hello. She walked with tiny steps, huddled over. At one point she was mistaken for a fifty-year-old. She lost twenty-five pounds in the first two months after Carl's death, and in her stomach she felt a constant physical pain. "A knot," she says. "A churning in my stomach and lungs, the way you feel before an important interview or exam. Except it didn't go away. Sometimes I would get a real pain in my heart as if all the heart muscles were clenched very tightly. I always felt I was building up to scream, cry, or gag. A wall of nausea always separated me from the people around me. I could see people move and smile, but they were in another world. If I had a conversation with someone, I could see he or she was making normal human gestures, but when I tried to react, I felt muffled. I was standing there talking but with the knowledge that something was wrong, all wrong."

Two months after Carl's death, Merryl made a list of what she believed were her options. She carried it with her wherever she went. The list read:

> suicide
> a hospital
> just refusing to move from bed—having them take me away
> going to the apt, lying on mattress, taking enough pills to be unconscious, away from the world indefinitely
> quitting job, moving to another city
> getting a different kind of job
> going on in these endless cycles of working/not working, staying in the city/staying at my parents' home—horrible, horrible

IV

THE O'ER-FRAUGHT
HEART

ALTHOUGH SHE DID NOT REALIZE IT, Merryl Maleska's eating and sleeping difficulties, her screaming, her stomach pains, her depression, even her suicidal thoughts were all normal responses to an abnormal situation. Behavior that has brought many mourners to psychiatrists with the fear that they are "going crazy" is considered within the standard range of grief reactions: "seeing" the dead person, "hearing" his key in the lock, calling out his name, dialing his office number and expecting him to answer. "Although mourning involves grave departures from the normal attitude to life, it never occurs to us to regard it as a pathological condition and to refer it to medical treatment," wrote Freud. "We rely on its being overcome after a certain lapse of time, and we look upon any interference with it as useless or even harmful." To Freud, grief's purpose was clear: "Mourning has a quite specific psychical task to perform: its function is to detach the survivors' memories and hopes from the dead."

Described like this, it sounds as clean and quick as a tonsillectomy, but in fact mourning has proved to be one of life's most painful, lengthy, and complex procedures. In 1984 a study by the National Academy of Sciences found that the 8 million Americans who lose a family member each year experience significant disturbance in their way of life for at least one year and as many as three. Of the 800,000 new widows and widowers each year, up to 20 percent remain clinically depressed a year after the death of their spouse. The death of a family member may increase a survivor's smoking, drinking, and drug use as well as the chance of serious physical and mental illness. Men who have lost a spouse or a parent are more likely to die from accidents, heart disease, some infectious illnesses, and suicide. For women, who are more apt to seek support, the loss of a loved one is less likely to increase mortality, though there is evidence that death rates from cirrhosis of the liver and from suicide may rise.

Although Freud laid the theoretical groundwork, it is generally agreed that the systematic study of grief did not begin until the Coconut Grove fire in 1942. Following a football game the Boston nightclub was packed beyond its legal capacity. A busboy accidentally ignited a decorative palm, and by the time the flames had been extinguished, nearly five hundred people were dead. From his work with the bereaved families Erich Lindemann, chief of psychiatry at Massachusetts General Hospital, wrote a groundbreaking paper, "The Symptomatology and Management of Acute Grief." He found that it was normal, indeed healthy, to experience such reactions as guilt, hostility, physical distress, preoccupation with the image of the lost loved one, and a sense of merely "going through the motions" of daily living. Grief that is delayed or repressed, suggested Lindemann, is morbid or abnormal. Only through the proper "grief work," preferably aided by psychotherapy, can someone emancipate himself from "bondage to the deceased" and move forward with life. Lindemann's observations have served ever since as the psychological model clinicians use to describe and treat grief.

In the last two decades increased interest in issues of death and dying, spearheaded by the work of Elisabeth Kübler-Ross and her concept of a "good death," has sparked a corresponding interest in bereavement and the concept of "good grief." At "grief institutes" and "bereavement centers" psychologists and social workers offer help to people who have lost loved ones. Researchers study physiological factors in grief and the biochemistry of tears while clinicians analyze the grief process. Under this renewed scrutiny Lindemann's model of normal grief has been refined. Rather than the relatively straight line Lindemann proposes, the path of grief is now being described by various experts as a circle, spiral, double-back, or zigzag. While they agree that mourners go through periods of shock, intense grief, and recovery, they have defined a variety of models. Some have adapted Kübler-Ross's five stages of dying—denial, anger, bargaining, depression, and acceptance—to grief. Others have catalogued as few as three or as many as twelve different stages. "There's a tendency for the novice to take the stages too literally," writes psychologist William Worden. "After her first book, *On Death and Dying,* many people expected dying patients literally to go through the stages she had listed. Some of them were disappointed when the stages were not passed through in some neat order."

Freud was the first to distinguish between grief and depression, which can have nearly identical symptoms. It is indeed difficult to draw the line beyond which mourning slips into depression. Many clinicians have tried to prescribe a length for normal mourning, and their estimates range from three months to six months, to "four full seasons," to two years, to forever. The NAS report suggested that professional intervention may be needed for those who show as much distress a year after the death as they did during the first month. As Lindemann suggested, the only sure sign of abnormal grief may be the *absence* of visible grief. "Sooner or later," wrote English psychoanalyst John Bowlby, "some of those who avoid all conscious grieving, break down—usually with some form of depression." A psychiatrist at Massachusetts General Hospital has estimated that 10 to 15 percent of the people who come to its mental health clinics are suffering from unresolved grief. Mere time, say grief experts, does not heal everything; the feelings must be talked out. "Give sorrow words," as Malcolm advised Macduff. "The grief that does not speak / Whispers the o'er-fraught heart, and bids it break."

Mourning is among the most primal and universal of responses, as researchers have found in observing grief reactions in animals from dolphins to ostriches to gorillas. One of the most haunting evocations of mourning ever written is Konrad Lorenz's description of bereavement in the Greylag goose:

> The first response to the disappearance of the partner consists in the anxious attempt to find him again. The goose moves about restlessly by day and night, flying great distances and visiting all places where the partner might be found, uttering all the time the penetrating trisyllabic long-distance call. . . . The searching expeditions are extended farther and farther, and quite often the searcher himself gets lost, or succumbs to an accident. From the moment a goose realizes that the partner is missing, it loses all courage and flees even from the youngest and weakest geese. As its condition quickly becomes known to all the members of the colony, the lonely goose rapidly sinks to the lowest step in the ranking order. . . . the goose can become extremely shy, reluctant to approach human beings and to come to the feeding place; the bird also develops a tendency to panic which further increases its "accident-proneness."

Lorenz has succinctly described some of the reactions commonly experienced by grieving humans: denial, searching, panic, loss of hope, vulnerability, social alienation, and isolation.

While any death is traumatic for survivors, some deaths are more traumatic than others. A sudden death may be more difficult than a death in which there has been some preparation, some chance to say good-bye. A violent death may be even harder. Murder, which is both sudden and violent, is more shattering still. But because it is sudden, often violent, and freighted with the added burdens of guilt and stigma, perhaps the most difficult of all deaths to resolve is suicide.

Suicide survivors pass through many of the responses common to all survivors, beginning with shock, numbness, and denial. Like Merryl they may have difficulty eating, sleeping, concentrating. They may have nightmares or anxiety attacks in which they endlessly replay scenes in their mind—particularly if the death was violent or if the survivor discovered the body. "The amount of blood hounded me," says a woman who found her lover after he had shot himself in the mouth. "I had dreams for a long time about red checkerboards, about typewriters with black and red keys. I had dreams where *I* was the blood pouring out of his head. I couldn't get that image out of my mind."

While survivors may deny that a suicide has occurred by hiding notes or insisting it was an accident, other forms of denial are less obvious. When one man returned home after the funeral of his younger brother who shot himself, he was reluctant to alter it in any way. "Every time I moved something, even just a dirty dish on the table, I'd think, 'This is the way it was before he died. If I move this chair or make this bed, he'll be even more dead. Everything I do is making him more dead." A woman who had not seen her husband's body after his suicide called his office repeatedly without identifying herself. "I needed to hear, 'No, I'm sorry, he's passed away,' because I couldn't believe it."

The pain may be temporarily deadened by shock. Some grief experts compare this phase to the "disaster syndrome" of emotional dullness, unresponsiveness, and sense of worthlessness experienced by survivors of earthquakes, plane crashes, and other mass catastrophes. Psychiatrist Robert Jay Lifton, in his study of survivors of the A-bomb at Hiroshima, described it as "psychic numbing," a turning off of emotions, "in which the survivor's responses to his environment are reduced to a minimum—often to those necessary to keep him alive—and in which he feels divested of the capacity either to wish or will." This sounds very much like one Ohio high school teacher's description of the first few months after her son hanged himself: "I was unable to function. I would drive the three miles to school, but I would forget how to get home. I would have to park the car until I could remember. I would go to the supermarket, but when I came out I could never find my car. Eventually, I gave up going to the store. I was indifferent to stop signs and red lights. I blocked out sound and sight. I became perfectly mute. And no one could penetrate it."

But eventually, like a patient coming out of anesthesia, the survivor awakens to the relentless enormity of the pain. "It was like a fist reaching into my stomach and closing tight," says one. "I feel as if he shot a hole bigger than me," says another. "I felt as if my heart had been torn from my chest and that I was bleeding to death as surely as my husband," says another. Others: "I felt like a skinned animal." "I felt as if my insides were nothing but smashed glass, and if you could peel my skin away, I would sift down into a pile of tinkling shards." "I am curdled with grief."

Feelings of guilt, common after any death, are vastly intensified after a suicide. Like a child poking his tongue in the hole left by a missing tooth, a survivor examines every interaction with the dead person, from the last contact back to the first. In light of the suicide every moment becomes evidence of failure. The guilt leads to what grief counselors call the "what ifs" and the "if onlys"—the words or actions they feel might have prevented the death: "If only I'd told her I loved her." "What if I hadn't gone out that night?" Survivors may feel guilt if they saw signs and did nothing, guilt if they saw signs and bent over backward to help, guilt if they failed to see any signs at all. Guilt may be especially intense for parents of suicides. Parents are supposed to die before their children. And in a society in which the "success" or "failure" of a child is often seen as a reflection of his parents' worth, a suicide may seem the ultimate evidence of bad parenting. Says one mother, "You tend to say, I have three children. Two are very successful; they did it all themselves. I have one child who killed himself; that was my fault."

If the suicide occurred during a time of conflict between the suicide and the survivor, guilt may be particularly acute. Suicide can be an act of anger directed at others, with the intent of producing remorse. The circumstances of the act—method, location, note—can be indelible expressions of that rage. "There's no way we can resolve it. He had the last word," says a woman whose son left a three-word suicide note: "Fuck you all." Another woman received a series of annoying phone calls from her husband after their separation. One day he telephoned to say he had a gun and was going to kill himself. Exasperated, the woman said before she hung up, "Go ahead." He did. Today, agonizing over the words she can never take back, the receiver she hung up, she says, "I feel as though I put down a revolver."

"Guilt is a way of bringing control back into a situation that seems out of control," says one grief counselor. "It comes from the perception that you could have done something to prevent it. There's something narcissistic about that because it suggests that you could singlehandedly have changed the outcome. It's not rational because you don't take that kind of responsibility for anyone's life while he is alive—otherwise you don't allow him to be a person. But when someone kills himself, you feel you should have been around him every waking minute. Everyone does. Everyone suddenly takes 100 percent responsibility for that person's life." In an article in *The Village Voice,* Sheila Weller described how after a friend's suicide thirty friends gathered to discuss the death. All thirty admitted that they felt in some way responsible. In that unanimity their guilt was eased, and they were able to realize that no one person can make someone die or stay alive.

Survivors of suicide tend to feel more anger than other mourners: at the deceased for rejecting and deserting them; at God for allowing it to happen; at themselves, their family, or the mental health profession for not preventing it; and at the world for not coming to a halt. "I see people who had far more problems than my brother did, and I get so angry," says a young man whose brother shot himself. "Why are *they* alive and my brother isn't?"

In the ancient Hebrew ritual of atonement, a live goat was driven out into the wilderness each year, symbolically laden with the sins of the people. Similarly, after a suicide survivors often select a scapegoat. The target may be unemployment, drugs, alcohol. It may be a psychiatrist, a boyfriend, a clergyman. Or it may be a member of the family. "There is an especially distressing tendency for the survivors of a suicide to look for a scapegoat," wrote Erich Lindemann and Ina May Greer. "And, as is the fate of most scapegoats, the victim is usually one of their own members and frequently the one least able to bear the added burden." Sometimes the scapegoat may even be the suicide himself, who is held responsible for all the family problems.

Anger at the dead person may be the most difficult to express. "I would be so full of rage if somebody killed my brother. And I would be enraged if my brother killed someone. But he's both those people—and I have both those feelings," says a man whose brother shot himself. At a meeting of survivors in Minneapolis a woman whose son killed himself blurted, "I'm so angry at him. . . . I could just kill him." Realizing what she had said, she burst out laughing. A woman whose seventeen-year-old son shot himself five years ago says, "My anger is with myself." She is quiet for a moment, then she adds, "And at God for letting my child die. And at the family for not seeing it . . . and at his friends, who didn't tell me he'd talked of suicide." Her voice begins to boil. "And at the school, who knew he was withdrawing but never called. I *know* it wasn't their fault. I *know* there's no one to blame." Her voice shakes. "But it's one thing to resolve anger in the mind, and it's another to resolve anger in the gut." She pauses, and when she speaks again, she is calm, apologetic. "I guess I need *someone* to place the blame on—anyone but him."

The suicide of an alcoholic, an abusive parent or spouse, a particularly troublesome child, or someone who has made repeated threats or attempts may be the culmination of an exhausting struggle for both the suicide and the survivor. "We all felt some relief," says one young man whose older brother's suicide followed four attempts, numerous hospitalizations, and a decade of manic depression that seemed impervious to drug therapy, electroshock, psychotherapy, and the love of his family. "He had been so unhappy, and now he was out of his pain. My mother said, 'He's at peace now.' I felt my brother had finally taken some sort of initiative and been successful at something." Arnaldo Pangrazzi, a hospital chaplain in Milwaukee who leads survivors' groups, writes, "Some feel guilty about experiencing relief, which implies neither a lack of love for the deceased nor happiness that he or she died. Rather, relief is the awareness that the tension, the waiting, the fear are over."

But merely to describe the shock, guilt, anger, and relief is to make them sound as if they were separate emotions with distinct boundaries. In grief they circle back endlessly on one another. A survivor feels angry for feeling guilty,

guilty for feeling angry, worthless for feeling guilty, angry for feeling worthless.

Through all these emotions the suicide survivor may be propelled by the question "why?" Finding a reason for the suicide can become an obsession. Survivors search for notes, read books about depression and suicide, interview friends, talk to therapists, consult psychics, and endlessly ask themselves questions, trying to make sense of a senseless act, to solve what centuries of professionals have been unable to solve. Survivors often believe that the pain would recede if only they could find an answer. They may latch onto a reason—the lost girlfriend, the unemployment, the alcoholism—but ultimately it dissolves under scrutiny into more questions. Says one grief counselor, "Even if there *is* a reason, that's never answer enough."

In the year following her husband's suicide one young woman looked everywhere for answers: therapists, survivor groups, suicide symposiums, books on suicide, workshops on holistic medicine, and psychics. She studied her husband's journal for an answer and stared at the next blank page, thinking that if she waited long enough, the answer might somehow appear. She drew up a two-page summary of possible factors, as much for herself as for friends who, baffled by the suicide, kept asking her "why?" Yet even her synopsis listed more reasons "why not." And she searched for answers in her dreams. "I've had dreams where I couldn't get his attention. I've had dreams where he'd say he was really alive, and I'd say, 'No, you're dead.' I've had dreams where I'm with him, and we have a wonderful time, and afterward I ask, 'But you died—aren't you going to tell me what happened?' But he'd go or I'd wake up. I've had dreams where he told me what happened and I forgot. One week for four nights I asked for favors. The first night I asked that he come and visit me in my dreams, and he did. The second, I asked that he come and talk. He did. The third night I asked that he come and make love to me, and he did. The fourth night I asked that he tell me why he killed himself. He didn't. He refused."

On the other hand, survivors may try to bury their questions and feelings along with the suicide. "A common response to suicide is to say, 'Let the dead lie," says family therapist Monica McGoldrick. "And when a suicide occurs, families tend to close down." Families may participate in a "conspiracy of silence," a kind of cold war in which communication is cut off, and each family member suffers alone, behind closed doors, avoiding mentioning the name of the departed, avoiding one another's gaze. After the suicide of one nineteen-year-old boy, an awkward, troubling silence settled over his parents and surviving siblings. "For months no one talked about him," says the boy's mother. "It was as if he'd never existed. Christmas came and went, and no one talked about it. That began to worry us." The family eventually decided to seek help. "In therapy we found out everyone had wanted to talk about it, but they didn't want to make other people unhappy."

A family's denial may take physical form. After a suicide some families build a "shrine" to the deceased, leaving the room exactly as it was, the bed unmade, the schoolbooks on the desk. When one couple bought a new house three months after the suicide of their sixteen-year-old son, the mother insisted on setting aside a bedroom for her dead child. Two years after his son shot himself, one man keeps his son's half-empty cereal boxes in the kitchen cupboard; in winter he sometimes checks his son's bedroom "to see if it's warm enough." Others try to erase all traces of the dead one from the house, throwing out all his possessions, "sanitizing" his room as if he had never been there. In his poem "The Portrait," Stanley Kunitz, whose father swallowed carbolic acid a few weeks before he was born, described such denial:

> My mother never forgave my father
> for killing himself,
> especially at such an awkward time
> and in a public park,
> that spring
> when I was waiting to be born.
> She locked his name
> in her deepest cabinet
> and would not let him out,
> though I could hear him thumping.
> When I came down from the attic
> with the pastel portrait in my hand
> of a long-lipped stranger
> with a brave moustache
> and deep brown level eyes,
> she ripped it into shreds
> without a single word
> and slapped me hard.
> In my sixty-fourth year
> I can feel my cheek
> still burning.

At some point almost everyone who has lost someone to suicide wrestles with suicidal thoughts of his own. To the survivor there is no statistic more chilling than the research that shows survivors to be at eight times higher risk for suicide than the general population. At survivor groups one of the most frequent questions is, "Is suicide inherited?"

While there is no convincing evidence that suicide is genetically transmitted, there are other reasons why survivors have an unusually high suicide rate. First, while people are not born with genes for suicide, some are born with a genetic susceptibility to certain forms of mental illness, including schizophrenia and manic depression, which are associated with heightened suicide risk. Second, after a death of *any* kind the risk of suicide increases. Widows and widowers, for instance, during the first year of bereavement have a risk of suicide two and a half times as high as married people in their age group. Third—and perhaps most important—once a suicide occurs in a family, it introduces itself as an option. "Before, we didn't live in a world where people killed themselves," says a man whose brother shot himself. "Intellectually, we did, but we didn't believe it really happened. Now, we live in that world where it does happen so we're more apt to think of that possibility." Suicidal thoughts may be prompted by an identification with the deceased, a yearning to join the lost loved one, or a desire to atone for feelings of guilt. Those thoughts, however fleeting, may make a survivor even more bewildered and frightened. "When my brother shot himself, I thought the world had gone crazy," says one young woman. "I felt a little crazy myself. In our family I was always 'the wild one' and my brother was 'the quiet one.' That terrified me because I thought, '*he* did it, and he seemed so much more together than me.' " She shakes her head. "I thought of suicide a lot. I was scared to death, but I wouldn't talk to anybody about it. I knew suicide wasn't hereditary, but I was afraid that one day I'd run off and shoot myself just like my brother."

Experts believe that suicide is more likely to occur in surviving families where the first suicide is not talked about and the guilt and anger are allowed to fester. If not dealt with openly, the influence of a suicide may be felt farther down the line. Suicide can be a learned reaction to stress, a coping technique that, once used in a family, can act as a sort of role model. Adults tend to repeat the type of violence—or the type of love—they experienced as children. Just as children physically abused by their parents tend to become abusive parents themselves, suicide by a parent tends to beget suicidal behavior in children. The poet John Berryman never forgave his father for killing himself when the younger Berryman was eleven. "I spit upon this dreadful banker's grave / who shot his heart out in a Florida dawn," he wrote in "Dream Song 384." In 1972, forty-six years after his father's death, Berryman jumped to his death from a Minneapolis bridge. "In a modesty of death I join my father," he had written in one of his later poems. In 1961, thirty-three years after his father shot himself, Ernest Hemingway shot himself at age sixty-one. Eleven years later his younger brother Leicester, who had been the one to find their father's body, shot himself, too. "Patterns become established in a family," says suicidologist Bruce Danto, "and these seem almost to predetermine the fates of individuals in successive generations." One year after her father's suicide a thirteen-year-old Illinois girl fatally stabbed herself, leaving a note, "I am drawn toward death like a bee toward honey, like Juliet toward Romeo, like a baby girl toward her Dada." Long after his suicide attempt, A. Alvarez realized that he had been introduced to the option of suicide in childhood:

I see now that I had been incubating this death far longer than I recognized at the time. When I was a child, both my parents had half-heartedly put their heads in the gas oven. Or so they claimed. It seemed to me then a rather splendid gesture, though shrouded in mystery, a little area of veiled intensity, revealed only by hints and unexplained, swiftly suppressed outbursts. It was something hidden, attractive and not for the children, like sex. But it was also something that undoubtedly did happen to grownups. However hysterical or comic the behavior involved—and to a child it seemed more ludicrous than tragic to place your head in the greasy gas oven, like the Sunday roast joint—suicide was a fact, a subject that couldn't be denied; it was something, however awful, that people did. When my own time came, I did not have to discover it for myself.

For some survivors the sense of identification with the suicide can become so strong that their own suicide seems almost inevitable, a destiny to fulfill; they don't choose suicide, suicide chooses them. That sense of identification was brought home when, at a suicide prevention conference, I met Jean, a chipper, frizzy-haired forty-nine-year-old Michigan woman who works with disturbed adolescents. When I asked what brought her to the conference, she answered brightly, "I come from a suicidogenic family." Seeing my questioning look, she explained. "My family produces suicides. It generates suicides. It passes them on."

Jean was thirty-one when her brother killed himself. Three years later her mother killed herself, leaving a note blaming her daughter. Jean's father was an alcoholic; her grandfather, who was overweight and had heart problems but refused to follow his prescribed medical regimen, "probably killed himself—after all, you don't have to put your neck in a noose to commit suicide." After her mother's death, Jean herself was twice hospitalized for suicide attempts. "Although I didn't want to die, I felt that killing myself was the right thing to do because my mother had done it. I felt it was my fate." After many years in therapy, Jean no longer believes that her suicide is inevitable, but she is convinced that suicide is part of her legacy. "It's not hereditary, but it's contagious," she says matter-of-factly.

While admiring Jean's frankness, I found her ready acceptance of her "suicidogenic" heritage unsettling and the word itself a bit frightening. The concept of "contagious" suicide may be the only way she can deal with her family's tragedies, but I wonder how thin the line may be between believing in that fate and embracing it.

On the other hand, for some survivors a suicide can actually serve a preventive role. They are steered away from suicidal thoughts by their firsthand knowledge of the pain their death would inflict on others. "Before my brother killed himself, I'd considered suicide myself," says a young musician who was twenty-five years old when his older brother shot himself. "I used to think my suicide would say to the world that life in the modern world is too much to bear. But my brother's death made me see how futile suicide is. It makes no statement, it just gives people grief. And now when I get depressed and thoughts of death come up, they don't continue long because I think how could I put my family through a second suicide?"

While a suicide loss is painful whether the survivor is a parent, child, or spouse, the nature of the loss may have a different quality for each. A parent may feel more guilt, a spouse, more anger. A sibling often feels confusion about his role in the family. Grandparent, friend, teacher, therapist—each role brings its own special kind of pain. But the effect on children may be the most destructive of all. Studies show that the loss of a parent in early childhood plays a key role in subsequent psychological development; if that loss is by suicide, it can be devastating. "For children," concluded the 1984 National Academy of Sciences report on grief, "the suicide of a parent or sibling not only presents immediate difficulties, but is thought by many observers to result in life-long vulnerability to mental health problems."

After a suicide children feel many of the same emotions as adults: denial, anger, confusion, and fear. Guilt can be intense. "Kids are apt to take the blame for any death," says Sandra Fox, director of the Family Support Center at the Judge Baker Guidance Center in Boston, which provides counseling for children and families coping with loss. "They feel they might have been responsible for it because of something they thought or wished or said or did or didn't do. And unconsciously, kids can very much wish their parents dead: 'Daddy, why don't you go play in traffic and die so I can carry off Mummy to a castle and marry her.' Now, if Daddy happens to die, the child thinks it's his fault." Children may have had hostile feelings toward the parent; they may have misbehaved immediately before the suicide; they may feel they might have prevented it—if only they hadn't quarreled with their brother, if only they had stayed home instead of going out to play. They may feel guilt because they didn't know whom to call after finding the body or didn't open the windows of a gas-filled room. Or they may feel guilt at merely being alive when their parent is dead. In his work with survivors of the Hiroshima bombings, psychiatrist Robert Jay Lifton described the "survivor guilt" felt by those who were not killed. The suicide of a parent, Lifton believes, may produce similar pangs in a child.

Children are even more apt to be left alone with their grief than adults. Intending to shield them from pain, well-meaning parents rarely level with their children about death. The subject is either avoided or explained in euphemisms, leaving children's imaginations to fill in the blanks. A study of thirty-six children who had lost a parent to suicide found that half of them were never told the truth; some learned the real story only when they over-heard adults talking about it or read the obituary in the newspapers. In a study of forty-five children between the ages of four and fourteen who had lost a parent to suicide, therapists Albert Cain and Irene Fast found that more than a quarter knew intimate details about the death yet were told it was from natural causes. One girl saw her father's body hanging in the closet; her mother insisted that he had died in a car wreck. A boy who had seen his father blow himself to pieces with a shotgun was told that he died of a heart attack. Two brothers who found their mother with her wrists slit were told she had drowned while swimming. When the children contradicted their elders, they were made to feel ashamed for making such statements and told they had merely had bad dreams or had confused reality with a television program.

Such lack of honesty following a suicide can be calamitous to a child. Cain and Fast found that distorted communication contributed to a broad range of symptoms: delinquency, running away, psychosomatic disorders, obesity, neurosis, and an incidence of psychosis three times that in other childhood bereavement cases. In addition, because the children had received the message that they should not know or talk about the suicide, they often felt conflict about knowing and talking in general, with resultant stammers, stutters, shyness, and learning disabilities. Other research has described the effect of unresolved grief in later life. Psychiatrist T. L. Dorpat, in a study of seventeen patients he began treating an average of sixteen years after a parent's suicide, found that unresolved grief had left a malignant residue: guilt, depression, arrested development, self-destructive behavior, and preoccupation with suicide.

Experts believe that the suicide of a parent need not be crippling if discussed openly and honestly. "What's mentionable is manageable," says Sandra Fox, who believes that early intervention with bereaved children can help avoid later problems. Fox encourages parents to explain clearly and directly what happened and why, giving honest information (appropriate to age) about the cause, helping children understand that the dead person is not coming back and that the child's sadness and anger are okay. Fox is often asked at what age a child should be told about a parent's suicide. As soon as they can talk? *"Before* they can talk," says Fox. "I don't mean you tell a two-year-old, 'Your daddy hung himself in the basement.' You start by explaining that Daddy died, and dying means we're not going to see him anymore the way we knew him here on earth. His body has stopped working. Then, as kids are ready and ask, 'How did he die?' or 'Why did he die?', you add the fact that it was a suicide. Children feel guilt after any death, and it's important to tell the child, 'You may think there's something you said or did that made your dad kill himself, but I want you to understand that's not what happened. Your dad killed himself because he had problems that he couldn't find any way to deal with.' "

Fox pauses. "You have to deal with it immediately although you certainly will have to rework it later, too, as kids understand more. But don't wait."

The devastating effect of a parent's suicide on a child—and the kind of communication that may best relieve it—is demonstrated in the story of Mary and Karen Vitelli. At noon on an exceptionally hot day in early fall, Mary and Karen were sitting with their mother, Linda, at the kitchen table in their apartment in a Boston suburb. Karen was five years old, Mary ten. A shy, intelligent girl who enjoyed helping out around the house, Mary had heated up Spaghetti-O's for lunch. Their mother was sewing a patch on a pair of Mary's pants so they would be ready in time for the new school year that began the following Monday. Mary would be entering fourth grade; Karen would be starting kindergarten. As Mary and Karen teased each other over lunch, their mother suddenly stopped sewing, threw the pants onto the table, hugged her daughters, and went upstairs.

After lunch Karen asked Mary to give her a shampoo. Mary said they had better ask their mother. They went upstairs and knocked on one of the two doors to her bedroom. There was no answer. That was strange—their mother never took naps during the day. They tried to open the door, but it was locked. They went to the other door, and by throwing all their weight against it, they were able to squeeze into the room. A couch had been pushed against the door. "Where's Mummy?" Mary said. Karen pointed to the other door and said, "Why are her feet hanging there?"

Their mother, her belt around her neck, her flip-flops still clinging to her feet, was hanging from the hinge on the door. "Why did you do this?" Mary screamed at her mother. "You promised you'd never leave us. Why did you do this?" She tried to lift her mother down, but she couldn't. Her shoulder ached for weeks. She ran to the telephone, looked up the number of the body shop where her mother's boyfriend Chris worked, and called him. "Come home," she said. "My mother's dead."

In fact, Linda was not quite dead. When Chris arrived, he gave her CPR while Mary called the ambulance. At the hospital Linda went into a coma. The children stayed with their grandmother Rose, and the three of them wept together. A few days later the doctors told Rose there was no chance that Linda would live, and it was agreed she would be taken off life-support equipment. When Rose told the children, Mary was furious. "You can't do that," she shouted. "You lied. Everybody lied. You said she was going to get better."

Although some of the family thought it would be needlessly traumatic, Mary and Karen insisted on seeing their mother's body, and the following day Rose took them to the hospital. Linda's body lay on a bed. The life-support systems had been disconnected. A psychiatric nurse was there to answer the children's questions. "Why did you make my mommy die?" Mary screamed. The nurse gently explained what had happened, but Mary continued to sob hysterically. Later, the nurse asked them whether they would like the clothes their mother had worn that day. "No, no, no, no," Mary whispered to her grandmother. "Don't take them." Rose asked the nurse, who was crying by now, to burn them.

Karen and Mary moved in with their grandmother, a compact, brisk, pragmatic woman who worked as a hairdresser. Divorced when Linda was five, Rose had raised three children on her own. She had been very close to Linda, her only daughter, who had married at sixteen and endured nine years of her husband's drinking and abuse before getting a divorce. In the past year Linda had found a new boyfriend and a new career, but the pressures of starting over at twenty-seven had apparently overwhelmed her. Though Rose was crushed by her daughter's suicide, her own grief was put on hold as she cared for her daughter's children. Karen seemed to be handling it well, but Mary was torn between her anger at and her love for her mother. Although she agreed to attend the wake, she refused to go to the funeral or to the cemetery, and when Rose tried to tell Mary how beautiful the service had been, she wouldn't listen. She asked Chris whether he would get a new girlfriend and he said yes, someday. "Well, never bring her here," Mary said. In fact, he never did get another girlfriend; a year later he shot himself near Linda's grave.

Over the following months Mary experienced the classic responses of stigma, fear, anger, and guilt. Three days after the funeral the new school year began, and Mary went back to school wearing the new clothes her mother had bought her. When she came home, she told Rose, "Some of the kids are coming up to me and saying, 'Your mother hung herself.' I want to go to a different school." Rose told her to hold her head high and deny it. Both Karen and Mary refused to go upstairs without their grandmother, and for several months the three of them slept in the same room, where they could comfort each other when one of them woke from a nightmare in tears. Mary was filled with anger. She didn't want anything around that her mother had given her. She refused to say anything nice about her mother, and if Rose mentioned Linda, Mary made an angry face. One day Rose overheard the children arguing. "I don't know why she did it," Karen was saying. "Because we were fighting," said Mary. Rose rushed in. "No," she said, "that's not it at all." She explained that their mother's death had nothing to do with them, that their mother had been troubled for reasons of her own. But Mary was filled with guilt for not saving her mother. "I tried to get her down, Grandma," she'd say, "but I couldn't. I just couldn't." Rose attempted to reassure her: "You're only ten—I couldn't have done it either," she said. "You did wonderfully to call Chris." Mary was unconvinced. She had recurring nightmares in which her mother came back to punish her for not saving her life.

One day the children's father, angry that Rose had won temporary custody, called Mary. "What are you and your grandmother trying to do? Do you want me to kill myself, too?" he said. Mary came into the kitchen, where Rose was fixing dinner. "He's going to kill himself," she said. Rose, numb and exhausted, said, "So what?" Mary was matter-of-fact. "Well, then you might as well kill yourself, and I might as well kill myself." Rose answered without thinking: "Not today—I have too much to do."

That afternoon Mary asked Rose if they could visit the grave. When they arrived, Karen laid the roses they had brought on the grave, but Mary, frightened, refused to go near. Nevertheless, Rose was encouraged. "When she asked to go to the grave, that's when I knew she was going to deal with things."

A few weeks after Linda's death the three of them began seeing a therapist, together and separately. Under his gentle questioning Mary opened up. By the second session she was describing every detail of her mother's death to him. She discussed her recurring nightmares and fears that her mother would come back and punish her for not saving her life. The therapist helped Mary and Karen practice what to say to their classmates when they were taunted about their mother hanging herself: "Mummy went to the hospital, went into a coma, and never came out of it." Over the following months he convinced them they were not responsible for their mother's death, and gradually their fears began to subside.

A year after their mother's death, the children's nightmares stopped. Mary and Karen were still afraid to go upstairs to the bathroom alone at night although they now did so in daylight. Mary's anger eased. She remained reluctant to go to the cemetery, and during a visit on her mother's birthday she kept her distance from the grave. When Mary was very young, her mother knit her a blue sweater, which Rose kept in the hope chest. One day, Rose took it out and asked Mary if she wanted to wear it. "No," said Mary. "Right now, I wouldn't want to wear it, but maybe someday I will."

V

MERRYL: THE JIGSAW PUZZLE

IN SEPTEMBER, Merryl began keeping a chart of how she felt. The chart's range was from "suicidal" to "bearable" to "acceptable," and Merryl's graph made precipitous daily zigzags. At the office she was still barely functioning. She couldn't concentrate; she spent all her time thinking about Carl. Gripped by a new worry, a "thought whirl" or a flash of guilt, she would call her mother and talk for an hour. The people in nearby offices heard her weeping but weren't sure what to do. "My supervisor was wonderful, but a lot of people didn't speak to me," she says. "I never felt ostracized, though. They just didn't know what to say." Neither did Merryl. "People asked me how I was, and I didn't know. I couldn't say 'fine,' and I couldn't say 'I want to be dead.' I couldn't say anything. I couldn't smile. For four months I never changed my expression. A friend told me it looked like a bomb had blown up in my face."

Merryl still thought of suicide—or, more accurately, of death. One day in Boston she stepped heedlessly in front of an oncoming trolley car. When she got on, the conductor shook his head and said, "Next time you do that, the insurance company will pay the fare." Merryl looked at him. "That's exactly what I want," she said. She moved slowly to the back of the car. "I didn't even know what I was doing," remembers Merryl. "But if I'd been hit, I wouldn't have minded." Merryl invented a game: Each day if she could think of one reason to be alive, she would put off dying until the following day. "One morning, I found myself thinking that the autumn leaves were pretty, and I thought, 'I would have missed that if I'd killed myself, so I'll stay alive until tomorrow.' "

Merryl moved into a room over her friend Judith's garage. Judith, an editor at Houghton Mifflin, had lost a close friend to suicide several years earlier and had been one of the first people to call Merryl after Carl's death. She seemed to know just what Merryl needed. Sometimes Merryl would go into her office and talk; other times she'd just huddle in a corner and cry quietly while Judith worked. Under her wing Merryl began to go out occasionally, to a lecture, a museum, or a concert. "I felt safe with Judith," says Merryl. "I could face things. She was like my seeing-eye dog." Sometimes Merryl sat at home with Judith's husband, an engineer, and listened to him discuss his work. "He could talk for hours about very boring subjects—the concrete used in making bridges, how to build the girders in a skyscraper—and it was just what I needed to hear." By late October the zigzags on Merryl's chart began to settle in the bearable/acceptable range. In November, Merryl laughed for the first time since Carl's death.

Meanwhile, Merryl continued trying to make sense of Carl's suicide. She started jotting down some thoughts about Carl on scraps of paper. Because she was having difficulty separating what had actually happened from what her guilt suggested had happened, she wrote down everything she could remember of those desperate final weeks. Gradually, she recorded many things: incidents she remembered, thoughts about Carl's personality, notes from her therapy sessions, raw expressions of wanting to die. Merryl sorted them into three piles: ideas about Carl's character, feelings of guilt, and the details of her day-to-day agony. If she felt strong, she might pick a piece of paper from a pile and pore over it. She dated all her notes. Often she would realize that a question she had written in November she had already asked in October—she had been over that same angle months before, but the wound had reopened. Soon she had hundreds of scraps of paper, which she kept in a black plastic bag she carried everywhere. She and Judith called them "Carl papers." Once, when she accidentally locked them into her car in a friend's driveway, she slept over that night so she could hear if someone tried to break into the vehicle.

Before Carl died it had never occurred to Merryl to read anything on the subject of death. Now her bedside table, once lined with books on maternity, was crowded with books on suicide, bereavement, and widowhood. Even the most basic information fascinated her—that, for instance, three times more men kill themselves than women. She quickly devoured the entries on suicide in her father's four encyclopedias. On weekly trips to the Brookline library she and Judith would meet at the checkout desk at closing time, Judith with eight books of poetry, Merryl clutching eight books on death. In Boston bookstores Merryl gravitated toward the psychology and sociology sections. Working in the college division at Houghton Mifflin, she had access to a room filled with shelf after shelf of psychology textbooks. She began to stay late after work, alone in the office, looking up Suicide in the index of each textbook and reading about depression, self-esteem, and personality theory. She filled another black plastic bag with copies of articles to reread. She read *Suicide in America* by Herbert Hendin, *Suicides* by Jean Baechler, *A Grief Observed* by C. S. Lewis, *Vivienne* by John Mack and Holly Hickler, *The Psychology of Self-Esteem* by Nathaniel Branden, *Widow* by Lynn Caine, among many other books. She learned about Freud and the death instinct, about anomic, egoistic, and altruistic suicide, about the wish to kill, the wish to be killed, and the wish to die, about lethality indexes, ambivalence, and the cry for help.

"I read everything about suicide I could get my hands on," says Merryl. "I was always hoping that the next book would have the answer and was always afraid it would do me in. . . . Only rarely did it help, and some of it hurt." Her mother had told her that hanging was a quick death, but in an encyclopedia she read that suicide by hanging usually takes eight minutes because the body does not fall from a height, as it would in an execution. Merryl couldn't stop shivering for days, thinking of the pain Carl might have felt. In *The Social Reality of Death* she read that a "validating significant other" can mean the difference between life and death for a suicidal person. Merryl was devastated, suddenly certain that she must not have been a "validating significant other." One day in August, browsing for suicide books, she found *Too Young to Die,* a book on adolescent suicide. She read parts of it in the bookstore and felt she was going to vomit. "It stressed the significance of external events and said that if you had recognized the clues, you could have saved the person," says Merryl. "I was frantic. This book seemed to say that it was really my fault after all, that I could have saved Carl." Merryl ran upstairs to her office and called three friends and her therapist before she began to calm down. "Everything I had put together in two months was coming apart," she says. She was back at square one, reminding herself that she *had* gotten him help, she *had* called a psychiatrist. Merryl gradually began to erect responses so that when a wave of guilt washed over her, she wouldn't be defenseless. One of the things that made her feel most guilty was the list she had given Carl in Chicago of the twenty-five states she was willing to move to. If she hadn't made those stipulations, she told herself, he'd still be alive—and she would buckle with feelings of guilt. But as she went over and over it, she began to respond more rationally to her self-accusations. She made a mental list of reasons why she should not feel guilty, and when guilt struck, she would recite the list to herself like a mantra:

1. Bad things could have eventually happened to Carl there (like not getting tenure), and he might have gone into despair at that point and killed himself.

2. If we had moved there, I might have been miserable. Then, if he'd

gone into despair and killed himself, I would have blamed myself even more for having complained.

3. I had a right to have some influence on where we would live. We had been in Chicago six years solely for his work.

4. Carl agreed to this plan; he could have insisted on his own plan or even moved on his own if it was that important.

5. I did become more flexible when things began going so badly in Boston, and was willing to put his career first completely—but who could know that by that point it would be too late? My perspective is all off now that I know his life was at stake. At the time I made the list I thought we were negotiating with usual and normal stakes and consequences.

But even as Merryl started to cope with the feelings of guilt, the sheer ache of missing Carl would flood her: the way his eyes lit up as he laughed; the determined way he walked; his boyish pleasure when he surprised her with a gift. And then there was the loss of the life they had been building together. "What hurt worst is that we were on the verge of so much," says Merryl. "Carl was finally finishing school after eight years of graduate work, and we were thinking of buying a house. Everything was so oriented toward life; there were books all over the house about pregnancy and motherhood. And then every one of my dreams was shattered in a split second, in one phone call. And because we'd been trying to have a child, it felt almost as if there had been two deaths." Guilt over the baby issue gnawed at Merryl. "One of the things I went over and over was if I had gotten pregnant, would Carl have stayed alive?" Later, her mother-in-law introduced her to a woman whose husband, a graduate student, had killed himself when she was three months pregnant. Her son was now seven. While this helped Merryl realize her pregnancy wouldn't have saved Carl, the overpowering feeling of loss remained—*she* wasn't pregnant, *she* didn't have a child, and now she'd never have Carl's child, maybe never have a child at all. "I was thirty-four and it seemed as if every woman in the world my age was pregnant," she says. "My best friend was pregnant, my two sisters-in-law were pregnant, and a half-dozen other friends were pregnant. We had all been on the same track together—college, career, marriage, babies, and here I was a widow and they were all pregnant." For a long time Merryl couldn't bear to think of Carl's nephew, and when she saw babies on the street she had to look away.

Christmas with Carl had always been special. They had lit candles in the windows, decorated trees with favorite ornaments, and opened the doors on Advent calendars together every December for eight years. This year Merryl spent Christmas with her parents, who had problems of their own. Her father was recovering from a hip replacement operation, and her mother was suffering pain from advancing cancer. The three of them, wanting to get far away from New England, flew to New Orleans. It was Merryl's first trip since she and Carl vacationed in Nova Scotia ten months before his death. On the way down, Merryl welcomed each sudden altitude drop or sharp tilt of the plane— "If I were taken away," she thought, "it would solve everything." In the elevator taking them to their room on the fortieth floor of an antiseptic downtown hotel, the bellhop said, "It's Christmas Eve; what are you doing here?" Her father answered quietly, "We're here *because* it's Christmas Eve."

The holiday was a nightmare. "We had an abysmal, horrible time," says Merryl. "I told my parents it was a good thing the windows were locked because we were on the fortieth floor and I really felt like leaping." The day after Christmas they went to the zoo. They made a pathetic trio. Merryl's father was in a wheelchair, pushed by Merryl's mother, who wheezed and occasionally cried out in pain. Merryl, hunched over, wrapped in a scarf, wearing glasses (since Carl's death she hadn't worn her contact lenses), looked as if she were in disguise. As they made their way slowly through the zoo, Merryl noticed a young couple strolling toward them, arm in arm, as chipper as a honeymoon couple in an advertisement. The man looked familiar; Merryl realized that she and Carl had known him at the University of Chicago. From the startled look in his eyes Merryl thinks he recognized her. But they passed each other without speaking. On the flight home, seated across from a young man who looked like Carl and was dandling an infant on his knee, Merryl broke into sobs so loud that people craned their necks to see what was wrong.

In January, Merryl moved back into the Brookline apartment. Nothing in it had changed since the day Carl died. The pencils on his desk were still sharp; his wastebaskets were still filled with notes from his work; his clothes still hung in the closet; his laundry still sat in the hamper; his shoes still sat under his desk; the novel he had been reading still lay on the night table, and the calendar in the bedroom was still turned to June 1982.

Over the following months Merryl spent as little time in the apartment as possible. She left the shades drawn except to admit enough light for Carl's plants to survive. She never went shopping, always ate takeout, never used the dishwasher, never vacuumed or dusted. She ignored the growing pile of second-class mail addressed to Carl. She never opened a closet or a dresser drawer; she kept her clothes in piles on the bed she had shared with Carl. She slept on a mattress in Carl's study, where she built a sort of cocoon in the shadow of his desk. Next to her pillow she kept Carl's pajamas and her nightgown from the last night they had slept together. Next to the mattress she arranged an intimate circle of belongings on the floor: her alarm clock, her journals, the notes and papers she was working on, her thirty-third birthday card from Carl, and a pad of paper on which she kept a daily tally of the number of days since Carl's suicide.

In many ways Merryl's own life had stopped at June 1982. For almost a year she didn't watch television, see a movie, or read a "normal" book. "Part of it was that everything seemed so trivial, but a lot of it had to do with the way Carl died," she says. "I couldn't pick up anything that had a story in it without wondering why *these* people didn't commit suicide." She never made phone calls although she didn't mind getting them. Faced with groups of people, she sought out a room's corners. "I lived a sort of marginal, weird existence. I was living out of shopping bags. If I met someone new and I was asked to explain my life, I would say that I worked at a publishing house and so on, but I really felt like screaming, 'You don't understand! I don't know who's who and what's what, and I don't know who I am.' "

To understand who she was, Merryl felt she had to understand who Carl was. Until she made some sense of his suicide, she knew she would be unable to move on. Each night after work she took out her "Carl papers" from the black plastic bag that by now was overflowing and spread the folded yellow pieces of paper on the dining room table, hoping that from all that raw material some answers would emerge. She would stay up late trying to fit together fragments of Carl's life like pieces of a giant jigsaw puzzle. "It would take me two hours to fit one little incident in," she says. She made flow charts with arrows swirling around events in Carl's life, trying to trace the path that had led to his death. Sometimes she went into the study or the bedroom and stood exactly where she had stood seven months earlier, and then she replayed aloud the words they had spoken. "I had this immense need to find out why this person would choose to die when there are so many people in the world who don't," says Merryl. "When a person commits suicide, all his qualities have to be reexamined in light of his death. And that's true only of this kind of death. Someone who dies in an accident is still the same person—you don't go back and analyze their character, wondering who they really were. All the characteristics of the person I'd lived with and loved for eight years—his gentleness, his amazing rapport with children—got thrown into the air. How did they fit in with someone taking his own life so violently? Everyone thought of that gentleness as a good thing, but now I wondered whether it was all just suppressed anger." Sometimes when Merryl passed Carl's portrait on the living room wall, she would stop and gaze at those eyes and wonder who this man really was.

Three times a week Merryl and her therapist talked about Carl. Her therapist helped Merryl realize that the qualities she loved in Carl had not been an illusion. "While there were times Carl should have spoken out, times when he was self-effacing and suffering from a lack of confidence, he had a very gentle, sincere, and responsible way of being," says Merryl. "And if he could have worked through it, if he could have lived, all those good qualities would still be there." Slowly, a picture of Carl began to take shape, of a thoughtful, caring, but troubled man whose high standards had led to great successes—and to great pain and loss of self-esteem when he believed he had fallen short of his ideals.

Merryl's therapist told her about something she called the "all or nothing" phenomenon. She explained that certain people, for various developmental reasons, see things as all or nothing situations. When they are flooded by negative feelings, any hopeful feelings are often completely forgotten. The person is swept by a black feeling of total hopelessness that may put him at risk for suicide. "As soon as she started talking about that, it clicked," says Merryl. "That's the way Carl was, with his projects, with his job search, and with his dissertation. That perfectionism came even in little things, like baking bread. If it didn't come out exactly right, he was deeply upset." That "all or nothing" quality was also evident in Carl's diary, which Merryl read after his death. In Paris, two nights before he was to fly home from his junior year abroad, Carl had written of the turmoil he felt at the thought of trying to reintegrate himself, with his growing political activism, into the campus he had left as an honors pre-med student. His life seemed to be changing faster than he could control. As he wandered through the streets of Paris that night, he thought of throwing himself into the Seine. He labeled that journal entry "I want to die."

Although the entry made her inexpressibly sad, it gave Merryl a small measure of understanding, even comfort, to know that Carl's thoughts of death had existed before she met him. "I've gone over all this with my therapist, and we feel that something snapped about ten days before he died when he became convinced that there was a fatal flaw in his dissertation," says Merryl. "And that if the dissertation was lost, he was, too. I think that ten days before his death—on some unconscious level—he'd made his decision to kill himself." Gradually, Merryl was able to separate her actions from Carl's. "In the last weeks of his life he was on a separate track. Although I wanted to believe that I could have some control over that, I really don't think I existed for him during that time. In a way that's a relief; understanding that helped ease my feelings of guilt and responsibility. But it's hard to come to terms with the idea that not only are you not responsible but that you probably didn't even matter to the other person at that point."

With the help of her therapist and her friend Judith, Merryl worked out a metaphor that helped put those last weeks into perspective. "It was as if Carl was under water, and his friends and family and I were on the surface, calling down to him. Occasionally, he would come up and communicate with us. But what was going on for him inside was the part of the water we never see: the undertow, a powerful force churning away down there that we couldn't touch. Suddenly, at the end, that undertow swept him away. It just literally overcame him."

Merryl became increasingly immersed in her exploration; at one point she planned to write an in-depth study of Carl's life. But in early February something nudged her from her obsession and eventually helped her to understand that she had come further along in her grieving than she had realized. On the subway to Harvard Square one day she bumped into an old acquaintance. The man, also an editor, had always liked Merryl, and after this chance encounter he asked her out. They began seeing each other. At times their dates were eerie when comparisons to Carl flew to her mind: Driving together in his car, Merryl would look over and be astonished that the man next to her wasn't Carl; walking the dogs, he would be dragged out the door the way Carl had been; when they kissed, she was surprised not to have to lift her head—Carl had been much taller. Merryl was frightened to be feeling something for someone other than Carl but was pleased to realize that she could feel at all. It was the first time since his death that she had thought for more than sixty minutes about something other than his suicide. Merryl began to take better care of herself: She had her hair cut and curled, she began wearing her contact lenses again, she ate more, and she went shopping. She had lost so much weight that none of her clothes fit, although she hadn't cared until now. As the relationship grew, all the things that had been ripped from Merryl by Carl's suicide seemed possible once more.

Two months after they met, the man left Merryl for a younger woman. Merryl was devastated, but the obsession of the larger grief had been relieved somewhat by the smaller, newer one. By the time the relationship was over, Merryl no longer kept a running tally of the number of days since Carl's death.

From what she had read, Merryl knew that the first anniversary of Carl's death might be difficult, so she made elaborate preparations. After an impromptu ceremony at the grave with her parents and Carl's family, she drove to Eastham, a small town on the Atlantic Ocean where she spent the night in a hotel. The next morning, exactly one year after Carl's death, she drove out to the beach with the contents of the suitcase Carl had taken to New York, which had been lying in her parents' basement, unopened, until this week. Now, sitting on the beach among the sunbathers, she spread these things on the sand in front of her: his watch, wallet, and wedding ring. She sang several of her favorite songs. She listened to the waves. She felt she had come a long way since the sight of the sea had meant only one thing: a way for her to die. She felt proud that she had gotten through the year.

In August, fourteen months after Carl's death, Merryl met a new employee at work whom she liked immediately. Ten days after they met he asked her out. Merryl accepted. On their first date Merryl told him about Carl. "I knew this man was probably going to mean something to me so I wanted it out on the table," she says. "He had to know how much it affected me. I was nervous about telling him, but he was very understanding. We talked a lot about the guilt I felt and the loneliness." Nathan was sympathetic; he had lived a quiet, solitary life in western Massachusetts and knew what it was like to be lonely.

Later on during that first date, he asked Merryl what she'd been reading lately. "Other than books about suicide," said Merryl, "nothing." It took a few minutes for the conversation to recover.

Merryl was more cautious this time. "I kept saying to myself, 'I don't want to get involved yet—I'm not ready for this, I'm still too vulnerable.' " But she had grown stronger in therapy, and the more she saw of Nathan, the more she was drawn to him. Like Carl he was sensitive, introspective, and well spoken. Like Merryl he was fascinated by writing and language. He was a computer buff, a sports nut, and an amateur historian. When he took Merryl to visit *Old Ironsides,* the American frigate from the War of 1812, Nathan was such a knowledgeable, enthusiastic guide that half a dozen tourists abandoned the official tour to follow him. One night Merryl and Nathan went to a showing of Hitchcock's *Rear Window.* As they kissed and hugged playfully in the dark theater, Merryl had a sudden sense of unreality. "Could I be enjoying life again?" she wondered. "Could this really be me?"

One day in October, about two months after they had met, they spent the day at the beach. At the end of the afternoon Nathan went ahead to get Merryl's car. As Merryl walked toward the car and saw a man's silhouette in the driver's seat, she had a moment of confusion. "I looked through the window, saw that silhouette, and thought, 'It's unbelievable seeing someone else drive the car that Carl and I bought together two years ago.' I had thought no one else would ever sit in that driver's seat. It was eerie. When I got in the car, I shook my head, almost to clear it. Then I looked over, and there was Nathan. I was happy to see him, and I touched his hair gingerly but affectionately." One night, so they wouldn't hear about it secondhand, Merryl called Carl's parents and told them she had met a man she was serious about.

In May, Merryl and Nathan decided to move in together. Merryl spent evenings and weekends in July packing up the Brookline apartment. Everything Carl owned was still untouched. Before she started, Merryl took photographs of the apartment, to record the way it had looked when she and Carl had lived there. And then she began to dismantle the scene of their life together, room by room. She started with the living room, which held the fewest memories. Next, she packed up the dining room, then the kitchen, then the bedroom. The bedroom wasn't too bad: Carl had kept his clothes in a closet in the study. After prolonged internal debate, every item wound up in one of three piles—one to go to the new apartment, one to be given to Goodwill, and one to be thrown away.

She saved the study until last. Almost everything Carl owned was in this room, undisturbed since the day he had died. From her reading she knew all about how bereaved people build shrines to the dead and get "stuck" in grief, but her therapist had agreed it would not be inappropriate for her to keep a box of Carl's clothes. Now Merryl sat on the floor holding up shirts and sweaters she knew so well, trying to decide which to keep, which she would never see again. She saved a green-and-blue-striped Indian bathrobe she had made him for Christmas four years before, one that he'd often studied in; she saved a soft green velour shirt that reminded her of their Chicago years, and a bathing suit she had made after they had first moved there; she saved a baggy white mohair sweater she had knitted him in 1969 that had started as a dressy sweater and, after several years in mothballs, had found a second life as a work sweater. When she had stuffed one large carton full and marked it "Carl's clothes," she realized she'd chosen something from each phase of their life together.

It was almost midnight by the time she turned to the old wooden desk where Carl had spent so much of his last eight years. Next to the desk stood the research for his unfinished dissertation—eighteen index card files, enough to catalogue a small-town library, crammed with white cards carefully hand-printed with quotations from psychology books, alphabetized and cross-referenced to other cards and to the books in Carl's vast library. Merryl sat on a packing crate and stared at the scene of Carl's failure, unable to face it, wishing she hadn't left it to the end. It was midnight, and the movers were due to arrive at eight. Merryl sat and stared some more, and then, carefully, as if handling precious, dangerous specimens, she transferred the contents of Carl's desk and files whole into boxes, without stopping to sort through it. The desk drawers took six boxes; the files filled eight. By three in the morning, when Merryl looked up, their home had been broken down to a skyline of stacked boxes. At four o'clock, exhausted, she drove to her new home in Cambridge.

Four hours later the movers arrived, and by that evening eight years of Merryl and Carl's shared life had been scattered to various destinations. A truckload went to the new house in Cambridge. Three carloads of clothes and shoes went to Goodwill, so much that it wouldn't fit into the hopper in a corner of the shopping mall. The elderly attendant refused to accept the overflow until Merryl, desperate, told him that her husband had recently died. His annoyance disappeared. "He must have been so young," he said sadly and waved her ahead. Their bed went to Merryl's brother, Carl's desk to her brother's girl-friend. The puppets Carl made for his dissertation research—the elephant, the pilot, the truck two feet long—went into a corner of her father's house at the Cape. Clothes too old for Goodwill, battered suitcases, dead plants, and a seven-foot stack of second-class mail addressed to Carl that had never been thrown out filled thirty green trash bags that lined the sidewalk in front of the Brookline apartment like a hedge two feet wide and thirty feet long. The Department of Public Works sent a special pickup because there was so much to haul away. When Merryl drove by the house the next morning, it was gone.

VI

A SAFE PLACE

"I'M MERRYL MALESKA. My husband committed suicide a year and a half ago."

"I'm Peter Courtney. Our daughter Lisa committed suicide six years ago just before Christmas."

"I'm Liz, Peter's wife."

"I'm Eileen Dowcett. My husband and I lost our son Philip five years ago."

"I'm Rona Marks, and my only daughter committed suicide three months ago."

"I'm Joyce Oldham, and my husband committed suicide thirteen months ago."

"I'm Bailey Barron, and our daughter committed suicide four years ago."

"I'm Stanley Barron."

"I'm Jean Clark. My husband committed suicide three years ago last January."

"I'm Tom Rossi, and my brother Rick committed suicide eight years ago."

On a Tuesday evening in January, eleven people are seated in a semicircle in a small room in Somerville, Massachusetts. They are members of Safe Place, a support group for survivors of suicide. Group "facilitator" Tom Welch, a slim, young Roman Catholic priest, begins tonight's meeting with his customary introduction: "Each of us comes to this circle with a private urgency, even agony and sorrow. Perhaps others we love are carrying their own burdens and aren't always available to comfort us. Let us use this time to create an opportunity for each to share, giving room for silence if that is appropriate, understanding that each has strengths to cope with his or her life, yet all are enriched by compassionate and understanding hearts."

Welch looks around the semicircle at each member of the group. "I wonder if someone might begin by sharing a concern they are presently dealing with."

There is a pause, then Bailey Barron, a middle-aged woman with short blonde hair, begins: "Fredi committed suicide four years ago . . . today," she says slowly, looking at her hands. "I didn't realize it before we came tonight. It was a Monday, a rainy Monday. . . . It brings back a lot of things. You go through the whole procedure again. Holidays are rough, anniversaries are rough." She shrugs. "Every day is rough."

Welch says gently, "Has anyone else recently experienced an anniversary?"

Peter Courtney, a compact, muscular man in a flannel shirt, nods. "We're coming very close. Lisa was on a Monday. It was snowing, cold and snowing. I was out on the boat, working, and when I came home, I found out. It's coming right back again now. A couple of weeks."

Joyce Oldham, a prim middle-aged woman in matching blue skirt and jacket, smiles politely. Her earrings tremble. "Just a month ago it was a year for me that my husband killed himself, and I was very depressed," she says. She gives an anxious, apologetic laugh and looks to either side for support. "Does it get any better after the years go by?" She scans the room nervously.

"Not better," says Bailey softly, staring at the floor. "Different."

Merryl Maleska was fortunate in having parents, relatives, friends, and a therapist who were unusually sensitive to her needs. Because the subject of suicide makes many people uncomfortable, survivors often have difficulty finding support. A survivor's need to analyze the suicide may seem unquenchable, and even the most sympathetic friend may eventually find it difficult to listen. But the need to talk may continue long after friends and family have had enough. Some survivors feel that even their closest friends cannot truly understand unless they have themselves lost someone to suicide. It was this need that drew Merryl to Safe Place.

More than four hundred survivors of suicide, ranging in age from twelve to eighty, have attended meetings of Safe Place since it started in 1978. They have come from as far away as Maine and Vermont to this three-story red brick building in Somerville, a densely populated blue-collar area of Boston. They represent a wide range of backgrounds; at tonight's meeting there are a lobsterman, a hairdresser, a housewife, a priest, and an editor. Some have lost parents, some husbands, some wives, some children, some grandchildren, some friends. For some the suicide occurred as recently as a week earlier; one woman came to the group twenty-three years after her husband killed himself. Safe Place, which is organized by Omega, a grief assistance program, meets the second and fourth Tuesday evenings of each month. People may attend as many or as few meetings as they like. Some come once, find it overwhelmingly painful, and never return; others attend every meeting for years. Most come for a year or so, then gradually stop, perhaps returning for meetings around birthdays, holidays, or the anniversary of the death, when wounds tend to reopen.

When they first hear about Safe Place from a friend or a counselor, survivors are often resistant to the idea, perhaps because of some stiff-upper-lipism, perhaps because they stigmatize others as they have been stigmatized them-selves—something *must* be wrong with the people in the group because, after all, someone in their family committed suicide. "When a friend told me about Safe Place, I said no thank you, my husband and I weren't up to it," remembers Arlene Feltz, whose son had hanged himself a few months earlier. "But deep down we felt we didn't belong to this kind of group. I don't know what kind of people we thought they would be—derelicts or something." She laughs. "Somehow I just felt they would look different." When the pain didn't let up, Arlene and her husband decided to try Safe Place. Sitting in a group of twelve people, Arlene, who had always been terrified of speaking in public, was anxious and mute. As the meeting started there was a pause, and suddenly, Arlene was shocked to hear herself talking about her son. "I don't even remember what I said, but that meeting was the biggest uplift since his death."

For many survivors, attending their first Safe Place meeting is like happen-ing upon an oasis. "It was literally my salvation," says a woman who came to the group two months after her husband shot himself. "It was the first time I felt that life might go on." It may be the first time new members have met anyone else who has lost someone to suicide. It may even be the first time they have ever said the word suicide out loud. Merely being in the same room with other survivors can be tremendously painful—and tremendously liberating. Tom Rossi, a young priest, came to his first meeting three years after his younger brother's suicide, still dogged by feelings of guilt and low self-esteem. "I looked around at the other people and thought it happened to them, and *they* look like nice, normal people so maybe I'm not such a horrible person, maybe *I* could be a nice person, too."

Merryl Maleska first came to Safe Place three weeks after Carl's death. She hated it. She said nothing, just sat there numb and stone-faced. "I was looking for someone like me, someone young who had lost her husband to suicide but who had come through it," she says. There was one woman close to Merryl's age whose husband, a psychology student, had shot himself, but after two years she still couldn't speak his name without weeping. Merryl left the meeting that night feeling more raw than she had when she arrived. Nevertheless, she continued to attend even though for many months it only seemed to depress her further. But Merryl had a vague idea it might be good for her someday.

And occasionally, lying in her bed or crying at work, she thought of the woman whose husband shot himself and felt a little less alone. "It helped me to know that this person was going through the same loss, the same torture. In the midst of my pain I would remember her face and think of how she had lost her husband, too. And that communion would somehow help me to make real, tangible, this event that was so unbelievable." After a while Merryl began to speak at meetings. "It was the one place I could talk about nothing but suicide for two hours and not feel guilty for taking up someone's time." Merryl's calendar that had once been so full now had only one appointment marked on it—meetings of Safe Place.

When Safe Place began in 1978, members of the Samaritans attended the meetings as observers. One night a survivor said that the presence of the Samaritans, whose work is based on the belief that suicide can be prevented, felt like an unspoken accusation. Since that night no one has been allowed in the room who has not lost a family member or close friend to suicide. (Tonight's is a special meeting in which Safe Place members have volunteered to be videotaped for educational purposes.) Otherwise, there are few rules. Safe Place has no agenda, no speakers, no required readings, and although people come looking for them, no answers. There is just a lot of what Welch calls "unloading"—talk, talk, and more talk. But even that is not required; some survivors attend faithfully for a whole season and never say a word. Safe Place meetings are not counseling sessions. There is no advice given. "People can respond to questions and share what works for them," says Welch, "but they can't suggest that someone else do this, too—it works for me, therefore it works for you." The goal, he explains, is to create "an atmosphere in which people can safely grieve."

Midway through tonight's meeting Welch turns to Rona, a divorced, middle-aged woman whose daughter killed herself three months ago. She is perched on her chair, lips tight, hands folded, as quiet and contained as an owl. She hasn't said a word all night; when someone speaks, she looks not at them but at a point on the floor in their general direction. Welch gently asks whether caring for her remaining children has left her any time for her own grief. Seven words into her answer Rona begins to weep. She cannot stop crying but she cannot stop talking, and a flood of anxieties gushes out: her children's fears, her son-in-law's drinking, her miserable Thanksgiving. ". . . And I tried to go through my daughter's things, but I couldn't go through them, so my son went through them and he said it's sad but he went through them and I just can't, and every day it's a different pain I have to face, I try to leave it in God's hands as much as I can, and that's helped, and I try to take it one day at a time, and that's helped with my pain, but it also, it . . . just . . . it doesn't . . . I just miss her so much."

As the words and tears pour out, the rest of the group is still. Although it is clear from their faces that they are deeply affected, no one gives her a handkerchief or moves to hug her or even touch her, although Liz Courtney, sitting next to her, unconsciously swings her arm up to rest on the back of Rona's chair. Later, I question Welch about their restraint. "If someone starts crying," he explains, "and you immediately pass the Kleenex or run over and hug the person, it stops the feeling. It may make the person feel that tears are inappropriate. Nothing should interrupt whatever someone is feeling. That's why refreshments aren't served until after the meeting. People need to be able to explore their pain without any interference—which is something they don't get to do at home."

Eventually, Rona's sobbing subsides into weeping, her words slow, and like an accordion that must be squeezed flat before all the notes can escape, she finally stops. ". . . And I know it's going to be even harder at Christmas, but my son said he would come over and put up the tree because my daughter always did that. And I find as time goes on it's gotten harder instead of easier." There is a long pause, as if the group is giving the spilled pain a chance to settle, and then Merryl says gently, "But three months is like yesterday, really." There are murmurs and nods of assent from the others. Bailey gives a wry smile. "In the beginning I thought that every day would make it better, every step would make it better," she says. "Well, it doesn't, and we all know that. You never go back to the beginning, but it isn't just a steady upward progress." Rona has stopped crying. She looks up at the faces of the group, meeting their eyes for the first time.

People feel comfortable at Safe Place talking about things they can't talk about anywhere else: the nightmares and gory details that friends want to be spared but a survivor can't shake, the fear that another family member might commit suicide, the sneaking suspicion they might be going crazy, the fear that they'll never be happy again. "It's amazing how many times I'll unravel an incident and people will say, 'That's how I feel,' or 'That happened to me,' " says a woman whose husband shot himself. A young woman whose lover killed himself a year ago can't tell friends that sometimes, when the pain is over-whelming, she gets in her car, rolls up the windows, and drives back and forth across a bridge, screaming. "You can say anything you want at Safe Place," she says, "and no one will ever laugh at you or think you're a jerk."

One of the most difficult issues for survivors to talk about is their own suicidal thoughts. "They need reassurance that it's okay to have those thoughts," says Welch. "In the group, people understand those feelings and so it gets said. No one gasps, no one faints." No Safe Place member has ever killed himself, and although Welch occasionally refers a troubled survivor to counseling, he is the first to admit that his interventions in the group are minimal. "I have a tremendous respect for the resiliency of humans," he says. More often the group's atmosphere encourages honesty on less dramatic ques-tions: "If friends ask me how I'm feeling and I say I'm feeling bad, they don't know what to say," says the mother of a boy who hanged himself. "So now

I just tell them I'm okay. But in group the other night, Father Welch asked me how I was feeling, and I said 'terrible.' " She smiles. "It felt good to be able to say that."

At Safe Place comfort comes in peculiar ways. No matter how awful a survivor's situation seems to be, at Safe Place there's always someone whose story sounds even worse. A mother plagued with guilt for not taking her son's suicide threats seriously meets a man who, hoping to shock his wife out of her threats, told her to go ahead and kill herself. A couple whose son shot himself in the heart meets a woman who found her husband shot in the head. A woman angry because her husband left no note meets a woman angry because her husband left a note. A young woman devastated by the suicide of her father meets a woman who lost both her father and her brother to suicide. "Measuring" can also work another way: Survivors for whom the wound is unbearably fresh can listen to a survivor whose loss is further in the past and realize that some day their pain may lessen. A woman whose son killed himself four years ago has never told *anybody* it was a suicide. Sitting in silence at Safe Place is the best she can do for now, but listening to survivors who are able to talk about the suicides in their families gives her a seed of hope. And those survivors are comforted to feel that their pain may be of use.

None of which means that a survivor will ever forget. "After five years I feel a lot better," says Liz Courtney to the group. Her hands cut quick geometric shapes in front of her as she speaks. "But still, it comes back. The waves keep coming." She looks toward her husband Peter, who nods. "Two weeks ago one of our daughters came home from St. Louis for some job interviews," she says, "and she was really excited. Our son had just bought a house, and our other daughter was getting along really well with her beau, and I was so happy that everybody was perking. But then when they left, I just dissolved. I couldn't put my finger on it at first and then I realized, 'Lisa isn't here to be part of this.' " Liz's hands fold tightly in her lap as if now that they've found each other they'll never let go. "I find I can get really upset about something and not have any idea what it's all about until I analyze it. And it always seems to come back to Lisa."

Safe Place was born because Liz and Peter Courtney, no matter where they turned, could not find quite enough room for their grief during the year after their daughter Lisa killed herself on the roof of a five-story building in Newburyport, a small town on the coast north of Boston.

One night, not quite six months after Lisa's death, Liz and Peter were at Peter's brother's house for dinner. Liz had been warned by friends who had been through deaths in their families that she would have six months to "get over" her daughter's death before people would expect her to "shape up her act." But Liz was still reeling with grief, and that night at dinner she began talking yet again about Lisa's suicide. Suddenly her brother-in-law interrupted. "Knock it off," he said. "Enough is enough." Liz was mortified but forced a smile. "Wait!" she said. "It's only been five and a half months—I still have two weeks!"

Liz and Peter Courtney laugh when they tell the story now. They laugh at their naiveté in thinking they could possibly "shape up their act" in five and a half or even six months. "Five *years* is when we began to feel better," says Liz, a tall, handsome woman who crafts lampshades. Her husband, Peter, a small, rugged-looking lobsterman, nods. "After five years the salt started to come out of the wound," he says. Seven years after their daughter's death, the pain still occasionally strikes without warning. For Peter the tears come as suddenly as a summer squall; they roll down his cheeks until his whole face is wet, and only when he has stopped crying does he pull a worn red bandanna from his pocket. Liz dabs delicately at her tears with a finger before they have a chance to travel far down her face. Recently, she and Peter were at a friend's house watching *Fanny and Alexander,* the film by Ingmar Bergman. In one scene a woman sees the body of her dead husband for the first time and howls like a jungle animal. "How awful," said one of the Courtneys' friends. "Who could make such a sound?" Liz didn't answer. She had flashed back to a moment seven years before, to the day her daughter died, when she had let out a howl exactly like that.

Lisa Courtney was "born with a crayon in her hand," as her mother says. At an early age she decided she wanted to be an artist; she edited the art quarterly in high school and attended an art school in Philadelphia. A slender girl with long blond hair and milky skin, Lisa was sensitive and shy, though, says Liz, "not painfully so." Liz and Peter were shocked when on Thanksgiving of her junior year at college they got a call from the school counselor at two in the morning telling them Lisa had been found by a night watchman, curled up and whimpering in a public bathroom cubicle. They took off in their station wagon for Philadelphia, terrified. "Lisa was sitting on a bed looking so pathetic," recalls Peter. "I felt so sorry for her. I thought, 'God, if I'd ever known this kid had been this tense . . .'" The doctor, who had given Lisa Thorazine, suggested they take her home for a rest.

Peter and Liz were determined to lick the problem as a family. Each week the three of them went to a husband-and-wife counseling team, and Lisa saw the wife for individual therapy. Over the next few years Lisa gradually seemed to emerge from her shell. She found an apartment, a good job as a jewelry designer, and a few friends. But each fall she went into a funk—a fog, as she called it—that she couldn't shake until Christmas.

The fall of 1977, when Lisa was twenty-three, a number of things went wrong: She felt she deserved more pay at her job but was too shy to ask for a raise; her car wasn't working; and worst of all, her boyfriend left her for his old girlfriend. One day Peter got a call. Lisa had stabbed herself, but she was going to be all right. Says Liz, "When we got to the hospital, we asked her what happened, and she said she'd gone out to Plum Island and that she just felt all this fog around her. She thought about stabbing herself out there, but she came back to her apartment and stabbed herself in the kitchen, fell to the floor and thought, 'Well, this is a dumb thing,' and then she drove herself to the hospital." Peter shakes his head. "I remember asking her why she'd done it," he says. "And she said, 'Well, I've never felt real pain, and I *had* to *find out* what *real pain* was *about*.' " Peter pounds the table with his fist at each word. He looks up, puzzled. "And I think that's what shook my boots." Liz speaks quietly: "I think she meant she'd cut herself because she was in such a fog that she needed to feel something sharp."

Lisa came home to live with her parents and went back to work part-time. Each evening the three of them sat by the fire and had "catch-up time," telling each other about their day. "It was a very tense time," remembers Peter, "hoping that Lisa would come out and say, 'This is what was good about the day, and this is what was lousy.' And trying to carry on a smooth conversation with somebody you knew was in a lot of pain." Three times a week they went to their therapists, who taped each session. Afterward, Liz, Peter, and Lisa listened to the tape at home, talking and searching and rehashing, trying to get to the bottom of this, whatever this was. It was an exhausting time for Peter and Liz as they tried to give Lisa enough room but not too much, to be cozy and caring but not suffocating. "It was twenty-four hours a day, it was all for Lisa, trying to help her save her life," says Liz. "And sometimes when I thought that we had done some good work, I felt so elated. I remember walking down the street one day feeling: 'My God, maybe we're really going to get to the root of this problem, maybe we're going to lift Lisa out of this . . .' "

But Lisa remained brittle and self-conscious. One day in her mother's studio, Lisa looked out the window and saw her old boyfriend and his new girlfriend walking down the street licking ice cream cones. "He never bought ice cream for me," Lisa said in a small voice. Another time she curled up under a table. "I didn't know the word 'regression' then," says Liz. "I didn't see until later it was a step on a long path of making her world smaller and smaller." Lisa worried that she was behaving peculiarly; one day she was mortified that she had driven out of a parking lot the wrong way. "You could always tell she felt a little raw," says Liz. "Her biggest problem was getting up in the morning. She was panicky—afraid to face the day. She'd cry and throw up. I'd hug her and say, 'Come on, let's go' or 'Don't get up if you don't want to.' " But it got worse. "One morning she said, 'I don't want to live anymore.' I said, 'But Lisa, just leave it until Friday, until we go back to the therapists.' "

Monday morning it snowed. When Lisa came downstairs, Liz asked her how she felt. "I'm fine," said Lisa. Liz told her daughter that she was going Christmas shopping and her father would be home at noon. "Is there anything you want to talk about now?" she asked. Lisa said no, she was okay, she was going to go to work.

"But Lisa never went to work," says Liz slowly. "She went to the building where I work. Her ex-boyfriend lives there, too, which is pretty heavy." Liz looks down at the table. "It's an enormous brick shoe factory that was made into artists' studios. And you can go all the way up to the fifth floor where there's a little room with a door that opens out on the roof. People sunbathe out there. Lisa used to go up there at lunchtime with her boyfriend. There's a beautiful view of the ocean. You can see Gloucester." Liz pauses. "Afterward, her ex-beau remembered hearing someone up on the roof, walking around this funny little room. He didn't know it was Lisa, he thought it was a kid. She'd gone up to that room where there was a lot of broken glass from kids busting windows over years and years and years, and she did all of this"—Liz makes a cutting motion at her wrists—"and this . . . and this"—her hand flashes at her legs, her arms, her neck—"I mean she really wanted *out.*" Liz looks away and begins to cry. "And then we assumed she just must have rolled off the roof."

In a coma, her skull fractured, her body covered with cuts and heavily bandaged, Lisa was kept on life-support systems while the family took turns sitting by her bed, talking softly to her, "just to let her know, whether she could hear us or not, that we were there," says Liz. But the doctors told the Courtneys it was hopeless, and they agreed the machines should be turned off. Friday evening they got a call from the hospital. Lisa was dead. "Saturday we saw her without any of the needles or the support systems, and that was a relief," says Liz. "I was glad she was at peace."

After the blur of friends and relatives arriving, the funeral service, friends and relatives departing, there was a sudden lull. Peter and Liz were alone. They talked about Lisa constantly. A sturdy, energetic man, Peter was drained and vulnerable. For weeks he couldn't finish a sentence without crying. About six weeks after the funeral he was painting the ceiling when he felt dizzy and fell off the sawhorse. He was able to telephone Liz, who rushed him to the doctor. Peter's heart had fibrillated; he was weak for weeks afterward.

Peter was angry at his daughter. Four weeks before her suicide, when she had stabbed herself in the stomach, Peter had asked Lisa to let him know if she ever felt like that again. "Don't leave me out of your act," he had said. Now he felt angry that she had broken her promise. Out on his boat he would suddenly cry, "Goddamn it, Lisa, why didn't you come to me?" When he was driving a truck with a load of lobsters into Boston, a sad tune would come over the radio, and he couldn't stop crying for half an hour. On his boat he would burst into sudden tears and then, just as quickly, it would be over.

Liz turned inward, wrestling with feelings of guilt. She felt she was a failure as a mother. One moment in particular haunted her, the morning before the suicide when Lisa had come downstairs in silence and Liz had said in frustration, "Please, for once, let me know how you're feeling—don't make me always have to ask."

Lisa had fallen from the tallest building in a small town, and her suicide made headlines in the local newspaper. "There wasn't anybody who didn't know, so there was no hiding, which made it easier in a way," says Liz. "But it also meant we were unable to hide if we wanted to. We knew everyone knew, and they knew we knew they knew." She gives a short, dry laugh. "Our close friends were great. Our medium friends were scared to death of us." Like many survivors, Liz and Peter often found themselves doing the comforting because their would-be comforters were so uncomfortable. Peter remembers one friend who crossed the street every time he saw him coming. "He could get from one side to another faster than a weasel in a chicken coop," says Peter, chuckling, shaking his head. "That went on for a long while, until one day there was a true traffic mess, and he couldn't make it across before I came upon him. I just said, 'Albert, how are you?' I knew he wanted to say something, but he just didn't know what the hell to say. So I said, 'Time's gone on and it's not easy for us, but it's getting better.' I just spilled that out to him, and I could see that just by my talking to him, it released some steam from his boiler."

While friends kept their distance, other survivors, some of whom they hardly knew, seemed to come out of the woodwork and immediately understand. Says Peter, "That spring a fellow fisherman came up to me. 'You've been through a bitch of a winter,' he said. 'My wife tried to kill herself so I know what you're going through, and it's a son of a bitch. The only difference is your kid didn't make it, my wife did.' " Peter taps his fingers on the table. "It was good to know a guy like that could understand."

Although Peter's need to talk about the suicide gradually diminished, for Liz the ache was continuous. She could still talk to Peter, to their children, and to Peter's brother and his wife. But after a while some of her friends grew weary. "People just didn't want to hear it," says Liz. "I tried to talk about it less, to be more careful about it," she says, giving a dry chuckle, "to grieve right." But her pain kept spilling over the edges. Years earlier she had been involved in several women's support groups, and now she kept wishing there were a group for this, a group where she could say what she wanted and people would listen whether it had been six months or six years.

Liz decided to look. A sixty-page notebook she kept that fall documents her exhaustive explorations. First she called the Boston Samaritans and talked to its director, Monica Dickens. Dickens was encouraging but knew of no groups for suicide grief; she suggested Liz try the Compassionate Friends, a support group for parents who have lost a child to death. Liz and Peter drove out to a church in Lynnfield one night for a meeting. It was comforting, but none of the other parents had lost a child to suicide. Suicide, Peter and Liz thought, seemed to need a special group of its own. Liz called Massachusetts General Hospital and was referred back to the Samaritans. She called McLean Hospital and was connected to a psychiatrist researching the biochemistry of suicide. She called a specialist in group therapy at Harvard who seemed surprised by the idea but wished her luck. She called a rabbi who had written books on suicide; he said if a group got started, he would love to write a book about it. She called an Episcopal minister who told her about Erich Lindemann and the importance of grief work. She called another minister who offered his church to the group if she ever found or founded one. She called a famous grief specialist who warned her to be careful because groups could be scary and someone might flip out.

After several months Liz had contacted a veritable Who's Who of bereavement. No one knew of anything in the area for suicide survivors, but they all knew of people who could benefit from such a group. Liz's notebook started filling up with these names—a woman from a farming town whose son had killed himself, a woman from a North Shore town whose son had killed himself. Liz talked to some of these people, and each survivor seemed to lead to another survivor who was looking for help. Then one morning Monica Dickens called and suggested she get in touch with Tom Welch, the young priest who had founded Omega, a two-year-old grief assistance program in Somerville that ran support groups for widows and widowers, and for the terminally ill and their families. Liz called Welch and they arranged to meet. Tom Welch was aware of survivors' needs to talk about a suicide, and he was aware of how often those needs went unmet. When he was in the seminary, a fellow priest had killed himself while on a retreat. It was never announced as a suicide. Welch only found out because word spread quickly. During his years at the seminary, two other priests took their lives. Each time there was no discussion or sharing of grief. "The seminary dealt with it very poorly," says Welch. "In fact, they didn't deal with it at all."

After meeting with Liz Courtney, Welch did some research of his own and found that although there were a handful of support groups for suicide survivors in the country, the closest was in Detroit, Michigan. "The groups were set up along the Alcoholics Anonymous model," Welch recalls. "In fact, one of them was called 'Suicides Anonymous.' The 'Anonymous' bothered me because it seemed to feed the idea that people need to be anonymous about suicide. It contributes to the conspiracy of silence and to society's inability to acknowledge that suicide is the way some people die. We didn't want to be anonymous about it, but we did want to be safe about it."

On November 9, 1978, almost one year after Lisa Courtney's death, nine people gathered in a small room at the Omega offices in Somerville. After Tom Welch spoke briefly about his ideas for the group, Liz described the research that had led her there. When she finished, there was an awkward pause. Then one man said that before they went any further, he wanted to know who everybody was and what had brought them there. One by one, people in the room introduced themselves. Then, as if a dam had burst, they began to talk about what it felt like to lose someone to suicide. For some of them it had been many years since the death, and talking about it was painful but freeing. At the end of the meeting, one woman stood. "I've said things here tonight that I've never been able to say anywhere else," she said. "This is a safe place."

Today, Safe Place is one of more than two hundred suicide survivor groups meeting in churches, kitchens, living rooms, and suicide prevention centers across the country. (Safe Place itself now has four chapters in Massachusetts.) The first group was started in 1971 in San Diego, and others—with names like LOSS, Heartbeat, Ray of Hope, Seasons, Life Line, Transition, and Life After Suicide—quickly followed. Many groups have informal roots. Two survivors meet, talk over coffee, begin to invite other survivors, and are soon gathering regularly to share their grief as well as advice on such practical matters as how to tell a child or what to do with the dead person's possessions. There are survivor conferences, survivor books, and survivor newsletters such as *Afterwords, Mayday,* and *The Ultimate Rejection,* which print poems, personal stories, and news about survivor research.

Because the concept of the "suicide-bereaved" as a special population is new, there is disagreement as to what approach best meets survivors' needs. While most of the groups, like Safe Place, are based on sharing personal experience, they range from intense weekly therapy sessions to irregular potluck dinners. One group leader runs "guided fantasies" in which she helps survivors reenact the mourning process—the funeral, the burial, and so on—in order to complete issues they may not have had a chance to resolve. Most groups meet once or twice a month and are open-ended, while others hold weekly sessions for two months, with agendas and reading lists. Some groups charge a fee, some pass the hat, most are free. Some prefer members to join as soon after the suicide as possible, others suggest they come three to six months later when the numbness has begun to wear off. Some groups are specifically for siblings, others just for mothers. There are a few groups for teenagers only, and in New Jersey there is a group for therapists who have lost patients to suicide. A group in Louisiana brings together survivors with people who have attempted suicide so that survivors may better understand what their loved ones felt, while attempters can see the pain they might cause if they were to commit suicide.

The growth of survivor groups has been so rapid and the variety so wide that in 1984 the American Association of Suicidology, recalling the unsupervised growth of prevention centers in the early seventies, appointed a committee to review survivor groups. The committee found that the main disagreement among groups was over the role of mental health professionals. While most use a therapist or counselor either as co-leader or consultant, some are led by survivors with no training. Some professionals worry that these "amateurs" may be in over their heads. "A few leaders don't recognize that they'll get involved with people who are severely troubled," says Sam Heilig, the social worker who chaired the AAS committee and for many years led a survivor group at the Los Angeles Suicide Prevention Center. "It's not uncommon for a suicide to trigger a series of underlying problems. In our group we've had people who are mentally ill, psychotic, severely depressed, and suicidal." Although the LASPC group has not had a survivor suicide, other groups have; a Detroit group (led by a mental health professional) has had two since starting in 1974. Heilig is among those who worry that survivor leaders may overlook people who need professional help. He feels that the LASPC group, co-led by a social worker and a survivor, offers the best of both worlds: The survivor can draw from personal experience, and the professional can answer questions about medication and statistics and act as a "safety net" so a survivor can feel safe falling apart.

Yet many survivors harbor great anger toward the mental health profession, especially if the person they mourn was in therapy. They may feel the "professionals" let them down. A few survivor-leaders insist there should be no professional involvement in groups. They say that they are capable of spotting problems and, when appropriate, of referring the survivor to professional help. "A lot of the literature writes up the pathological cases of survivors, so a few therapists think we're *all* basket cases," says one survivor-leader. "Many therapists look on us as a big pool of potential clients, but many survivors will never be able to go to a therapist." Explains one group leader, "The already stigmatized survivor may see needing therapeutic help as bringing them further stigma by labeling them as sick." At bottom, many survivors feel that no one who is not a survivor himself can understand. An Illinois social worker whose mother killed herself started a group when she realized that many survivors who were already in therapy seemed to need something more. "I feel so safe and warm and understood here," said a woman at her first meeting of the group. "I feel safe and warm at my shrink's office, too, but not always understood."

Whether a group leader is a trained therapist, an untrained survivor running a self-help group, or a counselor-priest like Tom Welch, working with survivors offers a unique perspective on suicide itself. Welch occasionally gets anonymous phone calls from people who are planning to kill themselves and, taking advantage of his reputation as a survivor expert, want to know how to make their suicide less painful for their families. What method should they use? Where should they do it? What should they say in their note? Welch listens carefully, suggests some options other than suicide, invites them to call him anytime, but tells them their questions are unanswerable. " 'There *is* no best way,' I say. I share with them what I learned from the group—that there is really no way to prevent the people who love them from feeling responsible for their death. They could leave them a thousand notes saying they're blameless, but it will never stop affecting them. Their lives will be forever changed."

As the Safe Place meeting continues, the ten survivors become progressively more animated and intimate, their voices more sure, their bodies leaning further into the circle. As I watch the videotape, I get an image of them— Peter, Liz, Merryl, Bailey, and the others—driving to Somerville from homes all over eastern Massachusetts, carrying their pain, coming to this room and pouring it out as if there were an almost palpable communal pile of shards of grief and guilt and anger on the floor in front of them. Each time their load becomes a little lighter although they know that no matter how much they unload, there will always be something left.

"We still have a few more moments," says Tom Welch, "and before we break from the group, I'm wondering if someone has something he'd like to share."

"Earlier, we were talking about the holidays," says Jean, whose husband shot himself three years ago. "One thing that has been helpful to me is to do something different each year. I haven't had a Christmas in my house or a tree, and that has been helpful. . . . I try to find a totally different scene over the holidays."

"It's a reminder of the happiness you can't participate in," says Welch.

"I don't ever want to have Christmas in my house again," murmurs Jean.

"I think one of the things about time is that even though the loss never goes away, other things come up, other things grow," says Tom Rossi. "It's like the pictures now of Mount St. Helens. There's life there, and things fill in some of the spaces that right now are just yawning wounds or huge horrible gaps that it doesn't look like you'd ever get over. So I try not to say that anything's forever—that I'll never celebrate again or that it'll never get any better." He pauses. "It'll never be like it was. But new things grow."

"Every Thanksgiving since Fredi's death, we've visited our cousins in North Carolina," Stanley says. "It's always been an escape. But every time we come home, it seems to come right back to that Monday after Thanksgiving when she took her own life." He looks at his wife. "I don't know why, but this Thanksgiving seemed to be the least difficult of all. This year I see things replacing the pain."

Peter nods. "Lisa's grave is down on Plum Island, not far from where we live," he says. "Every so often I go down there with some flowers I might find on the roadside on the way home from the fishing boat." He looks down at his lap. "For the first three or four years, I couldn't get to the gate without crying. By the time I spoke to the guard and went through the gate I was a basket case." He shakes his head. "But last time, I got all the way through the gate before I started crying!" He looks up, shaking his head, and smiles and everyone in the group begins to laugh with him.

After the laughter settles, Welch looks at the faces in the semicircle. "I'd like to make an opportunity for us to chat with one another for a while after we break from this group," he says, "but before that, why don't we spend a few moments in some quiet." And he, Peter, Liz, Merryl, Eileen, Rona, Joyce, Bailey, Stanley, Jean and Tom join hands, eyes closed, looking down. After a silence, Welch says, "Just feel all the warmth and support and comfort that's been here in this circle this evening. We can send out our good wishes, our hopes, our concern, our prayers. And remember always to take from this circle what we need for ourselves, to put all of that warmth and support into our own hearts."

VII

MERRYL: THE BUILDING
BLOCKS

SEVENTEEN MONTHS AFTER CARL'S DEATH Merryl Maleska spoke at an anniversary service held each November to which all Safe Place members, past and present, are invited. "For each of us in this room life has been torn open with such a shock that our deepest sense of trust in the world has been challenged," said Merryl. ". . . This would all be true of anyone who had lost a loved one in a tragic, sudden, totally unexpected way. For us, though, there are special, unique shadows to the distrust. It is not only the world, after all, that is unpredictable—not only the unforeseeable events of an accident— but the choice, the deliberate (in some sense) actions of our loved one that have so destroyed our sense of the world. Someone we loved terribly has rejected us, has told us we were not enough to stay alive for. Even if we *know* this was not at all his reason for doing what he did, it still *feels* like deep unutterable abandonment. How can we ever trust another human being with our caring? How can we make ourselves vulnerable again?"

Two years after Carl's death Merryl and Nathan settled into a five-room apartment on the first floor of a three-story frame house on a quiet side street in Cambridge. The furnishings were simple and comfortable; the apartment looked like that of many young professional couples just starting out, building a home. And for Merryl, in many ways, life was just beginning again. Once more she was excited by her work; she had recently been promoted to senior editor at Houghton Mifflin. A social life that had stopped for two years restarted, and her calendar became crowded with entries for movies, birthdays, dinner parties, and concerts. She and Nathan began to invite new friends over for dinner; Merryl began to shop in supermarkets again. "When I walked into Star Market for the first time in two years, I felt like someone from another culture," says Merryl. She gained back the twenty-five pounds she lost during her first year of grieving. She began to sew again; she made curtains for every room in the house and even knitted gifts for friends' babies. She started wearing jewelry again, resumed writing in her diary, and began, somewhat gingerly, to pick up "normal books." *War and Peace* was first, followed ten months later by *Dune.* "Both of them are set in other worlds," she says, "so they didn't seem as threatening." And when she and Nathan drove up through Maine to Quebec it was her first vacation since Carl's death.

As she builds a new home, another shared life, Merryl is occasionally swept by waves of fear. "The more I begin trusting someone again, the more afraid I am that I will lose everything again," she says. "Whenever Nathan is late coming home from a trip, I get worried. If he says he'll call at eight, I'm petrified by nine. I'm just waiting for the worst, for someone to call and say, 'There's been a problem.' We were at the beach not long ago. At the end of the afternoon when we got back to the car, I realized I'd lost an earring. Nathan went back to look for it. It was a long way back to where we'd been sitting, and it was getting dark. He was gone a long time. I got scared that he would disappear into thin air. It was totally irrational; I knew that, and he came back, of course, but I was terrified. When you've had things taken away from you, you are constantly reminded of how fragile life is."

Merryl was forcefully reminded of that when her mother died of cancer a year and a half after Carl's death. Although not unexpected, it was a shock. Merryl's father was overcome with grief, and Merryl made most of the funeral arrangements—with the same home that had handled Carl's death. "The funeral director couldn't believe I was back and that I was functioning," she says. "The last time he'd seen me I was prostrate on the floor." Her mother was buried next to Carl. "It's one of the most important pieces of land in the world to me," she says. "Before Carl died I was afraid of the word 'death,' and since then it seems as if I've lived in cemeteries." She chuckles wryly. "Now sometimes I feel more at home there."

For a year and a half Merryl had done little else but think about Carl's life and death. "My relationship with Carl spanned thirteen years, from 1969 to 1982—almost my entire adult life up to that point—and his suicide just blew my life open at the age of thirty-four when I was on the verge of so many things," she says. "I thought that Carl's suicide would define my life for a long, long time, but it's no longer primarily how I define myself. It's a major part of my life, but it's no longer the one thing I'm waiting to tell someone. There are lots of pure moments free of Carl—laughing with Nathan or at work. And that's a long way from the night I heard he died when I didn't think I'd be able to live."

In therapy Merryl is still piecing things together about Carl, but gradually she and her therapist have focused more on Merryl. For so long her life had seemed bound to Carl's life and his death. "My grief for Carl heightened a lot of the things I need to deal with in myself. I'm trying to come to terms with being a separate person and having a sense of my own self-worth. That's been a big part of separating myself from Carl and going on with life without him. I started feeling I was worth living for, whether or not I had Carl or any other man." Though she keeps the black plastic bag of "Carl papers" in her top desk drawer, she rarely looks at them. After not missing a meeting of Safe Place for more than a year, these days Merryl rarely attends. When she does, she is looked up to as a sort of role model, as someone who has come through. Sometimes she will see someone who has come to Safe Place for the first time, "looking like a waif," and she shivers, remembering her own first meeting.

Merryl still thinks of Carl every day. And though she no longer goes out of her way to talk about him, she doesn't go out of her way not to. "If somebody asks me where I got my car, I can say, 'Oh, Carl and I bought it,' " she says. "I don't unravel anymore. Or if I do start to unravel, I can put myself back together." When Nathan and Merryl were invited to the christening of Nathan's niece, Merryl was terrified she'd be undone by echoes of the christening party for Carl's nephew, the party that never took place. She was cautious but comfortable. She even held the baby. She is back in touch with Carl's brother and sister-in-law, who recently sent her a snapshot of Carl's nephew. "To me he looks a lot like Carl, which is a little eerie," she says. "But it didn't overwhelm me." One day she came across the pink bathrobe she had worn during her first months of mourning, and she touched the knots her nervous fingers had made of its stray threads. On weekends at her father's house on the Cape, Nathan likes to work in the study, Merryl's former "torture chamber." Merryl sometimes stands in the doorway and watches him. Though the studio couch is folded up, the clock with its insistent red digits still sits on its shelf. "And for a moment that hollow feeling at the pit of my stomach comes back. But then it's just a room again." She pauses, then adds, "But it'll never be *just* a room."

When Merryl visited New York for the first time since Carl's death she decided to walk past the hotel where Carl had died, which she had seen so many times in her imagination. As she stood on the sidewalk and looked at the small, ugly, gray building, she was flooded with sadness. Dirty curtains billowed out of open windows. A painted advertisement was peeling on the side of the hotel. "It was no place for a man of Carl's magnitude to die," says Merryl. "But painful as it was, I felt better having seen it. I felt I'd faced down a demon that had been haunting me."

Most of Carl's things that Merryl saved from the Brookline apartment lie in a corner of the basement. The suitcase Carl had taken to New York. The box marked "Carl's clothes." The portrait Merryl gave him for his thirty-second birthday. The inscribed glass biology prize Carl won as a sophomore at Tufts, his fraternity "paddle," his master's diploma. Ten eight-foot-tall card files with thousands of neatly lettered file cards. One dozen boxes marked "Carl's files," containing his dissertation. "I will part from these things eventually," says Merryl. "There will come a time in my life when I'm not going to cart around Carl's work, but that time hasn't come yet." Upstairs, in the right-hand drawer of her desk where she keeps the "Carl papers," Merryl keeps an envelope with a lock of Carl's hair she had saved. Recently, she opened it and held the brown curl in her hand. "I saw some gray in it, which I'd seen before, but it made me wonder—would his hair have been gray by now? What would he be like? He was only thirty-three—he had so many stages of his life to go through. He was a man who was still unfolding. What would he have been like when he was old?

"Carl will always be part of me," says Merryl, whose face still lights up when she talks about him. "I'll probably never know anyone else with his intensity and perception. He was so gentle, yet he had a way of cutting through things." She looks away. "I get a tremendous gripping feeling sometimes—at Christmas when I'm writing to his parents or when I'm looking at pictures of him. Suddenly, it will come back—that sense of what a good, rich, deep person he was. I think of the immense waste. It comes over me in an almost nauseating way. The loss of him not just from my world but from the whole world."

VIII

A PLACE FOR WHAT WE
LOSE

"WE FIND A PLACE FOR WHAT WE LOSE," wrote Sigmund Freud to Ludwig Binswanger after the death of his friend's son. "Although we know that after such a loss the acute stage of mourning will subside, we also know that we shall remain inconsolable and will never find a substitute. No matter what may fill the gap, even if it be filled completely, it nevertheless remains something else."

Some say survivors never recover from a suicide. "Life is back to normal, but normal is different now," says a man whose son hanged himself. "Normal will never be the normal it was before a year ago." A man whose teenage daughter killed herself two years ago says it helps him to think of his grief as a physical handicap: "Some people can't see, some people can't walk, and I can't seem to enjoy life," he says matter-of-factly. Says Tom Welch, "We never really essentially get over anything. We resolve it in such a way that we can go on."

Certainly, the sheer weight of the pain eases with time. In *Madame Bovary,* Flaubert describes a young widower's passage from suicidal depression to something approaching normalcy:

Ah well, slowly but surely, one day chasing another, spring on top of winter, autumn on top of summer, it leaked away, drop by drop, little by little; it left, it went away—it sank down, I should say, because there's always something stays, at the bottom, so to speak . . . a weight there, on the chest! But it's the same for all of us, we mustn't let ourselves go, and want to die just because others are dead.

During this slow process of healing, signs of recovery may seem minute. One mother visits her son's grave three times a week instead of daily; another dreams of her son once a week instead of every night. "For a year and a half my daughter was the first thing I thought of when I opened my eyes in the morning," says one woman. She smiles faintly. "Now I can make coffee before it hits me." Yet this gradual increase of pain-free moments may be fraught with its own dangers—the pangs of "recovery guilt" many survivors feel for not thinking about the suicide twenty-four hours a day. "It's like if I go on with my life, I must be an awful person," says Tom Rossi. "There's that tug that if things start to go well, then maybe I should punish myself, because what kind of person am I if I can be happy and he's dead?"

Even when the tide of everyday experience takes the edge off the pain, wounds are often reopened. The anniversary of the death may be particularly difficult; merely being asked how many children one has can be devastating. "Sometimes I say, 'I had three but I lost one,' " says a woman whose nineteen-year-old son hanged himself. "Sometimes I say two, but then I feel dishonest, as if I'm denying him." A year after their son killed himself, one couple was desolate when they received his license renewal application in the mail. Another couple, months after their son's suicide, received a Christmas card from his therapist, who had forgotten to remove the boy's name from his computer mailing list. The spring following the suicide of her daughter, a woman burst into tears when she saw purple tulips blooming in her yard; she had forgotten her daughter had planted them. "My hands are just like my mom's," says another woman. "Every time I look at them for the rest of my life I'm going to think of her suicide."

Three years after their daughter's suicide, Liz and Peter Courtney built a one-room addition to their house. As the contractors tore down the walls, Liz grew increasingly anxious. Some days she exploded at them for their seeming inefficiency; at other times she felt helpless, unable to answer their simplest question. She would come downstairs in the middle of the night, pacing off dimensions, fretting about what furniture would go where, calculating how the addition could be made less expensive, wondering whether the project was a mistake. One day Peter was horrified to find her beating her head on the banister. "I can't stand it," she moaned. "I want to give up. I want to die."

In retrospect, Liz, who went back to Lisa's therapists for help, believes she had a nervous breakdown. "I couldn't stand any more destruction," she says. "Lisa had hurt herself so badly, and I felt this house was being hurt, too." At the same time her despair helped her understand how her daughter must have felt. "I never wanted to take my life, but I sure wanted to get out of that pain.

And I thought, now I know what feeling awful feels like. Really awful. Really, really awful."

Six months later the addition was completed. "All of a sudden everything lightened," says Liz. "It was the climax; it just came out, and then the worst was over. I look back on it as being Lisa. It was the final hell. And I've felt so much better ever since."

Many grief counselors believe that healing after a suicide can begin only when the survivor realizes that the question "why" will never be answered. In a survey by Betsy Ross, the founder of an Iowa City support group called Ray of Hope, more than two hundred survivors were asked whether their explanation for the suicide had changed since the death. Over 70 percent said it had not, but they insisted that their relentless questioning was necessary regardless of the results. "I had to search for a reason even though I think I already knew I wouldn't find one," said one survivor. "He had to do it," said another. "I knew that then, and I know that now. I just didn't know why. I may never know why, but I couldn't accept that at first and I can now." Observes Tom Welch, "The search for the reason why is part of what people need to do, but finally they understand that no answer is ever enough. Healing and a sense of self-worth come only when one draws away from feeling responsible for the death. When people learn a way to let go, to give permission for what's already happened to them, only then will they be able to move on."

After a suicide, a person's entire life is seen through his final act, as if it discredits all the good things that came before. "The suicide totally changed the way I viewed our relationship," says a young woman a year after her husband hanged himself. "I really felt we were a model couple, and that's almost embarrassing now. I would like to be able to say to people, 'My husband and I had a great relationship,' but I feel too humiliated to do that." Says Tom Rossi, "I remember my brother as a happy person—he taught me more about life than anybody. Yet when I tell people about him, about all the good things, I have to have him commit suicide at the end. It's so odd. I have to create him and then destroy him." A more accurate balance is restored only as the survivor works back through the bad memories and the good memories begin to resurface. "It may be a picture or a movie or a piece of music," says the widow of a man who shot himself four years ago, "but now those things remind me of the good times, not the bad." As the widow of a man who jumped from an eleven-story building wrote, "I want Dick's death not to be bigger than his life."

Any death shakes our faith in our own world and in the order of the world around us. But suicide in particular forces survivors to question their most basic assumptions, a process in which they may ultimately learn some important things about the person they have lost and about themselves. "I thought I knew my husband," says a middle-aged lawyer. "I was so confident that I understood him and that I understood the world." She shakes her head. "My husband gave me the gift of my beginning to realize how powerless we are, how little we control, and how we have to accept that."

Some survivors speak of positive changes that emerge after a suicide, of families drawn closer together, of becoming more sensitive, loving, attentive, and compassionate. Some speak of the painful lesson of realizing that we can never truly know someone else, that in some way each of us is ultimately alone, and that life is a mystery. Some describe finding inner resources they did not know they had. "The pain I feel is offset by the knowledge that the very worst thing in life has happened to me, and I have survived," says one man. "Maybe we're never quite the same people we were before," says a woman whose son shot himself. "But maybe that's not all bad. Maybe we wouldn't *want* to be that person." In the four years since her son's death she has led a survivor group, returned to graduate school, and started to write. "I've become a kinder human being. I listen more closely to people. I try to use the positive approach." Her voice slows with each item on the list. "I'm aware of the good things, but I'd give them up in a minute if I could have him back."

IX

MERRYL AND CARL

___

FOUR YEARS AFTER CARL'S DEATH Merryl decided she was ready to sort through the eight cardboard boxes she had packed so hurriedly that final night in her Brookline apartment. And so every weekend for three months she sat in her study, door closed, sifting through the details of her past. Some of it she discarded, some she put aside to send to Carl's parents, and some she placed inside the steamer trunk she had bought to hold the memories she chose to save.

In one box Merryl found evidence of her first year of grieving: dozens of sympathy cards; stubs from bills she had paid; the program from a play she had attended with Judith; a diary she had bought and never written in; comforting letters from her mother. Other boxes held the fragments of the last few months of Merryl's shared life with Carl: dried flowers they had saved from Carl's sister's wedding; ticket stubs from Merryl's business trip to Chicago four weeks before Carl's death; notes for a speech Merryl had given that Carl attended; a baby picture of Carl grinning and splashing as his mother bathed him in the sink; a baby picture of Merryl that had faced Carl's on her bulletin board; a photograph of Carl's Swedish cousins that his mother had sent him a week before his death; pictures of Merryl and Carl at a family reunion; a card saying "Happy Sailing" that Merryl had been on the verge of mailing to Carl's recently remarried uncle; Merryl's work schedule for the months of June and July; Merryl's clipboard with a long list of things "To Do"; stray notes and clippings for his dissertation that Carl had thrown away in those last weeks; invitations for the christening party for Carl's nephew; tickets for a play they planned to see in July; the novel Merryl was reading at the time of Carl's death.

Then Merryl came across a thin white folder. She winced, knowing what was inside—Carl's picture from the "pigbook." When Carl's mother had learned how much Merryl loved that photograph, she had an enlargement made. Merryl had kept it in her desk in the Brookline apartment, and as she worked she occasionally took it out and looked at it. Now, as she held the folder in her hands, she shivered: "I knew I was going to look right into those eyes again." When she opened it, she felt blinded for a moment. There was Carl at age seventeen, looking exactly as he had looked twenty years ago when Merryl first found his picture and vowed to marry him. "When I looked into those eyes, I remembered Carl in the early way, how I worshiped him. And that shock of attraction and wonder all came back." She looked into Carl's eyes and thought, "How innocent, how soft, how full of hope, that faraway look, your eyes looking into me. I see in that look all the looks I was to come to know in you; you were a person coming to be. . . . How much did you know then? You cared so much about life, you wanted so much from it—why did it go awry for you? Those eyebrows, so full . . . oh, how you hurt me. And how I loved you."

Then Merryl took a deep breath and looked up. There was a current calendar on her wall. She heard the hum of cars on the street outside and the sound of Nathan puttering in the next room. She was surrounded by the details of her new life. She opened the trunk. "As I picked up the picture I looked into his eyes again, and it all began to recede. As I looked at him I thought, 'That was a different life, that was down another path.' And I closed the picture up. 'You suffered a lot, Carl,' I told him. 'But I have to put you away.' "

EPILOGUE

SINCE THE REPORTING of this book was completed, Merryl Maleska married Nathan and moved to a small town on the coast north of Boston. They are planning to adopt a child. Merryl attends occasional meetings of Safe Place and has written several articles about being a survivor of suicide.

In 1989, nearly seven years after his death, Merryl learned that Carl had left a suicide note. Believing it would do Merryl more harm than good, her parents and in-laws had withheld it from her. Merryl wrote to Carl's parents, who sent her a photocopy. In the four-line note, which began "She will get over it," Carl weighed the "misery" of staying alive against the "control" and "freedom" he would gain by killing himself. "I wish that the note had not been kept from me for so long," says Merryl. "Although reading the note gave me great pain—at seeing Carl's handwriting, at feeling more acutely his torturous state—the overall feeling was one of relief at having fuller knowledge and at knowing that I was in Carl's thoughts at the end."

In 1988, Americans Against Human Suffering, a political branch of the Hemlock Society, attempted to place legislation on the California state ballot that would permit a physician to assist a terminally ill person to die. They gathered fewer than one-half the 372,000 signatures required. The group has vowed to try again. Similar attempts are underway in Oregon, Washington, and Florida.

In 1989, Hemlock Society cofounder Ann Wickett was diagnosed with breast cancer. Two weeks after her mastectomy, her husband, Derek Humphry, left her. Wickett, who claims Humphry was so unnerved by the situation that he was unable to act rationally, is filing for a divorce. Humphry asserts that the marriage had been troubled for several years. In 1991, *Final Exit,* a book by Derek Humphry containing detailed instructions on how to take one's own life in the case of terminal illness, was published and within a few months had become a national bestseller.

On June 4, 1990, on a makeshift bed in the back of his 1968 Volkswagen van in a suburban Detroit park, retired pathologist Jack Kevorkian inserted an intravenous line into the arm of Janet Adkins, a fifty-four-year-old woman from Portland, Oregon, who was suffering from Alzheimer's disease. The line was attached to Kevorkian's "self-execution machine," which he had assembled for less than $30 from three intravenous bottles, plastic tubing, and a small motor. Kevorkian waited with Adkins, a Hemlock member who had read about Kevorkian's machine in a magazine article, as she pushed down a plunger that allowed thiopental sodium into her bloodstream, rendering her unconscious in twenty-five seconds, followed immediately by a lethal dose of potassium chloride that stopped her heart and brought death within six minutes. Kevorkian, who said he hoped to set up a clinic where physician-assisted suicides would become accepted medical practice, has been legally enjoined from using his machine.

On June 25, 1990, the United States Supreme Court ruled that the State of Missouri could require life support to be continued for thirty-two-year-old Nancy Cruzan, who has been in a "persistent vegetative state" since an auto accident in 1983. Cruzan's parents had sued to have their daughter's feeding tubes removed. Although the court, hearing a right-to-die case for the first time, recognized a "constitutionally protected liberty interest in refusing unwanted medical treatment," it ruled that the refusal must be expressed by a "competent" person, and that Cruzan had not made her own treatment wishes clear in advance. Its decision essentially left right-to-die rulings up to individual states.

In the mid-1980s control of the Los Angeles Suicide Prevention Center passed from clinicians and suicide experts to the business leaders who served on its board of directors. Nevertheless, the center grew increasingly troubled financially. In an effort to streamline the budget, several programs were cut and a third of the center's ninety staffers were laid off. When the board asked for the resignation of longtime LASPC staffer Sam Heilig, half of the crisis line counselors went on strike. A Committee to Save the Suicide Prevention Center was formed, and a petition was circulated calling for control of the center to be returned to the clinicians who had run it for so many years. The initiative failed. In 1989 the board voted to merge the LASPC into Family Services of Los Angeles, a vast social services agency. Norman Farberow and Robert Litman have resigned from the LASPC, although they continue to do suicide research. Edwin Shneidman, who left the LASPC in 1966, teaches at UCLA and writes books on suicide and thanatology.

In 1989 a Federal Task Force on Youth Suicide released a four-volume report on adolescent suicide, calling for further research on the topic.

In 1987, the latest year for which figures are available, 30,796 Americans killed themselves, a rate of 12.7 per 100,000, according to the National Center for Health Statistics.

ACKNOWLEDGMENTS

IN 1980, JOHN BETHELL, the editor of *Harvard Magazine,* of which I was then a contributing editor, asked me to write an article about suicide. That piece, which appeared in November 1983 as "The Enigma of Suicide," marked the beginning of my absorption in the subject. I have always been grateful for the care and patience shown to my work by the *Harvard Magazine* staff, and never was it more apparent or more necessary than during the gestation of that article. I thank John, Kit Reed, Jean Martin, and especially Gretchen Friesinger for their excellent editorial counsel.

I am grateful to Jim Silberman of Summit Books for seeing the germ of a book in the *Harvard Magazine* piece, and to Ileene Smith and Alane Mason of Summit for giving my manuscript the kind of meticulous line editing I had been told was no longer to be found among book editors. I owe a very special debt to my agent, Amanda Urban, who gave wise counsel and infectious enthusiasm at exactly the right moments.

I was fortunate to have friends both far and near who acted as clipping services, keeping me up to date with suicide news from across the country. I am particularly indebted to Phil Driscoll, June Goldberg, and John Neary. And to Campbell Geeslin, my former editor at *LIFE,* who accommodated my quixotic work schedule and provided wise editorial advice.

Although there are hundreds of people working in the field of suicide or suicide prevention to whom I owe thanks, I am particularly beholden to Patrick Arbore, Sam Heilig, Derek Humphry, Shirley Karnovsky, Joseph Lowenstein, Karen Dunne-Maxim, Julie Perlman, Charlotte Ross, Edwin Shneidman, Tom Welch, and Ann Wickett.

For translation, proofreading, hospitality, and help of other varieties, I thank Susan Brenholts, David Breskin, Naomi Cutner, Annalee Fadiman, Clifton Fadiman, Maureen Fitzpatrick, Peter Gradjansky, Eliza Hale, Nina Hale, Douglas Heite, Rob Larsen, Laura Natkins, Mark O'Donnell, Linda Pillsbury, Sam Pillsbury, Nancy Skinner, Rod Skinner, John Srygley, Jane Trask, and Lena Williams.

I cannot thank my parents and my brothers enough for their love and support, which has been as unwavering through the years I have worked on this book as it has been throughout my life.

I owe an enormous debt to my cousin and friend Henry Singer, a fine journalist who did the vast majority of the interviewing for Part One, and whose sensitivity and emotional generosity made him one of the few people I felt I could trust with such a delicate, difficult task.

Several months before deciding to write this book, I met Anne Fadiman, a writer who was herself in the midst of a long project on suicide, an examination of the right to die that won a National Magazine Award in 1987. We soon discovered that we had far more in common than our interest in suicide; during the course of my work on this book, we married and became parents. Anne's contributions to this book are varied and immense. She has been a gentle and exacting editor for each successive draft, showing as much care and enthusiasm for the last version as she had for the first. In living with me, she also, in a sense, lived with the people who inhabit this book, and not once did she complain about their presence. Without her editorial skill, this book would be less readable; without her love and support, it would have been unwritable.

I have often been asked, "Isn't it depressing to write a book on suicide?" The question never fails to surprise me, in large part because so many of the people I have met who have had first-hand experience with the subject—who have attempted suicide, or have struggled to cope with a suicide in the family, or have worked to prevent the suicide of someone they loved—are so courageous and admirable. I would like, lastly and most importantly, to thank those people whose voices and stories appear in this book,* who gave so generously of themselves, usually in the hope that by sharing their experiences, they might help someone else. I hope that I have not failed them.

*Some of these people, or their families, asked that their real names not be used in this book. This is a list of the pseudonyms I have given them. Part 1: Melinda; Dana Evans; Tammy; Lucy. Part 3: Peter, Barbara, Ruth, Sally, Kathy, Owen, and Gerald Newell; Bill; Anna; Lizzie; David Kinnell; Ellen Parker; Part 5: Fred and Holly Isham. Part 6: Mary, Karen, Linda, and Rose Vitelli; Chris; Rona Marks.

NOTES

PART 1
Chapter II

38 *believed to be far lower than the actual numbers* In *The Savage God,* A. Alvarez cites the perhaps apocryphal story of the Irish coroner who, returning a verdict of accidental death on a man who had shot himself, commented, "Sure, he was only cleaning the muzzle of the gun with his tongue." Alvarez, A. *The Savage God.* New York: Bantam, 1973, p. 82.

41 *a research project on adolescent suicide . . .* Salk, L., et al. "Relationship of Maternal and Perinatal Conditions to Eventual Adolescent Suicide." *The Lancet,* March 16, 1985, pp. 624–27.

41 *"What it suggests . . ."* Quoted in *USA Today,* March 19, 1985.

41 *the scant research on adolescent suicide* See Berman, A, Cohen-Sandler, R. "Childhood and Adolescent Suicide Research: A Critique" (1982). *Crisis,* 3, pp. 3–15. Most research on suicide is based on people who attempt the act "unsuccessfully"—and are thus available for study—and then generalized to include those who "complete" suicide. But attempted and completed suicide are believed to be psychologically different acts committed, by and large, by demographically different groups.

41 *This is probably the most primordial . . ."* Zilboorg, G. "Some Aspects of suicide" (1975). *Suicide,* 5(3), p. 135.

41 *In a study of fifty suicidal patients . . .* Moss, L. M., Hamilton, D. M. "The Psychotherapy of the Suicidal Patient" (1956). *American Journal of Psychiatry,* 112, pp. 814–19.

42 *A University of Washington study . . .* Dorpat, T. L., Jackson, J. K., Ripley, H. S. "Broken Homes and Attempted and Completed Suicide" (1965). *Archives of General Psychiatry,* 12, pp. 213–16.

42 *Comparing 505 children and adolescents . . .* Garfinkel, B. D., Froese, A., Hood, J. "Suicide Attempts in Children and Adolescents" (1982). *American Journal of Psychiatry,* 139(10), pp. 1257–61.

42 *parents of suicidal children were subject to intense mood shifts . . .* Pfeffer's extensive work with suicidal children is described in Pfeffer, C. R. *The Suicidal Child.* New York: Guilford Press, 1986.

42 *In a study of 159 adolescents...* Deykin, E. Y., Alpert, J. J., McNamarra, J. J. "A Pilot Study of the Effect of Exposure to Child Abuse or Neglect on Adolescent Suicidal Behavior" (1985). *American Journal of Psychiatry,* 142, pp. 1299–1303.

42 *over 40 percent of the suicidal youngsters...* Cited in Peck, M. "Suicide in Late Adolescence and Young Adulthood." In Hatton, C. L. Valente, S. M. (eds.) *Suicide: Assessment and Intervention.* Norwalk, Connecticut: Appleton-Century-Crofts, 1984, p. 222.

42 *science merely confirms common sense* My favorite example is the 1982 study comparing hospitalized suicidal adolescents with hospitalized nonsuicidal adolescents and with a control group of "coping" adolescents. The results? "Suicidals were found to experience the greatest total number of problems, nonsuicidals the next most, and controls the fewest." (Topol, P., Reznikoff, M. "Perceived Peer and Family Relationships, Hopelessness and Locus of Control as Factors in Adolescent Suicide Attempts" (1982). *Suicide and Life-Threatening Behavior,* 12(3), pp. 141–50.)

43 *"A baby repeatedly left to cry alone..."* Quoted in Giffin, M., Felsenthal, C. *A Cry for Help.* Garden City, New York: Doubleday, 1983, p. 195.

43 *"Nearly every suicidal child we've seen..."* Ibid., pp. 183, 215.

44 *children as young as three have taken their own lives* In 1980, according to NIMH, there were 3 suicides among children aged five to nine, and 139 aged ten to fourteen. (Estimates run far higher.) Each year some 12,000 children aged five to fourteen are hospitalized for deliberate self-destructive acts: stabbing, scalding, burning, jumping from high places, running into traffic. Of 50 depressed children treated over three years by psychiatrist Joaquim Puig-Antich of Columbia University, more than two-thirds had had suicidal thoughts and one-third had tried to kill themselves. He estimates that as many as one in every two hundred American prepubertal children have considered suicide. Fortunately, many children don't have a clear concept of what is lethal and may take a few aspirin or jump from a first-floor window.

Some suicidal children may be motivated by an attempt to escape an intolerable home life, others by self-punishment, others to rejoin a lost loved one—often recently dead—or to gain attention from a neglectful parent. Many have been physically abused by a family member. In a study of 662 preadolescent children treated at the Neuropsychiatric Institute over a five-year period, UCLA psychiatrists found that 5 percent were suicidal or "seriously self-destructive." Many came from families in which the concept of guilt was used to control the child's behavior. Suicide became not only a way of escaping family problems but a form of self-punishment. The child often blamed himself for family problems and came to believe that he deserved to die.

Such a dynamic is illustrated in the story of Sam, one of 70 suicidal children studied by psychiatrist Peter Saltzman at McLean Hospital over seven years. A ten-year-old fourth grader, Sam had a history of poor peer relationships, poor school performance, and a reputation as the class clown. His parents' marriage was troubled, and Sam felt he should try to keep his family together by staying home. (His parents separated three days after Sam's admission to McLean.) But Sam, who saw his nine-year-old sister as the family favorite, talked often of feeling unloved. One day after Sam accused his sister of stealing a nickel, his mother yelled at him and sent him to his room. He decided no one loved him and that he was better off dead. Leaving a note for his mother telling her not to worry about him anymore, he hanged himself. But his mother came in unexpectedly and found him. Rushed to the hospital, he was resuscitated. "I hanged myself because I didn't think anyone loved me," he told his therapist. Says Saltzman, "He could not be angry at the parent he was so dependent on for the possibility of any love."

44   *In a study of the health problems . . .*   Cited in Giffin and Felsenthal, *A Cry for Help,* p. 218.

45   *persistence of symptoms for at least two weeks*   After a suicide one often hears friends or family members say, "I don't understand it. He had problems, but he was getting over them. Lately, he seemed so happy." It is a common phenomenon that people kill themselves just when they appear to be coming *out* of a depression. It may be because they have made their decision to kill themselves, and their problems finally seem solved. Ironically, making the decision may help the depression to lift—and give them the energy needed to carry out the act.

47   *"They are like a trivial border incident . . ."*   Alvarez, *The Savage God,* p. 97.

47   *"If youth is the season of hope . . ."*   Eliot, G. *Middlemarch.* Cambridge: The Riverside Press, 1956, p. 398.

47   *"Nothing was more difficult . . ."*   Wordsworth, W. From the introduction to "Ode: Intimations of Immortality from Recollections of Early Childhood." In Perkins, D. (ed.) *English Romantic Writers.* New York: Harcourt, Brace, & World, 1967, p. 279.

47   *may not understand the permanence of death*   In a study of two hundred adolescents, one in five answered "yes" when asked if they could come back to life following a suicide. Such magical thinking is not limited to young people; some suicidal adults, too, describe death as a temporary state or believe that they will be able to observe the effect of their suicide on family and friends.

47   *"I thought death would be the happiest place to be . . ."*   *Newsweek,* August 15, 1983, p. 74.

48   *"I wandered the streets . . ."*   Quoted in Menninger, K. *The Vital Balance.* Harmondsworth, England: Penguin, 1977, p. 267.

50 *Cornell professor Urie Bronfenbrenner attached microphones...* Cited in Giffin and Felsenthal, *A Cry for Help,* p. 162.

50 *A sixteen-year-old whose family had moved from New Rochelle...* Ibid., pp. 125–127.

51 *"To be sure, the good parent of the 1950s..."* Winn, M. *The New York Times Magazine,* May 8, 1983, p. 21.

53 *A thirteen-year-old boy whose family had recently moved...* The Times (San Mateo), February 11, 1983, p. 10.

53 *"Television has brought about the virtual immersion..."* Quoted in Anderson, J. "An Extraordinary People." *The New Yorker,* November 12, 1984, p. 126.

54 *"Violence on television does lead to aggressive behavior..."* Ibid., p. 125.

54 *"Pediatricians need to take a 'TV history'..."* Quoted in *The Boston Sunday Globe,* Oct. 13, 1985, p. 46.

54 *A study comparing fears of fifth and sixth graders...* Cited in *U.S. News & World Report,* August 22, 1983, p. 43.

54 *"Many children feel they are living on the brink..."* The New York Times, October 16, 1984.

56 *Psychiatrist Paul Holinger graphed...* Holinger, P. C., Offer, D. "Prediction of Adolescent Suicide: A Population Model" (1982). *American Journal of Psychiatry,* 139(3), pp. 302–7. Offering further evidence of the cohort effect, studies have found that in countries which experienced post–World War II fertility trends similar to that of the United States, the youth suicide rate has followed those trends.

Chapter IV

80 *"contagious illness..."* Quoted in Bushman, D. "Cluster Suicides." *The Reporter Dispatch* (Gannett Westchester Newspapers), December 2, 1984, p. 1.

80 *In an article on the "Westchester suicides"...* Ibid., p. 16.

81 *Bruce Rounsaville and Myrna Weissman studied sixty-two patients* ... Rounsaville, B. J., Weissman, M. M. "A Note on Suicidal Behaviors Among Intimates" (1980). *Suicide and Life-Threatening Behavior,* 10(1), pp. 24–28.

82 *A letter to columnist Ann Landers...* The Reporter Dispatch (Gannett Westchester Newspapers), April 2, 1985.

84   *Then an article appeared in* The New York Times . . . Brody, J. E. " 'Auto-erotic Death' of Youths Causes Widening Concern." *The New York Times,* March 27, 1984, p. C1.

85   *"The most singular feature connected with suicide is . . ."* Winslow, F. *The Anatomy of Suicide.* London: Henry Renshaw, 1840, p. 108.

85   *"In the year of Grace 665 . . ."* Quoted in Coleman, L. *Suicide Clusters.* Boston and London: Faber and Faber, 1987, p. 17.

85   *"Some threw themselves out at windows . . ."* Quoted in Fedden, H. R. *Suicide: A Social and Historical Study.* New York: Arno Press, 1980, p. 150.

85   *"Very few of those who were attacked recovered . . ."* Quoted in Cavan, R. S. *Suicide.* New York: Russell & Russell, 1965, p. 69.

86   *"A strange and terrible affliction . . ."* Quoted in Fedden, *Suicide,* p. 299.

86   *"vanity, if not sanity, prevailed"* Alvarez, *The Savage God,* p. 104.

87   *"to abandon oneself to grief without resisting . . ."* Quoted in Wynter, A. *The Borderlands of Insanity.* London: Henry Renshaw, 1877, pp. 244–45.

87   *"The East African societies all destroy the tree . . ."* Bohannan, P. (ed.) *African Homicide and Suicide.* New York: Atheneum, 1967, p. 263.

87   *"A child is more open to suggestion . . ."* Friedman, P. (ed.) *On Suicide.* New York: International Universities Press, 1967, p. 57.

87   *"To all this may be added . . ."* Mathews, W. "Civilization and Suicide." *The North American Review,* April 1891, p. 484.

87   *"The sensational fashion in which so many newspapers . . ."* Freidman, *On Suicide,* p. 137.

88   *"One 'new Werther' shot himself . . ."* Friedenthal, R. *Goethe: His Life and Times.* Cleveland and New York: World Publishing Company, 1965, pp. 129–30.

88   *"the mischievous influence on popular opinions . . ."* Miller, S. *The Guilt, Folly, and Sources of Suicide.* New York: T. & J. Swords, 1805.

88   *"weakening the moral principles"* Winslow, *The Anatomy of Suicide,* p. 87.

89   *has been linked by researchers to forty-three Russian roulette deaths . . .* Cited in Coleman, *Suicide Clusters,* p. 126.

89   *"When the mind is beginning to aberrate . . ."* Quoted in Galt, J. M. *The Treatment of Insanity.* New York: Harper & Brothers, 1846, p. 212.

90   *"No fact is better established in science . . ."* Quoted in Phelps, E. B. "Neurotic Books and Newspapers as Factors in the Mortality of Suicide

and Crime" (1911). Reprinted from *Bulletin of the American Academy of Medicine,* 12(5), pp. 264–306 (pp. 2–3). This paper offers an extensive, if shrill, description of the controversy at the turn of the century.

90   *"inducing morbid people and criminals . . ."*   Quoted in Motto, J. A. "Suicide and Suggestibility: The Role of the Press" (1967). *American Journal of Psychiatry,* 124(2), p. 157.

90   *a "literary chamber of horrors . . ."*   These examples are found in Phelps, "Neurotic Books," p. 36.

90   *he found that suicides increased significantly . . .*   Phillips, D. P. "The Influence of Suggestion on Suicide: Substantive and Theoretical Implications of the Werther Effect" (1974). *American Sociological Review,* 39, pp. 340–54.

91   *compelling evidence linking suggestion and suicide . . .*   Since his study of the Werther effect, Phillips has further investigated the effect of mass media on aggressive behavior. In a 1979 study of California motor vehicle deaths, he found that front-page suicide stories may provoke an increase in auto fatalities. Three days after a story, fatal car crashes increase by more than 30 percent. The rate of single-car crashes is most affected, suggesting that some of the drivers may have had self-destructive motives. Again, the greater the publicity, the greater the rise in the number of deaths. In addition, he found significant similarities between the dead driver and the person described in the suicide story. Phillips has also linked murder-suicide stories to a rise in U.S. plane crashes. (Phillips, D. P. "Suicide, Motor Vehicle Fatalities, and the Mass Media: Evidence Toward a Theory of Suggestion" [1979]. *American Journal of Sociology,* 84[5], pp. 1150–74; Phillips, D. P. "Airplane Accident Fatalities Increase Just After Newspaper Stories About Murder and Suicide" [1978]. *Science,* 201, pp. 748–50.)

91   *two controversial and troubling studies . . .*   Phillips, D. P., Carstensen, L. L. "Clustering of Teenage Suicide After Television News Stories About Suicide" (1986). *The New England Journal of Medicine,* 315(11), pp. 685–89. Gould, M. S., Shaffer, D. "The Impact of Suicide in Television Movies: Evidence of Imitation" (1986). *The New England Journal of Medicine,* 315(11), pp. 690–94.

91   *after three of the four movies were broadcast*   Shaffer suggested that the fourth film, *Silence of the Heart,* did not trigger suicides because it portrayed suicide in a less sensational fashion. Educational materials and training guides were distributed to schools beforehand, suicide prevention hot line numbers were displayed during the broadcast, and a panel discussion on suicide prevention was aired immediately following the movie.

91   *"It is timely to ask whether there are measures . . ."*   Eisenberg, L. "Does Bad News About Suicide Beget Bad News?" (1986). *The New England Journal of Medicine,* 315(11), pp. 705–7.

91   *extended Phillips's study through 1984 . . .*   Milavsky, J. R., Kessler, R. C., Stipp, H. H. Paper presented at a joint meeting of the American Association of Suicidology and the International Association for Suicide Prevention, San Francisco, May 25–30, 1987.

91   *Phillips himself contradicted Gould and Shaffer's findings . . .*   Phillips, D. P., Paight, D. J. "The Impact of Televised Movies About Suicide: A Replicative Study" (1987). *The New England Journal of Medicine,* 317(13), pp. 809–11.

91   *Psychologist Alan Berman also questioned the data . . .*   Paper presented at a joint meeting of the American Association of Suicidology and the International Association for Suicide Prevention, San Francisco, May 25–30, 1987. Berman examined two of the films used in the Gould-Shaffer study, and a third film broadcast after their study had been completed.

92   *who nevertheless opposes censorship*   From time to time newspapers have been persuaded or pressured into suppressing stories about suicide. In the 1930s, for instance, Mussolini prohibited all reports of suicide in the Italian press; his vision of the modern fascist state did not include the possibility of suicide.

92   *The* Los Angeles Times *pointed out . . .*   Parachini, A. "An Alarming Picture of Youthful Suicides." *The Los Angeles Times,* August 19, 1984, part VI, p. 1.

Chapter V

96   *"Most people who commit suicidal acts . . .   "* Stengel, E. *Suicide and Attempted Suicide.* New York: Jason Aronson, 1974, p. 87.

97   *"The man up there is saying, 'Look at me . . .' "*   Quoted in *Time,* November 25, 1966, p. 49.

97   *"a desperate version of holding their breath . . ."*   Giffin and Felsenthal, *A Cry for Help,* p. 14.

97   *A thirteen-year-old Illinois girl . . .*   Ibid., p. 19.

97   *A Michigan youth hospitalized . . .*   Wrobleski, A. (1984). *Afterwords,* October 1984, p. 1. For more on attitudes of hospital staff toward attempters, see Welu, T. C. "Psychological Reactions of Emergency Room Staff to Suicide Attempters" (1972). *Omega,* 3(2), pp. 103–9.

98   *One young girl, after an argument . . .*   Klagsbrun, F. *Too Young to Die: Youth and Suicide.* New York: Pocket Books, 1981, p. 33–34.

98   *A lonely sixteen-year-old Minneapolis boy . . .*   Giffin and Felsenthal, *A Cry for Help,* pp. 30–31.

Chapter VI

114 *In a 1969 article on the prevention . . .* Cited in Ross, C. P. "Teaching Children the Facts of Life and Death: Suicide Prevention in the Schools." In Peck, M. L., Farberow, N. L., Litman, R. E. (eds.) *Youth Suicide.* New York: Springer Publishing Company, 1985, p. 153.

115 *"Our goal is to help youngsters . . ."* Breskin, D. "Dear Mom and Dad." *Rolling Stone,* November 8, 1984, p. 35.

116 *"Children, with a clearer understanding . . ."* Bernhardt, G. R., Praeger, S. G. "Preventing Child Suicide: The Elementary School Death Education Puppet Show." Unpublished paper, p. 6.

117 *"Any school administrator that stands in the way . . ."* Quoted in a letter sent by Donna-Marie Buckley, whose son had hanged himself, to President Reagan, June 1984.

119 *psychiatrist David Shaffer studied the effect of three different programs . . .* Paper presented at the twenty-first annual meeting of the American Association of Suicidology, Washington, D.C., April 13–17, 1988.

PART 2
Chapter I

129 *"Lo, my name reeks . . ."* Breasted, J. H. *Development of Religion and Thought in Ancient Egypt.* New York: Charles Scribner's Sons, 1912, pp. 163–69.

131 *"The Baganda were very superstitious . . ."* Roscoe, J. *The Baganda: An Account of Their Native Customs and Beliefs.* New York: Barnes & Noble, 1966, pp. 20–21.

132 *Primitive fear of the suicide's ghost . . .* Examples of primitive attitudes toward suicide are found in Westermarck, E. *The Origin and Development of the Moral Ideas.* London: Macmillan, 1912, pp. 229–64; Durkheim, E. *Suicide.* Trans. Spaulding, J. A., Simpson, G. New York: The Free Press, 1966, pp. 217–25; Dublin, L. I., Bunzel, B. *To Be or Not to Be.* New York: Harrison Smith and Robert Haas, 1933, pp. 137–53.

133 *For many years India . . .* For examples of revenge suicide in southern India, see Fedden, *Suicide,* pp. 45–46.

134 *"They are a nation lavish of their blood . . ."* Quoted in Durkheim, *Suicide,* p. 218.

134 *"They dwell on the red blaze . . ."* Quoted in Dublin and Bunzel, *To Be or Not to Be,* p. 145.

135   *"The king has a wooden scaffolding made . . ."*   Gaster, T. H. (ed.) *The New Golden Bough: A New Abridgement of the Classic Work by Sir James George Frazer.* New York: New American Library/Mentor, 1964, p. 281.

135   *"There is another world . . ."*   Quoted in Alvarez, *The Savage God,* p. 53.

136   *In Scythia, Herodotus tells us . . .*   Herodotus. *The Histories.* Trans. de Sélincourt, A. Harmondsworth, England: Penguin, 1988, p. 294.

136   *a "keen competition . . ."* Ibid., p. 342.

136   *"Should he outrage native custom . . ."*   Ellis, A. B. *The Tshi-Speaking Peoples of the Gold Coast of West Africa.* The Netherlands: Anthropological Publications, 1970, p. 287.

137   *In 1987 in the village of Deorala . . .*   *The Los Angeles Times,* October 10, 1987, part I, p. 1.

137   *Yet in Japan . . .*   My discussion of suicide in Japan owes much to Iga, M. *The Thorn in the Chrysanthemum: Suicide and Economic Success in Modern Japan.* Berkeley: University of California Press, 1986; Iga, M., Tatai, K. "Characteristics of Suicides and Attitudes Toward Suicide in Japan." In Farberow, N. L. (ed.) *Suicide in Different Cultures.* Baltimore: University Park Press, 1975, pp. 255–80; Seward, J. *Hara-Kiri: Japanese Ritual Suicide.* Rutland, Vermont, and Tokyo: Charles E. Tuttle, 1968.

137   *"The Japanese calendar of saints . . ."*   Griffis, W. E. *The Religions of Japan.* New York: Charles Scribner's Sons, 1895, p. 112.

138   *in a variety of circumstances . . .*   Durkheim noted that "a strange sort of duel is even reported there, in which the effort is not to attack one another but to excel in dexterity in opening one's own stomach." Durkheim, *Suicide,* p. 222.

139   *"The Japanese are an obstinate . . ."*   Quoted in Moore, C. *A Full Inquiry into the Subject of Suicide.* London, 1790, p. 140. In 1932, Henry Morton Robinson observed, "If the Samurai code existed in America today, Tammany Hall would be a catacomb of self-slain heroes." *The North American Review,* 234 (4), p.304.

139   *"the very shrine of the Japanese national . . ."*   Quoted in Kennan, G. "The Death of General Nogi." *Outlook,* October 5, 1912, p. 258.

139   *the almost 250 recorded cases . . .*   See Russell, O. D. "Suicide in Japan." *The American Mercury,* July 1930, pp. 341–44.

140   *"He mingles with the gods on high . . ."*   *Newsweek,* September 24, 1945, p. 58.

140   *jyoshi shinju continued to flourish . . .*   A recent article on Japan in *Time* described a jacket worn by a girl at Tokyo's Disneyland that read: IT IS ARGUED THAT DOUBLE SUICIDE IS THE SUBLIME CULMINATION OF LOVE.

141   *"My daughters and myself are so weak . . ."*   *Time,* March 1, 1976, p. 31.
In *The Thorn in the Chrysanthemum,* a study of suicide in modern Japan,
Mamoru Iga wrote, "The mother who commits suicide without taking her
child with her is blamed as an *oni no yō na hito* (demonlike person)." (Iga,
Thorn, p. 18.) In the United States the opposite is true. In 1985 in Los
Angeles, a thirty-two-year-old Japanese immigrant whose husband had
been unfaithful walked into the Pacific Ocean carrying her infant daughter
and four-year-old son. Although passersby managed to pull her from the
surf, her children drowned. Charged with voluntary manslaughter, the
woman told police that she had killed her children because she loved them
dearly. She was sentenced to eleven years in prison, but after intervention
by local Japanese groups, her sentence was reduced to three years' probation. She eventually returned to her husband.

141   *"the readiness of the Japanese to disembowel themselves . . ."*   Durkheim,
Suicide, p. 222.

141   *the suicide of Yukio Mishima*   My description of Mishima's suicide is
drawn from newspaper accounts and from Iga, M., and Tatai, K., "Characteristics of Suicides and Attitudes Toward Suicide in Japan," in Farberow, *Suicide in Different Cultures.* For further discussion of Mishima's
suicide see Lifton, R. J. *The Broken Connection.* New York: Touchstone/
Simon and Schuster, 1980, pp. 262–80.

142   *"a sadomasochistic homosexual . . ."*   Quoted in *The New York Times,*
November 9, 1974.

143   *psychiatrist Joost Meerloo told the story . . .*   Meerloo, J. A. M. *Suicide
and Mass Suicide.* New York: E. P. Dutton, 1968, pp. 93–94.

Chapter II

144   *"steep down from a high rafter . . ."*   Homer. *The Odyssey.* Trans. Fitz-
gerald, R. Garden City, New York: Anchor/Doubleday, 1963, p. 194.

145   *"thrusting into their throats the arrows . . ."*   Thucydides. *The History of
the Peloponnesian War.* In Hutchins, R. M. (ed.) *Great Books of the
Western World,* Chicago: Encyclopaedia Brittanica, 1952, vol. 6, p. 459.

145   *"went quite mad . . ."*   Herodotus, *The Histories,* p. 414.

145   *"to depart from their guard or station . . ."*   Quoted in Dublin and
Bunzel, *To Be or Not to Be,* p. 184.

146   *"If one of your own possessions . . ."*   Plato. *Dialogues of Plato.* Trans.
Jowett, B. Kaplan, J. D. (ed.) New York: Washington Square Press/
Pocket Books, 1951, p. 74.

146   *"in a spirit of slothful and abject cowardice . . ."*   Plato. *The Laws.* Trans.
Saunders, T. J. Harmondsworth, England: Penguin, 1975, p. 391.

146   *"To kill oneself to escape from poverty . . ."* Aristotle. *Ethics.* Trans. Thompson, J. A. K. Harmondsworth, England: Penguin, 1976 (revised edition), p. 130.

147   *"The many at one moment shun death . . ."* Epicurus. "Letter to Menoeceus." In Oates, W. J. (ed.) *The Stoic and Epicurean Philosophers.* New York: Random House, 1940, p. 31.

147   *"to weigh carefully . . ."* Quoted in Lecky, W. E. H. *History of European Morals from Augustus to Charlemagne* (two volumes). London: Longmans, Green and Co., 1869, vol. I, p. 226.

147   *"If one day, as well may happen . . ."* Quoted in Fedden, *Suicide,* p. 81.

147   *"as he had advanced so far . . ."* Quoted ibid., p. 80.

147   *"Such a discussion is tempered . . ."* Quoted in Moore, *A Full Inquiry,* vol. I, p. 238.

148   *"Nobody need complain . . ."* For the story of Vulteius, see Lucan. *Pharsalia.* Trans. Graves, R. Harmondsworth, England: Penguin, 1957, pp. 98–100.

148   *The noblest Roman suicide of them all . . .* For the story of Cato and his suicide, see Plutarch. *The Lives of the Noble Grecians and Romans.* Trans. Dryden, J. New York: The Modern Library, 1932, pp. 918–60.

149   *"when God himself shall give a just cause . . ."* and *"a noble lesson to mankind . . ."* Quoted in Dublin and Bunzel, *To Be or Not to Be,* pp. 186–87.

149   *"Jupiter himself could not have seen . . ."* Quoted in Choron, J. *Suicide.* New York: Charles Scribner's Sons, 1972, p. 22.

150   *"A resolution this . . ."* Pliny. *Letters* (two volumes). Trans. Melmoth, W. London: William Heinemann, 1915, vol. I, pp. 81–82.

150   *"Foolish man, what do you bemoan . . ."* Quoted in Fedden, *Suicide,* p. 79.

150   *"As I choose the ship . . ."* Ibid., p. 78.

150   *"Where had their philosophy gone . . ."* For the description of Seneca's death, see Tacitus. *The Annals of Imperial Rome.* Trans. Grant, M. London: Penguin, 1989, p. 376.

151   *For sheer exhibitionism . . .* The suicide of Peregrinus is described in Fedden, *Suicide,* pp. 66–67. For a more cynical account see *The Works of Lucian of Samosata* (four volumes). Trans. Fowler, H. W., Fowler, F. G. Oxford: Clarendon Press, 1905, vol. IV, pp. 79–95.

152   *Frazer reported that in Rome . . .* Cited in Fedden, *Suicide,* p. 84.

Chapter III

153 *There are six suicides in the Old Testament...* Quotations from the Bible are from *The Revised Standard Version.* New York: Thomas Nelson & Sons, 1946, 1952.

154 *"In the same manner..."* Quoted in Sprott, S. E. *The English Debate on Suicide from Donne to Hume.* LaSalle, Illinois: Open Court, 1961, p. 147.

154 *"the splendid martyrs of Christ"* Eusebius. *The History of the Church from Christ to Constantine.* Trans. Williamson, G. A. New York: New York University Press, 1966, p. 344.

154 *"No City escaped punishment..."* Quoted in Donne, J. *Biathanatos.* New York: Arno Press, 1977, p. 60.

155 *"rejoicing and exulting..."* Eusebius, *The History of the Church,* p. 202.

155 *"Amachus, give orders that our bodies..."* Quoted in Fedden, *Suicide,* p. 121.

155 *"Let fire and cross..."* Quoted in Eusebius, *The History of the Church,* p. 146.

155 *"When finally guilt is proved..."* Quoted in Fedden, *Suicide,* p. 120.

155 *"Unhappy men, unhappy men..."* Quoted in Strahan, S. A. K. *Suicide and Insanity.* London: Swan Sonnenschein, 1893, p. 18.

155 *the chosen fate of St. Simeon Stylites...* For an extensive and graphic description of martyrdom, see Menninger, K. *Man Against Himself.* New York: Harvest/Harcourt, Brace & World, 1938. Wrote Menninger, "Upon examination, the components of the self-destructive urge in asceticism and martyrdom are apparently identical with those which we found to determine actual suicide—the self-punitive, the aggressive, and the erotic" (p. 125).

155 *"Lo! For these thirty years and more..."* Ibid., p. 119.

156 *"many have destroyed themselves..."* Quoted in Fedden, *Suicide,* p. 125.

156 *"judged it the most prudent..."* Ibid., p. 126.

156 *"He that gelds himselfe..."* Quoted in Donne, *Biathanatos,* p. 133.

156 *"of all dreadful things the most unbearable"* Eusebius, *The History of the Church,* p. 342.

156 *"God cannot be offended with this..."* Quoted in Donne, *Biathanatos,* p. 148.

156 *"The rage of the Donatists..."* Gibbon, E. *The Decline and Fall of the Roman Empire.* New York: The Modern Library, 1932, vol. I, pp. 721–22.

157   *"If it is base to destroy others..."*   Cited in Westermarck, E. *Christianity and Morals.* London: Macmillan, 1939, p. 253.

157   *"monstrous"*   St. Augustine quotations are taken from St. Augustine. *City of God.* Trans. Bettenson, H. Harmondsworth, England: Penguin, 1984, pp. 26–39.

159   *"Let him who hath murdered himself..."*   Quoted in Dublin and Bunzel, *To Be or Not to Be,* p. 245.

159   *"The madman, or the idiot, or the infant..."*   Quoted in Fedden, *Suicide,* p. 138.

159   *"Life is a gift made to man ..."*   Aquinas's arguments against suicide are found in Aquinas, T. *Summa Theologiae.* Blackfriars. New York: McGraw-Hill; London: Eyre & Spottiswoode, 1975, vol. 38, pp. 30–37.

160   *written at the start of the fourteenth century ...*   Dublin and Bunzel pointed out that because of Church prohibitions, civil penalties, and the general stability of institutions and customs in the Middle Ages, individual suicide was practically unheard of during the eight hundred years between Augustine and Aquinas. Yet outside the tight framework of the Church there were sporadic bursts of self-destruction. In the Middle Ages demonic possession was the explanation for most mental disorder, and suicide was considered the ultimate evidence of the devil's work. In the 250 years prior to the end of the seventeenth century, at least 100,000 women were accused of witchcraft, tortured, and burned at the stake. Accused women often sought a less painful and humiliating end by taking their own lives. Ironically, their suicides were usually interpreted as proof of their collusion with the devil.

Chapter IV

161   *"Thou, constrained by no limits..."*   Pico della Mirandola, G. "Oration on the Dignity of Man." In Cassirer, E., Kristeller, P. O., Randall, J. H., Jr. (eds.) *The Renaissance Philosophy of Man.* Chicago: The University of Chicago Press, 1948, p. 225.

161   *"Death is a remedy against all evils ..."*   Unless indicated otherwise, quotes in this paragraph are from Montaigne. *The Essayes of Montaigne.* Trans. Florio, J. New York: The Modern Library, pp. 308–20.

162   *"All the wisdom and reasoning..."*   Cited in Noyes, R. "Montaigne on Death" (1970). *Omega,* 1(4), p. 315.

162   *"lest men far and wide commit suicide..."*   Erasmus, D. *The Colloquies of Erasmus.* Trans. Thompson, C. R. Chicago and London: The University of Chicago Press, 1965, p. 360.

162 *"people who lived next door to wisdom . . ."* Erasmus, D. *The Praise of Folly.* Trans. Hudson, H. H. Princeton: Princeton University Press, 1941, p. 41.

162 *"But yf the dysease be not onelye uncurable . . ."* More, T. *Utopia.* Collins, J. C. (ed.) Oxford: Clarendon Press, 1904, p. 100.

163 *"What if some litle paine the passage have . . ."* Quotations are from Spenser, E. *The Faerie Queene.* Bayley, P. C. (ed.) Oxford: Oxford University Press, 1966, Book I, pp. 195–99.

164 *As M. D. Faber has pointed out . . .* Faber, M. D. "Shakespeare's Suicides: Some Historic, Dramatic and Psychological Reflections." In Shneidman, E. S. (ed.) *Essays in Self-Destruction.* New York: Jason Aronson, 1967, pp. 30–58.

164 *"the disease of head-long dying"* This and the quotations in the following two paragraphs are from Donne, *Biathanatos,* pp. 62, 50, 47, 17–18.

165 *"thirst and inhiation . . ."* and *"because I had the same desires . . ."* Coffin, C. M. (ed.) *The Complete Poetry and Selected Prose of John Donne.* New York: The Modern Library, 1952, pp. 375–76.

165 *"I wonder if* Biathanatos *didn't begin . . ."* Alvarez, *The Savage God,* pp. 155–56.

165 *"because it is upon a misinterpretable subject"* Coffin, C. M., *The Complete Poetry and Selected Prose of John Donne,* p. 387.

166 *"hevy, thoghtful and wrawe . . ."* Chaucer, G. *The Canterbury Tales.* Skeat, W. (ed.) New York: The Modern Library, 1929, p. 581.

166 *"If there be a hell upon earth . . ."* For Burton quotations, see Burton, R. *The Anatomy of Melancholy.* New York: Empire State Book Company, 1924, pp. 281–88.

166 *"There be two sorts of voluntarie deathes . . ."* Quoted in Faber, M. D., "Shakespeare's Suicides," pp. 31–32.

167 *Protestant minister Johannes Neser preached three sermons . . .* A description of Neser's work can be found in Rosen, G. "History," in *A Handbook for the Study of Suicide.* Perlin, S., ed. New York: Oxford University Press, 1975, p. 18.

167 *an English country clergyman named John Sym . . .* Quotations in this paragraph are from Hunter, R., Macalpine, I. *Three Hundred Years of Psychiatry 1535–1860.* London: Oxford University Press, 1963, pp. 113–15, and Fedden, *Suicide,* p. 185.

167 *"as cruelly as possible . . ."* Quoted in Fedden, *Suicide,* p. 142.

168 *"brought through the town . . ."* Quoted in Dublin and Bunzel, *To Be or Not to Be,* p. 207.

168 *"harled through the town backwards . . ."* Cited in Westermarck, *Christianity and Morals,* p. 255.

168 *until he be persuaded . . ."* Quoted in Silving, H., "Suicide and Law." In *Clues to Suicide.* Shneidman, E. S., and Farberow, N. L. (eds.) New York: McGraw-Hill, 1957, p. 83.

168 *"The body is drawn out of the house . . ."* Quoted in Moore, *A Full Inquiry,* vol. I, p. 304.

168 *"that if any person, through temptation or melancholy . . ."* Quoted in Yorke, S. "Is Suicide a Sin?" *The North American Review,* Feb. 1890, p. 277.

169 *"If any person Inhabitant or Stranger . . ."* This quote and the case of Abraham Harris come from Noble, J. "A Glance at Suicide as Dealt with in the Colony and in the Province of the Massachusetts Bay" (1902). *Proceedings of the Massachusetts Historical Society,* 16, pp. 521–32.

169 *"Wheresoever you finde many . . ."* Donne, *Biathanatos,* p. 93.

169 *"is now growne so common . . ."* Quoted in Sprott, *The English Debate on Suicide,* p. 32.

169 *"Cato was not so much the wonder . . ."* and *"What Cato did . . ."* Quoted in Fedden, *Suicide,* pp. 240–41.

170 *of three hundred suicides in three English counties . . .* MacDonald, M. *Mystical Bedlam.* Cambridge: Cambridge University Press, 1981, p. 278.

170 *"These actions, considered . . ."* Quoted in Winslow, *The Anatomy of Suicide,* pp. 319–20.

Chapter V

171 *"To be* happy *or not to be . . ."* Quoted in Gruman, G. J. "An Historical Introduction to Ideas about Voluntary Euthanasia." (1970). *Omega,* 4 (2), p. 99.

171 *"When I am overcome by anguish . . ."* For quotations in this paragraph, see Montesquieu. *Persian Letters.* Trans. Betts, C. J. Harmondsworth, England: Penguin, 1987, Letter 76, pp. 152–54.

172 *"Every man has a right by nature . . ."* For Rousseau's discussion of suicide, see Letters 21 and 22 in *Julie ou La Nouvelle Héloise.* Paris: Garnier-Flammarion, 1967, pp. 278–91.

173 *"his goods are given to the King . . ."* Quoted in Fedden, *Suicide,* p. 224.

173 *"Each one has his reasons . . ."* Quoted in Ibid., p. 204.

173 *"We kill ourselves, too . . ."* Quoted in Ibid., p. 237.

173   *"It is a decision that I shall not take . . ."*   Quoted in Ibid., p. 205.

173   *"If suicide be criminal . . ."*   For Hume quotations, see Hume, D. "On Suicide." In *Essays Moral, Political and Literary.* London: Oxford University Press, 1963, pp. 585–96.

175   *"The carcass should have the Burial of an Ass . . .";* *"sons of perdition . . .";* and *"contribute somewhat to the advancement . . ."*   Quoted in Sprott, *The English Debate,* p. 122.

175   *"It might not only be refused . . ."*   Moore, C. *A Full Inquiry,* p. 339.

175   *"Nor let anyone plead . . ."*   Miller. *The Guilt, Folly, and Sources of Suicide.*

176   *"The text illustrated . . ."*   Herries, J. *An Address to the Public on the Frequent and Enormous Crime of Suicide: Recommended to the Perusal of All Who Are Distressed in Mind, in Body, or in Worldly Circumstances.* London: John Fielding, 1781.

176   *"Many of those who have maintained . . ."*   These and other quotes in this paragraph are found in Hey, R. *Three Dissertations; On the Pernicious Effects of Gaming, on Duelling, and on Suicide.* Cambridge: J. Smith, 1812, pp. 179–180, 208.

176   *"to resist temptations to suicide . . ."*   Quotes in this paragraph are cited in Cutter, F. "On Charles Moore's 'The Subject of Suicide' " (1970). *Omega,* 1(2), pp. 137–40.

177   *"Freedom, then, is not . . ."*   Quoted in Gruman, G. J. "An Historical Introduction to Ideas About Voluntary Euthanasia" (1973). *Omega,* 4(2), p. 97.

177   *"As for the morality of this act . . ."*   Quoted in Fedden, *Suicide,* p. 210.

177   *"The rule of morality does not admit . . ."*   Kant, I. *Lectures on Ethics.* Trans. Infield, L. Gloucester, Mass.: Peter Smith, 1978. p. 152.

177   *"might still serve as a model plea . . ."*   Fedden, *Suicide,* p. 220.

177   *"I have ever since repented . . ."*   De Staël quotations are drawn from de Staël, M. *The Influence of Literature Upon Society.* Hartford: S. Andrus & Son, 1844. pp. 99–112.

179   *"The excuse of not being in his senses . . ."*   Quoted in Moore, *A Full Inquiry,* vol. I, p. 324.

179   *"A penniless poor dog . . ."*   Ibid., pp. 323–24.

179   *partly the result of its reputation . . .*   For material in these two paragraphs, see Bartel, R. "Suicide in Eighteenth-Century England: The Myth of a Reputation." *Huntington Library Quarterly,* February 1960, pp. 145–158.

179 *"We do not find in history..."* Montesquieu. *The Spirit of Laws,* Trans. Nugent, T. New York: The Colonial Press, 1899 (revised edition) vol. I (Book XIV, Chap. 12), p. 231.

179 *In 1805, in a letter to a friend...* Lipscomb, A. A. (ed.) *The Writings of Thomas Jefferson.* Washington, D.C.: Thomas Jefferson Memorial Association, 1904 vol. XI, p. 64. In a letter dated February 8, 1805, Jefferson observed, "I prefer much the climate of the United States to that of Europe. I think it is a more cheerful one. It is our cloudless sky which has eradicated from our constitutions all disposition to hang ourselves, which we might otherwise have inherited from our English ancestors."

180 *"No urgent motive has prompted us..."* Quoted in Moore, *A Full Inquiry,* vol. I, p. 343.

180 *"in order to avoid the trouble..."* Cited in Winslow, *The Anatomy of Suicide,* p. 79.

180 *"With the greatest pleasure..."* Ibid., p. 133.

180 *"There are little domestic news..."* Lewis, W. S. (ed.) *Horace Walpole's Correspondence.* New Haven: Yale University Press, 1941, vol. XXXV, p. 236.

180 *"Life exists for the sake of death..."* Cited in Choron, J. *Death and Western Thought.* New York: Collier/Macmillan, 1973, p. 157.

181 *"By this conviction, I saved myself..."* Winslow, *The Anatomy of Suicide,* p. 86.

182 *"practised it as one of the most elegant of sports..."* Alvarez, *The Savage God,* p. 204. My discussion of the Romantics owes much to Alvarez's chapter "The Romantic Agony," pp. 194–205.

182 *"We swung between madness and suicide..."* Ibid., p. 204.

Chapter VI

183 *"hypertrophy of the poetic organ"* Quoted in Choron, *Death and Western Thought,* p. 159.

184 *"Whatever may be the cause of Anxiety..."* Hunter, R., Macalpine, I. (eds.) *A Treatise on Madness and Remarks on Dr. Battie's Treatise on Madness.* London: Dawsons, 1962, pp. 36–37.

184 *"Few, perhaps, are aware how frequently..."* Winslow, *The Anatomy of Suicide,* pp. 136–37. Of course, it is likely that many young suicides were caused not by masturbation but by guilt over the act.

185 *"Suicide presents all the characteristics..."* and *"The treatment of suicide..."* Quoted in Choron, *Suicide,* p. 63.

185   *"A lady, shortly after her accouchement . . ."*   For this and the following three quotations see Winslow, *The Anatomy of Suicide,* pp. 174–75, 198, 203.

185   *"A pint every hour . . ."*   Quoted in Galt, *The Treatment of Insanity,* p. 212.

185   *"Once in a while this was hard on the patient . . ."*   Quoted in Fuller, M. "Suicide Past and Present: A Note on Jean Pierre Falret" (1973). *Life-Threatening Behavior,* 3(1), p. 62.

186   *Van Helmont advocated holding the patient under . . .*   Cited in Bucknill, J. C., Tuke, D. H. *A Manual of Psychological Medicine.* London: John Churchill, 1858, p. 465. Referring to this treatment, Bucknill and Tuke quote Pinel approvingly: "One must blush at this medical delirium, worse, perhaps, than that of the madman whose reason it was to restore."

186   *"travelling, agreeable society, works of light literature . . ."*   Winslow, *The Anatomy of Suicide,* p. 166.

186   *"I should as soon think of recommending . . ."*   Quoted in Bucknill and Tuke, *A Manual,* p. 473.

186   *"How many females have come to the Salpêtrière . . ."*   Quoted in Galt, *The Treatment of Insanity,* p. 341.

187   *"As no rational being will voluntarily give himself pain . . ."*   Quoted in Winslow, *The Anatomy of Suicide,* p. 222. In the debate over whether suicides were insane, many nineteenth-century writers complained that suicides in their day lacked the heroism and cool rationality of the Ancient Greeks and Romans. One physician asserted that 10 percent of classical suicides were insane and 90 percent were rational, while 10 percent of nineteenth-century suicides were rational and 90 percent were insane.

187   *"I am far from supposing that all suicides . . ."*   Chevalier, T. *Remarks on Suicide.* London, 1824, p. 4.

187   *"The pathological and etiological history . . ."*   Griesinger, W. *Mental Pathology and Therapeutics.* Trans. Robertson, C. L., Rutherford, J. London: The New Sydenham Society, 1867, p. 253.

187   *"Two cases have occurred, one in Saxony . . ."*   Mathews, W. "Civilization and Suicide," *The North American Review,* April, 1891, p. 474.

187   *"We know, as a fact . . ."*   This and the following quotes in this paragraph are found in Strahan, *Suicide and Insanity,* pp. 188, 30, 75, 78.

188   *"All the superstitious fear . . ."*   Fedden, *Suicide,* p. 260.

188   *"Agnis Miller wieff of Jacob Miller . . ."*   Quoted in Shneidman, E. S. *Deaths of Man.* Harmondsworth, England: Penguin, 1974, pp. 115–16.

189   *"I dare ensure any man at this present . . ."*   This quote and information in this paragraph may be found in Graunt, J. *Natural and Political Observations made upon the Bills of Mortality.* Baltimore: The Johns Hopkins University Press, 1939, pp. 31–36.

190   *"The evil frequently appears among the Danes . . ."*   Masaryk, T. G. *Suicide and the Meaning of Civilization.* Trans. Weist, W. B., Batson, R. G. Chicago: University of Chicago Press, 1970, p. 48.

190   *"On this area of about 942,000 square kilomètres . . ."*   Morselli, H. *Suicide: An Essay on Comparative Moral Statistics.* New York: Arno Press, 1975, p. 37.

190   *"extremes of heat and cold lessen the prevalence . . ."*   Quoted in Strahan, *Suicide and Insanity,* p. 154.

190   *"Suicide and madness are not influenced . . ."*   Morselli, *Suicide,* p. 72.

190   *"A very low suicide frequency appears among clergymen . . ."*   Masaryk, *Suicide,* p. 42.

190   *"Certain it is that in the upper classes . . ."*   Morselli, *Suicide,* p. 249.

191   *"Nationality has a noticeable effect . . ."*   Masaryk, *Suicide,* p. 121.

191   *"The frequency of suicide in the various parts of Italy . . ."*   Morselli, *Suicide,* p. 102.

191   *"From whence this fact proceeds . . ."*   Ibid., p. 76.

191   *a German priest calculated the total number . . .*   Cited in Gargas, S. "Suicide in the Netherlands" (1932). *The American Journal of Sociology,* 37(5), p. 698.

191   *"The certainty of the figures . . ."*   Morselli, *Suicide,* p. 16. At that time it was believed that suicide was virtually unknown in "primitive" societies except in cases of "economic" suicide. Then in 1894, Alfred Vierkandt, a German sociologist, reported mass suicides among tribes in New Zealand and in Madagascar, and since then studies have found suicide in primitive societies throughout the world.

193   *"Lack of power, compelling moderation . . ."*   Durkheim, *Suicide,* p. 254.

194   *"suicide varies inversely . . ."*   Ibid., p. 209.

194   *"are very often combined . . ."*   Ibid., p. 287.

194   *"social facts must be studied as things . . ."*   Ibid., pp. 37–38.

194   *"When we learn that the most densely populated parts . . ."*   Friedman, P. *On Suicide,* p. 110.

194   *"Thus the unconscious creates a situation . . ."*   Ibid., p. 119.

194   *"the decisive factor here is erotic . . ."*   Ibid., pp. 71, 76.

195   *"No one kills himself who has never wanted . . ."*   Ibid., p. 87.

195   *"Let us suspend our judgement . . ."*   Ibid., p. 141.

195   *Robert Litman has pointed out . . .*   Much of my discussion of Freud is drawn from Litman, R. E. "Sigmund Freud on Suicide." In Shneidman, *Essays in Self-Destruction,* pp. 324–44.

195   *"I have long since resolved on a decision . . ."*   Quoted in Jones, E. *The Life and Work of Sigmund Freud,* vol. 1. New York: Basic Books, 1953, p. 132.

195   *"In the two opposed situations . . ."*   Freud, S. *Mourning and Melancholia* (1917). *Standard Edition of the Complete Psychological Works,* Strachey, J. (ed.) London: The Hogarth Press, 1953–1965, vol. 14, p. 252.

195   *"A patient over whom I had taken a great deal . . ."*   Freud, S. "The Psychopathology of Everyday Life" (1901). *Works,* vol. 6, p. 3.

195   *"We find that impulses to suicide in a neurotic . . ."*   Freud, S. "Totem and Taboo" (1913), *Works,* vol. 13, p. 154.

196   *"suicide is thus a kind of inverted murder . . ."*   Freud might also have agreed with the English comedy troupe Monty Python, who observed that "a murder is nothing but an extroverted suicide."

196   *"After long hesitancies and vacillations . . ."*   Freud, S. "An Outline of Psycho-Analysis" (1940). *Works,* vol. 23, p. 148.

196   *"We find that the excessively strong super-ego . . ."*   Freud, S. "The Ego and the Id" (1923). *Works,* vol. 19, p. 53.

Chapter VII

197   *In his 1895 address to . . .*   Quotations in this paragraph are from James, W. "Is Life Worth Living?" *Essays on Faith and Morals.* New York: Longmans, Green, 1947, pp. 1–31.

198   *"Have we a right to commit suicide? . . ."*   Zilboorg, G. "Considerations on Suicide, With Particular Reference to That of the Young" (1937). *American Journal of Orthopsychiatry,* 7, p.15.

198   *"The contemporary physician sees suicide . . ."*   Quoted in Szasz, T. *The Theology of Medicine.* Baton Rouge: Louisiana State University Press, 1977, p. 68.

198   *"Perhaps the greatest contribution . . ."*   Hastings, J. (ed.) *Encyclopaedia of Religion and Ethics.* New York: Charles Scribner's Sons, 1922, vol. 12, p. 24.

198   *In England . . .*   For a discussion of twentieth-century English suicide law, see Williams, G. *The Sanctity of Life and the Criminal Law.* New York: Alfred A. Knopf, 1957, pp. 278–83.

199   *"unless there is some outstanding feature . . ."*   Ibid., p. 279.

199   *"It is high time for the pulpit . . ."*   Quoted in *The Literary Digest,* July 16, 1932, p. 20.

199   *"At bottom, all the reasons . . ."*   Quoted in Choron, *Suicide,* p. 32.

200   *"Intentionally causing one's own death, or suicide . . ."*   Quoted in Larue, G. A. *Euthanasia and Religion.* Los Angeles: The Hemlock Society, 1985, p. 37.

200   *"There is but one truly serious philosophical problem . . ."*   Camus, A. *The Myth of Sisyphus and Other Essays.* Trans. O'Brien, J. New York: Vintage Books, 1955, p. 3.

200   *Andrew Henry and James Short examined fluctuations . . .*   Henry, A. F., Short, J. F., Jr. *Suicide and Homicide.* New York: The Free Press, 1964.

200   *Sociologists Jack Gibbs and Walter Martin refined . . .*   Gibbs, J. P., Martin, W. T. *Status Integration and Suicide: A Sociological Study.* Eugene: University of Oregon Press, 1964.

200   *Jack Douglas, in* The Social Meanings of Suicide . . .   Douglas, J. D. *The Social Meanings of Suicide.* Princeton: Princeton University Press, 1973.

201   *"A wealthy man is one day announced . . ."*   Menninger, *Man Against Himself,* p. 19.

201   *"To say that the death instinct gains the upper hand . . ."*   Zilboorg, G. "Considerations on Suicide," p. 17.

202   *Maurice Farber concocted a mathematical formula . . .*   Farber, M. L. *Theory of Suicide.* New York: Funk & Wagnalls, 1968, p. 75.

202   *a 1985 study of the Amish . . .*   Egeland, J. A., Sussex, J. N. "Suicide and Family Loading for Affective Disorders." *Journal of the American Medical Association.* (1985), 254 (7), pp. 915–18.

203   *One of the leading researchers . . .*   Much of the description of Asberg's work is drawn from Pines, M. "Suicide Signals" (1983). *Science 83,* October 1983, pp. 55–58.

204   *researchers at Wayne State University and at NIMH . . .*   These studies are summarized in *Science News,* May 29, 1982, p. 355.

204   *"Reducing suicide to a biological basis . . ."*   Quoted in *The New York Times,* October 8, 1985, p. C8.

PART 3
Chapter I

209   *"Whenever Richard Cory . . . "*   Robinson, E. A. "Richard Cory." In Matthiessen, F. O. (ed.) *The Oxford Book of American Verse.* New York: Oxford University Press, 1950, pp. 469–70.

Chapter II

222   *"No one ever lacks a good reason . . ."*   Pavese, C. *The Burning Brand: Diaries, 1935–1950.* Trans. Murch, A. E. New York: Walker, 1961, p. 99.

223   *the reported rarity of suicides and suicide attempts . . .*   Several death-camp survivors have pointed out that there were ways of killing oneself other than active suicide; one only had to draw near the barbed-wire fences to be shot by guards, or to relax one's struggle for survival to succumb. "We all had to fight constantly against the wish to go passively into death," a survivor told psychiatrist Joost Meerloo. "There is always a moment when a man surrenders, with his soul, with his will, and with his dreams. If that happened in the camps he was lost. Suicide was not even needed." (Meerloo, *Suicide and Mass Suicide,* p. 130.)

223   *"The day was dense . . ."*   Levi, P. *The Drowned and the Saved.* New York: Summit, 1988, p. 76.

223   *"It is impossible to think that I shall never . . ."*   Quoted in Enright, D. J. (ed.) *The Oxford Book of Death.* Oxford: Oxford University Press, 1983, p. 106.

224   *"There is no refuge from confession . . ."*   Quoted in Bartlett, J. *Familiar Quotations.* Boston: Little, Brown, 1980, p. 450.

224   *Manes pulled a knife from his kitchen drawer . . .*   Suicide was not an unfamiliar option for Manes; his father, despondent after his wife's death, killed himself, reportedly by stabbing, when Manes was a young man. Three years after Donald Manes's death, his twin brother, who had been in treatment for depression, attempted suicide, also by stabbing himself in the chest.

224   *he shot himself in the head . . .*   Kammerer's story is told in Koestler, A. *The Case of the Midwife Toad.* New York: Random House, 1972.

224   *"I have only myself to live with . . ."*   Quoted in *Time,* November 17, 1980, p. 94.

225   *"Dearest, I feel certain that I am going mad again . . ."*   Quoted in Woolf, L. *The Journey Not the Arrival Matters: An Autobiography of the Years 1939 to 1969.* New York: Harcourt Brace Jovanovich, 1969, pp. 93–94.

225 *"Paradoxical and tragic suicidal efforts . . ."* Kubie, L. S. "Multiple Determinants of Suicide." In Shneidman, *Essays in Self-Destruction,* p. 458.

226 *"To whom concerned . . ."* Friedman, P. "Suicide Among Police: A Study of Ninety-three Suicides Among New York City Policemen, 1934–1940." In Shneidman, *Essays in Self-Destruction,* p. 438.

226 *one study in Philadelphia . . .* Cited in Hendin, H. *Suicide in America.* New York: W. W. Norton, 1982, p. 96.

226 *A 1969 literature review . . .* Ibid., pp. 100–101.

226 *"Good creatures, do you love your lives . . ."* Housman, A. E. *Complete Poems.* New York: Henry Holt, 1959, p. 185.

226 *"If I commit suicide, it will not be to destroy myself . . ."* Quoted in Alvarez, *The Savage God,* p. 125.

227 *"Suicide always seeks to achieve something . . ."* Lifton's discussion of suicide is found in Lifton, *The Broken Connection,* pp. 239–61.

227 *The impulse to death . . ."* and *"for some, organic death . . ."* Hillman, J. *Suicide and the Soul.* Dallas: Spring Publications, 1985, pp. 63, 83.

227 *"The suicidal attempt . . ."* Kubie, L. S. "Multiple Determinants of Suicide." In Shneidman, *Essays in Self-Destruction,* p. 455.

228 *"Is it conceivable to murder someone . . ."* Quotations in this paragraph are found in Pavese, *The Burning Brand,* pp. 89, 48, 365, 366.

229 *"as if I were being stuffed . . ."* Quotations in this paragraph are taken from Plath, S. *The Bell Jar.* New York: Bantam, 1972, pp. 105, 152, 193.

229 *"an experience of harassment . . ."* Ringel, E. "The Presuicidal Syndrome" (1976). *Suicide and Life-Threatening Behavior,* 6(3), p. 131.

229 *"Everything was like a terrible sort of whirlpool . . ."* Shneidman, E. *Voices of Death.* New York: Harper & Row, 1980, pp. 15–16.

230 *"The logic of suicide is different . . ."* Alvarez, *The Savage God,* p. 116.

230 *"some standard domestic squabble"* The description of Alvarez's attempt and the quotes in this paragraph are from *The Savage God,* pp. 257–72.

Chapter III

233 *"Take a look at them . . ."* Cain, J. M. *Double Indemnity.* New York: Vintage Books, 1978, p. 67.

234   *"What a low-minded wretch . . ."*   Quoted in Moore, *A Full Inquiry,* vol. I, p. 357.

234   *"Hanging is a type of death . . ."*   Quoted in Fedden, *Suicide,* p. 231.

234   *"Not only have they made suicide more or less painless . . ."*   Alvarez, *The Savage God,* pp. 131–32.

234   *"Since many Norwegians live and work on the water . . ."*   Hendin, *Suicide in America,* p. 144.

235   *"Sexual experience, fighting, and drug usage . . ."*   Ibid., p. 145.

235   *a rash of ninety-three suicides by New York City policemen . . .*   Friedman, P. "Suicide Among Police." In Shneidman, *Essays in Self-Destruction,* pp. 414–49.

235   *people have committed suicide by . . .*   About half of this list is taken from a list compiled by George Kennan in an article for *McClure's* and quoted in Menninger, *Man Against Himself* (p. 55). The other, more recent examples are drawn from a variety of books and news clippings.

236   *On closer inspection . . .*   The nineteenth-century Parisienne who applied one hundred leeches to her body may well have been attempting to cure rather than kill herself, in an era when leeches were a common remedy for suicidal depression.

236   *"That the various means of suicide can represent . . ."*   Freud, S. "The Psychogenesis of a Case of Homosexuality in a Woman" (1920). *Works,* vol. 18, p. 162.

236   *"The choice of the manner of dying . . ."*   Quoted in Ellis, E. R., Allen, G. N. *Traitor Within: Our Suicide Problem.* Garden City, New York: Doubleday, 1961, pp. 125–26.

237   *"jumping out of the window may quite paradoxically . . ."*   Meerloo, *Suicide and Mass Suicide,* p. 74.

237   *psychiatrists Sidney Furst and Mortimer Ostow suggested . . .*   Cited in Hendin, *Suicide in America,* pp. 147–48.

237   *"Some suicides use their control . . ."*   Ibid., p. 149.

237   *"the multiplicity of methods helped this man . . ."*   Ibid., p. 149.

238   *"Suicides have a special language . . ."*   Sexton, A. *The Complete Poems.* Boston: Houghton Mifflin, 1981, pp. 142–43.

238   *go to great lengths . . .*   And they will go to great lengths to insist on suicide. Wrote Pavese: "There is nothing ridiculous or absurd about a man who is thinking of killing himself being afraid of falling under a car or catching a fatal disease. Quite apart from the question of the degree of suffering involved, the fact remains that to want to kill oneself is to want one's death to be significant, a *supreme* choice, a deed that cannot be

misunderstood. So it is natural that no would-be suicide can endure the thought of anything so meaningless as being run over or dying of pneumonia. So beware of draughts and street corners." (Pavese, *The Burning Brand,* p. 87.) Pity, then, poor Heliogabalus, a Roman emperor renowned for his eccentricity. Told by Syrian priests that he'd take his own life, he obtained a golden sword, a rope of imperial purple and gold, and a priceless ring filled with poison. And in case he decided on jumping, he ordered a pavement of jewels to be laid beneath one of his towers to receive his body. Unfortunately, before he had a chance to take advantage of his elaborate preparations, he was murdered by his guards.

238   *"A man who has attempted to drown himself . . ."*   Winslow, *The Anatomy of Suicide,* p. 210.

238   *A study of six people who survived leaps . . .*   Cited in Rosen, D. H. "Suicide Survivors: Psychotherapeutic Implications of Egocide" (1976). *Suicide and Life-Threatening Behavior,* 6(4), pp. 209–15.

239   *In one early project . . .*   For a brief summary of research on suicide notes, see Frederick, C. J. "Suicide Notes: A Survey and Evaluation" (1969). *Bulletin of Suicidology,* March 1969, pp. 17–26.

239   *In a study by psychologist Calvin Frederick . . .*   Frederick, C. J. "An Investigation of Handwriting of Suicide Persons Through Suicide Notes" (1968). *Journal of Abnormal Psychology,* 73(3), pp. 263–67.

240   *"Whether the writers of suicide notes differ . . ."*   Stengel, *Suicide and Attempted Suicide,* p. 44.

240   *Many note writers ask for absolution . . .*   Collections of suicide notes can be found in Shneidman, *Voices of Death,* pp. 41–76; Shneidman, Farberow. *Clues to Suicide,* pp. 197–215; Ellis and Allen, *Traitor Within,* pp. 170–85; Wolf, H. "Suicide Notes," *The American Mercury,* November 1931, pp. 264–72.

Chapter IV

245   *A six-year study recently undertaken . . .*   Paper presented at a joint meeting of the American Association of Suicidology and the International Association for Suicide Prevention, San Francisco, May 25–30, 1987.

245   *two years studying suicide in Scandinavia . . .*   Material in this and the following two paragraphs is from Hendin, H. *Suicide and Scandinavia.* Garden City, New York: Doubleday/Anchor, 1965.

247   *sociologist M. Harvey Brenner of Johns Hopkins University estimated . . .*   Cited in *The New York Times,* April 6, 1982, p. C1.

248   *"the struggle for existence is carried on . . ."*   "Suicide in Cities" (1905). *The American Journal of Sociology,* 10(4), p. 562.

248   *A study of Minneapolis suicides . . .*   Schmid, C. F. "Suicide in Minneapolis, Minnesota: 1928–32" (1933). *The American Journal of Sociology,* 39(1), pp. 30–48.

248   *In his 1955 district-by-district survey . . .*   Sainsbury, P. *Suicide in London: An Ecological Study.* London: Chapman and Hall, 1955.

249   *"It draws workaholics . . ."*   Quoted in *Time,* February 16, 1981.

249   *"A suicidal depression is a kind of spiritual winter . . ."*   Alvarez, *The Savage God,* p. 79.

250   *"You can't kill yourself by jumping . . ."*   Quoted in Seiden, R. H. "We're Driving Young Blacks to Suicide" (1970). *Psychology Today,* August 1970, p. 24.

250   *"Many of these young subjects . . ."* and *"It does not seem surprising . . ."* Hendin, H. *Black Suicide.* New York: Basic Books, 1969, pp. 139, 145.

251   *"To be a Negro in this country . . ."*   Quoted in Seiden, "We're Driving Young Blacks to Suicide," *Psychology Today,* August 1970, p. 28.

251   *"Young urban black men are subjected . . ."*   Ibid., p. 26.

251   *"They believe they have nothing to lose . . ."*   Quoted in *Time,* September 16, 1985, p. 33.

252   *"You ache with the need . . ."*   Ibid., p. 33.

252   *"The problem with such speculations . . ."*   Poussaint, A. F. "Black Suicide." Paper presented at "The Enigma of Suicide," a conference sponsored by the Samaritans in Boston, March 24, 1984, pp. 11–12.

252   *"There is a type of suicide the opposite . . ."*   Durkheim, *Suicide,* p. 276.

253   *"The Negro is subject to the imperatives . . ."*   Quoted in Seiden, R. H. "Current Developments in Minority Group Suicidology" (1974). *JBHP,* 1(4), p. 31.

253   *"As racial discrimination decreases . . ."*   Seiden, R. H. "Why Are Suicides of Young Blacks Increasing?" (1972). *HSMHA Health Reports,* 87(1), p. 5.

253   *"Perhaps these unifying social ties . . ."*   Ibid., p. 5.

253   *"The current increase in Black suicide . . ."*   Quoted in Seiden, R. H., "Mellowing with Age: Factors Influencing the Nonwhite Suicide Rate" (1981). *International Journal of Aging and Human Development,* 13 (4), p. 280.

253 *"A 1976 study by Alton Kirk . . ."* Kirk, A. R. "Socio-Psychological Factors in Attempted Suicide Among Urban Black Males" (1976). Unpublished Ph.D. dissertation, Michigan State University.

253 *"try to become more assimilated . . ."* Kirk, A. R. "Psycho-Social Modes of Adaptation and Suicide Among Blacks." Unpublished paper, Michigan State University, p. 10.

254 *"Their expectations of life . . ."* Poussaint, "Black Suicide," p. 12.

254 *"Blacks view suicide among blacks . . ."* Kirk, "Psycho-Social Modes," p. 11.

255 *One of the few large-scale studies . . .* Smith, J. C., Mercy, J. A., Warren, C. W. "Comparison of Suicides Among Anglos and Hispanics in Five Southwestern States" (1985). *Suicide and Life-Threatening Behavior,* 15(1), pp. 14–26.

256 *"After they were confined to the reservation . . ."* Dizmang, L. H. "Suicide Among the Cheyenne Indians" (1967). *Bulletin of Suicidology,* July 1967, p. 9.

256 *have found new ways to vent aggression . . .* The Native American death rate from cirrhosis of the liver is far higher than for any other race, especially among the young. The homicide rate is 7 percent higher than for the general population. The rate of violent accidents is surpassingly high.

257 *"Prior to the development of the gay movement . . ."* Rofes, E. E. *"I Thought People Like That Killed Themselves:" Lesbians, Gay Men and Suicide.* San Francisco: Grey Fox Press, 1983, p. 25. My discussion of gay and lesbian suicide owes much to this pioneering work.

257 *"The homosexual act in itself . . ."* Meerloo, *Suicide and Mass Suicide,* p. 72. Among the eminent psychiatrists who believed homosexuality to be inherently suicidal were Karl Menninger and Gregory Zilboorg. Zilboorg, in fact, suggested that male suicide was invariably connected to homosexuality. Pointing out that far more men than women kill themselves, Zilboorg suggested that "man's suicide has more to do with the inner struggles created by passivity and feminine strivings, i.e. by homosexuality. This would perhaps explain why more men shoot themselves than women, shooting having obviously something to do (symbolically) with passive homosexual wishes." (Zilboorg, G. "Considerations on Suicide, With Particular Reference to That of the Young" [1937]. *American Journal of Orthopsychiatry,* 7, p. 25.)

257 *"Homosexuality used to be a sensational gimmick . . ."* Cited in Rofes, *Lesbians, Gay Men and Suicide,* p. 11.

258 *"Have lesbians and gay men internalized the myth . . ."* Ibid., p. 14.

258   *"There is no doubt that suicide . . ."* Ibid., p. 21.

258   *"Less than two months ago I was told . . ."* Cited in Nelson, J. "Documentation Regarding Some Relationships Between Adolescent Suicide and Homosexuality." Unpublished paper, March 1987.

259   *two to three times more likely . . .* Cited in Gibson, P. "Gay Male and Lesbian Youth Suicide." Paper presented at a joint meeting of the American Association of Suicidology and the International Association for Suicide Prevention, San Francisco, May 25–30, 1987.

259   *a 1987 study by the Los Angeles Suicide Prevention Center . . .* Schneider, S., Farberow, N. L., Kruks, G. N. "Suicidal Behavior in Adolescent and Young Adult Gay Men." Paper presented at a joint meeting of the American Association of Suicidology and the International Association for Suicide Prevention, San Francisco, May 25–30, 1987.

260   *a study of AIDS patients in New York City . . .* Cited in *The New York Times,* March 4, 1988.

260   *"Gay men facing AIDS . . ."* Shilts, R. "Talking AIDS to Death." In Kaplan, J. (ed.) *The Best American Essays, 1990.* New York: Ticknor & Fields, 1990, p. 243.

260   *not only for those actually diagnosed with AIDS . . .* Some therapists have written about persons who engage in dangerous sexual practices in hopes of contracting AIDS and therefore killing themselves, and others who continue to engage in unsafe sex despite knowing the risks. In a study by the San Francisco AIDS Foundation, 3 percent of respondents admitted they knowingly engaged in unsafe sex practices.

Chapter V

262   *In his survey of the etymology . . .* Daube, D. "The Linguistics of Suicide" (1977). *Suicide and Life-Threatening Behavior,* 7(3), pp. 132–82. For much of the material in these three paragraphs I am indebted to this fascinating paper.

263   *A. Alvarez cites an earlier usage . . .* Alvarez, *The Savage God,* p. 48.

263   *"One barbarous word I shall produce . . ."* Quoted in Fedden, *Suicide,* p. 29.

264   *"eating to gluttony . . ."* Ibid., p. 184.

264   *"the daredevil who intentionally toys . . ."* Durkheim, *Suicide,* pp. 45–46.

264   *"I have now learnt . . ."* and *"When a member of my family . . ."* Freud, S. "The Psychopathology of Everyday Life" (1901). *Works,* vol. 6, pp. 178–82.

265   *"in the end each man kills himself . . ."*   Menninger, *Man Against Himself,* p. vii.

265   *Henri Barbusse once remarked that two armies at war . . .*   Cited in Meerloo, *Suicide and Mass Suicide,* p. 92.

265   *"The development of symptoms . . ."*   Menninger, K. "Expression and Punishment." In Shneidman, E. S. (ed.) *On the Nature of Suicide.* San Francisco: Jossey-Bass, 1973, p. 71.

266   *self-mutilation . . .*   In *Man Against Himself,* Menninger offers an extensive analysis of self-mutilation. For a brief but comprehensive summary of the syndrome, see Simpson, M. A. "Self-Mutilation and Suicide." In Shneidman, E. S. (ed.) *Suicidology: Contemporary Developments.* New York: Grune and Stratton, 1976, pp. 281–315.

267   *In a 1972 study of 147 suicidal male alcoholics . . .*   Cited in Hendin, *Suicide in America,* p. 127.

267   *"I didn't think I was worth anything . . ."*   Quoted in Giffin and Felsenthal, *A Cry for Help,* p. 53.

268   *Psychiatrist Melvin Selzer has demonstrated . . .*   Selzer, M. L., Payne, C. E. "Automobile Accidents, Suicide and Unconscious Motivation" (1962). *American Journal of Psychiatry,* 119, pp. 237–40.

268   *In a subsequent study . . .*   Cited in *The New York Times,* April 1, 1968, p. 35.

269   *"They use risk-taking behavior as a form of self-treatment . . ."*   The quote and a description of the study are taken from *The Washington Post,* June 9, 1987, Health Section, p. 5.

269   *"I would describe myself as having a life wish . . ."*   Quoted in Begley, M. "Risky Business" (1986). *Backpacker,* May 1986, p. 38. Yukio Mishima compared athletes who sought such extreme experience to kamikaze pilots. But most rock climbers, sky divers, and so on, are not, of course, suicidal. "Generally speaking, all dangerous activities (for example, auto racing, mountain climbing, acrobatics, etc.) *could* reflect suicidal tendencies," writes Jean Baechler. "There is no question of considering all race-car drivers as suicidal but simply of having available a form of suicidal behavior that is revealed in taking risks." (Baechler, J. *Suicides.* Trans. Cooper, B. New York: Basic Books, 1979, p. 19.) Some, however, may be attracted to such risky endeavors partially because of their self-destructive possibilities. The British climber Menlove Edwards was famous for his risky expeditions and bold routes. The feats that in public won him medals had a pathetic parallel in his private life. A homosexual who never found lasting love, he was tormented by depression. When depressed, he liked to row far out into the open sea in a battered boat, then ride huge waves to shore, scrambling to safety as they crashed on the rocks. At age thirty-four he suffered a breakdown and made three suicide attempts. He lived

the last fourteen years of his life as a recluse, cared for by his sister, although he continued to climb. In 1958 he committed suicide by swallowing potassium cyanide.

269   *"Life is impoverished, it loses in interest . . ."*   Quoted in Alvarez, *The Savage God,* p. 253.

269   *"Many soldiers have the fantasy . . ."*   Meerloo, *Suicide and Mass Suicide,* p. 75.

270   *In his 1950s study of murder . . .*   Wolfgang, M. E. "Suicide by Means of Victim-Precipitated Homicide." In Resnik, H. L. P. (ed.) *Suicidal Behaviors.* Boston: Little, Brown, 1968, pp. 90–104.

270   *A twenty-two-year-old babysitter who murdered . . .*   Quite the opposite of people who use murder as a means of suicide are those political prisoners who are murdered and called "suicides." During the 1930s when the National Socialists imprisoned and killed many of their opponents and insisted they were suicides, the French revived the caustic phrase *être suicidé*—to be suicided. More recently, this has occurred often among anti-apartheid prisoners in South Africa who are said to have killed themselves while in detention.

270   *creativity*   On the other hand, there are artists who make art of self-destruction, an aesthetic of asceticism. Like a contemporary St. Simeon Stylites, one New York performance artist spent five days and nights in a two-by-three-foot locker without food. Another sat on a shelf in an art gallery for twenty-two days. Then there was the man who lived in a cage for a year.

271   *"Most people are no longer alive . . ."*   Meerloo, *Suicide and Mass Suicide,* p. 19.

271   *"backing into the grave . . ."*   Quoted in Pretzel, P. W. "Philosophical and Ethical Considerations of Suicide Prevention" (1968). *Bulletin of Suicidology,* July 1968, p. 32.

271   *examples of self-destruction almost everywhere . . .*   Steincrohn, P. J. *How to Stop Killing Yourself.* New York: Ace Books, 1950.

271   *"One must be careful . . ."*   Baechler, *Suicides,* p. 18.

271   *"There is a little murder and a little suicide . . ."*   Quoted in Menninger, K. *Sparks.* Freeman, L. (ed.) New York: Thomas Y. Crowell Company, 1973, p. 142.

272   *"A thousand people . . ."*   Carroll, J. *The Winter Name of God.* Kansas City: Sheed and Ward, 1975, pp. 87–88.

PART 4
Chapter II

285   *"to the drowned, those suspended by the cord . . ."*   For material and quotations about the Royal Humane Society, see Gregory, G. *A Sermon on Suicide.* London: J. Nichols, 1797.

The Royal Humane Society made suicide prevention something of a spectator sport. Describing a despondent young woman who hanged herself but was restored to life after four hours, Society records noted: "Above one hundred spectators had the satisfaction of seeing this young woman restored to her friends, and to the most perfect composure of mind." In 1797, a year in which, according to society records, eleven would-be suicides were saved and "all of them were reconciled to life," the RHS held an anniversary celebration. The evening's highlight was "the Procession of the Persons restored to Life by the efforts of the Humane Society, and its Medical Assistants." Odes "To Sympathy" and "To Science" were recited, which seems appropriate considering that the society's good works were inspired as much by the spirit of scientific inquiry as by sympathy for the suicidal.

286   *In the nineteenth century . . .*   There were few organized prevention efforts in the nineteenth century. Like the Royal Humane Society, the Lemberg Volunteer Rescue Society (with a branch office in Budapest) was an emergency paramedical service whose cases included suicides and suicide attempts. According to a 1906 German newspaper article, the society had attended to 720 suicides and suicide attempts since its founding in 1893. Fedden reports that toward the end of the century an association was formed in Foochow, China, to keep four boats patrolling the Foochow bridge to save would-be suicides from drowning.

289   *founded by psychiatrist Erwin Ringel . . .*   Ringel frequently expressed his belief in the efficacy of such agencies by maintaining that "if Romeo had had a crisis intervention clinic handy, neither he nor Juliet would have died." (*The Washington Post,* January 21, 1973, p. C5.)

290   *"Prior to the 1950s . . ."*   Frederick, C. J. "Current Trends in Suicidal Behavior in the United States" (1978). *American Journal of Psychotherapy,* 32, p. 172.

295   *"Both of those have given way . . ."*   From *Psychiatric Clinics in Transition.* Tulipan, A. B., Feldman, S. (eds.) New York: Brunner-Mazel, 1969, p. 128.

299   *"The goal of the NIMH Center . . ."*   Shneidman, E. S. "The NIMH Center for Studies of Suicide Prevention." *Bulletin of Suicidology,* July 1967, p. 2.

299   *Suicidology—a word coined by Shneidman . . .*   Shneidman subsequently learned that the word "suicidologie" had been used in 1929 by Dutch professor W. A. Bonger.

300   *"massive public education"*   Shneidman, E. S. "A Comprehensive NIMH Suicide Prevention Program" (1966) (a 36-page memorandum to Stanley Yolles, then-director of NIMH), p. 14.

300   *"The 'early signs' of suicide . . ."*   Ibid., p. 2.

300   *"Just as there are fire stations . . ."*   Ibid., p. 7.

300   *"How to Set Up a Suicide Prevention Center"*   Allen, N. "How to Set Up a Suicide Prevention Center." *California's Health,* January 1970.

300   *While the LASPC served as the prototype . . .*   Much of the information on prevention centers in these paragraphs is drawn from Fisher, S. A. *Suicide Prevention and/or Crisis Services: A National Survey.* Canton, Ohio: Case Western Reserve University, 1972.

301   *Shneidman even pointed out . . .*   Shneidman, "A Comprehensive NIMH Suicide Prevention Program," p. 29.

301   *"One of the problems in the study . . ."*   Lester, D. "Spiritualism and Suicide" (1981). *Omega,* 12(1), pp. 45–49.

302   *A 1972 summary of research findings . . .*   Lester, D. *Why People Kill Themselves.* Springfield, Illinois: Charles C. Thomas, 1972.

302   *In one study psychologist Richard McGee . . .*   McGee, R. K., Richard, W. C., Bercun, C. "A Survey of Telephone Answering Services in Suicide Prevention and Crisis Intervention Agencies" (1972). *Life-Threatening Behavior,* 2(1), pp. 42–47.

302   *A 1970 CSSP-sponsored task force . . .*   Resnik, H. L. P., Hathorne, B. C. (eds.) *Suicide Prevention in the 70's.* Washington, D.C.: U.S. Government Printing Office, 1973, p. 3.

302   *When a 1968 study . . .*   Bagley, C. "The Evaluation of a Suicide Prevention Scheme by an Ecological Method" (1968). *Social Science and Medicine,* 2, pp. 1–14; Fox, R. "The Recent Decline of Suicide in Britain: The Role of the Samaritan Suicide Prevention Movement." In Shneidman, *Suicidology: Contemporary Developments,* pp. 499–524.

302   *But a subsequent, more carefully controlled study . . .*   Jennings, C., Barraclough, B. M., Moss, J. R. "Have the Samaritans Lowered the Suicide Rate? A Controlled Study" (1978). *Psychological Medicine,* 8, pp. 413–22.

302   *psychologist David Lester compared eight cities . . .*   Lester, D. "Effect of Suicide Prevention Centers on Suicide Rates in the United States" (1974). *Health Services Reports,* 89, pp. 37–39.

303   *the institute's top priority . . .*   At the same time, the federal government was at the height of its commitment to community mental health centers. Emphasis shifted from research to direct services. The government's goal was to reach more people for less money. With the move toward crisis intervention, direct services, and youth problems, suicide research received decreasing support, and the suicide prevention center *per se* was swallowed up in the extraordinary growth of hot lines of all varieties. By 1974 there were almost seven hundred hot lines in the United States; St. Louis alone was alleged to have ninety-three. There were hot line newsletters and hot line conventions. National magazines and TV melodramas offered histrionic accounts of tearful calls and heroic rescues. "At this very moment, thousands of hotlines are ringing" began a book describing the hot line phenomenon. "People are calling for help about problems that deal with pregnancy, illegal drugs, boy-girl problems, family hassles, alcohol abuse, suicide, loneliness, child abuse, runaways, rape, and more." The book, which included instructions on how to start a hot line, described the LASPC as "the grandfather of all hotlines." Its progeny now included Rap Shop, Some Body Loves You Baby, Awakening Peace, Fort Help, Mother, Need, the Way Out, Listening Post, Pulse, Inc., Oz, Yell Inc., Sunshine Line, and Tele-Mom (Hyde, M. O. *Hotline!* New York: McGraw-Hill, 1976.). In a 1972 issue of Romaine Edwards's *Hotline Newsletter,* the author, who claimed to have founded fifteen hot lines, captured the hot line fever: "The word got around quickly: You didn't need a battalion of degreed headshrinkers to start helping local folk with their big and little problems. . . . All you needed were a couple of phone numbers, a few friends, and a little publicity, and presto!"

303   *In a 1970 study of ten centers . . .*   Cited in Hendin, *Suicide in America,* p. 183.

303   *More than half of the four thousand calls . . .*   Cited in Lester, G., Lester, D. *Suicide: The Gamble with Death.* Englewood Cliffs, N.J.: Prentice-Hall, 1971, p. 162.

304   *a study by San Francisco psychiatrist Jerome Motto . . .*   Motto, J. A. "Evaluation of a Suicide Prevention Center by Sampling the Population at Risk" (1971). *Suicide and Life-Threatening Behavior,* 2(1), pp. 18–22.

304   *an eighteen-month follow-up program . . .*   Litman, R. E., Wold, C. I. "Beyond Crisis Intervention." In Shneidman, *Suicidology: Contemporary Developments,* pp. 525–46.

305   *A 1984 University of Alabama study . . .*   Miller, H. L., et al. "An Analysis of the Effects of Suicide Prevention Facilities on Suicide Rates in the United States" (1984). *American Journal of Public Health,* 74 (4), pp. 340–43.

Chapter III

308 *"People say, 'Well, how can these things happen . . .'"* Quoted in Giffin and Felsenthal, *A Cry for Help*, p. 41.

309 *Jerome Motto, in a follow-up study . . .* Motto, J. A., Heilbron, D. C., Juster, R. P. "Suicide Risk Assessment: Development of a Clinical Instrument." Paper presented at the World Psychiatric Association Seventh World Congress of Psychiatry, Vienna, Austria, July 10–16, 1983.

309 *A ten-year test of the Beck Depression Inventory . . .* Goleman, D. "Test Is Called Successful in Predicting Suicide." *The New York Times,* February 10, 1985, p. 35.

309 *Their "Reasons for Living Scale" . . .* Linehan, M. M., Goodstein, J. L., Nielsen, S. L. Paper presented at the Fourteenth Annual Meeting of the American Association of Suicidology, Albuquerque, N. M., 1981.

309 *In "Patient Monitoring of Suicidal Risk," . . .* Drye, R. C., Goulding, R. L., Goulding, M. E. "No-Suicide Decisions: Patient Monitoring of Suicidal Risk" (1973). *American Journal of Psychiatry,* 130(2), pp. 171–74.

310 *"Risk-Rescue Rating" . . .* Weisman, A. D., Worden, J. W. "Risk-Rescue Rating in Suicide Assessment" (1972). *Archives of General Psychiatry,* 26, pp. 553–60.

310 *devised the "SAD PERSONS" scale . . .* Patterson, W. M., et al. "Evaluation of Suicidal Patients: The SAD PERSONS Scale" (1983). *Psychosomatics,* 24(4), pp. 343–49.

310 *after his scale for suicide risk proved unsuccessful . . .* Pokorny, A. D. "Prediction of Suicide in Psychiatric Patients" (1983). *Archives of General Psychiatry,* 40, pp. 249–57.

311 *a computer proved more accurate . . .* Greist, J. H., et al. "A Computer Interview for Suicide-Risk Prediction" (1973). *American Journal of Psychiatry,* 130(12), pp. 1327–32.

311 *getting the person to that help may be difficult . . .* NIMH estimates that less than a third of those with depressive illness seek treatment, and of those who do, less than half see mental health professionals. And only about 12 percent of those who attempt suicide come to medical attention.

312 *"I did several things . . ."* Shneidman, E. S. *Definition of Suicide.* New York: John Wiley & Sons, 1985, p. 229.

312 *"Suicidal behaviors may be generated . . ."* Motto, J. A. "Recognition, Evaluation, and Management of Persons at Risk for Suicide." (1978). *Personnel and Guidance Journal,* 26, pp. 537–543.

312   *"Suicide proneness is primarily a psychodynamic matter . . ."* Buie, D. H., Maltsberger, J. T. "The Psychology and Assessment of Suicide." Unpublished paper, p. 18.

314   *what they call the "psychodynamic formulation" of suicide . . .* Described in Buie, D. H., Maltsberger, J. T. *The Practical Formulation of Suicide Risk.* Cambridge: The Firefly Press, 1983.

316   *"Gratifying results with depressive patients . . ."* Frederick, C. J., Resnik, H. L. P. "Interventions with Suicidal Patients" (1970). *Journal of Contemporary Psychotherapy,* 2(2), p. 105.

316   *Commenting on a 1970 study . . .* Mintz, R. S. "Basic Considerations in the Psychotherapy of the Depressed Suicidal Patient" (1971). *American Journal of Psychotherapy,* 25, p. 63.

316   *"In state hospitals, community mental health centers . . ."* Robitscher, J. *The Powers of Psychiatry.* Boston: Houghton Mifflin, 1980, p. 356.

316   *"Drugs are an essential part of medical management . . ."* Farberow, N. L. "The Suicidal Patient in Medical Practice" (1981). Reprinted from Spittell, J. A., Jr. (ed.) *Clinical Medicine,* 12, chap. 25. Philadelphia: Harper & Row, 1981, p. 6.

316   *Partly because they are the only mental health professionals . . .* As of 1988, more than a dozen states have moved to allow psychologists to admit patients to hospitals.

316   *They don't, says sociologist Donald Light . . .* See Light, D. *Becoming Psychiatrists: The Professional Transformation of Self.* New York: W. W. Norton, 1980; "Psychiatrists and Suicide." Unpublished paper; "Professional Problems in Treating Suicidal Persons" (1976). *Omega,* 7(1), pp. 59–67; "Treating Suicide: the Illusions of a Professional Movement" (1973). *International Social Science Journal,* 25(4), pp. 475–88.

317   *"Suicidal behavior is the most frequently . . ."* and *Psychiatrists, in fact, score no better . . .* Cited in Berman, A. L. "Notes on Turning 18 (and 75): A Critical Look at Our Adolescence" (1985). Paper presented at the Eighteenth Annual Meeting of the American Association of Suicidology, Toronto, Canada, April 18–21, 1985.

317   *"During the course of that epidemic . . ."* Stone, A. A. "Suicide Precipitated by Psychotherapy: A Clinical Contribution" (1970). Paper presented at the Ninth National Scientific Meeting of the Association for the Advancement of Psychotherapy, May 10, 1970.

317   *In a series of papers . . .* Stone, A. A., Shein, H. M. "Psychotherapy of the Hospitalized Suicidal Patient" (1968). *American Journal of Psychotherapy,* 22(1), pp. 15–25; Shein, H. M., Stone, A. A. "Psychotherapy Designed to Detect and Treat Suicidal Potential" (1969). *American Journal of Psychiatry,* 125(9), 141–45; Shein, H. M., Stone, A. A. "Monitoring

and Treatment of Suicidal Potential Within the Context of Psychotherapy" (1969). *Comprehensive Psychiatry,* 10(1), pp. 59–70.

318 *"These false axioms derive primarily from fear . . ."* Shein, H. M. "Suicide Care: Obstacles in the Education of Psychiatric Residents" (1976). *Omega,* 7(1), p. 77.

318 *"Some patients almost ready for suicide . . ."* Maltsberger, J. T., Buie, D. H., Jr. "Common Errors in the Management of Suicidal Patients" (1980). Unpublished paper, p. 14.

318 *Impressed with the jocular, Jewish-mother approach . . .* Described in Stone, "Suicide Precipitated by Psychotherapy," p. 5.

319 *In one of the few papers on the subject . . .* Maltsberger, J. T., Buie, D. H. "Countertransference Hate in the Treatment of Suicidal Patients" (1974). *Archives of General Psychiatry,* 30, pp. 625–33.

319 *In a 1967 study of six suicides . . .* Bloom, V. "An Analysis of Suicide at a Training Center" (1967). *American Journal of Psychiatry,* 123, pp. 918–25.

319 *William Wheat isolated several patterns . . .* Cited in Hendin, *Suicide in America,* p. 169.

320 *Robert Litman interviewed more than two hundred therapists . . .* Litman, R. E. "When Patients Commit Suicide" (1965). *American Journal of Psychotherapy,* 14, pp. 570–76.

321 *Shneidman and Farberow describe a man . . .* Farberow, N. L., Shneidman, E. S., Leonard, C. V. "Suicide Among Schizophrenic Mental Hospital Patients." In Farberow, N. L., Shneidman, E. S. (eds.) *The Cry for Help.* New York: McGraw-Hill, 1965, p. 90.

322 *"hundreds of ways"* Reynolds, D. K., Farberow, N. L. *Suicide: Inside and Out.* Berkeley: University of California Press, 1976.

323 *Half of all suicides at Metropolitan State Hospital . . .* Beisser, A. R., Blanchette, J. E. "A Study of Suicides in a Mental Hospital" (1961). *Diseases of the Nervous System,* 22, pp. 365–69.

323 *a study attributing a decline . . .* Woolley, L.F., Eichert, A.H. "Notes on the Problem of Suicide and Escape" (1941). *American Journal of Psychiatry,* 98, pp. 110–18.

323 *"State hospital patients, who as a group . . ."* Okin, R. L. "The Future of State Hospitals: Should There Be One?" (1983). *American Journal of Psychiatry,* 140(5), p. 579.

325 *In a 1967 survey of five Philadelphia medical schools . . .* Cited in Light, *Becoming Psychiatrists,* p. 30.

326   *In a poll reported in the* Journal of the American Medical Association
. . . Cited in Giffin and Felsenthal, *A Cry for Help,* p. 28.

327   *"Suicide can best be understood in terms of concepts . . ."* Shneidman,
Definition of Suicide, p. 226.

328   *psychologist Pamela Cantor appeared on ABC's "Nightline" . . .* Cited in
Giffin and Felsenthal, *A Cry for Help,* pp. 162–63.

Chapter IV

329   *One August day in 1937 . . .* For historical material on the Golden Gate
Bridge, see Brown, A. *Golden Gate: Biography of a Bridge.* Garden City,
New York: Doubleday, 1965.

330   *"almost any place in Japan . . ."* Russell, O. D. "Suicide in Japan"
(1930). *The American Mercury,* July 1930, p. 342.

330   *A study of 116 people who attempted suicide in Jukai . . .* Takahashi, Y.
"Aokigahara-Jukai: Suicide and Amnesia in Mt. Fuji's Black Forest".
Paper presented at a joint meeting of the American Association of
Suicidology and the International Association for Suicide Prevention, San
Francisco, May 25–30, 1987. In today's industrialized, westernized Japan,
several Tokyo skyscrapers have taken their places as suicide landmarks.
The Takashimadaira public housing complex, sixty-four apartment build-
ings on the edge of Tokyo, opened in April 1972. Within eight years, more
than seventy people leaped from its rooftops—some journeying from as
many as 120 miles away—earning it the nickname "Mecca for Suicide."

330   *the most powerful suicide magnet of all time . . .* The description of the
suicides at Mihara-Yama is drawn from newspaper and magazine accounts of the time, and from Ellis and Allen, *Traitor Within,* pp. 94–99.

331   *"At one time there seemed to be a growing propensity . . ."* Sweetser, W.
Mental Hygiene; or, an Examination of the Intellect and Passions. New
York: George P. Putnam, 1850, p. 292.

333   *gathered the names of 515 people . . .* Seiden, R. H. "Where Are They
Now? A Follow-up Study of Suicide Attempters from the Golden Gate
Bridge" (1978). *Suicide and Life-Threatening Behavior,* 8(4), pp. 203–16.

333   *psychiatrist David Rosen interviewed six of the eight people . . .* Cited in
Rosen, D. H. "Suicide Survivors: Psychotherapeutic Implications of Egocide" (1976). *Suicide and Life-Threatening Behavior,* 6(4), pp. 209–15.

333   *A second study by Seiden . . .* Seiden, R. H., Spence, M. C. "A Tale of
Two Bridges: Comparative Suicide Incidence on the Golden Gate and San
Francisco–Oakland Bay Bridges" (1982). *Crisis,* 3(1), pp. 32–40.

334   *the campaign for a barrier became a moot political issue . . .* In 1977, the
bridge's fortieth anniversary year, pro-barrier activists held a Memorial

Day rally on the bridge to commemorate the more than six hundred bridge suicides. Ironically, one of the speakers was Reverend Jim Jones, who arrived with three busloads of his Peoples Temple followers. "It is entirely fitting that on Memorial Day we are here on account of the hundreds of people who are not casualties of war, but casualties of society," he said. "For, in the final analysis, we have to bear collective responsibility for those individuals who could not find a place to go with their burdens, who came to that place of total helplessness, total despondency, where they took their own lives here on this beautiful bridge, this Golden Gate Bridge, a symbol of human ingenuity, technological genius but social failure." Eighteen months later he would lead 912 of his followers into mass suicide in the jungles of Guyana. The text of Jones's speech is reprinted in Seiden, R. H. "Reverend Jones on Suicide" (1979). *Suicide and Life-Threatening Behavior,* 9(2), pp. 116–19.

335   *"Much could be gained . . ."* Friedman, *On Suicide,* pp. 52–53. The opposite prevention strategy was proposed in the seventeenth century by Richard Capel. He suggested that instead of avoiding bridges that might tempt one to jump, one should march firmly across with a constant heart, and the urge would be conquered. "A false meanes is for a man to yeeld to much to feares, so as to thinke to avoid tentation, by declining, and not by resisting; as some dare not carry a knife about them, or when their knife is out, cast it from them, this is to yeeld too much to Satan: neither doth it helpe the matter, but rather keepe the tentation in. . . . The way to drive away our tentation is to keepe our knives about us . . . to fight it out against Satan, by setting the Word and Christ against him." (Quoted in Sprott, *The English Debate,* p. 46.)

336   *NIMH researcher Jeffrey Boyd scrutinized suicide rates . . .* Boyd, J. H. "The Increasing Rate of Suicide by Firearms" (1983). *The New England Journal of Medicine,* 308(15), pp. 872–74.

336   *A 1980 study found that the strictness of . . .* Lester, D., Murrell, M. E. "The Influence of Gun Control Laws on Suicidal Behavior" (1980). *American Journal of Psychiatry,* 137(1), pp. 121–22.

336   *In a study of eighty-two consecutive suicides . . .* Cited in Seiden, R. H. "Suicide Prevention: A Public Health/Public Policy Approach" (1977). *Omega,* 8(3), p. 271.

336   *In a 1986 study of firearm deaths . . .* Kellerman, A. L., Reay, D. T. "Protection or Peril? An Analysis of Firearm-Related Deaths in the Home" (1986). *The New England Journal of Medicine,* 314(24), pp. 1557–60.

336   *"If some persons would use slower methods . . ."* Quoted in Seiden, "Suicide Prevention: A Public Health/Public Policy Approach," p. 271.

337   *"It is unlikely that . . ."*   Hudgens, R. W. "Preventing Suicide" (1983). *The New England Journal of Medicine,* 308(15), pp. 897–98.

337   *"The NRA is not for gearing laws to the weakest element . . ."*   Quoted in Parachini, A. "Gun Deaths: Suicides Versus Murders." *The Los Angeles Times,* April 19, 1983, part V, p. 5.

337   *When the twenty-year-old manager of a Brooklyn clothing store . . .*   This and subsequent examples are taken from newspaper and magazine accounts.

338   *As a term project for "The Psychology of Death" . . .*   Moss, L. "Help Wanted: A Limited Study of Responses to One Person's Cry for Help" (1971). *Life-Threatening Behavior,* 1(1), pp. 55–66.

339   *the story of a young reporter . . .*   This story is repeated in Kobler, J. "Suicides Can Be Prevented" (1948). *The Saturday Evening Post,* March 27, 1948, p. 110.

Chapter VI

340   *"Suicide is a fundamental human right."*   Szasz, T. *The Second Sin.* Garden City, N.Y.: Anchor/Doubleday, 1973, p. 67.

340   *"If the psychiatrist is to prevent . . ."*   Szasz, T., in a speech given at a conference on "Suicide: What Is the Clinician's Responsibility?" Boston, February 1, 1985.

341   *"In fact, I firmly believe that psychiatric help . . ."*   Szasz, T., in a debate with Edwin Shneidman in 1972 at the University of California, Berkeley. Taped by Audio-Digest Foundation, 1930 Wilshire Blvd., Suite 700, Los Angeles, CA 90057.

341   *Abraham Lincoln, who was suicidally depressed . . .*   Psychiatrist Ronald Fieve has written that if Lincoln had been his patient today, he would insist on immediate "hospitalization, observation for suicidal intent, antidepressant drugs, and later, lithium as the treatment of choice." Lincoln survived his depression without such help; gun control seems to have been the form of suicide prevention he could most have benefited from.

341   *"The 'right' to suicide is a 'right' desired only temporarily . . ."*   Murphy, G. E. "Suicide and the Right to Die" (1973). *American Journal of Psychiatry,* 130(4), pp. 472–73.

341   *four people who survived six-story jumps . . .*   Hendin, *Suicide in America,* p. 210.

341   *"The right to kill oneself can be exercised quietly . . ."*   Hendin, *Suicide in America,* p. 225.

341 *"Suicide is not a 'right'..."* Shneidman, E. S. "Aphorisms of Suicide and Some Implications for Psychotherapy" (1984). *American Journal of Psychotherapy,* 38(3), p. 322.

342 *"Although such cases have not been studied..."* Wallace, S. E., "The Survivor's Rights." In Wallace, S. E., and Eser, A. (eds.) *Suicide and Euthanasia.* Knoxville: University of Tennessee Press, 1981, p. 67.

342 *"Suicidal persons are succumbing..."* Boldt, M. "The Right to Suicide" (1985). *Suicide Information and Education Centre Current Awareness Bulletin,* 1(2), p. 1.

342 *"the act [of suicide] clearly represents an illness"* Cited in Szasz, *The Theology of Medicine,* p. 68.

342 *"If a sociologist predicted..."* Cited in Brandt, A. *Reality Police: The Experience of Insanity in America.* New York: William Morrow, 1975, p. 146.

342 *"If a middle-aged lady goes to the doctor..."* From the debate between Szasz and Shneidman in 1972, University of California, Berkeley.

343 *"If everyone who evinces some abnormality..."* Friedman, *On Suicide,* pp. 84–85. The difficulty of drawing the line between sickness and health was described by Melville in *Billy Budd, Sailor:* "Who in the rainbow can draw the line where the violet tint ends and the orange tint begins? Distinctly we see the difference of the colors, but where exactly does the one first blendingly enter into the other? So with sanity and insanity. In pronounced cases there is no question about them. But in some supposed cases, in various degrees supposedly less pronounced, to draw the exact line of demarcation few will undertake, though for a fee becoming considerate some professional experts will. There is nothing namable but that some men will, or undertake to, do it for pay."

343 *"The argument connecting suicide and mental illness..."* In Green, B. R., Irish, D. P. (eds.) *Death Education: Preparation for Living.* Cambridge, Massachusetts: Schenkman Publishing Company, 1971, p. 120.

343 *A Harvard University study found that the highest estimate...* Cited in Hendin, *Suicide in America,* pp. 189–90.

343 *"Suicide is prejudged..."* Quotes in this paragraph can be found in Hillman, *Suicide and the Soul,* pp. 36, 37, 87, 93, 92.

344 *In a review of Hillman's book...* Litman, R. E. "Concern for Suicide: Before and After." In Shneidman, E. S., Farberow, N. L., Litman, R. E. (eds.) *The Psychology of Suicide.* New York: Science House, 1970, pp. 637–40.

344 *"In regarding the desire to live..."* Szasz, *The Theology of Medicine,* p. 81.

344   *"Some of the things that happen in these people's lives . . ."*   In Green and Irish (eds.), *Death Education,* p. 120.

345   *"If the person says, 'I'm going to kill myself . . .'"*   Ibid., p. 121.

PART 5

Chapter I

355   *"Among the Karens of Burma . . ."*   Westermarck, *The Origin and Development of the Moral Ideas,* p. 231.

355   *"Thus was he blessed with an easy death . . ."*   Suetonius, *The Lives of the Twelve Caesars.* Gavorse, J. (ed.) New York: The Modern Library, 1931, p. 115.

355   *"if any man labour of an incurable disease . . ."*   Cited in Fedden, *Suicide,* p. 72.

355   *"Just as a landlord who has not received his rent . . ."*   Quoted in Lecky, *History of European Morals,* vol. I, pp. 232–33.

355   *"I will not relinquish old age . . ."*   Ibid., p. 232.

356   *"do away with the sufferings of the sick . . ."*   Quoted in Humphry, D., Wickett, A. *The Right to Die: Understanding Euthanasia.* New York: Harper & Row, 1986, p. 4.

356   *"the most excusable cause . . ."*   Moore, *A Full Inquiry,* p. 270.

356   *might apply to the parish priest for the Holy Stone . . .*   Described in Gillon, R. "Suicide and Voluntary Euthanasia: Historical Perspective." In Downing, A. B. (ed.) *Euthanasia and the Right to Death.* Los Angeles: Nash Publishing, 1970, p. 182.

356   *Jonathan Swift, who suffered from Ménière's disease . . .*   Shapiro, S. L. "The Medical History of Jonathan Swift" (1969). *Eye, Ear, Nose and Throat Monthly,* 48, pp. 97–100.

356   *"I esteem it the office of a physician . . ."*   Bacon, F. *Selected Writings.* Dick, H. G. (ed.) New York: The Modern Library, 1955, p. 277.

356   *"We have very great pity for an animal . . ."*   Cited in Mannes, M. *Last Rights.* New York: William Morrow, 1974, p. 64.

356   *"should not torment his patient . . ."*   Quoted in Hendin, D. *Death as a Fact of Life.* New York: W. W. Norton, 1984, pp. 82–83.

357   *"in cases of incurable and painful illness . . ."*   Cited in Russell, O. R. *Freedom to Die: Moral and Legal Aspects of Euthanasia.* New York: Human Sciences Press, 1977 (revised edition), pp. 57–58.

357   *"practices of savages in all parts of the world."*   Ibid., p. 62.

357   *"Vast numbers of human beings are doomed . . ."*   Quoted in Twycross, R. G. "Voluntary Euthanasia." In Wallace, Eser, *Suicide and Euthanasia,* p. 88.

357   *"Some are proposing what is called euthanasia . . ."*   Cited in Kamisar, Y. "Euthanasia Legislation: Some Non-Religious Objections." In Downing (ed.), *Euthanasia and the Right to Death,* p. 115.

357   *This was only the beginning . . .*   "Of the five identifiable steps by which the Nazis carried out the principle of 'life unworthy of life,' coercive sterilization was the first," writes Lifton. "There followed the killing of 'impaired' children in hospitals; and then the killing of 'impaired' adults, mostly collected from mental hospitals, in centers especially equipped with carbon monoxide gas. This project was extended (in the same killing centers) to 'impaired' inmates of concentration and extermination camps and, finally, to mass killings, mostly of Jews, in the extermination camps themselves." Lifton, R. J. *The Nazi Doctors: Medical Killing and the Psychology of Genocide.* New York: Basic Books, 1986. Lifton's book offers a comprehensive description of the Nazi "euthanasia" program.

358   *Since then the word has been avoided . . .*   After World War II, several right-to-die groups dropped the word "euthanasia" from their titles. Most right-to-die activists also shy away from the word "suicide," with its unsavory associations.

358   *technological advances have been a mixed blessing.*   As machines capable of replacing human functions have developed, some ethicists question where the person ends and the machine begins. Thomas Szasz writes, "The final medical solution to human problems: remove everything from the body that is diseased or protesting, leaving only enough organs which—by themselves, or hooked up to appropriate machines—still justify calling what is left of the person a 'case'; and call the procedure 'humanectomy.' " Szasz, *The Second Sin,* p. 70.

358   *"For every illness, there is some procedure . . ."*   Quoted in *The New York Times,* January 18, 1985, p. B1.

358   *"The classical deathbed scene . . ."* and *"Where can we draw the line . . ."*   Fletcher, J. "The Patient's Right to Die." In Downing (ed.), *Euthanasia and the Right to Death,* pp. 65–66.

359   *doctors' dedication to life at any and all cost . . .*   It has been suggested that what one skeptical doctor calls "their crusade to slay the dragon of death" may be a function of doctors' neuroses as much as of their concern for patients; on psychological tests, doctors score high on death anxiety.

359   *"The dignity starts with . . ."*   Clark, B. *Whose Life Is It Anyway?* New York: Avon Books, 1980, p. 143.

359   *"We are discovering that saving life . . ."* Quoted in Hendin, *Death as a Fact of Life,* p. 79.

359   *One terminally ill seventy-eight-year-old . . .* This story is told in Barnard, C. *Good Life/Good Death.* Englewood Cliffs, New Jersey: Prentice-Hall, 1980, p. 88.

359   *passive euthanasia . . .* In active and passive euthanasia, the patient has requested to die; in "mercy killing," the "killer" takes matters into his or her own hands because the patient is no longer able to express his or her wishes, as in the case of a coma victim or someone suffering from Alzheimer's disease.

359   *"Thou shalt not kill; but need'st not strive . . ."* Gardner, H. (ed.) *The New Oxford Book of English Verse.* New York and Oxford: Oxford University Press, 1972, p. 682.

360   *"I have learned from my life in medicine . . ."* Barnard, *Good Life/Good Death,* p. 15.

361   *"What, morally, is the difference . . ."* Fletcher, J. "The Patient's Right to Die." In Downing (ed.), *Euthanasia and the Right to Death,* p. 68.

362   *According to a study reported . . .* Cited in *USA Today,* January 4, 1985, p. 1.

362   *"competent patients' decisions regarding medical treatment . . ."* Cited in Humphry and Wickett, *The Right to Die,* p. 126.

362   *"Basic to our considerations are two important precepts . . ."* Wanzer, S. H., et al. "The Physician's Responsibility Toward Hopelessly Ill Patients" (1984). *The New England Journal of Medicine,* 310, p. 955.

363   *"It is morally justifiable to withhold antibiotics . . ."* Ibid., p. 958.

363   *"When inevitable death is imminent . . ."* "The Vatican's Declaration on Euthanasia, 1980." Quoted in Larue, *Euthanasia and Religion,* p. 42.

364   *"In hospitals that have no rules . . ."* *Time,* April 9, 1984.

Chapter II

369   *announce the formation of the Hemlock Society . . .* Hemlock is one of thirty-two right-to-die societies in eighteen countries from Australia to Colombia to South Africa. Although most societies share a common goal—to guarantee people the right to choice in their own death—the groups disagree on the lengths to which they will go. The groups range from those that favor only passive euthanasia to those that, like Hemlock and the Voluntary Euthanasia Society, wish to legalize assisted voluntary euthanasia. In the United States there are three groups, two of which limit their focus to passive euthanasia. Concern for Dying, an "educational

council," tries to sensitize health professionals and the public about right-
to-die issues; it publishes a quarterly newsletter, hosts conferences and
seminars, runs a speakers bureau and film library, and distributes Living
Wills. The Society for the Right to Die favors a more active legislative
approach. In addition to issuing informational brochures and tracking
court decisions on right-to-die cases, it lobbies for changes in state laws
that would permit passive euthanasia. In pushing for the legalization of
assisted voluntary euthanasia, Hemlock is the most radical of the U.S.
groups. Many Hemlock members are former Society or Concern members
who wanted, as one recent convert says, "something a little stronger."

373   *"There is only one prospect worse . . ."*   Koestler, A. In *Exit: A Guide to
Self-Deliverance.* London: The Executive Committee of Exit, 1981, preface, p. 3

374   *no one had ever written a book on how to commit suicide.* A few books and
pamphlets have tackled the subject in a darkly comic mode, most notably
21 Delightful Ways of Committing Suicide, written and savagely illustrated by Jean Bruller and published in the U.S. in 1930.

375   *"It is the sovereign right of the individual . . ."*   *A Guide to Self-Deliverance,* p. 31.

375   *"We feel that the difficulties of decision-making . . ."*   Humphry, D.
"Order Book Now for May Delivery." In *Hemlock Quarterly,* April,
1981, p. 1.

376   *"I feel no remorse . . ."*   *The Boston Globe,* September 20, 1982.

Chapter III

382   *"whether it was logical to conscript . . ."*   Cited in Mannes, *Last Rights,*
pp. 62–63.

382   *"It seems unimaginable that either Schweitzer . . ."*   Fletcher, J. *Morals
and Medicine.* Princeton: Princeton University Press, 1954, p. 193.

382   *"Their argument turns . . ."*   Quoted in Battin, M. P. *Ethical Issues in
Suicide.* Englewood Cliffs, New Jersey: Prentice-Hall, 1982, p. 179.

382   *if shortening our lives interferes with God's will . . .*   In 1847, when ether
was first used in the delivery room, many people protested that labor pains
were divinely ordained and to use anesthetics went against God's will.

382   *"If it is for God alone to decide . . ."*   Rachels, J. *The End of Life:
Euthanasia and Morality.* Oxford: Oxford University Press, 1986, p. 163.

382   *"Human life consists in mutual service . . ."*   Cited in Mannes, *Last
Rights,* p. 141.

383   *"When life is more terrible than death . . ."*   Cited in Choron, *Suicide,* p. 78.

383   *"The final stage of an incurable illness . . ."*   Cited in Maguire, D.C. *Death by Choice.* New York; Schocken Books, 1975, p. 151.

383   *"Even if this is true . . ."*   Seneca, "Letter to Lucilius, No. 70." From *The Stoic Philosophy of Seneca.* Trans. Hadas, M. Gloucester, Massachusetts: Peter Smith, 1965, p. 203.

383   *a forty-four-year-old Maryland woman . . .*   Her story was told in *People,* October 13, 1986, pp. 43–44.

384   *In 1919, German psychiatrist Alfred Hoche . . .*   A year later Hoche co-authored *The Permission to Destroy Life Unworthy of Life.*

384   *philosopher Richard Brandt compared . . .*   Brandt, R. "The Rationality of Suicide." In *Suicide: The Philosophical Issues.* Battin, M. P., Mayo, D. J.(eds.) New York: St. Martin's Press, 1980, pp. 117–32.

384   *Some writers opposed to suicide in general . . .*   Battin, M. P. "Suicide: A Fundamental Human Right?" In Battin, Mayo, *Suicide: The Philosophical Issues,* p. 279.

384   *In one of the few articles on the subject . . .*   Jackson, D. L., Youngner, S. "Patient Autonomy and 'Death with Dignity': Some Clinical Caveats" (1979). *The New England Journal of Medicine,* 301, pp. 404–8.

385   *A study of uncompleted suicide pacts . . .*   Rosenbaum, M. "Crime and Punishment: The Suicide Pact." *Archives of General Psychiatry,* 40, pp. 979–82.

385   *They suggested that Cynthia had been emotionally coerced . . .*   If Koestler is to be blamed, however, the blame must be not for his wife's death but for her life. "A good man would have weaned her," wrote Barbara Grizzuti Harrison. ". . . I think it's fair to say he killed her." But to call Koestler a murderer seems as patronizing and demeaning to Cynthia as her husband may have been, denying her any volition of her own. "For a man in grave and failing health, self-deliverance was the final right," wrote Hemlock Society co-founder Ann Wickett. "For Cynthia, it was the final act of devotion. That too was her right. One regrets, however, less the nature of her death, than the nature of her life. She deserved more."

385   *"She was his appendix . . ."*   Quoted in Wickett, A. "Why Cynthia Koestler Joined Arthur." *Hemlock Quarterly,* January 1985, pp. 4–5.

385   *"It is hardly an exaggeration to say . . ."*   Ibid.

385   *mental health professionals and suicide experts are sympathetic . . .*   Some may discuss it as something other than suicide. "We need not argue the issue of whether it is rational for an individual with a painful terminal

illness to refuse extraordinary life-saving measures or to arrange more actively to end his life," writes Herbert Hendin (*Suicide in America,* pp. 214–15). "The person facing imminent death who is in intractable pain and arranges to end his life may be a suicide in the dictionary definition of the term, but not in the psychological sense." (Leading one to conclude that Hendin's psychological definition of suicide demands that the actor be irrational.) Many others in the field object to the right-to-die movement, while reserving the right to die for themselves. "I believe in suicide prevention, but I have Alzheimer's in my family, and I'm fearful of death without dignity," says a leader in suicide prevention. "If you're incompetent, they keep you from killing yourself. Well, the point at which I want out is when I *lose* competence. I have made a suicide pact with two of my sisters." Edwin Shneidman participated in the initial Hemlock think tank and delivered the keynote address at Hemlock's 1985 national conference. "I like Derek Humphry and I approve of what he does," he told the audience. "But I'm not a card-carrying Hemlock member, and I maintain some substantial differences with the goals of the organization." A friend of Shneidman's interprets: "Ed doesn't believe in rational suicide—except for himself."

385   *"From an intellectual standpoint I can appreciate . . ."*   Seiden, R. H. "Self-Deliverance or Self-Destruction?" Paper presented at the sixteenth annual meeting of the American Association of Suicidology, Dallas, Texas, 1983.

386   *"the limits are obscure . . ."*   Donne, *Biathanatos,* p. 216.

386   *"In his oft-quoted 1949 essay . . ."*   Alexander, L. "Medical Science Under Dictatorship" (1949). *The New England Journal of Medicine,* 241(2), pp. 39–47.

386   *"I think there is no way in which the right to die . . ."*   Quoted on "Rational Suicide?" produced by Barry Lando for "60 Minutes," CBS-TV, October 12, 1980.

387   *"Once any group of human beings is considered fair game . . ."*   Quoted in Humphry and Wickett, *The Right to Die,* p. 164.

387   *"Miss Voluntary Euthanasia . . ."*   Kamisar, Y. "Euthanasia Legislation: Some Non-Religious Objections." In Downing (ed.), *Euthanasia and the Right to Death,* p. 115.

387   *"I have seen the true wish for death among my patients . . ."*   Quoted in Wallace and Eser (eds.), *Suicide and Euthanasia,* p. 102.

387   *"Where is the sense . . . in telling a person . . ."*   Humphry and Wickett, *The Right to Die,* p. 313.

388   *"subscribed to the belief that . . ."*   Ibid., p. 14.

388   *"creatures born defective, whose present condition . . ."*   Ibid., p. 14.

388   *"Sentimental prejudice should not obstruct . . ."*   Ibid., pp. 14–15.

388   *"If a chronically sick man dies . . ."*   Slater, E. "Choosing the Time to Die." In Battin and Mayo, *Suicide: The Philosophical Issues,* p. 202.

388   *"there can be no possibility of an older person . . ."*   Barrington, M. R. "Apologia for Suicide." In Downing (ed.), *Euthanasia and the Right to Death,* p. 159.

389   *"They have one way only of determining . . ."*   Herodotus, *The Histories,* p. 128.

389   *The Tschuktschi of northern Siberia . . .*   Some of this list is drawn from Humphry and Wickett, *The Right to Die,* p. 2.

389   *The perhaps apocryphal story is told of some missionaries . . .*   Cited in Maguire, *Death by Choice,* p. 86.

389   *"Like leaves which fall off a tree . . ."* Quoted in *Time,* April 9, 1984, p. 68.

389   *"The time is not far off . . ."*   Lamm, R. D. "Long Time Dying" (1984). *The New Republic,* August 27, 1984, p. 21.

390   *"The postponement of an individual's death . . ."*   Cited in *The New York Times,* September 5, 1984.

390   *"creatively and honorably accepting aging . . ."* Callahan quotes are from *Time,* Nov. 2, 1987, p. 76.

390   *"Any sophisticated doctor would acknowledge . . ."*   *Los Angeles Times,* May 25, 1984, part V, p. 27.

391   *"Today, the needs of the individual . . ."*   Portwood, D. *Common-Sense Suicide.* New York: Dodd, Mead, 1978, pp. 46–47.

392   *"It is realistic to be concerned . . ."*   Seiden, "Self-Deliverance or Self-Destruction?" p. 10.

392   *"At best, the living old . . ."*   Butler, R. N. *Why Survive? Being Old in America.* New York: Harper Colophon, 1975, p. xi.

392   *"Many elders suffer a social death . . ."*   Levin, J., Arluke, A. "Our Elderly's Fate?" (1983). *The New York Times,* September 29, 1983, p. 27.

392   *the suicide rate of elderly Americans . . .*   Although the rate of elderly suicide has declined slowly over the last three decades, from 29.3 in 1950 to 17.1 in 1981, in recent years it has begun to climb again. In 1983 it stood at 19.2.

393   *Improved nursing home care is another . . .*   A 1986 report by the Senate Committee on Aging found that more than one-third of the nursing homes that serve the nation's most severely ill patients failed to meet minimum government standards. Even this low level of care can be difficult to

obtain; some nursing homes have waiting lists of two to three years. Steven Blum, an expert on nursing home care, urges the creation of more hospices and palliative care units. "There ought to be alternatives to the present choices," he says. "They are now limited to institutions. What institutions deny is choice; what the elderly seek is choice."

393   *"You don't have to kill the patient . . ."*   Quoted on "Rational Suicide?" produced by Barry Lando for "60 Minutes," CBS-TV, October 12, 1980.

393   *"If all the care were up to the standards . . ."*   Cited in Saunders, C. "Dying They Live: St. Christopher's Hospice." In Feifel, H. *New Meanings of Death.* New York: McGraw-Hill, 1977, p. 159.

393   *"Since the elderly depressed don't cause much trouble . . ."*   Quoted in *The Los Angeles Times,* November 13, 1984.

394   *A study of 136 elderly nursing home patients . . .*   Cited in *The New York Times,* July 16, 1982.

394   *"In general, where the 'geriatric case' is allowed to slip away . . ."*   Cited in Wrobleski, *Afterwords,* January 1985, p. 2.

394   *"Often people ask whether a human being . . ."*   In Speijer, N. "The Attitude of Dutch Society Toward the Phenomenon of Suicide." In Farberow, *Suicide in Different Cultures,* p. 164.

394   *"When an older woman leaves a social gathering . . ."*   Portwood, *Common-Sense Suicide,* pp. 17–18.

395   *"What we want, what our grandsons . . ."*   Quoted in Rolfe, G. B. "The Right to Die" (1893). *The North American Review,* 157(6), p. 758.

396   *"In a rational state of civilization . . ."*   Ibid., p. 758.

397   *"Robert Lowell once remarked . . ."*   Alvarez, *The Savage God,* p. 130.

397   *"People are going to help each other die . . ."*   Quoted in *USA Today,* May 15, 1985, p. 8A.

397   *"I believe that the classical philosophical argument . . ."*   Quoted in *The New York Times,* April 25, 1983, p. B8.

397   *"I myself believe that on moral grounds . . ."*   Battin, M. P. "Manipulated Suicide" (1980). In Battin and Mayo, *Suicide: The Philosophical Issues,* p. 179. For a lucid, thorough discussion of these issues, see Battin's *Ethical Issues in Suicide.*

PART 6
Chapter I

409   *"There are always two parties . . ."*   Toynbee, A. *Man's Concern with Death.* New York: McGraw-Hill, 1969, pp. 267, 271.

Chapter II

421   *In an eighteenth-century French engraving* . . . The engraving is reproduced in Delisle de Sales, J. B. C. I. *De la Philosophie de la Nature.* London, 1789.

422   *"decapitated . . . to render it harmless . . ."*   This list is taken partially from a similar list in Cain, A. C. (ed.) *Survivors of Suicide.* Springfield, Illinois: Charles C. Thomas, 1972, p. 29.

422   *In 1289, it is recorded* . . .   Fedden, *Suicide,* p. 138.

423   *"What punishment can human laws inflict . . ."*   Ehrlich, J. W. (ed.) *Ehrlich's Blackstone.* Westport, Connecticut: Greenwood Press, 1973, p. 838.

423   *In the case of Lancelot Johnson* . . .   Described in MacDonald, *Mystical Bedlam,* pp. 137–38.

424   *On two occasions the diarist Samuel Pepys* . . .   Fedden, *Suicide,* pp. 193–97.

424   *"They have run through his body . . ."*   Delisle de Sales, *De la Philosophie de la Nature,* vol. 5, p. 447.

424   *"our tenderness and compassion . . ."*   Cited in Cutter, F. "On Charles Moore's 'The Subject of Suicide' " (1970). *Omega,* 1(2), p. 137.

424   *In 1761, Marc-Antoine Calas* . . .   Described in Fedden, *Suicide,* pp. 231–32.

424   *"He plants a dagger . . ."*   Gregory, *A Sermon on Suicide,* pp. 12–13.

425   *"Stay then, guilty man! . . ."*   Miller, *The Guilt, Folly, and Sources of Suicide,* pp. 24–25.

425   *"The* Sorrow *which arises upon the Loss . . ."*   Hey, *Three Dissertations,* pp. 202–3.

425   *"With reference to suicide . . ."*   Winslow, *The Anatomy of Suicide,* p. 152.

426   *In 1901 at the Annual Meeting* . . .   Wood, J. M. S., Urquhart, A. R. "A Family Tree Illustrative of Insanity and Suicide." In Cain (ed.), *Survivors of Suicide,* pp. 40–43.

426   *George P. Mudge constructed a Mendelian pedigree* . . .   Mudge, G. P. "The Mendelian Collection of Human Pedigrees: Inheritance of Suicidal Mania." In Cain (ed.), *Survivors of Suicide,* pp. 44–51.

426   *"A man named Edgar Jay Briggs . . ."*   Reprinted in Cain (ed.), *Survivors of Suicide,* frontispiece.

427   *"Many are induced to think of suicide . . ."*   Winslow, *The Anatomy of Suicide,* pp. 96–97.

427   *"The suicide by his last act places the bar sinister . . ."*   Strahan, *Suicide and Insanity,* p. 90

427   *"in the hope that people may be induced . . ."*   Ibid., p. vi.

427   *A passage from James Joyce's* Ulysses . . .   Joyce, J. *Ulysses.* New York: Random House, 1961, p. 96.

428   *"Nothing lowered the prestige of a family as much . . ."*   Fedden, *Suicide,* p. 248.

428   *"he placed the mark of Cain upon me . . ."*   Lindemann, E., Greer, I. M. "A Study of Grief: Emotional Responses to Suicide" (1972). In Cain (ed.), *Survivors of Suicide,* p. 67.

429   *"I believe that the person who commits suicide . . ."*   Shneidman, E. S. "Foreword." In Cain (ed.), *Survivors of Suicide,* p. x.

429   *A 1967 study of a St. Louis center . . .*   Cited in Bergson, L. "Suicide's Other Victims" (1982). *The New York Times Magazine,* November 14, 1982, p. 104.

429   *"Given the present stage of our knowledge . . ."*   Resnik, H. L. P. "Psychological Resynthesis: A Clinical Approach to the Survivors of a Death by Suicide." In Cain (ed.), *Survivors of Suicide,* p. 177.

431   *A 1980 study compared the reactions . . .*   Calhoun, L. G., Selby, J. W., Faulstich, M. E. "Reactions to the Parents of the Child Suicide: A Study of Social Impressions" (1980). *Journal of Consulting and Clinical Psychology.* 48, pp. 535–36.

431   *"Even in the numbness of those hours . . ."*   Wechsler, J. A. *In a Darkness.* New York: W. W. Norton, 1972, p. 13.

Chapter IV

443   *"Although mourning involves grave departures . . ."*   Freud, S., "Mourning and Melancholia" (1917). *Works,* vol. 14, pp. 243–44.

443   *"Mourning has a quite specific psychical task . . ."*   Freud, S., "Totem and Taboo" (1913). *Works,* vol. 13, p. 65.

443   *a study by the National Academy of Sciences . . .*   Osterweis, M., Solomon, F., Green, M. (eds.) *Bereavement: Reactions, Consequences, and Care.* Washington, D.C.: National Academy Press, 1984.

444   *"There's a tendency for the novice . . ."*   Worden, J. W. *Grief Counseling and Grief Therapy.* New York: Springer Publishing Company, 1982, p. 32.

445   *"Sooner or later," wrote English psychoanalyst John Bowlby . . .*   Quoted in Ibid., p. 14.

445   *A psychiatrist at Massachusetts General Hospital . . .*" Ibid., p. 1.

445   *"The first response to the disappearance . . ."*   Lorenz, K. *On Aggression.* Trans. Wilson, M. K. New York: Harvest/Harcourt Brace Jovanovich, 1966, p. 208.

446   *described it as "psychic numbing" . . .* Lifton, R. J. *Death in Life.* New York: Random House, 1967, pp. 86–87.

447   *Sheila Weller described . . ."*   Weller, S. "Whose Death Was It, Anyway? Reflections on the Suicide of a Friend" (1981). *The Village Voice,* December 9–15, 1981, pp. 25–27.

448   *"There is an especially distressing tendency . . ."*   Lindemann, E., Greer, I. M. "A Study of Grief: Emotional Responses to Suicide." In Cain (ed.), *Survivors of Suicide,* p. 66.

448   *"Some feel guilty about experiencing relief . . ."*   Pangrazzi, A. "Suicide: How Christians Can Respond Today." *Catholic Update,* July 1984, p. 3.

450   *In his poem* "The Portrait" . . .   Kunitz, S. *The Poems of Stanley Kunitz, 1928–1978.* Boston and Toronto: Atlantic Monthly Press/Little, Brown, 1979, p. 86.

451   *suicide by a parent tends to beget . . .*   In his novel *God Bless You, Mr. Rosewater,* Kurt Vonnegut, Jr., wrote: "Sons of suicides seldom do well. Characteristically, they find life lacking a certain *zing.* They tend to feel more rootless than most, even in a notoriously rootless nation. They are squeamishly incurious about the past and numbly certain about the future to this grisly extent: they suspect that they, too, will probably kill themselves."

451   *"I spit upon this dreadful banker's grave . . ."*   Berryman, J. "Dream Song #384." In *The Dream Songs.* New York: Farrar, Straus, and Giroux, 1969, p. 406.

451   *One year after her father's suicide . . .*   Quoted in Giffin and Felsenthal, *A Cry for Help,* p. 173.

452   *"I see now that I had been incubating this death . . ."* Alvarez, *The Savage God,* p. 258.

452   *a suicide can actually serve a preventive role . . .*   The thought of a suicide's effect on survivors has long been a restraint on—and occasionally a spur to—potential suicides. Suffering from a bout of chronic catarrh, Seneca, who championed the idea of suicide as man's ever-available freedom, wrote, "Reduced to a state of complete emaciation, I had arrived at a point where the catarrhal discharges were virtually carrying me away with them altogether. On many an occasion I felt an urge to cut my life short there and then, and was only held back by the thought of my father, who had been the kindest of fathers to me and was then in his old age. Having in mind not how bravely I was capable of dying but how far from

bravely he was capable of bearing the loss, I commanded myself to live."
(Quoted in Battin, *Ethical Issues in Suicide,* p. 78.)

453   *"For children,"* concluded the 1984 National Academy of Sciences report
on grief . . .   Osterweis, Solomon, Green, *Bereavement,* p. 125.

453   *"Children are even more apt to be left alone . . ."*   Many parents mistakenly believe that a child is too young to grieve. "They think, 'She's only
three—she won't feel it,' " says Sandra Fox. Until recently, in fact, it was
believed that because they cannot comprehend the permanence of death
until about age nine, children are unable to mourn. Today, experts say that
children begin to sense separation and loss at six months and may be able
to grieve by age three. Children of any age express their grief differently
from adults, through physical symptoms such as restlessness, colds, and
upset stomachs, or through misbehavior, academic problems, and delinquency.

454   *In a study of forty-five children . . .*   Cain, A. C., Fast, I. "Children's
Disturbed Reactions to Parent Suicide: Distortions of Guilt, Communication, and Identification." In Cain (ed.), *Survivors of Suicide,* pp. 93–111.

454   *in a study of seventeen patients . . .*   Dorpat, T. L. "Psychological Effects
of Parental Suicide on Surviving Children." In Cain (ed.), *Survivors of
Suicide,* pp. 121–42.

Chapter VI

480   *"I feel so safe and warm . . ."*   Quoted in Slepicka, S. "The Role of
Support Groups in the Healing Process of Suicide Survivors." Unpublished paper.

Chapter VIII

487   *"We find a place for what we lose . . ."*   Quoted in Worden, *Grief Counseling,* p. 17.

487   *"Ah well, slowly but surely . . ."*   Quoted in Enright, *The Oxford Book
of Death,* pp. 113–14.

489   *"I want Dick's death not to be bigger . . ."*   Kenyon, K. "A Survivor's
Notes" (1979). *Newsweek,* April 30, 1979, p. 17.

SELECTED BIBLIOGRAPHY

The literature on suicide is massive. These are the books and papers I found most useful or thought-provoking in the preparation of this work.

BOOKS

Alcohol, Drug Abuse, and Mental Health Administration. *Report of the Secretary's Task Force on Youth* Suicide. (4 vols.) Washington, D.C.: U.S. Government Printing Office, 1989.

Alvarez, A. *The Savage God.* New York: Bantam Books, 1973.

Baechler, J. *Suicides.* Trans. Cooper, B. New York: Basic Books, 1979.

Barnard, C. *Good Life/Good Death.* Englewood Cliffs, New Jersey: Prentice-Hall, 1980.

Battin, M. P. *Ethical Issues in Suicide.* Englewood Cliffs, New Jersey: Prentice-Hall, 1982.

Battin, M. P., Mayo, D. J. (eds.). *Suicide: The Philosophical Issues.* New York: St. Martin's Press, 1980.

Bohannan, P. (ed.). *African Homicide and Suicide.* New York: Atheneum, 1967.

Bolton, I., with Mitchell, C. *My Son . . . My Son . . . .* Atlanta: Bolton Press, 1983.

Bruller, J. *21 Delightful Ways of Committing Suicide.* New York: Covici, Friede, 1930.

Bucknill, J. C., Tuke, D. H. *A Manual of Psychological Medicine.* London: John Churchill, 1858.

Buie, D. H., Maltsberger, J.T. *The Practical Formulation of Suicide Risk.* Cambridge: The Firefly Press, 1983.

Burton, R. *The Anatomy of Melancholy.* New York: Empire State Book Co., 1924.

Butler, R. N. *Why Survive? Being Old in America.* New York: Harper Colophon Books, 1975.

Cain, A. C. (ed.). *Survivors of Suicide.* Springfield, Illinois: Charles C. Thomas, 1972.

Callahan, D. *Setting Limits.* New York: Simon and Schuster, 1987.

Cavan, R. S. *Suicide.* New York: Russell & Russell, 1965.

Choron, J. *Death and Western Thought.* New York: Collier/Macmillan, 1973.

———. *Suicide.* New York: Charles Scribner's Sons, 1972.

Clark, B. *Whose Life Is It Anyway?* New York: Avon, 1980.

Coleman, L. *Suicide Clusters.* Boston and London: Faber and Faber, 1987.

Coser, R. L. *Training in Ambiguity.* New York: The Free Press/Macmillan, 1979.

Donne, J. *Biathanatos*. New York: Arno Press, 1977.

Douglas, J. D. *The Social Meanings of Suicide*. Princeton: Princeton University Press, 1973.

Downing, A. B. (ed.). *Euthanasia and the Right to Death*. Los Angeles: Nash Publishing Company, 1970.

Dublin, L. I. *Suicide: A Sociological and Statistical Study*. New York: Ronald Press, 1963.

Dublin, L. I., Bunzel, B. *To Be or Not to Be*. New York: Harrison Smith and Robert Haas, 1933.

Dunne, E. J., McIntosh, J. L., Dunne-Maxim, K. (eds.). *Suicide and Its Aftermath*. New York: W. W. Norton, 1987.

Durkheim, E. *Suicide*. Trans. Spaulding, J. A., Simpson, G. New York: The Free Press, 1966.

Ellis, E. R., Allen, G. N. *Traitor Within: Our Suicide Problem*. Garden City, New York: Doubleday, 1961.

Evans, G., Farberow, N. L. *The Encyclopedia of Suicide*. New York: Facts on File, 1988.

Exit. *A Guide to Self-Deliverance*. London: The Executive Committee of Exit, 1981.

Faber, M. D. *Suicide and Greek Tragedy*. New York: Sphinx Press, 1970.

Farberow, N. L. (ed.). *The Many Faces of Suicide*. New York: McGraw-Hill, 1980.

———. *Suicide in Different Cultures*. Baltimore: University Park Press, 1975.

———. *Taboo Topics*. New York: Atherton Press, 1963.

Farberow, N. L., Shneidman, E. S. (eds.). *The Cry for Help*. New York: McGraw-Hill, 1965.

Fedden, H. R. *Suicide: A Social and Historical Study*. New York: Arno Press, 1980.

Fisher, S. A. *Suicide Prevention and/or Crisis Services: A National Survey*. Canton, Ohio: Case Western Reserve University, 1972.

Friedman, P. (ed.). *On Suicide*. New York: International Universities Press, 1967.

Galt, J. M. *The Treatment of Insanity*. New York: Harper and Brothers, 1846.

Gates, B. T. *Victorian Suicide*. Princeton: Princeton University Press, 1988.

Gibbs, J. P., Martin, W. T. *Status Integration and Suicide: A Sociological Study*. Eugene, Oregon: University of Oregon Press, 1964.

Giffin, M., Felsenthal, C. *A Cry for Help*. Garden City, New York: Doubleday, 1983.

Goethe, J. W. *The Sorrows of Young Werther*. Trans. Mayer, E., Bogan, L. New York: Vintage Books, 1973.

Green B. R., Irish, D. P. (eds.). *Death Education: Preparation for Living*. Cambridge, Massachusetts: Schenkman, 1971.

Gregory, G. *A Sermon on Suicide*. London: J. Nichols, 1797.

Grollman, E. A. *Suicide: Prevention, Intervention, Postvention*. Boston: Beacon Press, 1971.

Guillon, C., LeBonniec, Y. *Suicide, Mode d'Emploi: Histoire, Technique, Actualité*. Paris: Éditions Alain Moreau, 1982.

Hankoff, L. D. (ed.). *Suicide: Theory and Clinical Aspects.* Littleton, Massachusetts: PSG Publishing Company, 1979.

Hastings, J. (ed.). *Encyclopaedia of Religion and Ethics.* New York: Charles Scribner's Sons, 1922.

Hatton, C. L., Valente, S. M. (eds.). *Suicide: Assessment and Intervention.* Norwalk, Conn.: Appleton-Century-Crofts, 1984.

Hayes, L., Kajdan, B. *And Darkness Closes In. . .National Study of Jail Suicides.* Washington, D.C.: The National Center on Institutions and Alternatives, 1981.

Hendin, D. *Death as a Fact of Life.* New York: W. W. Norton, 1984.

Hendin, H. *Black Suicide.* New York: Basic Books, 1969.

———. *Suicide and Scandinavia.* Garden City, New York: Doubleday/Anchor Books, 1965.

———. *Suicide in America.* New York: W. W. Norton, 1982.

Henry, A. F., Short J. F., Jr. *Suicide and Homicide.* New York: The Free Press, 1965.

Hewett, J. H. *After Suicide.* Philadelphia: Westminster Press, 1980.

Hey, R. *Three Dissertations; On the Pernicious Effects of Gaming, On Duelling, and on Suicide.* Cambridge: J. Smith, 1812.

Hillman, J. *Suicide and the Soul.* Dallas: Spring Publications, 1985.

Hoffman, F. *Suicide Problems.* Newark: Prudential Press, 1928

Hume, D. *Essays Moral, Political and Literary.* London: Oxford University Press, 1963.

Humphry, D. *Let Me Die Before I Wake.* Los Angeles: Hemlock, 1982.

Humphry, D., Wickett, A. *The Right to Die: Understanding Euthanasia.* New York: Harper & Row, 1986.

Hunter, R., Macalpine, I. *Three Hundred Years of Psychiatry, 1535–1860.* London: Oxford University Press, 1963.

Iga, M. *The Thorn in the Chrysanthemum: Suicide and Economic Success in Modern Japan.* Berkeley: University of California Press, 1986.

Jackson, S. W. *Melancholia and Depression.* New Haven: Yale University Press, 1986.

James, W. *Essays on Faith and Morals.* New York: Longmans, Green, 1947.

Kastenbaum, R., Aisenberg, R. *The Psychology of Death.* New York: Springer Publishing Company, 1976.

Klagsbrun, F. *Too Young to Die: Youth and Suicide.* New York: Pocket Books, 1981.

Knauth, P. *A Season in Hell.* New York: Pocket Books, 1977.

Kobler, A., Stotler, E. *The End of Hope.* New York: The Free Press of Glencoe, 1964.

Kushner, H. I. *Self-Destruction in the Promised Land.* New Brunswick, N.J.: Rutgers University Press, 1989.

Langone, J. *Death Is a Noun: A View of the End of Life.* Boston: Little, Brown, 1972.

———. *Vital Signs: The Way We Die in America.* Boston: Little, Brown, 1974.

Larue, G. A. *Euthanasia and Religion.* Los Angeles: The Hemlock Society, 1985.

Lecky, W. E. H. *History of European Morals from Augustus to Charlemagne.* London: Longmans, Green, 1869.

Lester, G., Lester, D. *Suicide: The Gamble with Death.* Englewood Cliffs, New Jersey: Prentice-Hall, 1971.

Lifton, R. J. *The Broken Connection.* New York: Simon and Schuster, 1980.

Light, D. *Becoming Psychiatrists: The Professional Transformation of Self.* New York: W. W. Norton, 1980.

Lukas, C., Seiden, H. M. *Silent Grief: Living in the Wake of Suicide.* New York: Charles Scribner's Sons, 1987.

MacDonald, M. *Mystical Bedlam.* Cambridge: Cambridge University Press, 1981.

Mack, J. E., Hickler, H. *Vivienne: The Life and Suicide of an Adolescent Girl.* Boston: Little, Brown, 1981.

Maguire, D. C. *Death by Choice.* New York: Schocken Books, 1975.

Mannes, M. *Last Rights.* New York: William Morrow, 1974.

Masaryk, T. G. *Suicide and the Meaning of Civilization.* Trans. Weist, W. B., Batson, R. G. Chicago: The University of Chicago Press, 1970.

Meaker, M. J. *Sudden Endings.* Garden City, New York: Doubleday, 1964.

Meerloo, J. A. M. *Suicide and Mass Suicide.* New York: E. P. Dutton & Co., 1968.

Menninger, K. A. *Man Against Himself.* New York: Harvest/Harcourt, Brace & World, 1938.

Miller, A. *Death of a Salesman.* New York: Bantam Books, 1951.

Moore, C. *A Full Inquiry on the Subject of Suicide.* London, 1790.

Morselli, H. *Suicide: An Essay on Comparative Moral Statistics.* New York: Arno Press, 1975.

Neale, R. E. *The Art of Dying.* New York: Harper & Row, 1973.

Norman, M. *'Night, Mother.* New York: Dramatists Play Service, 1983.

Osterweis, M., Solomon, F., Green, M. (eds.). *Bereavement: Reactions, Consequences, and Care.* Washington, D.C.: National Academy Press, 1984.

Pavese, C. *The Burning Brand: Diaries 1935–1950.* Trans. Murch, A. E. New York: Walker & Company, 1961.

Peck, M. L., Farberow, N. L., Litman, R. E. (eds.). *Youth Suicide.* New York: Springer Publishing Company, 1985.

Perlin, S. (ed.). *A Handbook for the Study of Suicide.* New York: Oxford University Press, 1975.

Plath, S. *The Bell Jar.* New York: Bantam Books, 1972.

Portwood, D. *Common-Sense Suicide.* New York: Dodd, Mead, 1978.

Reynolds, D. K., Farberow, N. L. *Suicide: Inside and Out.* Berkeley: University of California Press, 1976.

Roberts, A. R. (ed.). *Self-Destructive Behavior.* Springfield, Illinois: Charles C. Thomas, 1975.

Robitscher, J. *The Powers of Psychiatry.* Boston: Houghton Mifflin, 1980.

Rofes, E. E. *"I Thought People Like That Killed Themselves": Lesbians, Gay Men and Suicide.* San Francisco: Grey Fox Press, 1983.

Rollin, B. *Last Wish.* New York: Linden Press/Simon and Schuster, 1985.

Roman, J. *Exit House.* New York: Seaview Books, 1980.

Rosenfeld, L., Prupas, M. *Left Alive: After a Suicide Death in the Family.* Springfield, Illinois: Charles C. Thomas, 1984.

Russell, O. R. *Freedom to Die: Moral and Legal Aspects of Euthanasia.* New York: Human Sciences Press, 1977.

Shneidman, E. (ed.). *Death and the College Student.* New York: Behavioral Publications, 1972.

——. *Definition of Suicide.* New York: John Wiley & Sons, 1985.

——. *Voices of Death.* New York: Harper & Row, 1980.

Shneidman, E. S. *Deaths of Man.* Harmondsworth, England: Penguin, 1974.

——. (ed.). *Essays in Self-Destruction.* New York: Jason Aronson, 1967.

——. (ed.). *On the Nature of Suicide.* San Francisco: Jossey-Bass, 1973.

——. *Suicide Thoughts and Reflections, 1960–1980.* New York: Behavioral Sciences Press, 1981.

——. (ed.). *Suicidology: Contemporary Developments.* New York: Grune and Stratton, 1976.

Shneidman, E. S., Farberow, N. L. (eds.). *Clues to Suicide.* New York: McGraw-Hill, 1957.

Shneidman, E. S., Farberow, N. L., Litman, R. E. (eds.). *The Psychology of Suicide.* New York: Science House, 1970.

Sprott, S. E. *The English Debate on Suicide from Donne to Hume.* LaSalle, Illinois: Open Court, 1961.

Steincrohn, P. J. *How to Stop Killing Yourself.* New York: Ace Books, 1950.

Stengel, E. *Suicide and Attempted Suicide.* New York: Jason Aronson, 1974.

Stern, D. *The Suicide Academy.* New York: Arbor House, 1985.

Strahan, S. A. K. *Suicide and Insanity.* London: Swan Sonnenschein, 1893.

Szasz, T. *The Manufacture of Madness.* New York: Harper Colophon Books, 1977.

——. *The Theology of Medicine.* Baton Rouge: Louisiana State University Press, 1977.

Wallace, S., Eser, A. (eds.). *Suicide and Euthanasia.* Knoxville: The University of Tennessee Press, 1981.

Wechsler, J. A. *In a Darkness.* New York: W. W. Norton, 1972.

Weisman, A. D. *On Dying and Denying.* New York: Behavioral Publications, 1972.

Westermarck, E. *The Origin and Development of the Moral Ideas.* London: Macmillan, 1912.

Williams, G. *The Sanctity of Life and the Criminal Law.* New York: Alfred A. Knopf, 1957.

Winslow, F. *The Anatomy of Suicide.* London: Henry Renshaw, 1840.

Worden, J. W. *Grief Counseling and Grief Therapy.* New York: Springer Publishing Company, 1982.

PAPERS AND ARTICLES

Anonymous (1932). Ex-Suicide. *Harper's Monthly Magazine,* 165, pp. 426–35.

Applebome, P. Between Two Worlds (1985). *Texas Monthly,* January 1985, p. 104.

Asberg, M., Träskman, L., Thorén, P. 5-HIAA in the Cerebrospinal Fluid (1976). *Archives of General Psychiatry,* 33, pp. 1193–97.

Asimos, C. T. Dynamic Problem-Solving in a Group for Suicidal Persons (1979). *International Journal of Group Psychotherapy,* 29(1), pp. 109–14.

Atlas, J. The Survivor's Suicide (1988). *Vanity Fair,* January 1988, p. 78.

Baker, W. E. Diary of a Suicide (1913). *The Glebe,* 1(2).

Bakwin, H. Suicide in Children and Adolescents (1957). *The Journal of Pediatrics,* 50(6), pp. 749–69.

Bartel, R. Suicide in Eighteenth-Century England: The Myth of a Reputation (1960). *Huntington Library Quarterly,* February 1960, pp. 145–58.

Basescu, S. The Threat of Suicide in Psychotherapy (1965). *American Journal of Psychotherapy,* 19, 99–105.

Battin, M.P. Age Rationing and the Just Distribution of Health Care: Is There a Duty to Die? (1987). *Ethics,* 97, pp. 317–40.

———. The Least Worst Death (1983). *The Hastings Center Report,* 13(2), pp. 13–16.

Beck, A. T., Kovacs, M., Weissman, A. Assessment of Suicidal Intention: The Scale for Suicide Ideation (1979). *Journal of Consulting and Clinical Psychology,* 47(2), pp. 343–52.

Bergson, L. Suicide's Other Victims (1982). *The New York Times Magazine,* November 14, 1982, pp. 100–108.

Berman, A. L., Cohen-Sandler, R. Childhood and Adolescent Suicide Research: A Critique. *Crisis,* 3, 3–15.

Bernikow, L. Sickness Unto Death: Young Women and Suicide (1983). *Mademoiselle,* April 1983, p. 150.

Billings, J. H., et al. Observations on Long-Term Group Therapy with Suicidal and Depressed Persons (1974). *Life-Threatening Behavior,* 4(3), 160–70.

Blair, G. The Heart of the Matter (1984). *Manhattan, Inc.,* October 1984, pp. 72–79.

Blum, D. A Loss of Balance (1986). *New York,* January 13, 1986, pp. 32–37.

Bradley, K. A., Raffin, T. A. Life and Death Decisions: Ethical Decision Making When Resources Are Limited. Unpublished paper.

Breed, W. Five Components of a Basic Suicide Syndrome (1972). *Life-Threatening Behavior,* 2(1), pp. 3–18.

Breskin, D. Dear Mom and Dad (1984). *Rolling Stone,* November 8, 1984, p. 26.

Brown, G. L., et al. Aggression, Suicide, and Serotonin: Relationships to CSF Amine Metabolites (1982). *American Journal of Psychiatry,* 139(6), pp. 741–46.

Cantor, P. The Adolescent Attempter: Sex, Sibling Position, and Family Constellation (1972). *Life-Threatening Behavior,* 2(4), pp. 252–61.

Cantor, P. C. Personality Characteristics Found Among Youthful Female Suicide Attempters (1976). *Journal of Abnormal Psychology,* 85(3), pp. 324–29.

Cassity, J. H. Are You the Suicide Type? (1939). *The American Mercury,* October 1939, pp. 172–77.

Comstock, B. S. Suicide in the 1970's: A Second Look (1979). *Suicide and Life-Threatening Behavior,* 9(1), pp. 3–13.

Crocker, L.G. The Discussion of Suicide in the Eighteenth Century (1952). *Journal of the History of Ideas,* 13, pp. 47–72.

Danto, B. L. New Frontiers in the Relationship Between Suicidology and Law Enforcement (1979). *Suicide and Life-Threatening Behavior,* 9(4), pp. 195–204.

———. Practical Aspects of the Training of Psychiatrists in Suicide Prevention (1976). *Omega,* 7(1), pp. 69–73.

Daube, D. The Linguistics of Suicide (1977). *Suicide and Life-Threatening Behavior,* 7(3), pp. 132–82.

Eisenberg, L. Adolescent Suicide: On Taking Arms Against a Sea of Troubles (1980). *Pediatrics,* 66, pp. 315–20.

Emery, P. E. Adolescent Depression and Suicide (1983). *Adolescence,* 18(70), 245–58.

Engelhardt, H. T., Jr., Malloy, M. Suicide and Assisting Suicide: A Critique of Legal Sanctions (1982). *Southwestern Law Journal,* 36(4), pp. 1003–37.

Faber, M. D. Seneca, Self-Destruction, and the Creative Act (1978). *Omega,* 9(2), pp. 149–65.

———. Shakespeare's Suicides: Some Historic, Dramatic and Psychological Reflections. In Shneidman, E. S. (ed.). *Essays in Self-Destruction.* New York: Jason Aronson, 1967, pp. 30–58.

Fadiman, A. The Liberation of Lolly and Gronky (1986). *Life,* December 1986, pp. 71–94.

Farberow, N. L. Ten Years of Suicide Prevention—Past and Future (1970). *Bulletin of Suicidology,* 6, Spring 1970, pp. 6–11.

Farberow, N. L., MacKinnon, D. R., Nelson, F. L. Suicide: Who's Counting? (1977). *Public Health Reports,* 92(3), pp. 223–32.

Frederick, C. J. Current Trends in Suicidal Behavior in the United States (1978). *American Journal of Psychotherapy,* 32, pp. 172–200.

———. The Present Suicide Taboo in the United States (1971). *Mental Hygiene,* 55(2), pp. 178–83.

Frederick, C. J., Resnik, H. L. P. Interventions with Suicidal Patients (1970). *Journal of Contemporary Psychotherapy,* 2(2), pp. 103–9.

Freeman, W. Psychiatrists Who Kill Themselves: A Study in Suicide (1967). *American Journal of Psychiatry,* 124(6), pp. 154–55.

Garfinkel, B. D., Froese, A., Hood, J. Suicide Attempts in Children and Adolescents (1982). *American Journal of Psychiatry,* 139(10), pp. 1257–61.

Gibson, P. Gay Male and Lesbian Youth Suicide (1986). Paper presented at a joint meeting of the American Association of Suicidology and the International Association for Suicide Prevention, San Francisco, May 25–30, 1987.

Gould, M.S., Shaffer, D. The Impact of Suicide in Television Movies: Evidence of Imitation (1986). *The New England Journal of Medicine,* 315(11), pp. 690–94.

Gruman, G. J. An Historical Introduction to Ideas About Voluntary Euthanasia (1973). *Omega,* 4(2), pp. 87–138.

Gurland, B. J., Cross, P. S. Suicide Among the Elderly (1983). From Aronson, M. K., Bennett, R., Gurland, B. J. (eds.). *The Acting-Out Elderly.* New York: The Haworth Press, 1983, pp. 55–65.

Hackel, J., Asimos, C. T. Resistances Encountered in Starting a Group Therapy Program for Suicide Attempters in Varied Administrative Settings (1980). *Suicide and Life-Threatening Behavior,* 10(2), pp. 100–105.

Hansen, L. C., McAleer, C. A. Terminal Cancer and Suicide: The Health Care Professional's Dilemma (1983). *Omega,* 14(3), pp. 241–48.

Haughton, A. Suicide Prevention Programs in the United States—An Overview (1968). *Bulletin of Suicidology,* July 1968, pp. 25–29.

Havens, L. L. The Anatomy of a Suicide (1965). *The New England Journal of Medicine,* 272(8), pp. 401–6.

Heilig, S. M., et al. The Role of Nonprofessional Volunteers in a Suicide Prevention Center (1968). *Community Mental Health Journal,* 4(4), pp. 287–95.

Holinger, P. C., Offer, D. Prediction of Adolescent Suicide: A Population Model (1982). *American Journal of Psychiatry,* 139(3), pp. 302–7.

Holmes, J. H. Is Suicide Justifiable? (1934). *The John Day Pamphlets,* No. 42.

Jackson, D. L., Youngner, S. Patient Autonomy and "Death with Dignity: Some Clinical Caveats" (1979). *The New England Journal of Medicine,* 301, pp. 404–8.

Kastenbaum, R. On the Future of Death: Some Images and Options (1972). *Omega,* 3(4), pp. 319–30.

Kelly, W. A. Suicide and Psychiatric Education (1973). *American Journal of Psychiatry,* 130(4), pp. 463–68.

Kenyon, K. A Survivor's Notes (1979). *Newsweek,* April 30, 1979, p. 17.

Kirk, A. R. Psycho-Social Modes of Adaptation and Suicide Among Blacks. Unpublished paper.

Klein, J. A Mystery of Three Suicides (1977). *Rolling Stone,* February 10, 1977, pp. 34–39.

Klugman, D. J., Litman, R. E., Wold, C. I. Suicide: Answering the Cry for Help (1965). *Social Work,* 10(4), pp. 43–50.

Kobler, J. Suicides Can Be Prevented (1948). *The Saturday Evening Post,* March 27, 1948, p. 20.

Kovacs, M., Beck, A. T., Weissman, A. Hopelessness: An Indicator of Suicidal Risk (1975). *Suicide,* 5(2), pp. 98–103.

Lamm, R. D. Long Time Dying. *The New Republic,* August 27, 1984, pp. 20–23.

LeBlanc, A. N. "You Wanna Die with Me?" (1986). *New England Monthly,* December 1986, p. 76.

Light, D. Professional Problems in Treating Suicidal Persons (1976). *Omega,* 7(1), pp. 59–67.

———. Psychiatrists and Suicide. Unpublished paper.

———. Treating Suicide: The Illusions of a Professional Movement (1973). *International Social Science Journal,* 25(4), pp. 475–88.

Litman, R. E. Sigmund Freud on Suicide (1967). In Shneidman, E. S. (ed.). *Essays in Self-Destruction.* New York: Science House, 1967, pp. 324–44.

———. Suicide Prevention Center Patients: A Follow-up Study (1970). *Bulletin of Suicidology,* 6, Spring 1970, pp. 12–17.

———. When Patients Commit Suicide (1965). *American Journal of Psychotherapy,* 14, pp. 570–76.

Malcolm, A. H. Many See Mercy in Ending Empty Lives (1984). *The New York Times,* September 23, 1984, p. 1.

————. Some Elderly Choose Suicide Over Lonely, Dependent Life (1984). *The New York Times,* September 24, 1984, p. 1.

————. To Suffer a Prolonged Illness or Elect to Die: A Case Study (1984). *The New York Times,* December 16, 1984, p. 1.

Maltsberger, J. T., Buie, D. H. Countertransference Hate in the Treatment of Suicidal Patients (1974). *Archives of General Psychiatry,* 30, pp. 625–33.

————. The Devices of Suicide: Revenge, Riddance, and Rebirth (1980). *International Review of Psycho-Analysis.* 7, pp. 61–72.

Maris, R. Rational Suicide: An Impoverished Self-Transformation (1982). *Suicide and Life-Threatening Behavior,* 12(1), pp. 4–16.

Mathews, W. Civilization and Suicide (1891). *The North American Review,* April 1891, pp. 470–84.

McIntosh, J. L. Suicide Among the Elderly: Levels and Trends (1985). *American Journal of Orthopsychiatry,* 55(2), pp. 288–93.

————. Suicide Among Native Americans: Further Tribal Data and Considerations (1983). *Omega,* 14(3), pp. 215–29.

McIntosh, J. L., Hubbard, R. W., Santos, J. F. Suicide Facts and Myths (1983). Paper presented at the sixteenth annual meeting of the American Association of Suicidology, Dallas, Texas, April 21–24, 1983.

McIntosh, J. L., Santos, J. F. Changing Patterns in Methods of Suicide by Race and Sex (1982). *Suicide and Life-Threatening Behavior,* 12(4), pp. 221–33.

Menninger, K. Psychoanalytic Aspects of Suicide (1933). *International Journal of Psychoanalysis,* 14, pp. 376–90.

Miller, H. L., et al. Suicide Prevention Services in America (1979). *Alabama Journal of Medical Science,* 16(1), pp. 26–31.

Mintz, R. S. Basic Considerations in the Psychotherapy of the Depressed Suicidal Patient (1971). *American Journal of Psychotherapy,* 25, pp. 56–73.

————. Some Practical Procedures in the Management of Suicidal Persons (1966). *American Journal of Orthopsychiatry,* 36, pp. 896–903.

Moss, L. M., Hamilton, D. M. The Psychotherapy of the Suicidal Patient (1956). *American Journal of Psychiatry,* 112, pp. 814–19.

Motto, J. A. New Approaches to Crisis Intervention (1979). *Suicide and Life-Threatening Behavior,* 9(3), pp. 173–84.

————. Newspaper Influence on Suicide: A Controlled Study (1970). *Archives of General Psychiatry,* 23, pp. 143–48.

————. The Psychopathology of Suicide: A Clinical Model Approach (1979). *American Journal of Psychiatry,* 136(4B), pp. 516–20.

————. Rational Suicide and Medical Ethics (1981). From *Rights and Responsibilities in Modern Medicine,* 2, pp. 201–9. New York: Alan R. Liss.

Murphy, G. E. Suicide and the Right to Die (1973). *American Journal of Psychiatry,* 130(4), pp. 472–73.

Murphy, G. E., et al. Suicide and Alcoholism (1979). *Archives of General Psychiatry,* 36(1), pp. 65–69.

Noble, J. A Glance at Suicide as Dealt With in the Colony and in the Province of the Massachusetts Bay (1902). *Proceedings of the Massachusetts Historical Society,* 16, pp. 521–32.

Okin, R. L. The Future of State Hospitals: Should There Be One? (1983). *American Journal of Psychiatry,* 140(5), pp. 577–81.

Peck, M. L. Suicide Motivations in Adolescents (1968). *Adolescence,* 3(9), pp. 109–18.

———. Youth Suicide (1982). *Death Education,* 6, pp. 29–47.

Peck, M. L., Litman, R. E. Current Trends in Youthful Suicide (1974). In Bush, J. (ed.). *Suicide and Blacks: A Monograph for Continuing Education in Suicide Prevention.* Los Angeles: Fanon Research and Development Center, 1975, pp. 13–27.

Pepitone-Arreola-Rockwell, F. Death Anxiety: Comparison of Psychiatrists, Psychologists, Suicidologists, and Funeral Directors (1981). *Psychological Reports,* 49, pp. 979–82.

Phelps, E. B. Neurotic Books and Newspapers as Factors in the Mortality of Suicide and Crime (1911). *Bulletin of the American Academy of Medicine,* 12(5), pp. 264-306.

Phillips, D. P. The Influence of Suggestion on Suicide: Substantive and Theoretical Implications of the Werther Effect (1974). *American Sociological Review,* 39, pp. 340–54.

Phillips, D. P., Carstensen, L. L. Clustering of Teenage Suicides After Television News Stories About Suicide (1986). *The New England Journal of Medicine,* 315(11), pp. 685–89.

Pines, M. Suicide Signals (1983). *Science 83,* October 1983, pp. 55–58.

Pokorny, A. D. A Follow-up Study of 618 Suicidal Patients (1966). *American Journal of Psychiatry,* 122, pp. 1109–16.

———. Prediction of Suicide in Psychiatric Patients (1983). *Archives of General Psychiatry,* 40, pp. 249–57.

Pokorny, A. D., Davis, F., Harberson, W. Suicide, Suicide Attempts, and Weather (1963). *American Journal of Psychiatry,* 120, pp. 377–81.

Pretzel, P. W. Philosophical and Ethical Considerations of Suicide Prevention (1968). *Bulletin of Suicidology,* July 1968, pp. 30–38.

Raffin, T. A. The Right to Live, The Right to Die (1983). *Stanford Magazine,* Spring 1983, pp. 25–31.

Ringel, E. The Presuicidal Syndrome (1976). *Suicide and Life-Threatening Behavior,* 6(3), pp. 131–49.

Robbins, D., Conroy, R. C. A Cluster of Adolescent Suicide Attempts: Is Suicide Contagious? (1983). *Journal of Adolescent Health Care,* 3, pp. 253–55.

Robinson, H. M. The Case of Suicide (1932). *The North American Review,* 234(4), pp. 303–8.

Ross, C. P. Mobilizing Schools for Suicide Prevention (1980). *Suicide and Life-Threatening Behavior,* 10(4), pp. 239–43.

Ross, C. P., Motto, J. A. Group Counseling for Suicidal Adolescents (1984). In Sudak, H. S., Ford, A. B., Rushforth, N. B. (eds.). *Suicide in the Young.* Boston: John Wright–PSG Inc., 1984.

Ruggieri, C. Narrative of the Crucifixion of Matthew Lovat, Executed by His Own Hands, at Venice, in the Month of July, 1805 (1814). *The Pamphleteer,* vol. III, no. VI. London, 1814.

Saunders, J. M., Valente, S. M. Suicide Risk Among Gay Men and Lesbians: A Review (1987). *Death Studies,* 11, pp. 1–23.

Sayre, J. The Man on the Ledge (1949). *The New Yorker,* April 16, 1949, p. 34.

Scheinin, A.-G. The Burden of Suicide (1983). *Newsweek,* Feb. 7, 1983, p. 13.

Schuyler, D. Counseling Suicide Survivors: Issues and Answers (1973). *Omega,* 4(4), pp. 313–21.

Schwartz, A. J. Innacuracy and Uncertainty in Estimates of College Student Suicide Rates (1980). *College Health,* 28, pp. 201–4.

Schwartz, D. A., Flinn, D. E., Slawson, P. F. Suicide in the Psychiatric Hospital (1975). *American Journal of Psychiatry,* 132(2), pp. 150–53.

Seiden, R. H. Current Developments in Minority Group Suicidology (1974). *JBHP,* 1(4), pp. 29–50.

———. Self-Deliverance or Self-Destruction? (1983). Paper presented at the sixteenth annual meeting of the American Association of Suicidology, Dallas, Texas, 1983.

———. A Study of Student Suicide (1966). *Journal of Abnormal Psychology,* 71(6), pp. 389–99.

———. Suicide and Public Health: A Brief Appraisal (1972). *Life-Threatening Behavior,* 2(2), pp. 99–103.

———. Suicide Capital? A Study of the San Francisco Suicide Rate (1967). *Bulletin of Suicidology,* December 1967, pp. 1–10.

———. Suicide: Preventable Death (1974). *Public Affairs Report* (Bulletin of the Institute of Governmental Studies, University of California, Berkeley), 15(4), pp. 1–5.

———. Suicide Prevention: A Public Health/Public Policy Approach (1977). *Omega,* 8(3), pp. 267–76.

———. Where Are They Now? A Follow-up Study of Suicide Attempters from the Golden Gate Bridge (1978). *Suicide and Life-Threatening Behavior,* 8(4), pp. 203–16.

———. Why Are Suicides of Young Blacks Increasing? (1972). *HSMHA Health Reports,* 87(1), pp. 3–8.

Seiden, R. H., Spence, M.C. A Tale of Two Bridges: Comparative Suicide Incidence on the Golden Gate and San Francisco–Oakland Bay Bridges (1982). *Crisis,* 3(1), pp. 32–40.

Seiden, R. H., Tauber, R. K. Pseudocides vs. Suicides (1970). *Proceedings,* Fifth International Conference for Suicide Prevention, pp. 219–22.

Seligman, M. E. P. Giving Up on Life (1974). *Psychology Today,* May 1974, pp. 80–85.

Seligson, M. Are You Suicidal? (1972). *Harpers Bazaar,* August 1972.

Selkin, J. The Legacy of Émile Durkheim (1982). Paper presented at the fifteenth annual meeting of the American Association of Suicidology, New York City, April 15–18, 1982.

Selzer, M. L., Payne, C. E. Automobile Accidents, Suicide and Unconscious Motivation (1962). *American Journal of Psychiatry,* 119, pp. 237–40.

Shaffer, D. Suicide in Childhood and Early Adolescence (1974). *Journal of Child Psychology and Psychiatry,* 15, pp. 275–91.

Shaffer, D., Fisher, P. The Epidemiology of Suicide in Children and Young Adolescents (1981). *Journal of the American Academy of Child Psychiatry,* 20, pp. 545–65.

Shein, H. M. Suicide Care: Obstacles in the Education of Psychiatric Residents (1976). *Omega,* 7(1), pp. 75–81.

Shein, H. M., Stone, A. A. Monitoring and Treatment of Suicidal Potential Within the Context of Psychotherapy (1969). *Comprehensive Psychiatry,* 10(1), pp. 59–70.

Shneidman, E. S. Aphorisms of Suicide and Some Implications for Psychotherapy (1984). *American Journal of Psychotherapy,* 38(3), pp. 319–28.

———. The Suicidal Logic of Cesare Pavese (1982). *Journal of the American Academy of Psychoanalysis,* 10(4), pp. 547–63.

Siegel, K. Society, Suicide, and Social Policy (1982). *Journal of Psychiatric Treatment and Evaluation,* 4, pp. 473–82.

Singular, S. Local Hero (1984). *The Denver Post Magazine,* September 9, 1984, p. 11.

Stack, S., Haas, A. The Effect of Unemployment Duration on National Suicide Rates: A Time Series Analysis, 1948–1982 (1984). *Sociological Focus,* 17(1), pp. 17–29.

Stannard, D. E. Death and Dying in Puritan New England (1973). *The American Historical Review,* 78(5), pp. 1305–30.

Stearns, A. W. Suicide in Massachusetts (1921). *Mental Hygiene,* 5(4), pp. 752–77.

Stone, A. A. Suicide Precipitated by Psychotherapy: A Clinical Contribution (1970). Paper presented at the ninth national scientific meeting of the Association for the Advancement of Psychotherapy, May 10, 1970.

———. A Syndrome of Serious Suicidal Intent (1960). *Archives of General Psychiatry,* vol. 3, pp. 331–39.

Styron, W. Darkness Visible (1989). *Vanity Fair,* Dec. 1989, pp. 212–15, 278–86.

Terman, L. M. Recent Literature on Juvenile Suicides (1914). *Journal of Abnormal Psychology,* 9, pp. 61–66.

Tishler, C. L, McKenry, P. C., Morgan, K. C. Adolescent Suicide Attempts: Some Significant Factors (1981). *Suicide and Life-Threatening Behavior,* 11(2), pp. 86–92.

Toolan, J. M. Suicide in Children and Adolescents (1975). *American Journal of Psychotherapy,* 29(3), pp. 339–44.

———. Therapy of Depressed and Suicidal Children (1978). *American Journal of Psychotherapy,* 32(2), pp. 243–51.

Tucker, S. J., Cantor, P. C. Personality and Status Profiles of Peer Counselors and Suicide Attempters (1975). *Journal of Counseling Psychology,* 22(5), pp. 423–30.

Van Praag, H. M. Depression, Suicide and the Metabolism of Serotonin in the Brain (1982). *Journal of Affective Disorders,* 4, pp. 275–90.

Wanzer, S. H., et al. The Physician's Responsibility Toward Hopelessly Ill Patients (1984). *The New England Journal of Medicine,* 310, pp. 955–59.

Weaver, P., Jr. A Legal Suicide, 1996 (1896). *Overland Monthly,* 28, pp. 680–90.

Weis, S., Seiden, R. H. Rescuers and the Rescued: A Study of Suicide Prevention Center Volunteers and Clients by Means of a Death Questionnaire (1974). *Life-Threatening Behavior,* 4(2), pp. 118–30.

Weisman, A. D. Is Suicide a Disease? (1971). *Life-Threatening Behavior,* 1(4), pp. 219–31.

Weller, S. Whose Death Was It, Anyway? Reflections on the Suicide of a Friend (1981). *The Village Voice,* December 9–15, 1981, pp. 25–27.

Winegarten, R. On the Love of Suicide (1972). *Commentary,* August 1972, pp. 29–34.

Winn, M. The Loss of Childhood (1983). *The New York Times Magazine,* May 8, 1983.

Wold, C. I. Characteristics of 26,000 Suicide Prevention Center Patients (1970). *Bulletin of Suicidology,* No. 6, Spring 1970, pp. 24–28.

Wold, C. I., Litman, R. E. Suicide After Contact with a Suicide Prevention Center (1973). *Archives of General Psychiatry,* 28, pp. 735–39.

Wolf, H. Suicide Notes (1931). *The American Mercury,* November 1931, pp. 264–72.

Wrobleski, A. Rational Suicide: A Contradiction in Terms (1983). An address given at the First Unitarian Society, Minneapolis, Minnesota, February 27, 1983.

Wyden, P. Suicide (1961). *The Saturday Evening Post,* August 19, 1961, p. 18.

Zilboorg, G. Considerations on Suicide, With Particular Reference to That of the Young (1937). *American Journal of Orthopsychiatry,* 7, pp. 15–31.

———. Some Aspects of Suicide (1975). *Suicide,* 5(3), pp. 131–39.

INDEX

ABOUT THE AUTHOR

GEORGE HOWE COLT has an A.B. from Harvard and an M.A. in creative writing from Johns Hopkins. He was the inaugural Time, Inc., Fellow at *Johns Hopkins Magazine*, and has written for *The New York Times* and *Harvard Magazine*. He is currently a staff writer for *Life* magazine. His poetry has been published in *Ploughshares* and *Shenandoah*. His plays, *Origami* and *Holding Hands* were first produced at HB Playwrights Foundation. He lives in New York City with his wife, Anne Fadiman, a writer, and their daughter, Susannah.